The Correspondence of
Jonathan Swift

ESTHER JOHNSON (STELLA)

From an original drawing attributed to Dr. Thomas Parnell, Archdeacon of Clogher

The Correspondence of
Jonathan Swift

EDITED BY

HAROLD WILLIAMS

VOLUME II

1714–1723

OXFORD
AT THE CLARENDON PRESS

Oxford University Press, Ely House, London, W. 1

GLASGOW NEW YORK TORONTO MELBOURNE WELLINGTON
CAPE TOWN SALISBURY IBADAN NAIROBI LUSAKA ADDIS ABABA
BOMBAY CALCUTTA MADRAS KARACHI LAHORE DACCA
KUALA LUMPUR HONG KONG

134584

FIRST PUBLISHED 1963
REPRINTED, WITH CORRECTIONS, 1965

PRINTED IN GREAT BRITAIN

CONTENTS

LIST OF PLATES

VOLUME II

VOLUME III

LIST OF LETTERS

List of Letters

Correspondents	Date	Place	Original source	Printed source or transcript	Page
S. to E. of Oxford	19 July 1715	Dublin	B.M. Portland MSS. List 1		182
S. to Knightley Chetwode	2 Aug. 1715	,,		Forster copy	183
John Arbuthnot to S.	6 Aug. 1715	London	B.M. Add. 4805		184
Knightley Chetwode to S.	13 Aug. 1715	Woodbrooke		Forster copy	186
Rev. Robert Freind to S.	20 Sept. 1715	Westminster	B.M. Add. 4805		187
S. to Mrs. Chetwode	7 Oct. 1715	Dublin		Forster copy	188
Duchess of Ormonde to S.	17 Oct. 1715	Richmond (?)	B.M. Add. 4805		189
S. to Knightley Chetwode	17 Dec. 1715	Belcamp		Forster copy	189
Duchess of Ormonde to S.	23 Jan. 1716	Richmond (?)	B.M. Add. 4805		192
S. to Archdeacon Walls	26 Feb. 1716	Trim	Rothschild		193
S. to Bishop Atterbury	24 Mar. 1716	Dublin		Nichols 1801	193
Bishop Atterbury to S.	6 Apr. 1716	Bromley	B.M. Add. 4805		195
S. to Bishop Atterbury	18 Apr. 1716	Dublin		Nichols 1801	197
Viscountess Bolingbroke to S.	5 May 1716	London		Deane Swift 1768	199
S. to Archdeacon Walls	6 May 1716	Trim	Rothschild		201
S. to Archdeacon Walls	15 May 1716	Martry	Rothschild		202
S. to Archdeacon Walls	6 June 1716	Gaulstown	Rothschild		203
S. to Archdeacon Walls	14 June 1716	,,	Rothschild		204
S. to Archbishop King	17 June 1716	,,		Nichols 1801	205
S. to Archdeacon Walls	18 June 1716	,,	Rothschild		207
Archbishop King to S.	20 June 1716	Dublin	Library, Armagh		210
Pope to S.	20 June 1716	London (?)		Faulkner 1741	210
Viscountess Bolingbroke to S.	4 Aug. 1716	London	B.M. Add. 4805		212
S. to Pope	30 Aug. 1716	Dublin		Faulkner 1741	213
Duchess of Ormonde to S.	14 Sept. 1716	Richmond (?)	B.M. Add. 4805		216
S. to Archdeacon Walls	4 Oct. 1716	Trim	Rothschild		217
Viscount Bolingbroke to S.	23 Oct. [o.s. 12] 1716	Paris	B.M. Add. 4805		218
Charles Ford to S.	23 Oct. [o.s. 12] 1716	,,	B.M. Add. 4805		220

Correspondents	Date	Place	Original source	Printed source or transcript	Page
S. to Archbishop King	13 Nov. 1716	Dublin		Faulkner 1762	221
Archbishop King to S.	22 Nov. 1716	London	Rothschild		223
S. to Archdeacon Walls	6 Dec. 1716	Trim	Rothschild		228
S. to Archdeacon Walls	13 Dec. 1716	,,	Rothschild		229
S. to Archdeacon Walls	16 Dec. 1716	,,	Rothschild		231
S. to Archdeacon Walls	17 Dec. 1716	,,	Rothschild		232
S. to Isaiah Parvisol	18 Dec. 1716	,,	Rothschild		233
S. to Archdeacon Walls	19 Dec. 1716	,,	Rothschild		233
S. to Archbishop King	22 Dec. 1716	,,	Library, Armagh		235
S. to Esther Vanhomrigh	? Dec. 1716	,,	B.M. Add. 39839		239
S. to Archdeacon Walls	23 Dec. 1716	,,	Rothschild		240
S. to Archdeacon Walls	27 Dec. 1716	,,	Rothschild		241
S. to Archdeacon Walls	30 Dec. 1716	,,	Rothschild		242
S. to Archdeacon Walls	3 Jan. 1717	,,	Rothschild		243
S. to Archdeacon Walls	? Jan. 1717	—	Rothschild		244
S. to Archdeacon Walls	? Jan. 1717	—	Rothschild		244
Erasmus Lewis to S.	12 Jan. 1717	London	B.M. Add. 4805		245
Archbishop King to S.	12 Jan. 1717	,,		T.C.D. Letter-Book	247
S. to Archdeacon Walls	13 Jan. 1717	Trim	Rothschild		248
S. to Archdeacon Walls	24 Jan. 1717	,,	Rothschild		250
S. to Archdeacon Walls	27 Jan. 1717	,,	Rothschild		251
S. to Archbishop Walls	28 Jan. 1717	,,	Rothschild		252
S. to Archdeacon Walls	31 Jan. 1717	,,	Rothschild		252
S. to Archdeacon Walls	3 Feb. 1717	,,	Rothschild		253
S. to Archbishop King	2 Mar. 1717	Dublin		Faulkner 1762	255
Archbishop King to S.	2 Mar. 1717	London		T.C.D. Letter-Book	257
S. to Archbishop King	9 Mar. 1717	Dublin		Faulkner 1762	258
Archbishop King to S.	12 Mar. 1717	London		T.C.D. Letter-Book	260

List of Letters

Correspondents	Date	Place	Original source	Printed source or transcript	Page
Archbishop King to S.	21 Mar. 1717	London		T.C.D. Letter-Book	261
S. to Archdeacon Walls	28 Mar. 1717	Trim	Rothschild		263
S. to Archdeacon Walls	30 Mar. 1717	,,	Rothschild		264
S. to Archbishop King	1 May 1717	Magheralin		Faulkner 1762	265
Archbishop King to S.	13 May 1717	Bath		T.C.D. Letter-Book	267
S. to Archdeacon Walls	19 May 1717	Magheralin	Rothschild		268
S. to Archdeacon Walls	23 May 1717	Trim	Rothschild		269
Erasmus Lewis to S.	15 June 1717	London	B.M. Add. 4805		270
Erasmus Lewis to S.	18 June 1717	,,	B.M. Add. 4805		272
Erasmus Lewis to S.	2 July 1717	,,	B.M. Add. 4805		273
S. to Robert Cope	9 July 1717	Dublin		Nichols 1779	274
S. to E. of Oxford	9 July 1717	,,	Longleat xiii		276
S. to Joseph Addison	9 July 1717	,,	Berg Collection, New York Public Library		276
S. to E. of Oxford	16 July 1717	,,	B.M. Portland MSS.		278
S. to Bishop Atterbury	18 July 1717	,,		Nichols 1801	278
Matthew Prior to S.	30 July 1717	Westminster	B.M. Add. 4805		280
E. of Oxford to S.	6 Aug. 1717	Wimpole (?)	B.M. Add. 4805		282
S. to Archdeacon Walls	19 Aug. 1717	Ardsallagh	Rothschild		282
Matthew Prior to S.	24 Aug. 1717	Heythrop	B.M. Add. 4805		283
S. to Knightley Chetwode	Summer 1717	—		Forster copy	284
Marquess of Wharton to S.	7 Jan. 1718	Dublin	B.M. Add. 4806		285
Joseph Addison to S.	20 Mar. 1718	Holland House	B.M. Add. 4805		286
Lord Harley to S.	24 Apr. 1718	Wimpole (?)		Hawkesworth 1766	287
Matthew Prior to S.	1 May 1718	London	B.M. Add. 4804		288
S. to Lord Harley	17 May 1718	Dublin	B.M. Portland MSS.		289
Matthew Prior to S.	29 May 1718	London	B.M. Add. 4085		290
S. to Charles Ford	20 Aug. 1718	Laracor or Trim	Rothschild		291

List of Letters

Correspondents	Date	Place	Original source	Printed source or transcript	Page
Rev. Thomas Sheridan to S.	22 Dec. 1722	Dublin		Dodsley *Miscellanies* 1745	440
S. to John Gay	8 Jan. 1723	,,		Longleat xiii, ff. 92–93	441
S. to the Duke of Grafton	24 Jan. 1723	,,		Hawkesworth 1766	444
John Gay to S.	3 Feb. 1723	London	B.M. Add. 4805		445
S. to Knightley Chetwode	12 Feb. 1723	Dublin		Forster copy	448
S. to Rev. Thomas Wallis	12 Feb. 1723	,,		Duncombe	449
S. to Archbishop King	22 Feb. 1723	,,		Faulkner 1762	450
S. to Knightley Chetwode	25 Feb. 1723	,,		Forster copy	451
Knightley Chetwode to S.	26 Feb. 1723	,,		Forster copy	451
S. to Robert Cope	11 May 1723	,,		Nichols 1779	452
S. to Knightley Chetwode	May 1723	,,		Forster copy	455
S. to Robert Cope	1 June 1723	,,		Nichols 1779	455
S. to Knightley Chetwode	2 June 1723	,,		Forster copy	457
Pope to Swift	Aug. 1723	—		Transcript at Cirencester	457
Viscount Bolingbroke to S.	Aug. 1723	La Source		Curll 1736	460
S. to Rev. Thomas Sheridan	3 Aug. 1723	Clonfert		Dodsley *Miscellanies* 1745	463
S. to Pope	20 Sept. 1723	Dublin		Longleat xiii	464
S. to Rev. Thomas Sheridan	12 Oct. 1723	,,		Nichols 1779	467
S. to E. of Oxford	6 Nov. 1723	,,		Portland MSS.	467
John Arbuthnot to S.	7 Nov. 1723	London	B.M. Add. 4805		469
Duchess of Ormonde to S.	9 Dec. 1723	—	B.M. Add. 4805		471
Viscount Bolingbroke to S.	25 [o.s. 14] Dec. 1723	—	B.M. Add. 4805		472
S. to Knightley Chetwode	Dec. 1723	Dublin		Forster copy	474
Archbishop King to S.	19 Dec. 1723	,,		No copy in T.C.D. Letter-Book	475

Primate Lindsay to Swift

Jan: 5th 1713[-14.]

S^r

Yours I received the second instant[1] and immediatly got Mr Justice Nutly to write to the Bishop of Killala, at Kells to know of him whither if we could get him translated to the Bishoprick of Raphoe, he would accept of it; And this day we received his answer that it was not worth his while to carry his family so far Northwards for so little advantage as that Bishoprick would bring him, his own being upwards of a thousand a year and Raphoe not much above eleven hundred.[2]

The reason why I got Judge Nutley to write, was, because I apprehended it might seem irksome to him to be persuaded by my self to accept of what I left, though at the same time I can assure you I have done little more than saved myself whole by that Bishoprick and he might, if he pleased, in a little time have received sixteen or seventeen hundred pounds for fines; so that if this comes time enough to your hands, you will prevent any farther motion that way, but if Meath drops, I believe it would be an acceptable Post,[3] and the truth is he hath always in the worst of times voted honestly, and behaved himself as a true son of the Church—In the mean time, be assured, the Judge knows not that you are concerned in this affair—

There is a gentleman whom I believe you must have heard of Dr Andrew Hamilton Archdeacon of Raphoe, a man of good learning and abilities, and one of great interest in that Country, whom I could wish you could move for (since the Bishop of Killala refuses) to succeed me in Raphoe, as one that is most likely to do good in that part of the country, of any man I know.[4]

[1] The Queen's letter appointing Lindsay to the primacy was signed two weeks before and the patent had been issued the previous day.

[2] William Lloyd, Bishop of Killala, was on friendly terms with both Swift and Stella. He had held the bishopric of Killala since 1691. Raphoe was considered of greater importance, and an almost certain step on the ladder of further preferment.

[3] William Moreton by whom Swift was ordained. He died in 1715 (*Fasti Eccl. Hib.* ii. 45, 234; iii. 121).

[4] Dr. Hamilton, who was a native of that part of Ireland, and probably related to the Earl of Abercorn, remained Archdeacon of Raphoe until his death. He had been appointed to that dignity when only twenty-one years of age, and held it during the unprecedented period of sixty-four years.—Ball.

And now be pleased to accept my thanks for the great services you have done me, and as you have contributed much to my advancement, so I must desire you upon occasion, to give me your farther assistance for the service of the Church.

The Parliament is prorogued to the 18th instant but the Whigs continuing obstinate and deaf to all persuasions to carry on the Queens business with peace & gentleness we conclude it must be dissolved.[1]

If this should not come time enough to your hands, to prevent the Bp of Killala's letter for a translation to Raphoe I will labour all I can to make him easy.

Address: For the Reverend Dr. | Swift Dean of St. | Patricks in Dublin | to be left at Mr Rasmus | Lewis at Mr. Bromleys Office | London
Endorsed by Swift: Ld Primate of Ireld | June.[2] 5. 1713

4804

Viscount Bolingbroke to Swift

[7 January 1713-14.]
Thursday Morning | Two aclock[3]

Tho' I have not seen you, I did not fail to write to Lord Treasurer. Non tua res agitur dear Jonathan. 'tis the Treasurers cause, 'tis my Cause, 'tis every mans cause who is embark'd in our bottom.

[1] The Government sought unsuccessfully that if Parliament was allowed to meet again the attack on Phipps should be dropped.

[2] Thus erroneously written by Swift.

[3] Ball assumes that this letter, like that of Swift to the Earl of Oxford, Feb. 1712 (see i. 288), refers to the vacant deanery of Wells. William Graham, Dean of Wells, had just died. This letter, as Professor Firth has shown (*Review of English Studies*, 1926, ii. 7-8), related to the office of *Historiographer*, which Swift was anxious to secure, and it was written in Jan. 1713-14. In Jan. 1713 Swift saw Bolingbroke and Oxford almost daily. Bolingbroke went to Windsor on 24 Dec. 1713, and, owing to the Queen's illness, remained there till 5 or 6 Jan. He wrote two letters to Shrewsbury on 5 Jan. In one letter he says that he 'was confined to this place' for a fortnight while the rest of 'the Queen's servants' were for the most part in London, and he adds 'I have not had so much opportunity of talking to the Lord Treasurer.' Swift was also in London and Bolingbroke had not seen him for two weeks. Bolingbroke urges Shrewsbury (as Lord Chamberlain) to appoint Swift to the post of Historiographer vacated by the death of Thomas Rymer (Bolingbroke's *Letters*, 1798, ii. 574, 579-81). The date of this letter may then be safely conjectured. Bolingbroke left Windsor on Wednesday, 6 Jan., spent the first part of the night dealing with business awaiting him in London, and finished at two on Thursday morning by writing a brief note to Swift.

depend upon it that I never will neglect any opportunity of shewing that true esteem, that sincere affection, & honest friendship for you which fill the breast of your faithful | servant,

Bolingbroke

Address: Dr Swift

King's Letter-book[1]

Archbishop King to Swift

Dub: Jan: 13th 1713[-14.]

S^r

I have before me yours of the 31 of Decem— last, which came not to my hands till yesterday, I am heartily obliged to you for the frankness and plainness of it.

As to the first thing, that it is impossible for the two Kingdoms to proceed long upon a different scheme of politicks I believe it is true, but withall I think it impossible to set the two parties on the same foot in Ireland as in England, for our division is founded on the right of our Estates which are all claimed by the forfeiters and nothing can restore them but the Pretender nor any thing take them from us but bringing him in, whereas all your contests so farr as I understand them have no other foundation, but who shall have the ministry and employments the gaining these has no connexion with the Pretender, you may have them without him or under him. But you see the case is widely different with us and here is the true source of the zeal and violence of the Protestants of Ireld. Remove the fear of the Pretender, and you may lead them like a dog in a string.

I know you will say there is no danger of him but you must allow people whose all is at stake to be jealous of every step made to their ruin. I must not tell you what they reckon steps towards this, but they have lists of them, such I mean as they want steps and such as put them out of their wits.

As to your computation of the House of Commons. I do not wonder you computed wrong, for so did everybody here, and I amongst the rest. But many of those that I reckoned on as Torys

---

[1] The letter-book copy in Trinity College, Dublin (N. 3. 4. 243-6) is not wholly legible.

prove on this occasion Whigs, and let me tell you, that if the weight of the Government were not on them many more would declare themselves on that side, I my self can count near 30: One when they lost the Speaker, being asked how the matter went, answered with an air of pleasure, as God would have it, the vote went against us, and I never saw men better pleased by being worsted. I took some pains in the matter of the Speaker and had by connivance half a dozen of the chief of them at my chamber, where I represented to them the great hazard and danger they run and with more arguments than I have yet heard from any other.[1] They could not answer me, but only told me that if they could have any assurance or hopes that their grievances wou'd be removed they would drop their Speaker and insist on nothing but the removall of my Ld Chancellor and quieting the city of Dublin. I cou'd say nothing to these, and then they said they wou'd proceed their own way and if undone they had rather it should be the act of others than their own. However I found this effect, that 6: or 7 deserted and either absented themselves or voted for Sir Richard Levinge.

There are in the Parliament about 70: officers about 9: or 10: converts and as many more expectants or dependents as make up an hundred. I believe as much art and as many methods have been used to make a Parliament as well could be, and this is the effect. I do not think it difficult to get a Parliament that will be in the interest of the Church and Queen, but twill not be so easy to get one, that will come into all measures as desired.

I remembered when you assisted to procure the first Fruits and 20th parts and gave us some hope of getting the Crown rents I thought you greatly in the interest of the Church; but the highest Torys were of another opinion. You are well aware from this and many more examples that the interest of the Church is very different from that of particular persons, as is that of the Government from particular servants.

As to our representations from hence, I suppose you have seen that of the Convocation and of the House of Lords concerning Mr. Molesworth.[2] The fact was thus, being in the Presence Chamber

---

[1] The chief argument of the Government was that the Speaker had always been nominated by the Court, and that the defeat of Sir Richard Levinge would show disrespect to the Queen and the Lord Lieutenant.—Ball.

[2] As already mentioned (Swift to King, 31 Dec. 1713) Robert Molesworth was an active member of the opposition.

4

when the Convocation made their addresses, he saw Mr. Percival[1] with others at the head of the Lower House, who a few days before had appeared at the head of a riotous and mutinous mob with laurels in their hats; this moved the spleen of the peevish man, and he whispered to one by him that those that have turned the world upside down are likewise come hither, some overheard him, and you see what a turn is given it.[2]

As to my self I heartily opposed and protested against some votes in the House of Lords particularly their sending two Lords to bring away the Councill books without asking leave of the Government,[3] which I called Rappareeing them and reckoned to be a great insult on the Government and Crown and an ill precedent.

I likewise dissented from their voting my Lord Chancellor to have acquitted himself with honour and integrity, in the several stations he had been in,[4] because the Commons were then examining into his management, and we had actually before us the City business and it seemed to me a prejudicing the matter which we were to examine, and on which for ought we knew an impeachment might come up the next day, nor could I come into an address to her Majesty to continue him lest it might give a precedent to the Commons to address against him, as it actually did, for before they seemed and indeed promised only to make a representation of their grievances, and humbly lay them before her Majesty, and refer themselves to her goodness for redress, but the Lords proceedings put them out of all patience, and made them conclude, that it was no more a fault in them to address to remove him, than in the Lords to continue him.

Neither did I like the handle taken to bring this matter before the Lords. It was thus, one Crow, as I think his name is, was by motion called before the House and gave evidence that sometime in August

[1] According to the Whigs Archdeacon Percival was guilty of fomenting a disastrous riot during the Dublin election, exciting to excesses 'a party already influenced by hot liquors' (*Mr. Molesworth's Preface, with Historical and Political Remarks, to which is added a True State of his Case with respect to the Irish Convocation*, London, 1714).

[2] The Lower House of Convocation represented to the House of Lords that Molesworth was guilty of profanity in designing to represent Convocation as a seditious body.

[3] When the proceedings with regard to the election of civic officers in the city of Dublin was under consideration in the House of Lords, two peers were sent, while the House sat, to bring the minute books from the Council Chamber.

[4] In an address conveying this vote to the Queen the Lords praised Phipps, and asked her not to believe reports in his disfavour.

last, one Nuttall, discoursing and indeed bantering with a child, spoke to the child scandalous words of the Lord Chancellor, which I suppose you have seen.[1] It appeared by the man's confession that he owed money to this Nuttall, and that he had a suit, then depending before my Lord Chancellor. In my own opinion these circumstances were such that they could not justly found such votes, besides I thought Nuttall ought to have been called and heard what he could say for himself, which could not be obtained. For my own part I know no wisdom but truth and honesty if these support me well and good, but if not it will be my wisdom patiently to submit to the will of God, which has been the method I have taken all my life, and I hope no temptation shall ever prevail with me to forsake it in my old age.

I cou'd never understand the policy of Governours taking on them selves the faults or odium of their Servants, and there are many examples where it has produced ill consequences.

As to the sherrifs calling in the guard to assist them when oppressed by a Mobb, I am not lawier enuff to say anything to it but I think there was something like it done in suppressing a Mobb when I was last in London. only not 13: Soldiers were wounded before they shot, and a great part of the Crowd were [not] Papists, that had nothing to do there.

If you have a mind to see the depositions taken in the Lords' House, or the votes, let me know and those and such other papers as I think may be for your diversion shall be sent you.

I told you nobody can answer for a House of Commons, nor can I now engage they will give money, I believe if they sit again which I do not expect, they will make a more regular and I hope, more mannerly representation of their grievances, but hope likewise they will not be so far enemies to themselves as to deny money.

If you had seen what I have done, you would not wonder that what is done here is imputed to one man.[2]

---

[1] The reference is to needless and absurd consideration given by the Lords to an alleged puerile conversation between a certain Richard Nuttall and a child three years old.

[2] i.e. Sir Constantine Phipps.

Sir Constantine Phipps to Swift

Dublin 15 Jany 1713[-14.]

Dear Sr

Many of my letters from London tell me how much I am obliged to you for your friendly sollicitation on my Sons behalf, wch will be always remembered by us both wth the same Gratitude as if it had succeeded.[1] I had congratulations from the Duke of Ormonde, my Ld Bolingbroke, & others, on acct of my Sons have the place, for they sent me word it was actually don & severall other persons had Letters of it & our friends were extreamly rejoyced at the well timing of it & it was a great addition to the mortification of the Whigs & the disappointment will be a cause of great joy to them. but in this & in all other things I submit to the Judgmt of my Superiors who know best wht is fit to be don. As to looking out for any thing else for my Son there is nothing else here that I know is fit for him & if any thing worth his having falls in England, it will be dispos'd of before I can have notice of it.

We are told by every body, that the rest of our vacant Bishopricks[2] will be fill'd to our Satisfaction. If they are you must be one of them. But if you are resolv'd that you will not yet Episcopari there give me leave to recommend to you an affair of my Ld Abercorns wch is that you would consent to the Agreemt the Vicars Chorals have made wth him for renewing his Lease[3] I am inform'd there are some misunderstandings between you. tis very unhappy there should be any difference between two such sure & great friends to the Common Cause I do assure you, we are very much obliged to my Ld Abercorn for his great service in these times of difficulty he is as good a Friend as any in the world and as bad an enemy, and I am very sure if you would make him a Compliment & oblige him in this matter you would gain an entire true friend of him for the future & oblige a great many of your Friends here who have all a great value & esteem for him.

I heartily congratulate you on her Majesty's Recovery[4] & the good effect it has had in uniting our friends that together with the Resolu-

---

[1] Phipps to Swift, 9 Nov. 1713.
[2] Raphoe, Kilmore, Ardagh, and Derry.
[3] Swift to Worrall, 31 Dec. 1713.
[4] After the election, but before the meeting of her last Parliament, the Queen

tion that is taken to support the Church Interest will, without doubt in a little time render all things easy & quiet in both kingdoms. though as yet our Whigs here are as obstinate & perverse as ever the Commons are resolv'd they will give no money bill till I am remov'd & the Aldermen will not own my Ld Mayor nor proceed to any Election notwithstanding the opinion of all the Judges here, & of the Attorney Generall & all the Queen's Counsel (except Sir Joseph Jekyl)[1] in England.[2]

I wish you many happy New years & should be very proud to receive your Commands here being with the utmost sincerity and esteem | Your most obedient | humble servt |

Con. Phipps

Endorsed by Swift: Ld Chanc^llr Ireld | Jany. 15th 1713

4804

The Earl of Anglesey to Swift

Dublin, Jan. 16, 1713–14.

Mr Dean[3]

You judged extremly right of me that I shou'd with great Pleasure receive wt you tell me, that my endeavours to serve Her Majestie in this Kingdom are agreeable to my Ld T— & the rest of the Ministers: I have formerly so freely expressed to You the honor I must always have for his Lordship, that I cannot explain my self more

fell dangerously ill. While at Christmas she lay between life and death at Windsor Bolingbroke was in attendance. The Tories were in despair; the Whigs pleasurably excited. Temporarily the Queen recovered (*H.M.C., Portland MSS.* v. 374–6, 381).

[1] Called to the bar in 1687; a persistent Whig; he was knighted in 1700; and in 1717 he became Master of the Rolls. Satirized by Pope in 'Epilogue to the Satires', Dialogue I, pp. 38–40.

[2] On a fresh representation the English law officers agreed that the Lord Mayor of Dublin could remain in office for another year.

[3] The writer of this letter, Arthur Annesley, succeeded his brother John as fifth Earl of Anglesey. He was a Fellow of Magdalene College, Cambridge, and represented the University in Parliament, 1702–10. He was Joint Vice-Treasurer and Treasurer at War in Ireland, 1710–16. His family connexions with that country, his ability, and his Tory convictions led to the expectancy of his appointment as Lord Lieutenant. The hope was frustrated by the death of Queen Anne (*Poems,* p. 978 n.). He is frequently mentioned in *The Journal to Stella;* and Swift often dined with him. He died in 1737.

fully on that subject. But, what his Lordship has already done for the Church and the Church Interest here, and what we have assurance will soon be done, will give his Lordship so entire a command in the affections of all honest men here (which are not a few) that I am persuaded, he will soon find Ireland an easy part of the administration. for it is my firm opinion, that steady and vigorous measures will so strengthen the Hands of our Friends in both Kingdoms that after the efforts of Despair (which never last long) are over Her Majestie, & Her Ministers will receive but little trouble from the Faction either on this or on your side of the Water. You are very kind to us in your good Offices for Mr Phipps, because a mark of Favour so seasonably, as at this time, conferred on Ld Chanc's son will have a much greater Influence & reach farther than his Lordship's Person. I am preparing for my journey. And I hope I shall be able to lay such a State of this Kingdom before my Ld Treasurer, as may prevent future Disappointments when it shal be thought necessary to hold a Parliam^t. If this Parlmt is not to sit after, the present prorogation, I do think, were I with you, I cou'd offer some reasons why the filling the vacant Bishopricks should be deferr'd for a little time. I praise God for his great Goodness in restoring Her Majestie to Her Health, the Blessing of wch, if we had no other way of knowing, we might learn from the mortification it has given a certain set of men here. I shal trouble you with no Compliments, because I hope soon to tell you how much | I am Dear S^r | Yrs |

Anglesey

Endorsed by Swift: Ld Anglesey | Jany. 16. 1713–14

Rothschild[1]

Swift to Archdeacon Walls

London. Feb. 2^d; 1713

S^r

I have some Letters of yours to acknowledge, and a great deal of thanks to give you for your great love of my Affairs. I shall be glad if you think it convenient, to begin paying my first-Fruits, for the sooner I am out of debt, the better, and if you paid the Bp of Dromore 100^{ll} to begin with. I came yesterday from Winds^r with L^d T^r, and

[1] Previously in the possession of Sir John Murray. Since 1935 in Lord Rothschild's Library.

thought the 4 Bishop^ks1 would have been disposed of; but he sd
nothing to me so I conceive other Business stopt it. We are here in
odd Circumstances. Few of the Whigs will allow the Queen to be
alive, or at best that she can live a Month. She yesterday writ a
Letter to the Ld Mayor concerning these Reports[2] which I suppose
will be printed in the Gazette of to day (for I write this in the morning) Our Stocks are fallen 6 or 7 per cent, and it is a plain Argumt
how much they would fall if she really had dyed. She is now very
well, Sate in Council long on Sunday, and signed above 40 Papers
yesterday for L^d T^r3 and I hope she will be in Toun by the 16 at the
opening of the Parlmt.[4] I have done all I could for Mr Manley;[5] I
have had abundance of ill will by being his Friend. I durst not ask
directly to continue him; but that he and his Family might not
starve. I s^d a great deal of this to L^d T^r a fortnight ago, when I was
with him alone in his Coach going to Winds^r, in so much that when
at Supper there, severall were wishing to have him out; L^d T^r s^d
openly, the Dean is not of your Opinion &c. I have staved it off (as
I believe) but it is impossible to think, that he can hold it; and he
would have been out 2 years ago, if I had not battled for him. Y^r
Argum^ts are pure ones; he has lost a kind Brother &c: Why his
Brother[6] was a Beast and did him ten times more harm than good.

---

[1] Raphoe, Derry, Kilmore, and Ardagh. The possibility of preferment was in
Swift's mind.

[2] In this letter the Queen announced her intention of opening Parliament in
person, and expressed her hope that the citizens of London would put a stop to
those malicious rumours which prejudiced the public credit and tranquillity. In
writing to the Queen, Bolingbroke informed her that the conduct of the Whigs
at that time displayed 'the ingratitude and disloyalty' that 'they always had at
heart'.—Ball.

[3] Lord Treasurer, Harley.

[4] Parliament met on the 16th of the month; but the formal opening by the
Queen did not take place till 2 Mar.

[5] Stella's friendship with Isaac Manley, Postmaster-General in Ireland, in
whose house she took her place at card parties, induced Swift to regard him
leniently, although he was an active Whig, and was suspected by the Tories of
illegally intercepting letters. See *Journal*, pp. 12, n. 6, 29, 483; *Bath MSS.*
i. 244–5. Manley succeeded in retaining his position until superannuated, and
died in Dublin in 1735.

[6] The brother was John Manley, M.P. for Bossiney borough. He had drawn
his cousin, Mrs. Mary de la Rivière Manley, author of *The New Atlantis*, into a
false marriage, while his wife was living. Swift's characterization of him as 'a
Beast' was probably due to his knowledge of this misdemeanour. He had died
quite recently.

London. Feb 11ª / 14 1713

My Affairs not suffering me to return to Ireld as soon as I intended, I must desire the favour of you, to renew my Licence of Absence for half a year longer, and I will order my Agent Mr Parvisol to attend you with the Charges of it. I think you told me that England was not expressed in the Licence of Absence, of which I am glad, because I would not be limited in point of Place. The Qu— was very well on Monday noon last, & on the Birthday entertained Company above 3 hours. We are all doing as well as we can, and I hope the Effects will make you approve our Management. Dury and Ossay were disposed of last Monday, as I suppose you must know, the rest are yet deferred though expected every week, but there are some Difficulties, we I may tell you 6 Months hence, I wish our Friends of Ireld both here and there would be a little more uncnanimous in their Churches, and some of them more Charitable. It is impossible to please them all. You see I write in a most cursory Style, but you may guess the Reason. I hope the Qu will be in Town in a Week. I am

Your most obedient
humble servt.
J: Swift.

Pray burn this, & let me
know you have received it.

Swift to Joshua Dawson. 11 February 1713

You know Mr Manley has been the most violent Party-man in Ireld, and what can be s^d in behalf of such a Man:—My Service to Gossip Doll: I hope my God-child is well—. . .¹

Address: To | The Reverend Mr Archdeacon Walls | at his House in Queen Street | over against the Hospital | Dublin | Ireland

Frank: E. Lewis.

Postmark: 2 FE

Rothschild

Swift to Joshua Dawson

London Febr 11th 17$\frac{14}{13}$

S^r2

My Affairs not suffering me to return to Ireld as soon as I intended, I must desire the Favor of You, to renew My Letters of Absence for half a year longer, and I will order My Agent Mr Parvisol to attend you with the Charges of it.³ I think you told me that *England* was not expressed in the Letters of Absence, of which I am glad; because I would not be limited in point of Place.⁴ The Qu— was very well on Monday now last, and on Her Birthday entertaind Company above 3 hours. We are all doing as well as we can, and I hope the Effects⁵ will make you approve our Management. Derry and Ossory were disposed of last Monday,⁶ as I suppose you must know, the rest are yet deferred though expected every week, but there are some difficultyes, which I may tell you 6 Months hence,

¹ Two lines are torn off here.

² A facsimile of this letter appeared in the *Autographic Mirror* for 1865, the text differing slightly from the original. Ball states that his text was taken from Swift's autograph, then in the possession of Mrs. Lambart of 66 Park Mansions, Knightsbridge, London. It was sold at Sotheby's, 24 May 1938, Lot 559, and is now in Lord Rothschild's Library, No. 2285.

³ Dignitaries of the church and civil officials were obliged to obtain licence for absence from Ireland. This involved payment of fees to Dawson as permanent secretary. When leaving Ireland Swift had paid £5. 19s. 1d. for his licence.

⁴ Ball suggests that Swift may have had in mind 'the need of refuge if the authorship of *The Publick Spirit of the Whigs*, which was published on the opening of Parliament, became known'. This may, perhaps, be considered unlikely.   ⁵ Effects] efforts *Ball.*

⁶ The bishopric of Derry was filled by the translation of John Hartstonge from Ossory; and in his room Thomas Vesey, Bishop of Killaloe, and eldest son of Archbishop Vesey, was appointed.

I wish our Friends of Ireld both here and there would be a little more unanimous in their Characters, and some of them more Charitable. It is impossible to please them all. You see I write in a most cursory Style but you may guess the Reasons. I hope the Qu will be in Town in a Week. I am | Your most obedient | humble Servt |

J: Swift.

Pray burn this, & let me know you have received it.

Address: To Joshua Dawson Esqr | at the Castle of | Dublin | Ireland

4804

The Earl of Oxford to Swift

Wensday[1]
night [3 March 1713–14.]

I have heard that some honest men who are very innocent, are under troble touching a Printed pamphlet. a friend of mine, an obscure person, but charitable, puts the enclosed Bill in y^r hands to answer such exigencys as their case may immediatly require. and i find he wil do more, this being only for the present.

If this comes safe to your hands it is enough.

Endorsed by Swift: Ld Tres^r, Oxford to | me in a Counterfeit hand | with the Bill when the | Printers were prosecutd by | the House Lds for a Pamphlet. | Mar. 13th 1713–14.
and: Lett^r with Bill 100^ll. | Rx Mar. 14.[2] 17$\frac{14}{13}$
and at the head of the letter. I was then in London

[1] From 22 Oct. 1713 onwards Steele's forthcoming pamphlet was heralded by successive announcements. At length on 19 Jan. 1713–14 *The Crisis* was published. Swift ridiculed the absurdity of continuous advertisement and protracted delay. See *Poems*, pp. 179–80. Swift's reply to Steele's *Crisis* appears to have taken him more trouble and time than he anticipated. At last, on 23 Feb., *The Publick Spirit of the Whigs* appeared. For *The Crisis* and two other pamphlets Steele was in trouble with the House of Commons; and now angry complaint came from the Lords against Swift's pamphlet on account of paragraphs in which he had spoken contemptuously of the Scottish nobility and the union of the two kingdoms. The peers voted the pamphlet a 'false, malicious, and factious Libel'. The Ministry recognized that a breach of parliamentary privilege had been committed. John Morphew, the publisher, and John Barber, the printer, were taken into custody; and a proclamation was issued for the discovery of the author. The first edition of the pamphlet was withdrawn and another substituted from which the objectionable passages were removed. See *Prose Works*, ed. Temple Scott, v. 309–57; ed. Davis, viii. 27–68.

[2] Doubtless a mistake for 4 Mar.

The Earl of Peterborough to Swift

March the 5th [O.S. 22 February] 1713–14.

Queries for Dr. Swift next Saturday at Dinner.

Whether any great man, or Minister have favour the Earle of Peterborow with one single Line since he left England,[1] for as yett he has not received one word from any of them, nor his friend of St Patrick?

Whether, if they doe not writte, till they know what to writte, he shall ever hear from them?

Whether any thing can be more unfortunate, then to be overcome when strongest, outwitted having more witt, & baffled having most money?[2]

Whether betwixt two Stools The . . . to the ground (Reverend Dean) be not a good old proverb, which may give subject for dayly meditation, & mortification?

I send Thee Lazy Scribbler a letter from the Extremity of the Earth,[3] where I passe my Time, admiring the humility & patience of that power heretofore so Terrible, and the new scene which we see, To Witt, The most Christian King waiting with so great resignation, and respect to know The Emperor's pleasure as to Peace or warr.

Where I reflect with admiration upon the politicks of those, who, breaking with the old Allies, dare not make use of the new ones, who pulling down the old Rubbish & Structure, doe not erect a new fabrick upon solid foundations, but this is not so much to the purpose, for in the world of the moon, provided Toasting continue, the Church, & State can be in noe Danger.

But, alas in this un merry Countrey, where we have Time to think, and are under the necessity of thinking, where impiously we make use of reason, without a blind resignation to providence, the bottle, or chance, what opinion think you we have of the present

---

[1] In the latter part of 1711 Peterborough was abroad busying himself at Frankfort with matters outside his instructions, and was moved to Italy on a nominal mission. In Jan. 1712–13 he was back in England in serious ill health (*Journal*, 14 Mar.). In November he was sent as ambassador extraordinary to the Duke of Savoy, now King of Sicily. The accession of George I brought to an end his official career. The last surviving letter from Swift to Peterborough, prior to Mar. 1713–14, dates as far back as 4 May 1711.

[2] Villars and Eugene negotiated the peace between Louis and the Emperor Charles which was signed at Rastadt in Mar. 1714.   [3] i.e. Sicily.

management in the refined parts of the world, where there are just motives of fear, when neither Steadinesse nor conduct appears, & when the Evil seems to come on apace, can it be believed, that Extraordinary remedies are not thought of.

Heavens what is our fate, what might have been our portion, & what doe we see in the Age we Live in, France & England, the Kings of Spain, & Sicily perplext, & confounded by a head strong youth,[1] one who has lost so many Kingdoms by pride & folly, and all these powerfull nations att a gaze, ignorant of their Destiny, not capable of forming a Scheme which they can maintain against a Prince who has neither Shipps, money, nor Conduct, some of the ministers assisted, & supported power, others with a Parliament att their disposal, & the most inconsiderable of them, with the Indies att their Tayle.

And what doe I see in the center as it were of ignorance & bigottry, The first request of a Parlament to their King is to employ effectuall means against the increase of Priests The idle Devourers of the fatt of the Land,[2] we see churches shutt up by order from the Pope,[3] sett open by Draggons to the general content of the people, To conclude it fell out that one of your acquaintance[4] found him self att a great table, the only unexcommunicated Person by his Holinesse, The rest of the company Eating, & Toasting under anathemas, with the Courage of a Hardened Heretick.

Look upon the Piece I send you, soe neverthelesse what a sneaking Figure he makes att the foot of the Parson,[5] who could expect this from him, but He thinkes, resolves, & executes.

If you can guesse from whence this comes, adresse your letter to him. a Messieurs Rafnell et Fretti Sacerdotti Genoa.

March the 5th.

Address: For the Reverend Dr Swift Dean of | St. Patrick.
Endorsed by Swift: E of Peterborow | From Sicily Mar | 5th—1714
   and: Ld Peterborow | Rx about May 1st 1714. | Answered 20th.

[1] Charles XII of Sweden.

[2] King Victor Amadeus revived the Monarchia Sicula, which practically excluded the Pope from any authority over the Church in Sicily.

[3] Pope Clement XI answered the King's establishment of the Monarchia by bann and interdict.

[4] It has been suggested that Berkeley, whom Peterborough had taken with him as chaplain, was the person indicated; but he remained in Italy while Peterborough went to Sicily, and the allusion is probably to Peterborough himself.

[5] Ball suggests that this was probably a cartoon upon the King's declining papal investiture on ascending the throne.

Rothschild[1]

Swift to Archdeacon Walls

London. Mar. 6th 17$\frac{14}{13}$

I think I writt to you since I heard from You; I am now under a great deal of uneasy Business, which I hope to get over;[2] in the mean Time, I must desire you to step to Mr Dawson at the Castle, and let him know I writt to him above three weeks ago to renew my Lettr of absence[3] which ends just about the End of February, the half year being then just out. I desired he would let me know, he had received my Letter, and had taken out a new Licence for another half Year; but I have not heard from him. I likewise writt to Parvisoll with Orders to pay Mr Dawson the Charges of the Licence. Parvisol has writt to me this Post but said nothing of that Affair: Pray if it be not done already, get it done now, and pay Mr Dawson. I had a short Lettr from Dr Raymd just now; I will write to him soon. I am in mighty hast, but however give my Service to our Doll, & my God-child | Yrs |

Jonath: Swift.

Address: To the Reverend, Mr Archdeacon | Walls, at his House in Queen-street | over against the Hospitall in | Dublin | Ireland
Postmark: ? MR
Later endorsement: Dr Swift | March 6th 17$\frac{13}{14}$

[1] Previously in the possession of Sir John Murray. Since 1935 in Lord Rothschild's library.

[2] On the previous day Morphew and Barber had been before the House of Lords, and on the motion of Lord Wharton the examination of Barber had been adjourned to the next day, when nine of his employees were ordered to be in attendance. The proceedings were, however, then abruptly closed, on the Earl of Mar informing the House that he had instituted criminal proceedings against Barber (*Journals of the House of Lords* and *Parliamentary History*, vi. 1262). It is to this incident Swift alludes in the lines:

> While innocent, he scorns ignoble Flight;
> His watchful Friends preserve him by a Sleight.

Poems, p. 196.

[3] See ii. 11.

Rothschild[1]

Swift to Archdeacon Walls

London Mar. 27. 1714

I had yrs of the 6th instant, and am much obliged to you for yr Care with Parvisol. As for the Bishops goods,[2] I can say nothing, if our Dol, and goody Stoit, and the St Mary Ladyes would consult about what I should take, and the Price, I would be content, & leave it to them, but the St Mary Ladyes being not in Toun, if our Doll & Stoit would do it alone, I am satisfied. what can I do more at this Distance, I am teazing about yr Bishoprick;[3] but you rail at one another so, that it is hard to settle; and besides ⟨we are not in a humour to mind you: we are in a confounded⟩ situation at present; fit only to talk of some years hence by the fire side.[4] Y^r Schemes about yr self are all Spleenatick,[5] is there no place on Earth to fitt you but Mala—what dy call it.[6] I know not whether Jephson[7] will be dropt or no . . .; as Meath, Tuam, &c. but we must divide the Bishopricks, . . . My Service to Gossip Dol, goody Stoit & Catherine.

Address: [To] the Rev^d | Mr Archdeacon Walls | over against the bluecoat | Hospital in | Dublin
Frank: C Ford   *Postmark:* 27 MR
Later endorsement: Dr Swift | March 27th 1714

[1] Rothschild No. 2281 (8). The paper is torn affecting the address, but not the text of the letter, which is, however, in part scored out. The portion enclosed within angular brackets can be deciphered with reasonable certainty. Later portions, as indicated, are illegible.

[2] Stearne was still in occupation of the Deanery.

[3] yr Bishoprick] the bishoprics.—Ball. Swift certainly wrote the singular. The bishoprics were Raphoe, Derry, Kilmore, and Ardagh.

[4] For Swift's considered opinion, 'by the fire side', of the state of affairs, see his *Enquiry into the Behaviour of the Queen's Last Ministry.* He admits that 'all agreed to blame and lament' Oxford's 'Mysterious and procrastinating Manner in acting; which the State of Affairs at that Time could very ill admit'. Furthermore, the differences between Oxford and Bolingbroke 'split the Court into Parties' (*Prose Works*, ed. Davis, viii. 152).

[5] Spleenatick] splendid—Ball. The word is certainly 'Spleenatick'.

[6] The reference is to Malahidert, a parish adjoining Castleknock. The prebend was then held by the Hon. John Moore, and Walls probably hoped that in the changes then pending Moore might be promoted and he succeed to the stall.

[7] William Jephson, who held the deanery of Lismore for twenty years, was one of the persons suggested for preferment to the episcopal bench, but his promotion was opposed by Lord Anglesey (*Portland MSS.* v. 403). The portion of the obliterated sentences which remain show that Swift was referring to his scheme of severing Ardagh from Kilmore (i. 419).

Lady Betty Butler to Swift

19 April 1714

most provoking unkle[1]

if I was inclined to beleive good news, I shou'd be very glad since I'm quite out of your memory, that you are going post out of yr wits, but that, was a fine fetch indeed to solve yr Lasyness, I expected you wou'd have given me a few cautions of this dangerous place which considering my great Beauty might be necesary, I have been so good to deliver yr mesage, but if my mother will take my advice she wont care a fig for yr love, perhaps you may think me pert to say this to my uncle, but I hate to be particular and tis the fashion to show the most disrespect | to those that may Claim the greatest Deference

my service to   Aprill the 19
Doctor pratt[2]
    I am yr afronted | neice |

Eliz Butler

Endorsed by Swift on second verso: Lady Betty Butler | Ap[r] 19. 1714

4804

The Duchess of Ormonde to Swift

Ap: the 24th 1714

Brother

I shou'd sooner have thank't you for yr letter, but that I hope't to have seen you here by this time.[3] you can't imagine how much I

---

[1] This, which appears to be the only extant letter from Lady Betty Butler to Swift, was discovered in the Public Record Office, S.P., 63/370, by Dr. Irvin Ehrenpreis. The curious form of address is explained by the fact that Lady Betty Butler's father, the Duke of Ormonde, was a fellow member with Swift of the Brothers' Club. The Duchess found pleasure in a pretence of relationship between herself and members of the family with Swift. She was his 'sister', her daughter, his 'niece'. Lady Betty was on visiting terms with the Vanhomrighs, and appears to have entertained sincerely friendly feelings for Swift. She died unmarried in 1750.

[2] Dr. Benjamin Pratt, Provost of Trinity College, Dublin, who enjoyed the social life of London.

[3] The Duchess may have been in attendance on the Queen at Kensington, or

am greived wⁿ I find people I wish well to, run counter to their own interest, and give their enemyes such advantages, by being so hard upon their freinds, as to conclude, if they are not wth out fault, they are not to be supported, or scarce convers't wth,[1] Fortune's a very prety Gentlewoman, but how soon she may be chang'd, no body can tell, freting her wth the seeing all she dos for people, only makes 'em despise her, may make her so sick, as to alter her complection, but I hope our freinds will find her constant in spight of all they do, to shock her, & remember the story of the Arrows, that were very easily broke, singly, but wⁿ tyed up close together, no strength of man cou'd hurt 'em,[2] but that you may never feel any ill consequences from w^tever may happen, are the sincere wishes of | Brother | y^{rs} wth all sisterly | Affection

Endorsed by Swift at head of letter: Dutchess of Ormonde
On verso of second leaf: Dutchess of Ormonde | Ap^r 24. | 1714

P.R.O., State Papers of Ireland

The Rev. John Geree to Swift

Letcombe, 24 April 1714.

Mr Dean[3]

Yesterday was Sennight arriv'd here very safe the noble Present of Wine You were pleas'd to make us: in a Flask of wch my Wife &

she may have been writing from Richmond, where Ormonde then owned the Lodge which later became a royal residence. In the *Journal*, 17 June 1712, Swift alludes to dining with the Duchess at Richmond, which he calls by its earlier name 'Sheen'.

[1] While the Queen lay ill, the report of her death seeming imminent, Swift used his best endeavours to cultivate the 'strictest Friendship' between Oxford and 'the General', that is Ormonde, for the 'Advantage such an Union must be to her Majesty's Service' (*Prose Works*, ed. Davis, viii. 155).

[2] Swift's poem 'The Faggot' may have drawn its hint from this letter. See *Poems*, pp. 188–91.

[3] The Rev. John Geree, who is said to have lived 'in Sir William Temple's family' (*Portland MSS*. vii. 186), became a fellow of Corpus Christi College, Oxford, and was presented by his college to the living of Letcombe Bassett, Berkshire. Despairing of the political situation Swift retired there in the summer of 1714, reaching the rectory, apparently, on 3 June. He remained there till he left for Ireland on 16 Aug. See *Poems*, pp. 191–2. In 1734 Geree was appointed a canon of Hereford. He died in 1761. *Alumni Oxonienses*, E.S., ii. 558.

I drank your Health, after it was a little settled, & think it to be so
extraordinary good, that we shall readily comply wth your Orders not
to be too prodigal of it, nor produce it to any but our best Freinds.
We return You our most humble Thanks for it; & wish You would
give us Leave to take it for an Earnest, that You intend Yourself to
follow in a little Time, and honour our poor Habitation wth your
Presence: where You will have a Horse, & Garden, and pretty good
Study of Books, & the Master & Mistress entirely at your Service:
Tho' I doubt that, at last, the Happiness of entertaining such a Guest
as Mr Dean, must be owing to (w^t I dare not wish for) the Divisions
& Mis-understandings at Court, wch may drive him into these Parts.
I am, S^r, extreamly oblig'd to you for so frankly repeating the Assurances You formerly gave me of your Readiness & Desire to do me
some good Offices wth the Ld Chancellor; tho' I purposely declin'd
any Sollicitations of this kind, for fear of being troublesome; especially since I was very well assur'd, that w^never a favourable Opportunity sh^d offer itself, You w^d not be wanting to my Interests.[1] In the
mean time, S^r, I sh^d be much oblig'd to You, if You w^d please to
encourage my School, by recommending some young Gentlemen
hither. I w^d certainly take all the Care of them I could: & I think I
might undertake to further them more in their Learning for the
Time, than others do at the common, or ev'n the great Schools;
partly on Acc^t of the Method I take with them: & partly, of the
small Number I propose to have the charge of: wch being but ten or
twelve at the most, I shall have leisure to consider every One's
Capacity, & apply my self to it accordingly; making Things plain
to slower Apprehensions, & setting forward those of more quick &
pregnant Parts, as fast as their Genius will carry them. I hope the
Mention of my taking young Gentlemen to Board, will not frighten
you from making this the Place of your Residence, w^n ever You
think fit to retire: Since I am confident you w^d find no manner of
inconvenience from those I have already, wch are only four (besides
a Nephew of mine) & those very orderly & good:[2] And I want only
the Revenue, wch more w^d supply me with, to make such Conveniences about me, that my Number (when compleat) sh^d not be offensive. And therefore I hope that this Consideration will be no Bar to

---

[1] Harcourt promised Swift 'the first convenient Living' for Geree (*Journal*,
p. 585).
[2] For an account of Swift's manner of spending his time, when at Letcombe,
see Pope to Arbuthnot, 11 July 1714 (Sherburn, i. 233).

the Happiness of seeing You here: & that no other may be so, is the hearty wish of | S^r | Y^r most obedient, and | oblig'd, & most humble Servt |

John Geree

My Wife, S^r, presents | her humble Service to You
Letcomb Apr. 24, | 1714.

Address: To | The Rev^d the Dean | of St Patrick's | P^{e}sent

Deane Swift 1765

Swift to the Earl of Peterborough

London, May 18, 1714.

My Lord,

I had done myself the honour of writing to your Excellency, above a month before yours of March the 5th came to my hands. The Saturdays' dinners have not been resumed since the Queen's return from Windsor; and I am not sorry, since it became so mingled an assembly, and of so little use either to business or conversation:[1] so that I was content to read your quieries to our two great friends. The Treasurer stuck at them all; but the Secretary acquitted himself of the first, by assuring me he had often written to your Excellency.

I was told, the other day, of an answer you made to somebody abroad, who inquired of you the state and dispositions of our Court: That you could not tell, for you had been out of England a fortnight. In your letter, you mention the world of the Moon, and apply it to England; but the moon changes but once in four weeks. By both these instances, it appears you have a better opinion of our steadiness than we deserve; for I do not remember, since you left us, that we have continued above four days in the same view, or four minutes with any manner of concert. I assure you, my Lord, for the concern I have for the common cause, with relation to affairs both at home

---

[1] It seems to be implied here that Peterborough was an early attendant of the Saturday Club dinners, although in the *Journal*, 9 Jan. 1712–13, Swift says: 'I was of the Originall Clubb when onely poor Lord Rivers, Ld Keeper, & Ld Bolinbr came.' In time 'other Rabble' intruded. See also *Memoirs relating to that Change in the Queen's Ministry* (*Prose Works*, ed. Davis, viii. 124), where Swift tells us that as the company grew more numerous the meetings 'became of less consequence; and ended only in drinking and general conversation'.

and abroad, and from the personal love I bear to our friends in power, I never led a life so thoroughly uneasy as I do at present.[1] Our situation is so bad, that our enemies could not, without abundance of invention and ability, have placed us so ill, if we had left it entirely to their management. For my own part, my head turns round; and after every conversation, I come away just one degree worse informed than I went. I am glad, for the honour of our nation, to find by your Excellency's letter, that some other Courts have a share of frenzy, though not equal, nor of the same nature with ours. The height of honest men's wishes at present is, to rub off this session; after which, no body has the impudence to expect, that we shall not immediately fall to pieces: Nor is anything I write the least secret, even to a Whig footman.

The Queen is pretty well at present; but the least disorder she has, puts all in alarm; and, when it is over, we act as if she were immortal. Neither is it possible to persuade people to make any preparations against an evil day. There is a negotiation now in hand, which, I hope, will not be abortive: The States-General are willing to declare themselves fully satisfied with the peace and Queen's measures, &c., and that is too popular a matter to slight. It is impossible to tell you whether the Prince of Hanover intends to come over or no. I should think the latter, by the accounts I have seen; yet our adversaries continue strenuously to assert otherwise, and very industriously give out, that the Lord Treasurer is at the bottom; which has given some jealousies not only to his best friends, but to some I shall not name; yet I am confident they do him wrong. This formidable journey is the perpetual subject both of Court and coffee-house chat.[2]

[1] In *An Enquiry into the Behaviour of the Queen's Last Ministry* Swift recounts the difficulty he had in prevailing upon the Queen, through Oxford, to fill the vacancies in the Irish bishoprics. Oxford told him that he had tried frequently without effect, 'and that He found His Credit wholly at an End' (*Prose Works*, ed. Davis, viii. 159).

[2] On 12 Apr. 1714 Schütz, the Hanoverian representative, abruptly demanded from Harcourt a writ summoning the Electoral Prince, afterwards George II, as the Duke of Cambridge, to take his seat in Parliament. That night a cabinet council was held in the Queen's presence, who was furiously angry. Bolingbroke played up to the Queen supporting her view that the writ should be refused. Oxford and the other Ministers realized the legality of the claim and the writ was issued. The Elector George showed better understanding, repudiated the affair, and insisted on the recall of Schütz. Oxford had, however, lost all favour with the Queen (Trevelyan, *England under Queen Anne*, iii. 277–9).

Our mysterious and unconcerted ways of proceeding have, as it is natural, taught every body to be refiners, and to reason themselves into a thousand various conjectures. Even I, who converse most with people in power, am not free from this evil: And particularly, I thought myself twenty times in the right, by drawing conclusions very regularly from premises which have proved wholly wrong. I think this, however, to be a plain proof that we act altogether by chance; and that the game, such as it is, plays itself.

By the present enclosed in your Excellency's letter, I find the Sicilians to be bad delineators, and worse poets.[1] As sneakingly as the Prince looks at the Bishop's foot, I could have made him look ten times worse, and have done more right to the piece, by placing your Excellency there, representing your Mistress the Queen, and delivering the crown to the Bishop, with orders where to place it. I should like your new King very well, if he would make Sicily his constant residence, and use Savoy only as a commendam. Old books have given me great ideas of that island. I imagine every acre there worth three in England; and that a wise prince, in such a situation, would, after some years, be able to make what figure he pleased in the Mediterranean.

The Duke of Shrewsbury, not liking the weather on our side the water, continues in Ireland, although he formally took his leave there six weeks ago.[2] Tom Harley is every hour expected here, and writes me word, he has succeeded at Hanover to his wishes. Lord Strafford writes the same, and gives himself no little merit upon it.[3]

Barber the printer was, some time ago, in great distress, upon printing a pamphlet, of which evil tongues would needs call me the author: he was brought before your House, which addressed the Queen in a body, who kindly published a proclamation, with 300*l*. to discover.[4] The fault was, calling the Scots a fierce poor northern people. So well protected are those who scribble for the Government. Upon which, I now put one query to your Excellency, What has a man without employment to do among ministers, when he can neither serve himself, his friends, nor the public?

---

[1] The cartoon, or printed document, enclosed with Peterborough's letter of 5 Mar., O.S., 1714.

[2] Adverse winds delayed Shrewsbury's return to England.

[3] Thomas Harley, Oxford's cousin, had been sent to Hanover to assure that Court of the Government's good faith in respect to the succession. After the cabinet meeting, mentioned above, Oxford had sent him an admirably drafted letter. Lord Strafford was at The Hague.   [4] See p. 12, n. 1.

In my former letter, which I suppose was sent to Paris to meet you there, I gave you joy of the government of Minorca.[1] One advantage you have of being abroad, that you keep your friends; and I can name almost a dozen great men, who thoroughly hate one another, yet all love your Lordship. If you have a mind to preserve their friendship, keep at a distance; or come over and shew your power, by reconciling at least two of them; and remember, at the same time, that this last is an impossibility. If your Excellency were here, I would speak to you without any constraint; but the fear of accidents in the conveyance of the letter, makes me keep to generals. I am sure you would have prevented a great deal of ill, if you had continued among us; but people of my level must be content to have their opinion asked, and to see it not followed; although I have always given it with the utmost freedom and impartiality. I have troubled you too much; and as a long letter from you is the most agreeable thing one can receive, so the most agreeable return would be a short one. I am ever, with the greatest respect and truth, | my Lord, |

Your Excellency's | most obedient, and | most humble servant.

4804

Chiverton Charleton to Swift

22 May 1714.

Sir[2]

Hearing from honest John[3] that you still persist in your resolution of retiring into the country[4] I cannot but give you my thoughts of it, at the same time that I am sensible how intruding it may appear in me to trouble you with what I think; but you have an unlucky quality which exposes you to the forwardness of those who love you, I mean good nature from which, tho I did not alwaies suspect you guilty of it I now promise my self an Easy pardon, so that with out being in much pain as to the censure you may pass upon my

[1] Peterborough's appointment as Governor of Minorca had been announced in April. Owing to the death of the Queen he never assumed office.

[2] Chiverton Charleton held the office of Lieutenant of the Yeomen of the Guard. The postscript suggests that he had some connexion with the Ormonde family. He may have been writing from their Lodge at Richmond.

[3] i.e. John Barber.

[4] In despair at his inability to heal the differences between Oxford and Bolingbroke, Swift had by this time resolved to leave London.

assurance I shall go on gravely to tell you I am entirely against your design. I confess a just indignation at several things and particularly at the returns your services have met with may give you a disgust to the court and that retirement may afford a pleasing prospect to you who have lived so long in the hurry & have born so great a share of the load of business & the more so at this Juncture when the distraction among your friends is enuff to make any one sick of a Courtier's life. but on these very accounts you shou'd choose to stay and convince the world that you are as much above private resentment where the Publick is concerned, as you are incapable of being tyred out in the Service of your country and that you are neither afraid nor unwilling to face a storm in a good cause.

It is true, you have less reason, than any one I know, to regard what the world saies of you for I know none, to whom the world hath been more unjust, yet since the most generous revenge is to make the ungratefull appear yet more ungratefull you should still persecute the publick with fresh obligations; and the rather, because some there of a temper to acknowledge benefits, & it is to be hoped the rest may not alwaies continue stupid; at least (suppose the worst) the attempt to do good carries along with it a secret satisfaction, with which if you are not sensibly affected, I am at a loss how to account for many of your actions. I remember very well what you have sometimes said upon this subject, as if you were now grown useless &c. To which I have this to answer that tho your efforts are in vain to day, some unforeseen incident may make them otherwise to morrow & that should you by your absence lose any happy opportunity you will be the first to reproach your self with running away & be the last man in the world to pardon it. If I had denyed self-Interest to be at the bottom of all I have said, I know you wou'd think I had lyed villainously & perhaps not think amiss neither, for I still flatter my self with the continuance of that favour you have on many occasions been pleased to shew me & am vain enuff to fancy I should be a considerable loser if you were where I could not have an opportunity of clubbing my shilling with you now & then at *good Eating.* but as much as I am concerned on this account I am not so selfish to say what I have done if it were not my real opinion which whether you regard or not I cou'd not deny my self the satisfaction of speaking it & of assuring you that I am with the utmost sincerity & respect Sir | your most obliged, and | most faithfull servant |

                                 Ch. Charleton

ye 22ᵈ of May 1714

My Lady Duchesse I can answer for her, is very much your servant tho I have not her commands to say so, She is gone to see the Duke of Beaufort who is ill tis fear'd he cannot recover.¹ She went away this morning so early I have had no particular account how he is but am told he does nothing but doze. the messenger came to her at three in the morning & she went away immediateley afterwards.

Lady Betty² desires me to thank you for your letter & wou'd be glad, Since the Provost³ is graciously pleased to stay her Majesty's time, to know where it is he designs to stay.

Honest Townshend⁴ & I have the satisfaction to drink your health as often as we do drink together: whether you approve of your being toasted with the Bishop of London⁵ & such people I cannot tell but at present we have disposed you in the first list of Rank Tories.

A servant is just now come from the Duchesse of Ormonde and gives such an account of the Duke of Beaufort that tis thought he cannot possibly recover

Address: To | the Reverend Dean Swift
Endorsed by Swift: Mʳ Charleton | May 22. 1714
and: May. 22ᵈ. 1714 | Mʳ Ch— | On my intentions to | retire

B.M., Add. MS. 39839

Swift to Miss Esther Vanhomrigh

Upper Letcomb near Wantage in Berkshire.
Jun. 8. [1713] 1714⁶

You see that I am better than my Word, and write to you before I have been a week settled in the House where I am.⁷ I have not much

---

¹ Henry Somerset, 1684–1714, second Duke of Beaufort, nephew of the Duchess of Ormonde. He died in his thirty-first year through drinking a quantity of small beer after over-heating himself.

² Lady Betty, Ormonde's only surviving child.

³ Provost Pratt expected to receive one of the vacant bishoprics, but he was disappointed.

⁴ Not identified.

⁵ Bishop Robinson, the Utrecht plenipotentiary, had been in this year translated from Bristol to London.

⁶ The correct date is '1714'. Swift mistakenly wrote '1713'.

⁷ On Monday, 31 May, Swift left London and travelled to Oxford by coach.

news to tell you from hence, nor have I had one Line from any body since I left London; of which I am very glad. But to say the Truth, I believe I shall not stay here so long as I intended; I am at a Clergyman's house, an old Friend and Acquaintance, whom I love very well, but he is such a melancholy thoughtfull man partly from Nature, and partly by a solitary Life that I shall soon catch the Spleen from Him.[1] Out of Ease and Complaisance, I desire him not to alter any of his Methods for me; So, we dine exactly between twelve and one, at eight we have some Bread and Butter, and a Glass of Ale, and at ten he goes to Bed. Wine is a Stranger, except a little I sent him, of which one Evening in two, we have a Pint between us. His wife has been this Month twenty miles off at her Fathers, and will not return this ten days, I never saw her, and perhaps the House will be worse when she comes. I read all day or walk, and do not speak as many words as I have now writt, in three days. So that in short I have a mind to steal to Ireland, unless I find my self take more to this way of living, so different in every Circumstance from what I left. This is the first Syllable I have writt to any body since you saw me.[2] I shall be glad to hear from you, not as you are a Londoner but a Friend. For I care not threepence for News, nor have heard one Syllable since I am here, The Pretender or Duke of Cambridge[3] may both be landed and I never the wiser. But if the place were ten times worse, nothing shall make me return to Toun while Things are in the Situation I left them. I give a Guinnea a week for my Board, and can eat any thing. I hope you are in good Health and Humor. My Service to Moll—My Cold is quite gone.

A vous &c

There he stayed several days. On 3 June William Stratford, Canon of Christ Church, wrote to Edward Harley, Lord Oxford's son: 'The Dean of St. Patrick's came hither on Monday: . . . He was in the College on Tuesday, . . . He is gone to Mr. Gery's, who has a parsonage near Wantage.' And on 5 June he wrote: 'The Dean of St. Patrick's left not Oxford till Thursday morning' (*Portland MSS.* vii. 186).

[1] For the Rev. John Geree see p. 18, n. 3. The parish of Letcombe Bassett lies on the north side of the Berkshire Downs. To this day it is a comparatively remote spot. The chancel of the church dates from the twelfth century; but from the end of the thirteenth century onwards the building has undergone many changes. See *Victoria County Hist., Berkshire*, iv. 217–22.

[2] The first person to whom Swift wrote, after leaving the disturbed political scene, was Vanessa, a testimony to the continuance of their intimate friendship.

[3] The English title conferred on the Electoral Prince of Hanover, afterwards George II.

I send my Man 2 miles with this to the Post Toun so if there be a Letter by chance from you, I shall not be able to tell you so now. I hope our maid carryed you your Band box with the Papers and deeds

Address: To Mrs Esther Van-homrigh, at her | Lodgings over against the Surgeon's in | Great Rider Street, near St James's Street | London
Endorsed: 1st

4804

John Gay to Swift

London. June 8th [1714]

S^rI

Since you went out of Town my Lord Clarendon was appointed Envoy Extraordinary to Hanover in the room of Lord Paget,[2] and by making use of those Friends which I entirely owe to you, He hath accepted me for his Secretary. this day by appointment I met his Lordship at Mr Secretary Bromley's office, ⌐eer⌐[3] he then order'd me to be ready by Saturday. I am quite off ⌐from⌐ the Dutchesse of Monmouth.[4] Mr Lewis was very ready to serve ⌐me⌐ upon this occasion as was Dr Arbuthnot & Mr Ford. I am every day attending my Lord Treasurer for his Bounty in order to set me out, which he hath promised me upon the following Petition which I sent by Dr Arbuthnot.

[1] In the *Journal*, 14 May 1711, Swift refers to *The Present State of Wit*. This pamphlet, dated 3 May 1711 and signed J.G., was probably written by John Gay. Swift, though praised, was not wholly pleased for he took the author to be a Whig. He had only lately made the acquaintance of Gay, probably through Pope or one of the other friends mentioned in this letter.

[2] Edward Hyde (1661-1724), the third Earl of Clarendon, was Governor-in-Chief of New York, 1701-8. He was appointed Envoy Extraordinary to Hanover in place of Henry, seventh Baron Paget, who was unwilling to accept office until he received a step in the peerage. On 19 Oct. 1714, after the accession of George I, he was created Earl of Uxbridge.

[3] Part of the right hand of the sheet is frayed. Indicated by half brackets.

[4] Gay had been appointed secretary to the Duchess of Monmouth whose husband had been executed in 1685. Apparently she preferred using the forfeited honour instead of the title of Duchess of Buccleuch which she held in her own right.

The Epigrammatical Petition of John Gay.[1]

I'm no more to converse with the Swains
But go where fine People resort
One can live without Money on Plains,
But never without it at Court.

If when with the Swains I did Gambol
I arrayed me in silver and blue
When abroad & in Courts I shall ramble
Pray, my Lord, how much Money will do?

We had the Honour of the Treasurer's Company last Saturday when we sate upon Scriblerus.[2] Pope is in Town & hath brought with him the first Book of Homer.[3] I am this evening, to be at Mr Lewis's with the Provost Mr Ford Parnell & Pope. 'tis thought my Lord Clarendon will make but a short stay at Hanover. if 'twas possible, that any recommendation could be procur'd to make me more distinguish'd than ordinary during my Stay at that Court I should think myself very happy if you could contrive any Method to procure it. for I am told that their Civilitys very rarely descend so low as the[4] Secretary. I have all the reason in the World to acknowledge this as wholly owing to you, and the many favours I have receiv'd from you purely out of your Love for doing Good assures me you will not forget me in my absence; as for myself whether I am at home or abroad, Gratitude will always put me in mind of the Man to whom I owe so many Benefits

I am | Your most obliged | Humble Servt

J Gay

Address: For the Reverend Dr Swift Dean | of St Patricks.
Endorsed by Swift at head of letter: The Dean sent Gay abroad Gay
  Below address: Gay | Jun. 8. 1714

[1] This petition to Lord Oxford appeared, with a slight variant in the sixth line, in *Additions to the Works of Alexander Pope*, i. 104. See *Poetical Works of John Gay*, ed. G. C. Faber, p. 212.

[2] For the Scriblerus Club, of which Pope, Swift, Arbuthnot, Gay, and Parnell were members, see *Poems*, p. 184; and *Memoirs of the Extraordinary Life Works and Discoveries of Martinus Scriblerus*, ed. Charles Kerby-Miller.

[3] Pope's agreement with Bernard Lintot for a metrical translation of the *Iliad* was signed on 23 Mar. 1714; whereas the agreement for Tickell's rival translation was signed with Jacob Tonson on 31 May 1714. At the time this letter was written neither poet was near to a publication date. Twelve months were to pass before the two translations of the first book of the *Iliad* appeared. See *The Early Career of Alexander Pope*, George Sherburn, pp. 128–48.

[4] as the] as to the *Ball*.

John Barber to Swift

London, June. 8. 1714.

Dear S^r

I have inclos'd all the Letters that have come to my Hands: I saw my Lord Treasurer to day, who ask'd me where you were gone? I told his Lordship you were in Berkshire. He answer'd it is very well, I suppose I shall hear from him. My Lord Bol— was very merry with me upon your Journey, and hop'd the World would be the better for y^r Retirement; and that I should soon be the Midwife. The Schism Bill was read the 2^d time yesterday, and Committed for to morrow without a Division.[1] Every Body is in the greatest Consternation at your Retirement, and wonder at the Cause. Mr Gay is made Secretary to my Lord Clarendon, and is very well pleased with his Promotion. The Queen is so well, that the Sicilian Ambassador hath his Audience to night: She can walk, Thank God, and is very well recover'd. . . .

Si^r | Y^r most Obedient humble | Servt |

Tyrant.[2]

I forgot to tell you, that I saw Mr Harley,[3] who told me he would instantly send for the Horse from Herefordshire; but that he being at Grass, had ordered his Man not to Ride hard; but that you should have him with all convenient Speed.

Endorsed by Swift at the head of the letter: John Barber
  At end: June 8th 1714 | Jon Barber | Aldm

[1] The Schism Act made it illegal for anyone to teach, in institutions or in private houses, unless he had obtained a licence from the Bishop, and unless he qualified by taking the Sacrament according to the rites of the Church of England. The Bill, after heated debate, was passed by a majority of 111 in the Commons and 5 in the Lords. It was to come into force on the first of Aug. On that day Queen Anne died, virtually rendering the Act inoperative. It was not repealed, however, till the winter of 1718–19.

[2] To the left of the word 'Tyrant' Swift has written 'John Barber'. A sentence before the subscription has been obliterated. 'as does Sir' can be read. Words written over seem to be 'beyond consent I will appoint the happy day'.

[3] Thomas Harley, Oxford's cousin.

Swift to Archdeacon Walls

June. 11th 1714

[1]I think it is long since I wrote to you;[2] or you to me; I am now retired into the *Country* weary to death of Courts and Ministers, and Business and Politicks; I hope to be in Ireld if possible by the End of *the Summer*, sooner I can not, having many Papers to look over and settle while I am here. I was six weeks compassing the great Work of leaving London, and did it at last abruptly enough; but go I would; the Reasons I may live to tell you, or perhaps you will guess them by their Effects *before I see you.* I shall say no more, but that I care not to live in *Storms, when I can no longer* do Service in the ship, and am able to *get out of it.* I have gone thro my Share of Malice and Danger, and will be as quiet the rest of my *days, as I can*——So much for Politicks—I should hope Parvisol might have payd in enough to discharge the Bp of Dromore 300^{ll}; He sett the Tyths of the Deanry for 430^{ll}, of which I had 30^{ll}: my other Livings cannot be much less (I hope) than 200^{ll} of which 140, or 150^{ll} may come to my share after paying Warburton & other things; & he had large Arrears upon Laracor, of which I think you sent me word he had brought in some part.[3] here is above 500^{ll} besides the Arrears; and I never had one Bill from him since I came here; but have lived upon some other money I brought over with me, upon a little Principall I melted, & some Interest I receavd, and money I have borrowed & the rest upon the Revenues of our two *Friends at Trim*, which I received here, and gave them Bills on Parvisol, which Article (with 20^{ll} I now give them Bills for in the inclosed, thô I have not yet received the money out of the Exchequer) will not amount, I am sure to 100^{ll}. So that he ought to have payd you in above 400^{ll} unless he hath suffered the Farmers of the Deanry to run in Arrear, which under the late Dean they never used to do. As for the Land-rents of the Deanry, I have ordered Parvisol not to receive them, nor design to do it, till I examine into the Leases, which shall be as soon as I come over.

---

[1] Lord Rothschild's Library, No. 2281 (9).
[2] See 27 Mar. 1714.
[3] 'And *Parvisol* discounts Arrears,
   By Bills for Taxes and Repairs.' *Poems*, p. 174.

I have in the . . .[1] belongs to three Friends, but left to my Managemt; it is worth now about . . . English, (for it has fallen of late) and that returned to Ireld, with a little Addition would make. . . . To tell you a Secret, I think as times are like to be, I should be glad to have my money in another Place, and would willingly make some Purchase in Ireld, if I could hear of any between Dublin and Trim, or near thereabouts; and if you would joyn with me, we would purchase together, and You should either have the Land for Security, or be a joynt Purchaser as you pleased—This I say, because I think you have told me that yr money lyes in severall hands at Interest, which is lyable to Accidents; if you approve of this, pray enquire, if not, do it for me, and I will purchase for my self, as far as 1000 or 1500[11], because I could borrow money on the Land, & pay it by degrees, or pay the Interest as I pleasd. But when you enquire name no names.

I have sent over six Boxes with Books by long Sea; I suppose they will come in a little time; pray be so kind to leave word for them at the Custom-house: yr Neighbor Craven[2] will do me that good Office. You must pay the Freight of them, but let them ly in the Custom house till I come over, because I will wrangle hard about the Custom, for they are all old Books, and half of them very bad ones bought at Auctions only to make a shew as a Dean of St Patricks should.

My Service to Gossip Doll. I hope my Godchild is well, & pray give my Service to Alderman Stoit, & Goody, & Katherine; & Mr Manly & Lady.

Tell Dr Synge[3] I have his Lettr of May 24 just now come to me; I will answer it in some time. at present you may let him know that I am fully resolved to call the Vicars to Account to the utmost I am able.[4] he wants to see the Books belonging to the Dean and Chapter. I know not who has the Key of the Cabinet, in which Cabinet I suppose is the Key of some Chest of Drawers where the Books are: I believe either you or Mrs Brent[5] has it: pray see. He tells me Mr

---

[1] The greater part of a line is here obliterated in ink and illegible. Ball professes to read 'South Sea Stock one thousand pounds'; but this accounts for only thirty letters, whereas there must have been over fifty letters in the space covered by the obliteration. There are two lesser obliterations, as indicated, in the next two lines.

[2] Named again in a letter to Walls, 30 Mar. 1717, but otherwise unidentified.

[3] Samuel Synge, Precentor of St. Patrick's. The letter is missing. No letter from Synge to Swift has survived.

[4] See Swift to Worrall, 31 Dec. 1713.   [5] Swift's housekeeper.

Fetherston[1] is gone to Lusk, and that my Sermons cost 20ˢ every five weeks, very dear that. Dol and you shall pay for it. | Yʳˢ | &c.

Address: To the Revᵈ | Mʳ Arch Deacon Wall over | against the Hospitall in | Queen street | Dublin[2]
Postmark: ? 12 IV
Frank: C Ford
Later endorsement: Dʳ Swift | June 11ᵗʰ 1714

Rothschild[3]

Swift to Charles Ford

12 June 1714.

Pray be so kind to direct the inclosed[4] to the Reverend Mʳ Archdeacon Wall, over against the Hospitall in Queen-street Dublin. I hope they sent you my Scrutore. I gave the Key of it at Oxford to Mʳ Trap, to deliver to You. I am going on with the Discourse of which you saw the Beginning;[5] but not a Word of it for your Life. Did I steal away without telling you? No I remember I told you where to direct to me. I am at a Parsons House 52 miles from You, putting some Papers in order. And you may be as mad as you all please for me. I write this Post to Mʳ L—.[6] I drink nothing but ale, and read and write and walk all day. I reckon I shall get the Spleen, but that is nothing. I long till your Session is over, but what have I to do with Politicks. Our Strawberryes are ruined for want of rain, and Our Parsons Pigs have done ten Shillings worth of Mischief upon Goodman Dickens's Corn. Tis thought the Tyth-farmer must answer for it. I was tother day to see Parson Hunsden[7] at lower Letcomb. He is very ill with a Ptisick, but his Wife looks strong and

---

[1] Presumably the Rev. Thomas Fetherston (see i. 390) had been preaching in Swift's place. His absence at Lusk would necessitate the employment of a substitute. Lusk lies on the coast in the north of county Dublin.

[2] This letter, written at Letcombe Bassett, was sent to Ford in London, who addressed and franked it.

[3] Lord Rothschild's Library, No. 2282 (6).

[4] The previous letter, addressed and franked by Ford in London.

[5] *Some Free Thoughts upon the Present State of Affairs*, first printed in 1741. See Swift's letter to Ford of 18 July.

[6] Lewis.

[7] John Hunsdon (1649–1715) of Queen's College, Oxford, vicar of Letcombe Regis since 1676. He died in the following March.

lusty. Will you have any more of this? Well, Chuse, and adieu. I sent last Post a Letter to J. Barb—[1] under your Cover.

June 12ᵗʰ 1714.

Our publick news is that Princess Sophia is dead.[2]

Address: To Charles Ford Esqʳ, at | His Office at White-hall ǀ London
Postmarks: W[ant]age *and* 11
                              IV

Royal College of Surgeons of England[3]
Swift to John Gay

June. 12ᵗʰ 1714

I wonder how you could have the Impudence to know where I am;[4] I have this Post writt to Mʳ Harley,[5] who is just come from Hanover, to desire he would give you a Letter; I have described you to him, and told him I would write to you to wait on him, which will do you no hurt neither about your Affair in the Treasury. You begin to be an able Courtier, which I know from two Instances, first for giving me thanks for your Prefermᵗ, to which I onely contributed by saying to Dʳ Arbuthnot and Mʳ Lewis that I wished it. Secondly for wheedling My Lᵈ Treasʳ with an Epigram, which I like very well, & so I am sure will he, and I reckon you will succeed; but pray learn to be a Manager, and pick up Languages as fast as you can, and get Aristotle upon Politicks, and read other Books upon Governmᵗ; Grotius de Jure belli et pacis, and accounts of Negotiations & Treatyes &c. and be a perfect Master of the Latin, and be able to learn every thing of the Court where you go; and keep correspondence with Mʳ Lewis, who if you write Letters worth shewing, will make them serviceable to you with Lᵈ Treasʳ; & take Mʳ Lewis's advice in all Things, and do not despise mine, and so God bless you, and make you able to make my Fortunes—I am glad Mʳ Pope has made so much dispatch, My Service to him & the Parnelian.[6]

¹ John Barber.
² The Electress of Hanover. She had died 28 May.
³ This letter is one among others in the Hunter-Baillie Collection in the Royal College of Surgeons of England, Lincolns Inn Fields, London.
⁴ Letcombe Bassett.   ⁵ Lord Oxford's cousin, Thomas Harley.
⁶ Parnell, the poet.

John Arbuthnot to Swift

St. James's June 12ᵗʰ, 1714

Dear Brother

I am glad your proud Stomach is come down, & that you submitt
to write to your freinds, I was of opinion that if they managd yow
right they might bring yow to be fond even of an article of the post
boy or flying post.¹ As for the present state of our Court affairs, I
thank God I am allmost as ignorant as yow are to my great ease, &
comfort, I have never enquird about any thing, since MLM told the
Dragon, that she would carry no more Messages nor medle nor
make, &c.² I don't know whether things were quite so bad when yow
went. The D—n manages this Bill, pretty well, for yow know that
is his forte,³ & I beleive at the Rate they go on, they will do Mischief
to themselves & good to no body else. Yow know that Gay gos to
Hanover, and My Lord Treasurer has promis'd to equipp him.
Munday is the day of departure, & he is now dancing attendance, for
money to buy him shoes stockings & linen.⁴ The Duchess has turnd
him off⁵ which I am affraid will make the poor Man's Condition
worse instead of better. The Dragon was with us on Saturday night
last after having sent us really a most excellent copy of verses, I really
beleive when he lays down he will prove a very good poet. I remember the first part of his verses was complaining of ill usage & at last
he concludes

¹ George Ridpath was publisher of the Whig *Flying Post*, Abel Roper of the
Tory *Post-Boy*. In *The Dunciad* Pope brackets them together:

> There Ridpath, Roper, cudgell'd might ye view;
> The very worsted still look'd black and blue.

Swift and Pope regarded both as libellous journalists. See *The Dunciad*, ed.
Sutherland, pp. 118, 302.

² MLM stands for 'My Lady Masham'. 'The Dragon' was an appellation of
Lord Oxford used by Swift and his circle. Unfortunately a coolness had arisen
between Lady Masham and Oxford, which led to a decline in his favour with the
Queen (*Portland MSS.* v. 403).

³ For the Schism Bill see p. 29. Oxford's handling of the situation was
irresolute and scarcely justifies Arbuthnot's judgement. He was, however, in a
difficult situation.

⁴ Arbuthnot was writing on Saturday. In two days Gay was due to depart.
The time was short to complete his preparations. On Thursday Gay had written
to Oxford to remind him of his needs (*Portland MSS.* v. 457).

⁵ The Duchess of Monmouth whom he was serving as secretary.

he that cares not to rule, will be sure to obey,
    when summon'd by Arbuthnot, pope parnell & Gay.[1]

Parnell has been thinking of going chaplain to My lord Clarendon, but they will not say whether he should or not. I am to meett our Club at the pall mall coffee house about one to day, wher we can not fail to remember yow The Q—n is in good health much in the same circumstances wt the Gentleman I mention'd, in attendance upon her Ministers for some thing she can not obtain. My Lord & My Lad[y] Masham & Lady Fair[2] remember you kindly, & none with more sincere respect than | Your affectionat Brother & | humble servant |

Jo: Arbuthnott

Address: For | The Reverend The | Dean of S^t patricks
Endorsed by Swift: Jun. 12th 1714 | Dr Arbuthnot

Royal College of Surgeons of England
Swift to John Arbuthnot

Jun. 16th, 1714

Dear Brother[3]
    My Stomack is prouder than You imagine, and I scorned to write till I was writt to. I have already half lost the Idea's of Courts and Ministers I dine between 12 and one, and the whole house is a bed by ten and up at six, I drink no wine, and see but one dish of meat. I pay a Guinea a week for dieting and lodging my self and Man, with an honest Clergyman of my old Acquaintance, and my paying is

---

[1] Oxford's lines, in his own hand, in answer to a Scriblerian invitation, are to be found at Longleat (Portland Papers, xiii. f. 71):
June 5th: 1714
In these Dangerous times when Popery is Flagrant
And ye servants of Oxford would choose to be vagrant
When Mercury *Dukes* set up for Physitians
Or wch is the same for state Polititians
He that cares not to rule will not fail to obey
    When Summoned by Arbuthnot, [A. Deacon *deleted*] Pope, Parnel & Gay
'A. Deacon', for Parnell, is deleted.
[2] Lady Masham's sister, Alice Hill.
[3] Printed inaccurately in Peter Cunningham's edition of Johnson's *Lives of the Poets*, iii. 203; and more carefully from the original by Aitken, *Life and Works of Arbuthnot*, pp. 61–63. The original is in the Royal College of Surgeons.

forced, for he has long invited me; I did not know till last Night that the Princess Sophie was dead,[1] when my Landlord and I chanced to pay a Visit to a Farmer in a Neighboring Village, and was told so over a Mug of Ale, by a brisk young Fellow just come from London, who talked big and looked on us with great Contempt. I thank you for your Kindness to poor Gay. Was the Money paid, or put off till they [*sic*] day after he went? I reckon by what you tell me, that it is now a high season to be very merry in Lady fair's[2] Lodgings. I heartily pity you in particular: Look after your Mistress and your self grow rich, and since nothing better can be done, let the World vadere I have a mind to live in Yorkshire for a year,[3] in order to put my self out of Memory and Debt. The Fashion of this world passeth away, however I am angry at those who disperse us sooner than there was need. I have a Mind to be very angry, and to let my anger break out in some manner that will not please them, at the End of a Pen.[4] I wish you could get Ldy M— to give you those Hints[5] we have often spoke off, & to muster up your own, for the Dragon I despair he will do that, any more than any thing else; and indeed you are all of you Dragons more or less, for I am sure it is above 3 years since I have spoke to Lady M— and you about this. My humble Service to My Lord and Her, whom I love as much as you do, though I have greater Obligations to them. and my humble Service[6] & thanks to the Qu— of Prudes[7] for remembering me . . . You are a Sett of People drawn almost to the Dregs; You must try another Game; this is at an End. Your Ministry is fourscore and ten years old, and all you can endeavour at is an Euthanasia, or rather it is in a deep Consumption at five and twenty.—I approve Lady M—s conduct, and think all she can now do in relation to the Dragon, is to be passive; for the rest, to cultivate her own Credit to the utmost. Writing to you much would make me stark mad; judge his condition who has nothing to keep him from being miserable but endeavoring to forget those for whom he has the greatest Value, Love, and Friendship. But you are a Philosopher and a Physician, & can over-come by your Wisdom and Your Faculty those Weaknesses which

---

[1] The Electress died 28 May.   [2] Alice Hill.

[3] Swift mistakenly believed his family to be connected with Yorkshire.

[4] *Some Free Thoughts upon the Present State of Affairs, Prose Works*, ed. Davis, p. 73.

[5] Presumably hints for the writing of the *Four Last Years of the Queen*.

[6] 'and' scrawled out before 'Service'.

[7] Alice Hill.

other men are forced to reduce by not thinking on them—adieu &
love me half as well as I do you—

Address: To Dr Arbuthnot

Rothschild

Swift to Charles Ford

Jun. 16. 1714[1]

I thank you kindly for your Letter, it was welcom because it came
from You, but I value not your News a farthing, nor any publick
You can tell me. I hear you grow madder and madder; that I can
know at the distance I am. I would ensure a Pitcher for a year that
a child carryes nine times a day to a Well, sooner than your M—ry.
Trap has the Key of my Ecritoire, and was desired to give it you.
Pray God bless you—adieu.

I write this Post to M^r. L. Dr A.,[2] and others.

Address: To Charles Ford Esqr, at | His Office at Whitehall | London
Postmark: 18 IV

Faulkner 1741

Alexander Pope to Swift

June 18, 1714.

Whatever apologies it might become me to make at any other time
for writing to you, I shall use none now, to a man who has own'd
himself as splenetick as a Cat, in the country. In that circumstance,
I know by experience a letter is a very useful, as well as amusing
thing: If you are too busied in State-affairs to read it, yet you may
find entertainment in folding it into divers figures, either doubling
it into a pyramidical, or twisting it into a Serpentine form to light a
pipe:[3] or if your disposition should not be so mathematical, in taking

---

[1] Lord Rothschild's Library.

[2] Mr. Lewis, Dr. Arbuthnot. That to the latter is the previous letter written
on this same day.

[3] 'to light a pipe' occurs in Pope's clandestine volume and in Faulkner 1741,
vii. 1. Pope omitted it from London texts supervised by him, 1741-2.

it with you to that place where men of studious minds are apt to sit longer than ordinary; where after an abrupt division of the paper, it may not be unpleasant to try to fit and rejoyn the broken lines together. All these amusements I am no stranger to in the country, and doubt not but (by this time) you begin to relish them in your present contemplative situation.

I remember a man, who was thought to have some knowledge in the world, us'd to affirm, that no people in town ever complained they were forgotten by their friends in the country: but my encreasing experience convinces me he was mistaken, for I find a great many here grievously complaining of you, upon this score. I am told, further, that you treat the few you correspond with in a very arrogant style, and tell them you admire at their insolence in disturbing your meditations, or even enquiring of your retreat: but this I will not positively assert, because I never receiv'd any such insulting Epistle from you. My Lord Oxford says you have not written to him once since you went: but this perhaps may be only policy, in him or you; and I, who am half a Whig, must not entirely credit any thing he affirms. At Button's[1] it is reported you are gone to Hanover, and that Gay goes only on an Ambassy to you. Others apprehend some dangerous State-treatise from your retirement; and a Wit who affects to imitate Balsac,[2] says, that the Ministry now are like those Heathens of old, who received their Oracles from the woods. The Gentlemen of the Roman Catholick persuasion are not unwilling to credit me, when I whisper that you are gone to meet some Jesuits commissioned from the Court of Rome, in order to settle the most convenient methods to be taken for the coming of the Pretender. Dr. Arbuthnot is singular in his opinion, and imagines your only design is to attend at full leisure to the life and adventures of Scriblerus. This indeed must be granted of greater importance than all the rest; and I wish I could promise so well of you. The top of my own ambition is to contribute to that great work, and I shall translate Homer by the by. Mr. Gay has acquainted you[3] what progress I have made in it. I can't name Mr. Gay, without all the acknowledgements which I shall

[1] A coffee-house frequented by Addison and his 'little senate', a coterie of Whig wits. It was situated in Russell Street, opposite Will's. The name was derived from Daniel Button, the proprietor.

[2] Jean Louis Guez de Balzac, 1594–1654.

[3] Gay had informed Swift (8 June 1714) that Pope had brought to town with him 'the first Book of Homer'.

ever owe you, on his account. If I writ this in verse. I would tell you,
you are like the sun, and while men imagine you to be retir'd or
absent, are hourly exerting your indulgence, and bringing things to
maturity for their advantage. Of all the world, you are the man
(without flattery) who serve your friends with the least ostentation;
it is almost ingratitude to thank you, considering your temper; and
this is the period of all my letter which I fear you will think the most
impertinent. I am with the truest affection | Yours, *&c.*

4804

Thomas Harley to Swift

19 June 1714

S^{r1}

   Your letter gave me a great deal of pleasure. I do not mean only
the satisfaction one must allways find in hearing from so good a
friend who has distinguished himselfe in the world & formed A new
Caracter which no body is vain enough to pretend to imitate. but
you must know the moment after you disapeard I found it was to no
purpose to be unconcernd & to slight (as I really have done) all the
silly storys and schemes I met with every day, the effects of selfe
conceit & frightend hasty desire of gain. they asked me has not the
Dean left the Town is not Dr Swift gone into the Country? yes and
I would have gone into the Country too if I had not learnt one canot
be hurt till one turns ones back (for which reason I will go no more
on their Errants) but seriously you never heard such bellowing about
the Town of the state of the Nation, especially among the sharpers
sellers of Bearskins² and the rest of that kind nor such crying pissing
& squalling among the Ladys, insomuch that it has at last reached

   ¹ The writer of this letter was Thomas Harley, cousin to the Lord Treasurer,
and a Secretary of the Treasury. During the reign of Queen Anne he was M.P.
for Radnorshire, but lost his seat on the change of government; and thereafter
lived in retirement. He died in 1738. In 1712 he was sent with instructions to the
plenipotentiaries at Utrecht. He had now returned from a mission to Hanover
to reassure that Court on the succession. See *Portland MSS.* iii–vii *passim*.

   ² The equivalent word (Stock Exchange) would now be 'bear'. In its present
sense, 'speculator for a fall', it may have come into use at the time of the South
Sea. This use may have arisen from the proverbial saying 'to sell the skin of a
bear before one has caught it'. See *O.E.D.* and Brewer's *Dictionary of Phrase and
Fable*.

the house of Comons which I am sorry for because tis hot & uneasy sitting there in this season of the year, but I was told to day that in some Countrys people are forced to watch day & night to keep wild beasts out of their corn do not you pity me, for yeilding to such grave sayings to be stifled every day in the house of Comons? when I was out of England I used to receive 5 or 6 letters each post, with this passage—(As for what passes here, you will be informd by others much better therefore I shall not trouble you with any thing of that sort) you will give me leave to use it now, as my excuse to you for not writeing news. I hope honest Gay will be better supplyd by some friend or other. before I received your direction I had ordered My servant who comes next monday out of herefordshire, to leave your horse[1] at the Crown in Farrington,[2] where you can easily send for him, I hear he was so fat they could not travel him till he was taken down & I orderd he should go short Journeys, he is of A good breed & therefore I hope will prove well, if not use him like a bastard & I will choose another for you | I am sr your most faithfull | Humble servt |

                                                    T: Harley

Endorsed by Swift: Jun. 19ᵗʰ 1714 | Tom: Harley.

4804

William Thomas to Swift

                                                    22 June 1714
Revᵈ Sʳ

It was with difficulty, that I prevailed with myself to forbear acknowledging your very kind Letter. I can only tell you, it shall be the Business of my Life to endeavour to deserve the Opinion you express of me, & thereby to recommend my self to the Continuance of yʳ Friendship.[3]

---

[1] For a previous mention of this horse see John Barber to Swift, 8 June 1714.
[2] About nine miles from Letcombe. Oxford used to stay at this inn when travelling from his seat in Herefordshire.
[3] The endorsement shows that the writer was a secretary of Lord Oxford. So far as is known Swift, after retiring from London, wrote no letter to Oxford before that of 3 July, which survives in the original. Swift's absence from the scene was generally noted. On the very day of this letter Sir John Perceval, later first Earl of Egmont, wrote to his cousin Dan. Dering in Ireland: "Tis generally

My Ld. Tr. does upon all occasions do Justice to your Merit, & has exprest to all his friends the great Esteem he has for so hearty & honest a friend and particularly on occasion of the Letter you mention to have lately writ to him and all his friends can inform you with what pleasure he communicated it to them.

And now for Business, I am to acquaint you that last Thursday I recd the 50ll., (which now waits your Ordrs) & dated your Rect. accordingly wch I delivered to Mr Whetham who payd me the Money.[1] I do not pretend to tell you how matters go. Our fr—d says very bad. I am sanguine enough to hope, not worse. I am, with all possible Esteem Ever yrs

Endorsed by Swift: Mr Thomas | Rx. Jul. 24 | 1714
   and: Jun. 22d 1714 | Mr Thomas Secrty | to Ld Trear

4804

John Arbuthnot to Swift

Kensington: June 26. 1714

D: Brother

I had allmost resolvd not to write to yow, for fear of disturbing so happy a state as you descrybe; on the other hand, a little of the divill, that cannot endure any body should enjoy a paradise, almost provok'd me to give you a long, & melancholy state of our affairs for yow must know, [that] is just my own case, I have with great industry endeavourd to live in ignorance, but at the same time would enjoy Kensinton Garden,[2] & then some busy discontented body or another comes just cross me: & beginns a dismall story, & befor I go to supper, I am as full of greivances as the most knowing of them: I will plague you a little by telling you that the Dragon dy's hard He is now kicking & cuffing about him like the divill. & you know parliamentary manaagement is the forte but no hopes of any settlement between the two champions. The Dragon said last night to

expected the Treasurer will give way to his Antagonist very soon, to whom the other Friends fall frequently off; I was told that of late Swift is not so frequent at the Treasurer's levy as he us'd to be, insomuch as the other twitted him with the Comparison of a Rat which leaves a falling house' (B.M. Add. MS. 47087).
   [1] The reference is to the business between Mr. Fetherston and Baron Scrope (see i. 390). Whetham, who was first commissioner of excise, appears to have been connected by marriage with Scrope.—Ball.
   [2] The Queen was at this time residing at Kensington Palace.

My L M—m,[1] & me that it is with great industry he keeps his freinds, who are very numirous from pulling all to pieces, Gay had a hundred pound in due time, [and] went away a happy man. I have sollicited both Ld Tr & Ld Bolingbroke strongly for the parnelian,[2] & gave them a memorial t'other day. Ld Trs speaks mighty affectionatly of him, which yow know is an ill sign in Ecclesiastical preferments. witness some, that yow know, & I know, wher the contrary was the best sign in the world.

Pray Remember Martin,[3] who is an innocent fellow, & will not disturb your solitude. The ridicule of Medicin is so copious a subject that I must only here & ther touch it. I have made him study physick from the Apothecarys bills, wher ther is a good plentifull field for a satyr upon the present practice; one of his projects was by a stamp upon blistering plaisters & melilot by the yard, to raise money for the Govert & to give it to R—ff[4] & others to farm, But ther was like to be a petition from the inhabitants of London & Westminster who had no mind to be flead. There was a probleme about the doses of purging Medecins published four years ago showing that they ought [to] be in proportion to the bulk of the patient. from thence, Martin endeavours to determin the question about the Weight of the Ancient men, by the doses of physick that were givn them. one of his best inventions was a map of diseases for the three cavitys & one for the external parts, just like the four quarters of the world. Then the Great diseases are like capital Citys with their symptoms all like streets & suburbs, with the Roads that lead to other diseases it is thicker sett with Towns than any flanders Map yow ever saw. R—ff is painted at the corner of the Map, contending for the universal empire of the world, & the rest of the physicians opposing his ambitious designs with a project of a Treaty of partition to settle peace. Ther is an excellent subject of ridicule from some of the German physicians, who sett up a sensitive soul as a sort of a first Minister to the rational. Helmont[5] calls him Archaeus,

---

[1] Lady Masham.   [2] The poet Parnell.

[3] The allusion is to the *Memoirs of Martinus Scriblerus* (see p. 28, n. 2). Arbuthnot here outlines a scheme for its continuation.

[4] Radcliffe was not held in favour by Swift (*Journal*, 10 Apr. 1711), nor by many of his contemporaries, who regarded him as a clever empiric. His medical experience, however, won him many remarkable cures. He amassed a large fortune which he bequeathed to public purposes.

[5] Jean Baptiste van Helmont, 1577–1644, whose works entitled *Ortus Medicinae* were published four years after his death by his son.

Dolaeus[1] calls him Microcosmetor. he has under him severall other Genii that reside in the particular parts of the body, particularly Prince Cardimelech in the heart. Gasteronax in the stomach, & the plastick prince in the organs of Generation. I believe I could make yow laugh at the explication of distempers from the wars & Ally-ances of those princes & how the first Minister getts the better of his Mistress anima rationalis The best is that it is making a reprisal upon the politicians, who are sure to Allegorize all the animal oeconomy into state affairs. Pope has been collecting high flights of poetry, which are very good, they are to be solemn nonsense.[2] I thought upon the following t'other day as I was going into my Coach, the dust being troublesome:

> The dust in smaller particles arose
> than those which fluid bodyes do compose.
> Contrarys in extremes do often meett.
> 'twas now so drye, that you might call it wett

I dont give yow these hints to divert yow but that yow may have your thoughts & work upon them. I know yow love me heartily & yet I will not own that yow love me better than I love yow. My ld & lady Masham love yow too & read your letter to me with pleasure. My lady says she will write to yow, whether yow write to her or not. D freind Adieu

Endorsed by Swift: Jun. 26th 1714 | Dr Arb—

Rothschild

Swift to Charles Ford

1 July 1714.

[3]Here it is,[4] read it, and send it to B—[5] by an unknown hand, have nothing to do with it, thô there be no Danger. Contrive he may not

---

[1] Johann Dolaeus.

[2] Used by him in Περι Βαθους: *Or, Martinus Scriblerus his Treatise of the Art of Sinking in Poetry*, which appeared in the Pope and Swift *Miscellanies. The Last Volume*, 1727.

[3] Lord Rothschild's Library, No. 2282 (8).

[4] *Some Free Thoughts upon the Present State of Affairs.* As will appear from subsequent letters the printed text of 1741 differs widely from what Swift sent to Ford.

[5] Barber, the printer.

shew it Mʳ L— yet how can you do that? For I would not have him
know that you or I had any concern in it. Do not send it by the
Penny post, nor your Man, but by a Porter when you are not at your
Lodgings. Get some Friend to copy out the little Paper, and send it
inclosed with the rest, and let the same Hand direct it, and seal it
with an unknown Seal. If it be not soon printed, send to Dunstons[1]
in the name desired.—Spend an hour in reading it, and if the same
word be too soon repeated, vary it as you please, but alter your
Hand. adieu. Jul. 1. 1714. I would fain have it sent on Saterday night,
or Sunday[2] because of the date, that it might not be suspected to
come from here. If you think any thing in the little Letter suspicious,
alter it as you please.

Address: To Charles Ford Esqʳ | at His Office at White-Hall | London
Postmarks: Wantage *and* 2 IY

B.M., Portland MSS. List I

Swift to the Earl of Oxford

July. 3ᵈ 1714.[3]

When I was with you, I have said more than once, that I would
never allow Quality or Station to make any reall Difference between
Men. Being now absent and forgotten, I have changed my Mind.
You have a thousand People who can pretend they love you, with as
much appearance of Sincerity as I, so that according to common
Justice I can have but a thousandth part in return of what I give.
And this difference is wholly owing to your Station. And the Misfortune is still the greater, because I always loved you just so much
the worse for your Station. For in your publick Capacity you have
often angred me to the Heart, but, as a private man, never once.[4] So

---

[1] St. Dunstan's Coffee-house, Fleet Street.

[2] Sunday was 4 July.

[3] The original of this letter is among the Portland papers now deposited in the
British Museum. There it is dated 3 July; and thus also endorsed by Oxford
himself. The letter was first printed by Deane Swift, *Essay*, 1755, pp. 338–40,
and next among the letters collected by him in 1765, in both instances dated
'July 1'.

[4] This letter appears to be intended as an apology for *Some Free Thoughts*
which Swift had begun in May, before leaving London. It was, as the previous
letter shows, finished and sent to Ford on 1 July. Ford replied on the 6th,

that if I only looktd towards my self I could wish you a private Man to morrow. For I have nothing to ask, at least nothing that you will give, which is the same Thing, and then you would see whether I should not with much more willingness attend you in a Retirement, whenever you pleased to give me leave, than ever I did at London or Windsor. From these sentiments, I will never write to you (if I can help it) otherwise than as to a private Person, nor allow my self to have been obliged by you in any other Capacity. The Memory of one great Instance of your Candor and Justice, I will carry to my Grave; that having been in a manner domestick with you for almost four Years, it was never in the Power of any publick or concealed Enemy to make you think ill of me, though Malice and Envy were often employd to that End. If I live, Posterity shall know that and more, which, though you and somebody that shall be nameless, seem to value less than I could wish,¹ is all the Return I can make you. Will you give me leave to say how I would desire to stand in your Memory; As one who was truly sensible of the honor you did him, though he was too proud to be vain upon it. As one who was neither assuming, officious nor teazing, who never wilfully misrepresented Persons or Facts to you, nor consulted his Passions when he gave a Character. and lastly, as one whose Indiscretions proceeded altogether from a Weak Head, and not an ill Heart. I will add one thing more, which is the highest Compliment I can make, that I never was afraid of offending you, nor am now in any Pain for the manner I write to you in. I have said enough, and like one at your Levee having made my Bow, I shrink back into the Crowd.²

Endorsed by Lord Oxford: Dean of | St Patrick | July 3: 1714

reporting that he had sent it to the printer on Sunday. Before sending it he made a few corrections. Then Barber, the printer, sent the manuscript to Bolingbroke, who would have altered some passages, and during the delay the Queen died. On 15 June 1737 Swift handed another manuscript copy to Mrs. Whiteway. Four years later, in May 1741, it was printed by George Faulkner, not from this copy, but from the copy which had been preserved by Barber. See *Prose Works*, ed. Davis, viii, pp. xxiii–xxv, 73–98, 205–9.

¹ Swift is referring to his application for the office of Historiographer. The 'somebody that shall be nameless' was the Queen.

² Deane Swift's printing of this letter is faithful to the original, save for pointing and two insignificant variants.

Swift to John Arbuthnot

Jul. 3. 1714.

I reckoned you would have held up for one Letter and so have given
over, that is the usuall way I treat my best absent Friends when I am
in London. Did I describe my self in a happy State here? Upon my
faith you read wrong; I have no happyness but being so far out of
the Way of the Dragon and the rest—Lewis reproaches me as one
who has still an Itch to the Court, only because I asked him how the
Summa rerum went. Was not that unjust. and quotes upon me, Quae
lucis miseris tam dira Cupido.[1] I do assert that living near a Court
with some Circumstances is a most happy Life, and would be so still
if the Dragon did not spoyl it. I find the Triumvirate of honest
Councellors is at an end, I am gone, Lewis says he lives in Ignorance
in his Castle, and you meddle as little as you can. One thing still lyes
upon you, which is to be a constant Adviser to Ldy M—. The Game
will of course be playd into her hand. She has very good Sense, but
may be imposed upon. And I had a whisper, that the Squire[2] plyes
there again. Tis as you say, if the Dragon speaks kindly of Parnel,
he is gone. tis the Ossoryes that get the Derryes,[3] & the Chesters the
Yorks.[4] To talk of Martin in any hands but yours, is a Folly. You
every day give better hints than all of us together could do in a
twelvemonth; And to say the Truth, Pope who first thought of the
Hint has no Genius at all to it, in my Mind. Gay is too young;
Parnel has some Ideas of it, but is idle; I could putt together, and
lard, and strike out well enough, but all that relates to the Sciences
must be from you. I am a vexed unsettled Vagabond, and my
Thoughts are turned towards some Papers I have, and some other
things I would fain get from you and Ldy M— and would have had
from the Dragon, but that is impossible till he is out, and then I will
go to him to Herefordshire and make him give me Hints.[5] I have got

[1] *Aen.* vi. 721.

[2] i.e. Bolingbroke.

[3] The bishopric of Derry had recently been filled by the translation of John
Hartstonge, Bishop of Ossory.

[4] Sir William Dawes had been translated from Chester to York on the death
of Archbishop Sharp.

[5] For the *Four Last Years of the Queen*. Swift had submitted the manuscript
of this work, or the major part of it, to Sir Thomas Hanmer (*Journal*, 27 Feb.
1712–13). Was the mention of Bromley a slip on Swift's part?

my History[1] from Sec^try Bromley; and they shall never have it again; and it shall be an altered thing if I live.

The hints you mention relating to Medicine are admirable; I wonder how you can have a Mind so degagé in a Court where there is so many Million of things to vex you. You must understand, I have writt this Post to the Dragon, but you must not take notice of it, nor I fancy will he. For what I writt is very odd and serious. I think to go and Ramble for a Month about Herefordshire & those Parts. Ask the Dragon whether he will order his People at his Castle to receive me. Why do you not send your Pal^mt a grazing. What do you mean by your Proclamations and 5000[11]? Till I hear Reasons I dislike your Politics. Why do I talk of it say you? Why did that Puppy Barber write it to me? But the Commons offer 100000[11] If I was the Pretender I would come over my self, and take the money to help to pay my Troops.[2] They had better Put out a Proclamation that whoever discovers the Pretender or the Longitude[3] shall have 100000[11]—This Strain is a Sacrifice to Hanover, the Whigs, and the Qu—'s State of Health. It will neither satisfy H—ver, silence the Whigs, nor cure the Gout. Give him a Pension, & oblige him to live beyond the Alps. What's become of y^r Project to make it high Treason to bring over foreign Troops?[4] I wish a little care was taken for Securing the Kingdom as well as the Succession—

But country Politicks are doubly insupportable, and so I have done; and retire to lament with my Neighbors the want of Rain, and dearness of Hay. Farmer Tyler says, the white Mead at Chawdry has not been so bad in the memory of Man, and the Summer Barley

---

[1] Further to Oxford's association with Herefordshire Swift's desire to visit the county may have arisen from recollections of Thomas Swift, vicar of Goodrich near Ross.

[2] At the instigation of the Lords a proclamation was issued offering a reward of £500 for the apprehension of the Pretender should he land in England. The Commons proposed that it should be increased to £100,000.

[3] The exact determination of the longitude by vessels at sea long presented insuperable difficulties, and the government offered a substantial reward for the discovery. In the *Journal*, 28 Mar. 1712, Swift alludes to a 'Projector' who claimed to 'have found out the Longitude'. He may have been the heterodox divine William Whiston, who pursued mathematical studies. In 1714 he published, in collaboration with Humphry Ditton, *A New Method of Discovering the Longitude*.

[4] Oxford proposed a bill for that purpose. Nothing more was heard of it, for it would have proved contrary to the interests of both the house of Hanover and of the Pretender.

is quite dryed up; but we hope to have a pretty good Crop of Wheat.
Parson Hunsdon[1] tis thought must stick to his Bargain, but all the
Neighbors say the Attorney was an arrand Rogue. We cannot get a
Bitt of good Butter for Love or Money. I could tell you more of the
State of our Affairs, but doubt your Tast is not refined enough for it.
Address: To Dr. Arbuthnott

Rothschild[2]

Swift to Archdeacon Walls

July. 3[d] 1714

I received yrs of Jun. 24[th3] just now, and heartily thank you for it,
and for the Pains you and M[r] Forbes are at about my rotten Affairs.
I have made that Parvisol a Rogue by my own Carelessness, and
trusting to his Accounts; and have denyed my self many a necessary
thing hoping to have some money in bank agst I wanted it. I look
upon him as a Knave, and I beg you will do so too: and if you are of
Opinion to take a new Manager for My Deanry and Livings this
year, I believe the Power I left with you will suffice, for as I remember it was as large as I could make it. I leave it all to you; his sinking
the 35[11] odd moneys of this last year is insupportable. He never was
allowed above twelvepence a pound in all for my other Livings, both
setting and receiving. He always getts setting money besides, which
is a considerable perquisite; and that twelvepence is never allowed
by me but by the Tenant; except in Rathbeggan[4] where by an old
Custom (I think) the Minister pays it, in the Deanry and Laracor &c,
the Tenant always pays it.—For his Quantums and his Merit he is
a Rascal; He knows how much I have remitted to him & given to
him severall years. Must I be a Loser by giving him the Deanry
to sett. Can I not hire a hundred would be glad to be employd;
If he takes Journeyes are they above a dozen miles, and is he not
pd for them by his Place. Let him give me a clear Account, and
then talk of Merit. For my own Part; I think the best way would be
to seize on himself and all his Books, and force him to the best

[1] The Rev. John Hunsdon, vicar of Letcombe Regis.
[2] Lord Rothschild's Library, No. 2281 (10).
[3] Missing. Evidently a reply to Swift's letter of 11 June.
[4] The outlying parish of the Laracor union, separated from the others. See
Landa, *Swift and the Church of Ireland*, pp. 42–43.

48

Account we can, and employ somebody else this coming year. But I leave it to you. I am in no fear of being thought a hard Master; and if you think it the wisest way, I will take the Blame of the unmercifull Part: For I think such a Rascal deserves nothing more than rigorous Justice. He has imposed upon my Easyness; and that is what I never will forgive; and therefore I beg you will not do the least Thing in regard to him, but meerly for my Interest, as if I were a Jew, and let who will censure me. I have been often told I have been too easy with that Fellow, and was led by him; But yet no body would particularly advise me to shake him off, or recommend me to another. I must be a blind Puppy indeed to be led by him. Pize on it talk so mealy-mouthed of a Scroundel whom I kept with his Family a dozen years from starving, as if you fear getting ill will by complaining. What you would do in your own Case, do in mine, onely be something less mercifull, because he deserves no other Mercy than what is for my Interest. So, again—tender of doing him ill Offices; I am sure you are tenderer of doing them to me. I shall hate you if you talk at that rate, tenderer of a Rascal that by his Pride Vanity and Carelessness is ruining me, when I am loaden with Debts, and the Court will not give me a Penny to pay them.—I am above 150^{ll} in Debt in London since I came. I have been in the Country these 5 weeks, and probably shall return to Toun no more. I design to be in Ireld I hope by the End of Summer. I am weary of Ministers; I stole from them all, and have here a little Quiet, and have somewhat recovered my Health, which I had sufficiently shaken among them. I sett abundance of People at a Gaze by my going away; but I layd it all on my Health, and now the nine days Wonder is over. They expect I will return, but I mean to balk them, and take a ramble for some weeks about Hereford-shire[1] &c, and to Ireld. I would be with you sooner, but that I wait the Issue of some things. My Servide to y^r Trim Ladyes when you write to them. I intend to write to them in some time.

Ld Kingstons[2] Affairs are all Chimaeraes; besides I hope I have done with Courts for ever. My Service to Gossip, & Stoits & Manleys. I hope my God child is well.

---

[1] As noted previously the attraction to Herefordshire was Lord Oxford's residence at Brampton, and possibly also Goodrich.

[2] John, third Lord Kingston, who, after attaching himself to the fortunes of James II, had returned to Ireland and gained a free pardon in 1694. He died in London, 17 Feb. 1727-8.

I think by the Account, that Parvisol's Arrears are greater than when I left Ireld.

Why should I give him Allowances for Journeys, when I can have a Manager in Dublin or on the Spot who will do it for the common Perquisites, as the last Dean had.

In that, he is a cursed Villain, and if it will not hurt my Interest, I shall be glad to be rid of him; which if you and Forbes agree to do; there must be some Concert with Mr Warburton who is his Overseer^1 & [at] Laracor, & I think Dr Raymd, I have forgot. Do as you please, but let no regard to him influence you. I will take all the blame of Hardship on my self: And lay it on me as strong as you please.

Address: To the Rev^d | Mr ArchDeacon Walls | over against the Hospitall | in Queen street | Dublin^2
Frank: C Ford
Postmark: 6 IV
Later endorsement: Dr Swift | July 3^d 1714

4804

Charles Ford to Swift

London July 6 [1714]

If B.^3 be not a very great Blockhead, I shall soon send you a letter in print, in answer to your last. I hope it may be next post, for he had it on Sunday.^4 I took care to blot the e's out of onely, and the a's out of Scheame,^5 which I suppose is the meaning of your question whether I corrected it. I don't know any other alteration it wanted, and I made none except in one Paragraph that I chang'd the present to the past tence four times, and I am not sure I did right in it neither. There is so great a tenderness and regard shewn all along to the —^6 that I could have wish'd this expression had been out, [the uncertain timorous nature of the—] But there was no striking it out

---

^1 The original has no resemblance to the word 'broker', as read by Ball.
^2 This letter, written at Letcombe Bassett, was sent to Ford in London, who addressed and franked it.
^3 Barber. Swift has written 'arber' above the line.
^4 4 July.
^5 Swift's normal spellings.
^6 The Queen. The expression does not appear in the printed text of 1741.

without quite spoiling the beauty of the passage, and as if I had been the Author myself, I preferr'd beauty to discretion. I really think it is at least equal to any thing you have writ, and I dare say it will do great service as matters stand at present. The Collonel[1] and his friends give the game for lost on their side, and I believe by next week we shall see L. B.[2] at the head of affairs. The B^p. of Roc—r[3] is to be Ld Privy Seal. They talk of several other alterations as that my Ld Trevor is to be President of the Council, Ld Abingdon Chamberlain, Ld Anglesey L^d L^t of Ireland, that Mr Bromley is to go out, and a great many more in lesser employments. I fancy these reports are spred to draw in as many as they can to oppose the new Scheme. I can hardly think any body will be turn'd out of the Cabinet, except the T—r, and the P—y S—l.[4] Perhaps my Ld Pau—t[5] may lay down. Certainly the Sec—ry[6] may continue in if he pleases, and I don't hear that he is dispos'd to resign, or that he is so attach'd to any Minister, as to enter into their resentments. What has John of Bucks[7] done? and yet the report is very strong, that he is to be succeeded by my L^d T—or. The Duke of Shrewsbury was one out of eight or nine Lords, that stood by my Ld Bol—ke yesterday in the debate about the Spanish Treaty, and spoke with a good deal of spirit. Is it likely he is to be turn'd out of all?[8] The Lords have made a Representation to the Queen, in which they desire her to surmount the insurmountable difficultys the Spanish Trade lyes under by the last Treaty.[9] It is thought there was a Majority in the House to have prevented such a Reflection upon the Treaty, if they had come to a division. The clamour of the Merchants, Whig and Tory, has been too great to have pass'd a Vote in vindication of it, as it stands rati-

---

[1] Oxford.   [2] Bolingbroke.   [3] Atterbury.

[4] The Earl of Dartmouth, Lord Privy Seal.

[5] Earl Poulett, Lord Steward of the Household.

[6] William Bromley, Secretary of State (Southern Department). The office holders named can, on the whole, be regarded as friendly to Oxford.

[7] The Duke of Buckingham.

[8] The offices of Lord Chamberlain and Viceroy of Ireland.

[9] On 2 July the Lords took into consideration the three explanatory articles which had been added at Madrid to the Treaty of Commerce with Spain signed at Utrecht, and for which Bolingbroke and Arthur Moore were mainly responsible, and after long debate, in which Oxford said that the articles were not beneficial, it was resolved to refer the papers to the Queen. Her answer was reported on the 5th, and regarded as unsatisfactory; whereupon the difficulties which attended the Spanish trade were represented to her. See Boyer's *Political State*, July 1714, pp. 564–72.

fyed, but my Ld Anglesey and his Squadron seem'd willing to oppose any censure of it, and yet this Representation was suffer'd to pass no body knows how. To day they are to take into consideration the Queen's answer to their Address, desiring to know who advis'd her to ratify the Explanation of three Articles. She sent them word she thought there was little difference between that, and what was sign'd at Utrecht. When they rise, I will tell you what they have done. The last money Bill was sent up yesterday, so that in all probability the Parliament will be up in two or three days,[1] and then we shall be entertain'd with Court Affairs. I hope you got mine last post, and one a fortnight ago. Will the change of the Ministry affect Elwood?[2] He is in pain about it, and I am told the people of Ireland are making a strong opposition against the present Provost.

The consideration of the Queen's answer is deferr'd till to morrow. I am now with my Ld Guildford,[3] and three other Commissioners of Trade, who were examin'd to day at the Bar of the H: of L^ds. They are prodigiously pleas'd with what has been done, but I don't understand it well to give you an account, for the rapture they are in hinders them from explaining themselves clearly. I can only gather from their manner of discourse that they are come off without censure.

Endorsed by Swift at the beginning: Mr Ford | Affairs go Worse—
    At the end: Jul. 6. 1714 | Ch—F—

4804

William Thomas to Swift

6 July 1714

Rev^d S^r

I should not have presumed to break in upon your Retirem^t nor so much as enquire for your Address had not the Enclosed given me a fair Occasion to ask after your health.[4] I need not add any thing to

---

[1] Parliament was prorogued on 9 July.

[2] John Elwood hoped to succeed Benjamin Pratt as Provost of Trinity College, Dublin. Pratt was waiting in vain for a bishopric.

[3] Francis North, second Baron Guildford, whom Swift regarded as 'a mighty silly fellow'. No reason for 'rapture' is discoverable in the report of the examination of Moore and the other Commissioners given in Boyer's *Political State*.

[4] This letter evidently refers, like the writer's preceding one (see 22 June), to the business between Fetherston and Baron Scrope.

w^t the Papers will inform you touching that affair. The person mentioned in the Baron's Letter has not yet called upon me. When you
have Endorsed the Letter of Attorney, please to return that & the
Baron's Letter that I may punctually follow his Directions. I dare
not mention anything of Politicks to one that has purposely withdrawn himself from the Din of it. I shall only tell you that your
friends applaud your Conduct with relation to your own Ease, but
they think it hard you should Abdicate at a juncture your friendship
seems to be of most use to them. I am sure some of them want your
advice as well as assistance. You will forgive this Digression from
Business when I tell you I shall not repeat this trouble not having so
much as kept a Copy of your Direction. You may Direct your Commands to me under Cover to our Common Friend.[1] I hope you
believe me too sensible of Obligations to need formall assurances of
the sincere respect wherewith I am | Revd S^r | Your most Obed^t &
most | humble Servt

W^m: Thomas

Endorsed by Swift: July. 6th 1714 | Mr Thomas, Sec^rty | to Ld Treas^r
   and: Mr Thomas. | Jul. 6. 1714

4804

Erasmus Lewis to Swift

Whitehall | July 6. 1714

You give me such good reasons for your desire of knowing what
becomes of our grand affair, that to oblige you and perhaps to give
my self vent I'le tell you w^t I think on't. the two Lady's[2] seem to
have determin'd the fall of the Dragon, and to entertain a chimerical
notion, that there shall be no Monsr le Premier, but that all power
shall reside in one, and profit in the other. the man of mercury[3]
soothes them in this notion, with great dexterity and reason, for he
will be mons^r le premier then of course, by virtue of the little seal. his

---

[1] i.e. Erasmus Lewis.

[2] The Duchess of Somerset, still Mistress of the Robes, and Lady Masham,
both exercised at Court an influence hostile to Oxford. Ball suggests, with
probability, that the Duchess had no friendly feelings for Bolingbroke, but she
believed that in the event of the Queen's death a Whig government would almost
certainly replace that in power if Bolingbroke was chief Minister and not Oxford.

[3] Bolingbroke.

character is to bad to carry the great Ensigns, therefore he takes another method and I think it very artfull, viz. to continue his present station, to wch. the power may altogether be as properly attach'd as to the wand. in this brangle I am no otherwise concernd, than that I must lose part of the pleasure I had in the conversation of my friends, and that I am really apprehensive the two Lady's may suffer by the undertaking, for the man, of mercury's bottom is too narrow, his faults of the first magnitude, and we can't find, that there is any scheme in the world how to proceed. mercurialis complains that the Dragon has usd him barbarously, that he is in with the Democraticals, and never conferred a single obligation upon him since he had the wand. le temps nous eclaircira.

I propose to move on the 2d of August to Bath, and to stay there or goe from thence according as our Chaos settles here, I believe I shall not go to Abercothy[1] otherwise I would attend you. shan't we meet at Bath, before I begun this Paragraph I sh'd have added something to the former, wch is, that the Dragon is accusd of having betray'd his friends yesterday upon the matter of the three Explanatory articles of the Spanish treaty of Commerce,[2] wch he allowd not to be beneficial, and that the Qu. might better press for their being changd if it was the sense of the house they ought to be so. the Address then passd without a negative.

I thank you for the account you give me of the farm in Buckinghamshire. I could like the thing and the price too very well, but when it comes to a point I own my weakness to you I can't work my self up to a resolution whilst I have any hope of the 200^l a year I told you [of] in my own parish it lies now at sale. if I miss I wd catch greedily at the other.

When I am at the Bath, I'le set down the hints you desire.

Above Lewis's letter Swift has written: Ld Treasurer Oxford begins to decline at Court

And at end: Lewis July. 6th 1714

[1] Lewis's birthplace near Caermathen.
[2] See i. 397, n. 1.

John Barber to Swift

London, July 6. 1714

Hon^d S^{r1}

I had yrs of the 3^d Instant, and am heartily glad of yr being in Health, which I hope will continue. Pray draw what Bills you please, I'll pay them at demand. I will take Care of Mrs Rolt's affair:[2] I wish you would write to her. I had a Visit from one M^{rs}. Brackley[3] to day; she gives her humble Service, and desired my Assistance with Gen. Hill. I told her it was best to stay till there was a *Master*, and I did not doubt but that something would be done. I fortunately met Ld Bol. yesterday, the minute I had yr Letter; I attack'd him for some wine, & he immeediately order'd you two dozen of Red Fr. wine, and one dozen of strong Arazina White wine: The Hamper will be sent to Morrow by Robt Stone the Wantage Carrier, and will be there a Friday: I am afraid it will cost you 5^s to George, my Lord's Butler, but I would do nothing without Order. My Lord bid me tell you this Morning that he will write to you, and let you know, That as great a Philosopher as you are, you have had the Pip: That the Publick affairs are carried on with the same Zeal and quick Dispatch as when you was here; nay, that they are improv'd in several Particulars. That the same good Understanding continues: That he hopes the World will be the better for yr Retirement: That yr *inimitable Pen* was never more wanted than now; and more, which I can't remember: I believe he expects you should write to him. He spoke many affectionate and handsome Things in yr Favour. I told him yr story of the *Spaniel*, which made him laugh heartily.

---

[1] No address, but at the head of the letter Swift has written 'J— B—r'.

[2] The exact relationship of Patty Rolt to Swift cannot be traced. She is frequently mentioned in the *Journal* and in his letters. Her first husband appears to have fled abroad. In indigent circumstances she moved from one cheap lodging to another. She married as her second husband a servant of the Earl of Sussex called Lancelot; but Swift was still giving her financial assistance in 1735.

[3] Probably this was the Mrs. Bradley mentioned in the *Journal*, 18 Sept. 1711. She was a servant to Lady Giffard (Julia Longe, *Martha Lady Giffard*, p. 213).

Swift to Miss Esther Vanhomrigh

July. 8. 1714[1]

I find you take heavily that touch on your Shoulder;[2] I would not have writt to you so soon, if it were not to tell you that if you want to borrow any money, I would have you send to Mr Barber or Ben Took,[3] which you please, and let them know it, and the sum, and that I will stand bound for it, and send them my Bond. I did not know that our Posts went on Tuesday[4] else I would have writt 2 days ago to tell you this. I do not see how you can be uneasy when the year is out, for you can pay onely what you receive, you are answerable for no more. And I suppose you have not given Bonds to pay your Mothers Debts. As to your 2¹¹ 5ˢ that you gave your note for, if that be all it is a Trifle, and your owning it with so much Apology looks affected; if you have no more secret Debts than that, I shall be very glad. But still, I cannot understand how any of those Creditors of your Mother can give you the least Trouble, unless there be some Circumstance that I do not know the Bottom of. I believe I shall not stay here much longer, and therefore, if you want to borrow money I would have you do it soon, and of the two rather of Ben Took; because I have just drawn a Note upon Barber for thirty Guinneas for my own Expences. I believe a Bond had better be sent to me down to sign, and I will send it back to you, and you may give it Ben. You may speak freely to Ben of this; and if he has no money

---

[1] Vanessa's mother had died before this letter was written, and numerous debts were contracted both by Vanessa and her sister Mary (who though six or seven years the younger, seems to have been decidedly the more extravagant of the two in the matter of drapery). It was probably on this occasion that Vanessa borrowed £50 at 5 per cent. from Ben Tooke. The interest was apparently never paid, and the accumulated sum was one of the many claims which were showered upon Berkeley, her executor, when he was in London in 1726–7. Vanessa had voluntarily made herself responsible for a number of her mother's debts, whereof one, it is interesting to note, was for coffee supplied from the St. James's Coffee-house. On 28 Jan. of this year (1713–14) she gave to one Katherine Hill a promissory note for £33. 7s. 6d., being a debt of her mother's; and before leaving London in October she had pawned some jewels to John Barber (see Swift to Barber 15 Oct. 1720).—Freeman.

[2] The touch on the shoulder may imply an encounter with a bailiff.

[3] Benjamin Tooke is referred to frequently in the *Journal*. Swift had secured for him the appointment of publisher of the *Gazette*.

[4] Swift was writing on Thursday.

by him we must apply to Barber. I am forced to conclude in hast because the Post house is 2 Miles off, and it[1] will be too late if I stay longer; adieu.

My Service to Molkin.

Address: To Mrs Van-Homrigh, at M^r | Handcook's House in little Ryder Street | near St James's Street | London
Postmark: Wantage 9 [J] y
Endorsed: 3

4804

John Arbuthnot to Swift

Kensington July 10th | 1714[2]

Dear Brother

I have talk'd of your affair to no body but My Lady M–m, she tells me that she has it very much at heart, & would gladly do it for her own sake & that of her freinds but thinks it not a fitt season to speak about it.[3] We are indeed in such a strange Condition as to politicks that no body can tell now who is for who. it were worth the while to be here four & twenty hours, only to consider the oddness of the scene. I am sure it would make yow relish your country life better. The Dragon holds fast with a dead grype the little Machine[4] if he would have taken but half so much pains to have done other things, as he has of late to Exert him self against the Esquire,[5] he might have been a dragon, instead of a dagon. I would no more have suffered & done what he has, than I would have sold my self to the Gallys. haec inter nos. however they have gott now rid of the parlimt & may have time to think of a scheme, perhaps they may have one allready. I know nothing but 'tis fitt to rally the broken forces under some head or another They really did very well the last day but one in the house of Lords. but yesterday, they were in a flame about the Queens answer, till the Queen came in & putt an end to it.[6] The Dragon showd me your letter[7] & seemd mightily pleasd with it. he

---

[1] A word is obliterated between 'and' and 'it'.

[2] At the head of the letter Swift has written: 'Affairs still Worse.'

[3] The reference is apparently to Swift's application for the position of Historiographer.

[4] The symbol of his office.   [5] Bolingbroke.

[6] Parliament had been prorogued the previous day.

[7] That of 3 July.

has pay'd ten pounds for a manuscript of which I beleive ther are
severalls in town, it is a history of the last invasion of Scotland.[1]
wrote just as plain, tho not so well as another History which yow &
I know, with characters of all the men now living, The very names
& invitation that was sent to the pretender, This by a flaming Jacobite
that wonders that all the world are not so. perhaps it may be a Whig
that personates a Jacobite. I saw two sheets of the beginning which
was treason every line. if it go's on at the same rate of plain dealing,
it is a very extraordinary piece, & worth your while to come up to
see it only. Mr Lockhart they say ownes it it is no more his than it
is mine.[2] dont be so dogged, but after the first Shower, come up to
town for a week or so. it is worth your while. your friends will be
glad to see yow, & none more than my self   adieu.

Address: For | The Reverend the | Dean of S^t patricks
Endorsed by Swift: Jul 10. 1714 | Dr Arbuthnot

4804

Charles Ford to Swift

London July 10

What answer shall I send? I am against any alteration, but additions I think ought by no means to be allow'd. I wish I had call'd
sooner at St Dunstan's, but I did not expect it would have come out
till thursday, and therefore did not go there till yesterday. Pray let
me know what you would have done. B.[3] was a Blockhead to shew
it at all, but who can help that? Write an answer either for yourself
or me, but I beg of you to make no condescentions.

Yesterday put an end to the Session and to your pain. We gain'd
a glorious victory in the House of Lords the day before. The attack
was made immediately against A. M—re, who appear'd at the Bar
with the other Commissioners of Trade. The South Sea Company

---

[1] Arbuthnot is referring to *Memoirs of the Affairs of Scotland from Queen
Anne's Accession to the Throne to the commencement of the Union of the two
Kingdoms of Scotland and England*, written by George Lockhart (1673–1731) of
Carnwath, and published anonymously. He was an active Jacobite and agent of
the Stuarts.

[2] Arbuthnot was mistaken.

[3] Barber.

had prepar'd the way[1] by voting him guilty of a Breach of trust, and uncapable of serving them in any office for the future. This passed without hearing what he had to say in his defence, and had the usual fate of such unreasonable reflections. Those who propos'd the resolutions were blam'd for their violence, and the person accus'd appearing to be less guilty than they made him, was thought to be more innocent than I doubt he is. The Whigs propos'd two Questions in the H: of L^ds against him and lost both, one by 12 and the other I think by 18 votes.

Court affairs go on as they did. The cry is still on the Captain's[2] side. Is not he the person B. means by one of the best pens in England? It's only my own conjecture, but I can think of no body else. Have you the Queen's Speech, the L^ds Address &c. or shall I send them you, and do you want a comment? Have Pope and Parnell been to visit you as they intended?[3] I had a letter yesterday from Gay who is at the Hague,[4] and presents his humble service to you. He has writ to Mr Lewis too but his respect makes him keep greater distance with him, and I think mine is the pleasanter letter, which I am sorry for. We were alarm'd by B. two days ago. He sent Tooke word our friend was ill in the country, which we did not know how to interpret till he explain'd it. It was M^rs M—[5] he meant, but she is in no danger. Pray write immediately that there may be no further delay to what we ought to have had a week ago.

Endorsed by Swift: M^r F—d. | R̃ Jul. 12 | 1714

[1] 'for a censure' is crossed out after 'way'. Arthur Moore rose from humble beginnings to remarkable business ability and wealth. He antagonized the merchant class of London; and at this time he was under attack for clandestine trade and breach of trust.

[2] Bolingbroke's.

[3] Pope and Parnell went over from Binfield to Letcombe on Sunday 4 July, and stayed with Swift some days. Pope describes the visit in an amusing letter written to Arbuthnot (Sherburn, i. 233).

[4] Gay was Secretary to Lord Clarendon, Envoy Extraordinary to Hanover. Gay's letter to Ford is printed on p. 221 of Nichol Smith's *Letters of Swift to Ford*.

[5] Mrs. Manley was now living in poverty at Finchley. See *Portland MSS.* v. 458, 491.

John Barber to 'Samuel Bridges'

Lambeth Hill, July 6. 1714

[*Enclosure*]

S^r

I thankfully acknowledge the receipt of a Packet sent last Sunday: I have shewn it only to one Person, who is charm'd with it, and will make some small Alterations and Additions to it, with your leave: You will the easier give leave, when I tell you, that it is one of the best Pens in England. Pray favour me with a Line. I am | S^r Yr most Obedient Servt. |

Jn: Barber

Address: To | Samuel Bridges,[1] Esqr; | at St Dunstans Coffee-house | Fleet-street
Endorsed by Swift: July. 6th 1714 | J— B—rs Letter | about the Pamphlet

Rothschild[2]

Swift to Charles Ford

July. 11. 1714

I thank you for your long kind Letters. B—[3] writt to me since, but took no notice of any thing come to his hand, perhaps he will not venture without advice, and advice will ruin it. Why did you not blot out whatever you had a Mind; as for Service it will do, a Fiddlestick. It will vex them, and that's enough. Your Letters will make good Memoirs; I have putt up your last among my Papers, I have had all you sent me before.[4]—No, I hope and belive Elwood[5] will be safe; but who knows any thing in such a Confusion. Some of the Changes you mention, were what we were scheaming severall months ago; particularly that of L^d Tr—or and upon second reading, I think none else; for the rest seems wild to me, but strange things may happen in our land in less than six weeks.

[1] Ford's pseudonym.
[2] Lord Rothschild's Library No. 2282 (9).
[3] Barber's letter, 6 July, see p. 55.
[4] Ford's letter of 6 July, the first now preserved. The letter of 10 July had not yet been received.
[5] Elwood was hoping to be appointed Provost of Trinity College, Dublin.

The inclosed.   To the Revrd Mr Archdeacon Wall
over against the Hospitall in Queen Street
Dublin.¹

Wall tells me Parvisol is playing the Rogue with me in my Accounts, and run in great Arrears. I shall be ruined with staying here.

Address: To Charles Ford Esqr | at His Office at White-hall | London
Postmarks: Wantage *and* 12 IY

4804

Viscount Bolingbroke to Swift

[13 July 1714.]

I never laugh'd my Dear Dean, att your leaving the Town; on the contrary I thought the resolution of doing so, att the time when you took it, a very wise one.² But I confess I laugh'd, and very heartily too, when I heard you affected to find within the village of Letcombe all your heart desir'd. in a word I judg'd of you just as you tell me in your letter that I should judg. if my grooms did not live a happyer life, than I have done this great while, I am sure you would quit my service. Be pleas'd to apply this reflexion.

Indeed I wish I had been with you with Pope and Parnel, quibus neque animi candidiores. in a little time perhaps I may have leisure to be happy. I continue in the same opinions & resolutions as you left me in, I will stand or fall by them.

adieu no alteration in my fortune or circumstances can ever³ alter that sincere friendship with which I am Dear Dean yrs

July 13 | 1714

I fancy you will have a visit from that great Politician & Casuist, the Duke.⁴ He is att Oxford with Mr Clarke.⁵

Endorsed by Swift at the head of the letter: Lord Bolingbroke on my Retiring
   On verso of second leaf: July. 13th 1714 | Lord Bolingbroke.

---

¹ The enclosure, dated 3 July, was safely received by Walls.
² Probably Swift had written to Bolingbroke on receiving the message contained in Barber's letter of the 6th.   ³ Ball mistakenly prints 'even'.
⁴ The Duke of Ormonde, who was Chancellor of Oxford as well as of Dublin University.
⁵ George Clarke, 1661–1736, a politician and virtuoso. He had been long known to Ormonde, for when attending King William in Ireland as Secretary

61

Pierpont Morgan Library[1]

Swift to John Arbuthnot

July. 13th 1714.

Dear

I wonder how you came to mention that Business to L^{dy} M[asham],[2] if I guess right, that the Business is the Histor—'s[3] Place; It is in the D^e of Shr—'s[4] Gift, and he sent Ld Bol. word, that thô he was under some Engagem^t, he would get it me &c, since which time I never mentioned it, thō I had a Memoriall some Months in my Pocket, which I believe you saw but I would never give it Ldy M— because things were embroyld with her.[5] I would not give two Pence to have it for the Value of it; but I had been told by L^d P—[6] Ldy M— and you, that the Qu— had a Concern for her History &c: and I was ready to undertake it. I thought Ld Bol— would have done such a Trifle, but I shall not concern my self, and I should be sorry the Qu— should be asked for it, otherwise than as what would be for her Honor and Reputation with Posterity &c. Pray how long, do you think I should be suffered to hold that Post in the next Reign. I have inclosed you the originall Memoriall as I intended it; and if Ld Bol— thinks it of any moment, let him do it; but do not give him the Memoriall, unless he be perfectly willing: For I insist again upon it, that I am not asking a Favor; and there is

at War he had lived most of his time in the Duke's castle at Kilkenny. In 1680 he was elected a fellow of All Souls, and retained the fellowship for the rest of his life. He served as a Tory M.P. for the University and several constituencies at intervals. He was a man of taste, of wealth, and a notable benefactor of Oxford.

[1] Ball (ii. 178) notes this draft letter without supplying the text, stating that it was 'a few years ago in the possession of Mr. Sabin of 172, New Bond Street'. The original, and other Swift letters, passed to the Pierpont Morgan Library. It has been printed by Maxwell B. Gold in the Appendix, pp. 176–8, of his *Swift's Marriage to Stella*, 1937; and in the *Gazette of the Grolier Club*, Apr. 1946, pp. 184–5.

[2] In his letter to Swift of 10 July Arbuthnot said, 'I have talk'd of your affair to no body but my Lady M—m'.

[3] Historiographer's.

[4] Duke of Shrewsbury's. The post was in his gift as Lord Chamberlain. Bolingbroke wrote to the Duke, 5 Jan. 1713–14 (*Letters of Bolingbroke*, ii. 581), soliciting the appointment for Swift. On the day before this letter was written Thomas Madox had been sworn into the office (B.M. Add. MS. 4572, F. 108).

[5] As mentioned before Swift was now out of favour with Lady Masham.

[6] Peterborough.

an end of that Matter, only one word more, that I would not accept it if offered, onely that it would give me an Opportunity of seeing those I esteem and love, the little time they will be in Power. You desire me to come to Toun, indeed I will not: I am overcoming you by Absence as fast as I can, and you would have me come and break my Heart. Shall I not be miserable to stand by and see things going every day nearer to ruin; can I (as I have repeated to you often) do the least good to my self, my Friends, or the Publick: and do you think much Spirit to continue when I have no Call, and be wholly insignificant. You and Friend L[ewis] entirely approved of my Retiring for these very Reasons, and you two onely know how often our fairest schemes & hopes have come to nothing—Do you really think the Dragon was at Bottom—pleased with my Lett^r;[1] I sh be apt to doubt it. He will be hanged before he will answer me. I should be glad to see that Manuscript about the Invasion: & I think I ought to have a Copy of it.[2] I must repeat it again—that if Ld Bol— be not full as ready to give this Memoriall inclosed, as you are to desire him, let it drop; for in the present View of Things I am perfectly indifferent: for I think every Reason for my leaving you is manifestly doubled within these 6 weeks by your own Account as well as that of others.—Besides I take it perfectly ill that the Dragon who promised me so solemnly last year to make me easy in my Debts has never done the least thing to it;[3] so that I can safely say I never received a Penny from a Minister in my Life; and tho I seem to complain, yet to you I will speak it, that I am very uneasy that I am likely to lose near 300^ll beside the heavy debts I ly under at a Season of my Life when I hoped to have no Cares of that Sort.— and this puts me in mind of something M^r L[ewis] writt to me, that I should get the Secr^tys to contribute 50^ll[4] (they promised a great deal more) to sett a certain troublesome matter right, that you know of. I protest I cannot get so many shillings, neither do I think they expect I should do it. I conceive Ld Bol— would be ready to do it

[1] Swift's letter to Lord Oxford of 3 July.

[2] Lockhart's *Memoirs Concerning the Affairs of Scotland* mentioned by Arbuthnot in his letter to Swift of 10 July.

[3] Swift is here alluding to the heavy expenses in which he was involved by his induction to the Deanery of St. Patrick's; and to the £1,000 promised by Oxford towards defraying them. In this letter it is noticeable that Swift writes more kindly of Bolingbroke than of Oxford.

[4] Presumably this was the £50 which he owed Fetherston, Prebendary of St. Patrick's. See Swift's letter to Archdeacon Walls, 8 Aug. 1714.

for asking, if you would give your self the Trouble, for I cannot do it & I hope M^r L— would get one Moiety from Sec^{try} Bar[ber][1] will you concert it with M^r L— The Dragon did his Part in it very handsomely Pardon me for speaking to you of this; but M^r L— will satisfy you how it stands. My Humble Service to L^d & L^{dy} M— & Mrs Hill.

Deane Swift 1768

Charles Ford to Swift

London, July 15. 1714.

You see I was in the right; but I could wish the booby had not convinced me by naming my Lord *Bolingbroke*,[2] and then I should have dealt well enough with him. Since it has happened so, the best remedy I could think of, was to write him a very civil answer; in which, however, I have desired to see the alterations: this is mentioned with great respect to my Lord. Though he is promised to have it again to-morrow, it is probable he may be disappointed, and there may be time enough for me to receive your directions what I shall do, when I get it into my hands. If the alterations are material, shall I send it to some other printer as it was first written? Reflect upon every thing you think likely to happen, and tell me beforehand what is proper to be done, that no more time may be lost. I hate the dog for making his court in such a manner.

I am very sorry you have had occasion to remove your premier minister.[3] We are told now, we shall have no change in ours, and that the Duke of *Shrewsbury* will perfectly reconcile all matters. I am sure you will not believe this any more than I do; but the *Dragon* has been more chearful than usual for three or four days; and therefore people conclude the breaches are healed. I rather incline to the opinion of those who say he is to be made a Duke, and to have a pension. Another reason given why there is to be no change is, because the Parliament was not adjourned to issue new writs in the room of those who were to come in upon the new scheme, that they

---

[1] So described on account of the kindly secretarial duties he discharged for Swift.

[2] Ford must have enclosed a second letter from Barber, stating that Bolingbroke was the person altering *Some Free Thoughts*.

[3] Parvisol.

might sit in the house at the next meeting. But I can't see why an adjournment may not do as well at the beginning as at the end of a session; and certainly it will displease less in *January* or *February*, than it would have done in *July*. The Whigs give out the Duke of *Marlborough*[1] is coming over, and his house is actually now fitting up at *St. James*'s. We have had more variety of lies of late than ever I remember. The history we were formerly talking of would swell to a prodigious size, if it was carried on.[2] There was a fire last night on *Tower-Hill*,[3] that burnt down forty or fifty houses. You say nothing of coming to town. I hope you don't mean to steal away to *Ireland* without seeing us.

Deane Swift 1768

Charles Ford to Swift

London July 17. 1714.

A second to-morrow is almost past, and nothing has been yet left at *St. Dunstan*'s. *B.*[4] will lose by his prodigious cunning; but that is nothing to the punishment he deserves. Had it been only his fear, he would have chosen somebody else to consult with; but the rogue found out it was well written, and saw the passages that galled. I am heartily vext at the other person, from whom one might have expected a more honourable proceeding. There is something very mean in his desiring to make alterations, when I am sure he has no reason to complain, and is at least as fairly dealt with as his competitor. Besides, a great part of it is as much for his service as if he had given directions himself to have it done. What relates to the Pretender is

[1] Marlborough and the Duchess were reported in the newspapers to be at Ostend on 18 July. They landed at Dover on 2 Aug., and arrived in London on Wednesday, 4 Aug.

[2] For writings supplementary to the *Four Last Years of the Queen* see *Prose Works*, ed. Davis, vol. viii.

[3] 'This morning about Two of the Clock a Dreadful Fire began at a Cane Chair-Makers in Gravel Lane in Hounds-Ditch, they being Boiling of Varnish; and before it could be Extinguished Burnt down near 20 of those Houses besides 5 next the Street in Hounds-Ditch.' *Dawks's News Letter*, 15 July 1714. The *Evening Post* says 'above Thirty Houses, besides many more very much damaged'.

[4] Barber; the 'other person' is Bolingbroke.

of the utmost use to him;[1] and therefore I am as much surprized at his delay, as at his ungenerous manner of treating an unknown author, to whom he is so much obliged. But perhaps I may wrong him, and he won't desire to turn the whole to his own advantage. If it had come to me yesterday, or to-day, I was resolved to have sent it to some other printer without any amendment; but now I shall wait till I have your directions. I wish you had employed somebody else at first; but what signifies wishing now? After what *B*. writ in his last, I can hardly think he will be such a —— as not to let me have it: and in my answer I have given him all manner of encouragement to do it. He has as much assurance as he can well desire, that the alterations shall be complied with, and a positive promise that it shall be returned to him the same day he leaves it at *St. Dunstan*'s.

I can't imagine why we have no mischief yet. Sure we are not to be disappointed at last, after the bustle that has been made. It is impossible they[2] can ever agree, and I want something to make my letters still entertaining. I doubt you will hardly thank me for them, now the parliament is up; but as soon as any thing happens you shall know it.

The Queen has not yet appointed the time for removing to *Windsor*. My Lord Chief Baron *Ward*[3] is dead, and we have already named seven successors, among whom is our Lord Chancellor *Phips*. *Frank* Annesley was to have had his place under my Lord *Anglesey*,[4] so that it is well for him[5] we have provided him with another for life.

[1] Neither Swift nor Ford knew that Bolingbroke was at this time treating with the Pretender.

[2] Oxford and Bolingbroke.

[3] Sir Edward, Chief Baron of the Exchequer since 1695. He was succeeded by Sir Samuel Dodd.

[4] Anglesey was expected to succeed Shrewsbury as Lord Lieutenant of Ireland (*Portland MSS.* vii. 192). Phipps was succeeded as Lord Chancellor by Alan Brodrick, and returned to practice at the English Bar. Francis Annesley (1663–1750), who was Anglesey's cousin, was a Bencher of the Inner Temple, and at this time M.P. for Westbury. In May 1711 he promoted the Bill for the building of fifty new churches in London, saw it through the House of Commons, and thereafter he was one of the commissioners for the building of the churches.

[5] i.e. Phipps.

Erasmus Lewis to Swift

Whitehall | July. 17. 1714.

I am sorry to find by those [that] have fresher advices from you than yours of the 11th to me, that Parvisol's conduct puts you under a necessity of changing the Administration; for it will probably draw you to Ireland whether you will or no, However I hope to see you at Bath three weeks hence, whatever happens. I meet with no man or woman who pretend upon any probable grounds to judge who will carry the great point. our *female friend*[1] told the Dragon in her own house last thursday morning, these words, you never did the Q. any service, nor are you capable of doing her any, He made no reply, but supped with her and mercurialis[2] that night at her own house, his revenge is not the less meditated for that, he tells the words clearly & distinctly to all mankind, those who range under his banner, call her ten thousand bitches & kitchen-wenches. those who hate him doe the same, and from my heart I grieve that she sh'd give such a loose to her passion, for she is susceptible of true friendship, and has many social & domestick virtues.[3] the Great Attorney[4] who made you a sham offer of the Yorkshire Living, had a long conference with the Dragon on thursday,[5] kisd him at parting & curs'd him at night, he went to the Countrey yesterday, from whence some conjecture nothing considerable will be done soon. Lord Harley & Lady Harriot[6] went this morning to Oxford, he has finish'd all matters with Lord Pelham,[7] as far as can be done without an act of Parliamt.

---

[1] Lady Masham.

[2] Bolingbroke.

[3] Swift entertained the same opinion of her. Lord Dartmouth's opinion of her was: 'She was exceedingly mean and vulgar in her manners, and of a very unequal temper, childishly exceptious and passionate' (Burnet's *History*, Oxford, 1833, vi. 37).

[4] Lord Chancellor Harcourt. There is evidence (*Portland MSS.* vol. v) that Harcourt had been essaying the difficult part of a mediator.

[5] The 15th.

[6] Lady Henrietta Cavendish Holles, daughter and sole heiress of John, Duke of Newcastle. Her marriage with Edward Harley, Oxford's son, had taken place in the previous year. Before 'went' the words 'into the country yesterd' are scored out.

[7] To his nephew Thomas, second Baron Pelham, the future Duke of Newcastle, Lord Harley's father-in-law, bequeathed the greater part of his vast possessions.—Ball.

the composition was sign'd by the Auditor[1] & Naylor[2] brother in law to Lord Pelham this day se'night Lord Harley is to have the whole of the Cavendish Estate[3] which is valued at 10000l. pr. an. and has upon it 40000l pounds worth of timber, but three of this ten thousand a year he had by the will, he remits to Lord Pelham the 20000l charg'd for Lady Harriots fortune that lie convenient for him to the value of about 20000l more. according to my computation Ld Harley gets by the agreement (if the timber is worth 40000l) 140,000, and when the joyntures fall in to him will have 16000l a year, but the Cant is, 26,000. Lord Pelham will really have 26,000l a year from the Newcastle family wch with his Paternal [estate] will be twice as much as Lord Harley, the Estate of the later is judgd to be in the best condition, and some vain glorious friends of ours say it is worth more than the others, but let that pass. adieu.

Endorsed by Swift: Mr L— | Rx. Jul. 19. | 1714
At the head of the letter Swift has two notes: (a) The Dragon Lord Treasurer Oxford so called by the Dean. by Contraryes, and for he was the mildest, wisest and best Minister that ever served a Prince. *(b)* Mrs Masham was the Queen's Favorite, fell out in a Rage, reproaching Lord Oxford very injuriously.

4804

Lord Harley to Swift

17 July 1714

Brother Swift,[4]

Your sister has at last got rid of her lawyers. We are just setting out for Oxford, where we hope to see you. I am, | Your affectionate brother |

Harley.

[1] Oxford's brother, Edward Harley, M.P. for Leominster.
[2] George Naylor, M.P. for Seaford.
[3] To which John Holles, Duke of Newcastle, had succeeded through his wife, one of the daughters of Henry Cavendish, second Duke of Newcastle of the first creation.—Ball.
[4] Lord Harley was an original member of the Brothers' Club. The 'sister' was his wife, Lady Henrietta Cavendish Holles, whom he had married about a year before. The lawyers had, presumably, been engaged with financial terms relating to the marriage.

John Arbuthnot to Swift

London: July 17 1714

Dear Brother

I thought it necessary to speak to L M—m[1] about that affair,[2] because I believe it will be necessary to give her Majesty the same notion of it which the memoriall dos, & not that yow are asking a little scandalous sallary for a sinecure. Lewis despairs of it & thinks it quite over since a certain affair. I will not think so. I gave your letter with the enclosed Memorial[3] Cavalierement to L B—ke[4] he read it, & seemd concernd at some part of it expressing himself thus, that it would be amongst the eternal scandals of the govert to suffer a man of your character, that had so well deservd of them to have the least uneasy thought, about these matters. as to the 50[11] he was ready to pay it;[5] & if he had had it about him would have givn it me: The Dragon all the while was walking with the Duke of Sh—berry,[6] so my L B—ke told me, I *would imm*ediatly stir*rin this* matter, but *I know not how I stand with some folks* (for the D S—rry is taken him self to the Dragon, in appearance) *I know how I stand w*[t] *that man,* (pointing to the Dragon) but *as to the other I cant tell.* however, I *will claim his promise.* & so he took the Memorial. Dont think I make yow a bare compliment in what I am going to say for I can assure you I am in earnest I am in hopes to have two hundred pounds before I go out of town, & yow may command all or any part of it yow please as long as you have occasion for it I know what yow will say, *to see a scoundrell pretend to offer to lend me money.* our scituation at present is in short thus they have rompu en visiere with the Dragon, & yet dont know how to do w[t]out him M L M—m has in a Manner bid him defyance without any scheme, or Likeness of it in any form or shape as far as I can see. notwtstanding he visits cringes flatters &c. which is beyond my comprehension. I have a very comical accompt of Letcomb, & the D of S[t] patricks from pope,[7] with an Episode of the Burning glass. I was going to make an Epi Gramm upon the

---

[1] Lady Masham.

[2] The position of Historiographer. Five days before the date of this letter Thomas Madox had been appointed to the office. The salary was £200 a year.

[3] The Memorial, dated 15 Apr. 1714, was printed by Deane Swift in 1765. See *Prose Works*, ed. Temple Scott, v. 477.

[4] Bolingbroke.   [5] See p. 41.   [6] Shrewsbury.

[7] As noted before, p. 59. Pope and Parnall paid a visit to Swift at Letcombe.

imagination of your Burning your own History w^t a^1 Burning glass. I wish pope or parnell would putt it into Rhyme. the thought is this, Apollo speaks that since he had inspired yow to reveal those things which were hid ev'n from his own light such as the feeble springs of some Great events, & perceaving that a faction who could not bear their deeds to be brought to light had condemnd it to an ignominious flame, that it might not perish so, he was resolv'd to consume it w^t his own a celestial one & then yow must conclude with some simile Thus &c. Ther are two or three that will fitt it. Whetstone has at, last publish'd his project of the longitude; the most ridiculous thing that ever was thought on, but a pox on him he has spoild one of my papers of Scriblerus', which was a proposal for the longitude not very unlike his to this purpose, that since ther was no pole for East & west that all the princes of Europe should joyn & build two prodigious poles upon high mountains with a vast Light house to serve for a pole Star. I was thinking of a calculation of the time charges & dimensions. Now you must understand his project is by light houses & explosion of bombs, at a certain hour. Lewis invited me to dinner to day, & has disappointed me. I thought to have said some thing more about yow. I have nothing more to add but my Dear friend a Dieu.

Endorsed by Swift: D^r Ar— | Rx Jul. 19. | 1714

Deane Swift 1765

Swift to the Duke of Ormonde

July 17th, 1714.

My Lord,

I never expected that a great man should remember me in absence, because I knew it was unreasonable, and that your Grace is too much troubled with persons about you,[2] to think of those who are out of the way. But, if Dr. Pratt[3] has done me right, I am mistaken, and your Grace has almost declared that you expected a letter from me; which you should never have had, if the Ministry had been like you:

----

[1] Ball prints 'the'.
[2] Swift hoped that Ormonde's influence would still save the Ministry.
[3] Evidently Pratt was still in London.

For then I should have always been near enough to have carried my own messages. But I was heartily weary of them; and your Grace will be my witness, that I despaired of any good success, from their manner of proceeding, some months before I left town; where I thought it became me to continue no longer, when I could do no service either to myself, my friends, or the public. By the accounts I have from particular friends, I find the animosity between the two Great Men does not at all diminish: Though I hear it is given out that your Grace's successor[1] has undertaken a general reconcilement. If it be true, this will succeed like the rest of his late undertakings.[2]

I must beg your Grace's pardon, if I intreat you, for several reasons, to see Lady Masham as often as you conveniently can: And I must likewise desire you to exert yourself in the disposal of the bishopricks in Ireland. It is a scandal to the Crown, and an injury to the Church, that they should be so long delayed. There are some hot headed people on the other side the water, who understand nothing of our Court, and would confound every thing; always employed to raise themselves upon the ruins of those characters they have blasted. I wish their intermeddling may not occasion a worse choice than your Grace approved of last winter. However, I beg you will take care that no injury be done to Dr. Pratt, or Dr. Elwood,[3] who have more merit and candour than a hundred of their detractors. I am, with the greatest respect, | My Lord, | Your Grace's most obedient, and | Most obliged humble servant, |

J. S.

Rothschild

Swift to Charles Ford

July. 18th. 1714

Here's a Splutter with your nasty Pamphlet; I fancy, one of L^d B—'s alterations will be to soften a Particular that seems to fall hard upon him: *Whether others have not contended for a greater Part in the*

---

[1] The Duke of Shrewsbury, Ormonde's successor as Lord Lieutenant.
[2] The allusion is to Shrewsbury's failure to reconcile party differences in Ireland.
[3] Pratt hoped for a bishopric; and Elwood hoped to succeed Pratt as Provost of Trinity College, Dublin.

Direction of Affairs &c., *than either Friendship, Gratitude, or*[1] &c. The Word *Gratitude* seems hard there, and may be left out; but I will not have any thing harder on the Dragon than it is; and if you dislike the Alterations, take back the Thing, and either burn it or send it to some other Printer as you think best. If the last, leave out the Word *Gratitude*, and let all the rest be as at first except what you think fit to change, for I rely altogether on your Judgment; and will not write one word more about it, say what you will. The D— of Shr— would certainly be a proper man to reconcile People, but I doubt it is too far gone: The D— would make a great Figure in doing it; but he wants the Circumstances of Courage and Truth. Ld Bol— writt to me last Post[2] and hints quite otherwise that Things are as bad as ever, or worse; so he did in an Ironicall message he sent me by B—r.[3] Barb— has writt to me thrice this last week and never said a Word of the Pamphlet, so I hope neither he nor L^d B— smoak. As to my coming to Town, I have no Thoughts of it, unless they send for me, as I am sure they will not; or unless they make me Historg^r4 which I am sure they never think of, and I shall not ask. I intend to take a Ramble into Herefordshire &c. about a fortnight hence, and for ought I know to Ireland about Michalmas. The Letter I writt to the Dragon was in the Style of a Parting. He has shewn it to Dr Arb^t— and pretends to be pleased with it: I nippt him a little in it. I believe you never paid the Sempstress in Westminster hall, nor took my Hankerchiefs. I ow her 3 or 4 shillings of an old Debt. She must stay till next Sessions like her Betters.

M^r L— writes me word that 50^11 should be got from the Secr^tys to finish that Troublesom Business you know of.[5] I have desired D^r A— to speak to Ld B. for his part, and it would be kind in M^r L— to speak to Mr Bromly for tother part. What can I do? I have no money; and I think it would be hard if they do not sett me right in such a Trifle as they promisd.

Upon second thoughts, how comicall a Thing was it to shew that Pamphlet to Ld Bol— of all men living. Just as if *the Publick Spirit* had been sent to Argyle for his Approbation—adieu.

Address: To Charles Ford Esqr | at his Office at White-hall | London
Postmarks: Wantage *and* 19 IY

---

[1] The passage is not in the printed text of *Some Free Thoughts.*
[2] Letter of 13 July.   [3] Barber's letter of 6 July.
[4] Historiographer.
[5] Lewis with reference to the Fetherston business.

Charles Ford to Swift

London July 20, 1714

Who would ever do any thing for them, when they are so negligent of their own interest? The Captain[1] must see what use it would be to him to have it publish'd, and yet he has not return'd it. You have another copy by you, I wish you would send it, and if you don't care it should appear in your own hand, I will get it transcrib'd. My Secretary is a boy of ten or eleven years old, and no discovery can be made by him. I don't know what my L^d Bo— may do, but I dare say Bar— do's not suspect from whence it comes. However I wonder he has not mention'd it to you.

I thought you had heard the Historiographer's place had been dispos'd of this fortnight. I know no more of him who has it, than that his name is Madocks. It would be imprudence in them to send for you, but I hope you will come. A reconcilement is impossible, and I can guess no reason why matters are delay'd, unless it be to gain over some Lords who stick firm to the Dragon, and others that are averse to the Captain. The D. of S—y declares against him in private conversation, I suppose because he is against every chief Minister, for it's known he has no kindness for the Collonel.[2] Ld Ang— rails at the Chancelor, for some opinion the Attorney and Solicitor G^l. have given relating to Ireland.[3] Who can act, when they have so much caprice to deal with.

Mr L. says he will speak to Mr Bromley for his part, and will engage it shall be paid as soon as Ld Bolingbroke has given his.[4] But it was mention'd before my Ld Treasurer, and he immediately took the whole upon himself. If they liv'd near one another, and a house between them was on fire, I fancy they would contend who should put it out, till the whole street was burnt. M^r L— goes into Wales the week after the next. I shall have the whole Town to myself. Now

---

[1] Bolingbroke.   [2] Oxford.

[3] On the question whether the Lord Mayor of Dublin could hold office for another year the opinions of six counsel, besides the Attorney and Solicitor-General, were taken. Four were found in favour of the Irish executive, and four in favour of the Dublin Corporation (Ball, *Judges in Ireland*, ii. 48–50; *Portland MSS.* v. 473).

[4] A reference apparently to the £1,000 promised to pay Swift's induction expenses.

it's my own, I begin not to value it. Pope and Parnell tell me you
design them a visit.[1] When do you go? If you are with them in the
middle of a week, I should be glad to meet you there. Let me know
where you are to be in Herefordshire, and I will send you some claret.
It is no compliment, for I am overstock'd, and it will decay before I
drink it. You shall have either old or new, I have too much of both.
I paid the woman for your handkerchiefs, but should not have given
her so much, if she had not assur'd me you agreed with her. I think
you may very well strike off the old debt, and she will have no reason
to complain. So I told her, but if you would have me I will pay her.

Pray send me the other copy,[2] or put me in a way of recovering
the former.

Endorsed by Swift: Rx Jul. 22. 1714 | Ch— F—

Forster copy[3]

Swift to John Grigsby

[20 July 1714]

Mr Grigsby

Pray pay to Mr John Barber My Dividend on one thousand pounds
being all my stock in the South Sea Company's Books, for half a
year's interest due at Midsummer last: and this shall be your sufficient Warrant.

Jonath: Swift

July 20. 1714

[1] At Binfield.
[2] Of *Some Free Thoughts.*
[3] Forster Collection: Red Box F. 44. E. 1. Forster does not state whence he
took the transcript. It was probably the item which appeared at the John Dillon
sale, No. 920, 10 June 1869, and was purchased by Waller for £1. 13s. 0d. This
same document again appeared at the American Arts Association Sale, Anderson
Sale, 2–3 May 1934. Cf. Swift to John Grigsby, accountant for the South Sea
Company, 15 Sept. 1713, at which time the stock stood at £500. The stock was
held by Swift on behalf of three friends. See his letter to Archdeacon Walls of
11 June 1714.

Hunter-Baillie Collection[1]

Swift to John Arbuthnot

Oxford. July. 22^d 1714

How came I here? why, L^d H—y writt to me,[2] and so I came to
have his Company and his L$^{dy's}$ 2 or 3 days. They go to morrow, and
I return to my Country place, where I will not stay a fortnight, and
then I will ramble somewhere else. The Language spoken to me
now, is that the Dragon will be out in a few days; and perhaps is
already, because Ld Chancell^r was summoned from his Country-
house 2 days ago by Ld Bol— in great hast, and they conceive it may
be, to put a finishing Stroak: I cannot heartily pardon your giving
over to advise L^{dy} M— who in my opinion is going on upon a very
dangerous Adventure without one Creature to direct her. I am told
that L^{dy} M— is much broke with the Dragon, as Ld Bol. and what
she s^d to the Dragon a week ago is of so desperate a Strain, that I can
not think her in a Temper to be at the Head or the Bottom of a
Change; nor do I believe a Change accompanyed with such Passion
can ever succeed. For God sake do not leave her to her self: Your
Post keeps you allways near her, and she cannot but think you her
Friend. I am quite struck with Accounts given me by those I am
now with. What can be your new Scheam, What are your Provoca-
tions. Are you sure of a Majority; Will not the Dragon when he is
out be able to draw off y^r Friends. Ld Bol—'s Language to me was
quite contrary to his present Proceedings; Therefore I do not approve the last, I know not what to say; but if I were to be of necessity
allways at Court like you, I would never let People run mad telling
and warning them sufficiently: You act^d a great Part a year ago
under the first Change; & will you not hinder men from kicking
down all if you can.—Pray write to me soon, and excuse y^{r}self, &
tell me how Things are   adieu—

[1] The original of this letter is contained in the Arbuthnot Letter Book, fol. 5,
Hunter-Baillie Collection, vol. 1, Royal College of Surgeons of England.

[2] While at Oxford Lord Harley stayed with Dr. William Stratford, Canon
of Christ Church. He had been Oxford's chaplain, and watched over Lord
Harley during his college course. From that time he carried on a continuous
correspondence with Harley. The letters are printed *H.M.C. Portland MSS.*
vol. vii.

4804

The Duke of Ormonde to Swift

July 22^d 1714.

S^r

I am very glad to hear from you[1] I thought you had hid your selfe from the world, and given over all thoughtes of your friends, I am very sorry for the reason of your retirement, I am witness to your endeavours to have made up, what I believe the Great Man you mention will hardely compas, I am of your opinion, that it is shameful that the Vacant Bishopricks are not disposed off, I shall doe all that lyes in my power to serve the Gentlemen that I have allready mentioned to the Queen, and hope, with good success.

for the Lady[2] you mention I shall endeavour to see her as often as I can, she is one, that I have a very greate esteem for,

I send you some Burgundy, which I hope you will like, it is very good to cure the Spleene, believe me with greate truthe | S^r | your most affectionat friende | and humble servant |

Ormonde

Endorsed by Swift: July 22^d 1714 | Duke of Ormonde

4804

Erasmus Lewis to Swift

Whitehall
July. 22. 1714

I receiv'd a Letter from you last Monday for my Lord Treasurer in a blank cover.

last Friday[3] Ld Chancellor went into the Countrey with a design to stay there to the 10th of Aug. but last tuesday he was sent for Express by Ld Bolingbroke. next tuesday the Queen goes to Windsor. w^t changes we are to have will probably appear before she goes. Dr Arbuthnot dines with me to day, & in the evening we goe to Kensington.

Endorsed by Swift: M^r L— | Rx Jul. 24 | 1714

[1] 17 July.   [2] Lady Masham.
[3] The 19th.

Charles Ford to Swift

22 July 1714.
London July 22ᵈ.

Pray send me the other copy,[1] and let us have the benefit of it, since you have been at the trouble of writing. Unless ——[2] be serv'd against his will, it is not like to be done at all, but I think you us'd to take a pleasure in good Offices of that kind, and I hope you won't let the cause suffer, tho I must own in this particular, the person who has the management of it, do's not deserve any favour. Nothing being left for me at St. D—n's,[3] I sent to B.[4] for an answer to my last. He says it is not yet restor'd to him, as soon as it is, I shall have it. This delay begins to make me think all Ministers are alike, and as soon as the Captain[5] is a Collonel,[6] he will act as his Predecessors have done.

The Queen goes to Windsor next tuesday,[7] and we expect all matters will be setled before that time. We have had a report, that my Lᵈ P—y S—l[8] is to go out alone, but the learned only laugh at it. The Captain's friends think themselves secure, and the Collonel's are so much of the same opinion that they only drink his health while he is yet alive. However it's thought he will fall easy with a pension of 4000 a year, and a Dukedom. Most of the stanch Torys are pleas'd with the alteration, and the Whimsicals[9] pretend the cause of their disgust was because the Whigs were too much favour'd. In short we propose very happy days to ourselves as long as this Reign lasts, and if the *uncertain timorous nature of* ——[10] do's not disappoint us, we have a very fair prospect. The Dragon and his Antagonist meet every day at the Cabinet: they often eat, and drink, and walk together as if there was no sort of disagreement, and when they part, I hear they give one another such names, as no body but Ministers of State could bear without cutting throats. The D. of M——gh is expected

---

[1] Of *Some Free Thoughts*.   [2] Bolingbroke.
[3] St. Dunstan's.   [4] Barber, the printer.
[5] Bolingbroke.   [6] Chief Minister.
[7] 27 July. She did not leave London; on that day she was present at the protracted meeting of Council at which Oxford ended his political career.
[8] Dartmouth.
[9] The group of Hanoverian Tories led by Sir Thomas Hanmer.
[10] The Queen.

here every day.[1] Dr Garth says he comes only to drink the Bristol
waters for a Diabetis. The Whigs are making great preparations to
receive him, but yesterday I was offer'd considerable odds that not
one of those who go out to meet him, will visit him in half a year.
I durst not lay, tho I can hardly think it. My Ld Marr[2] is marryed
to L^y Frances Pierrepoint, and my Ld Dorchester[3] her father is to
be marry'd next week to Lady Bel Bentick. Let me know if you go
to Pope's, that I may endeavour to meet you there.

Endorsed by Swift: M^r F—d | Rx Jul. 24. | 1714

4804

Charles Ford to Swift

24 July 1714.
London July 24.

We expected the great affair[4] would have been done yesterday, and
now every body agrees it will be to night. The Bishop of London,[5]
Ld Bathurst,[6] Mr. Bridges,[7] Sr Wm Wyndham,[8] and Campion,[9] are
nam'd for Commissioners of the Treasury, but I have not sufficient

[1] Marlborough's return was given out to be due to bad health and bad
weather. He crossed on the day of the Queen's death, and reached London on
Wednesday, 4 Aug.

[2] The Earl of Mar, appointed third Secretary of State in September 1713,
married as his second wife Lady Frances Pierrepoint (sister of Lady Mary
Wortley Montagu) on 20 July 1714.

[3] The Marquess of Dorchester, created Duke of Kingston 1715, married as
his second wife Lady Isabella Bentinck, fifth daughter of the Earl of Portland,
on 2 Aug. 1714.

[4] The dismissal of Oxford, which did not take place till 27 July. The Treasury
was not put into commission; the Duke of Shrewsbury succeeded Oxford on
the 30th.

[5] John Robinson.

[6] Allen Bathurst, one of the twelve peers created 1 Jan. 1712; the friend of
Swift and Pope.

[7] James Brydges, son of Lord Chandos of Sudeley, created Earl of Carnavon
Oct. 1714; 'the princely Chandos', the supposed original of Pope's Timon.

[8] Chancellor of the Exchequer.

[9] Henry Campion, member at this time for Sussex. He was a leading member
of the October Club. Boyer's *Political State*, Feb. 1712, pp. 117–21, gives a list
of its 159 members.

Authority for you to depend upon it. They talk of the D: of Ormond for our L^d L^t. I can't get th[e] pamphlet[1] back, what shall I do? I wish y[ou] would send me the other copy. My Ld Anglesey go's next monday to Ireland. I hear he is only angry with the Chan—r, and not at all with the Captain.[2]

Address: To the Rev^d | Dr Swift Dean of St Patrick's
Endorsed by Swift: Mr F— | Rx Jul·26·1714
   and July. 24th 1714 | Ch— F—

Williams

William Thomas to Swift

24 July 1714

Rev^d S^r[3]

You see how troublesome you make your friends by owning them. You will hear by this post what circumstances we are in here, and Mr L.[4] presses me to give you this trouble upon my own acc^t. & your friendship leaves me no room to doubt of your favour in it if you think it convenient. It is that you would second him in his application to Lady Masham in my behalf. you know there was an Equivalent given my Predecessor not in money but in an Office of 500^ll P ann for 32 y^rs as Comptroller of one of the Lotterys. If her Ladyship does not think me fit to be trusted, I may hope by your Intervention for some Compensation. But I leave you to concern for me as far as you think you may safely do. You may be assur'd I shall never betray my Trust, I hope the Service will not suffer if I am continued in my present Employmt, & it is for that Our friend believes your Assistance will be successful if you will give yourself

---

[1] 'pamphlet' (i.e. *Some Free Thoughts*) obliterated in the manuscript.

[2] i.e. angry with Phipps, the Irish Chancellor, not with Bolingbroke.

[3] This letter has not previously been printed. Formerly the property of D. A. Talbot Rice, Esq., it came up for sale at Sotheby's on 8 July 1959, and was purchased by the editor of these volumes. Two previous letters were addressed to Swift by William Thomas, secretary to Lord Oxford, 22 June and 6 July 1714. Of these the former, as well as the above letter, were unsigned.

[4] Erasmus Lewis. See the next letter.

trouble to write by next Post. Believe me to be in all Circumstances, most sincerely yours.

Address: For | The Reverend | The Dean of St Patrick[1]

4804

Erasmus Lewis to Swift

Whitehall | July. 24. 1714.

I saw Ld H. this morning he tells me that he left you horridly in the Dumps,[2] I wish you were here for after giving a quarter of an hours vent to our grief for the departure of our Don Quixote,[3] we sh'd recover our selves, and receive consolation from each other. the triumph of the Enemy makes me mad I feel a strange tenderness within my self, & scarce bear the thoughts of dating Letters from this Place, when my old friend is out whose fortune I have sherd for so many Years, but fiat voluntas tua, the damn'd thing is we are to doe all dirty work, we are to turn out Monckton,[4] & I hear we are to pass the new Commission of the Treasury: for god sake write to Lady Masham in favour of poor Thomas, to preserve him from ruin.[5] I'll second it. I intended to have writt you a long letter, but the moment I had turn'd this page, I had intelligence that the Dragon has broke out into a fiery passion with my Lord Ch.[6]—sworn a thousand oaths that he w'd be reveng'd, &c. this impotent womanish behaviour vexes me more than his being out. this last stroke shews

---

[1] This letter is written on the first and second page of a sheet folded to quarto size. The address appears on the fourth page on which are also two endorsements by Swift: 'July 24th. 1714 Mr Thomas Secr^{ty} to Ld Treas^r', and 'Mr Thomas. Rx Jul. 25., 1714.'

[2] After their meeting at Oxford. See Swift to Arbuthnot, 22 July.

[3] i.e. Oxford.

[4] Robert Monckton, one of the commissioners for trade and plantations, who had given information against Arthur Moore, one of his brother commissioners, for accepting a bribe from the Spanish court, to get the treaty of commerce continued.—Hawkesworth.

[5] Mr. Thomas had been secretary under the old commission of the treasury, and he wrote to the Dean, by the same post, for a recommendation to Lady Masham, either to be continued in the same office under the new commissioners, or to be considered in some other manner, by way of compensation.—Hawkesworth.

[6] Harcourt.

quantula sint hominum corpuscula. I am determined for the Bath on the 2ᵈ or the 9ᵗʰ of Aug. at farthest.

Endorsed by Swift: Mʳ L— | Rx July 26 1714.

4804

John Arbuthnot to Swift

[24 July 1714.]

D Brother

I suppose yow have reced[1] the Account of Sᵗ Kilda. Ther is an officer ther who is a sort of a tribunus plebis, whose office it is to represent the Greivances of the people to the laird of Mᶜleod who is suppos'd to be their oppressor, he is bound to contradict the laird till he gives him three Strokes wᵗ a cane over the head, & then he is at liberty to submitt.[2] This I have done & so has your friend L—s[3] it has been said that we & the Dean were the Authors of all that has since happend by keeping the Dragon in when there was an offer to lay down,[4] I was told to my face[5] that what I said in this case went for nothing, that I did not care if the great persons[6] affair's went to entire ruin so that I could support the interests of the Dragon. that I did not know the half of his proceedings, particularly it was said tho I am confident it was a mistake that he had attempted the removing her[7] from the favour of a Great person. in short the fall of the Dragon dos not proceed alltogether from his old friend but from the Great person, whom I perceave to be highly offended by little hints

---

[1] Hawkesworth and Ball have 'received'. Scott has 'read', which makes better sense. The manuscript looks like 'reced'.

[2] Scott has a note, xvi. 188, part of which is here quoted: 'The officer in question was a sort of deputy-lieutenant under the steward of the Laird of Macleod, from whom, and not from the hand of the laird himself, he was subject to receive castigation. "This officer, as such, is obliged to adjust the respective proportions of lands . . . and what else could be claimed by virtue of the last tack or lease, which is never longer than for three years, condescended to by the steward."' Martin's *Voyage to St. Kilda*, London, 1753, 8, p. 50.

[3] To Lady Masham.

[4] Presumably a reference to the ministerial crisis in March.

[5] Evidently by Lady Masham.

[6] i.e. the Queen.   [7] i.e. Lady Masham.

that I have receav'd. In short The Dragon has been so ill us'd, & must serve upon such terms for the future if he should, that I swear I would not advyse Turk jew nor infidel to be in that state. come up to town & I can tell you more. I have been but indifferently treated my self by some body at Court in small concerns, I can't tell who it is! but mum for that. adieu

Endorsed by Swift: D^r Ar— | Rx Jul. 26. | 1714.

Hunter-Baillie Collection[1]

Swift to John Arbuthnot

July. 25th 1714

You are every way too kind;[2] as to the Hist's place, I now hear it has been disposed of these 3 weeks to one Madocks. I wonder Ld Bol— knew nothing of it So there is an end of that, and of twenty Reflections one might make upon it. If the Q— is indifferent in those Matters, I may well be so too. I was 3 days last week in Oxford with L^d and L^{dy} H— & Dr Str—d. Our Talk was of the Dragon's being out, as a Thing done. So no more Reflections on that neither. Qu'est que l'homme. And so you will lend me all your Money. The mischief is, I never borrow money of a Friend. You are mightily mistaken: All your Honor, Generosity, good Nature, good Sense, Witt, and every other Praiseworthy Quality, will never make me think one Jott the better of You. That time is now some years past, and you will never mend in my Opinion. But really Brother you have a sort of Shuffle in your Gate: and now I have s^d the worst that your most mortall Enemy could say of you with Truth. I defy Pope and his Burning glasses, a Man cannot amuse himself 50 miles from London after four years jading himself with Ministers of State, but all the Town must hear of it. However if Pope makes the right use of your Hint for an Epigram or a longer Copy, I shall not be angry—It was a malicious Satyr of yours upon Whiston, that what you intended as a Ridicule, should be in any way struck upon by him for a Reality.— Go on for the sake of Witt and Humor, and cultivate that Vein which no Man alive possesses but your self, and which lay like a Mine in the Earth, which the Owner for a long time never knew of.

[1] In the Hunter-Baillie Collection, Royal College of Surgeons.
[2] See Arbuthnot to Swift, 17 July.

L ^{dy} M—m who talked of writing to me first has not answered my Letter. Put her not in mind I beg you. I believe she has heard of my Letter to the Dragon,[1] and dislikes it as partiall. I hear he has shewn it to every living Soul, & I believe has done so in *Malice* as the French understand that word. My humble Service to L^d and L^{dy} M— & Mrs Hill. By what I heard at Oxford, Ld Trevor[2] is fallen off with the rest, & indeed the Circle of the Dragon's Friends seemed very narrow, by the loss they were at for Healths, we came to yours 6 Glasses before the usuall time. adieu

Rothschild

Swift to Charles Ford

25 July 1714.

July. 25th 1714.[3] I had yours[4] and accordingly inclose the Pamphlett, and do with it as you please. It will now do nothing to the Cause for I hear from others hints of what you say plainly, that the Dragon must out. I was three days last week at Oxford with Ld H. and his L^{dy}, at Dr Stratfords,[5] and they all said the same thing; and sett as hard on L^{dy} M— as on Ld Bol. I find you are not much displeasd; nor I perhaps with the Dragons being out; but with the manner of it; and the dispositions of those who come in; and perhaps their Crede Scheam.[6] I shall not go to Pope's[7] but entre nous I will sett out for Ireland to morrow Sennight.[8] Say nothing of it yet. Dr A. knows nothing of the Histor.'s place being disposed of; and has gravely mentiond it to Ld Bol— who intended as gravely to speak to D. Shrew^y. I am satisfied; let them take their own Course; perhaps it may produce a History they will not like. And I will tell you

[1] Of 3 July 1714.

[2] Thomas Trevor, Lord Chief Justice, who was suggested for the office of Lord President of the Council.

[3] Lord Rothschild's Library 2282 (11). The manuscript appears to bear the date '1712'.

[4] The letter of 22 July. The pamphlet is the second copy of *Some Free Thoughts*.

[5] See p. 75. Swift to Arbuthnot, 22 July. Swift returned to Letcombe on the 23rd. See also *Portland MSS*. vii. 195.

[6] For the Schism Act see p. 29, n. 1.

[7] See Ford to Swift, 20 July *ad fin*.

[8] Monday, 2 Aug. Swift remained at Letcombe till 16 Aug.

one Hint when I have more time. Have you got the Cambrick Hanckercheifs? otherwise you have paid her for nothing.[1] I wish you would send them down by the Carrier on Wednesday morning early. Barber will tell you where. No, Send them by your Man to Robert Stone[2] at the Saracen's head in Friday street near Cheapside, directed to me.—I think when you send the inclosed to a Printer you should prefix the following Letter,[3] which should be printed before it.

Mr (name his name). The annexed Papers were sent a month ago to a very cautious Printer, with leave to shew them to any one Friend he had a Mind: The Person he shewed them to has kept them ever since in order to make some Alterations, and the time is almost lapsed wherein they might have done any Service. I shall no longer wait the Leisure either of that Printer or his Friend; If you do not think them worth a Publication, pray return them immediatly. I am S^r &c.

And you may chuse the same or any other place to have them sent to you. They will cost some time transcribing; and I think it is not prudent to let them be in my Hand.

Address: To Charles Ford Esqr, | at His Office at White-hall | London
Postmark: 26 IY

Deane Swift 1765

Swift to the Earl of Oxford

July 25th, 1714.

My Lord,

To-morrow se'en-night I shall set out from hence to Ireland; my licence for absence[4] being so near out, that I can stay no longer with-

---

[1] See Ford to Swift, 20 July *ad fin.*

[2] The Wantage carrier. According to the 'List of all the Stage Coaches', &c., in *New Remarks of London*, 1732, p. 195, the Wantage wagon left the Saracen's Head, Friday Street, on Wednesdays. There was a second Wantage wagon, which left Oxford Arms, Warwick Lane, on Thursdays.

[3] The events of the following week put an end to all thoughts of publishing *Some Free Thoughts*. The pamphlet was printed in 1741 from the manuscript which had been sent to Barber. See *Prose Works*, ed. Davis, viii, pp. xxiii–xxviii, 205–9.

[4] See Swift's letter to Joshua Dawson, 11 Feb. 1713–14, and note.

out taking another. I say this, that, if you have any commands, I
shall have just time enough to receive them before I go. And, if you
resign in a few days, as I am told you design to do, you may possibly
retire to Herefordshire,[1] where I shall readily attend you, if you soon
withdraw; or, after a few months stay in Ireland, I will return at the
beginning of winter, if you please to command me. I speak in the
dark, because I am altogether so; and what I say may be absurd.
You will please to pardon me; for, as I am wholly ignorant, so I have
none of your composure of mind. I pray God Almighty direct and
defend you, *&c.*

4804

The Earl of Oxford to Swift

July.27.1714[2]

If I tell my Dear Friend the value I put upon his undeserved
friendship, it wil look like suspecting you or my self: Though I have
had no power since July 25: *1713*[3] I believe now as a Private man I
may prevaile to renew your Licence of Absence conditionally you
wil be present with me. For to morrow morning I shall be a Private
Person, when I have setled my Domestic affairs heer, I go to
Wimple;[4] thence alone to Herefordshire; If I have not tir'd you
tête-a-tête fling away so much time upon one who loves you, & I
believe in the mass of souls ours were plac'd neer each other
I send you an imitation of Dryden
as I went to Kensington

To serve with love
And shed your Blood
Approved is above

---

[1] To his own seat, Brampton Castle.

[2] There is a facsimile of this letter in vol. i of Wilson's *Swiftiana*, 1804.

[3] The date is not a slip of the pen. For a year past co-operation between
Oxford and Bolingbroke had ceased. Although he had lost his power Oxford was
not actually dismissed by the Queen till the very day on which he wrote this
letter. On that same afternoon she gave him a kindly interview of farewell
(*Portland MSS*. v. 480–1). Bolingbroke was to enjoy only two full days of power
as Secretary of State; and he was at a loss, with no effective plans in mind.

[4] His son's seat in Cambridgeshire.

But heer Below
The Example[s] shew
tis fatal to be Good[1]

Endorsed by Swift: July 27th 1714 | Earl of Oxford | Just before the | Loss of his
   Staff.

4804

Erasmus Lewis to Swift

Whitehall | July. 27. 1714.

I have yours of the 25th you judge very right 'tis not the going out,
but the manner that enrages me. the Q. has told all the Lords the
reasons of her parting with him.[2] viz. that he neglected all business,
that he was seldom to be understood, that when he did explain himself, she could not depend upon the truth of what he said; that he
never came to her at the time she appointed, that he often came
drunk, that lastly to crown all he behav'd himself towards her with
ill manner indecency & disrespect.[3] Pudet haec opprobria nobis.[4] &c.
I am distracted with the thoughts of this, & the pride of the Conqueror,[5] I wd give the world I could goe out of town to morrow, but
the Secretary[6] saith, I must not goe till he returns wch will not be
till the 16th of Aug. or perhaps the 23. but I am in hopes I may goe
towards Bath the 16. the runners are already employd to goe to all
the Coffee houses. they rail to the pit of hell, I am ready to burst for
want of vent.

the stick is yet in his hand, because they cannot agree who shall
be the new Commssrs. we suppose the blow will be given to night
or to morrow morning, the sterility of good & able men is incredible
when the matter is over I'le wait upon our she friend,[7] if she receives
me as usual, I'le propose to her that I will serve where I doe, provided I may be countenanc'd & at full liberty to pay my duty to all

---

[1] Oxford was so much pleased with this rhyme that he sent it to his sister two
days later (*Portland MSS.* v. 477).

[2] i.e. Oxford.

[3] Whether these words, if spoken at all, were uttered in public or private, it
is difficult to reconcile them with the nature of the farewell which the Queen
vouchsafed to Oxford. On her side the parting can hardly be interpreted as
insincere in character.

[4] Cf. Ovid, *Met.* i. 758.   [5] Bolingbroke.
[6] i.e. Bromley.   [7] Lady Masham.

the Harleian family, in the same manner I used to doe. if that is not allow'd me in the utmost extent, consistent with my trust here, I'le propose an employment in the revenues, or to goe out without any thing, for I will be debarr'd going to him, if she does not receive me as she us'd to doe, I will never goe again, I flatter my self she will be so friendly as to enter into the consideration of my private circumstances, & preserve her old goodness to me.

there is no seeing the Dragon till he is out, and then I'le know his thoughts about your coming to Brampton. I hear he goes out of town instantly to Wimple, and my Lady to Brampton, that he'l joyn her there after a few days stay at Wimple. adieu.

Endorsed by Swift: M^r L— | Rx July. 23. 1714

4804

Lady Masham to Swift

July, 29 1714.

My Good freind

I own it looks unkind in me not to thanke you in all this time for your sincere kind letter; but I was resolved to stay till I cou'd tell you the Q—n had gott soe far the better of the Dragon as to take her Power out of his hands, he has been the most ungrateful man to her and to all his best freinds that ever was born; I cannot have soe much time now to write all my mind because my Dear Mistress is not well; and I think I may lay her illness to the charge of the Treasurer who for three weeks together was teasing and vexing her without intermission; and she cou'd not gett rid of him till tuesday last.[1] I must put you in mind of one passage in your letter to me, which is, I pray God send you wise and faithfull freinds to advise you at this time when there are soe great difficultys to struggle with; that is very plain and true; therefore will you who have gone through soe much and taken more than any body pains and given wise advice (if that wretched man had had sense enough and hones[ty] to have

---

[1] The 27th. After Oxford had surrendered his staff on that day the Council continued till two o'clock in the morning in a vain endeavour to come to agreement upon the appointment of commissioners to take his place. The Queen remained to the end, and her fatal illness has been attributed to this severe physical and mental strain. Lady Masham's letter should not be interpreted as a trustworthy statement. She was now governed by an intense dislike of Oxford.

taken it) I say will you leave us and goe into Ireland, noe it is impossible; your goodness is still the same, your charity and compassion for this poor lady who has been barbarously us'd wont lett you doe it; I know you take delight to help the destressd and there cannot be a greater object than this good lady who deserves pitty; pray Deare friend stay here and dont believe us all alike to throw away good advice and dispise every bodys understanding but theire own; I cou'd say a great deal upon the subject but I must goe to her, for she is not well, this comes to you by a safe hand[1] soe neither of us need be in any pain a bout it; my Ld and Bro[2] are in the countrey, my sister[3] and Girls are your humble Servants

Endorsed by Swift: July 29th 1714 | Ldy Masham

4804

Erasmus Lewis to Swift

Jul. 29. [1714]

I have yours of the 27. I write this in the morning, for I goe in the evening to Kensington,[4] if I am well received I'le continue my homage, if not they shall hear of me no more. where shall I write to you again, for I cannot stir from hence till the 16 of Aug. at soonest. nothing could please me more than to pass a few months with you at Abercothy,[5] but I am yet uncertain whether I shall go there at all. all I am sure of is that I will goe out of town to some place for some time, first to the Bath. for I can't bear staying in this room. I want physick to help my digestion of these things, thô the squire[6] is kinder to me than before. I am not mortify'd at what you tell me of Mercurialis,[7] only I w'd know whether any disrespectfull conduct of mine has bro't it upon me, or whether it is onely a general dislike of me, because I am not a man of parts, or because I am in other Interests.

they would not give the Dragon the least quarter, excepting onely

---

[1] That of John Barber, who then intended to visit Swift at Letcombe. See Barber to Swift, 31 July.

[2] Jack Hill.　　　　　　　　　　　　　　　　　　　　　[3] Alice Hill.

[4] To see Lady Masham. See Lewis's letter of the 27th.

[5] Lewis's birthplace in Wales.

[6] The reference may be either to Bromley or to Bolingbroke.

[7] i.e. Bolingbroke.

a pension, if he will work journey-work by the quarter. I have long thought his parts decay'd, & am more of that opinion than ever. the new Commission is not yet nam'd, wd not the world have roared ag't the Dragon for such a thing. Mercurialis entertain'd Stanhope, Craigs Pulteney & Walpole,[1] wt if the Dragon had done so. D. of Somerset dines to day with the fraternity at Greenwich with Withers[2] nobody goes out with the Dragon, but many will sit very loose. some say the new men[3] will [be] Lexington,[4] Wyndham,[5] Strangeways,[6] Sr John Stonhouse[7] & Campion.[8]

Endorsed by Swift: Mr L— | Rx July 29/30. 1714

Rothschild[9]

Swift to Archdeacon Walls

July. 29th 1714

This day I received yrs of the 20th instant. You know I suppose that two Months ago I retired to the Place where I now am, above 50 Miles from London, foreseeing the Storm that would happen. This day I had a Letter from my Ld Treasr to let me know he was just going to give up the Staff, which I suppose he did yesterday.[10] He says he is going in a Week or two to retire to his House in Herefordshire, and begs I would stay with him some time there. I cannot possibly refuse his Request, therefore I must intreat you to go to Mr Dawson, and desire him to renew my Licence when the last is expired, which will be at the End of August. I have writt to him this

---

[1] The future Whig ministers.

[2] Sir William Withers, one of the Tory members for the City of London.

[3] The commissioners of the Treasury, which eventually was not placed in commission.

[4] Robert Sutton, second Baron Lexington, who had been Ambassador to Madrid. Swift in his note on Macky's *Characters* dismissed him as possessed of 'A very moderat degree of Understanding'. *Prose Works*, ed. Temple Scott, x. 280.

[5] William Wyndham, Chancellor of the Exchequer.

[6] Thomas Strangways, M.P. for Dorsetshire.

[7] Controller of the Household, and a parliamentary representative for Berkshire.

[8] Henry Campion, M.P. for Sussex and an extreme Tory.

[9] Lord Rothschild's Library 2281 (11).

[10] As noted before, Oxford was dismissed and surrendered the staff on Tuesday the 27th.

Post to the same Purpose.[1] I had fixed my Journey to Ireld to the 2^d of August 4 days hence, And my Trunk with all my Cloaths and Linnen was sent last week to Chester, and I am almost in Rags. I hope to be in Ireld by the End of Autumn: Pray direct yr Letters no more to Mr Lewis (who is retiring upon this Occasion) but to Charles Ford Esqr, at his Office at White-hall. You may let Parvisol still expect me In Ireld till he knows the contrary, or tell him as you please. And for the rest I leave the whole to you and Mr Forbes, turn him out, keep him, hang him, save him, just as you please.[2] I am ashamed to give you all this Trouble, and I am now a poor cast Courtier. M^r (the young Parson I forget his name that gave me the Scaremt[3] at I don't know where, the Sunday after I was installd) I have received his 50 Pound; it is in a Friends hand, and shall be pd to his Order when he pleases—O, Mr Fetherston,[4] that's his name, pray tell him this when you see him. Service to our Doll, I thought to have been so merry with you a fortnight hence. Service to Goody Stoit, Catharine, & the Manleys. I served Manley while I was able, I said to L^d T^r I would not let him turn him out without a Pension, and so it stuck, and so he has lingerd on,[5] he should now I believe look out for some other Friends: & if you are great there, you should hint it to him. I shall lose all favor with those now in power by following Ld Oxf^d in his Retreat. I am hitherto very fair with them, but that will be at an end.

Address: To the Rev^d | Mr ArchDeacon Wall over | against the Hospitall in
          Queenstreet | Dublin[6]
Frank: C Ford
Postmark: 31 IY
Later endorsement: Dr Swift | July 29th 1714

   [1] See the following letter.
   [2] See Swift's letter to Walls of 3 July.
   [3] i.e. Sacrament.
   [4] Fetherston was then vicar of Crumlin, a village three miles to the south-west of Dublin.—Ball.
   [5] See Swift's letter to Walls of 2 Feb. 1713-14.
   [6] This letter, written from Letcombe Bassett, was sent to Ford in London, who addressed and franked it.

Swift to Joshua Dawson

July 29, 1714.

Sir,[1]

I have been these two months fifty miles from London, to avoid the storm that has happened at Court. The news will tell you a post or two before this of my Lord Ox.'s laying down; he was to do it yesterday. He has sent to desire I would stay some time with him at his house in Herefordshire, which I am not likely to refuse, though I may probably suffer a good deal in my little affairs in Ireland by my absence. This makes it necessary for me to desire you would please to renew my licence of absence, which expires about the end of August. As soon as it's expired, I should hope so much from your friendship, that, though any accident might happen to prevent your timely notice, you would do me such a favour whenever there is occasion. I had fixed my journey to Ireland to be on the second of August, when this incident changed it. I think it is about this time two years[2] that you came to my lodgings with Mr. Pratt,[3] to tell me the news of Lord Godolphin's going out, which was as joyful to me as this is otherwise. I believe you will reckon me an ill courtier to follow a discarded statesman to his retirement, especially when I have been always well with those now in power, as I was with him. But to answer that would require talking, and I have already troubled you so much who are a man of business. I am Sir, |
Your most obedient humble servant, | J. Swift.

Pray let the absence be general as before. I was very near wanting it some months ago with a witness.[4] I know not what alterations this change may make in the scheme for Irish promotions. I hear Dr. Pratt and Elwood are secure.

[1] Cf. Swift's letter to Dawson, 11 Feb. 1713-14.
[2] *Recte* four years.
[3] Captain John Pratt, the Provost's brother.
[4] When writing to Dawson about the renewal of his licence, 11 Feb. 1713-14, Swift hinted that it should be in general terms, perhaps with a mind to the possible need of a refuge if the authorship of *The Public Spirit of the Whigs* became known.

John Barber to Swift

July 31. 1714.
6 at night

Dear S^r ————

I am heartily sorry I should be the Messenger of so ill News, as to tell you, the Queen is dead, or dying; if alive, 'tis said she can't live 'till Morning. You may easily imagine the Confusion we are all in on this sad Occasion. I had sett out yesterday to wait on you, but for this sad Accident, and should have brought Letters from L— B. and L—y M. to have prevented yr going.[1] Pray don't go, for I will come to you when I see how Things stand. My Lord Shrewsbury is made Lord Treasurer; and every thing is ready for the Proclaiming the Duke of Brunswick, King of England. The Parliam^t will set[2] to Morrow, and choose a new Speaker, for Sr Tho. is in Wales.[3] For God's Sake don't go, but either come to London, or stay till I come to you.

Address: To the Revd Mr Geree, | at Upper Letcomb near | Wantage. | in | Berks
Frank: Free W. Withers.
Endorsed by Swift (below address): Ba—r | Rx. Aug. 1. 1714 | Q—s. dying.
   (and later): July. 31st 1714 | J—B—r

4804

Erasmus Lewis to Swift

Kensington.[4]
Saturday. Jul. 31. 6. in the Evening.

At the time I am writing the breath is said to be in the Queen's nostrills but that is all, no hope left of her recovery.

Lord Oxford is in Council, so are the Whigs.[5] we expect the

---

[1] To Ireland.   [2] 'set' *sic.*

[3] Hanmer was, however, sent for, and the House of Commons adjourned on meeting after the Queen's death until he came.

[4] The letter is written on a folio sheet, the upper and lower parts of which are badly soiled.

[5] Lewis's letter refers to details of the Council meeting held on 30 July. Of those who received and answered the summons only three were strong Hanoverians: Shrewsbury, Robinson, Bishop of London, and Oxford's friend Lord

demise to night. there is a prospect that the Elector will meet with
no opposition, the fr. having no fleet nor being able to put one out
soon. L^{dy} M.¹ did receive me kindly, poor woman I heartily pity her,
now is not the Dragon born under a happy planet to be out of the
scrape. D^r Ar. thinks you sh'd come up. you will not wonder if all
my Countrey resolutions are in suspense pray come up to see how
things goe.²

Endorsed by Swift: M^r L— | Rx Aug. 1. 1714 | Qu— dying

4804

Charles Ford to Swift

London   July 31. [1714]
Three in the afternoon

I don't doubt but you have heard the Q— is dead,³ and perhaps
we may be so unfortunate before this comes to you. But at present
she is alive, and much better than could have been expected. I am
just come from Kensington, where I have spent allmost these two
whole days. I am in great hast, but till dinner comes up, I will write
to you, and give you as full an account as I can of her illness. Her
disorder began between eight and nine yesterday morning. The Doctors order'd her head to be shav'd, and while it was doing, she fell
into a Fit of Convulsion, or as they thought an Apoplexy. This lasted
near two hours, and she was speechless, and shew'd little sign of life
during that time, but came to herself upon being blouded. As soon
as she recover'd, my Ld Bol— went to her, and told her the P—y
Council was of opinion, it would be for the publick service to have
the D. of Shrewsbury made Ld Treasurer. She immediately con-

Dartmouth. The leading Jacobites—Bolingbroke, Wyndham, Ormonde, Buckinghamshire, and Lansdowne—had no plans, and were afraid to show their
hands too readily. Argyle and Somerset had not been summoned, but after a
visit paid to Bothmar, the Elector's representative, they entered the chamber in
which the Council was to meet, exercising their rights as Privy Councillors
(Trevelyan, *England under Queen Anne*, iii. 302).

¹ Lady Masham.   ² No address.

³ At six o'clock on the morning of Sunday, 1 Aug., Dr. Shadwell announced
that the Queen could not live another two hours. Messages were sent out to
members of the Council. Shrewsbury and a few others quickly arrived, presently
to learn that the Queen had died at half past seven o'clock. See *Wentworth
Papers*, pp. 407–8; Boyer's *Political State*, 14 July, 627–35; *Portland MSS*. v. 480.

sented, and gave the Staff into the Duke's hands.[1] The Great Seal was put to the Patent by four a clock. She continued ill the whole day. In the evening I spoke to Dr. A—[2] and he told me he did not think her distemper was desperate. Radcliffe[3] was sent for to Cass—n about noon, by order of the Council, but said he had taken Physick, and could not come. In all probability he had sav'd her life, for I am told the late Ld Gower[4] had been often in the same condition with the gout in his head, and Rad— kept him alive many years after. This morning when I went there before nine, they told me she was just expiring. That account continued above three hours, and a report was carried to town that she was actually dead. She was not prayd for even at her own Chapel at St. James's, and what is most infamous Stocks rose three per cent upon it in the city.[5] Before I came away she had recover'd a warmth in her breast and one of her arms, and all the D^rs agreed she would in all probability hold out till to morrow, except Mead who pronounc'd several hours before she could not live two minutes, and seems uneasie it did not happen so. I did not care to talk much to A— because I heard him cautious in his answers to other people, but by his manner I fancy he do's not yet absolutely dispair. The Council sat yesterday all day and night, taking it by turns to go out and refresh themselves. They have now adjourn'd upon what the D^rs said till five. Last night the Speaker[6]

---

[1] Tradition is divided as to how far the Queen was conscious when she handed Shrewsbury the Treasurer's staff. In the *Wentworth Papers*, p. 408, it is stated that the Lord Chancellor guided her hand. At a much later date (1788) the Marquis of Buckingham averred that her consent was 'never given, but only supposed' (*H.M.C. Fortescue*, i. 364). Lansdowne, who was present at the scene, declared that she was 'perfect in her senses' (*Portland MSS.* v. 477).

[2] Arbuthnot.

[3] Anne had entertained an aversion to Radcliffe for twenty years past. Ford is alone in saying that he was now summoned 'by order of the Council'. The *Political State* says by the Duke of Ormonde; Radcliffe himself thought by Lady Masham. When the message came he was suffering from a severe attack of gout, and from a report sent by Mead he knew that nothing more could be done. His conduct in refraining from attendance was discussed in the House of Commons. The affair appears to have preyed on his mind, and he died three months later, on 1 Nov. See Pittis, *Dr. Radcliffe's Life and Letters*, pp. 72–76; and *Wentworth Papers*, p. 410.

[4] Sir John Leveson-Gower, created Baron Gower of Sittenham 1703. He died in 1709, aged thirty-four.

[5] *The Evening Post*, 29–31 July, quotes South Sea Stock at 81½—84¾, Bank Stock 120½–123¼.

[6] Sir Thomas Hanmer did not return from Wales till the 4th. Bromley's

and my Ld C. Justice Parker[1] were sent for, and the Troops from Flanders.[2] This morning the Hanover Envoy[3] was order'd to attend with the black box,[4] and the Heralds to be in a readiness to proclaim the new King. Some of the Whigs were at Council yesterday, but not one fail'd to day, and most of the Members of that Party in each House are already come to town. If any change happens before the Post go's out, I will send you word in a Post[s]cript, and you may conclude her alive, if you hear no more from me and have no better authority than Post Letters to inform you of the contrary. For God's sake, don't think of removing from the Place where you are till matters are a little setled. Ireland is the last retreat you ought to think of, but you can never be better than you are now till we see how things go.

I had yours with the printed Pamphlet as well as the other, and should have sent it away to morrow. Pray let me hear from you. [*Six lines heavily obliterated.*][5] Have you had all mine? I have fail'd you but one post, (I think it was the last,) for a fortnight or more.

Eleven at night.

The Queen is something better, and the Council is again adjourn'd till eight in the morning.

Endorsed by Swift: M^r F—d | Rx Aug. 1. 1714 | Qu— dying

letter summoning him is printed in *The Correspondence of Sir Thomas Hanmer*, ed. Bunbury, 1838, p. 169.

[1] Sir Thomas Parker, Lord Chief Justice, 1710–17, afterwards Lord Chancellor and Earl of Macclesfield.

[2] Seven of the ten battalions then in Flanders were recalled.

[3] Kreienberg.

[4] Containing the names of the Lords Justices nominated by the Elector, who with the seven great officers named in the Act of 1705 formed the Regency.

[5] Ford has scribbled out some words, and disguised others by inserting letters or writing new ones over them. The passage, as Swift found, is very difficult to read, but runs thus: 'Bar— was order'd by my Ld Bol— to go down & endeavour to bring you to town. He undertook for the—if this had not happen'd. I really believe he is very sincere in what I hear he has profess'd of you. B— I suppose will tell you all. He told me, and I desired him to write you word of it.'

B.M. Add. MS. 39839

Swift to Miss Esther Vanhomrigh

Aug. 1. 1714

I have had now two Letters of yours to answer;[1] I am pleased to see you picqued about my dearness to Ben and John.[2] They are worthy Subjects; There are some words I never use to some People; let that satisfy. How many Gentlemen, says you, and fine young Gentlemen, truly, would be proud to have you desire so much of them. Who told you, I was going to the Bath[3]—no such Thing. I had fixed to sett out to morrow for Ireld; but poor Ld Oxford desires I will go with him to Herefordshire: and I only expect his answer whether I shall go there before, or meet him hereabouts, or go to Wimple (His Sons house) and so go with him down; and I expect to leave this in 2 or 3 days, one way or other; I will stay with him till the Parlmt meets again, if he desires it. I am not of your Opinion about Ld Boling—perhaps he may get the Staff: but I cannot rely on his Love to me.[4] He knew I had a Mind to be Historiographer, though I valued it not but for the publick Service, yet it is gone to a worthless Rogue[5] that no body knows. I am writt to earnestly by some body to come to toun, and joyn with these People now in Power, but I will not do it. Say nothing of this, but guess the Person. I told Ld Oxford I would go with him when he was out, and now he begs it of me; and I cannot refuse him. I meddle not with his Faults as he was a Minister of State; but you know his personall Kindness to me was excessive; he distinguished and chose me above all other

---

[1] These letters are missing. No letters from Vanessa addressed to Swift at Letcombe have been preserved.

[2] Scott in a footnote, *Works*, xix. 415, suggests that this familiar style was in common use by Swift when writing to Benjamin Tooke and John Barber, and that Vanessa was jealous 'of a distinction never paid to her'. This is an improbable suggestion. The mode of address was never used by Swift.

[3] Lewis very probably informed Vanessa that he had suggested to Swift (6 July 1714) that he should accompany him to Bath.

[4] Swift wronged Bolingbroke in thinking him indifferent to his desire for the post of Historiographer. On 5 Jan. 1713–14 Bolingbroke addressed a letter to Shrewsbury averring to him that Swift was fitter for the office 'than any man in the Queen's dominions'. There is also good reason to believe that Bolingbroke was not unmindful of the £1,000 expected by Swift for his induction expenses, and that he caused an order to be signed in his favour.

[5] Thomas Madox, 1666–1727, far from being a 'worthless Rogue' was an erudite, industrious antiquary, who produced works of lasting value. See *D.N.B.*

Men while he was great; and his Letter to me tother day was the most moving imaginable. The Knife handles[1] should surely be done up in Silver, and strong, I believe Brandreth my Toyman in Exchange Alley would deal most honestly by me. Barber knows him. Where's your discretion in desiring to travell with that Body[2] who I believe would not do it for a thousand Pounds, except it were to Italy. Pray God send you a good Deliverance through your Accounts; 'Tis well you have been a Lawyer so long.—You will be two hours reading this Letter it is writt so ill.[3] When I am fixed any where perhaps I may be so gracious to let you know; but I will not promise. Service to Moll. adieu

Address: To Mrs Van-Homrigh, at M^r | Handcock's, in little Rider-street, | near St James's Street | London
Postmark: Wantag[e] 2 AU
Endorsed: 5

4804

The Rev. John Birch to Swift

1 August 1714.

Mr Dean![4]
   At twelve-a-clock Ld Bolingbrokes man Rid through Wantage to Call Mr Packer[5] to London, The Queen being Dead:[6] I am Con-

---

[1] In his edition of Swift's *Works*, 1814, this letter was printed twice by Scott, xvi. 202–3 and xix. 415–16. The passage, 'The knife handles . . . it is writt so ill', does not appear in the earlier printing. A footnote at xix. 416 says, 'The passage within brackets is restored from Mr. Berwick's manuscript'.

[2] Barber. Doubtless Vanessa was anxious to accompany him to Letcombe.

[3] On the contrary it is neatly written and easily legible. Swift was in the habit of disparaging his handwriting.

[4] The Rev. John Birch had been vicar of Wantage for over twenty years.

[5] Robert Packer, of Shellingford Castle, near Faringdon. His wife and Bolingbroke's were sisters, daughters of Sir Henry Winchcombe. He was member for Berkshire from July 1712 (in succession to Bolingbroke, called to the Upper House) till his death in Apr. 1731.

[6] The messenger, who could not have left till seven-thirty o'clock at the earliest, had covered the fifty-nine miles from London in extraordinarily good time. Presumably changes of horses were waiting.

founded at the melancholy news: yet could not forbear sending it
You: | Yʳ Truly humble Servant

Jo: Birch

Wantage One-a-Clock August 1ˢᵗ | 1714

Address: To | The Reverend the Dean of | Sᵗ Patrick, Letcomb
Endorsed by Swift, below address: Mʳ Birch of Wantage. | Rx ½ hour after one,
    on Sunday | afternoon—Aug. 1. 1714 | Queen's death. | She ⌜died at 7 that
    morning⌝¹

4804

Erasmus Lewis to Swift

Tuesday
Aug. 3. 1714

I am overwhelmed with business, & therefore have onely time to
tell you I receiv'd your's of Aug. 1. & think you sh'd come to town
to see how the world goes. for all old schemes designs projects journey's &c: are broke by the great event. we are ill prognisticators.
every thing goes on with a tranquillity we durst not hope for. E.
Berkeley commands the fleet.² Ld Dorset compliments the King.³
D. of Bolton Lᵈ Lieut Southampton.⁴ Addison Secʳʸ to the Regents.⁵

Address: To | The Revᵈ the Dean of Sᵗ | Patricks at Mʳ Gery's | at upper
    Letcomb near | Wantage | Berks.
Frank: E. Lewis.
Endorsed by Swift above address: Mʳ L— | Rx Aug. 4. 1714

¹ The words in half-brackets are mostly cut away.
² James, third Earl of Berkeley, was the son of Swift's old patron. He served
with distinction in the navy. He was Vice-Admiral of the Blue, 1707–8, of the
Red, 1709, and First Lord of the Admiralty, 1717–27.
³ Lionel Cranfield Sackville, 1688–1765, the only son of Charles, sixth Earl
of Dorset. He was created Duke of Dorset in 1720. In 1730 he was appointed
Lord Lieutenant of Ireland, and became one of Swift's correspondents.
⁴ Charles Paulet, or Powlett, 1661–1722, second Duke of Bolton and seventh
Marquis of Winchester. He held minor offices during the reigns of William III
and Anne. From 1717 to 1719 he was Lord Lieutenant of Ireland. Macky,
Characters, wrote of him, 'Does not now make any figure at court'. Swift added
'a great Booby'.
⁵ As the Whigs were in a majority amongst the Regents, none but members of
that party were selected for the duties mentioned.

Swift to Charles Ford

Aug. 3. 1714

You are more constant than all my Correspondents together; and I wonder you are not ashamed of it. We had an account of the Queen at noon on Sunday by a Servant of Ld Bol—s who rode through Wantage to Mr Packer.[1] It was what I monthly expected, thô not daily, and I laughed at their new Ministry for that very Reason, before this happened; I fancy the Qu— dyed about 5 on Sunday morning. She was alive at two, as we hear by a Postscript to the Postmasters Letter at Wantage. I writt a week ago to Mr Dawson at the Castle of Dublin, to desire he would renew my Licence of absence when it expires, which will be the End of this Month; Lest it should miscarry, I beg you will write to him to the same Purpose, and desire his Answer, which will serve us both. I desire it may be a Licence of Absence in generall, without specifying England; because, who knows, &c. My Trunk with Cloaths and Linnen is gone to England,[2] and I am here in Rags, intending to have sett out yesterday for Ireland; if the Dragon's Fall had not first stopt me, and then the Qu—'s Death.—Were the Whigs at Council when D— Sh— was recommended to be Tr—[3] You want hands. I think Ratcliff[4] acted right, they would never distinguish him by any honorary Pension, but send for him at a Plunge when he could onely lose Credit. For the Qu—'s case seems not to have been the Gout in her Head, But Histericks, Convulsive, or Apoplectick, but I judge at distance. Poor Ar—[5] was glad to hope as long as possible. The Manuscript you have, may lye by now: Some Hints in it may serve for a help to future Memoirs, or burn it, as you please.[6] I have [been] plaguing my self to read 5 or 6 lines you blotted out. That is human Nature. I have done the Imitation of Hoc erat in votis.[7] Tis pretty well, and will serve in some scurvy Miscellany. Pray send me the

---

[1] Cf. Birch to Swift, 1 Aug.

[2] A mistake for 'Ireland'.

[3] See p. 94, n. 1.

[4] Cf. Ford to Swift, 31 July.

[5] Arbuthnot.

[6] In his next letter Swift asks Ford to return the manuscript.

[7] Horace, *Satires*, II. vi. Swift's imitation of 'Hoc erat in votis' was first printed in the Pope and Swift, *Miscellanies. The Last Volume*, 1727. For notes on Pope's extension of the poem as printed in folio, 1738, see *Poems*, pp. 197–202.

Gazette of Tuesday next, if it contains any thing materiall of these Things. adieu.

Address, on separate cover: To Charles Ford Esqr. at | His Office at White-hall | London
Postmarks: Wantage *and* 4 AV

4804

John Barber to Swift

Aug. 3. 1714

Hon^d. S^r.

You may easily imagine the concern we were all in on the sudden surprise of the Queen's death. I have hardly recover'd it yet. L. B. told me last Friday[1] that he would reconcile You to Lady S. and then it would be easy to set you right with the Q. and that You should be made easy here, and not go over;[2] He said 20 Things in yr favour, and commanded me to bring You up, whatever was the Consequence: He said further, he would make clear Work with them. But all vanish'd in a minute; and he is now threatned and abus'd every day by the Party, who publickly rejoice, and swear they will turn out every Tory in England.

Inclosed you have a Letter from my Lord; he desires you would come up, and be any where Incog. The Earl of Berkley is to command the Fleet to fetch over the King, and the Duke of Argyle is to go to Scotland. I send you the list of 25 Kings.[3] Poor Lady Mash—

[1] 30 July.

[2] Bolingbroke knew well that Swift's lampoon on the Duchess of Somerset, *The Windsor Prophecy* (*Poems*, pp. 145–8), had, by the influence of the Duchess with the Queen, deprived him of any hope of preferment in England. Before this Archbishop Sharp had called the Queen's attention to 'A dang'rous Treatise', i.e. *A Tale of a Tub*; but he appears subsequently to have expressed his regret. Even, however, in the peaceful retirement of Letcombe, Swift failed to restrain himself from a savage attack on the Duchess of Somerset. 'The Author upon Himself', though first printed by Faulkner in 1735, was written there.

[3] The Lords Justices consisted of the seven officers of state, viz. the Archbishop of Canterbury, the Lord Chancellor, the Lord Treasurer, the Lord President of the Council, the Lord Privy Seal, the First Commissioner of the Admiralty, the Chief Justice of the King's Bench, and nineteen peers nominated by the Elector. Shrewsbury was one of the latter, and owing to his appointment as Lord Treasurer the number of Lords Justices was reduced to twenty-five.— Ball.

is almost dead with Grief;[1] . . . The Parliam^t meets to Morrow which will hinder me from coming down for 3 or 4 days, but if you resolve to go in the Country farther[2] I will certainly come down, for I must needs see you. Pray favour me with a Line. I am | S^r | Y^r most Obedient | humble Ser^t

Pray come up.[3] When my Lord gave me the Letter,[4] he sd he hop'd you would come up, and help to save the Constitution, which with a little good managem^t might be kept in Tory Hands

Endorsed by Swift: M^r B—r | Rx. Aug. 3^d . 1714

4804
Viscount Bolingbroke to Swift

Aug: the 3^d 1714.

Dear Dean.[5]

The Earl of Oxford was remov'd on Tuesday, the Queen dyed on Sunday . . what a world is this, & how does fortune banter us?

John Barber tells me you have set your face towards Ireland. pray don't go. I am against it, but that is nothing. John is against it. Ireland will be the scene of some disorder, att least it will be the scene of mortification to yr friends. here every thing is quiet & will continue so. besides which as prosperity divided, misfortunes may perhaps to some degree unite us.[6] the Torys seem to resolve not to be crush'd, and that is enough to prevent 'em from being so. Pope has sent me a letter from Gay. Being learned in Geography he took Binfield[7] to be the ready way from Hanover to Whitehall.

adieu. But come to London if you stay no longer than a fortnight.

Ever yours Dear | Jonathan most sincerely.

I have lost all by the death of the Queen but my Spirit, & I protest

---

[1] Some words are here obliterated. Peter Wentworth (*Wentworth Papers*, p. 408) questions the genuineness of Lady Masham's tears.

[2] To stay with Oxford.

[3] The words 'Pray come up' are enclosed within lines.

[4] The following letter.

[5] This was enclosed in the previous letter.

[6] It may be accepted, without question, that this would not for Bolingbroke mean union with Oxford.

[7] Where Pope lived.

to you I feel that encrease upon me. the Whigs are a pack of Jacobites. that shall be the cry in a month if you please.[1]

Endorsed by Swift: Ld Bolingbroke | Aug. 3^d 1714

4804

Charles Ford to Swift

London Aug: 5th 1714

I have writ to Dawson[2] for a license of absence for you, but you know you must take the oaths in Ireland within three months. There are a great many here in the same circumstances, and in all probability some of them will desire an Act of Parl^t to have leave to do it here. In that case it will be no difficult matter to have you included. M^r L—[3] tells me he writ to you to come up to town, and I see no reason why you should not. All matters go on very quiet, and we are not apprehensive of any disturbances. Stocks never rose so much in so few days.[4] This is imputed to the hatred of the old Treas—r and the Popularity of the new one. The Whigs were not in Council, when he was recommended.[5] L^d B— propos'd it there, as well as to the Queen, and I hope they two are upon very good terms, tho M^r L— seems positive of the contrary. I never heard of any pique the D: had to him, but that he was to be chief Minister, and that being at an end, why may not they be reconcil'd? The Dragon was thought to shew more joy upon proclaiming the King, than was consistent with the obligations he had receiv'd from ——.[6] He was hiss'd all the way by the mob, and some of them threw halters into his coach.[7] This was not the effect of Party, for the D: of Or—d was huzza'd throughout the whole city, and follow'd by a vast crowd to his own house, tho he us'd all possible endeavours to prevent it. There was an

---

[1] Bolingbroke means if Swift would lend the assistance of his pen.

[2] Ford's letter to Dawson was in the P.R.O., Dublin.—Ball.

[3] Lewis's letter of 3 Aug.

[4] South Sea Stock rose from 81½ on 30 July to 89½ on 5 Aug., and 92½ on 6 Aug. Bank Stock from 120½ to 127½ and 130 (the *Evening Post*).

[5] As Privy Councillors, Somerset and Argyle were present.

[6] The Queen.

[7] The King was proclaimed at several sites in London. According to Boyer's *Political State*, Aug. 1714, p. 119: 'No manner of Disturbance was given to the Ceremony; nor was any Disorder committed in it; save only, that some of the Mobb hiss'd at and insulted the Lords Ox—d and B—ke.'

attempt to affront the Captain[1] in the Cavalcade, but it did not succeed, and tho a few hiss'd, the acclamations immediately drown'd their noise. Not a single man shew'd the least respect to the Collonel[2] and last night my Ld Bingley[3] was beaten by mistake coming out of his house. I doubt he has disoblig'd both sides so much, that neither will ever own him, and his enemys tell storys of him that I shall not believe, till I find you allow them. The L^ds Justices made a Speech to the Parl^t to day. If it comes out time enough I will send it you, but I hear it only contains their proceedings upon the Queen's death, that they have yet receiv'd no directions from the King, and to desire the Commons to continue the funds, which are expir'd. I am told our R—ts[4] are already divided into four Partys. The greatest use they have yet made of their Power is to appoint my Ld Berkeley[5] to command the Fleet which is to bring over the King, and to make the D: of Bolton[6] L^d L^t of Hampshire. I send you a Gazette, tho I am asham'd to have it seen.[7] I had writ a great deal more of the Queen's illness, an account of her Birth &c. But I could not find out M^r L— and had no body to consult with, and therefore chose rather to say too little, than any thing I doubted might be improper. Yesterday the Duke of Marl—gh made his Publick Entry through the city. First came about 200 horsemen three in a row, then a Company of train bands with drums &c. His own Chariot with himself and his Dutchess. Then my Dutchess[8] follow'd by 16 Coaches with 6 Horses, and between 30 and 40 with two horses.[9] There was no great mob

---

[1] Bolingbroke.   [2] Oxford.

[3] Robert Benson, created Baron Bingley July 1713, Chancellor of the Exchequer 1711 to 1713 (succeeded by Wyndham). 'On Wednesday last 4 August Mr. Man, the woollen draper, went to the Earl of Oxford's house in York Buildings, and called his Lordship all to naught, so soon as he went out of the house he met the Lord Bingley and insulted him' (News-letter, *Portland MSS.* v. 485).   [4] Regents.

[5] See p. 98, n. 1.   [6] See p. 98.

[7] Ford's account of the Queen's illness and death, in the *Gazette* of 31 July to 3 Aug., runs to only a dozen lines: 'This Day, at half an Hour past Seven in the Morning, died our late most Gracious Sovereign Queen Anne, in the Fiftieth Year of her Age, and the Thirteenth of Her Reign; a Princess of exemplary Piety and Virtue. Her Majesty complained on Thursday last of a Pain in Her Head: The next Day She was seized with Convulsion Fits, and for some time lost the use of Her Speech and Senses, which tho' She afterwards recovered upon the Application of proper Remedies, She continued in a very weak and languishing Condition till She expired.'

[8] The Duchess of Montagu.

[9] In the *Wentworth Papers*, p. 410, it is stated that Marlborough was conscious

when he pass'd through the Pellmall, but there was in the city, and he was hiss'd by more than huzza'd. At Temple Bar I am assur'd the noise of hissing was loudest, tho they had prepar'd their friends to receive him, and the gathering of others was only accidental. You may guess how great a Favourite he is by some old storys of his behaviour at the Camp when ——[1] was there, and afterwards at Han—r, and by the share he and his Family have in the Regency.[2] But to be sure this discreet action will endear him more than any subject in England. We had bonfires &c. at night. From the List of L^{ds} Justices, and some other things, we imagine to ourselves there wo'n't be many changes, but that the vacancys for some time will be fill'd up with Whigs.

What I blotted out in my last was something that pass'd between the Captain and B—r relating to you. After I had writ, they told me all letters would be open'd, which made me blot out that passage. B—r says he gave you some account of it tho not a full one.[3] I really believe L. B— was very sincere in the professions he made of you, and he could have done any thing. No Minister was ever in that heigth of favour, and L^y M—[4] was at least in as much credit as she had been in any time of her life. But these are melancholy reflections, pray send me your Poem Hoc erat &c.[5] or bring it up yourself. B— told me he had been several hours with the Captain upon a thing that should have come out, but was now at an end.[6] He did not tell what it was, and I would not ask many questions for fear of giving him suspicion.

Endorsed by Swift: Aug. 5. 1714 | C.F.

that his entry into London was too triumphal in character, and that he offered his regrets to the city.

   [1] The King. He had not been informed by Marlborough and Eugene of their plans for the campaign of 1708 and refused to act on the offensive; and in May 1710 he resigned his command.

   [2] Neither Marlborough nor the Earl of Sunderland, his son-in-law, was included in the Regency. But the King's first official act when the news of Anne's death reached Hanover was to appoint Marlborough Captain-General.

   [3] See Barber to Swift, 3 Aug., in which Bolingbroke is said to have expressed the hope of reconciling the Duchess of Somerset to Swift and setting him right with the Queen.

   [4] Lady Masham.

   [5] Swift's imitation of Horace's *Satires*, II. vi (*Poems*, p. 197).

   [6] Swift's *Some Free Thoughts*.

Gay to Swift or Arbuthnot

Hanover, 16 August [o.s. 5], 1714

Dear Sir.

You remember, I suppose, that I was to write you abundance of Letters from Hanover;[1] but as one of the most distinguishing Qualities of a Politician is Secrecy, you must not expect from me any Arcanas of State; there is another thing that is necessary to establish the Character of a Politician which is, to seem always to be full of Affairs of State, to know the Consultations of the Cabinet Council, when at the same time all his Politicks are collected from Newspapers. which of these two causes my Secrecy is owing to, I leave you to determine, there is yet one thing more that is extreamly necessary for a foreign Minister which he can no more be without than Artisan without his Tools, I mean the Terms of his Art, I call it an Art or a Science, because I think the King of France hath establish'd an Academy to instruct the young Machivillians of his Country in the deep and profound Science of Politicks. to the end that I might be qualified for an Employment of this Nature, and not only be qualified myself, but (but to speak in the Stile of Sr John Falstaff) be the cause of Qualification in others;[2] I have made it my business to read Memoires, Treatys, &c.[3] and as a Dictionary of Law terms is thought necessary for young Beginners so I thought a Dictionary of terms of State would be no less usefull for young Politicians. the Terms of Politicks being not so numerous as to swell into a Volume especially in time of Peace, for In time of War the terms of Fortification are included; I thought fit to extract them in the same Manner for the benefit of young Practitioners, as a famous Author hath compiled his Learned Treatise of the law called The Doctor and Student.[4] I have not made any great Progress in this Piece, but however I will just give you a Specimen of it, which will

---

[1] See Gay to Swift, 8 June 1714, *ad fin.*, 'as for myself whether I am at home or abroad, Gratitude will always put me in mind of the Man to whom I owe so many Benefits'.

[2] 'I am not only witty in myself, but the cause that wit is in other men', *2 Hen. IV*, I. ii.

[3] See Swift to Gay, 12 June 1714.

[4] A legal treatise by Christopher Saint-Germain, 1460?–1540, for the use of students, first published in Latin, 1523. In 1531 an English translation appeared. There were many subsequent editions.

make you in some manner a judge of the Design, and Nature of this Treatise.

Politician.

What are the Necessary Tools for a Prince to work with?

Student.

Ministers of State.

Politician.

What are the two great Qualities of a Minister of State?

Student.

Secrecy and Dispatch.

Politician.

Into how many parts are the Ministers of State divided?

Student.

Into two. first Ministers of State at home. secondly. Ministers of State abroad, who are called foreign Ministers.

Politician.

very right. now as I design you for the latter of these Employments, I shall wave saying any thing of the first of these. What are the different Degrees of foreign Ministers.

Student.

The different degrees of foreign Ministers are as follows first Pleni-potentionarys, Second Embassadors Extraordinary, third, Embassa-dors in Ordinary, fourth, Envoys Extraordinary, fifth Envoys in Ordinary, sixth, Residents, seventh, Consuls, and Eighth Secretarys.

Politician.

How is a Foreign Minister to be known?

Student.

By his Credentials.

Politician.

When are a foreign Ministers Credentials to be delivered?

Student.

Upon his first admission into the Presence of the Prince to whom he is sent, otherwise called his first Audience.

Politician.

How many kinds of Audiences are there?

Student.

Two, which are called, a Publick Audience and a Private Audience.

Politician.

What should a Foreign Minister's Behaviour be when he has his first Audience?

Student.

He should bow profoundly, speak deliberately, and wear both sides of his long Periwig before.

&c.

by these few Questions and Answers you may be able to make some judgment of the usefullness of this Politick Treatise. Wiquefort[1] tis true, can never sufficiently be admired for his Elaborate Treatise of the Conduct of an Embassador in all his Negotiations. but I design this only as a Compendium, or the Embassador's Manual or Vade Mecum. I have wrote so far of this Letter, and do not know who to send it to. but I have now determined to send it either to Doctor Arbuthnot or the Dean of St Patricks, or to both. My Lord Clarendon is very much approved of at Court, and I believe is not dissatisfied with his Reception. We have not much variety of Diversions, what we did yesterday & to day we shall do to morrow, which is, go to Court and walk in the Gardens at Heernhausen. if I write any more my Letter will be just like my Diversions, the same thing over and over | again so | Srs. | Your most obliged Humble | Servt

J Gay.

Hanover | Aug. 16. 1714

I would have writ this Letter over again but I had not time, correct all Erratas.

Address: For Dr Arbuthnot or the | Dean of St Patricks.
Endorsed by Swift: Gay | Hanover 16th | 1714.

4804

Erasmus Lewis to Swift

Whitehall | Aug. 7. 1714

'tis true you have nothing to doe here, but what have you to doe any where else, till you goe to Ireland where you must indeed be

---

[1] *L'Ambassadeur et ses fonctions*, La Haye, 1680, by Abraham de Wicquefort.

before three months end, in order to qualify your self.[1] the law requires it as much as if your Deanry was but now conferr'd upon you.

Arbuthnot is remov'd to Chelsea & will settle there.[2]

The town fils every moment. we are as full in the House of Commons as at any time. we are gaping & staring to see who is to rule us. the Whigs think they shall engross all. we think we shall have our share. in the mean time we have no divisions at Council or in Parliament.

I sent twice to Kensington to enquire after Lady Masham's health. next week I'le goe to see her, and will keep up my acquaintance in all events if she thinks fit. I doubt she and her Sister[3] are not perfectly easy in their affairs, but you forgot one that is worse than either, that is Mr Hill who has not a sous.[4]

I stay here till our commission is either renew'd to us or given to an other. I am yrs—

Endorsed by Swift: M^r L— | Rx. Aug. 8.

Deane Swift 1765

Swift to Lady Masham

August 7th, 1714

Madam,

I had the honour of a letter from your Ladyship a week ago; and the day after, came the unfortunate news of the Queen's death, which made it altogether unseasonable, as perhaps it may be still, to give your Ladyship this kind of trouble. Although my concern be as great as that of any other good subject, for the loss of so excellent a Princess; yet I can assure you, Madam, it is little to what I suffer upon your Ladyship's particular account. As you excel in the several duties of a tender mother, a true friend, and a loving wife, so you have been the best and most faithful servant to your Mistress,

---

[1] By taking the oaths in Ireland.

[2] Subsequent references make it appear that Arbuthnot held some office in connexion with Chelsea Hospital.

[3] Alice Hill.

[4] Lewis entertained an exaggerated view of Lady Masham's money difficulties; and her brother, Major-General Jack Hill, when he died in 1735, was in a position to leave a fair legacy to his nephew Samuel, second Baron Masham.

that ever any Sovereign had.[1] And although you have not been re-warded suitable to your merits, I doubt not but God will make it up to you in another life, and to your children and posterity in this. I cannot go about to comfort your Ladyship in your great affliction, otherwise than by begging you to make use of your own piety, and your own wisdom, of both which you have so great a share. You are no longer a servant, but you are still a wife, a mother, and a friend; and you are bound in conscience to take care of your health, in order to acquit yourself of these duties, as well as you did of the other, which is now at an end.

I pray God to support your Ladyship, under so great a share of load, in this general calamity: And remain, with the greatest respect and truth, Madam,

Your Ladyship's | Most obedient, and | Most obliged servant.

I most heartily thank your Ladyship for the favourable expressions and intentions in your letter, written at a time when you were at the height of favour and power.

Deane Swift 1765

Swift to Viscount Bolingbroke

August 7th, 1714.

My Lord,

I had yours of the third, and our Country-post is so ordered, that I could acknowledge it no sooner. It is true, my Lord, the events of five days last week might furnish morals for another volume of Seneca. As to my Lord Oxford, I told him freely my opinion before I left the town, that he ought to resign at the end of the session. I said the same thing often to your Lordship and my Lady Masham, although you seemed to think otherwise, for some reasons;[2] and said

[1] As has been noted already opinions of Lady Masham's character varied widely. Swift entertained a sincere regard for her. The three letters which have survived, addressed to him by Lady Masham, reflect a woman of good education. The disparagement of her character in the *Wentworth Papers* is clearly dictated by personal dislike, and should not be taken at face value.

[2] As early as the autumn of 1713 Harley had formed a resolution to resign. He was, however, persuaded by his friends to stay on. Before Swift retired to Let-combe it had become clear that Oxford was no longer fit for office. Even Swift advised him to resign. Inspired, however, by dull antagonism to his rival he

so to him one afternoon, when I met you there with my Lord Chancellor. But, I remember, one of the last nights I saw him, (it was at Lady Masham's lodgings) I said to him, that, upon the foot your Lordship and he then were, it was impossible you could serve together two months; and I think I was just a week out in my calculation. I am only sorry, that it was not a resignation, rather than a removal; because the personal kindness and distinction I always received from his Lordship and you, gave me such a love for you both, (if you great men will allow that expression in a little one) that I resolved to preserve it entire, however you differed between yourselves; and in this I did, for some time, follow your commands and example. I impute it more to the candour of each of you, than to my own conduct; that, having been, for two years, almost the only man who went between you, I never observed the least alteration in either of your countenances towards me. I will swear for no man's sincerity, much less for that of a Minister of State: But thus much I have said, wherever it was proper, that your Lordship's proposals were always the fairest in the world, and I faithfully delivered them as I was empowered: And, although I am no very skilful man at intrigue, yet I durst forfeit my head, that, if the case were mine, I could either have agreed with you, or put you *dans vôtre tort*. When I saw all reconciliation impracticable, I thought fit to retire; and was resolved, for some reasons (not to be mentioned at this distance) to have nothing to do with whoever was to be last in. For, either I should not be needed, or not be made use of. And let the case be what it would, I had rather be out of the way. All I pretended was, to speak my thoughts freely, to represent persons and things without any mingle of my interest or passions, and, sometimes, to make use of an evil instrument,[1] which was like to cost me dear, even from those for whose service it was employed. I did believe there would be no further occasion for me, upon any of those accounts. Besides, I had so ill an opinion of the Queen's health, that I was confident you had not a quarter of time left for the work you had to do; having let slip the opportunity of cultivating those dispositions she had got after her sickness at Windsor.[2] I never left pressing my Lord Oxford with

retained the Treasurer's staff; and Bolingbroke continued his intrigues with Jacobite plotters.

[1] i.e. the press.

[2] When in the winter of 1713 the Queen was lying seriously ill at Windsor, and she heard that the expectancy of her death roused frequent and undisguised

the utmost earnestness, (and perhaps more than became me) that we might be put in such a condition, as not to lie at mercy on this great event; and I am your Lordship's witness that you have nothing to answer for in that matter. I will, for once, talk in my trade, and tell you that I never saw any thing more resemble our proceedings, than a man of fourscore, or in a deep consumption, going on in his sins, although his physician assured him he could not live a week. Those wonderful refinements, of keeping men in expectation, and not letting your friends be too strong, might be proper in their season. *Sed nunc non erat his locus.*[1] Besides, you keep your bread and butter till it was too stale for any body to care for it. Thus your machine of four years modelling is dashed to pieces in a moment: And, as well by the choice of the Regents, as by their proceedings, I do not find there is any intention of managing you in the least. The whole nineteen[2] consist either of the highest party-men, or, (which mightily mends the matter) of such who left us upon the subject of the peace, and affected jealousies about the succession.[3] It might reasonably be expected, that this quiet possession might convince the Successor of the good dispositions of the Church-party[4] towards him; and I ever thought there was a mighty failure somewhere or other, that this could not have been done in the Queen's life.—But this is too much for what is past; and yet, whoever observed and disliked the causes, has some title to quarrel with the effects. As to what is to come, your Lordship is in the prime of your years, *plein des esprits qui fournissent les espérances*; and you are now again to act that part, (though in another assembly) which you formerly discharged so much to your own honour, and the advantage of your cause. You set out with the wind and tide against you; yet, at last, arrived at your port, from whence you are now driven back in open sea again. But, not to involve myself in an allegory, I doubt whether, after this disappointment, you can go on with the same vigour you did in your more early

expressions of joy among the Whig leaders, she determined, writes Swift, to take 'all just and proper Methods that her Ministers should advise her for the Preservation and Continuance' of the constitution 'in Church and State' (*Prose Works*, ed. Davis, viii. 154–5).

[1] Horace, *Ars Poet.* 19.

[2] The number of the peers nominated by the Elector.

[3] The Hanoverian Tories.

[4] Swift's hope was that in a Ministry established under the new régime emphasis on the support of the Church would secure recognition and the inclusion of some of his friends.

youth. Experience, which has added to your wisdom, has lessened
your resolution. You are now a general, who, after many victories,
hath lost a battle, and have not the same confidence in yourself or
your troops. Your fellow-labourers have either made their fortunes,
or are past them, or will go over to seek them on the other side.—
Yet, after all, and to resume a little courage: To be at the head of the
Church-interest is no mean station; and that, as I take it, is now in
your Lordship's power. In order to which, I could heartily wish for
that union you mention;[1] because, I need not tell you, that some are
more dexterous at pulling down their enemies than, *&c.* We have
certainly more heads and hands than our adversaries; but, it must
be confessed, they have stronger shoulders and better hearts. I only
doubt my friends, the rabble, are at least grown trimmers; and that,
setting up the cry of Trade and Wool, against Sacheverell and the
Church,[2] hath cooled their zeal. I take it for granted, there will be
a new Parliament against winter; and, if they will retain me on the
other side, as their counsellor, I will engage them a majority. But,
since it is possible I may not be so far in their good graces, if your
Lordship thinks my service may be of any use in this new world, I
will be ready to attend you by the beginning of winter. For the misfortune is, that I must go to Ireland to take the oaths; which I never
reflected on till I had notice from some friends in London. And the
sooner I go the better, to prevent accidents, for I would not willingly
want a favour at present. I think to set out in a few days, but not
before your Lordship's commands and instructions may reach me.

I cannot conclude without offering my humblest thanks and
acknowledgments, for your Lordship's kind intentions towards me,
(if this accident had not happened) of which I received some general
hints.—I pray God direct your Lordship: And I desire you will
believe me to be what I am, with the utmost truth and respect, |
Your Lordship's most obedient, *&c.*

[1] In his letter to Swift of 3 July.
[2] The party cries of the last general election. The Whig candidates wore in
their hats locks of wool, signifying devotion to trade and prosperity. The oak leaf
'sported by their rivals, appealed successfully to the hearts of thousands of rustic
voters' (*History of the Reign of Queen Anne*, Wyon, ii. 471).

Swift to Charles Ford

Aug. 7th. 1714

The Inclosed,[2] | To the Reverend M^r
Arch-deacon Wall, over against the Hospitall
in Queen-street. Dublin.

I had your long kind Letter of the 5th: I never once dreamt of
taking the Oaths: but the sooner I do it the better: and travelling
will soon grow bad; so that I design to sett out on Monday sennight
the 16th instant, and if they want me, I can return in Winter, when
I suppose you will have a new Parlm^t, for this is not for your Purpose. To include my self in an Act, will not be decent, unless I were
unable to travell; and besides I have some good Friends among the
L^{ds} who would be glad to mortify me with their Negative. I have
writt this Post a very long Letter to Ld Bol—[3] and told him my Call
for Ireland; and that I would come back if I were wanted. I wish he
and the Dragon would write. I believe M^r L is in the right about the
Captain and D. of Shr— I have been long afraid that we were losing
the Rabble[4]—As for Ld Bingl—[5] I will not be [h]is Guarantee.—I
think the Regents agree pretty well in their Choice of Persons, and
that we are this moment under the Height of a Whig Administration.
You do not mention Addison; who M^r L says is Secretary to the
Regency.[6] Your Gazette is perfectly right, and what is said of the
Queen very decent and proper: had there been more it might have
been better; and indeed I know no body has a better Style for Letters
or Business than you: which considering your Lazyness, you may
be said to have acquired in spight of your Teeth. I do not conceive
the D. of M. will be a Favorite. I believe your Dutchess lookt very
sawcy and handsom. When did the Rabble get this Trick of Hissing;
they learnt it at the Play-house in the upper Gallery. How a div—l
do you gather from the List of R—ts that there will not be many
removalls; they are all of the rankest Whigs, except 4 or 5 Proselytes,

---

[1] Lord Rothschild's Library, No. 2282 (13).

[2] The following letter, dated 8 Aug.

[3] The previous letter.

[4] It will be noticed that writing to Bolingbroke in the previous letter Swift
says: 'I only doubt my friends, the rabble are at least grown trimmers.'

[5] See p. 103, n. 3.

[6] Stated in Lewis's letter of 3 Aug., the day on which Addison was appointed
(*Political State*, Aug. 1714, p. 142).

which is worse; at least such as quarrelled about the Peace and Treatyes, and Danger of the Succession.[1]

I will bring you my Poem my self—when I return from Ireland: It is not yet sufficiently corrected to my Mind, thô I have labored it much. But I am not now that way turned. I am breeding another Pamphlet, but have not writt a Word of it. The Title will be something like this—Some Considerations upon the Consequences apprehended by the Qu—s Death.[2] If I have humor I will write it here and upon the Road, and send it you from Ireland.

If you have the Manuscript I sent you last, pray return it me by next Post, for I may have use for some Passages in it.[3]

I must desire you to receive 50[11] from M[r] Thomas[4] of the Treasury; which belongs to a Clergy-man in Ireland, to whom I have this Post sent a Bill. With part of this money, pay your self the 20 Guineas I ow you, and for the Handkerchiefs you bought, there will then remain six or seven and twenty Pounds; out of which pay thirty Guinneas to M[r] Barber, besides for hatts, Nightgown, Books &c. whatever his Account is. How will you do this? Why: he is to receive 30[11] of mine from the South-Sea,[5] which I hope will overdo it a great deal, and keep the Remainder in your Hands. Take up Barbers Note for the thirty Guinneas and cancell it. Can you do this silly debt without perplexing your self?

And pray tell M[r] Thomas I writt to him this Post under cover to M[r] L—

Address: To Charles F[. . . . .][6]
            his Office at [. . . . .]

---

[1] The 'Proselytes' among the nineteen Regents were the 'Whimsicals', or Hanoverian Tories—the Archbishop of York, the Duke of Roxburgh, and the Earls of Anglesey, Nottingham, and Abingdon.

[2] Swift never proceeded far with this pamphlet, dated 'Aug. 9. 1714' and headed 'Some Considerations upon the Consequences hoped and feared from the Death of the Queen'. The original manuscript in the Forster Collection consists of two leaves only. It was first printed by Deane Swift in 1765. See *Prose Works*, ed. Davis, viii, pp. xxix–xxx, 99–104, 210.

[3] *Some Free Thoughts*, second copy.

[4] For William Thomas, Lord Oxford's secretary, and the clergyman, who was Thomas Fetherston, Prebendary of St. Patrick's, see pp. 41, 50, 79.

[5] Swift had £1,000 in South Sea Stock.

[6] Damaged and postmarks torn off.

Swift to Archdeacon Walls

Letcombe, August 8, 1714.[1]

If I had but fixed a week sooner for my journey to *Ireland*, I should have avoided twenty inconveniencies that have since happened to me, and been with you at the time I am now writing. Upon the Earl of *Oxford*'s removal, he desired I would go with him into *Herefordshire*; which I consented to, and wrote you word of it, desiring you would renew my licence of absence at the end of this month, for I think it then expires. Two days after, I had earnest invitation from those in power, to go up to town, and assist them in their new Ministry; which I resolved to excuse: but, before I could write, news came of the Queen's death, and all our schemes broke to shatters. I am told I must take the oaths in *Ireland* in three months; and I think it is better travelling now than later: and although I am earnestly pressed by our broken leaders to come up to town, I shall not do it; but hope to set out on the sixteenth[2] instant towards *Ireland*, and if it please God, be with you in nine or ten days after this comes to your hands. However, let my licence be renewed before it expires. I think I answered yours in my last.[3] I leave all things entirely to you and Mr. *Forbes*. My service to gossip *Doll*, goody *Stoyte* and *Martha*,[4] and Mr. *Manley*[5] and lady. Mr. *Manley* is, I believe, now secure in his post; and it will be my turn to solicit favours from him. I have taken up Mr. *Fetherston*'s money, to pay some debts in *London*;[6] I desire you will pay him fifty pounds, with the usual exchange, at twenty days sight; or later, if it be inconvenient.

[1] This letter, enclosed in Swift's letter to Ford of 7 Aug., was first printed by Nichols in his *Supplement to Swift's Works*, 1779.

[2] Among the *Portland MSS.* in the British Museum, 3rd Deposit, Packet 3, is a note in Swift's hand, dated 'Friday morning'. 'My things are all packt up, and in the city . . . I shall set out for Ireland on Monday next.' Aug. 16 was a Monday.

[3] 29 July.

[4] Mrs. Stoyte's sister.

[5] Isaac Manley, Postmaster-General in Ireland.

[6] See p. 90.

Erasmus Lewis to Swift

Whitehall
Aug. 10. 1714

I never differ'd from you in opinion in any point so much as in your proposal to accommodate matters between the Dragon and his quondam friends.[1] I will venture to goe so far with you as to say, he contributed to his own disgrace by his petitesses more than they did or ever had it in their power to doe, but since they wd admit of no terms of accommodation when he offred to serve them in their own way,[2] I had rather see his dead Carcass than that he sh'd now tamely submit to those who have loaded him with all the obloquy malice could suggest & tongues utter. have not Charteris[3] Brinsden[4] & all the runners been employd to call him Dog, villain sot & worthless, & shall he after this joyn them to w^t end? I have great tenderness for Lady — & think her best way is to retire & enjoy the Comforts of a domestick Life, but sure the earth has not produced such monsters as Mercur—[5] and his companion[6] & the Prelate.[7] The last openly avows he never had obligation to the Dragon, loads him with 10000 crimes, thô his greatest in reality was preferring him. but to come out of this rant, w^t sh'd they be friends for, cui bono? are we in a dream, is the Qu. alive again, can the lady[8] hereafter make any figure but a persona muta in the drama. if the Dragon declares ag^t the man of mercury he may strike in with the tertium quid that will probably arise, but with him he can never be otherwise than spurn'd & hated. the natural result of this is, that however I may for my private satisfaction desire to see you here, I cannot but think you sh'd goe to Ireland to qualify your self, then return hither, when the Chaos will be jumbled into some sort of order. if the King keeps

---

 [1] This reads as if Swift had written to Lewis proposing the possibility of going to London to attempt a reconciliation between Oxford and Bolingbroke. This, however, hardly seems credible.

 [2] Lewis was undoubtedly right in his belief that towards the end Oxford obstinately clung to office.

 [3] Colonel Francis Charteris, 1675–1732, the notorious scoundrel, and the subject of Arbuthnot's famous epitaph. See Pope and Swift, *Miscellanies. The Third Volume*, pp. 61–63; also *D.N.B.*

 [4] Said to be an oculist who attended Prince Eugene when in England.

 [5] Bolingbroke.   [6] Harcourt.

 [7] Bishop Atterbury.   [8] Lady Masham.

some Tory's in employment the notion of whig & Tory will be lost, but that of Court & Countrey will arise.

The regency has declar'd in favour of the whigs in Ireland.[1]

I believe W. Thomas[2] will stand his ground.

We shall be disolv'd as soon as we have settled the Civil List.

we have no appearance that any attempt will be form'd by the Pretender.

Endorsed by Swift: M^r L | Rx. Aug. 11. 1714

4804

Viscount Bolingbroke to Swift

Aug. 11th 1714

I swear that I did not imagine that you could have held out thro' two pages, even of small paper,[3] in so grave a stile. your state of late passages is right enough. I reflect upon 'em with indignation & shall never forgive myself for having trusted so long to so much real pride & awkward humility, to an air of such familiar friendship, & a heart void of all tenderness, to such a temper of engrossing business & power, & so perfect an incapacity to manage one wth such a tyrannical disposition to abusing [the] other &c but enough of this, I cannot load him as a Kn—,[4] without fixing fool on myself.

for you I have a most sincere & warm affection, and in every part of my life will shew it.

go into Ireland, since it must be so, to swear, & come back into Britain to bless. to bless me and those few friends who will enjoy you.

Johannes Tonsor[5] brings you this: From him you will hear what is doing. adieu, Love me, & love me the better because after a greater

---

[1] The long-drawn dispute between the Irish Executive and the Corporation of Dublin was in course of accommodation. The Corporation had been ordered to proceed to the election of a Lord Mayor and Sheriffs, and the Council to approve those who were elected.

[2] Oxford's secretary. Ball has 'Mr.' for 'W.

[3] Unfortunately Swift's long and important letter of 7 Aug. is not forthcoming in the original. If he compressed it within two pages of small paper it must have been difficult to read; but probably by 'pages' we are to understand 'leaves'.

[4] i.e. Oxford, 'as a Knave'.

[5] i.e. John Barber.

blow than most men ever felt I keep up my spirit, am neither dejected att what has pass'd nor apprehensive at what is to come. meâ
virtute me involvo.[1]

Endorsed by Swift: Aug. 11ᵗʰ 1714 | Lord Bolingbroke

Rothschild[2]

Swift to Charles Ford

Aug. 12. 1714

I have received the Pacquet;[3] by the same Token, some scoundrel
of the Post office either here or there, scratched out your name, and
indorsed it, *this is no right Frank, but must pay 2 shill.* I have orderd
my Man to inquire to morrow, whether it were done at Wantage.—
Sure the Dragon intends to strike in with the new World; by his
treating the Kings.[4] He thinks he has a kind of Merit by his ill
Usage, and may think right for ought I know. I sett out early on
Monday next[5] for Ireland, be so kind if any Letters come to me
inclosed to You or Mʳ L— to send them to Dublin; but not till you
are sure I am as far as Chester.—Confound all Politicks. Have I had
enough of them or no? We had news here that Lᵈ Bol— was sent to
the Tower, and this Night a Servant from Wantage brings word,
that a Stranger who spread that Report there, is taken up for it. You
are to know that Wantage is a Whig Town. You are incorrigeable in
that Fault of giving more than I would have. Between the Time that
I desired your Wine and your granting it me, things altered so, that
I shall hardly have a Tast of it; But I sent Mʳ Geree a Chest of
Florence,[6] and have drunk it out since I came here; so yours must

---

[1] Horace, *Odes*, III. xxix. 54–55.

[2] Lord Rothschild's Library, No. 2282 (14).

[3] Containing, presumably, the second copy of *Some Free Thoughts.*

[4] Swift echoes a phrase in Lewis's letter of 10 Aug., 'if the Dragon declares
agᵗ the man of mercury he may strike in with the tertium quid that will probably
arise'. In addition to showing joy upon proclaiming the King, Oxford had on
6 Aug. drafted a letter to the King expressing his zeal and devotion (*Portland
MSS.* v. 484). The reading is difficult; perhaps 'friends' or some such word has
been omitted after 'Kings', and 'treating' is not certain.

[5] 16 Aug. He reached Dublin on Tuesday, 24 Aug.

[6] Geree had acknowledged on 24 Apr. 'the noble present of wine' which
Swift had sent him when arranging for his visit to Letcombe.

requite him. I knew not how to buy, nor since the Change where to beg; and living without it would hurt my Health. Be assured I will never repay you. I have writt a good piece of the Thing I told you I was breeding.[1] I shall be quiet some time or other. I reckon the King has by this time received his Condoleance and Congratulation, Grief in one hand &c, Or rather Joy in one hand, and Gladness in the other. The Dragon told me confidently and often, that all foreigners Peers, such as Portland &c ceased to be Peers, on the Queen's Demise: by the Act of Settlement. Sure he was mistaken.[2] I had a short melancholy Letter from Dr Prat,[3] he and the rest are hardly used. How shall I look Elwood[4] in the Face. I have no Interest even with the Footmen of any body now in Power. This is a bad Stroak for the H. of L^ds in Ireland; and consequently for our Friends here. I sollicited that matter 800 times; but that cursed Delay ruined all.

Adieu, and now I am going, believe I love you very well—

Address: To Charles Ford Esqr, at his | Office at White-hall London
Postmarks: Wantage *and* 13 AV

4804

Charles Ford to Swift

London Aug: 12 [1714]

Our Justices sit several hours every day, without affording us the least news. I don't hear any thing they have done worth mentioning except some Orders they have given about the dispute in the City of Dublin.[5] You may be sure they are not such as will please our friends,

---

[1] *Some Considerations upon the Consequences hoped and feared from the Death of the Queen.*

[2] The Act of Settlement 1701 (12 & 13 Will. III, c. 2) enacted that 'no Person born out of the Kingdoms of England Scotland or Ireland or the Dominions thereunto belonging although he be naturalized or made a Denizen (except such as are born of English parents) shall be capable to be of the Privy Councill or a Member of either House of Parliament or to enjoy any Office or Place of Trust either Civill or Military or to have any Grant of Lands Tenements or Hereditaments from the Crown to himself or to any other or others in Trust for him'.

[3] Benjamin Pratt.

[4] John Elwood, Vice-Provost of Trinity College, Dublin.

[5] See p. 117, n. 1. 'Orders are sent to Dublin to require Sir Samuel and the aldermen of that city to meet, and elect forthwith a Lord Mayor and Sheriffs, and the Lords Justices and Council are to approve of the persons so elected' (*Portland MSS.* v. 486).

but I think you and I agreed in condemning those Proceedings in our own people. My Lᵈ Derby¹ is made Lᵈ Lieuᵗ of Lancashire. That and Hampshire² are the only vacant Employments they have fill'd up, I suppose under pretence of their being maritime Countys. If the Whigs had directed the List of Regents Marl— Sund— and Whar— had not been left out.³ There are five Torys too that would not have been in.⁴ Tho they were a little whimsical for three or four days about the Succession, they seem'd to recant and own themselves in an Error by later Votes. Every one of them approv'd the Peace, and were for the Address at the end of the last Session that it was safe, honourable, and advantagious. Considering what Ministers were employed here by the Court of Hanover, and that the King himself had little information but what he receiv'd from them, I think his List shews no ill disposition to the Torys, and they say he is not apt to be hasty in removing the persons he finds in Employment. The Bill is brought in for granting him the old Dutys for the Civil List.⁵ One Wikes of Northampton mov'd to tack the place Bill to it, but no body seconded him, and he was extremely laugh'd at.⁶ He happens unluckily to be a Tory.

Did you receive your Papers last post?⁷ The first copy is not yet left at St. D—n's,⁸ should I send to B—r for it, in L. B's name? I have writ to him to bring in his Bill, and as soon as he comes I will pay him.⁹ I suppose I shall see him to morrow. I wish you a good journey to Ireland, but if I hear Saterday's post comes into Wantage

¹ James Stanley, tenth Earl of Derby.

² The Duke of Bolton was made Lord Lieutenant of Hampshire.

³ Cf. a letter by Lord Berkeley of Stratton, 3 Aug. 1714, in *Wentworth Papers*, p. 409: 'It was a surprise to me, and I fancy will be not be less soe to himself, not to see My Lord Wharton's name in the list, and My Lord Sunderland look'd very pale when the names were read.'

⁴ For the five Torys see Swift to Ford, 7 Aug., and note.

⁵ The grant amounted to £700,000. A Tory motion that the sum should be raised to £1,000,000 was allowed to drop.

⁶ 'Hereupon John Wykes, Esq; Member for the Town of *Northampton*, proposed the *Tacking* to it the *Bill*, which had so often miscarry'd, *for limiting the Number of Officers in the House of Commons*: But no Body seconded that Motion' (*Political State*, Aug. 1714, pp. 151–2). The name is given as William Wykes, or Wickes, in the Parliamentary Returns.

⁷ The second copy of *Some Free Thoughts* had been returned by Ford; the first remained in Barber's hands.

⁸ St. Dunstan's, the Coffee-house in Fleet Street.

⁹ See Swift to Ford, 7 Aug., *ad fin.*

on Sunday, I may trouble you again. Pray let me know when you land in Ireland, that I may write to you if any thing happens worth while. I shall be very impatient for what you promise me from thence. I should be very glad to hear from you while you are on the road.

Ld Anglesey came to town last tuesday. They are all here now, except Pembroke and Strafford.[1]

Charles Eversfield[2] is making his Court to the D: of Somerset, and Argyle. He declares he will keep his place if he can, and that he will not stir for Campion's election in the County of Sussex. Campion and he have had some high words upon that account. Ld Orford[3] told the Commis^rs of the Admiralty, they were ignorant, negligent of their duty, and wanted zeal for the King's service.

4804

John Arbuthnot to Swift

London: Aug. 12 1714

My Dear Friend[4]

I thank yow for your kind Letter, which is very comfortable upon such a melancholy occasion My Dear Mistress's days were numbred even in My imagination & could not exceed such certain Limits but of that small number a great deal was cutt off by the last troublesome scene of the contention amongst her Servants. I beleive sleep was never more welcome to a weary traveller than death was to her, only it surprised her too suddainly before she had sign'd her will, which no doubt her being involvd in so much business hindr'd her from finishing. it was unfortunate that she had been persuaded as is

---

[1] The Earl of Anglesey returned from Ireland, Tuesday, 10 Aug. He was one of the Regents nominated by the Elector; so also was the Earl of Pembroke. The Earl of Strafford, who was First Lord Commissioner of the Admiralty, a Regent *ex officio*, was at The Hague (*Wentworth Papers*, p. 414).

[2] Charles Eversfield was at this time member for Horsham. In June 1712 he had been made Treasurer and Paymaster of the Ordnance. For Campion see Ford to Swift, 24 July; he was not re-elected for Sussex. They had both been leading members of the October Club.

[3] Edward Russell, Earl of Orford, one of the Lords Justices, First Lord of the Admiralty 1709–10 and 1714–17.

[4] The ink of this letter is faded. Arbuthnot's hand, in any event, is difficult to decipher.

supposd by Lowndes[1] that it was necessary to have it under the great Seal. I have figurd to myself all this Melancholy Scene & even if it be possible worse than it has happened twenty times, so that I was prepard for it. My Case is not half so deplorable as that of poor Lady Mashams[2] & severalls of the Queen's servants, some of whom have no chance for their bread but the generosity of his present Majesty which severall people that know him very much commend. so far is plain from what has happen'd in publick affairs that what one party affirm'd of the settlement has prov'd true, & that it was firm, that it was in some measure an advantage to the successor not to have been here & so obligd to declare him self in severall things in which he is now at liberty. & indeed never any prince in this respect came to the Crown with greater advantages. I can assure you the peacable scene that now appears is a disappointment to more than one sett of people. I have an opportunity calmly & philosophically to consider that treasure of vileness & baseness that I allways beleived to be in the heart of man, & to behold them exert their insolence & baseness, every new instance instead of surprising & greiving me really diverts me & in a manner improves my Theory. Tho I think I have not mett with it in my own case except from one man & he was very far mistaken for to him I would not abate one grain of my proud Spirit. Dear Freind the last sentence of your letter quite kills me: never repeat that melancholy tender word that you will endeavour to forgett me. I am sure I never can forgett yow, till I meett with, (what is impossible) another whose conversation I can so much delight in as Dr Swifts & yet that is the smallest thing I ought to value you for. That hearty sincere freindship That plain & open ingenuity in all your commerce, is what I am sure I never can find in another alas. I shall want often, a faithfull monitor one that would vindicate me behind my back & tell me my faults to my face. god knows I write this with tears in my eyes. yet do not be obstinate, but come up for a little time to London, & if you must needs go, we may concert a manner of Correspondence wherever we are. I have a letter from Gay just before The Queen's death, is he

---

[1] William Lowndes, 1652–1724, successively M.P. for Seaford, St. Mawes, and East Looe, was Secretary to the Treasury from 1695 till his death. He is credited with having invented the enduring phrase 'Ways and means'. Gay addressed some verses to Lowndes (*Poetical Works*, ed. Faber, p. 174).

[2] As previously mentioned the financial affairs of Lord and Lady Masham were not so unhappy as was commonly believed.

not a true poet who had not one of his own books to give to the princess that askd for one.[1]

Endorsed by Swift: D^r A | Aug. 13. 1714 | About the Queen

B.M. Add. MS. 39839
Swift to Miss Esther Vanhomrigh

Aug. 12th 1714[2]

I had y^r Letter last Post, and before you can send me another, I shall set out for Ireld: I must go and take the Oaths, and the sooner the better. I think since I have known you I have drawn an old house upon my Head. You should not have come by Wantage for a thousand Pound. you used to brag you were very discreet; where is it gone?[3] It is probable I may not stay in Ireland long; but be back by the beginning of Winter. When I am there I will write to you as soon as I can conveniently, but it shall be allways under a Cover; and if you write to me, let some other direct it, and I beg you will write nothing that is particular, but what may be seen, for I apprehend letters will[4] be opened and inconveniences will happen. If you are in Ireld while I am there I shall see you very seldom. It is not a Place for any Freedom, but where every thing is known in a Week, and magnifyed a hundred Degrees. These are rigorous Laws that must be passed through: but it is probable we may meet in London in Winter, or if not, leave all to Fate, that seldom cares to humor our Inclinations. I say all this out of the perfect Esteem and Friendship I have for you. These Publick Misfortunes have altered all my Measures, and broke my Spirits. God Almighty bless you;[5] I shall, I hope be on horseback in a day after this comes to y^r Hand. I would

---

[1] As will be seen from Arbuthnot's letter to Swift of 19 Oct. 1714, the Electoral Princess, the future Queen Caroline of England, appears to have given Gay some reason to believe that she would befriend him.

[2] Hawkesworth and Scott (xvi. 224) print only part of this letter.

[3] There seems to be little doubt that Vanessa had paid Swift a visit at Wantage, or even Letcombe.

[4] For 'will' Ball reads 'may'.

[5] Ball omits the words 'God Almighty bless you'.

not answer your Questions for a Million; nor can I think of them with any Ease of Mind. adieu.

Address: To Mrs Van-Homrigh, at M^r | Handcock's in little Rider Street | near
St James's Street | London
Postmarks: Wantage *and* 13 AU
Endorsed: 6

4804

Charles Ford to Swift

Aug 14th [1714]

I hope you did not pay the two shillings for Postage. If you did, pray send me the cover, that I may enquire into the meaning of it. I suppose you expect news upon Crags's return from Hanover,[1] but I don't hear a word more than what you have in the L^ds Justices Speech. Yesterday morning after he came the Whigs look'd dejected, and our friends very much pleas'd, tho I don't know any reason for either, unless it was expected by both sides that he would have brought Orders for Alterations. It seems the Dragon's entertainment was upon a family account upon the agreement between Ld Harley and Ld Pelham,[2] and only those who were concern'd in their affairs were invited. But slighter grounds would have serv'd to raise a story at this time, and it was sufficient that my Ld Townesend and Ld Cooper[3] din'd at his house. However we look upon him as lost to our side, and he has certainly made advances of civility to the Whigs, which they have return'd with the utmost contempt. I am told Dismal[4] begins to declare for his old friends, and protests he was really afraid for the Protestant Succession, which made him act in the manner he did. The forreign Peers are certainly deprived of their

[1] James Craggs, the younger, had been sent to Hanover on 31 July (before the Queen's death) with a letter from the Council to the Elector desiring him to hasten over to England, and he arrived back on 13 Aug.

[2] The greater part of Newcastle's estates had gone to his nephew, the second Lord Pelham (created Duke of Newcastle 1715). The agreement between Harley and Pelham is described in Erasmus Lewis's letter to Swift of 17 July.

[3] Viscount Townshend succeeded Bolingbroke as Secretary of State on 17 Sept.; Lord Cowper, afterwards Earl Cowper, succeeded Harcourt as Lord Chancellor on 22 Sept. Both were Lords Justices.

[4] The Earl of Nottingham.

right of voting by the express words of the Act of Succession,[1] and it appears it was the intention of the Legislature at that time, for Prince George of Den—k was excepted by name. But it's thought the Lords will interpret it otherwise when it comes to be tryed. They don't lose the other Privileges of Peerage, and their Posterity born here may sit in the House. The same clause extends to the House of Commons, and no Foreigner can enjoy any Employment civil or military. They may be favourable to the Lords, who are all Whigs, but I doubt poor Duke Disney will lose his Regiment.[2]

I suppose B[r] has given you an account of L. B's Pamphlet.[3] If you and he are not come to an eclaircissement upon it, shall I send to him for it? I long for the other. Yesterday the Commons voted Nem. Con. to pay the Hanover Troops that deserted us in 1712.[4] To day S[r] W[m] Wyndham, Campion, and two or three more gave some opposition to it, for which they are extremely blam'd. I think they had acted right if they had spoke against it yesterday, but it seems they were not then in the House. They had not strength enough to day to come to a division. Once more I wish you a good journey, and a quick return, and I hope you will find things go better than you expect.

Endorsed by Swift: Aug. 12, and 14, 1714 | Ch. F— | Memd. I left | Ledcomb[5]
Aug. 16. 1714 | in order to Ireld.

[1] See p. 119, n. 2.

[2] Henry Desaulnais, a French Huguenot, who anglicized his name as Disney, or Desney. In 1694 he was an ensign in the First Foot Guards, and was promoted lieutenant, 15 Feb. 1695. He became captain in Colonel Meredyth's regiment of foot, 23 Apr. 1706, captain of the Foot Guards, 13 Mar. 1708, and colonel of Alnut's regiment of foot, 23 Oct. 1710. On 25 July 1715 he sold his colonelcy. On 25 Dec. 1725 he became colonel of the 29th Foot (Dalton's *Army Lists*, v. 44, 241, pt. ii. 6; *George the First's Army*, i. 365; ii. 400). Disney died 21 Nov. 1731 and was buried in the east cloister of Westminster Abbey. He was a friend of Bolingbroke. See further Gay's *Mr. Pope's Welcome from Greece*, ll. 29–32; *Wentworth Papers*, p. 108; Lady M. W. Montagu's *Works*, 1817, v. 176.

[3] Swift's *Free Thoughts* as revised by Bolingbroke. But Barber had not spoken of it in his letter to Swift of 3 Aug. The 'other' which Ford longs for is *Some Considerations*.

[4] When Ormonde acted on St. John's secret instructions to 'avoid engaging in any siege or hazarding a battle till you have further orders from her majesty'. On 13 Aug. 1714 Horatio Walpole moved 'to impower the Lord High Treasurer, or Commissioners of the Treasury for the Time being, to issue the sum of 65022*l.* 8*s.* 8*d.* (being the Arrear due to the Troops of *Hanover*, for their Service in the *Low Countries* in the Year 1712)'. Boyer, *Political State*, Aug. 1714, p. 155.

[5] 'Ledcomb' written over 'Wantage' crossed out.

B.M. Portland MSS., List 2
Swift to the Earl of Oxford

Aug. 15. 1714

My Lord.

This great Event of the Queen's death, as it has broken your Measures of retiring, and called you back again into Affairs[1] so it has affected me so far as to force me into Ireland to take the Oaths. I sett out to morrow morning, and shall have no Thoughts of returning, unless some Juncture of Affairs shall make my Friends think it may be of any use. I wish your Lordship good Success in this new Scene, and that you may have Credit enough with the King to sett him right in his Opinions of Persons and Things. I am almost tempted to think it was by the peculiar Favor of Providence, that your Lordship gave up your Employment before Her Majesty's Death. At least it is thus I judge at Distance, from the Leavings of the little I knew when I came from Toun. However, I conceive you have still as hard a Game to play as any Man now in England. and will be as much obnoxious to Censure as when you were at the Head of the Ministry; though perhaps less to Danger; and though I know you value neither, yet I could wish to see you always exempt from both, as far as human Prudence can place you: At least, a good Man should onely be threatened by Cowards and censured by Fools, and then he will be safe enough in his Person and Reputation. | I am with the greatest Respect | Your Lordship's &c

Endorsed by Lord Oxford: Aug: 15ᵗʰ | 1714 | D: Sw. | Rx Aug: 19.(?)

Rothschild[2]
Swift to Charles Ford

[August 1714]
Dublin. Septr. 1714.[3]

I have been hindred by perfect Lazyness, and Listlessness, and anneantissement to write to You since I came here; which was

---

[1] Oxford (and Bolingbroke) entertained a misguided hope that they would find a place in the councils of the new sovereign. Instead therefore of retiring to his Herefordshire seat Oxford lingered on in London. He even approached some of his former colleagues in order to secure their support when the summons came (*H.M.C. Rept*, 11, Appt., pt. v, p. 321).   [*For notes 2, 3 see opposite.*

Tuesday the 24 instant. I am now hunting after a Horse to ride. I know not what to say to You. I cannot think nor write in this Country: My time passes in doing nothing, which makes me so busy that I have not leisure for any thing else. I have not added one Syllable to the Thing I was about;[1] which at London or Letcomb would have now been finished. Tell Barber I will write to him in a few days. I have already to M^r L—.[2] I cannot stop my Ears when People of the wisest sort I see (who are indeed no Conjurers) tell me a thousand foolish Things of the Publick: But I hope I shall keep my Resolution of never medling with Irish Politicks. It is hoped by those of our Side, that the K— will not answer altogether the Expectation of the Whigs, the Chancellor here[3] tells me he has been informed so from England. But I can believe nothing at this distance, when I know that there is no trusting to any thing three yards from the Court. I wish the Honeymoon may not make the Parlm^t give up any thing they will repent of. I shall judge of what will happen by the great or little Pains to manage by the Court against next Elections; without much Pains and Pence the Whigs cannot have a Majority; and without a Majority, I think they cannot prudently take any large steps.

This is the Summ of my Politicks: L^d B— would fain have me come over soon.[4] I will not do it, till I am fully convinced that my coming may be of use. For I care not to fight against Sea and Wind so late in my Life; and having been beaten with all Advantages on our side, makes me a greater Coward than ever. L— and you shall deal very fairly with me; For my Fortunes will not suffer me to make an idle Journey. And therefore when I am presst to go over, I will have both your impartiall Opinions, if you will give them to me. Being in England onely renders this Place more hatefull to me, which Habitude would make tolerable. I can say no more now, and what I have said is not worth a Rush. Pray order Barber to settle my Accounts, and let him send them to me—

Y^rs.

[1] *Some Considerations.*
[2] The letter to Barber (if written) and the letter to Lewis are not preserved.
[3] Sir Constantine Phipps.
[4] See Bolingbroke's letter to Swift of 11 Aug.

[2] Lord Rothsdhild's Library, No. 2282.
[3] Swift has mistaken the month. 'Sept^r' should be 'August', as is shown by 'the 24 instant' and by the London postmark (Aug. '30' or '31'). The letter was posted at Trim.

I believe the Bp of Clogher[1] is in | Town, and D[r] Prat or others
know | where to send to Him

Address, on separate cover: To Charles Ford Esq[r], | at His Office at Whitehall |
London
Postmarks: Trim *and* 3 [?] AV

Deane Swift 1765

Swift to Viscount Bolingbroke

Dublin. September 14th, 1714

I hope your Lordship, who were always so kind to me while you
were a servant, will not forget me now in your greatness.[2] I give you
this caution, because I really believe you will be apt to be exalted
in your new station of retirement, which was the only honourable
post that those who gave it you were capable of conferring. And as,
in other employments, the circumstances with which they are given,
are sometimes said to be equally valuable with the gift itself, so it was
in your case. The sealing up your office, and especially without any
directions from the King,[3] discovered such sentiments of you in such
persons, as would make any honest men proud to share them.

I must be so free to tell you, that this new office of retirement will
be harder for you to keep, than that of Secretary: And you lie under
one great disadvantage, beside your being too young, that whereas
none but knaves and fools desire to deprive you of your former post,
all the honest men in England will be for putting you out of this.

I go on in writing, though I know not how to send you my letter.
If I were sure it would be opened by the sealers of your office, I
would fill it with some terms of art, that they would better deserve,
than relish.

[1] St. George Ashe.
[2] Bolingbroke had been dismissed from office a fortnight before the date of
this letter, but the fact was only known in Ireland on 11 Sept. when the *Dublin
Gazette* announced that on 31 Aug. 'the Right Hon. the Lord Bolingbroke was
removed from being one of his Majesty's Principal Secretaries of State, and his
Office sealed up'.
[3] Boyer (*Political State*, viii. 187) declares that Bolingbroke was dismissed
under the direct order of George I sent from Hanover. The wording of the
announcement in the *Dublin Gazette* may have led Swift to infer that Bolingbroke
was removed by the Lords Justices.

It is a point of wisdom too hard for me, not to look back with vexation upon past management. Divines tell us often from their pulpits, that half the pains which some men take to be damned, would have compassed their salvation: This, I am sure, was extremely our case. I know not what motions your Lordship intends; but, if I see the old Whig-measures taken in the next elections, and that the court, the bank, East-India, and South-sea,[1] act strenuously, and procure a majority, I shall lie down and beg of Jupiter to heave the cart out of the dirt.

I would give all I am worth, for the sake of my country, that you had left your mantle with some body in the House of Commons, or that a dozen honest men among them had only so many shreds of it.—And so, having dispatched all our friends in England, off flies a splinter, and knocks two Governors of Ireland dead.[2] I remember, we never had leisure to think of that kingdom. The poor dead Queen is used like the giant Lougarou in Rabelais.[3] Pantagruel took Lougarou by the heels, and made him his weapon to kill twenty other giants; then flung him over a river into the town, and killed two ducks and an old cat. I could talk very wisely to you, but you would regard me not. I could bid you, *non desperare de republicâ*; and say, that *res nolunt diu male administrari*. But I will cut all short, and assure you, that if you do not save us, I will not be at the pains of racking my invention to guess how we shall be saved; and yet I have read Polybius.

They tell me you have a very good crop of wheat, but the barley is bad.[4] Hay will certainly be dear, unless we have an open winter.

---

[1] In his *Examiner*, No. 35, 5 Apr. 1711, Swift wrote: 'One Thing I might add, as another acknowledged Maxim in that Party, and in my Opinion, as dangerous to the Constitution as any I have mentioned; I mean, That of preferring, on all Occasions, the *Moneyed* Interest before the *Landed*.'

[2] The Lords Justices of Ireland were unwilling to comply with the orders sent them from England in relation to the civic dispute (p. 117, n. 1). The English Lords Justices retorted by superseding Primate Lindsay and Lord Chancellor Phipps, and appointing in their room Archbishop King and the Earl of Kildare. Archbishop Vesey, presumably on account of his great age, was continued as a Lord Justice.   [3] Book ii, chap. xxix.

[4] The *Dublin Gazette* had mentioned that Bolingbroke had retired to 'his seat at Bucklebury in Berkshire'. It was likely that on hearing this news that Swift sat down to write to him. Three years before Swift had visited Bolingbroke at Bucklebury, an estate he enjoyed in the right of his wife, eldest daughter of Sir Henry Winchcombe, Bt. Swift described Bolingbroke at Bucklebury as 'a perfect country gentleman' who 'smoakt tobacco with one or two neighbours; he

I hope you found your hounds in good condition, and that Bright has not made a stirrup-leather of your jockey-belt.

I imagine you now smoking with your humdrum squire, (I forget his name) who can go home at midnight, and open a dozen gates when he is drunk.

I beg your Lordship not to ask me to lend you any money. If you will come and live at the Deanry, and furnish up an apartment, I will find you in victuals and drink, which is more than ever you got by the Court: And, as proud as you are, I hope to see you accept a part of this offer before I die.

The ——— take this country; it has, in three weeks, spoiled two as good sixpenny pamphlets, as ever a proclamation was issued out against.[1] And since we talk of that will there not be [* * * *].[2] I shall be cured of loving England, as the fellow was of his ague, by getting himself whipt through the town.

I would retire too, if I could; but my country-seat, where I have an acre of ground, is gone to ruin. The wall of my own apartment is fallen down, and I want mud to rebuild it, and straw to thatch it.[3] Besides, a spiteful neighbour has seized on six feet of ground, carried off my trees, and spoiled my grove.[4] All this is literally true, and I have not fortitude enough to go and see those devastations.

But, in return, I live a country-life in town, see no body, and go every day once to prayers; and hope, in a few months, to grow as stupid as the present situation of affairs will require.

Well, after all, parsons are not such bad company, especially when they are under subjection; and I let none but such come near me.[5]

---

enquired after the wheat in such a field; he went to visit his hounds; and he knew all their names' (4, 5 Aug. 1711, *Journal*).

[1] *Some Free Thoughts* and *Some Considerations*.

[2] 'Here are two or three words in the manuscript totally erased and illegible.'— Deane Swift.

[3] This description illustrates the humble character of Swift's parsonage house at Laracor.

[4] In his imitation of Horace, Lib. ii, Sat. 6, Swift refers to the grove:

> A Terras Walk, and half a Rood
> Of Land set out to plant a Wood.

Poems, p. 198. The neighbour was John Percival of Knightsbrook in the parish of Laracor.

[5] His circle of clerical friends was indeed limited at that time. So far as his correspondence shows Archdeacon Walls, Dr. Raymond, his vicar, Worrall, and his curate, Warburton, were alone allowed to come near him.—Ball.

However, pray God forgive them, by whose indolence, neglect, or want of friendship, I am reduced to live with twenty leagues of salt water between your Lordship and me, &c.

Rothschild

Swift to Charles Ford

Dublin. Sep^ber. 27. 1714

I have had your three Letters,[1] and have no Excuse for not ackno-ledging them beside the generall Langour this Country gives one, and the want of Matter to furnish what may be worth any body's reading; For if an Account of the Factions here deserved writing, you may be pretty confident I mingle not with them, thô after fourty miles riding over Welch mountains,[2] I might amuse my self with two Parsons whom I met with a Friend, I might amuse my self with giving half an hours way to their Impertinences. I know not how your Speculations and Conjectures tend, or what Hopes you can form, for my Part since their Treatment of Ld Bol—[3] and some other Pro-ceedings I expect the worst the[y] can compass, and that they will be able to compass it; if the Crown thinks fitt at the Head of the Stocks to exert it self upon the next Elections. If any thing witholds the Whigs from the utmost Violence, it will be onely the fear of provoking the Rabble, by remembring what passt in the Business of Sacheverell. Our Ld Chancellor has writt for leave to go for England and waits it impatiently because he knows he must be out, which is not yet done by some Incident, which it seems you had not heard of when You writt your Letter.[4] I believe [h]is elder Brother on your side[5] will hardly meet with better Quarter, let him make what sub-missions he pleases; I believe every thing you can say of him, and that nothing but Guinneas can influence him. Give my service to Mr Domvile,[6] I am glad I had Credit enough to make a Letter from me do him a Pleasure; He is but an half dippt Whig; pray advise him to a little Violence on one side or other, else he will be a very insigni-

---

[1] Not now known.
[2] Presumably between Chester and Holyhead.
[3] See the previous letter.
[4] Phipps was not succeeded by Alan Brodrick, afterwards Viscount Midleton, till 30 Sept. See *Political State*, Sept. 1714, p. 280, and Oct., p. 338.
[5] Lord Harcourt.　　　　　　[6] William Domvile, M.P. for co. Dublin.

ficant Gentleman. There is a way of charming an Ague into Dogs; can you not contrive to charm your Infectious Distemper from the Cows and Sheep into Whigs, a much more infectious Cattle.

Yes, I have other Reasons for Staying in Ireland besides saving money, or else I should have none at all. I would first know how your Elections are like to run; besides, I stay here out [of] a *Publick Spirit*; And I stay here because of Ld Bol's Treatment; And I stay here to forget England and make this Place supportable by Practice, and because I doubt whether the Present Government will give me a Licence. These I take to be good Reasons; However, if I can get leave, I will come when I am calld, and not till then.—I know not why you should give up till you are forced.[1] I remember the Whig Ministers advised all their Friends against it some years ago. I think the King is now arrived,[2] (for I know no News) and one would see the new World a little before one left it. Judge Nutley[3] is just come over to us; I onely talkt a minute to him at his Coach side; He and most of us despond; Quo fata vocant[4]—adieu.

What do you talk of writing in this Country, I can as easily fly.

—28th. By the Bonfires I guess the Pacquets are come in, but I have not yet received my Letters, if there be any for[5] me.

No address: separate cover lost.

Forster copy

Swift to Knightley Chetwode

Dublin, 27 September, 1714.[6]

Sir,[7]

The Person who brought me your letter delivered it in such a Manner that I thought I was at Court again, and that the Bearer

---

[1] The office of Gazetteer.

[2] The King arrived at Greenwich on 18 Sept. and made his entry into London on the 20th.

[3] In 1714 Richard Nutley had been superseded as a Puisne Justice of the Queen's Bench by James Macartney. See Ball, *Judges in Ireland*, ii. 39, 72, 86.

[4] Cf. Virgil, *Aen*. vi. 147, x. 472.

[5] MS. 'from'.

[6] This is the first letter of a correspondence between Swift and Knightley Chetwode, or Chetwood, of Woodbroke, near Portarlington, covering the years 1714 to 1732, by far the greater proportion consisting of letters written by Swift.

[*For continuation of note 6, and note 7, see opposite.*

wanted a place; and when I received it, I had my answer ready to give him after perusal, that I would do him what service I could. But I was easy when I saw your hand at the bottom, and then I recollected I was in Ireland, that the Queen was dead, the Ministry changed, and I was only the poor Dean of St. Patrick's. My Chapter joins with me: we have consulted a lawyer, who (as it is usuall) makes ours a very good case; my desires in that point are very moderate, only to break the lease, and turn out nine singing men.[1] I should have been with you before this time, if it had been possible for me to find a horse; I have had twenty sent to me; I have got one, but it is good for nothing, and my English horse[2] was so ill I was forced to send him to grass. There is another evil, that I want a stock of hay, and I cannot get any. I remember Prince Butler[3] used to say: 'By

[1] The dispute between Swift and the Vicars Choral as to the lease from the latter to the Earl of Abercorn (see i. 427, n. 4) was evidently not yet terminated.

[2] Presumably 'Bolingbroke', the horse Swift brought with him when he came over for his institution.

[3] Otherwise Brinsley Butler, who became the second Lord Newtown-Butler

---

These letters formed the text of George Birkbeck Hill's *Unpublished Letters of Dean Swift*, 1899. These were printed from a transcript. We have no certain information as to who made the copy. The transcriber, it is clear, was not wholly reliable or a faithful reader; although he was anxious to reproduce Swift's spelling, capitalization, and general habits in letter-writing. The number of letters copied was fifty-eight. In the Forster Collection (No. 589) the record of a long correspondence between Edward Wilmot Chetwode and Forster extending from 1855 to Dec. 1871 leads up to a differing and more thorough transcript. Forster tells us that Chetwode made a copy of the letters with his own hand and subsequently invited him to Woodbroke to collate it with the originals. This Forster did; but the date of his visit is not stated. Subsequently the letters were stowed in a specially constructed vault under the study floor at Woodbroke. When again examined it was found that damp had reduced them to pulp. The Forster transcript contains sixty-seven letters; and on the whole, with some reservations, appears to be a safer guide. It has been decided, therefore, to use this transcript, in the main in Elrington Ball's conventionalized form, for the reproduction of the Swift–Chetwode correspondence. It would be a mistake to attempt conjectural modifications.

[7] Knightley Chetwode was descended from a long line of English gentry holding estates first in Buckinghamshire and later in Northamptonshire. His nearer ancestors suffered financial misfortune, and his grandfather came over to Ireland in the hope of mending his affairs. In this he was evidently successful for Swift's friend owned considerable estate in Ireland with two country residences, one in co. Meath about twelve miles north of Laracor and the other in Queen's County.

my Soul there is not a drop of water in the Thames for me.' This is my case; I have got a fool to lend me fifty pounds, and now I can neither get hay nor horse, and the season of the former is going. However if I cannot soon get a horse, I will send for my own from grass, and in two days endeavour to reach you; for I hear October is a very good month.

Jourdain[1] has been often telling my agent of some idle pretence he has to a bit of one of my parishes worth usually about five pounds per annum, and now the Queen is dead perhaps he may talk warmer of it. But we in possession always answer in those cases, that we must not injure our successors. Those idle claims are usual in Ireland, where there has been so much confusion in parishes, but they never come to anything. I desire my humble service may be presented to Mrs. Chetwode.[2] I am, | Your most obedient | humble Servant, |

Jon: Swift.

Sept. 28. This was writ last night not knowing the post day: I now tell you that by noise and bonfires I suppose the packets are come in with account of the King's arrival.[3]

Address: To Knightley Chetwode Esq., at his house near Portarlington, in the Queen's County. Per post.

and first Viscount Lanesborough. He and his elder brother Theophilus, on whom the barony of Newtown-Butler was conferred by George I, were college contemporaries of Swift. It was for the latter that the three manuscript volumes, 'The Whimsical Medley', containing transcripts of contemporary verse were compiled (Barrett's *Essay*, p. 85; *Poems*, p. xlviii).

[1] The Rev. John Jourdain held the parish of Dunshaughlin for more than half a century. The parish adjoined Rathbeggan, the outlying parish of the union of Laracor. See Landa, *Swift and the Church of Ireland*, pp. 42–43. Cf. also Swift to Chetwode, 21 June 1715.

[2] Chetwode's wife, to whom he had been married fourteen years, was the daughter of Richard Brooking of Devonshire. Her father had come to Ireland under the protection of Sir Richard Reynell, Bt., Chief Justice of the King's Bench, also a member of a Devon family (Ball, *Judges in Ireland*, i. 354–5). Through her mother Mrs. Chetwode was a niece of Godfrey Boate, a judge of the King's Bench (*Poems*, p. 284).

[3] Although the King had landed at Greenwich on Saturday the 18th contrary winds had prevented the news reaching Dublin for ten days. The news was then received with manifestations of public rejoicing (*Dublin Gazette*).

Swift to Knightley Chetwode

Dublin, 6 October, 1714.

Sir,

I acknowledge both your letters, and with any common fortune might have spared you the trouble of reading this by coming myself. I used to value a good revenue, because I thought it exempted a man from the little subaltern cares of life; and so it would if the master were wise, or servants had honesty and common sense. A man who is new in a house, or an office, has so many important nothings to take up his time that he cannot do what he would. I have got in hay; but my groom offended against the very letter of a proverb, and stacked it in a rainy day, so that it is now smoking like a chimney.¹ My stable is a very hospital for sick horses. A joiner who was to shelve a room for my library has employed a fortnight, and yet not finished what he promised in six days. One occasion I have to triumph, that in six weeks time I have been able to get rid of a great cat,² that belonged to the late Dean, and almost poisoned the house. An old woman under the same circumstances I cannot yet get rid of, or find a maid. Yet in spite of all these difficulties, I hope to share some part of October at Woodbrooke.³ But I scorn your coach; for I find upon trial I can ride.

Indeed I am as much disquieted at the turn of public affairs as you or any men can be.⁴ It concerns us spiritual men in a tender temporal point. Everything is as bad as possible; and I think if the Pretender ever comes over, the present men in power have traced

---

¹ Owing to the humidity of the climate the getting in of hay in Ireland is often no easy matter. It would appear that Swift's groom, a Scotsman, should have known better.

² There is ground for believing, however, that Swift was not without a weakness for cats.—Ball.

³ By combining the last syllable of his own name with the first of his wife's Chetwode had found an appropriate name for his Queen's County residence. The name is now spelled without the final 'e'; but as appears from an autograph letter (Civil Correspondence, P.R.O. of Ireland) Chetwode adopted the spelling used here.—Ball.

⁴ Swift, as we have seen in earlier letters, had entertained a hope that some of his Tory friends would be retained in the Ministry, and was unprepared for the complete transfer of power to the Whigs in Ireland as well as in England.

him the way. Your servant is just come for this, and I am dressing
fast for Prayers. | Your most obedient &c. |

J. S.

Address: To Knightley Chetwode Esq.

4805

John Arbuthnot to Swift

Octobr: 19. 1714

Dear Brother

Ev'n in affliction your letter made me melancholy, & communicated some of the spleen which yow had when yow wrote it, and
made me forfeilt some of my reputation of cheerfullness & temper
under afflictions. however I have so many subjects among my freinds
& fellow servants to be greivd for, that I can easily turn it off my
self with credit.[1] The Queens poor servants are like so many poor
Orphans, exposed in the very streets, & those whose past obligations
of gratitude & honour ought to have engagd them to have represented their case pass by them like so many abandon'd creatures,
without the possibility of ever being able to make the least return
for a favour, which has added to my Theory of human Virtue. I wish
I did not only haunt yow in the obliging & affectionat sense yow are
pleasd to express it but were personally present with you, & I think
it were hardly in the power of fortune not to make some minutes
pleasant. I dine with My lord and lady Masham to-day, where we
will, as usually, remember yow. Yow have read ere this time the
History of the white Staff,[2] which is either contriv'd by an enimy
or by himself, to bring down vengeance, & I have told some of his
nearest freinds so. all the Dragon can say will not give him one single

[1] On 7 Sept. Arbuthnot wrote to Pope: 'I have seen a letter from Dean Swift;
he keeps up his noble spirit, and tho' like a man knock'd down, you may behold
him still with a stern countenance, and aiming a blow at his adversaries' (Sherburn, i. 251). The letter from Swift to which Arbuthnot refers has been lost.
It was probably at this time that Swift, despondent at the turn of political events
and sick at heart on parting from his English friends, wrote the lines 'In Sickness' (*Poems*, p. 203).

[2] *The Secret History of the White Staff*, of which four editions appeared in
1714, was written by Defoe with knowledge which can only have been gained
from Lord Oxford; and, despite what Arbuthnot says, was regarded by some as
a defence of the late Lord Treasurer. That Minister's connexion with Defoe was
not realized by Swift.

freind amongst the whole party, & therefore I even wonder at him, which yow will say is a strange thing. The very great person[1] of all can hardly speak of him with patience. the Condé[2] acts like a Man of spirit, Makes up to the K & talks to him & would have acted with more sense than any of them could he have had any body to have acted along with him nos numerus sumus[3] &c The Man yow speak off is just as you describe so I beg pardon Shadwell says he will have my place of Chelsea.[4] G—th told me his meritt was, giving intelligence about his Mistris health. I desired he would do me the favour to say that I valud my self upon quite the contrary & I hopd to live to see the day when his Majesty would value me the more for it too. I have not seen any thing as yet to make me recant a certain inconvenient opinion I have, that one cannot pay too dear for peace of mind. Poor philosopher Berkley;[5] has now the idea of health, which was very hard to produce in him, for he had an idea of a strange feaver upon him so strong that it was very hard to destroy it by introducing a contrary one. poor Gay is much were he was only out of the Duchesses[6] family & service he has some confidence in the Princess[7] and Countess of Picbourg.[8] I wish it may be significant to him. I advycd him to make a poem upon the princess before she came over descrybing her to the English ladys, for it seems the princess does not dislike that; (she is really a person that I beleive will give great content to every body) but Gay was in such a groveling condition, as to the affairs of the world, that his muse would not stoop to visit him. I can say no more of newes than that you will find the proceedings hitherto have been comparatively gentle. adieu.[9]

Endorsed by Swift: D^r A— | Oct^tr (18?) 19 1714

[1] i.e. the King.

[2] i.e. the Earl of Peterborough, who had then just returned from Italy.

[3] Hor. *Ep.* I. ii. 27, 'nos numerus sumus et fruges consumere nati'.

[4] As Ball observes the allusion is evidently to an office held by Arbuthnot in connexion with Chelsea Hospital. Sir John Shadwell, like Sir Samuel Garth, was a Whig, but was a physician to Queen Anne, and attended her in her last illness.

[5] Berkeley had returned from Italy with Peterborough.

[6] i.e. the Duchess of Monmouth.

[7] i.e. the future Queen Caroline, who had landed in England on 11 Oct.

[8] A lady-in-waiting to the Princess.

[9] On the same piece of paper, the third page of the sheet, additional matter is written, beginning 'I thank you kindly' and ending 'I will add no more, being to write on the other side to the Dean; which pray forward'. Hawkesworth, 1766, prints this as if written by Arbuthnot to Swift. Nichols, 1801, xi. 425, prints it correctly as addressed by Arbuthnot to Ford.

Forster copy

Swift to Knightley Chetwode

Dublin, 20 October, 1714.

Sir,

The Bishop of Dromore is expected this night in town on purpose to restore his cat,[1] who by her perpetual noise and stink must be certainly a Whig. In compliance to your observation of old women's tenderness to each other, I have got one as old and ugly as that the Bishop left, for the ladies of my acquaintance would not allow me one with a tolerable face though I most earnestly interceded for it. If I had considered the uncertainty of weather in our climate, I should have made better use of that short sunshine than I did; but I was amusing myself to make the public hay and neglected my own. Do you mean my Lady Jenny Forbes that was?[2] I had almost forgot her. But when love is gone, friendship continues. I thought she had not at this time of day been at a loss how to bring forth a child. I find you are readier at kindling other people's bonfires than your own. I had one last night *par manière d'acquit*, and to save my windows.[3]

Your closet of eighteen foot square is a perfect gasconade. I suppose it is the largest room in your house or rather two rooms struck out into one. I thank you for your present of it, but I have too many rooms already; I wish you had all I could spare, though I were to give you money along with them. Since you talk of your *cave de brique*, I have bought forty-six dozen bottles and want nothing but the circumstance of wine to be able to entertain a friend. You are mistaken, I am no coy beauty but rather with submission like a wench who has made an assignation and when the day comes, has not a petticoat to appear in. I am plagued to death with turning away and taking servants; my Scotch groom ran away from me ten days ago and robbed me and several of the neighbourhood. I cannot stir from hence till a great vessel of Alicant is bottled, and till my horse is in a condition to travel and my chimney piece made. I never wanted so much a little country air, being plagued with perpetual

[1] See p. 135, n. 2.

[2] She was the daughter of the second Earl of Granard, and had married Major Josiah Champagne, who lived at Portarlington near Woodbrooke. See Forbes's *Memoirs of the Earls of Granard*.

[3] Swift was writing on the day of the King's coronation, which, as the *Dublin Gazette* records, was celebrated with elaborate musical and military honours, bonfires, and fireworks.

colds and twenty ailments,[1] yet I cannot stir at present as things stand. | I am your most obedient &c.

Address: To Knightley Chetwode Esq., at Woodbrooke, near Portarlington.

Forster copy

Knightley Chetwode to Swift

[24 October, 1714]

I am favoured with your letter,[2] but not a great deal pleased with its contents: I mean that anything should ail you whom I so much value. If air would remove it as you say, I am sorry you will not believe that air and prospects were as beneficial and agreeable as those on each side your door streetward. If it be worth while, as you pleasantly say, for a Whig-drove Bishop to make a journey to restore his cat, sure it will be worth his endeavour to get a day set apart on the occasion. I will expect for the future the 20th of October in our calendar in lieu of the 29th of May. The ladies of your acquaintance are I confess a little hard upon you in regard to faces to tie you down to ugliness and age. But you know best if it be not just.[3]

The lady I mention is the veritable Lady Jenny Forbes, your quondam acquaintance; she was more at a loss to bring forth [than] would easily be believed, and so diffident lest it should prove *une grossesse de vent* that nothing but seeing and feeling could convince, even after so much pain and so much danger. You banter your country friends strangely; but nevertheless though your bottles do, yet my *cave de brique* does not want the circumstance of wine to enable me to entertain a friend. You are either a great deal diffident or not at all so, otherwise you would see, judge, try if my eighteen foot square be a gasconade. I wish I could take what rooms you say you could spare; for aught I know it might not only serve you and me but both our successors. I really at first apprehended you had discovered a bit of extravagance of mine when you mention your chimneypiece; for I had sent for one of marble to my closet. I

[1] See p. 136, n. 1.
[2] The previous letter. The above letter from Chetwode is missing in Birkbeck Hill's volume.
[3] The following words are struck out: 'Since the world says you may command a very agreeable one and yet defer it.'

thought you [who] said so much of the Scotch could not so easily forget the thistle motto. It is plain in your case what has been often said to me by Sir Edward Seymour[1] does not hold true, that no one ever got anything from that nation but what stuck to them; [for] your groom did not stick to you though he robbed you. Pray let me know if your great vessel of Alicant be bottled. I have some in bottles which I will pretend to put in competition with it.

I am afraid your inclinations are not as good as your horse's condition to travel. Pray let me know if I may hope to see you manage these difficulties, and when; if you will let me hope for it in a reasonable time, I will delay going to my winter quarters,[2] which for a month past nothing but my expectation of you has made me defer. Mrs. Chetwode who is much your admirer and humble servant, bade me tell you, your not coming hither is owing to your fears of being upbraided with being an old bachelor. You great men never say a word of news to little ones, otherwise you would have mentioned my Lord Bolingbroke as I desired, for I am more attached to him than, I believe, you know of. I have not to add, but to desire *toujours avoir l'honneur de votre amitié*, for I am, with all imaginable respect, | Your faithful friend and obedient servant.

Hawkesworth 1766

Swift to Sir Arthur Langford

Trim, Oct. 30, 1714.

Sir,[3]

I was to wait on you the other day, and was told by your servant that you are not to be seen till towards evening, which, at the distance I am at this time of the year,[4] cannot easily be compassed. My prin-

---

[1] Sir Edward Seymour (1633–1708), Speaker of the House of Commons 1673–9. In the reign of Anne he became Comptroller of the Queen's Household; but in Apr. 1704 he was abruptly dismissed. His staunch Tory politics would commend him to Chetwode, who had evidently known him personally.

[2] His residence in co. Meath lay about twelve miles to the north of Laracor.

[3] For an account of Sir Arthur Langford see Swift to Dean Stearne, 17 Apr. 1710 *ad fin*. Descended from a Devonshire family he had migrated to Ireland and established himself in Swift's parish of Laracor. In his new surroundings he had imbibed devout Presbyterian sympathies.

[4] The reference is to the greater distance of Summerhill, Langford's seat, from Trim than from Laracor.

cipal business was, to let you know, that since my last return from *England* many persons have complained to me, that I suffered a conventicle to be kept in my parish, and in a place where there never was any before. I mentioned this to your nephew *Rowley*[1] in *Dublin*, when he came to me with this message from you; but I could not prevail with him to write to you about it. I have always looked upon you as an honest gentleman, of great charity and piety in your way, and I hope you will remember at the same time, that it becomes you to be a legal man, and that you will not promote or encourage, much less give a beginning to a thing directly contrary to the law. You know the Dissenters in *Ireland* are suffered to have their conventicles only by connivance, and that only in places where they formerly used to meet. Whereas this conventicle of yours is a new thing, in a new place entirely of your own erection, and perverted to this ill use from the design you outwardly seemed to have intended it for. It has been the weakness of the Dissenters to be too sanguine and assuming upon events in the State which appeared to give them the least encouragement; and this, in other turns of affairs, hath proved very much to their disadvantage. The most moderate Churchmen may be apt to resent when they see a sect, without toleration by law, insulting the established religion. Whenever the legislature shall think fit to give them leave to build new conventicles, all good Churchmen will submit; but till then we can hardly see it without betraying our Church. I hope, therefore, you will not think it hard if I take those methods which my duty obliges me, to prevent this growing evil, as far as it lies in my power, unless you shall think fit from your own prudence, or the advice of some understanding friends, to shut up the doors of that conventicle for the future.[2] I am, with true friendship and esteem, Sir, your most obedient humble servant,

B.

---

[1] Hercules Rowley, who represented Londonderry in the Irish Parliament.

[2] Swift was evidently unsuccessful in securing the closure of the conventicle, for Langford, who died in less than two years, left substantial bequests for the upkeep of the chapel and the maintenance of a Presbyterian minister.

Swift to Miss Esther Vanhomrigh

Philips-town Nov^br 5th 1714[1]

I met yr Servant when I was a mile from Trim, and could send
him no other Answer than I did; for I was going abroad by Appointment; besides I would not have gone to Kildrohod to see you for all
the World.[2] I ever told you, you wanted Discretion. I am going to a
Friend upon a Promise, and shall stay with him about a fortnight:
and then come to Town, and I will call on you as soon as I can, supposing you lodge in Turnstile Alley[3] as your Servant told me, and
that your Neighbours can tell me whereabouts. Y^r Servant said you
would be in Town on Monday;[4] so that I suppose this will be ready
to welcome you there. I fear you had a Journey full of fatigues; pray
take Care of your health in this Irish air to which you are a Stranger.
Does not Dublin look very dirty to You, and the country very miserable. Is Kildrohod as beautifull as Windsr, and as agreeable to you
as the Prebends Lodgings there;[5] is there any walk about you as
pleasant as the Avenue, and the Marlborough Lodge.[6] I have rode
a tedious Journy to day,[7] and can say no more. Nor shall you know
where I am till I come, & then I will see you. A Fig for yr Letters
and Messages: Adieu—

Address: To Mrs Van-homrigh, at her | Lodgins in Turn-Stile Alley, | near
          Colledge-green | Dublin
Postmark: 6 NO
Endorsed: 1st

[1] Swift was on his way from Trim by way of Philipstown to visit Chetwode.
Philipstown was the assize town of the King's County.

[2] Some communication between Vanessa and Swift had probably occurred
since he left England in August; but of this there is no evidence. Presumably she
had concluded that he entertained no intention of an early return to England and
resolved to follow him to Ireland. She settled at Celbridge, earlier known by its
Irish name as Kildrought. Here she is said to have inherited a house from her
father. Celbridge lies about eleven miles to the west of Dublin.

[3] Adjoining the Houses of Parliament in College Green. Afterwards known as
Parliament Row.   [4] The 8th.

[5] See *Journal*, 7 Aug. 1712: 'Windsor is a most delightfull Place, . . . My
Lodgings there look upon Eaton and the Thames, I wish I were Owner of them,
they belong to a Prebend.'

[6] The residence of the Duchess of Marlborough in right of the rangership of
Windsor Park.—Ball.

[7] The journey from Trim to Philipstown is one of twenty-five Irish miles.—
Ball.

Forster copy

Swift to Knightley Chetwode

> Woodbrooke, 6 November [1714]
> past one in the afternoon.

Not to disturb you in the good work of a godfather nor spoil your dinner, I only design Mrs. Chetwode and you would take care not to be benighted; but come when you will you shall be heartily welcome to my house.[1] The children's tutor is gone out and so there was no pen and ink to be had.

Endorsed: A pencil note from Woodbrooke where he came in K.C's absence dining out.

4805

John Arbuthnot to Swift

> [November 1714]

Dear Brother

I send yow the scrape of a letter begun to yow by the whole Society[2] because I suppose yow ev'n value the fragments of your freinds. The Honest Gentleman at whose lodgings we wrote is gone for ffrance, I really value your judgement extreamly in chusing your freinds I think worthy Mr Foord is an instance of it being[3] an honest sensible firm friendly man, & qaulis ab incaptu processerat &c,[4] tho by the way praising your judgement is a little compliment to myself, which I am apt to fall into of late, no body now being at the trouble of doing it for me. The parnelian, who was to have carried this letter seems to have changd his mind, by some sudden turn in his affairs but I wish his hopes may not be the effect of some accidental thing

---

[1] Swift had evidently arrived early at Woodbrooke, which is only about ten Irish miles from Philipstown, and had found his host and hostess out attending a christening feast in the neighbourhood. This note was probably sent in the carriage which was to bring them home.—Ball.

[2] The Scriblerus Club.

[3] Six words struck out before 'being'.

[4] Horace, *Ars Poetica*, 127. Within a few weeks of the accession of George I Ford ceased to be Gazetteer. He remained in London, however, till the spring of 1715. He is known to have been in France before the end of April. On his return to England during the summer he was arrested. See Nichol Smith, *Letters of Swift to Ford*, pp. xvi–xvii.

working upon his spirits, rather than any well grounded project.¹ If it be any pleasure to you I can assure you that you are remember'd kindly by your freinds & I beleive not altogether forgott by your Enimys. I think both is for your reputation. I am told that I am to lose my little preferment² however I hope to keep a little habitation warm in town. I cannot but say, I think ther is one thing in your Circumstance that might make any man happy which is a liberty to preach; such a prodigious priviledge, that if it did not border on Simony I could really purchase it for a summ of money, for my part I can never imagine any man can be uneasy that has the opportunity of venting himself to a whole congregation once a week, & yow may pretend what yow will I am sure yow think so to, or yow don't judge right as for newes I never enquire about any fuimus troes &c sed nunc ferox Jupiter transtulit omnia ad Argos.³ My present politick is to give no disturbance to the present folks in the due exercise of their power for fear of forcing them to do very strange things rather than part with what they love so well. untoward reports in the country will make elections dearer, which I am sorry for The Dragon I am affraid will be struck at. adieu in Hast. I must not forgett to tell you a passage of the pretenders declaration to this purpose, that he had no reason to doubt of his Sisters good intention towards him, which made him sitt quiet in her time, but was now dissapointed by the deplorable accident of her sudden death.⁴

Endorsed by Swift at head of letter: Dʳ Ar— | Rx Decʳ 2. 1714

Rothschild⁵

Swift to Archdeacon Walls

Novembr. 23. [1714.]

I writt to you or some of Your Crew the day before I left Trim; I have been here ever since at Mʳ Chetwoods, where I am used very well, and ride out whenever the weather will let me, and have been

¹ In September Parnell and Pope were in Bath together. At the end of the year or early in 1715 Parnell returned to Ireland.
² The word 'preferment' is followed by a heavy deletion—? 'Chelsea College'.　　　　　　　　　³ *Aen.* ii. 325–7.
⁴ The concluding paragraph—'I must not . . . sudden death'—was omitted by Hawkesworth.
⁵ Lord Rothschild's Library, No. 2281 (12).

in tolerable Health, though realy I think I used more Exercise in Dublin, for in this Country of Ireld there is no walking in Winter. I have been in 3 or 4 Neighboring Touns all better than Trim, and here is a great deal of Wood and Hedges hereabouts, so that in Summer it would be a sort of England onely for the Bogs: I have waited for good Weather and Opportunity to see my Lands near Athy¹ which is but ten miles off, and that besides my Lazyness and Welcom has kept me so long here, and may still a Week longer. Yʳ Letter to Portarlington was rightly directed if you had added in the Queens county;—Why the whole room painted?² is it not enough to have onely the new Panels & Edges of the Shelves painted; Do what you will, but pray let it be done before I come, that the Smell may go off. Is the Chimney-piece up, or onely finished at the Man's House? I am sorry the Bishop³ went out of Toun before I came. Read that last Sentence to Mʳˢ Johnson and observe whether she turns up her Forhead and dabs her hand on the Table, or on her Knee.⁴ I desired that Mʳˢ Brent⁵ might be spoke to to⁶ have the Groom cover the Wine with Litter to prevent Frost, & to take Care not to shake the Vessel, some Litter should be under an[d] over: But pray do not let him fill the whole Cellar with it, onely just enough to keep out the Frost. My Service to Gossip, and the Ladyes of Sᵗ Mary's—what does Gossip do for want of a Gamester:⁷ Pray give the Groom & Maid some Board-wages. If you can not read this yʳ Lodgers can. What news of Bolton⁸ & yʳ Living?

Address: To the Reverend Mʳ Archdeacon | Wall, over against the Hospitall | in
      Queen-street | Dublin
Stamp: PORTARLINGTON
Late endorsement: Dʳ Swift | Novʳ 23ᵈ 1714

   ¹ The corps of the deanery of St. Patrick's included the rectory and some part of the lands of the parish of Kilberry near the town of Athy, in the county of Kildare. In his letter to Chetwode of 3 Jan. 1714–15 Swift describes them at length.—Ball.
   ² A reference to work being executed for Swift in the deanery house.
   ³ Stearne, the Bishop of Dromore.
   ⁴ Ball suggests that this is 'doubtless an allusion to some practice of Stella when playing cards'.
   ⁵ Mrs. Brent, the housekeeper, did not at this time reside in the deanery.
   ⁶ to to] to and   *Ball.*
   ⁷ Ball suggests that 'Swift was probably Mrs. Walls's partner at cards, and provided the stakes'.
   ⁸ Theophilus Bolton was installed Chancellor of St. Patrick's 7 May 1722. In September of the same year he was raised to the bishopric of Clonfert; in 1724

Swift to Knightley Chetwode

Dublin, 3 December, 1714.[1]

Sir,

Mr. Graves[2] never came to me till this morning, like a vile man as he is. I had no letters from England to vex me except on the public account.[3] I am now teased by an impertinent woman, come to renew her lease; the Baron[4] and she are talking together. I have just squired her down, and there is at present nobody with me but—yes, now Mr. Walls is come in—and now another—you must stay. Now I am full of company again and the Baron is in haste;[5] I will write to you in a post or two. Manley is not Commissioner nor expects it.[6] I had a very ingenious Tory ballad sent me printed, but receiving it in a Whig house I suddenly read it, and gave it to a gentleman with a wink, and ordered him to burn it, but he threw another paper into the fire. I hope to send you a copy of it. I have seen nobody since I came. Bolton's patent for St. Werburgh's is passed,[7] and I believe I shall find difficulties with the Chapter about a successor for him. I thought to give the Baron some good coffee, and they made it so bad, that I would hardly give it Wharton.[8] I here send some snuff to

he was transferred to Elphin; and in 1729 he was promoted to the archbishopric of Cashel. He died in 1744 leaving a valuable library for the use of the clergy. He had been nominated by Stearne to the incumbency of St. Nicholas Without, and, as will be seen by the next letter, it is to this living that Swift refers. Cotton, *Fasti Eccl. Hib.* i. 18, ii. 52.

[1] As the superscription shows Swift had returned from Woodbrooke to Dublin.

[2] Not identified.

[3] Chetwode's reply, 8 Dec. 1714, suggests that there had been some announcement in the newspapers about Swift.

[4] Robert Rochfort, born in Ireland about 1652, had a distinguished legal career. Since 1707 he had been Chief Baron of the Irish Court of Exchequer. In 1714 he was superseded. In his earlier years a Whig he became an uncompromising Tory. A close friend of Chetwode he probably owed to him his introduction to Swift. The Rochforts, and their family home, Gaulstown, figure prominently in Swift's verses. See Ball, *Judges in Ireland*, ii. 68–69; *Poems, passim*.

[5] The Baron was going to Woodbrooke and was taking Swift's letter.

[6] This observation suggests a rumour that Manley was to be made a Commissioner of the Revenue.

[7] Theophilus Bolton was Chancellor of St. Patrick's Cathedral, and the parish of St. Werburgh's in Dublin was part of the corps of the Chancellorship.

[8] On the Hanoverian accession Wharton's name was omitted from the list of Lords Justices; but he was made Privy Seal.

Mrs. Chetwode; the Baron will tell you by what snatches I write this paper, I am, | Yours &c.

My humble service to Dame Plyant.¹

Address: To Knightley Chetwode Esq., per messenger.

B.M. Add. MS. 39839

Swift to Miss Esther Vanhomrigh

[? November 1714]

I will see you to morrow if possibly, you know it is not above 5 days since I saw you, and that I would ten times more if it were at all convenient; whether your old Dragon² came or no, whom I believe my People cannot tell what to make of, but take him for some Conjurer, adieu

    Tuesday morn³

      10.

Address: To Mistress Van^r
Endorsed: 3rd

B.M. Add. MS. 39839

Swift to Miss Esther Vanhomrigh

[? End of 1714]⁴

I will see you in a day or two, and believe me it goes to my Soul not to see you oftner. I will give you the best Advise, Countenance

¹ Apparently Swift was applying to Chetwode's wife the name of the 'soft and buxom widow' of Ben Jonson's *Alchemist*.

² Vanessa's servant.

³ The date of this brief note is quite uncertain. The content and the endorsement suggest that it may not be out of place before the letter next following. Scott places it at xix. 438 and Ball among Supplemental Letters to vol. iii.

⁴ There is no external evidence for assigning an assured date to this letter. It seems, however, to belong to the preceding two letters and those following. This and the subsequent letter are both endorsed '4th', and on this ground have been placed side by side. Scott, xix. 422, places it after the letter dated 'Dublin 1714' and beginning 'Well now I plainly see'; Ball, ii. 260, prints it after the letter also dated 'Dublin 1714' and beginning 'You cannot but be sensible'. He also assigns the conjectural date '[*December* 6, 1714]', which would be a Monday.

& Assistance I can.—I would have been with you sooner if a thousand Impediments had not prevented me. I did not imagine you had been under Difficultyes, I am sure my whole Fortune should go to remove them. I can not see You I fear to day having Affairs of my Place to do; but pray think it not want of Friendship or Tenderness which I will allways continue to the utmost

Monday morn.

Address: To Mrs Hessy Van
Endorsed: 4th.

B.M. Add. MS. 39839

Miss Esther Vanhomrigh to Swift

Dublin 1714 [? December]

You cannot but be sensible (at least in some degree) of the many uneasiness's I am a slave to a wretch of a Brother[1] cunning Executors and importunate creditors of my mothers things I can in no way avoid being subject to at present and weighty enough to sink greater spirits than mine without some support once I had a friend that would see me some times and either commend what I did or advise me what to do[2] which banished all my uneasiness. but now when my misfortunes are increased by being in a disagreable place amongst strange prying deacitful people whose company is so far from an amusement that it is a very great punishment you fly me and give me no reason but that we are amongst fools and must submit I am very well satisfied that we are amongst such but know no reason for haveing my happiness sacrificed to their caprice. you once had a maxime (which was to act what was right and not mind what they

---

[1] In his will, made that year, Bartholomew bequeathed to his sisters a life interest in his estate. Owing to his early death they had, before many months passed, succeeded to it.

[2] In his letter to Vanessa from Letcombe, 12 Aug. 1714, Swift had warned her that if she came to Ireland he would seldom see her, for it was a place where everything would be known in a week and magnified in the telling.

[*sic*] world said)[1] I wish you would keep to it now pray what can be wrong in seeing and advising an unhappy young woman I cant imagine you cant but know that your frowns make my life insuportable you have taught me to distinguish and then you leave me miserable now all I beg is that you will for once counterfeit (since you won't otherwise) that indulge⟨ent⟩[2] friend you once were till I get the better of these difficultys for my sisters sake for were not she involved whô I know is not so able to manage them as I am I have a nobler soul then sitt struggling with misfortunes when at the end I can't promise my self any reall happyness forgive me and I beg you'd believe it is not in my power to avoid complaining as I do

Endorsed: 4th

B.M. Add. MS. 39839

Swift to Miss Esther Vanhomrigh

[? 27 December 1714]

I received y[r] Letter when some Company was with me on a Saturday night; and it put me in such confusion, that I could not tell what to do.[3] This morning a Woman who does Business for me, told me she heard I was in —— with one —— naming you, and twenty

---

[1] See *Cadenus and Vanessa*, ll. 606-13:

> Two Maxims she could still produce,
> And sad Experience taught their Use:
> That Virtue pleas'd by being shown,
> Knows nothing which it dare not own;
> . . . .

Poems, pp. 705-6. Hawkesworth, 1766, prints only part of this letter: 'You once had a maxim . . . these difficulties.'

[2] Paper torn.

[3] The chronological placing of this letter is extremely difficult. The endorsement, '6th', suggests that it was written near the end of 1714. On the other hand it may be supposed that Swift and Vanessa had both been in Ireland longer than a few months to prompt the repetition of empty tittle-tattle. Swift, however, had warned Vanessa that in Ireland everything was known in a week. 'I said to you long ago' suggests two or three years in Ireland, unless it be taken to refer to a conversation in England. The allusion to 'that little master' is puzzling. Does it indicate the schoolboy 'commonly reported to be the Dean's son by Mrs. Johnson' (Nichols, *Works*, 1801, xix. 230)? If not written in 1714 this letter may be assigned conjecturally to 1717.

particulars, that little master and I visited you, & that the A—B[1] did so; and that you had abundance of wit &c. I ever feared the Tattle of this nasty Toun; and I told you so; and that was the Reason why I said to you long ago that I would see you seldom when you were in Ireld. and I must be easy if for some time I visit you seldomer, and not in so particular a manner. I will see you at the latter end of the week if possible. These are Accidents in Life that are necessary and must be submitted to —— and Tattle by the help of Discretion will wear off

    Monday morn
       10 a clock.

Endorsed: 6th

B.M. Add. MS. 39839

Miss Esther Vanhomrigh to Swift

Dublin 1714[2]

    Well now I plainly see how great a regard you have for me. you bid me be easy, and you'd see me as offten as you could gett the better of your inclinations, so much. or as offten as you remembred there was such a one in the world. if you continue to treat me as you do, you will not be made uneasy by me long. tis impossible to describe what I have suffer'd since I saw you last, I am sure I could have bore the Rack much better than those killing, killing, words of yours. some times I have resolved to die without seeing you more, but those resolves to your misfortune did not last long. for there is something in humain nature that prompts one so to find relief in this world. I must give way to it. and beg you'd see me and speak kindly to me, for I am sure you'd not condemn any one to suffer what I have don could you but know it the reason I write to you, is because I cannot tell it you, should I see you. for when I begin to complain then you are angry, and there is some thing in your look so awful, that it strikes me dumb. oh that you may but have so much regard for me left that this complaint may touch your soul with pitty. I say as little as ever I can, did you but know what I thought, I am

    [1] Archbishop King.
    [2] The letter may have been written during the last three months of the year old style.

sure it would move you. Forgive me and believe I cannot help telling
you this & live

Endorsed: 6th

Forster copy

Knightley Chetwode to Swift

Woodbrooke, 8 December, 1714.

I received your letter[1] by the Baron and the Plyant Dame's snuff,
for both which favours we are thankful to you. I stayed another day
at Naas[2] and from thence went to Mount Air. I brought the historian
of that family home with me. We had some discourse of you and
drank your health; I shall acquaint you when I see you of a good deal
passed whilst I stayed there. I am glad you received nothing from
England to vex you which regarded your private. I can assure you
my pains on that head were not a few. Yours makes me easy in the
point, though it is said in the public Gazette which I read.[3] This
place I hate since you left it; I will go off Monday eight days. I have
been diligent for some days past to get some work done you advised;
I flatter myself it is to your satisfaction.[4] I have been this day upwards of nine hours at the same sort of work you were at one day, am
pretty much fatigued, [and] am glad it is night to get victuals and
ease.

I must let you know I have the Baron's faithful promise about
your affair; all the directions I could give was Kilberry and the lands
adjoining belonging to the Dean of St. Patrick's.[5] I know not if these
instructions be sufficient; if not I pray send me fuller, and the other
denominations if more there be. I am in great hopes of the aforesaid
ballad you mention; pray send it me. The Baron tells me I am not
longer Mr. Justice.[6] Dame Pliant and I join in our requests that you

---

[1] 3 Dec. 1714. The above letter is missing from Birkbeck Hill's volume.

[2] Chetwode had apparently accompanied Swift on his way to Dublin as far as
Naas, co. Kildare, lying half-way between Woodbrooke and Dublin.

[3] Neither the London nor Dublin *Gazettes* disclose the subject of this allusion.

[4] Swift considered himself an authority on the scenic layout of estates. He had
probably been making suggestions for the improvement of the grounds at
Woodbrooke.

[5] See p. 145, n. 1.

[6] i.e. in the Commission of the Peace.

will so order your affairs to be with us at Martry[1] this Christmas. According to what I hear from you we will concert the method of getting you conveyed thither. There is good hay [there], though wanted here. I hear you will meet with great difficulty with your Chapter; I hope I am misinformed. Pray hint to me if you confide in Manley.[2] If you see him, and believe it worth while, you may please to let him know I am his humble servant. All here are entirely devoted to your service, and I am with the utmost respect and affection, | Your faithful and obedient &c.

Rothschild[3]

Swift to Archdeacon Walls

Belcamp.[4] Mond. morn. Dec[br] 27 [1714].

Some Business kept me in Toun an Hour longer than I thought and I was forced to come back to the Deanry for something I had

---

[1] Chetwode's residence in the county of Meath, which took its name from the parish in which it is situated. The latter lay not far from the parish of Ardbraccan, of which Knightley Chetwode's father, who was in Holy orders, had been rector.—Ball.

[2] Judging from the fact that his letters to Chetwode were generally sent by private hand, it is evident that Swift did not trust Postmaster Manley; and, as appears later on, had good reasons for his suspicions.—Ball.

[3] Lord Rothschild's Library, No. 2281 (13).

[4] Swift now appears for the first time as a guest in the ancestral home of Ireland's great son, the illustrious Henry Grattan. Belcamp was then the residence of the mother of Swift's seven famous friends. She was the widow of the Rev. Patrick Grattan, a senior fellow of Trinity College, Dublin, who on his marriage had obtained a stall in St. Patrick's Cathedral as Prebendary of Howth, the well-known promontory in the Bay of Dublin, and discharged the cure of souls in his prebendal parish, which lies not far from Belcamp, as well as in others adjacent to it. Of her sons the eldest, Henry, who was the grandfather of the patriot, was seated in Cavan; the second, William, who had been like his father a fellow, held a college living in the north of Ireland; the third, James, was a Dublin physician; the fourth, Robert, who was in Holy orders, held his father's prebend in Swift's cathedral; the fifth, John, who was also in Holy orders, was rector of a parish adjacent to Belcamp; the sixth, Richard, who became Lord Mayor of Dublin and was knighted, was a merchant; and the seventh, Charles, to whom there has been reference in connexion with the loss of his fellowship (i. 342), was master of Portora, a school of royal foundation in the north of Ireland (see *The Family of Grattan*, by G. D. Burchaell, Athlone Pursuivant, in *The Irish Builder*, xxx. 225).—Ball. Belcamp lies five miles north of Dublin, to

forgot. It was near 3 before I crosst the Ferry. There Tom and the Groom waited, and my Horses were standing at a Shop where Brandy is sold: at the door of it, I used to take Horse. I observed the two Loobyes put on my Cloak the wrong side outwards, and I found Will was drunk: I rode on, and found Tom did not come up,[1] I stayd, he galloped up; I chid him, he answered foolishly, he was drunk as a Dog, tottered on his Horse, could not keep the way, sometimes into the Sea, then back to me, swore he was not drunk, I bid him keep on, lasht him as well as I could, then he vowed he was drunk, fell a crying, came back every moment to me. I bid him keep on, at last with galloping and turning backwards & forwards Bolingbroke[2] grew mad, & threw him down, I came up, & called a Boy and Man to get the Horse from him, he resisted us all 3, was stark mad with drink, at last we got the Bridle from him, the Boy mounted, and away we rode, Tom following after us; what became of him I know not, I fancyed he would reel hither. The Bearer is the Boy that came with me; I beg you would step to the Deanry, & see lest Tom should come there, & perhaps in his desperate humor rob me. I would have his great Coat, Boots & Whip taken from him; let him have a Crown in part of his Wages, and the rest he shall have when I come, and his Account is given up. Let him leave the House immediatly, with a Charge to the Maid & Gilespy not to let him come into the doors. I was an Hour going between the Ferry & the red harp,[3] but got here before it was dark. My humble Service to the Ladyes. Tom has my Quill & Brush for my Teeth, I believe in his Pocket, for I can not find it among my Things; get it from him and I will send for it to y^r House for I want it mightily. Pray enquire for some Lad for a Servant; I will also turn off Will when I come: Remember to send my Letters to night.

My Service to Gossip & the Ladyes. The Bearer is the Boy who came with me. I have given him a Shilling. adieu.

Address: To the Reverend Mr Archdeacon | Walls in Queen street
Late endorsement: Dr Swift | Decr 27th 1714

the west of the road leading to Malahide. In Swift's time the shortest way was by a ferry which crossed the Liffey. To save time Swift had sent his horses round by one of the two bridges then available, to await him at the ferry.

[1] Swift loved to ride attended by two servants, preceded by a groom and followed by a valet. In 'The Duty of Servants at Inns' (*Prose Works*, xi. 360) exact instructions are given them.　　　　　　[2] The horse's name.

[3] This fine expanse of sand frequented by Dublin equestrians has been mentioned previously.

Forster copy

Swift to Knightley Chetwode

3 January, 1714–15.

I have had a letter of yours[1] by me these three weeks, which among others has lain unanswered, because I left off my old custom of answering letters before the post-day; and it happened that upon post-day I never had leisure; but besides I waited till I could hear you had got to Martry. I know not what you observed in the public Gazette about that business I was uneasy at: for I never heard of anything, and had letters since from the person chiefly concerned. I am afraid the Dean's field[2] will be quite spoiled in your absence. I had made an extract out of the lease of Kilberry, of the denominations, but feared you had no correspondence with the Baron since you left the neighbourhood. However I will here annex it. Ay, the ballad; I cannot for my life tell where it is at present, but a copy shall be sent or brought to you.[3]

I had gone thus far when company came in, and I was forced to leave off, and go abroad to a Christmas dinner, where I stayed till eleven, and at coming home my maid told me that one of your servants were here to know whether I would go down to Martry, and that he will call to-morrow morning; therefore I resolve to finish this letter to-night, and am glad of the opportunity, not knowing where to direct to you better than by Navan.[4] I believe you may be out of the peace, because, I hear almost all our friends are so. I am sorry Tories are put out of the King's peace; he may live to want them in it again. My visitation is to be this day sennight, after which I soon intend for the county of Meath; I design great things at my visitation, and I believe my Chapter will join with me. I hear they think me a smart Dean; and that I am for doing good. My notion is, that if a man cannot mend the public he should mend old shoes if he can do no better; and therefore I endeavour in the little sphere I am placed to do all the good it is capable of.

[1] 8 Dec. 1714.

[2] Presumably Swift had allowed his name to be attached to one of the Woodbrooke fields.

[3] Ball suggests that the ballad may have been one entitled *Britannia's Tears: A Satyrical Dirge by way of a Lamentation on the Deplorable Death of Her late Gracious Majesty Queen Anne*, printed in Dublin, 1714. There is a copy in the library of the Royal Irish Academy.

[4] Martry lies a few miles north-west of Navan, co. Meath.

As for judicious John, he is walked off. Your cursed good ale ruined him. He turned such a drunkard and swaggerer, I could bear him no longer: I reckon every visit I make you will spoil a servant. I shall come with two servants and three horses, but a horse and a servant I shall leave at Trim. I hear an universal good character of Mr. Davis; but however I shall have my eye over him and the lads.[1] As for news, the d——l a bit do I ever hear, or suffer to be told me. I saw in a print that the K[ing] has taken care to limit the clergy what they shall preach;[2] and that has given me an inclination to preach what is forbid: for I do not conceive there is any law yet for it. My humble service to Dame Plyant. You talk of your hay but say nothing of your wine. I doubt it is not so good as at Woodbrooke: and I doubt I shall not like Martry half so well as Woodbrooke.

Now for the lands at Kildare:—The manors, lordships and townships of Kilberry, Castleriddy and Cloney; also the prebend of Kilberry, with the lands, tenements and tithes whatsoever appertaining to the said prebend, rectory, churches, and towns of Kilberry, Bert, Cloney, Srowland, Kilcolman, Oldcourt, and Tullygorey, Prusselstown, Shanraheen, Tyrrellstown, Clonwannir, and Russellstown. The land without the prebend and all those cursed Irish names is 1700 and odd acres; supposing the land to be a crown an acre at full rent the whole is worth

per annum	£425	0	0
Supposing the prebend and tithes of all those hard names worth	50	0	0
The whole will be worth at full rent	£475	0	0
And it pays me only	£120	0	0

There was a great deal of young wood which has been horribly abused.

If the Baron could contrive that I might have some account of this land &c: he would do me a great favour.

Address: To Knightley Chetwode Esq., per private hand.

[1] Probably Chetwode's sons received their early education in Dublin. He had three sons surviving infancy—John born in 1706, Valentine born in 1708, and Crewe born in 1710. Davis was presumably the name of their schoolmaster. Valentine matriculated in Trinity College, Dublin, in 1725 (*Alum. Dub.*, p. 149).

[2] On 11 Dec. the King issued directions to the Archbishops and Bishops for the 'preserving of unity in the Church and the purity of the Christian Faith, concerning the Holy Trinity; and also for preserving the peace and quiet of the State'.

Erasmus Lewis to Swift

[January 1714–15]

I have one Letter from you to ackowledge, wch I will do very soon, in the mean time I send this[1] to acquaint you, that if you have not already hid your papers in some private place in the hands of a trusty freind, I fear they will fall into the hands of your[2] Enemy's. sure you have already taken care in this matter by w^t the publick prints told you of the proceedings of the great men towards the Earle of Strafford[3] & Mr Prior,[4] however for greater caution this is sent you by—— |

Address: To the Reverend | Doctor Swift Dean of | St Patricks Dublin | Ireland
Postmark: 4 MR
Endorsed by Swift: 1714— | Mr Lewis | about Sep^{tb}

4805

Swift to Monsieur Giraldi

De Dublin en Yrlande, | Fevrier 25me 1714–15
Monsieur[5]

Je prens la libertè de vous presenter le porteur de cellecy Monsieur Howard,[6] Gentilhomme savant et de condition de ce pais cy, qui

[1] This letter, previously to Ball, has been erroneously dated 4 Nov. 1714; but as the contents show this cannot be correct. The incidents referred to indicate Jan. 1714–15. Lewis's closing words inform Swift that the letter is being conveyed to him by a private hand. Nevertheless there is a postmark showing the 4th of March, which suggests that in the end Lewis, or his intermediary, was compelled to use the post. Swift's endorsement is clearly inaccurate. For clarity the letter has been lightly punctuated.

[2] The correct reading. Previous editors read 'our'.

[3] Lord Strafford had been recalled from his embassy at The Hague; and in Jan. 1715 he was ordered to surrender his papers.

[4] The Earl of Stair arrived in Paris on 12 Jan. 1715 to supersede Prior as envoy to the French court, directing him also to surrender his papers. On his return to England in March Prior was impeached.

[5] This is a copy by Swift, not the original carried by Howard. Giraldi was secretary to the Duke of Tuscany. How Swift knew him is not known.

[6] Robert Howard, 1683–1740, a fellow of Trinity College, Dublin, in 1726 became Bishop of Killala, and in 1729 was translated to Elphin.

pretend de faire le tour d'Italie, et qui etant Chanoine en mon Doyennè et professeur de college ici, veut en voyageant parmi les Catholiques s'opiniatrer le plus dans son Heresie: et après tout Monsieur, c'n'est que juste, que puisque vous avez derobè notre franchise Angloise pour l'ajouter à votre politess Italienne, que quelques-uns de nous autres tramontanes devoient en voyageant chez vous, faire des represailles. Vous me suffrirez aussi de vous prier de presenter mes tres humbles Devoirs à son Altesse Royale le grand Duc.

Pour mon particulier, Monsieur je prens la libertè de vous dire que deux mois devant la morte de la Reyne, voyant, qu'il étoit tout à fait impossible de r'accommoder mes amis du Ministere, Je me retirè à la campagne en Berkshire, d'ou apres ce triste evenement, Je venois en Yrlande, ou je demeure en mon Doyennè et attens avec le Resignation d'un bon Chretien la Ruine de notre Cause et de mes amis, menacès tous les jours par la Faction Dominautè. Car ces Messieurs sont tout à fait resolus de trancher une demy douzaine de tetes des meilleures d'Angleterre, et que vous avez fort bien connus et estimè. Dieu sait quel en sera l'evenement. Pour moy j'ay quitte pour jamais la Politique, et avec la Permission des bonnes gens qui sont maintenant en Vogue, je demeureray la reste de ma vie en mon hermitage pour songer à mon salut.

Adieu Monsieur, et me faites la Justice de croire, que je suis, avec beaucoup de Respect | Monsieur | Votre — &c

Endorsed by Swift: Copy | a Mons Giraldi | Fev^r 24. 1714

Rothschild 2286

Swift to Matthew Prior

Dublin. March. 1st 17¹⁵⁄₁₄

S^ri

Give me leave to recommend Mr Howard[2] the bearer of this, to your Favor and Protection, whether he finds you still at Paris pre-

---

[1] This is a letter hitherto unprinted. It was sold at Sotheby's, 5 Mar. 1934, Lot 201, and is now in Lord Rothschild's Library, No. 2286. The catalogue describes the letter as addressed to Bolingbroke. It is in fact addressed to Prior. After St. John was raised to the peerage Swift always, when any formula is recorded, addressed him as 'My Lord' or 'My Dear Lord'. The dates and

[For continuation of note 1, and note 2, see overleaf

paring for your Return, or already arrived at London to the great
Satisfaction of your Friends and your Enemyes. He is brother to
your old Acquaintance Mr Howard the Painter;[1] a Senior Fellow of
our College; and more than all one of My Prebendaryes: and for the
rest, worthy to be recommended ever to you; and will want it the
more at this time because he intends to travel.

Since I came here I never received a Line from any Friend of
Consequence, and some of mine thō sent with Caution, I hear have
been opened, so that I know nothing further with Relation to you
than what those People tell me who read News papers. That you
lost your Employment so soon, and were afterwards forced to stay
in France so long, are Politicks out of my Depth. You have the
Honor to be used ill with the best Men of the Kingdom, and to have
been highly instrumental in a Work to which Your Enemyes perhaps
principally on[2] their Establishment; yet I confess I often wished you
at home about a twelvemonth ago. I have no Concern at present
about you but with Relation to your Fortune. You and some others
have convinced the World that a Man of Business may be a Man of
Witt, but I will swear he ought not to be a Philosopher too, at least

---

[1] Hugh Howard, 1675–1737, after three years spent in Italy returned to
England, practising as a portrait-painter. An accomplished student of art he
succeeded in collecting prints, drawings, medals, &c., on a lavish scale. He left
his collections to his brother Robert, by that time Bishop of Elphin, who removed
them to Ireland. See *D.N.B.*

[2] Thus written by Swift for 'own'.

---

content of the letter point decisively to Prior. On 25 Feb. 1714–15 Swift wrote
a letter to Giraldi in favour of Robert Howard who was about to travel abroad.
On 1 Mar. he wrote the letter under discussion in the belief that the addressee
might still be in Paris. He would rightly believe Bolingbroke still to be in England, for it was not till 27 Mar. 1715 that he fled the country in disguise. Prior
was under recall from Paris; but he did not reach London till later than the first
of March. At this time Swift was very short of news from England, knowing
little about the movement of events. The reference to Hugh Howard, the
portrait-painter, is significant. Prior did know this Howard, brother of the
prebendary, and wrote 'To Mr. Howard: An Ode', printed in his *Poems on
Several Occasions*, 1709, p. 209. This letter, beyond question, was addressed to
Prior.

[2] As will have been noted previously, 25 Feb., Swift had already furnished
Robert Howard with a letter of introduction to serve him on his travels abroad.
Although at this time Swift entertained a warm regard for Howard, Prebendary
of Maynooth in St. Patrick's Cathedral, their relations became less friendly. See
Landa, *Swift and the Church of Ireland*, pp. 87–93.

he ought to suspend that Part of Philosophy which teaches the Contempt of Money, and resume it when he can get no more. I know you can retire as gracefully as any man from six footmen and a gilt Chariot to Jonathan and your Cloak, but I pronounce whatever Court suffers it is not a Christian one.

Now you come from making Peace abroad, I wish you would make it among our Friends at home.—But I will say no more, for I am so entirely ignorant of all Affairs that I should in three Lines be in danger of talking very absurdly: all I know proper for me to add is, that no Man loves or esteems you more than | Y^r | most obedient | &c &c Brother |

J. S.

Will you tell our Friends that I am just alive, and that is all.

Portland MSS., B.M. Deposit, List I

Swift to Lord Harley

Dublin, Mar. 1. 17$\frac{15}{14}$

My Lord

Since I left England I have not seen a News-paper, nor have above three or four times heard any body talk of what passes in the World. It is the only Receit I have to possess any Degree of Quiet. Tother day I was told it was in the printed Papers that the best Lady in the World had lately brought one of her own Sex into it:[1] for which I do most heartily congratulate with Your Lordship and her. And I hope to live long enough to send you half a dozen Letters of Congratulation upon the same Account; onely My Lady must take care now and then to vary the Sex. I hope Her Ladyships Health is by this time quite reestablished and that she can run up to the Nursery to visit her little Infant. I could be almost angry that Your Lordship did not consider what a Part I take in everything that concerns you, at whatsoever distance I am; for then you would have contrived I might have known a Thing of so much Importance by a surer way then common Report. But a Circumstance shall not make me quarrell with what I like: And since you want no Addition of Fortune or

[1] Edward, Lord Harley's only surviving child, the 'Lady Marget' of Swift's letters, was born on 11 Feb. In 1734 she was married to William Bentinck, second Duke of Portland.

Honor, I shall pray God to preserve your Health, and Encrease your Family. I must say one thing more, that though these are not Times for Raillery, I am impatient to see my little Niece.

Pray tell my Lady that I have broke my Heart with breaking her Snuff box. I put it in a close pocket, when I was on Horseback, and forgot to remove it when I alighted, and so overlayd it as a Mother does a Child she is too fond of. But the Matter cannot rest thus. I tax her Ladyship with 5 Guineas, which she must lay out on an Etuy just such a one as yr Lordship's, with Shagrin outside and Silver Instruments. I cannot easily break that: Pray let my Lady buy it immediately with her own Hands. Or if she will not do that; let me have 2 small Copyes of Her Picture and yr Lordship, They will not come to above 5 Pounds each, for I am tender of your Purse.

Another thing you must both promise me, that whenever these Gentlemen in Power shall think fit to destroy the Church, and abolish Bishopricks and Deanries as wicked and useless; you will settle on me 50[11] a year to live in Guernsey; for there I am determined; because Wine and Vittals are cheap in that Island, and I promise when I am an old Gentleman to come back and be a Tutor to your Children. Perhaps I am not so much in jest as you may believe; for there is nothing too bad to be apprehended in my opinion, from the present Face of Things. I am with the greatest respect and truth, my Lord, Your Lordship's most obedient and most humble Servt |

Jon. Swift.

Will your Lordship present | my most humble Services | to My Ld Oxford, and to My | L^d and L^dy Dupplin.[1]

Address: To the Right Honerable | the Lord Harley in | London.
Endorsed: Dr Swift Dublin | March 8: 171$\frac{4}{15}$

---

[1] Oxford's daughter and son-in-law. George Hay, Viscount Dupplin, as Baron Hay of Pedwardine, was one of the twelve new peers created by Anne in Dec. 1711. In 1709 he married Abigail, Oxford's second daughter. In 1719 he succeeded his father in the earldom of Kinnoul.

Swift to Knightley Chetwode

Dublin, 31 March, 1715.

Sir,

I have been these ten weeks resolving every week to go down to Trim, and from thence to Martry; and have not been able to compass it, though my country affairs much required my presence. This week I was fully determined to have been at Trim, but my Vicars hinder me, their prosecutions being just come to an issue,[1] and I cannot stir from hence till the end of April, when nothing but want of health or horses shall hinder me. I can tell you no news. I have read but one newspaper since I left you and I never suffer any to be told me. I send this by my steward,[2] who goes to Trim, to look after my rents at Laracor. Pray present my most humble service to Dame Plyant. I suppose you do not very soon intend to remove to the Queen's county. When I come to Trim I shall after a few days there, stay awhile with you, and go thence to Athy;[3] and thence if possible to Connaught and half round Ireland. I hope your little fire-side is well. I am with great truth and esteem | Your most obedient humble servant |

J. S.

Is it impossible to get a plain easy sound trotting Horse?

Address: To Knightley Chetwode Esq (private hand).

Knightley Chetwode to Swift

5 April, 1715

Dear Sir,

Though I am to be yet three weeks longer without you and of consequence as long unhappy, yet did I with the greatest pleasure

---

[1] See p. 133.

[2] Gillespy, mentioned by Swift in his last letter to Walls, 27 Dec. 1714, seems temporarily to have succeeded Parvisol in the collection of Swift's tithes and rents; but before long Parvisol was again in Swift's employment.

[3] To see his lands of Kilberry.

receive yours from Trim[1] since you think of me and with kindness. Love, which is ever jealous, made me fear I had lost that share in your regards I most covet to possess; it is my greatest satisfaction you give me to know it is otherwise. I have confined myself to Martry closely, lest I should be out of the way when you should arrive, which I daily expected, till some days ago I started to Rowly Singleton[2] and Dean Cox at Drogheda[3] where I drank your health as I do daily, but there particularly in company of Mr. Whaley, Lord Primate's chaplain.[4]

I hope nothing will divert your purpose of seeing me this month. Do you preserve health? I will procure you horses. There is a grey gelding in my neighbourhood in a mad fellow's custody—nothing the better of that you will say—which I like and have offered money for; he is strong, young, tolerably handsome, and I am told sound, trots well, has good spirit, but I think him too dear. He asks sixteen pounds for him and swears he refused twelve pounds, which I am not willing to believe the more for his swearing it, or because it is against my interest. I have broke a young mare since you left me, which abounds in mettle, trots finely, and carries tolerably well, but I fear is not comely enough for his Grace of St. Patrick's. If you like her she is yours. If this does not please, the bay mare you rode to Powerscourt[5] has got so much flesh and spirit that she has forgot to trip. Say which of these three will be most to your *goût*.[6]

I do not intend Dame Pliant and the family shall see Woodbrooke this long time, though I have sent several workmen up thither and have appointed carpenters to meet me there Passion week to agree for to prepare to build the dwelling house which I am impatient to

---

[1] The preceding letter was doubtless sent by hand by way of Trim. The above letter is missing from Birkbeck Hill's volume.

[2] A member of a family long associated with Drogheda. Edward Singleton, alderman of that town, was father of Prime Serjeant Singleton, one of the executors of Swift's will.

[3] Thomas Cox, Dean of Ferns, Rector of Drogheda (J. B. Leslie, *Armagh Clergy*, p. 239).

[4] Primate Lindsay had been a fellow of Wadham College, as was also Nathaniel Whaley, and doubtless this association accounted for his appointment as chaplain to the Archbishop.

[5] Viscount Powerscourt's estate in co. Wicklow.

[6] Chetwode was evidently a lover of horseflesh. In the *Dublin Gazette* of 4–8 Nov. 1707, there is a curious advertisement from him describing a 'very handsome English mare', a 'broad squat black mare', and a 'well fore-hand black mare', that had been stolen off the lands of Martry.—Ball.

begin. I am now upon taking my Lord Meath's house in this county till my own house and deer park be finished;[1] finding this house too small I propose to let it, and the house I am about to take being but fifteen miles from Dublin, I the better like it.

I heard from some friends in England since I saw you. Upon it I postpone my journey thither till I have answers to letters I sent by a private hand to several of my friends there; I did not judge the messenger being a lady so proper for you or she should have called for your commands.[2] This bearer, my steward's son, going to Dublin with some money to Doctor Travers,[3] I have given the Doctor the hint of printing the second scene of the fourth act of Shakespeare's Henry the Eighth, with no title, [as] a parallel case.[4] I will not be out of the way the latter end of the month, by which time I hope to have it in my power to apprise you of my English friends' sense of my journey, and shall regulate myself in the affair by your advice.

If you go or progress, as you hint, I shall esteem it an honour if you take me into your train. I hope the Baron has found means to satisfy you in a certain affair; I pressed him again on that head but a few weeks since. If I could by any means contribute to your service or satisfaction I think myself happier than you perhaps believe, for I am *toujours jusqu'au tombeau, mon cher Monsieur et digne ami, tout à vous du meilleur de mon cœur.*

K. C.

[1] This house, which had been formerly known as New Hall or Tara Hall and was then called Brabazon Lodge, was situated near the hill of Tara, the seat of supreme sovereignty in ancient Erin.—Ball.

[2] Subsequent letters show that Chetwode was in correspondence with a leading member of the Tory party in England, presumably the Duke of Ormonde, who within four months fled to France and joined the Pretender.

[3] The Rev. John Travers, vicar of St. Andrew's, Dublin, and a member of Swift's Chapter.

[4] Ball suggests that Chetwode's proposal was to apply Queen Katherine's character of Cardinal Wolsey to Bishop Burnet who had died on 17 Mar. of this year.

Forster copy
Swift to Knightley Chetwode

Dublin, 6 April, 1715.

Sir,

Your messenger brought me your letter[1] when I was under a very bad barber's hands, meaning my own. I sent for him, because I heard he was something gentlemanish, and he told me he returned to-day; so that I have only time to thank you for your letter, and assure you, that bar accidents I will be in Trim in a fortnight. I detest the price of that horse you mention, and as for your mare I will never trust her. My grandmother used to say that good feeding never brings good footing. I am just going to church, and can say no more, but my humble service to Dame Pliant. I believe the fellow rather thinks me mad than is mad himself: sixteen pounds—why it is an estate; I shall not be master of it in sixteen years.

I thought that passage out of Shakespeare had been of my own starting, and that the magistrate of Martry would not have imagined it. How can you talk of going a progress of 200 miles? I know nothing of any shoes I left.[2] I am sure they are not paid for, and so at least I shall be no loser whatever you may be. Adieu.

Address: To Knightley Chetwode Esq.

Forster copy
Knightley Chetwode to Swift

Trim, 25 April, 1715.[3]
Dr. Raymond's parlour, Two o'clock.

Dear Dean,

I am just alighted here from Woodbrooke where I doubted not of finding his Grace of St. Patrick's, but you are so in love with synodical bear-gardens,[4] that you would no more leave Dublin before Wednesday[5] than you would send me news-pamphlets or ballads. I

---

[1] The preceding letter.
[2] Chetwode's letter makes no reference to shoes.
[3] This letter is missing from Birkbeck Hill's volume.
[4] The diocesan Synod to which Chetwode refers was doubtless that of Meath for which Dublin was the most convenient centre.
[5] 27th.

bade Tom Warburton[1] tell you I said you were a sad fellow, because I durst not be so free to write it; I prevailed on him since he had a budget on each side of him, to add your letter to the bulk. If you were a great Prince you would I believe imprison half your subjects, for you have confined me to Martry near four months for so [I have been] since but expecting you.

Well now a few words *seria mixta jocis*; Tommy, little Tommy, pretty Tommy is gone like Judas *ad locum proprium suum*; Galloway also stone dead; you and Gay Mortimer have brought a rot among the wicked; as for Mortimer, I do not expect much from him, but I thought you as a churchman would allow him time to repent, which, however, upon the whole matter I saw little hope of from any but horn mad Sunderland from marrying.[2] The Baron[3] will see you to-morrow or at the Synod, and will give you account of his commission. I am so angry with you, if it were not for offending Dame Pliant, and that I know you would have your frisk like the Berkshire acquaintance without consequence,[4] I would go to Dublin with Tom Warburton. This town since Wharton's death is like hell, nothing but weeping, wailing, and gnashing of teeth.[5] For God sake do somewhat to comfort Joe, and send him back contented; tell him you will make the next his friend, keep him from melting his tallow, help him in his longitude,[6] do anything to keep him alive.

Dinner appears, I am hungry, Mrs. Raymond as prodigiously civil as ugly, and I forced to conclude, with the assurance of this truth from a good hand that I am, | Yours.

[1] Swift's curate who was evidently going to Dublin to attend the Synod.

[2] Chetwode is giving his opinions on the political situation in terms not easy to be understood by an ordinary reader into whose hands the letter might fall. The Whig cause had been weakened by the deaths of Burnet, here called Galloway, in March, and Wharton, called Tommy, on 12 Apr. Neither Chetwode, nor Swift, trusted Oxford, here called Mortimer, as a leader. Strangely, for his part, Chetwode placed hopes on the Whig Charles Spencer, third Earl of Sunderland.

[3] Rochfort, Chief Baron of the Exhequer in Ireland.

[4] This may be a reference to Vanessa's visit to Letcombe.

[5] Wharton was alleged to have interfered with the liberties of Trim in the election of a mayor (*Journal*, 30 Nov. 1710).

[6] Joe Beaumont's loss of reason was attributed to his calculations about the longitude.

Blenheim Palace
The Duke of Ormonde to Swift

[3 May 1715.]¹

Hon^d and ever, Dear Dean.

You need not have added new favours to endear you to my heart
and remembrance you are too precious to both which makes me continually regret We have lost you for so long a time. I receive with all
the respect and thankfullness imaginable the Present Mr Took made
me on your part and which came very seasonably. I wish it were in
my power to deserve your goodness. We have been continually
alarmed with Reports concerning you, some say your papers were
seized, then Messengers were sent to fetch you over, which we could
not help being pleas'd at, as not doubting your innocency, which we
knew so much of your prudence. But we lov'd our selves so well as
to compound for a Little uneasiness to you rather than Miss so great
a satisfaction as the sight of you would be to all your Friends. How
is your health, how the giddiness of your head? I can se[e] no body
that can tell me those minute Circumstances that are so necessary
to our quiet. Common Report bespeaks you retired and melancholy,
conversing with few persons hating Ireland and yet making no
attempt to come to England. Corinnikin² & myself drink your health
daily; she is come to love a Glass of Wine much better than she did,
but with this remark, that it happens in the very worst time. We
have no new favourite nor never can; you have left so sweet a relish
by your Conversation upon all our pleasures that we can't bear the
thoughts of intimacy with any person,³ a faint Copy of a most agree-

---

¹ This letter and the following were seized by the Irish executive. As appears
from letters which will be found in Appendix XI, two packets addressed to
Swift, in one of which these letters were enclosed, were given by the Duchess of
Ormonde's chaplain, Mr. Charleton, to a Mr. Jeffreys, who is described as an
agent of Bishop Hartstonge, to bring to Ireland. On landing in Ireland Jeffreys
was searched, and the packets being found, they were brought to the acting
Lords Justices, Archbishop King and the Earl of Kildare. The Lords Justices
opened the packets and sent off the letters that evening to Stanhope. The next
day copies were sent to Sunderland, as Lord Lieutenant, who was then at Bath.
Clerical copies of this and the following letter have found their way into the
muniments of the Duke of Marlborough at Blenheim Palace. Only a portion of
each letter is reproduced by Ball.

² The Duchess of Ormonde. Her real name was Mary.

³ During his latter days in London, before the death of the Queen, Swift

able original is to be found in a certain reverend Divine whom you introduced to our acquaintance,[1] but it will not do even with the advantage of youth. We see him once a Week of Commemorating our common Loss in your Conversation. Tyrant[2] has undertaken to furnish you by this same hand with all the news. I hear that you desire none. If I knew your inclination I would endeavour to be agreeable, but I have still thought that you would not have your friends write & set the Example. Corinnikin sends you her love and service. I give you her very words. I acknowledge my self to be most humbly, | yours &c.

May 3. 1715.

Blenheim Palace

John Barber to Swift

London May 3[d] 1715—

Hon[d] Sir,

I rejoice at this occasion of sending a letter by a safe hand to the Dean of S[t] P— my best Friend and Patron. I beg you will believe it was not want of Duty or Respect, that made me silent so long but a tedious Confinement of near 5 Months on one hand and fear of Miscarriage on the other. Two days before the *Captain*[3] went abroad he sent for me, and amongst other things, asked me with great earnestness, If there was no possibility of sending a Letter safe to your hands. I answer'd, I knew but of one way and that was to direct to you under cover to M[rs] Van—.[4] He reply'd no way by Post wou'd do. I then said tho I was lame and ill, I would go over with it myself if he pleased. He thanked me, and said I should hear from him in a Day or two, but I never saw him more

Sir W. Wyndham[5] had a letter yesterday from him dated about 8 days ago; he was then very well and M[r] Ford[6] with him. His

seems to have enjoyed frequent intercourse with the Duke and Duchess of Ormonde.

[1] Possibly Berkeley.   [2] i.e. Barber.
[3] Bolingbroke had crossed to France on 27 Mar.
[4] The reference is to Vanessa. Mrs. Vanhomrigh had died before this time.
[5] With him in politics Bolingbroke was closely associated.
[6] Ford is known to have been in France before the end of April. That he nursed sympathies with Bolingbroke can hardly be questioned. For letters addressed to Ford by Bolingbroke see *Letters of Swift to Ford*, pp. 231–40.

motions depend upon the report from the Secret Committee, and the Brin[sde]n[1] (with the last instructions from his friends here) will go over, by which he will confirm himself. You have seen a letter which bears his name.[2] I will tell you a secret; it was written by Bishop Atterbury. It hath done a great deal of good, and we have not lost a man by his going. It was a great suprize at first, but everybody is now convinced he would have been sacrificed had he staid. The *Colonel*[3] is the most contemptible Creature in the Kingdom, both Part'es are continually cursing him. He gives himself Airs of being the greatest Tory in the world and wou'd fain be at the head of them. But I believe they will never trust him again.

We are in daily expectation of the Secret Committee's Report, they threaten very much, but it is believed they will make nothing of it, they are divided among themselves, for Jekyll[4] has absolutely refused to go near them, & Vernon, Hambden and Sir Richard Onslow[5] have declered they will never sign the Report. Among other things I send you the Duke of Ormond's Conduct.[6] which tis hopd will do that great man service. He is in the highest esteem here, and last Fryday, being his Birthday, two hundred of his Grace's Friends dined at the Devil's at Temple Barr, and at night there were two bonfires on that occasion, one in Newgate Market and the other in the Pallmall. Mr. P[rio]r is despised by all honest men for giving up his letters, yours among the rest.[7] Dr. Arb[uthno]t was turned out on that score. M[r] L[ewi]s is come to town, much provok'd & full of Spleen. I have a hundred things to say to you. How is your Health? and how do you bear up under the Load? We have 20 frightfull Accounts of your being sent for up, and your papers seized, for you are the reputed Author of every good thing that comes out on our side.

[1] See p. 116, n. 4.

[2] This letter, dated as if written at Dover, challenges production of any criminal correspondence on his part. [3] Lord Oxford.

[4] Sir Joseph Jekyll (1663–1738) was one of the committee of secrecy appointed to investigate the cases of Bolingbroke and Oxford. *D.N.B.*

[5] Sir Richard Onslow, speaker of the House of Commons in Queen Anne's third Parliament, was a man of moderate Whig principles.

[6] *The Conduct of his Grace the Duke of Ormonde in the Campagne of 1712*, London, 1717.

[7] The important diplomatic position held by Prior in Paris during the previous reign naturally led to distrust of him by the government. His papers were impounded; but this does not mean that he voluntarily surrendered private personal letters. Nor can Arbuthnot be accused of a like practice.

Lord Wharton's death hath extremely mortifyed the Whigs. Sunderland is very ill, has been mad for some time, and is going to the Bath. Walpole is in a very bad way, and Stanhope is the Bully.[1]

I have little to do, and if you don't come over this summer, pray give me leave to come over to see you. I shall than be a Traveller and have some thing to talk on.

I shall say nothing of the Ladies they write for themselves.

Our Friends here and all the Kingdom over are in great Spirit. we shan't always groan under the Burden. I wish I might speak out.

My best respects to Dear Lady Van— Mr Provost, Dr Par— & all I have the Honour to know on your side.

All your Friends here are well and wish you among them; I saw Lady M— & Dr Arb—t yesterday & Duke Disney to Day, who all mentioned you with the utmost respect.

There is not a Day but We have ——— publisht. I wish you would let me know how I might send you every thing with safety. I am, | D^r S^r | Your most obed^t humble | ser^t, | &c

Rothschild[2]

Swift to Archdeacon Walls

Trim. May. 5th 1715

Since y^r Inmates[3] are so lazy & sawcy that they make you their Secretary, I will take no notice of them. I would have Gillespy[4] come down as soon as he has putt the Affair of his new Farm in such a way as not to suffer by his Absence, and I thought that would have been by Monday next.

If your Scheme of Winn[5] can be brought about I will do my part fully in it; as for Chamb[erlain] or the A— Bp— or Bolton working any of theirs, they shall be deceived as far as all my Power reaches: and they shall not find me altogether so great a Cully as they would willingly make me.[6] Whenever you see me fail in any part relating

---

[1] Tory hopes grounded upon these suppositions were soon dispelled.
[2] Lord Rothschild's Library, No. 2281 (14).
[3] Stella and Mrs. Dingley.   [4] See p. 161, n. 2.
[5] Ball reads 'moves', which cannot be correct. The word is 'Winn'.
[6] The reference is to the desire of Walls for the vacant benefice of St. Nicholas Without, a project to which Swift lent his support. Archbishop King preferred the appointment of Philip Chamberlain, a canon of St. Patrick's, who held the

to you I desire I may hear of it, and if you be mealy mouthed, do it by whom you please. And whenever you think any step I can make will be for y^r Service, tell it me freely, and I will either comply or shew you why I cannot. No body is so stiff as an easy man put upon his mettle, and they shall neither fool me nor you, at least in this Point.

Well, but however my Service to Doll and the Ladyes—

Adieu

Jo's[1] Respects to all | Mr Chetwood[2] presents y^u his Service

Address: To the Reverend Mr Archdeacon | Walls over against the Hospitall | in Queen-street | Dublin

Postmark: Illegible. *Post office stamp:* TRIM

Late endorsement: Dr Swift | May 5th 1715

'Rothschild[3]

Swift to Archdeacon Walls

Wood-brook Mr Chetwoods House. Sund. May. 22. 1715

[I came] here on Friday last from Mr Rochforts where I stayed [f]our days with Mr Chetwood, very well entertained, and a very fine place.[4] I go hence to morrow (God willing) to the Deanry Lands near Athy about 12 miles off,[5] and on Wednesday night intend to be at Trim. We have had perpetuall ill weather ever since I left you except one or two days, yet I have seldom failed being on horseback, and have my health well enough.—Gillespy[6] is to meet me at Athy,

---

prebend of St. Audoen. A protracted conflict was finally settled by the appointment of Chamberlain, while Walls was consoled with a minor rectory. See Landa, *Swift and the Church of Ireland*, pp. 79–82.

[1] Joe Beaumont.

[2] Chetwode had evidently joined Swift at Trim, whence, as appears from the next letter, they set out to pay a visit to the Rochforts.—Ball.

[3] Lord Rothschild's Library, No. 2281 (15). The manuscript has been torn, damaging the first three lines of the letter.

[4] The 'very fine place' was Gaulstown House, the seat of the Rochfort family, which lay between the town of Trim and Woodbrooke, the home of Knightley Chetwode. Gaulstown and its inmates form the subject of Swift's poem 'The Journal', written by him during a visit to the place in 1721 (*Poems*, pp. 276–83). Satirical verses on the discomforts of the house, written by Delany, will be found in *Whartoniana*, 1727, i. 30–31.

[5] See p. 145.   [6] See p. 161.

and from thence I suppose will go to Dublin about Thursday; but
for my own Return, I can yet say nothing. However I desire you will
finish the Machine for dining sub dio: I hope we shall have some
merry dinners under it this Summer. I will send Bolingbroke to
Clem Barry[1] if I can get another Horse. He is very fat and well, but
I hate riding him. As *to my Wine in the* Hogshead I would have it
filled up when it wants, but I will not have it forced. Mr Rochfort
sent y^r Letter after me. I thank you for your care about it, but no
Messenger has been here yet from the Governmt,[2] nor will I hope
till I get to Athy; for I should be sorry to go back till I see the Land.
My humble Service to Gossip Doll and the Ladyes; I suppose they
want a third at Ombre sometimes by way of Stop-gap, and miss me.
Pray press Gillespy to get money from the Deanry, & receive it from
him, and let Mrs Brent go now and then into the Celler to prevent
Accidents in my Wine. If any thing happens about St Nicholas let
me know about it at Trim. I am yrs &c |

                                                                    J.S.

Address: To the Reverend Mr Archdeacon | Walls, over against the Hospitall | in
          Queen-street | Dublin
Postmark: 31 MA   *Stamp:* PORTARLINGTON
Late endorsement: Dr Swift | May 22^d 1715

Rothschild[3]

Swift to Archdeacon Walls

                                              Trim. June. 15. 1715

   I am here at the Fair to buy a Horse,[4] but cannot succeed. I had
all y^r Letters; As for Tailer[5] he may go hang himself if he pleases;
I hope he will leave us, & then I will have a better; but I will not
turn him out without y^r Leave. I hope Gilespy has got you some

---

   [1] Clement Barry, mentioned in 'The Journal', lived at Saggart near Dublin.
He was a distant cousin of the then Lord Santry. In *Gulliveriana* he is described
as 'Mr. Barry, chief Favourite and Governour of *Gallstown*'.
   [2] Walls had evidently acquainted Swift with the seizure of his letters (p. 166).
   [3] Lord Rothschild's Library, No. 2281 (16).
   [4] Swift had evidently come there with Chetwode from either Woodbrooke
or Martry. See the two preceding letters.—Ball.
   [5] The reference is probably to one of the Vicars-Choral of St. Patrick's
Cathedral—Charles Taylor, who had been a member of the choir for over
twenty years.—Ball.

money; I wonder he has not writt to me. It is time for him to reckon the Sheep & Lambs; I think he should have done it in these Livings when he was here; but it was out of my Head. Pray speak to him about it; I know not whether he is used to those sort of Tythes, being onely practice in Impropriations; but you must talk to him of it. I will not have any Rents received from Smith or Benson till I give you notice. My Service to Gossip Doll and yʳ Inmates. Mʳ Chetwood presents his Service to You; so does Dʳ Raymd Warburton & Jo to You and the Ldyes. Bolingbroke is very well. I have just writt to the Bp of Clogher, who I yesterday hear is arrived.¹ But I hope Mʳˢ Brent sees the Celler sometimes. I would have the Vessel of Wine filled if it wants; but by no means forced or touched by a Wine cooper.

Address: To the Reverend Mʳ Archdeacon | Walls, over against the Hospitall | in
      Queenstreet | Dublin
Late endorsement: Dʳ Swift | June 15ᵗʰ 1715

Forster copy

Swift to Knightley Chetwode

Dublin, 21 June, 1715.

I was to see Jourdain,² who tells me something but I have forgot it; it was, that he had a letter ready and you were gone, or something of that kind. I had a terrible hot journey and dined with Forbes,³ and got here by nine.

I have been much entertained with news of myself since I came here: it is said there was another packet directed to me, seized by the Government, but after opening several seals it proved only plum-cake. I was this morning with the A. Bp: who told me how kind he had been in preventing my being sent to &c.⁴ I said I had been a

---

¹ The opening sentence of Swift's letter to Pope of 28 June 1715 shows that Bishop Ashe had been in London.

² See p. 134, n. 1.

³ The Rev. Thomas Forbes, rector of Dunboyne, who managed some of Swift's local affairs.

⁴ Swift was probably under no illusions as he listened to King. Ball discovered in the P.R.O. among the State Papers relating to Ireland a letter, 19 May 1715, directed by the Archbishop and the Earl of Kildare, Lords Justices, to Stanhope, Secretary of State, informing him of papers addressed to Swift, and suspected of being treasonable, which had been seized at the Custom House. In this matter

firm friend of the last Ministry, but thought it brought me to trouble myself in little parties without doing good, that I therefore expected the protection of the government, and that if I had been called before them, I would not have answered one syllable or named one person. He said that would have reflected on me. I answered I did not value that, and that I would sooner suffer more than let anybody else suffer by me, as some people did. The letter which was sent was one from the great lady you know, and enclosed in one from her chaplain.[1] My friends got it, and very wisely burned it after great deliberation, for fear of being called to swear; for which I wish them half hanged. I have been named in many papers as proclaimed for five hundred pounds.

I want to be with you for a little good meat and cold drink; I find nothing cold here but the reception of my friends. I said a good deal more to the Archbishop not worth telling at this distance. I told him I had several papers, but was so wise to hide them some months ago. A gentleman was run through in the playhouse last night upon a squabble of their footmen's taking places for some ladies. My most humble service to Dame Plyant; pray God bless her fireside. They say the Whigs do not intend to cut off Lord Oxford's head, but that they will certainly attaint poor Lord Bolingbroke.[2]

Address: To Knightley Chetwode Esq. at Martry near Navan in the County of Meath.

Forster copy

Swift to Knightley Chetwode

Dublin, 28 June, 1715.

I write to you so soon again, contrary to my nature and custom which never suffer me to be a very exact correspondent. I find you

King can hardly be accredited with acting quite frankly. Nothing, in the end, came from an examination of the papers; but it is evident that if a case could have been made out against Swift his friends could not have prevented a prosecution.

[1] The great lady was the Duchess of Ormonde, whose chaplain, Charleton, handed papers to a Mr. Jeffreys, Bishop Hartstonge's agent (who was being examined at the Customs) with an instruction that he was to 'deliver them carefully into the Dean of St. Patrick's hands'.

[2] On 10 June the House of Commons had voted the impeachment of both Oxford and Bolingbroke.

passed your time well among ladies and lions and St. Georges and
dragons. Yesterday's post brought us an account that the Duke of
Ormond is voted to be impeached for high treason. You see the plot
thickens.[1] I know not the present disposition of people in England,
but I do not find myself disposed to be sorry at this news. However
in general my spirits are disturbed, and I want to be out of this town.
A Whig of this country now in England has writ to his friends, that
the leaders there talk of sending for me to be examined upon these
impeachments. I believe there is nothing [in] it; but I had this
notice from one who said he saw the letter or saw somebody that
saw it.

I write this post to Dr. Raymond to provide next Sunday for Mr.
Sub,[2] so I suppose he may be at ease, and I wish I were with him.
I hope Dame has established her credit with you for ever, in the
point of valour and hardiness. You surprise me with the account of
a disorder in your head; I know what it is too well and I think Dame
does so too. You must drink less small beer, eat less salad, think less,
walk and drink more, I mean wine and ale, and for the rest, emetics
and bitters are certainly the best remedies. What length has the river
walk to thirty foot breadth? I hope 8 thousand at least. If Sub had
no better a taste for beef and claret than he has for improvements of
land, he should provide no dinners for me. Does Madam gambol
now and then to see it? How is the Dean's field? So it cost a bottle
of wine, extra dry, to dry poor Sub. I hope he sometimes loses his
eyes to please Dame.

There is a collegian found guilty of speaking some words; and I
hear they design in mercy to whip or pillory him.[3] I went yesterday
to the Courts on purpose to show I was not run away.[4] I had warning
given me to beware of a fellow that stood by while some of us were
talking. It seems there is a trade going of carrying stories to the

---

[1] The impeachment of Ormonde had been voted on the 21st of this month.
[2] This evidently means that Raymond was to take Warburton's duty at
Laracor.
[3] At that time several members of Dublin University were expelled or
admonished for disloyalty (Stubbs, *Hist. of Univ. of Dublin*, p. 156). On 27 June
three had been expelled; one a master of arts, for making a copy of a pamphlet
called *Nero Secundus*, and two, both bachelors of arts, for disrespectful language
about the King.—Ball.
[4] In London it had been rumoured, as Boyer relates (*Pol. State*, ix. 455), that
'the famous libeller Swift', hearing that search was to be made for him, had
absconded.

government and many honest folks turn the penny by it. I cannot yet leave this place but will as soon as possible. Tom this minute brought me up word that the Baron's man was here, and that his master[1] is in town. I hope to see him, and give him half a breast of mutton before he goes back. He is now with a lawyer. I believe old Lombard Street is putting out money.

The Report of the Secret Committee is published.[2] It is a large volume. I only just saw it at Manly's. It is but a part, and probably there will be as much more. I do not believe or see one word is offered to prove their old slander of bringing in the Pretender. The treason lies wholly in making the peace. Charles Ford[3] is with Lord Bolingbroke in Dauphiné within a league of Lyons, where his Lordship is retired, till he sees what the Secret Committee will do. That is now determined and his Lordship will certainly be attainted by Act of Parliament. The impeachments are not yet carried up to the Lords. I suppose they intend to make one work of it.

Address: To Knightley Chetwode, Esq., at Woodbrooke, near Portarlington, Queen's County.

---

[1] Chief Baron Rochfort.

[2] The *London Gazette* thus announces its appearance: 'Just Published, A Report from the Committee of Secrecy, appointed by order of the House of Commons to examine several Books and Papers laid before the House relating to the late Negotiations of Peace and Commerce, &c. Reported on the 9th of June 1715, by the Right Honourable Robert Walpole, Esq.; Chairman of the said Committee. Together with an Appendix, containing Memorials, Letters, and other Papers referred to in the said Report. Publish'd by Order of the House of Commons. Printed for Jacob Tonson, Timothy Goodwin, Bernard Lintot, and William Taylor.'—Ball.

[3] During the period Ford had been acting as editor of the *Gazette*, 1 July 1712 to 25 Sept. 1714, he had resided continuously in London. For six months thereafter his movements remain uncertain. Bolingbroke, as previously noted, fled the country on 27 Mar. 1715. Ford is known to have been in France before the end of April; and here Swift, apparently from information upon which he could rely, says that he was with Bolingbroke. Later in the summer he returned to England and was arrested. In a letter written to the second Lord Oxford, 14 Aug. 1725, Swift said that Ford was 'long in confinement'. See further *Letters of Swift to Ford*, ed. Nichol Smith, Introduction, pp. xv–xviii.

Faulkner 1741

Swift to Pope

Dublin, June 28, 1715.

My Lord Bishop of Clogher gave me your kind letter full of re-proaches for my not writing.[1] I am naturally no very exact correspon-dent, and when I leave a country without probability of returning, I think as seldom as I can of what I lov'd or esteem'd in it, to avoid the *Desiderium* which of all things makes life most uneasy. But you must give me leave to add one thing, that you talk at your ease, being wholly unconcerned in publick events: for, if your friends the Whigs con-tinue, you may hope for some favour; if the Torys return, you are at least sure of quiet. You know how well I lov'd both Lord Oxford and Bolingbroke, and how dear the Duke of Ormond is to me: do you imagine I can be easy while their enemies are endeavouring to take off their heads?[2] *I nunc, & versus tecum meditare canoros*[3]—Do you imagine I can be easy, when I think of the probable consequences of these proceedings, perhaps upon the very peace of the nation, but certainly of the minds of so many hundred thousand good subjects? Upon the whole, you may truly attribute my silence to the eclipse, but it was that eclipse which happened on the first of August.[4]

I borrowed your Homer from the Bishop (mine is not yet landed) and read it out in two evenings. If it pleases others as well as me, you have got your end in profit and reputation: Yet I am angry at some bad Rhymes and Triplets,[5] and pray in your next do not let me have so many unjustifiable Rhymes to *war* and *gods*. I tell you all the faults I know, only in one or two places you are a little obscure; but I expected you to be so in one or two and twenty. I have heard no soul

---

[1] Bishop Ashe, who had been in London, had returned to Ireland about two weeks earlier. See Swift's letter to Archdeacon Walls, 15 June 1715.

[2] In actual fact the Whigs in power found it a relief when Bolingbroke fled to France in March and Ormonde in June. On 16 July Oxford was committed to the Tower, where he remained till July 1717, when further proceedings against him were dropped. He was set at liberty, but excepted from the Act of Grace.

[3] Horace, *Ep.* ii. ii. 76. In a footnote Faulkner translates: 'Go now and meditate the tuneful Song.'

[4] The date of Queen Anne's death. An exceptionally dark eclipse of the sun, causing great alarm in itself and as a portent of calamities, occurred on 22 Apr. 1715. Pope had probably alluded to this in the lost letter which Swift was here answering.

[5] Swift entertained a lifelong objection to triplets.

talk of it here, for indeed it is not come over; nor do we very much abound in judges, at least I have not the honour to be acquainted with them. Your Notes are perfectly good, and so are your Preface and Essay.[1] You were pretty bold in mentioning Lord Bolingbroke in that Preface.[2] I saw the Key to the Lock[3] but yesterday: I think you have changed it a good deal, to adapt it to the present times.

God be thanked I have yet no parliamentary business,[4] and if they have none with me, I shall never seek their acquaintance. I have not been very fond of them for some years past, not when I thought them tolerably good, and therefore if I can get leave to be absent, I shall be much inclin'd to be on that side, when there is a parliament on this: but truly I must be a little easy in my mind before I can think of Scriblerus.

You are to understand that I live in the corner of a vast unfurnished house; my family consists of a steward, a groom, a helper in the stable, a foot-man, and an old maid, who are all at board-wages, and when I do not dine abroad, or make an entertainment, (which last is very rare) I eat a mutton-pye, and drink half a pint of wine: My amusements are defending my small dominions against the Arch-Bishop, and endeavouring to reduce my rebellious Choir.[5] *Perditur haec inter misero lux.*[6] I desire you will present my humble service to Mr. Addison, Mr. Congreve, and Mr. Rowe, and Gay. I am, and will be always, extreamly yours, &c.

[1] The first volume of Pope's *Homer*, containing the first four books of the *Iliad*, had just been published. The prefatory 'Essay . . . on Homer' was written by Parnell, and did not wholly satisfy Pope.

[2] In his Preface to the *Iliad*, among other acknowledgements, Pope made reference to 'my Lord *Bolingbroke*, not more distinguished in the great Scenes of Business than in all the useful and entertaining Parts of Learning, [who] has not refus'd to be the Critick of these Sheets, and the Patron of their Writer'. The last words, written at a time when Bolingbroke had fled the country, might seem bold. The Preface may have been in print before the flight to France.

[3] *A Key to the Lock* is listed in Lintot's *Monthly Catalogue* (p. 79) as published in Apr. 1715. Evidently from Swift's remark here it was written and seen by him before he left England in 1714.

[4] It is not easy to follow the exact meaning of this paragraph. 'Parliamentary business' refers, doubtless, to the Irish Parliament, with which, as yet, he had no associations. He held it in little regard, and says that when it was sitting he would prefer to be in England; but, with due regard for his safety, this could hardly be contemplated for the time being.

[5] Archbishop King was at issue with Swift about his assertion of decanal prerogatives.

[6] Horace, *Sermones*, II. vi. 59.

Forster copy

Knightley Chetwode to Swift

Woodbrooke, 2 July, 1715.[1]

I consulted Mr. Whalley's almanac[2] for the day of the month and casting my eye lower I find that he says on the 19th begin the dog days, but of no influence with us; he is a dog for saying so, for the dog days began sooner, and a great deal influence us as I think. Now comes Laughlin to tell me the Dean of St. Patrick's and the Baron are coming into the court, and so I leave off writing.

Two hours after I writ the above lines I go on with my letter. The Baron leaves me with a parson, his brother-in-law,[3] who has got Philipstown living on Lightburne's death. Baron tells me you entertained him well, that some business of the Church keeps you in town, that you remember the Dame and Squire, and made him believe you intended us the greatest and most agreeable kindness to come down; for God sake persist in that good resolution, make me happy and leave the town.

Sub is here and *sub sigillo* is the worst improver of land alive; if it were not ungenerous since he came up in kindness and at my request, I would send you his journal, for I can tell with exactness what he will do every minute of the twenty-four hours of every day. But let that pass, to answer your queries. The Dean's field flourishes, the quicks are cleared and grow well; it is a fine thing to have a good lawn, they talk of mowing it, I assure you. Your river walk is thirty feet wide, has in all its windings and meanders, as we suppose, about five thousand foot in length. Madam with her long green legs, gamboled twice to see it, got several falls, laughed at her own ill-footing squalled with a tolerable grace, rose and so proceeded. For the regard you express for my health, I am infinitely obliged to you. Your recipes guide me. I drink wine more, small beer less, eat no salads, walk so much that Sub pronounces me distracted, complains of his forehead sweating, to be like somebody, when alas!

[1] This letter is not printed in Birkbeck Hill's volume.

[2] Whalley was a Dublin astrologer who died 17 Jan. 1724. Gilbert (*Hist. of Dublin*, i. 188) states that several lines of Swift's elegy on Partridge (*Poems*, p. 97) were distributed in Dublin as an epitaph on Whalley. In actual fact the whole, with the exception of ll. 95–102, was adapted and reprinted as a broadside.

[3] Rochfort's wife was the daughter of an ancestor of Lord Castlemaine. She had two brothers in holy orders, Matthew Handcock, Archdeacon of Kilmore, and Stephen Handcock, Dean of Clonmacnoise.—Ball.

> Before, behind, behind, before,
> He puffs and blows and sweats all o'er;

declaims against men of fortune making themselves slaves, mentions Percival,[1] and at last recollects it is two o'clock.

The Baron brought me a bond for two hundred pounds lent by me to Ruler Benjamin,[2] not a word of the quondam ten pounds he refused to lend me. He brought me [also] a written newsletter from London, with an account of your brother of Gloucester having prated in Convocation against tumults more than against preferment ecclesiastical; for God sake is the account true, I cannot believe it.[3]

To be a little serious: I hate your account of one man, who saw another man, who saw a letter, which said you would be sent for. I do not a great deal like matters. I should, indeed, think less unless I could think better or serve the world more. I wish my spirits were but barely disturbed. I am sometimes half-mad. The treason of making a peace seems as absurd to me as the articles against the peers which we have in the prints. I wish this provoking courage may end well; I never liked it. What the disposition of people in England is at present I do not so well know as I should do were there fewer dogs and rascals in the offices for letters. I shall long to see the Report; I hear many ill-reports, but I long to see the worst of all reports. I wish our friends in the neighbourhood of Lyons continuation of life, welfare, honour, and to surmount the present difficulties. I hope and earnestly trust that in this great scene all our friends will show and approve themselves great men. I stay here till the week after next, bar accidents. I am always desirous to know how I could contribute to your service or satisfaction for I am, *toujours, Votre,* &c.

---

[1] See p. 130, n. 4.

[2] A younger brother of Knightley Chetwode's father, the Rev. John Chetwode. He acted as solicitor to the Revenue Commissioners of Ireland.

[3] Knightley Chetwode, 1650–1720, a successful careerist. After taking orders he was successively chaplain to the Earl of Dartmouth, the Princess of Denmark, and to James II. He missed the see of Bristol, to which he had been nominated, by the abdication of the King. In 1689 he was appointed chaplain to all the English forces in Holland under Marlborough's command. In 1707 he became Dean of Gloucester. He was also a friend of Roscommon and Dryden and made a modest literary reputation for himself. His speech in Convocation, to which Swift alludes, attacked the High Church party and was calculated to gratify the Whigs. See *D.N.B.*

Swift to Knightley Chetwode

Dublin, 7 July, 1715.

I had your letter[1] the other day by Mr. Foxcroft[2] who was so kind to call on me this morning, but would not stay and dine with me though I offered him mutton and a bottle of wine. I might have been cheated of my ginger-bread for anything you said in your letter, for I find you scorn to take notice of Dame's kind present; but I am humbler and signify to her that if she does not receive by Mr. Foxcroft a large tin pot well crammed with the Duke of Ormond's snuff, holding almost an ounce, she is wronged. I wish Laughlin[3] had not been mistaken when he saw me coming into your court. I had much rather come into it than into the Court of England. I used formerly to write letters by bits and starts as you did when Laughlin thought I was coming; and so now I have been interrupted these three hours by company, and have now just eaten a piece of beef-steak spoiled in the dressing, and drunk a cup of sour ale, and return to finish my letter. Walls sat by me while I was at my dinner, and saw me finish it in five minutes, and has left me to go home to a much better.

I find by your journal of Sub's life for one day, that he was more careful of finding manure for your land in the nasty Scotch meaning than in showing satisfaction or skill in what you are doing. Sure you stretch your walk when you talk of 5000 foot, but your ambition is to have it longer than Mr. Rochfort's canal, and with a little expense it will be made a more beautiful thing. Are you certain it was Madam's green legs you saw by the riverside, because I have seen in England a large kind of green grasshopper, not quite so tall but altogether as slender, that frequent low marshy grounds.

The Baron told me he was employed here by you in an affair of usury, of which I give you joy, but did not tell me the particulars. I believe the affair of your English uncle[4] is true, I have had it from many hands. How is that worse than the Bishop of London's[5] letter to his clergy and their answer, both owning that the tumults were in order to bring in popery and arbitrary power, a reproach which the rabble did not deserve, and has done us infinite hurt. I have not seen the articles; I read no news and hear little. There is no mercy for the

---

[1] The previous letter.   [2] Not identified.
[3] Not identified.   [4] The Dean of Gloucester.
[5] John Robinson, formerly plenipotentiary at Utrecht.

poor collegian, and indeed as he is said to have behaved himself, there could none be expected. The Report is printed here but I have not read it. I think of going for England, if I can get leave, when Lord Sunderland comes over,[1] but not before unless I am sent for with a vengeance. I am not much grieved at your being out of the peace; I heard something of it the day I left you, but nothing certain. Major Champagne has hard usage, and I am truly concerned for him and his lady.[2] I am told here that some of our army is to be transported for England.

I had a letter this day from thence, from the person who sent me one from a lady, with great satisfaction that hers to me was not seized.[3] That letter talks doubtfully of the Duke of Ormond; that the Parliament resolves to carry matters to the highest extremes, and are preparing to impeach the Duke of Shrewsbury which the King would not suffer at first, but at length has complied with;[4] that Prior is kept closer than Gregg,[5] to force him to accuse Lord Oxford though he declares he knows nothing, and that it is thought he will be hanged if he will not be an evidence;[6] and that Lord Oxford confounds them with his intrepidity etc.

I think neither of your places[7] is remote enough for me to be at, and I have some project of going further, and am looking out for a horse. I believe you will be going for England by the time I shall be ready to leave this. Nasty foolish affairs of the deanery keep me thus long here. My humble service to Dame; pray God bless her and her fireside. The Baron gave me hopes of doing something about Kilberry. Did he tell you how I pulled Tom's locks the wrong way for holding a plate under his armpit and what cursed bacon we had with our beans? Adieu.

Address: To Knightley Chetwode Esq.

[1] Lord Sunderland had been appointed Lord Lieutenant, but he never crossed to Ireland, alleging the poor state of his health. On 28 Aug. 1715 he exchanged the viceroyalty for the office of Lord Privy Seal.

[2] See p. 138, n. 2.

[3] The Duchess of Ormonde.

[4] A false rumour.

[5] William Gregg, the clerk in Harley's office, who entered into treasonable correspondence with the French Ministry. Even under severe pressure he refused to inculpate Harley. See *Journal*, 24 Aug. 1711, and note.

[6] On his return from France Prior had been examined before the Secret Committee; but he succeeded in dispelling doubts of his good faith.

[7] i.e. Woodbrooke or Martry.

Portland MSS., B.M. Deposit, List I

Swift to the Earl of Oxford

July. 19th. 1715

My Lord

It may look like an idle or officious Thing in me to give Your Lordship any Interruption under your present Circumstances.[1] Yet I could never forgive my self if, after having been treated for several Years with the greatest Kindness and Distinction, by a Person of Your Lordship's Virtue and Wisdom, I should omitt making You at this time the humblest Offers of my poor Service and Attendance. It is the first time I ever solicited You in my own behalf, and if I am refused, I think it will be the first Request You ever refused me. I do not conceive my self obliged to regulate my Opinions by the Proceedings of a House of L^{ds} or Comm^s; and therefore however they may acquitt themselves in Your Lordship's Case, I shall take the liberty of thinking and calling You, the ablest and faithfullest Minister, and truest Lover of Your Country that this Age hath produced. And I have already taken Care that you shall be so represented to Posterity, in spight of all the Rage and Malice of Your Enemyes.[2] And this I know will not be wholly indifferent to Your Lordship, who, next to a good Conscience, did always esteem Reputation Your best Possession. Your Heroick and Christian Behaviour under this Prosecution astonisheth every one but me, who know You so well, and know how little it is in the Power of human Actions or Events to discompose you. I have seen Your Lordship labouring under greater Difficultyes and exposed to greater Dangers, and overcoming both, by the Providence of God, and Your own Wisdom and Courage. Your Life has been already attempted by private Malice, as it is now by publick Resentment. Nothing else remained: You were destined to both Tryals; and the same power which delivered you out of the Paws of the Lyon and the Bear, will I trust, deliver you out of the hands of the uncircumcized.

I can write no more. You suffer for a good Cause, for having pre-

---

[1] Oxford was confined in the Tower, to which he had been committed by the House of Lords.

[2] The reference is to *An Enquiry into the Behaviour of the Queen's Last Ministry*. This tract was not, however, printed till 1765. Two manuscripts are extant. See *Prose Works*, ed. Davis, vol. viii; and the pamphlet as edited by Irvin Ehrenpreis, 1956, Indiana Univ. Press.

served Your Country, and for having been the great Instrument under God, of His present Majesty's peacable Accession to the Throne. This I know; and this Your Enemyes know; and this I will take Care that all the World shall know; and future Ages be convinced of.

God Almighty protect You, and continue to you that Fortitude and Magnanimity he hath endowed you with. Farewell,

J.S.

Forster copy

Swift to Knightley Chetwode

2 August, 1715.

Considering how exact a correspondent you are, and how bad a one I am myself, I had clearly forgot whether you had answered my last letter, and therefore intended to have writ to you to-day whether I had heard from you or no, because Mr. Warburton told me you were upon your return to Martry. Though it be unworthy of a philosopher to admire at anything, and directly forbidden by Horace, yet I am every day admiring at a thousand things. I am struck at the Duke of O— flight.[1] A great person here in power read us some letters last night importing that he was gone to the Pretender, and that upon his first arrival at Calais he talked of the King only as Elector etc. But this is laughed at, and is indeed wholly unlike him, and I find his friends here are utterly ignorant where he is, and some think him still in England. —

Aug. 4. I was interrupted last post, but I just made a shift to write a few words to the Baron. The story of an invasion is all blown off; and the Whigs seem to think there will be no such thing. They assure us of the greatest unanimity in England to serve the King, and yet they continue to call the Tories all Jacobites. They say they cannot imagine why any Tory should be angry, since there never was the least occasion given; and particularly they cry up their mercy shown to Bingley.[2] There is no news of any more people gone off, though

[1] The Duke of Ormonde had crossed to France a few days earlier. The news could have only just reached Swift.

[2] This allusion is surprising, for Lord Bingley, Chancellor of the Exchequer 1711–13, was not a pronounced party man. See Ford's letter to Swift, 5 Aug. 1714.

Lord Shrewsbury was named. The suspending the Habeas Corpus Act has frightened our friends in England. I am heartily concerned for poor Joe,[1] and should be more so if he were not swallowed up by his betters.

Give my service to Dame Plyant, and desire her to let me know what quantity of cherries she has for brandy; you may steep them in just enough to keep them alive, and I will send you some very good if I can and you will tell me how much. But here I want Joe. I hope Dame found the boys well, and that she gave them good counsel upon the subject of gooseberries and codlings, for I hear the eldest has been a little out of order.

I am glad to hear you and the Doctor are grown so well together, and was not Mrs. Raymond the civilest thing in the world? I find you intend to take some very sudden resolution, and truly I was like to be as sudden, for I was upon the balance two hours whether I should not take out a license of absence immediately upon a letter I received;[2] but at last I thought I was too late by a week for the design; and so I am dropped again into my old insipidness, and the weather has been so bad, that together with my want of a horse, and my steward urging one every day about my tithes, I have not been a mile out of town these five weeks, except once on foot.

I hear Major Champagne was left half pay, and consequently that he will now have whole; so that he may yet eat bread. God preserve you and Dame and the fire-side, believe me, ever, | Entirely yours &c.

Address: To Knightley Chetwode Esq., at Martry, near Navan, County of Meath.

4805

John Arbuthnot to Swift

Aug: 6th

I receaved your very Heraclitian letter; I am kinder than yow I desire to hear your complaints, and will allways share them, when I cannot remove them. I should have the same concern for things as yow, were I not convinc'd that a comet will make much more strange revolutions upon the face of our Globe, than all the petty

---

[1] Beaumont.
[2] Perhaps Chetwode contemplated joining Ormonde, and Swift was anxious to dissuade him from so dangerous a course.

changes that can be occasiond by Goverts & Ministrys and yow will
allow it to be a matter of importance to think of methods to save ones
self & family in such a terrible shock when this whole earth will turn
upon new poles & revolve in a new orbite. I consider my self as a
poor passenger, & that the earth is not to be forsaken nor the rocks
remov'd for me. but yow are certainly some first minister of a great
Monarch, who for some Misbehaviour are condemnd in this revolution of things to govern a chapter & a quire of singing men. I am
sure I should think my self happy if I had only such a province as
the latter. Certainly your chapter is too peacable, and not like other
chapters else they would give yow more occupation. yow see I begin
with philosophy as to business, I this moment sawe the Dragon. he
had your letters & shewed them to me some time ago, and seems to
be mighty fond of the project, only he is to be at Wimple & not in
Herefordshire & it is but a step further. & he is to write this night
if yow beleive him to that very purpose, nay I am to have the letter
to enclose & I intend to keep mine open till eleven. It is strange that
yow should imagine the Dragon had cast his exuviae in his Den, or
that Confinement is a Cure for inactivity so far from it. all these
habits are ten times stronger upon him than ever. [Lewis][1] will
furnish yow with a collection of new storys that are as far beyond
the old ones as yow can imagine. therefor I say again come & yow
will be far from finding such dismall scenes as yow describe. your
own letter will furnish yow with topicks to conquer your Melancholy
for in such mutability, what is it that must not in time cast up even
the return of that Brother[2] you mention and as philosophical as I am
I should be very sad if I did not think that very probable & feasible.
As to your freinds, though the world is changed to them, they are
not changd to yow and yow will be Caressed as much as ever and
by some that bore yow no good will formerly. do yow think there is
no pleasure in hearing the H—r[3] club declaim upon the clemency &
gentleness of the Late Reign, and a thousand stranger things as for
the Constitution it is in no more danger than a strong man that has
gott a little surfeit by Drunkenness. all will be well & people recover
their sober senses every day. severall of your friends dine with me to
day L Ma—, Jo. Drummond[4] The Judge &c when yow will be

---

[1] Injury to the paper.   [2] i.e. Bolingbroke.
[3] Hanover.
[4] Lady Masham, John Drummond. Swift had made the acquaintance of the
latter, Oxford's financial agent at The Hague, during his last visit to England.

remembered. I wish I could return your compliments as to my wife and Bairns. Sure you are a very ill Husband for you had the compleat Thousand[1] when you was in England & six pence of another thousand given by the Dragon, I remember that full well. L[2] is gone his progress I shall be at Bath in a fortnight come that way. adieu. I really think the person I recommended will do well, he will be quite another thing befor Michaelmas, with Roseingraves[3] teaching. & he has a good voice.

Address: For | The Reverend D^r | Swift Dean of | S^t patricks | Dublin
Endorsed by Swift: Dr Arbuthnot | Aug. 5th 1715

Forster copy
Knightley Chetwode to Swift

Woodbrooke, 13 August, 1715.[4]

Though this leaves me perplexed beyond expression, and that I do not know you can extricate me, yet I would not omit to write to you, for sometimes imparting lessens affliction. My hurrying to this country, as I did, was to have an interview with an old lady,[5] whom I was directed to see, and by whose directions I was to form all my present measures. Either I am faulty in deferring it so long, or she is sooner called away than I expected. Be it whether it will, her being gone leaves me a great deal in the dark, pretty irresolute, and under all possible confusion. But if I resolve anything, it is to pursue my first resolution. I wish I were certain you knew her, or had seen her ere she embarked, but you are pleased to be sometimes so politic and dark that I never had reason from you to believe you of her acquaintance.

I hope to see you soon, so soon that I was in suspense if I should not have been the porter of this letter.[6] Your former resolution which

[1] A reference to the £1,000 promised to Swift to meet his expenses on installation as Dean of St. Patrick's.
[2] Lewis.
[3] The organist at St. Patrick's.
[4] This letter is missing from Birkbeck Hill's volume.
[5] In a note appended to the copy of this letter by Forster's friend, Edward Wilmot-Chetwode, it is suggested that 'old lady' was a pass-word for the Duke of Ormonde. Nothing is known of Ormonde's visiting Ireland at this time; and it is most improbable.
[6] The letter now becomes an answer to Swift's of 2 Aug.

you laid aside for being a week too late, would have been better, in my opinion, pursued, since three weeks would be allowed. You take me, I dare say, without further *éclaircissement*. I have seen about sixteen of the clergy since I left you. I find them chagrined and disobliged a good deal with some late steps made by your friend, whom you call Proverb;[1] how justly or unjustly I do not pretend to enter into. I writ to Dame about the cherries. I cannot inform you of the fit quantity you say you want, for that you cannot eat your cake and have your cake; if he be swallowed up by as many of his betters as step aside, I cannot tell you what to say to it. I sent for the Baron[2] to come to me; he has promised, but I have not yet seen him. I had a letter this morning from quondam Lady Jenny to come to her. I could not go. She tells me *Monsieur le Major* was to [take] post at Holyhead for London the day I dined with you, his post not at that time given away notwithstanding reports. I will see her to-morrow, and you before Tuesday's post; I will not add more now, and wish I have not said too much, but of this I am certain that I am with the utmost affection and truth, ever, | Entirely yours.

4805

The Rev. Robert Freind to Swift

Westr | Sep. 20. 1715

Mr Dean[3]

I am much oblig'd to Lady Kerry[4] for giving you an occasion of writing, and shall always be pleas'd to receive any commands from You. Mr Fitzmorris is very promising, and a favourite of mine already, I had never seen nor heard from any one that was concern'd

---

[1] Perhaps the reference is to Provost Pratt; and the 'late steps made' signify the action taken by the authorities about disloyalty in the College.

[2] Rochfort.

[3] The writer of this letter was Robert Freind who had been under-master of Westminster School since 1698. He became headmaster in 1711; and the school prospered under his headship, which ended with his retirement in 1733. Swift records a dinner of several friends at his house (*Journal*, 1 Feb. 1711–12).

[4] Anne, Lady Kerry, frequently mentioned in the *Journal*, was the daughter of Sir William Petty. In 1693 she married Thomas Fitzmaurice, Baron of Kerry. Evidently she had asked Swift to commend her younger son to Freind. He had already concerned himself about the entrance of her elder son into Christ Church, Oxford, where he matriculated on 10 Mar. 1712–13 (*Journal*, 24 Feb. 1712–13).

for him till I had the favour of Yours, but as I had taken particular notice of him on his own account, I shall now do it much more upon yours. This will be brought to you by yr kinsman Mr Rolt,[1] I am glad I can tell you, that he has behav'd himself very well here, He is not of the brightest sort, but is very sober and industrious and will work out his way, and I believe deserve any incouragement you are pleas'd to give him. Things are in an odd posture with us at present, and the state of banishment you are in may be endur'd without much regrett, however I shall hope in a little time to see you here when more of yr friends are in town, The Bp[2] and my Br[3] are much yours, and very desirous of a happy meeting with You, before this can be with you, you will be able to guess how soon that may happen, may it be as soon as is wisht by | Sr | Yr most obedient and faithfull | humble Servant |

R. Freind

Endorsed by Swift: Dr Robt Freind | Sept. 20. 1715

Forster copy

Swift to Mrs. Chetwode

7 October, 1715.

Madam,

I find you are resolved to feed me wherever I am. I am extremely obliged to your care and kindness, but know not how to return it otherwise than by my love and esteem for you. I had one letter from Mr. Chetwode from Chester,[4] but it came late, and he talked of staying there only a week. If I knew where to write to him I would. I said a good deal to him before he went, and I believe he will keep out of harm's way in these troublesome times. God knows what will become of us all. I intend when the Parliament meets here,[5] to retire somewhere into the country. Pray God bless and protect you, and your little fire-side. Believe me to be ever, with true esteem, Madam, | Your most obedient, humble Servant, |

J. Swift.

[1] Possibly a son of Swift's relative, Pat Rolt.
[2] i.e. Atterbury.   [3] John Freind, the physician.
[4] Chetwode had evidently determined to throw in his lot with the Duke of Ormonde.
[5] The first Irish Parliament of George I met on 12 Nov.

The Duchess of Ormonde to Swift

Oct: the 17ᵗʰ 1715

Sʳ

I was extreamly pleased to find you had not forgot yr. freinds, wⁿ tis so hard for 'em to write to you, & by their concern for you put you in mind of them, but I find no misfortunes can lessen yr freindship, wch is so great as to blind you of the side of their faults, & make you beleive you see virtues in 'em, it were happy for 'em they enjoyed in any degree, for I am sure some of those you named are much wanted at this time, I was as you heard, very well pleased that my freind¹ was safe as to his person, but very uneasy at seeing his reputation so treated, as to his fortune, it is yet in dispute, however, as long as he is well I am satisfied, tis wth dificulty I do hear, but now & then, a stragling body brings me an account of him, for there has bin no incouragemt to write by the post, all letters miscarrying that either he or I writ that way, that we have given it over now, & trust to accident for newes of each other, I hope I shall hear from you oftener then I have don for some months past, for no freind you have has more respect for you than | yr most faithfull | humble servant

Yr neice Betty² is yr humble servant

Endorsed by Swift: Dutchess of Ormd | Octᵇʳ 17 1715

Forster copy

Swift to Knightley Chetwode

17 December, 1715.

I have had three letters from you, one from Chester, another round a printed paper, and the third of the 6th instant. The first I could not answer for it came late, and you said you were to leave Chester in a week, neither did I know how to direct to you till your second came, and that was so soon followed by the third that now I answer both together. I have been miserably ill of a cruel cold, beyond the common pains, and so as to threaten me with ill conse-

---

¹ i.e. Ormonde.
² Lady Betty Butler, the Duchess of Ormonde's daughter.

quences upon my health, else you should have heard from me three weeks sooner. I have been ten days, and am still at Mr. Grattan's four miles from the town,[1] to recover myself, and am now in a fair way.

I like the verses well. Some of them are very well though against my friends, but I am positive the town is out in their guess of the author. I wonder how you came to see the Dragon, for I am told none of his nearest relations have that liberty, nor any but his solicitors. Had I been directed to go over some months ago, I might have done it, because I would gladly have been serviceable, but now I cannot, and agree with you and my other friends that I am safer here. I am curious to know how he carries himself, whether he is still easy and intrepid; whether he thinks he shall lose his head, or whether it is generally thought so.

I find you have ferreted me out in my little private acquaintance, but that must be *entre nous*. The best of it is you cannot trace them all. My service to them, and say I [would] give a great deal to be among you. I do not understand the rebus. I would apply it to myself, but then what means 'narrow in flight'? I am sorry at heart for poor Ben.[2] He has in his life been so splenetic that it was past a jest. He should ride, and live in the country and leave off his trade, for he is rich enough. As much as I hate news, I hear it in spite of me, not being able to govern the tongues of your favourite and some others. We are here in horrible fears, and make the rebels ten times more powerful and the discontents greater than I hope they really are; nay it is said the Pretender is landed or landing with Lord knows how many thousands.[3] I always knew my friend Mr. Attorney[4] would be as great as he could in all changes. When Cole of the Oaks comes to town assure him of my humble service, and that when storms are over I will pass some time with his leave among his plantations. Dame Pliant and I have had some commerce, but I have not been able to go there, by foolish impediments of business here. She has been in pain about not hearing from you. I lately heard your boys were well. The Baron called to see me here in the country yesterday, and said you had lately writ to him.

---

[1] Belcamp.   [2] Benjamin Tooke, Swift's publisher.

[3] In December the Old Pretender, accompanied by only six attendants, sailed in a small vessel from Dunkirk, and on the 22nd made a safe landing at Peterhead.

[4] Harcourt, Lord Chancellor, until superseded by Earl Cowper on the accession of George I.

There is one period in your letter very full of kind expressions, all to introduce an ugly suspicion of somebody that told you I know not what. I had no acquaintance with you at all till I came last to this kingdom, and it is odd if I should then give myself the liberty of speaking to your disadvantage. Since that time you have used me so well, that it would be more than odd if I gave myself that liberty. But I tell you one thing, that when you are mentioned by myself or anybody else, I presently add some expressions, that he must be a rude beast indeed who would lessen you before me, so far am I from doing it myself, and I should avoid it more to you than another, because you are a man anxious to be informed, and have more of punctilio and suspicion than I could wish. I would say thus much to few men. Because generally I expect to be trusted, and scorn to defend myself; and the Dragon thought it the best compliment to him he ever heard, when I said I did not value what I said to him, nor what I said of him. So much upon this scurvy subject.

You may direct to S. H. at Mrs. Holt's over against the Church in Bride's Street. The Parliament here are as mad as you could desire them; all of different parties are used like Jacobites and dogs. All conversation with different principles is dangerous and troublesome. Honest people get into corners, and are as merry as they can. We are as loyal as our enemies, but they will not allow us to be so. If what they said were true, they would be quickly undone. Pray keep yourself out of harm's way. It is the best part a private man can take unless his fortune be desperate, or unless he has at least a fair hazard for mending the public. My humble service to a much prouder man than myself; I mean your uncle.[1] Dr. P[ratt][2] showed me a letter from you about three weeks ago. He is well, I suppose, for I am a private country gentleman, and design to be so some days longer. Believe me to be ever, with great truth and esteem, | Yours &c.

I direct to the Pell Mell coffee-House, because you mention changing Lodgings.

Address: To Knightley Chetwode, Esqr. at the Pell mell Coffee-house, in Pell-mel—London.

[1] The Dean of Gloucester.
[2] Provost of Trinity College.

The Duchess of Ormonde to Swift

Jan the 23^d 17$\frac{16}{15}$

S^r

Yr letter[1] was a great while upon the road before I had the good luck to have it, I think I was happy that it ever arrived here, for it is the second letter I have received out of Ireland in above seven months, either those few freinds I have there are afraid of taking notice of me or my enemyes won't let me have the comfort of thinking I have any left, & therefore stop my letters. I give you a thousand thanks for so kindly remembring an absent freind, as you alwayes think right, I don't wonder you are of the opinion our freind[2] has not all his good offices very well returned, but who lives[3] in this world must arm themselves with patience, & a resolution able to bear ingratitude,[4] reproach, poverty, & afflictions of all kinds, or submit to the discipline of Bedlam, I have not heard from my master[5] these many months, I hope he is well because the good nature of the world wou'd take care I shou'd hear, if he were otherwayes,

The Lady you name in yr letter lives at her house in Berkshire[6] I can't entertain you, with so much, as the tittall tattells of the town, having not seen it these four months, nor scarce any thing but frost & snow, wch. makes me converse most wth Robin redbreasts, that do me the favour to come in at windows to see me, yr neice[7] is yr humble servant, but not well, having a Rash

I beleive by this time you wish you had not provok't me to write, since you are troubled with so long a scrall from me who am with great truth | sr | yr most sincere | freind & humble servant

Endorsed by Swift: Dutchess of Orm— | Jan^r 23. 1715

[1] Probably a reply to her letter of 17 Oct.
[2] i.e. Oxford.
[3] *Sic.* Ball prints 'live'.
[4] 'with' is blotted out before 'ingratitude'.
[5] i.e. Ormonde.
[6] Bucklebury in Berkshire, an estate inherited by Lady Bolingbroke from her father.
[7] Lady Betty Butler.

Swift to Archdeacon Walls

Trim. Febr. 26ᵗʰ. 1715–16

I lay at Forbes's² friday night,³ he had no Horse to lend me, one was lame, & tother sick, so I was forced to bring yʳ Scrub with me; You have reason to complain of Bolingbroke's shyness, Your Horse was like to cast Will half a dozen times.⁴ I was very weary with my Journy yesterday, but thank God am well to day, and as bad as the Weather is, I read Prayers and preached at Laracor. For poor Warburton (who could believe it) is layd up with the Gout. The Roads were abominably bad from Dunboine⁵ hither; My Mare is brisker after the Journey than before—I design to ride every day, I hope Bolingbroke carryed you well this day to Castle-knock. I saw the Gardens at Laracor, and the Grove too (tell Mʳˢ Johnson that) and they all look sadly desolate. My Land lord & Land lady⁶ give their Service to you and Gossip Doll & the Ladyes: I am very much theirs; and hope our Doll is better. Shift as you can without your nag till I return, he shall fare as well as the rest: My Duty to My Lᵈ Bishops of Cloghʳ & Dromore⁷ | Yrs—

Address: For | the Revd Mʳ Archd | Walls | in Queen-street | Dublin
Postmark: 27 FE   *Poststamp:* TRIM
Later endorsement: Dʳ Swift | Feb 26ᵗʰ 17¹⁵⁄₁₆

Nichols 1801

Swift to Bishop Atterbury

Dublin, March 24, 1715–16

My Lord,
As much of your Lordship's thoughts and time are employed at present,⁸ you must give me leave to interrupt them, and, which is

¹ Lord Rothschild's Library, No. 2281 (17).
² See p. 172, n. 3.
³ Swift had evidently left Dublin on Friday the 24th.—Ball.
⁴ Swift had exchanged Bolingbroke for a horse of Walls.
⁵ Forbes was rector of Dunboyne. He had been a chaplain to the Duke of Shrewsbury when the duke was Lord Lieutenant in 1713.
⁶ Dr. and Mrs. Raymond.
⁷ Bishops Stearne and Ashe were then in Dublin for the meeting of the Irish Parliament.—Ball.   *[For note 8 see overleaf*

worse, for a trifle; though, by the accidents of time and party, of some consequence and great vexation to me. I am here at the head of three and twenty dignitaries and prebendaries, whereof the major part, differing from me in principles, have taken a fancy to oppose me upon all occasions in the chapter house:[1] and a ringleader among them has presumed to debate my power of proposing, or my negative, though it is what the deans of this Cathedral have possessed for time immemorial, and what has never been once disputed. Our constitution was taken from that of Sarum; and the knowledge of what is practised there in the like case would be of great use to me. I have written this post to Dr. Younger, to desire he would inform me in this matter;[2] but having only a slender acquaintance with him, I would beg your Lordship to second my request, that the Dean would please to let me know the practice of his cathedral, and his power in this point. I would likewise desire your Lordship to let me know how it is at Westminster, and the two other cathedrals, with whose customs you may be acquainted.[3]

Pray, my Lord, pardon this idle request from one that loves and esteems you, as you know I do. I once thought it would never be my misfortune to entertain you at so scurvy a rate, at least not at so great a distance, or with so much constraint:

> Sis felix, nostrumque leves [I do not like *quicunque*] laborem:
> Et quo sub coelo tandem, quibus orbis in oris
> Jactemur, doceas.[4]

---

[1] For a discussion of the involved relations of Swift with his chapter see Landa, *Swift and the Church of Ireland*, chap. ii. In March of 1715–16 Swift had proposed a member of his chapter as proctor for the ensuing year, but he was outvoted by eight to six; and when he proposed himself he was rejected by the same count.

[2] Dr. John Younger was Dean of Salisbury and prebendary of St. Paul's. Apparently he gave Swift the same advice as that contained in Atterbury's letter printed below.

[3] Swift probably referred to Carlisle and Christ Church, Oxford, of which Atterbury had been successively Dean before his appointment to the bishopric of Rochester and deanery of Westminster.

[4] Virgil, *Aen.* i. 330–3. 'quicunque' is called for as an adaptation from the 'quaecunque' of Virgil.

---

[8] Swift refers to the part taken by Atterbury in opposing latitudinarian tendencies in the Church encouraged under the new régime. His brilliant gifts as an orator qualified him as a champion of the high-church party; and gradually as a pronounced supporter of the Jacobite cause.

The greatest felicity I now have is, that I am utterly ignorant of the most publick events that happen in the world: *multa gemens igno-miniam plagasque, &c.*[1] I am with the greatest respect and truth, my Lord,

Your lordship's most dutiful and most humble servant,

J. Swift.

4805

Bishop Atterbury to Swift

Bromly. | Apr. 6. 1716.

Good Mr Dean,

My Gout kept me so long a Prisoner at West[r] this Winter, that I have fixed at Bromly[2] this Spring much sooner than ever I yet did: for wch reason my meeting with Dr Younger will be more difficult, than it would be, had I been still at the Deanery.[3] The best (or rather the worst) is, that I beleive, he can say nothing to you upon the matter about wch you write, which will please you. His Deanery is of the Old Foundation; & in all such Foundations, the Deans have no extraordinary Powers or Priviledges, & are nothing more than Residentiarys, with a peculiar Corpse belonging to them as Deans; the first of the Chapter, but such whose Presence is not necessary towards the Dispatch of any one Capitular Act; the Senior Residentiary supplying their Absence, in every case, with full Authority. Thus I say, the case generally is in the Old Deanerys; unless where the Local Statutes may have expressly reservd some peculiar Power or Priviledge to the Deans of those Churches. But none of them, I dare say have a Negative either by Canon-Law, Custome, or Local Statute.

Thus much to shew you that a nice Search into the Peculiar Rights of the Dean of Sarum, will be needless, if not mischievous to you.

The three Deanerys wch I have had, are all of the New Foundation by H. 8. or Q. El. In the Charters of, all there is a Clause, impowering the Dean to make, punish, & unmake all the Officers. In the Statutes of one of them (Carlisle) the D[s] Consent in all the Graviores Causae is made expressly necessary; & in the other Two,

[1] Virgil, *Georg.* iii. 226.
[2] The palace of the Bishop of Rochester.   [3] Of Westminster.

nothing from the Foundation of those Churches, ever passd the Seal, without the Dean's Sigilletur, first written on the Lease, Patent, Presentation &c wch is a manifest and uncontested Proof of his Negative.

As to the Power of Proposing, that I apprehend not to be Exclusive to the other Members of Chapters. It is a point chiefly of Decency, & Convenience; the Dean being the Principal Person, & supposd best to be acquainted with the affairs of the Church, & in what Order they are fittest to be transacted. But if any One else of the Body will propose any thing, & the rest of the Chapter will debate it, I see not how the Dean can hinder them; unless it be by leaving the Chapter: & that it self will be of no moment in Churches, where his Absence doth not break up, & dissolve the Chapter; as it dos, where his Consent to any thing there treated of is expressly requird before it can pass into an Act. Where indeed he is allowd such a Negative, he is generally allowd to make all proposals, because it would be to no purpose for any one to make a Proposition, wch he can quash by a Dissent: but this is not, I say, a matter of Right, but Prudence.

Upon the whole, the best Advice I can give you, is, whatever your Powers are, by Statute, or Usage, not to insist on them too strictly in either of the Cases mentioned by you, unless you are very sure of the Favor & Countenance of your Visitor. The Lawyers, you will find, whenever such Points come before them for a Decision, [are] very apt to disregard Statute & Customs in such Cases; & to say, that their Books make the Act of the Majority of the Corporation the Legal Act of the Body, without considering whether the Dean be among the Minority, or no. And therefore your utmost Dexterity & Address will be necessary, in order to prevent such a Tryal of your Right at Common Law; wch it is ten to one, (especially as things now stand) will go agst you. If the Refractory part of your Chapter are stout, & men of any Sense, or supported underhand, (the last of these is highly probable) You had better make use of expedients to decline the Difficulty, than bring it at present, to a Decision. These are the best Lights, & this the best Advice I can give you, after a long Experience of the natural Consequences of such Struggles,[1] & a careful Search into the Foundation of the Powers & Priveledges claimd & disputed on the one side, & the other.

I wish I could say any thing more to your satisfaction, but I

[1] The moderation and sound sense of Atterbury's advice to Swift is the more

cannot; & I think, in all such Cases, the best Instance I can give you of my Friendship, is not to deceive you.

There is a Statute in the latter End of H. 8. reign[1] worthy of your perusal—The Title of it relates to the *Leases of Hospitals* &c & the Tenor of it did, in my apprehension seem always to imply, that without the Dean, Master &c nothing could be legally done by the Corporation: but the Lawyers will not allow this to be good Doctrine—& say, that Statute (notwithstanding the constant Phrase of it) determines nothing of this Kind: & at the most, implys it onely as to such Deanerys &c where the Dean, Master &c has the right of a Negative, by Statute or Usage—And few Lawyers there are, who will allow even thus much. I cannot explain my self farther on that head: but when you peruse the Statute, you will see what I mean; thô, after all, it dos not I beleive, include Ireland. However, I look upon it as a declaration of the Common Law here in England.

I am sorry, You have any Occasion to write to me on these heads, & much sorrier that I am able to give you any tolerable Account of them. God forgive those, who have furnished me wth this knowledge, by involving me designedly into those Squabbles; I thank God, I have forgiven them!

I will enter into nothing but the Enquirys of your Letter: & therefore add not a word more, either in English or Latin, but that I am, with great Esteem, | Good Mr Dean | Your very aff^t | humble Servant | Fr. Roffen.

Endorsed by Swift: Bp Rohst | Rx Apr. 12. 1716
  (*and later*): About my | dispute with | the Chap^tr

Nichols 1801

Swift to Bishop Atterbury

April 18, 1716.

My Lord,

I am extremely obliged to your Lordship for the trouble you have given yourself in answering at length a very insignificant letter.[2] I shall entirely follow your Lordship's advice to the best of my skill.

noteworthy in that he was himself from early days a born controversialist. He was in serious difficulties with his own chapters of Carlisle and Christ Church. Smalridge who succeeded him at both these places described himself as coming with a 'bucket of water' to quench the fires started by his friend Atterbury.

[1] 33 Hen. VIII, cap. 37.   [2] His letter of 24 Mar.

Your conjectures from whence my difficulties take their rise are perfectly true. It is all party. But the right is certainly on my side, if there be anything in constant immemorial custom. Besides, though the first scheme of this Cathedral was brought from Sarum, yet, by several subsequent grants, from Popes, Kings, Archbishops, and Acts of Parliament, the dean has great prerogatives. He visits the chapter as ordinary, and the Archbishop only visits by the dean. The dean can suspend and sequester any member, and punishes all crimes except heresy, and one or two more reserved for the Archbishop. No lease can be let without him. He holds a court leet in his district, and is exempt from the Lord Mayor, &c. No chapter can be called but by him, and he dissolves them at pleasure. He disposes absolutely of the petty canons and vicars-choral places. All the dignitaries, &c. swear canonical obedience to him. These circumstances put together, I presume, may alter the case in your Lordship's judgment. However, I shall, as your Lordship directs me, do my utmost to divert this controversy as much as I can. I must add one thing, that no dignitary can preside without a power from the dean, who, in his absence, makes a sub-dean, and limits him as he pleases. And so much for deaneries, which I hope I shall never trouble your Lordship with again.

I send this enclosed, and without superscription, to be sent or delivered to you by a famous friend of mine, and devoted servant of your Lordship's.

I congratulate with England for joining with us here in the fellowship of slavery. It is not so terrible a thing as you imagine; we have long lived under it, and whenever you are disposed to know how you ought to behave yourself in your new condition, you need go no farther than me for a director. But, because we are resolved to go beyond you, we have transmitted a bill to England, to be returned here, giving the government and six of the Council power for three years to imprison whom they please for three months, without any trial or examination; and I expect to be among the first of those upon whom this law will be executed. We have also outdone you in the business of Ben Hoadley;[1] and have recommended to a bishopric one whom you would not allow a curate in the smallest of your parishes.[2] Does your Lordship know that, as much as I have been

---

[1] Benjamin Hoadly was appointed to the bishopric of Bangor on 21 Dec. 1715.

[2] The allusion is said to be to Dr. Charles Carr, who was then chaplain to the

used to lies in England, I am under a thousand uneasinesses about some reports relating to a person that you and I love very well? I have writ to a lady upon that subject, and am impatient for an answer.[1] I am gathering up a thousand pounds, and intend to finish my life upon the interest of it in Wales.

God Almighty preserve your Lordship *miseris succurrere rebus*, whether you understand or relish Latin or no. But it is a great deal your fault if you suffer us all to be undone; for God never gave such talents without expecting they should be used to preserve a nation. There is a doctor[2] in your neighbourhood, to whom I am a very humble servant. I am, with great respect,

Your Lordship's most dutiful, &c.

J. Swift.

Some persons go this summer for England; and if Dr. Younger be talked with, I hope you will so order it that it may not be to my disadvantage.[3]

Deane Swift 1768

Viscountess Bolingbroke to Swift

London, May 5, 1716.

Mr. Dean,[4]

Your letter came in very good time to me,[5] when I was full of vexation and trouble, which all vanishes, finding that you were so

Irish House of Commons. Swift's depreciatory remark may have been due to a sermon preached by him designed to appeal to the temper of the new régime. Many years later, however, when Carr was Bishop of Killaloe, he was noted with favour by Swift as one of the three bishops who voted against the Bills of Residence and Division (*Poems*, p. 804).

[1] From July 1715 to March 1716 Bolingbroke had been acting as Secretary to the Pretender. He was dismissed on grounds of incompetence and even treachery. He surrendered his papers, which would all go into 'a letter-case of moderate size'. For a full account of the transactions see Bolingbroke's *Letter to Sir William Windham*, composed in 1717 but not published till 1753. The reply of the lady, otherwise Lady Bolingbroke, follows.

[2] Dr. Robert Freind of Westminster School.

[3] That they may not be supplied with precedents for his chapter to use against him.

[For notes 4, 5 see overleaf.]

good to remember me under my afflictions, which have been not greater than you can think, but much greater than I can express. I am now in town; business called me hither, and when that is finished I shall retire with more comfort than I came. Do not forsake an old friend, nor believe reports which are scandalous and false. You are pleased to enquire after my health; I can give you no good account of it at present, but that country, whither I shall go next week, will, I hope, set me up. As to my temper, if it is possible, I am more insipid and dull than ever, except in some places, and there I am a little fury, especially if they dare mention my dear Lord without respect, which sometimes happens; for good manners and relationship are laid aside in this town; it is not hard for you to guess whom I mean.[1] I have not yet seen her Grace,[2] but design it in a day or two: we have kept a constant correspondence ever since our misfortunes, and her Grace is pleased to call me sister. There is no body in the world has a truer respect and value for her than myself. I send this to my friend *John*,[3] and beg you, when you do me the favour of an answer, to send it to him, who will take care to convey it to me in the country; for your letter lay a long while before it came to my hands. I beg you to look with a friendly eye upon all my faults and blots in this letter, and that you will believe me, what I really am, your most faithful humble servant,

F. B.

[1] The reference may be to Bolingbroke's father Sir Henry St. John who succeeded his father in a baronetcy in 1708. He was raised to the peerage as Baron St. John of Battersea and Viscount St. John in 1716. Despite dissolute habits he lived to his ninetieth year, dying in 1742.

[2] The Duchess of Ormonde.

[3] John Barber.

_____

[4] Bolingbroke's first wife, whom he married 22 May 1701, was Frances, first daughter and co-heiress of Sir Henry Winchcombe, second baronet of Buckle-bury. She was a very handsome woman (Hearne's *Collections*, vi. 252), who retained her loyalty to her husband despite his unfaithfulness. She was a 'great favourite' of Swift (*Journal*, pp. 237, 326).

[5] See the previous letter.

Rothschild[1]

Swift to Archdeacon Walls

Trim. May. 6. 1716

I am at the Doct[rs] House,[2] where with great Difficulty I have got half a Sheet of Paper to write to You. I was so hurt in my Thigh with riding, that being on horseback made my sore enflame, & I can now neither ride nor walk but am mending, and hope to be on horseback in 2 or 3 days. Pray take some opportunity of seeing Tom Stanton, and what he has done with M[r] Pratt about my Papers.[3] Desire Mrs Brent to gett the Cellar Window where the Hogsheds are, close stopt, and the other if it wants. Gillespy talked of his intending to be here in great Hast; I hope he has given you some Money in all this time. Tell Robin Grattan[4] I had his Letter, and thank him for his Manuscript which has been printed in every News Paper. My humble Service to Gossip Doll & the Ldys, are our two Bishops come to Toun? will Clogher take Tuam as the News says?[5] I am going to dinner—Adieu

I have done dinner, and have nothing further to say to You D[r] Raymd gives his Service to You & the Ladyes—so does Warburton & M[r] Preston[6]—

Address: To the Reverend M[r] Archdeacon | Walls, at his House over against | the Blew-coat Hospitall in | Queen-street | Dublin
Postmark: 7 MA   *Poststamp:* TRIM
Later endorsement: D[r] Swift | May 6th 1716.

[1] Lord Rothschild's Library, No. 2281 (18).
[2] Raymond's. Swift appears to have been away from Dublin for some days.
[3] From a subsequent reference it is evident that the business related to a loan of money. Owing to his official position the Provost's brother would be specially qualified to advise in such a matter. Someone, perhaps Walls, has used the outer fold of this letter for working out additions, the meaning of which is not plain.
[4] See p. 152, n. 4.
[5] Archbishop Vesey (p. 129, n. 2) had died on 28 Mar. Neither Ashe nor Stearne benefited by his death.
[6] John Preston, father-in-law of Peter Ludlow.

Rothschild[1]

Swift to Archdeacon Walls

Martry.[2] May 15 [1716.]

If any thing happen, to make you easy, aliquid malo fuit usus in illo. If the Sinecure be as you say and that you are sure of it, and Your Friends advise you, and that after mature thinking, it will make you perfectly easy, I believe I shall be brought to comply that Chamberln should have St Lukes and Dopping St Nicholas.[3] If that could be compassed, it would be a real Pleasure to me, because I might have an Opportunity of obliging a Brother of Sam Dopping whom I love and esteem above most men,[4] & therefore I beg you will push it, but you may trust me I will not be backward in straining a Point to do you good.

Pray be so kind to press Mr Staunton to finish that Affair with Mr Pratt, and if he does not like the Security, I empower him to act as he would in his own Case or the Case of a Client, and I shall be extreemly thankfull and obliged to him.[5] Mr Bindon[6] promised to preach a Turn for me, I believe mine is Sunday next or the following .. Some of the Farmers at Laracor pretended they could not pay me till Gillespy came down; and a hint has been given me that the Reason[7] was he had some dealings with them for Corn, which if it be true, will breed a Perplexity in my Affairs that I shall not endure,

[1] Lord Rothschild's Library, No. 2281 (20). The first line is heavily blotted out and illegible.

[2] Evidently Swift had recovered from the soreness induced by riding, mentioned in the previous letter, and had been able to proceed from Trim to Martry.

[3] Walls had been promised a benefice in the south of Ireland due to become vacant by Charles Carr's elevation to the bishopric of Killaloe, if Swift would appoint Chamberlain to the vacant cure of St. Nicholas. This Swift was unwilling to do, and proposed to transfer Anthony Dopping, a brother of Swift's friend, Sam Dopping, from St. Luke's parish to that of St. Nicholas and give the former to Chamberlain.

[4] Sam Dopping had proved himself a stout Tory and was one of Chancellor Phipps's great allies. In the *Long History of a Short Session* the Chief Secretary is censured for not nominating him as Speaker when Levinge was rejected, instead of consenting to the election of Brodrick.—Ball.

[5] See previous letter.

[6] Thomas Bindon, a fellow of Trinity College, Dublin, was later appointed Dean of Limerick.

[7] Several words relating to the alleged 'Reason' are here smudged with ink, but remain legible.

Pray tell him what I say, and know the bottom of it, and give him a little Advice. I go to Morrow to Rochforts if it be fair, when you write, pray direct to me there, to Mr Rochforts at Gallstown in Westmeath, if there be a more particular Direction Robin Gratton will tell you, to whom send the inclosed to Abbey street.[1] This Weather hath kept me from riding; The Farmers here say the Rain is come too late for the Winter corn. You must be so kind to send the Maid 3 shill a week to live on: My humble Duty to the 2 Bishops, and Service to Gossip Doll and the Ladyes. I would fain have Sam Holt[2] pd his 25^ll he lent me to buy Wine.

Address: To Mr Archdeacon Walls
Later endorsement: Dr Swift | May 15th 1716

Rothschild[3]

Swift to Archdeacon Walls

Gallstown. June. 6. 1716

I had Yours this day sent me by Express from Trim, I suppose there is no great Hast about the Instrument from me.[4] The Governmt may lodge a Warrant for a Fiant for you in Chamberlins Hands, & then all will be safe; But I would have you enquire a little more carefully into the Value and Nature of the Sinecure: For it would vex me to the Heart to give that Man a Living without any Substantiall Benefit to You. I hear it is near Cork,[5] it will be easy for you to get an Answer from thence: and there can be no possible Inconvenience if the Warrant for the Fiant be in Chamberlins keeping. I do here promise, and will give it under my Hand that if the Sinecure be what can be thought sufficient, I will nominate him. And I have not been yet taxed with breaking my Word. You may have sufficient Information in ten days or a fortnight. I speak purely for your Interest. And when you are satisfyed in the Value of the Thing by

---

[1] A former approach to the Abbey of St. Mary's, Dublin.
[2] Sam Holt, a son-in-law of Isaac Manley, was later to receive a plurality of Church preferment, including a prebend of St. Patrick's.
[3] Lord Rothschild's Library, No. 2281 (21). Part of the lower portion of the letter is torn away. Conjectural words are supplied within brackets.
[4] See the previous letter.
[5] The rectory of Castlehaven in the county of Cork.

good Hands and that the Warrant for the Fiant is drawn, I will come to Town my self, or give sufficient Power. Worral has my Seal.

This is a plain Path for the Matter to go in [and any] body can tell you that there is no need of any [kind of] Hurry. If the Fiant it self was drawn there . . . Consequence in it; but I would have no Step [taken without] better Information; and lett Carr[1] tell you what he k[nows.]

My Service to Gossip Doll & the Ladyes

Address: To Archdeacon Walls
Later endorsement: D[r] Swift | Jan. 6th 171$\frac{6}{7}$[2]

Rothschild[3]

Swift to Archdeacon Walls

Gallstoun. Jun. 14. 1716,

I am not of opinion that Your Affair requires so much hast as you speak of;[4] If M[r] Chamberln has the Warrant by him in Your Name, it may keep this Month without any manner of Consequence, or a great deal longer, which I know very well, and My Lord chief Baron now confirms to me. I have severall Reasons to keep me from returning till Tuesday sennight,[5] when I intend God willing, to be in Toun. You may count upon it, that it lyes very much at my Heart to make you easy, I write by Paddy to the Bp of Dromore, to have his Judgmt in one Point; after which I will absolutely determine, and it is of no Consequence at all when the Duke[6] or Ar. Bishop[7] go for England. My Service to Gossip Doll

Address: To M[r] Archdeacon Walls
Later endorsement: D[r] Swift | June 14th 1716

   [1] He was the former holder of the sinecure.
   [2] The endorsement thus gives the date inaccurately both as to month and year.
   [3] Lord Rothschild's Library, No. 2281 (22).
   [4] See previous letter.   [5] The 26th.
   [6] The second Duke of Grafton, then one of the Lord Justices of Ireland. He had been appointed to that position together with the Earl of Galway. Grafton returned to Ireland in 1720 as Lord Lieutenant.
   [7] The absence of friendliness at this time between Swift and Archbishop King has already been mentioned. As Ball observes, the appointment of Bolton as Chancellor of St. Patrick's was obviously due to the Archbishop's desire to have an ally and observer in the Chapter. In writing to Lord Sunderland, 29 Oct. 1714, King stated frankly that, unless he had a person like Bolton in the chapter he was afraid his affairs there would not go well.

Swift to Archbishop King

Gallstown, June 17, 1716.

My Lord,

I have an account by this post that your Grace intends in two or three days to go for England. I heartily wish you a good voyage, and a speedy return, with a perfect recovery of your health, and success in all your undertakings for the service of the Church. I lately applied myself to some persons who I thought had credit with your Grace, that they would prevail on you to consent that Mr. Dopping should have St. Nicholas, and that Mr. Chamberlain, upon surrendering a sinecure (fallen by the late promotion) to Mr. Walls, might succeed to St. Luke's;[1] and having heard your Grace was not disinclined to this scheme, I thought you had authority enough to make it go down with Mr. Chamberlain, who would be a gainer by the exchange, and, having already a plentiful fortune, would have as good an opportunity of showing his abilities in one parish as in the other. I should add my humble entreaties to your Grace to consent to this proposal, if I had not so many reasons to apprehend that it would succeed just so much the worse for my solicitation. I confess, every friend I have discovered long before myself that I had wholly lost your Grace's favour, and this to a degree that all whom I was disposed to serve were sure to thrive the worse for my friendship to them; particularly, I have been assured that Mr. Walls would not have failed of the prebend of Malahidert, if he had not been thought too much attached to me;[2] for it is alleged, that according to your Grace's own scheme of uniting the prebends to the vicarages it would almost have fallen to him of course; and I remember the poor gentleman had always a

---

[1] King and Swift possessed interrelated rights of preferment in connexion with St. Patrick's. Soon after Swift's installation political antagonisms began to play their part; and with the change of power differences between the two were accentuated. Furthermore, the recent appointment of Lindsay to the primacy, favoured by Swift, cannot have been pleasing to King, nor the elevation of Theophilus Bolton to the chancellorship of St. Patrick's to Swift. In addition the two put forward opposing candidates for the cure of St. Nicholas Without. See Landa, *Swift and the Church of Ireland*, pp. 78–87. Difficulties within the chapter were undoubtedly fomented by King; and, as Ball writes, 'Swift's expostulation in this letter cannot be considered other than a temperate and deserved rebuke'.

[2] John Moore, who held the prebend of Mulhuddart, had died on 1 June.

remote hope of that prebend whenever Dr. Moore should quit it. Mr. Walls came lately down to me to Trim upon that disappointment, and I was so free as to ask him, whether he thought my friendship had done him hurt; but he was either so meek, or so fearful of offending, that he would by no means impute his misfortune to any thing beside his want of merit, and some misrepresentations; which latter I must confess to have found with grief, to have more than once influenced you against some, who by their conduct to your Grace have deserved a quite different treatment. With respect to myself, I can assure your Grace, that those who are most in your confidence make it no manner of secret, that several clergymen have lost your Grace's favour by their civilities to me. I do not say any thing of this by way of complaint, which I look upon to be an office too mean for any man of spirit and integrity, but merely to know whether it be possible for me to be upon any better terms with your Grace, without which I shall be able to do very little good in the small station I am placed. The friendship I had with the late Ministry, and the trust they were pleased to repose in me, were chiefly applied to do all the service to the Church that I was able. I had no ill designs, nor ever knew any in them. I was the continual advocate for all men of merit without regard of party; for which it is known enough that I was sufficiently censured by some warm men, and in a more particular manner for vindicating your Grace in an affair where I thought you were misrepresented, and you seemed desirous to be set right.[1] And upon the whole, this I can faithfully assure your Grace, that I was looked upon as a trimmer, and one that was providing against a change, for no other reason but defending your Grace's principles in Church and State; which I think might pass for some kind of merit in one who never either had or expected any mark of your favour. And I cannot but think it hard, that I must upon all occasions be made uneasy in my station, have dormant prebends revived on purpose to oppose me,[2] and this openly acknowledged by those who say they act under your Grace's direction. That instead of being able to do a good office to a deserving friend, as all my predecessors have been, it is thought a matter of accusation for any one to cultivate my acquaintance. This I must think to be hard treatment, and though I regard not the consequences as far as they are intended to affect

---

[1] The report that King had compared Harley to Piso; see i. 228, n. 2.
[2] The reference is to the prebend of Timothan, to which no appointment had been made from the reign of Queen Elizabeth till then.—Ball.

myself, yet your Grace may live to lament those which from thence may happen to the Church.

When I was first made dean, your Grace was pleased, in a very condescending manner, to write to me that you desired my friendship:[1] I was then in the service of the Ministry, and the peace was made: and if I had any share in their ill designs I was then guilty, but I do not know that I have ever done anything since to forfeit your good opinion. I confess I lost many friends by the Queen's death, but I will never imagine your Grace to be of the number.

I have given your Grace too long a trouble. I humbly beg your blessing, and shall remain ever, with the greatest truth and respect, my Lord, | Your Grace's most dutiful | and most humble servant, |

Jonath. Swift.

Rothschild[2]

Swift to Archdeacon Walls

Galls-toun Jun. 18. 1716

I sate up till four this morning writing Dispatches by Mr Rochfort who left us about 2 hours ago, and is not very certain that he may not go for Engld to morrow about an Appeal in some Tryall there. With him went a large Pacquet directed to You, containing Letters to the A. Bp. of Dromore. Dr Travers,[3] and Mrs Johnson; but not a word to Your self, because I had no mind to say any thing to you, and am now in no Condition to write, being quite disorderd with scribbling over a dozen Letters at a Heat, and want of sleep, which I shall endeavour to make up after I have answered some Parts of y^r Lettr.

I should be very glad to serve Mr Dopping on his Brothers Account,[4] and the Man himself hath been always personally obliging to me, and I believe him an honest Man that loves his own Interest, but would not do an ill or base Thing to compass it, and being a man acceptable to that Party I was glad of the Opportunity; but you must needs suppose that if it were res integra, I would certainly give it to y^r self to hold with Castleknock, or if that were not possible

---

[1] King to Swift, 16 May 1713.
[2] Lord Rothschild's Library, No. 2281 (23).
[3] See p. 163, n. 3.
[4] See p. 202, n. 4.

that I have severall People whom I love very well, and know much bett^r than I do Mr Dopping, and who want it much more. Then in my Conscience I think Mr Chambrln doth not deserve such a Living nor is equall to such a Cure being a man of very low Parts and understand[ing], with a very high Conceit of himself, and party-mad into the Bargain.[1] I have let the Ar Bp know my mind very freely in a long Letter,[2] I have drawn up all his ill Treatment of me, and shewn him the Injustice and Ingratitude of it, how he is governed by Favorites who misrepresent Things and Persons to him, and that if the Queen had lived, he and his Favorites would have used me better. I have reproached him with the Dormant Prebend and other Steps on purpose to oppose me; that his Favorites openly profess that no man who is well with me shall have any Encouragment: That severall Persons assured me nothing else *could have hindred you from Malahiddert, wherein he broke his own Scheam on purpose because you were my Friend*; that I taxed you with it, but y^r great meekness or fears of offending made you impute y^r disappointment onely to y^r Want of Merit, or Misrepresentations of y^r Enemyes. I minded him how many Friends I had lost or at least gained Enemyes by supporting & defending his Character in the late Reign, that my Intimacy and Confidence with the late Ministry could be no just reason for his using me ill; because he had writt to me upon my being made Dean to desire my Friendship and then the Peace was made, and all the Mischief done, if I had a hand in any. I said it was impossible for me to do any good in my Station while I was upon this Foot with him—With twenty other Things I now forget, as that he might make Chamberln comply if he pleased, &c.

It is impossible for Dougat[3] to keep his Honesty in the way and Company he is.

The Bp Drom^{re} did not move this matter of Dopping to me, but I wholly to him, & I blame him for dropping it, and that he hath not Zeal enough to make the Ar-Bp cram it down Chamberlns Throat. How would it be inconvenient to the Ar. Bp to remove Chamberln

---

[1] On the other hand, the Archbishop says Chamberlain was a good man and an excellent preacher, and was not fairly used by the Tory government (King to Addison, 18 Dec. 1714).—Ball. [2] See p. 205.

[3] Robert Dougatt, a nephew of Archbishop King, was appointed Prebendary of Swords in 1709. In 1715, through the offices of the Archbishop, he was appointed Archdeacon of Dublin, and four years later he became Precentor of St. Patrick's. He proved himself a troublesome member of Swift's chapter. See Landa, *Swift and the Church of Ireland*, pp. 74, 83–84, 89, 92.

from his present Cure of St Nicholas, he may have a thousand Whig Curates in Dublin. I told the Ar. Bp that Chamberln was rich and onely wanted an Opportunity to shew his Parts which he might do as well at St Lukes. I own he would get little by it, but he hath a further Dependance on the Ar. Bp. and obligation to him, and therefore if his Grace pleased the matter might easily be compassed.

If Mr Bolton apprehends I do him a Kindness and will give me any Ironicall Thanks on that Score, I shall either bear them or return as well as I am able.

I know not what Scheams you could form for Mr Dopping unless St Nicholas were not attended with a Law suit. In that Case I could wish Dopping had St Nicholas & the Sinecure, Chamberlayn had Castleknock, and you Dopping's Country Living and St Lukes but as things are now, this is all but Vision.

I have sent my last Determination in the Pacquet directed to you this morning. I have but two Intentions, the first to do you a Service, and the other to take some Care of my own Credit and the good Opinion of my Friends. It is not hatred to Chamberln or Love to Mr Dopping that makes me Refractory, I could soon get over both of these.

I believe you are uneasy enough, and so am I, upon your Account as well as my own, I am certain, Chamberln has made good use of what he has picked from you by y^r Fears and Uneasyness. He thinks I have personall malice to Him, but he does him self too much honor, I do not so much as despise him. My Ends were to make as good a Bargain for you as I could, and to have some Regard to my own Credit.

I have sd all I can think on; Tis now between 8, and 9, and I doubt I shall not pay my self in Sleep. I leave the rest to your black privy Councellr—be not frightened, I mean onely Mrs Johnson.

My humble Service to Gossip Doll & the Ladyes.

I just now had a Let^{tr} from Bp Dromore, it was kept by going to Molingar instead of Kinnigad,[1] My Duty to me,[2] what I writt this morning to him in the Pacquet directed to you must serve for an answer—Pray send the inclosed to Dr Coghill[3]

Address: To Mr Archd. Walls.
Late endorsement: Dr Swift | June 18th 1716

---

[1] Mullingar is the assize town of Westmeath, and Kinnegad a village on the main road from Dublin to it.—Ball.   [2] me] Ball incorrectly 'him'.
[3] Dr. Marmaduke Coghill, the Judge of the Prerogative Court.

The Library, Armagh, MSS. Hibernica, vol. i. 60

Archbishop King to Swift

Dublin June 20th 1716

Revd Sir

I was[1] favoured with yours of 17 inst., by which I am heartily sory. to find that there are some very industrious to sow dissention between you and me, and do not wonder at it because the same was much laboured in y^r predecessors time as he himself can tell you, but he was aware of the Snare and avoided it. I entreat you to do the like and not give any credit to those false misrepresentations that self interested persons make. Assure y^r self they are neither yr frends nor mine nor the Churches. pray therefore give no ear to such Whisperers as separate chief frends.

As to the Business of Dr Wall, Mr Chamberlain and Mr Dopping, I am conscious to myself, that in order to give you satisfaction, I have gone as farre as either prudence or Justice will allow me, and I am afraid a little further. I never used my authority with any Clergyman to oblige him to go further than was consistent with his inclinations and Interest, nor do I believe it is advisable I shou'd. I shou'd be glad of an opportunity to convince you of the reality of my earnest desire and intention to live in all good understanding with you as being sensible it is necessary for our common quiet and good, and therefore again entreat you to lay aside all surmises and believe that I am Sincerely | Revd Sir y^r etc.

W. D.

I intend for the Bath God willing Tuesday[2] or Wednesday next, if you have any service for me in England you may command me.

Address: To Dean Swift.

Faulkner 1741

Alexander Pope to Swift

June 20, 1716[3]

I cannot suffer a friend to cross the Irish seas without bearing a testimony from me of the constant esteem and affection I am both

---

[1] Ball reads 'am'.   [2] The 26th.

[3] The date of this letter is in doubt. Pope may have supplied 'June 20' when

obliged and inclined to have for you. It is better he should tell you than I, how often you are in our thoughts and in our cups, and how I learn to sleep less[1] and drink more, whenever you are named among us. I look upon a friend in Ireland as upon a friend in the other world, whom (popishly-speaking) I believe constantly well-disposed towards me, and ready to do me all the good he can, in that state of separation, tho' I hear nothing from him, and make addresses to him but very rarely. A protestant divine cannot take it amiss that I treat him in the same manner with my patron Saint.

I can tell you no news, but what you will not sufficiently wonder at, that I suffer many things as an Author militant: whereof, in your days of probation, you have been a sharer, or you had not yet arrived to that triumphant state you now deservedly enjoy in the Church. As for me, I have not the least hopes of the Cardinalat, tho' I suffer for my Religion in almost every weekly paper. I have begun to take a pique at the Psalms of David (if the wicked may be credited, who have printed a scandalous one in my name.)[2] This report I dare not discourage too much, in a prospect I have at present of a post under the Marquess de Langallerie,[3] wherein if I can but do some signal service against the Pope, I may be considerably advanced by the Turks, the only religious people I dare confide in. If it should happen hereafter that I should write for the holy law of Mahomet, I hope it will make no breach between you and me; every one must live, and I beg you will not be the man to manage the controversy against me. The Church of Rome I judge (from many modern symptoms, as well as ancient prophecies) to be in a declining condition; that of England will in a short time be scarce able to maintain her own family: so Churches sink as generally as banks in Europe,[4] ⌜and 'tis time to look out for some better security⌝.

---

printing in 1741, forgetting that Curll published his objectionable parody of the first Psalm, under the title *A Roman Catholic Version of the First Psalm, for the Use of a Young Lady, by Mr. Pope* ten days after 20 June. But the date cannot be far wrong, for Ford carried the letter over, and he spent July and August in Ireland. See Ault, *New Light on Pope*, p. 158, n 1. Sherburn, i. 341, n. 2.

[1] Alluding to his constant custom of sleeping after dinner.—Warburton, 1751.

[2] In the *Post-Man*, 28–31 July 1716, Pope hypocritically repudiated *The First Psalm*.

[3] A French officer (1656–1717) who served under Louis XIV, Prince Eugene, the King of Poland, the Landgrave of Hesse, and at this time proposed to lead Turkish forces against Italy. In 1717 he died in prison.

[4] In the clandestine volume sent by Pope to Ireland and in the 1741 octavo

I don't know why I tell you all this, but that I always loved to talk to you; but this is not a time for any man to talk to the purpose. Truth is a kind of contraband commodity which I would not venture to export, and therefore the only thing tending that dangerous way which I shall say, is, that I am and always will be with the utmost sincerity, | Yours, &c.

4805

Viscountess Bolingbroke to Swift

London Aug ye 4th 1716

Dear S^r

I wish y^r last[1] had found me in the countrey, but to my misfortune, I am still kept in towne, solliciting my unfortunate business,[2] I have found great favour from his majesty, but form is a tedious thing to wait upon, since tis my fate I must bear it with patience, & parfect it if I can, for there is nothing like following business one selfe, I am unwilling to stir without the seales, wch I hope to have soon, I have been very ill, this place never agreeing with me, & less now then ever, it being prodigious hot weather, I know not[3] what to say to one part of yrs, only this that you will forgive the fears of a woman if she sayes she is glad tis as tis, tho' it has almost ruin'd her[4] I hope one time or other his majesty will find my Lord has been misrepresented & by that means, he may be restored to his Countrey once more, with honour, or else however harsh it may sound out of my mouth, I had rather wear black. this are[5] my real sentiments, I never thought my

printed by Faulkner the text was as printed here. In later Pope editions the clause in half brackets was omitted, and after the word 'Europe' the following was substituted: 'and for the same reason; that Religion and Trade, which at first were open and free, have been reduced into the Management of Companies, and the Roguery of Directors.'

  [1] Probably Swift's reply to her letter of 5 May. Untraced.
  [2] Lady Bolingbroke was doubtless seeking indemnification of her Bucklebury estate from the consequences of her husband's attainder. She had brought him a large fortune, much of which had been spent, or given to him when he left the country.
  [3] 'not' is written above the line.
  [4] Bolingbroke was living at the time in association with the Marquise de Villette, who became his second wife.
  [5] 'are' first written, then 'is' above the line.

selfe nor my health of any consequence till lately, & since you tell me tis soe, to the unworthy, as you please to term it, I shall take care of it, for the worthy, wch I once thought soe they are good for nothing, but to neglect distresst friends, those few friends I meet with now are worth a thousand Relations, that I found long agoe, wee have the happiness of odd halfe witted Relations, & silly obstinate opiniative friends, that are a severe plague to me, I never could have the pleasure of talking one moment to the D of O,[1] she had alwaies company, & some that I wish she had not, she is now out of towne & wee doe not Corrispond at present, I wish her all happiness, & in better handes as to her business, you have a much better opinion of me then I deserve but, I will study all I can to merit y^r favour, wch you are soe kind to assure me of, I wish it were possible for us two, to meet, that I might assure you in person that I am | yrs most faithfully &c

Yrs came safe, I hope this will too you, there is a Lady who never forgets you, & a particular friend to me, & has been a great cumffort to me in my trouble, I mean my tenant, she is now in the countrey to my griefe.

Endorsed by Swift: Lady Bol— | Aug. 4. 1716

Faulkner 1741

Swift to Alexander Pope

Aug. 30, 1716

I had the favour of yours by Mr. F.[2] of whom, before any other question relating to your health, or fortunes, or success as a poet, I enquired your principles in the common form, 'Is he a Whig or a Tory?' I am sorry to find they are not so well tallied to the present juncture as I could wish. I always thought the terms of *Facto* and *Jure* had been introduced by the Poets, and that Possession of any sort in Kings was held an unexceptionable title in the courts of Parnassus. If you do not grow a perfect good subject in all its present

---

[1] The Duchess of Ormonde.
[2] Charles Ford, who was setting out on a journey to Rome, evidently carried over this letter to Pope. See Ford's letter to Swift from Paris, *infra* 23 Oct. N.S.

latitudes, I shall conclude you are become rich, and able to live without dedications to men in power, whereby one great inconvenience will follow, that you and the world and posterity will be utterly ignorant of their virtues. For, either your brethren have miserably deceiv'd us these hundred years past, or Power confers virtue, as naturally as five of your Popish sacraments do Grace.—You sleep less and drink more.—But your master Horace was *Vini somnique benignus*:[1] and as I take it, both are proper for your trade. As to mine, there are a thousand poetical texts to confirm the one; and as to the other, I know it was anciently the custom to sleep in temples for those who would consult the Oracles, 'Who dictates to me slumbring, &c.[2]

You are an ill Catholick, or a worse Geographer, for I can assure you, Ireland is not Paradise, and I appeal even to any Spanish divine, whether addresses were ever made to a friend in Hell, or Purgatory. And who are all these enemies you hint at? I can only think of Curl, Gildon, Squire Burnet, Blackmore, and a few others whose fame I have forgot: Tools[3] in my opinion as necessary for a good writer, as pen, ink, and paper. And besides, I would fain know whether every Draper doth not shew you three or four damned pieces of stuff to set off his good one? however, I will grant, that one thorough bookselling Rogue is better qualified to vex an author, than all his contemporary scriblers in Critick or Satire, not only by stolen Copies[4] of what was incorrect or unfit for the publick, but by downright laying other mens dulness at your door. I had a long design upon the Ears of that Curl, when I was in credit, but the rogue would never allow me a fair stroke at them, though my penknife was ready and sharp. I can hardly believe the relation of his being poisoned, though

---

[1] Horace, *Satires*, ii. 3. 3. 'Indulgent to himself in Sleep and Wine'—Faulkner's footnote.

[2] *Paradise Lost*, ix. 23. In the manuscript list of his books made by Swift in 1715 is the following entry: 'Milton's Paradise Lost. Lond · 1711 · small volume.' This book disappeared before the sale in 1745, and no copy of the work replaced it. Nichols, however, in his edition of Swift's *Works*, 1801, xix, p. vi, refers to a copy once in the possession of J. C. Walker, the Irish antiquary, with marginal notes by Swift, 'for the use of Mrs. Johnson and her friend Mrs. Dingley'.

[3] Elwin emended to 'Fools'. But as Pope in the London text added 'are' before 'as', it is improbable that he would have overlooked 'Tools' if it was not the word he intended.

[4] This is notoriously False, Mr. *Pope*'s being handed to the Press by a Gift of his Friend, Henry Cromwell, Esq.; to Mrs. Thomas, as is now well known.—Curll (1741).

the Historian pretends to have been an eye-witness:[1] But I beg pardon, Sack might do it, though Rats-bane would not. I never saw the thing you mention as falsely imputed to you; but I think the frolicks of merry hours, even when we are guilty, should not be left to the mercy of our best friends, until Curl and his resemblers are hanged.

With submission to the better judgment of you and your friends, I take your project of an employment under Langallerie to be idle and unnecessary: Have a little patience and you will find more merit and encouragement at home by the same methods. You are ungrateful to your country; quit but your own Religion, and ridicule ours, and that will allow you a free choice for any other, or for none at all, and pay you well into the bargain. Therefore pray do not run and disgrace us among the Turks by telling them you were forc'd to leave your native home because we would oblige you to be a Christian; whereas we will make it appear to all the world, that we only compelled you to be a Whig.

There is a young ingenious Quaker[2] in this town who writes verses to his mistress, not very correct, but in a strain purely what a poetical Quaker should do, commending her look and habit, &c. It gave me a hint that a sett of Quaker-pastorals might succeed, if our friend Gay could fancy it, and I think it a fruitful subject; pray hear what he says. I believe further, the personal[3] ridicule is not exhausted; and that a porter, foot-man, or chair-man's pastoral might do well. Or what think you of a Newgate pastoral, among the whores and thieves there?[4]

Lastly, to conclude, I love you never the worse for seldom writing to you. I am in an obscure scene, where you know neither thing nor person. I can only answer yours, which I promise to do after a sort whenever you think fit to employ me. But I can assure you the scene

---

[1] The reference is to Pope's folio pamphlet (Griffith, *Bibliography*, No. 52), published in April 1716: *A Full and True Account of a Horrid and Barbarous Revenge by Poison, on the Body of Mr. Edmund Curll, Bookseller; . . . Publish'd by an Eye-Witness.* This was reprinted in *Miscellanies. The Third Volume*, 1732, pp. 17-27. See also *Prose Works of Alexander Pope*, Norman Ault, pp. xciv-xcvii, 257-66.

[2] Said by Faulkner to be George Rook, a linen draper. In the *Journal to Stella*, 13 Dec. 1712, p. 582, Swift speaks of expecting a visit from 'the Son of Coz Rooks eldest Daughter'. See also Swift's letter to Thomas Swift, 6 Dec. 1693. The young Quaker may, therefore, have been related to Swift.

[3] personal] Pastoral *1740*.

[4] This suggestion may have led to the writing of Gay's *Beggar's Opera* (1728).

and the times have depressed me wonderfully, for I will impute no defect to those two paltry years which have slipt by since I had the happiness to see you. I am with the truest esteem, | Yours, &c.

4805

The Duchess of Ormonde to Swift

Sept: the 14ᵗʰ/1716

Sʳ

I had the ill fortune to miss of that letter you upbraid me wth,[1] I had deserved any reproaches you cou'd make me, if it had come to my hands, & yr. inquiryes after me, I'l make you wish you'd not bin so angry wth me, for I will scrall out my self, wt you'd rather Betty or my maid had, for they wou'd have made shorter work of it, but I will answer every part of yrs, that you obliged me wth, by Mr Ford,[2] first as to the Lady[3] you mention, The reason I had not seen her in a great while was my being in the country, to tell you the truth I believe her husband has bin a better courtier then either she or any of her sex cou'd be, because men have it in their power to serve, & I believe hers, has effectually don what lay in him,[4]

you kindly ask how my affairs go, there is yet no end of 'em, & God only knows wn there will be, for wn every thing was thought don, a sudden blast had blown all hopes away, & then they give me fresh expectations, in the mean time I am forct to live upon the borrow, my goods all taken away, that I shan't so much as have a bed to lye upon but wt I must buy, & no money of my own to do that wth, so that you may imagine me in a chearfull way, I pray God support me,

The gentleman[5] you inquired after is very well now, the illness you heard he had he has bin subject to a good while, wt you desire, I wish it were in the power of either his brother[6] or I, but all will

---

[1] Probably a reply to her letter of 23 Jan.

[2] This letter delivered by Ford is not forthcoming.

[3] i.e. Lady Bolingbroke.

[4] The implication seems to be that Bolingbroke by treachery to the Pretender earned favour for his wife from George I with regard to her estate

[5] i.e. Ormonde.

[6] The Earl of Arran, 1671–1758, second son of Thomas, Earl of Ossory, eldest son of the first Duke of Ormonde, was created Earl of Arran in the peerage

go from both of us of every kind, only they say, that the clothes upon my back, I may perhaps call my own, & that all, I was obliged to leave the country I was so ill there that if I had not come to the physician I can't tell wt might have happened, my daughter is yr most humble servant, & is pretty well in health, am not I one of my word, & troubled you twice as long as you'd have wisht, but you'l find by this, that a womans pen shou'd no more be set at work, then her tongue, for she never knowes wn to let either of 'em restt, but my paper puts me in mind, that I have but just room to tell you, I wish much to see you here, if it cou'd be with yr satisfaction, & that I am, with great sincerity sr | yr faithfull | humble servant

Endorsed by Swift at head of letter: Dutchess of Ormd | Sep^{br} 14th. 1716

Rothschild[1]

Swift to Archdeacon Walls

Trim Oct^{br}. 4th 1716

It was very foolish in Jo[3] to allarm you as if I was in danger, as the D^r[4] tells me, thô he would not shew me[5] yr Lett^r, nor do I know a word in it I was ill but 3 days, and have been well since yesterday morning. I hope Gossip Doll is so; the D^r tells me she is brought to bed, but not the Sex, he therefore supposes it a Girl. The Weather

of Ireland in 1693, and in 1694 Baron Butler in the English peerage. In Macky's *Characters* he was described as possessed of 'very good sense, though [he] seldom shows it'. Swift observed: 'This is right; but he is most negligent of his own affairs.' Cf. an interesting letter addressed to him by Swift in 1739.

[1] Lord Rothschild's Library, No. 2281 (24).

[2] Swift's correspondence at this point raises an interesting question—the date of his marriage to Stella, on the assumption that the marriage ever took place. Archbishop Bernard, a believer in the secret marriage, examines (*Prose Works*, ed. Temple Scott, xii. 98) the question of probable dates for the ceremony. If at Clogher he concludes that it must have taken place between 28 July and 4 Oct. 1716, or between 5 Dec. and 18 Mar. 1717. In his introduction to Ball's edition of the *Correspondence* (p. xxiv, n. 2) the Archbishop, with more letters before him from which to judge, concludes that if the marriage took place at Clogher in 1716 it must have been between 30 Aug. and 4 Oct. when we have a gap in the correspondence. As Ball remarks, however, 'the references to Bishop Ashe in the correspondence afford some ground for the conclusion that the only meetings between the Bishop and Swift took place in Dublin'. See also Gold, *Swift's Marriage to Stella*, p. 95.

[3] i.e. Beaumont.   [4] i.e. Raymond.   [5] me] om. *Ball.*

mends and I have yet thoughts of going to Mʳ Rochforts,¹ if it continues fair; Pray spur up Gillespy to get some Arrear money. the Dʳ
sd he expected you here last night, I should have thought you mad;
Do you not believe, that if I had any Sickness of Consequence, I
should have got a coach to come to Town, or sent there for a Doctor.
I assure you I have been very careful of my self, and so have my
friends been of me . . . I wish I had the Deeds,² or I shall lose all
this years opportunity of planting. My Service to the Ladyes I hope
they are well. Do you hear any thing of Jarvis's going. For I hate to
be in Toun while he is there³— | Yʳˢ &c

Address: To the Reverend Mʳ Archdeacon | Walls, at his house over against | the
blue-coat Hospitall, in | Queen street | Dublin
Postmark: ? OC
Later endorsement: Dʳ Swift ¦ Octʳ 4ᵗʰ 1716

4805

Viscount Bolingbroke to Swift

Octob: 23 [O.S. 12] 1716

It is a very great truth that among all the losses which I have
sustained, none affected me more sensibly than that of yr company
and correspondence, and yet even now, I should not venture to write
to you, did not you provoke me to it.⁴ A commerce of letters between
two men who are out of the world, and who do not care one farthing
to return into it again, must be of little moment to the State; and yet
I remember enough of that world to know, that the most innocent
things become criminal in some men, as the most criminal pass ap-
plauded in others.

Your letter breathes the same spirit as your conversation att all

¹ i.e. Gaulstown.
² Swift had arranged to purchase from Percival twenty acres of land as an
addition to the Laracor glebe. The purchase had been approved by the Board of
First Fruits on 22 June (Minutes in P.R.O. of Ireland). In connexion with this
transaction the editor has a document, signed and sealed by Percival and Swift,
showing the extent and layout of the ground.
³ Swift's desire to avoid Jervas may have been roused by the latter's Whig
politics or by possible demands on his time for sittings. During visits to Ireland
Jervas seems to have painted Swift more than once. See Falkiner's essay, *Prose
Works*, ed. Temple Scott, xii. 12–13.
⁴ Swift had evidently sent a letter to Bolingbroke by Ford's hand.

times inspir'd, even when the occasions of practising the severest rules of virtuous fortitude seem'd most remote; if such occasions could ever seem remote to men, who were under the direction of your able & honest friend Sr Roger.[1]

To write about myself is no agreeable task, But yr commands are sufficient att once to determine & excuse me. Know therefore that my health is far better than it has been a great while. that the money which I brought over with me will hold out some time longer, and that I have secur'd a small fund which will yield in any part of the globe[2] a revenue sufficient for one, qui peut se retrancher meme avec plaisir dans la mediocrité. I use a French expression, because I have not one that pleases me ready in English. During several months after my leaving that obscure retreat, into which I had thrown myself last year, I went thro' all the mortifying circumstances imaginable. att present I enjoy, as far as I consider myself, great complacency of mind. But this inward satisfaction is embitter'd when I consider the condition of my friends. they are got into a dark hole where they grope about after blind guides, stumble from mistake to mistake, jostle against one another, & dash their heads against the wall, & all this to no purpose for assure yrself that there is no returning to light, no going out but by going back. my stile is mystick, but it is yr trade to deal in mysterys, & therefore I had neither comment nor excuse. you will understand me, & I conjure you to be persuaded, that if I could have half an hours conversation with you, for which I would barter whole hours of life, you would stare, haul yr wigg, & bite paper more than ever you did in yr life. Adieu Dear Friend may the kindest influence of Heaven be shed upon you, whether we may ever meet again, that Heaven only knows, if we do what millions of things shall we have to talk over! in the mean while believe that nothing sits so near my heart as my country and my friends, and that among these you ever had, and ever shall have, a principal place.

if you write to me, direct a Monsr Charlot chez Monsr Cantillon Banquier Rue de l'Arbre Sec. Once more Adieu.

Endorsed by Swift: Lord Bolingbroke | Octb. 23^d 1716

[1] i.e. Oxford.   [2] Previous editors print 'world'.

Charles Ford to Swift

Paris Oct: 23. [O.S. 12, 1716][1]

If I was to see you again, you would give twice as much as you offer'd six weeks ago[2] not to have seen me. By the same rule you might afford something not to hear from me, but the enclos'd[3] came this morning to me, and I could not send it away without adding a few lines in the cover. They are not to put you again into the spleen, but only to ask how you do, and how you employ yourself. Do the great designs go on at Laracor,[4] or have the rains put a stop to your improvements, as well as to my journey? It will cost you but a penny, and a few minutes to answer these questions, and in return you shall know any thing you desire to know of me in my travels. I shall go on as soon as we have five or six days sunshine to dry the roads, and make the finest country in the world supportable. I am laugh'd at here when I talk of travelling, and yet of waiting for fair weather, but to me the journey is the greatest part of the pleasure; and whereas my companion[5] is continually wishing himself at Rome, I wish Rome was a thousand leagues farther off that I might have more way to pass in France and Italy. If you will do me the favour to write to me direct to be left with Mr Cantillon Banker in Paris.

Address: To the Rev^d | Dr Swift Dean of St Patrick's | at his house in | Dublin, | par Londres   Ireland
Postmark: 23 OC
Endorsed by Swift: The Squire | Rx Nov^{br} 7th 1716
   and: Paris. Oct^{br} 23^d 1716

---

[1] By editors prior to Nichol Smith the date has been given wrongly as 'October 28'.
[2] As noted before Ford had spent July and August in Ireland and set out for Rome at the beginning of September.
[3] Bolingbroke's letter to Swift of 23 [o.s. 12] Oct. 1716.
[4] Swift's purchase of land from Percival already noted.
[5] 'Mr. Wight.' Ford has left a long account of 'an adventure that happened to Mr Wight and me at Siena' on 12 Oct. 1717.

Swift to Archbishop King

Dublin, Nov. 13, 1716.

My Lord,[1]

The Reason I never gave your Grace the Trouble of a Letter, was, because it could only be a Trouble without either Entertainment or Use; for, I am so much out, even of this little World, that I know not the commonest Occurences in it; neither do I now write to your Grace upon any Sort of Business, for I have nothing to ask but your Blessing and favourable Thoughts; only, I conceived it ought not to be said, that your Grace was several Months absent in *England*, without one Letter from the Dean to pay his Respects. My Schemes are all circumscribed by the Cathedral and the Liberties about it, where nothing of Moment hath happened since your Grace left it, except the Election of Mr. *Chamberlain* to St. *Nicholas*, which passed quietly while I was in the Country. I am purchasing a Glebe by the Help of the Trustees,[2] for the Vicarage of *Laracor*; and I had Vanity enough to desire it might be expressed by a Clause in the Deeds, as one Consideration, that I had been instrumental in procuring the first Fruits, which was accordingly inserted; but, Hints were given it would not pass.[3] The then Bishops of *Ossory* and *Killaloe* had, as I am told, a Sum of Money for their Labour in that Affair, who, upon my Arrival at *London* to negociate it, were one of them gone to *Bath*, and the other to *Ireland*:[4] But it seemeth more reasonable to give Bishops Money for doing nothing, than a private Clergyman[5] Thanks for succeeding where Bishops have failed. I am only sorry I was not a Bishop, that I might at least, have got Money. The Tory Clergy here seem ready for Conversion, provoked by a Parcel of obscure Zealots in *London*, who, as we hear, are setting up a new

---

[1] Until the close of this letter Swift ignores the content of his letter to King of 17 June 1716 to which King had replied briefly on the 20th.

[2] Of the First Fruits.

[3] At a meeting of the Board of First Fruits on 12 Oct. the deeds were ordered to be engrossed. There was no mention in the minutes of the meeting to the part which Swift had played in procuring the First Fruits.

[4] Swift's commission to solicit the remission of the First Fruits, 31 Aug. 1710, was addressed to the Bishops of Ossory and Killaloe, who had preceded him to London. When he arrived he found they had left having achieved nothing.

[5] Clergyman] gentleman *Ball*.

Church of *England* by themselves.¹ By our Intelligence it seemeth to be a Complication of as much Folly, Madness, Hypocrisy, and Mistake, as ever was offered to the World. If it be understood so on your Side, I cannot but think there would be a great Opportunity of regaining² the Body of the Clergy to the Interest of the Court; who, if they were persuaded by a few good Words to throw off their Fears, could never think of the Pretender without Horror, under whom it is obvious that those Refiners would have the greatest Credit, and consequently every Thing be null since the Time of the Revolution, and more Havock made in a few Months, than the most desponding among the Tories can justly apprehend from the present Management in as many Years. These, at least are, as I am told, the Thoughts and Reasonings of the High-Church People among us: But, whether a Court, in the Midst of Strength and Security will conceive it worth their While to cultivate the Dispositions of the People in the Dust, is out of my Reach.

The Bishop of *Dromore*³ hath never been in Town since he went to his Diocese, nor doth he say any Thing of coming up. He is in good Health.

I was told, a Week or two ago, a confused Story of the Anatomy Lecturer at the College turned out by the Provost, and another put in his Place.⁴ I know not the Particulars; but, am assured, he is blamed for it, both by the Prince⁵ and your Grace.⁶ I take the Provost to be a very honest Gentleman, perfectly good natured, and the least inclined to speak ill of others, of almost any Person I have known. He hath very good Intentions; but, the Defect seemeth to be, that his Views are short, various and sudden; and, I have Reason to

---

¹ In 1713 George Hickes, non-juror and titular Bishop of Thetford, induced two Scottish bishops to take part with him in the consecration of three successors, alleging that all the Catholic bishops of the English Church, except he himself, had died; and these three consecrated two more.

² regaining] regarding *Faulkner*.

³ The Irish Parliament was prorogued on 20 June. Presumably the Bishop of Dromore had then gone down to his diocese; and there remained.

⁴ Pratt, as has been noted, gave inadequate attention to his duties as Provost of Trinity, spending a large part of his time in London. He was also censured by Archbishop King and others for failure to suppress Jacobite intrigues. A doctor who delivered lectures in anatomy was superseded; but, nevertheless, reappointed in the following year.

⁵ The Prince of Wales had been appointed Chancellor of the University in place of Ormonde.

⁶ As Archbishop of Dublin King was one of the visitors.

think, he hardly ever maketh Use of any other Counsellor than himself. I talked to him of this Matter since it was done, and, I think, his Answers satisfied me; but, I am an ill Retainer of Facts, wherein I have no Concern; my humble Opinion is, that it would be much to his own Ease, and of theirs who dislike him, if he were put into another Station; and, if you will not afford him a Bishoprick, that you will let him succeed some rich Country Dean. I dare be confident the Provost had no other End in changing that Lecturer than a Design of improving Anatomy as far as he could; for, he would never have made such a Step as chusing the Prince Chancellor, but from a Resolution of keeping as fair as he possibly could with the present Powers, in Regard both to his Ease and his Interest; and, in Hopes of changing a Post, wherein to say the Truth, he hath been used by Judges and Governors like any Dog, and hath suffered more by it in his Health and Honour, than I, with his patrimonial Estate would think it were worth. Here hath been one *Whittingham*,[1] in an Ordination Sermon, calling the Clergy a thousand dumb Dogs, and treating Episcopacy as bad as *Boyse*,[2] yet, no Notice at all shall be taken of this, unless to his Advantage upon the next vacant Bishoprick, and Wagers are laid already, whether he or one *Monk*[3] will be the Man. But, I forgot myself, and therefore shall only add, that I am with the greatest Respect and Truth, | My Lord, | Your Grace's most dutiful, | And most humble Servant, |

Jon. Swift

Rothschild 2287

Archbishop King to Swift

London Suffolk Street
Novr 22. 1716

R^{vr} Sir[4]

⟨I read yours of the 13 ins^t with great satisfaction, it is not only an advantage to me & you, that there should be a good correspondence

---

[1] Charles Whittingham had been appointed to the prebend of Mulhuddart which brought him into the chapter of St. Patrick's, strengthening opposition to the Dean.   [2] The Rev. Joseph Boyse. See i. 107, n. 3.

[3] Probably the Rev. Thomas Monck, educated at Trinity, who held a living in the south of Ireland (*Alum. Dub.*, p. 585).

[4] Editors prior to Ball, beginning with Faulkner, 1746, viii. 364, print only

between us, but also to the publick, & I assure you I had much ado to persuade people here, that we kept any tolerable measures with one another, much less that there was any thing of a good intelligence, & therefore you judged right that it ought not to be s^d that in some,[1] many months, that I had not received any letters from you.

I do a little admire, that those that shou'd be yor fastest frends shou'd be so opposite to acknowledge the service you did in procuring the 20th parts & first fruits, I know no reason for it, except the zeal I shewed to do you justice in that particular from the beginning, but since I only did it, as obliged to bear testimony to the truth in a matter, wch I certainly knew, & wou'd have done the same for the worst enemy I had in the world, I see no reason why you shou'd suffer because I among others was yor witness. but be not concerned, ingratitude is warranted by modern & ancient custom, & 'tis more honour for a man to have it asked why he had not a suitable return to his merits, than he was overpaid, *bene facere et male audire* is the lot of the best men, if Calumny or ingratitude cou'd have put me out of my way, God knows where I should have wandered by this time.

I am very glad the business of St Nicholas is over any way my inclination was Dr Wall, that I might have joined the vicaridge of Castleknock to the prebend of Malaheidort,[2] wch wou'd have made a good provision for one man, served the cures better & yielded more then to the incumbent, than it can do now when in different hands, but I cou'd not compasse it without using more power over my Clergy, than I am willing to exert, but as I am thankfull to you for your condescention in that affair, so I will expect that these wth w^m you have complyed shou'd shew their sense of it by a mutual return

about one-quarter of this letter, the first three paragraphs and the last two, here enclosed in angular brackets. Ball printed the letter in full, as it appears in the clerical transcript in the manuscript room in Trinity College, Dublin. Lord Rothschild's Library, No. 2287, contains Archbishop King's autograph, which was closely reproduced by the scribe. The letter is here printed from the Rothschild manuscript. At the head of King's letter, which occupies both sides of two leaves, $12\frac{1}{2} \times 7$ in., and the recto of a third, two notes appear in an unidentified hand, one calling attention to the fact that the letter as printed in the 'Works' represents only a 'small Part' of the whole.

[1] some] so *Ball*.

[2] King, writing to Addison, 18 Dec. 1714, speaks of Walls as a grave and good man. When he suggested that Walls should be nominated to the prebend by the Crown it was evidently with the hope that Swift might be persuaded to relinquish his own right and that of his chapter.

of the like complyance, w^n there shall be occasion Such reciprocal kind offices are the ground of mutual confidence and frendship, & the fuel that keeps them alive, & I think nothing can contribute more to our common ease & the publick good than maintaining these between you & wth the Clergy.⟩

As to the zealots here, that you observe are setting up a new Church of England, 'tis true the word is new but the thing has been all along, but kept close wth the utmost secresy,[1] in so much that Mr Dodwell[2] did not know of it & but very few of their own party, but when they supposed their Game sure by the late rebellion, they took courage & spoke out, Dr Hicks[3] was made suffragan Bp of Thetford above 20 years ago & there are others but not known, they have published lately some of the D^{rs} letters, of wch I have got a sight, & they go on such principles as these.

That the pretender is the only true & lawfull King of these Realms & all that have occupied the throne since meer usurpers.

That all persons owe allegiance to the pretender under pain of damnation.

That to own the King is a damnable sin & to pray for him like the sin of Balaam, if he had cursed Israel, that to be present at the prayers made for him is the like sin.

That all the present Bps & clergy, that own the King are in a state of damnation & that all the acts they perform are of no use or benefit to the people, & all people, that join with them are in the case of those that joined with Corah &c against Moses &c.

That they must continue in this case till they do penance, confess their guilt & be admitt[ed] to their respective offices, either by new ordination or laying on of hands for confirmation, as the non-juring church shall think fit.

That many of the English laws are unchristian, such as that patronages are lay fees, that Tiths may become lay fees, that the King is supreme ordinary, that canons can't be made, & oblige without the Kings consent. Quare impedits & prohibitions & lastly appeals to the King in chancery are of the same nature.

That the revolution is founded on the doctrine that Resistance is lawfull, & that Bps may be deprived by meer lay power, wch are

---

[1] For 'secresy' Ball reads 'fury'.
[2] Henry Dodwell, 1641–1711, non-juror and voluminous writer. In 1710 he returned to the established Church.
[3] See p. 222, n. 1. Hickes had died in 1715.

heresyes, & that those who were deprived, suffered that on account of their duty.

That w^n a Kingdom is conquered by a greater power, the subjects are not to make the best conditions with the conqueror they can, but rather suffer all their throats to be cut, than own him.

That it is better to be present at the popish prayers to sts,[1] than at the service w^{re} the King is prayed for.

I suppose that the present Government do not ow many good words to men of such principles, or that there wou'd be much good done by them.

But as to the rest of the Clergy, that own the government, & are under a malediction & excommunication according to these mens opinion the acts, sacraments & prayers void & null, or at best of no use or benefit till they repent & turn Jacobites, they may expect not only a few good words but also many good acts of favour & kindness.

I verily believe the bulk of these never designed to bring in the pretender, but those that were reall in the design, over reached them by persuading them that if they wou'd keep together & stand obstinatly against the King & his ministry they wou'd be able to force him to come into their measures & by endeavouring this, they not only encreased the number of the Jacobites, but brought matters to such a pass, that the Jacobite plot had more than an even lay for Success; in order to this great care was taken to prejudice the people not only against the ministry but likewise against the Kings person & Royal family; vile libels, false absurd & monstrous calumnys & slanders were raised, handed about & fomented, & the danger of the church rung from most pulpits, & at last an actual rebellion raised. 'Tis by these encouragements that these zealots ventured to shew themselves, profess openly their principles, & Dr Hicks book that lay dormant was printed & dispersed about Sep^{tr} 1715 amongst the party.

This by meer accident, that one of them came to be seised last summer, & an abstract of its principles published in the daily curront, as I take it, it has put both y^r universities here & the Bps & clergy in a great ferment, all parties think themselves obliged to answer it & several answers have already come abroad; they seem to have the same sense of it that the clergy wth you have according to yor representation; the court seems mightily pleased with the effect of it & have resolved to cultivate the opportunity of gaining the

---

[1] i.e. Saints.

clergy by all good offices on their part, as being sensible that this is the best & surest method to fix the government on the affection of the people. The Prince manages himself with great civility to all people taking particular care that no reputed Tory shall have cause to complain of his reception.

I have no fear but upon this ground I have observed, that an injured person can easily forgive, & I frequently have observed such forgiveness to be sincere but it is much harder for the wrong doer to be reconciled effectually: now it is manifest that the Clergy have highly injured, affronted & abused the court, but the court has no ways injured them & therefore tho I am morally certain that the court is ready & desirous to forgive them yet I doubt w^{thr} the reconciliation will be so easy on the other hand.

If these Gentlemen shou'd get their pretender it will fare with them as it did with the cavaliers on the restoration of King Charles the 2^d; but to be sure what ever favour they might have at first, the whole tide as it soon did then woud turn into Popery.

As to the Provost's affair I heard a great deal of it, but was resolved not to take it from suspected or insufficient persons & therefore writ to Dr Coghill[1] for an account of it, I recd one from him and saw the provost's account to Mr Molineux[2] & recd a letter likewise from him, I frame no Judgment on the whole because I am not sure, but it may come before me in another way.

Only I can't but take notice of one passage. Mr Molineux has bin & is still the provosts best frend, he writ him a letter with the freedom of a frend, gave him his sense of his proceedings & his reasons, the provost instead of answering the objections & giving such grounds of his acting as might justify himself, falls on some free & easy expressions in the letter & scolds him most heartily, this shews w^t you surmise, that he consults only his own passions in w^t he do's & those are evil counsellors, but Mr Molineux is wiser than to break with him on this account.

The scheme you mention for him[3] is the very thing I had projected & as I believe had secured but how it will be after this, I can't say, but to be sure I will do my endeavour.

⟨We have a strong report that My Ld Bolingbroge will return here

---

[1] Dr. Coghill was one of the members for the University.
[2] Samuel Molyneux, 1689–1728, astronomer and politician. He was at this time secretary to George, Prince of Wales.
[3] 'him' written above the line.

& be pardoned, certainly it must not be for nothing, I hope he can tell no ill story of you.[1]

I think you have enuf for once & I add only my prayers for you & am | R S^r | yor Most Humble | Ser^t & B^r | Will. Dublin⟩

Rothschild[2]

Swift to Archdeacon Walls

Trim. Dec^br 6. 1716.

I never was so weary in my Life as this last Journey and so were my Horses I struck in at Galtrim[3] not being able to go further. I find, Warburton had writt to me not to come here because the small pox was still in this Toun, but it appears there is onely one Woman has it, so I shall continue here. I wonder that Rascall Gillespy does not come down;[4] I beg you will enquire after him, What can the Rascall mean? I go this morning to inspect and settle the Bounds of the Lands at Laracor. Poor Jo is much out of the Graces of every body here.[5] I vindicate him sometimes, and sometimes drop him. This is noble weath^r for you to walk in. I hope the Boys picture is finished by this Time;[6] My Service to Friend Jarvis, I heartily wish him a good Voyage: pray send Sweet-heart some money to keep her alive.[7] Every body here is well, and Mrs Raymd & [Mrs] Chetwood most particularly give you their Service, and the former insists you should come down for a few days and be merry with us this Christmas; do if you can. Remember Sunday Sennight is my Turn at St Patricks— Y^rs | J. S.

Address: To the Reverend M^r | Archdeacon Walls at his House | over against the Blue-coat Hospitall in Queen-Street | Dublin
Postmark: 7 DE
Later endorsement: Dr Swift | Decr 6th 1716

[1] A singularly uncalled for and offensive observation.
[2] Lord Rothschild's Library, No. 2281 (24).
[3] A parish near Trim.
[4] In May Gillespy had talked of intending to be at Trim 'in great haste'. Cf. Swift to Walls, 6 May.   [5] Cf. Swift to Walls, 4 Oct.
[6] It appears by Swift's letter to Walls, 19 Dec. 1716, that a portrait of Walls's son had been painted by Jervas.
[7] Delany (*Observations*, pp. 186–7) describes Swift's cook as a woman 'of a large size, and very robust constitution: and such a face, as in the stile of Ladies, would be termed *plain:* that is, much roughed with small-pox, and furrowed by age'.

Swift to Archdeacon Walls

Trim Dec[br] 13th 1716

I had yrs yesterday. Gillespy has been with me, I have dispatched him and allowed him His Wages and Boardwages to this *very day*. I desire you will take notice of my kindness to him in as strong a manner as You can. I have given him a conditionall note for 22[ll] *odd* money. I forgot to speak to him to deliver up his *Parchment bound Folio* of Accounts, and *all the rest of his Papers* relating to my Livings I here send you a List of the *Bonds*[2] *of Laracor* for 1715 which he sett, and which I ought to have had down with me, and which M[r] Gillespy says *You have*, though *you have not sett down the Sums* of any one of them in y[r] great Book; I cannot imagine how I came to forget bringing down those Bonds of Laracor which Gillespy set for this year, I protest I do not remember any of them, but understood that he said that D[r] Raymd had taken care of all Laracor this year, whereas upon examining he said he had set all those which I here send you a list of, and that you have the Bonds, I will there fore contrive to send some body to you by whom they may be safely returned. I hope the Messenger was with you early yesterday morning with the Map of the Glebe to be purchased;[3] I have given Gillespy a Note upon you for 1[ll] 3[s] which he payd by D[r] Raymonds Order. I shall not have the Countenance to give any more trouble to M[r] Staunton, since we cannot prevail on him to take any Acknoldgment.

As for going to Dromore,[4] the matter is so that I have not a Horse strong enough to carry me there, as I found by coming down here, and I know not where to get one; besides I cannot Stir till I have settled this Business of the Glebe, and likewise till I have contrived some means to order my Affairs now Gillespy hath left me: For I must have some body to get in my Arrears, and my present dues. Pray pay your self what I ow you, and let me not be troubled with yr lowsy Debt; for I believe you are as great a Beggar as I.

The Tyths let by Gillespy at Laracor for this year 1716 of which he says you have the Bonds are as follows. Some of the Tenants may

---

[1] Lord Rothschild's Library, No. 2281 (25).
[2] For the farm of the tithe.
[3] From Percival. See Swift to Walls, 4 Oct. 1716.
[4] Subsequent letters show that Stella, Rebecca Dingley, and Gossip Doll spent that Christmas with Bishop Stearne at Dromore.

perhaps be changed but you will know the Denominations of the Lands.

	Sett in the year 1715		
Numb^r 1.	Part of Knockbeg. Nicholas Dolon	8. 5.0	6- 0-0
2.	Part of Summerstown. Mich. Heaps & Pat Connel		1- 1-6
3.	Part of Summerstown. Jam Murphy		1- 1-6
4.	Part of Summerstown. Patr. & Morrice Murphy.		9-15-0
5.	Part of Summerstown. John Fay	1:14:3	1-10-0
6.	Clondogan. Archibald Alexand^r	16:16:0	16- 4-0
7.	Part of Summerstn Patr. Connel & Hugh Reily	2-12-0	2-10-0
9.	Part of Summer hill. George Bowsman		0-15-0
14.	Both Guennets. Mr Wm Steer	11: 5:0	10- 0-0
17.	Part of Dingan Rich^{dr} Babington	0.14.0	0-13-6
20.	Summer hill. Mr George Dennis	11- 0-0	10- 0-0
23.	Part of Summerhill John Fagan		2-10-0
25.	Laracor, Stokestown, Reedstown M^r J^n & Mark Tews	16. 0.0	20- 0-0
			82- 0-6[1]

These are bonds Gillespy says you have, and these are the Summs they were let for in the year 1715 as I find in your Book, perhaps they may not be sett now in the same manner. For Instance, *Summerstown* which is now in five Parcells you may have for this year in one; and Tenants names may be changed; however you will easily see whether they be the same Tythes, and compare the Summs.

The Doctor & Mrs Raymond insists to have you whipt down this Christmas upon Condition, that you and Mrs Brent will put 2 *dozen* Bottles of Wine into a large Hamper and send it down before you: 1 *dozen* of Gross Lee and the other Dozen of the Wine last drawn: but with a nick to distinguish, and I will likewise have a dozen of ten shilling Wine for vulgar Company, that must be marked too

Each Bottle must be bundled in its own bitt of Hay.—

Gillespy has a Horse of mine in my Stable, which he has so lamed as it will be never good for any thing; Therefore I have *given it to*

---

[1] Ball suggests that the figures in the second column represent possibly the rate for the preceding year.

him, and will have it removed immediatly from my Stable, where it has ruined me in Hay and Oats. You will see Gillespy on Saturday as he says.

I wish you would put the Provost[1] in mind of doing something for himself in case the Bp of Killalla should dye.[2] | Service to Friend Jarvis.

Address: To the Reverend Mr Archdeacon | Walls, at his House over against | the Blue-coat Hospitall in Queen-street | Dublin
Postmark: ? 14 TRIM
Later endorsement: Dr Swift | Decr 13th 1716

Rothschild[3]

Swift to Archdeacon Walls

Trim Dec^{br} 16th 1716

Your messenger came by noon when I was at Laracor[4] but I had Your Post Letter before, and am disappointed in not having the hon^r of Paddy's Company. To morrow we all go to Mr Percivalls[5] and if there be no Difficultyes started, I will send Will on Tuesday (who shall be a Wittness) Dr Raymond desires you will keep the Trim Charity money till one of the Church wardens waits on you to receive it, and gives you an Acquittance. Whatever you agreed to pay yr Messenger, let him have it, and I give him a Shilling into the Bargain. You will know more I hope on Tuesday night. I am sorry you disturbed yr self so early this morning as 4 a clock, I doubt you were ready to sleep at Y^r own Sermon. All here give your Service and are angry you mention nothing of Your coming down. Pray put up those Bonds you have of Laracor 1716 which Gillespy sett, and

---

[1] Dr. Benjamin Pratt.

[2] William Lloyd, Bishop of Killala, friend of Stella and Swift, had died two days before.

[3] Lord Rothschild's Library, No. 2281 (26).

[4] Swift was writing on a Sunday.

[5] To execute the lease of the land taken from Percival for the glebe. On 5 Dec. the Committee of the Board of First Fruits had ordered the deeds to be sent down to be executed, with a direction that the Vicar-General of the diocese of Meath and two credible witnesses should see and attest the due perfection thereof.— Ball.

return them to me by the Messenger I shall send; for now is my Time of gathering Money if I can. adieu

Address: To the Reverend M^r | Archdeacon Walls
Later endorsement: Dr Swift | Decr 16th 1716

Rothschild[1]

Swift to Archdeacon Walls

Trim Decbr. 17. 1716

Every thing is done as you ordered, and Will Geddes goes with this to morrow morning early;[2] Mr Percivall keeps his own part of the Deed, and I send you the other with the Lease to give to Dr Coghill.[3] I thought the Board[4] had no more to do with it, however they can now have it on Wednesday[5] to do what they please. I think all your particulars have been observed. Will is a Witness and can swear what you please.

Pray send by Will (and see him put them up carefully,) the Bonds which Gillespy set for Laracor this year 1716: because I want the Money. Will is to wait Your Orders about his Return.

Some people here say there ought to be a Memoriall sent in order to have the Deeds Registered[6] but since you onely say a Witness sworn is sufficient, & that Mr Percivall says so to, I have not done it.

Address: To the Reverend | Mr Archdeacon Walls
Later endorsement: Dr Swift Decr 17th 1716.

[1] Lord Rothschild's Library, No. 2281 (27).
[2] The lease had been executed that day.
[3] Judge of the Prerogative Court.
[4] Of First Fruits.
[5] Swift was writing on Monday.
[6] The reference is to the system of registering deeds in Ireland which was established early in that century. As Swift found subsequently, a memorial reciting the contents of the deed is necessary, and one was lodged on 5 Feb. following (*Registry of Deeds*, Bk. 18, p. 119). The deeds were witnessed by Anthony Raymond, Jonathan Preston, a notary public, and Swift's servant, William Geddes, who made the affidavit accompanying the memorial.—Ball.

Swift to Isaiah Parvisol

[18 December 1716.][2]

Mr Parvisol

As you go into Town[3] pray call upon Archdeacon Walls and desire him to send immediatly to Mrs Brent, that she would cover the Hogsheads of wine with Straw and Litter to prevent their being hurt by the Frost, not onely the three *Hogsheads* in my Cellar, but those two which are in the *Bishop's* Cellar: I hope the Paper will be sent to us by Mr Meight[4] so as to sent by us by nine to morrow morning, therefore you need not stay, but desire Mr Walls to be at home at nine or ten a Clock to morrow morning, for we design to send the Map to him to be sent to Dr Coghill or his Clerk.

Tuesd morn   Yr Asst | J. Swift

Leave [this] line for the Archdeacon if he be not [at home].[5]

Address: For Mr Parvisol.

Rothschild[6]

Swift to Archdeacon Walls

Trim. Decbr. 19th 1716

I hope Will got safe and timely to You yesterday; I have since been thinking to propose it to you whether it might not be proper to order him to ride to the Deanry,[7] and there give notice to some of the principall Farmers (that is to say those who ow most, of whom you may give him a List both as to their Names & habitations) that

---

[1] Lord Rothschild's Library, No. 2281 (28).

[2] This letter was probably written on Tuesday, 18 Dec. 1716, while negotiations for the purchase of the glebe lands were continuing.

[3] Dublin.

[4] For 'Mr Meight' Ball reads 'the Mite'.

[5] The paper is torn, and three words of the postscript are missing.

[6] Lord Rothschild's Library, No. 2281 (29).

[7] By 'the Deanry' Swift means land in the possession of the Dean of St. Patrick's in the southern part of the county of Dublin. In his letter to Archbishop King of 16 July 1713 he alludes in the same sense to 'my Deanry'. An ancient castle, formerly used for a country residence of the Deans, stood on the property.

Gillespy hath left me, and that I require those who have their money ready would on the next Market day pay their money to You who have their Bonds, and can give them Receits on the back of them; Will may likewise find out old Barnwell[1] & say the same thing to him, & let old Barnwell inform the Farmers. This will be usefull that the Farmers should know, and also help me to get a little money, who have not a Farthing to bless my self. Do not be frighted as if I intended to constitute You my Receiver, but you know I am at a loss what to do. I wish also that Will had a List of those Deanry men who ow me Arrears, to give to Barnwell, who might tell those People, that I shall proceed against them if they will not come and clear their old Debts. The Gentlemen of the Deanry might be likewise desired to send their money by any servant who comes up to Market, and you might draw up a Paper of Instructions pursuant to this for Will to give to Barnwell. I suppose he knows or can find out where Barnwell lives; and you must let Will have what Shillings he shall want to maintain himself, while he stays, for I could only give him eighteen pence. If you think what I say materiall, you will please to do it, or alter it in whatever Method you think fit.

I wish with the Bills of Laracor for this Year 1716, you would send me in a Paper separate, the Bills of Arrears for Laracor of which I find a list in y^r Book, from Parvisol; to see if I can pick up any thing out of them.

Is Jarvis gone? Has he finished Jacky's Picture?[2] Will you come down this Christmas, and send some Wine before you? Have you payd y^r self your own debt, out of the 70^{11}? When Jarvis is gone you must take Jacky's Picture home.

Do you know that one of the great Packets you had for me was nothing but a scoundrell sermon of that Rascall Smedley,[3] sent me

---

[1] The Barnewalls, an Anglo-Norman family, descended from the De Dernevals of Brittany, had long settled in co. Meath. For several generations they held important judicial positions in Ireland. In 1461 Robert Barnewall was created Baron of Trimleston. One of their family seats, Drimnagh Castle, was adjacent to the Deanery property; but long before the time at which Swift was writing it had passed out of their possession, and the family was only represented by persons in humble circumstances. See *D.N.B.*

[2] See p. 228.

[3] Jonathan Smedley, born 1671, was probably responsible for the famous verses (*Gulliveriana*, p. 77), said to have been affixed to the door of St. Patrick's Cathedral at the time of Swift's installation as Dean. The 'scoundrell sermon' was presumably that preached by Smedley in London in this year in his capacity of an army chaplain. It was printed in London. Although in addition to a com-

either by himself or some other dog on purpose to put me to charge and Vexation? another large one was from the Arch-Bp, and it is a civil Letter and friendly except in one Article, for which I will be revenged by an Answer;[1] he says tis confidently reported that L^r Bolingbroke is returning, that the Consideration must be to discover secrets, and his Grace hopes that My L^d has no ill things to say of me, By which the Arch-Bp plainly lets me know that he believes all I have s^d of my self and the last Ministry with relation to the Pretender to be Court Lyes. My Service in y^r next, to our Dromore Friends. I hope they are well.[2] I writ a Thew to measure out my Ground and prepare for some other things relating to it:

Address: To the Reverend | Mr Archdeacon Walls | Queenstreet
Later endorsement: Dr Swift | Decr 19th 1716

The Library, Armagh

Swift to Archbishop King

Trim Dec^{br} 22^d 1716.
My Lord.[3]

I have been here some days to finish the Purchase of a Glebe for my Country Parish.[4] I have prevayled on a Gentleman to alienate 20 Acres for 200^{ll} to be had from the Trustees of the first Fruits. He then sets me twenty Acres[5] for 999 years. Upon the last 20 Acres, I am by Agreement to lay out the s^d 200^{ll} in Building, and to give the Gentleman immediatly 55^{ll} out of my own Pocket, and to pay

mon Christian name Swift and Smedley's lives ran a somewhat parallel course, it is doubtful if they were ever personally acquainted. Smedley was educated at Trinity College, Dublin (*Alum. Dubl.*, p. 756), took orders, and was presented to the small country living of Ringcurran, co. Cork. In 1718 he elicited the favour of Lord Townshend, Secretary of State, and was presented to the deanery of Killala. This he resigned in 1724; and on 24 June of the same year was instituted Dean of Clogher. He developed violent Whig proclivities; and an irrepressible hatred of Swift and Pope was manifested in the miscellanies of *Gulliveriana*, 1728. Pope, thereupon, gave him a place in *The Dunciad*, ii. 291–4. In 1729 Smedley sailed to seek his fortune in Madras. See *Poems*, pp. 360–1; *D.N.B.*; *H.M.C.* Eleventh Report, part iv, p. 130.

[1] See p. 228, 22 Nov. 1716; and Swift's answer in his letter of 22 Dec.
[2] Bishop Stearne, the St. Mary Ladies, and Gossip Doll.
[3] This is the sixth of the autographs preserved in the Record room at Armagh.
[4] See p. 218.   [5] Ball has '23'.

him 14[11] per anñ for ever which is nearly the value of the whole 40
Acres; These last 20 Acres after I have built and improved, I design
to leave my Successors; who will then have 40 Acres of good Glebe,
with House Gardens &c for 14[11] per anñ.[1] I reckon to lay out of my
own Money about 250[11], and so to be an humble Imitator of your
Grace. longo intervallo. This Expedient was a Project of Dr. Raymond Minister of this Town to deal with a Jew[2] who would not
lessen his Rent-roll to save all the Churches in Christendom; Dr.
Coghill[3] and everybody else approves the Thing, since it is a good
Bargain to the Church, a better to the Gentleman, and only a bad
one to my self; and I hope Your Grace will have the same Thoughts.

Since I came down here I received the Honor of a large and therefore an agreeable Letter, from Your Grace of No[br] 22[d] I have reason
to think my self hardly dealt with those of the side in Power, who
will not think I deserve any Place in your good Thoughts, when they
cannot but know, that, while I was near the late Ministry I was a
common Advocate for those they called the Whigs, to a degree that
a certain great Minister told me I had always a Whig in my sleeve;
neither did I ever fayl to interpose in any Case of Merit or Compassion, by which means severall Persons in England, and some in
this Kingdom, kept their employmts, for I cannot remember that
My Lord Oxford ever refused me a Request of that kind. And
for the rest, Your Grace may very well remember that I had the
Honor of corresponding with you during the whole Period with some
degree of Confidence. Because I knew that Your Grace and I had
wished the same Things, but differed only in opinion about the
Hands that should effect them. It was on Account of this Conduct
that certain warm Creatures of this Kingdom then in London and
not unknown to Your Grace had the Assurance to give me broad
hints that I was providing against a Change, and I observe those
very men are now the most carefull of all others, to creep as far as
they can out of harm's way.

The System of the new Zealots which Your Grace hath extracted,
must be very suitable to my Principles who was always a Whig in
Politicks. I have been told that upon the Death of the last Non-
juring Bishop,[3] Dodwell and his followers thought the schism at an
end. My Notion was that these People began to sett up again upon

---

[1] The arrangement for the additional land was not carried through.
[2] Percival.
[3] Ken.

despair of their cause by the Rebellion being brought to an end, else their Politicks are if possible worse than their Divinity. Upon the whole it is clear that the Game is entirely in the Hands of the King and his Ministers, and I am extremely glad of Your Grace's Opinion, that it will be played as it ought: Or if we must suffer for a name, however I had rather be devoured by a Lyon than a Rat.

That maxim of the injuring Person never forgiving the person injured is, I believe true in all Particulars, but not of Communityes. I cannot but suppose that the Clergy thought there were some Hardships, and Grounds for Fears, otherwise they must be very wicked or very mad: to say more would be to enter into dispute upon a Party subject: A Dog or a Horse knows when he is kindly treated; and besides a wise Administration will endeavor to remove the vain as well as the real Fears of those they Govern.

I saw the Provost yesterday in this Neighbourhood, and had some little talk with him upon the Occasion of the Bp of Killala's Death;[1] I believe he would accept of the Deanry of Derry, if Dr. Bolton the Dean should be promoted but I said nothing of it to him; I believe he hath wrote to Mr Molyneaux, I find, since he cannot be trusted with a Bishoprick, that he desires to leave his Station with as good a Grace as he can, and that it may not be thought that what he shall get is onely to get rid of him. I said in generall that such a Circumstance as things stood was hardly worth the Quiet of a Man's whole Life, and so we parted, onely with telling him, I intended to write to Your Grace, in answer to a Letter I had from you.

I should be sorry to see My Lord Bolingbroke following the Trade of an informer, because he is a Person for whom I always had and still continue a very great Love and esteem.[2] For I think as the rest

[1] See p. 231, n. 2.

[2] King's previous letter to Swift, written from London and dated 22 Nov. 1716, ended with allusion to a 'strong report' that Bolingbroke was returning to England and would be pardoned. In continuation King ungraciously expressed the hope that he would have no 'ill story' to tell of Swift. Part of this letter, including the final reference to Bolingbroke, was first printed by Faulkner, 1746, viii. 364–6. Faulkner followed it immediately with a reply from Swift, dated 16 Dec. 1716, comprising the latter part of the above letter. A draft of this portion of the letter, in Swift's handwriting, preserved in Lord Rothschild's Library (No. 2287), is dated 'Trim December ye 22^d | 1716'. Swift's letter to Archdeacon Walls of 19 Dec. 1716 makes it quite clear that at the time of *that* letter he had not replied to King, although he tells Walls that he will be 'revenged by an answer' to the Archbishop for his observation upon Bolingbroke and himself. Faulkner's date must be wrong; and the letter printed by Ball, dated 'December 16' (ii. 348–9),

of Mankind do, that Informers are a detestable Race of People, though they may be sometimes necessary. Besides I do not see whom his Lordship can inform against, except himself. He was 3 or 4 days at the Court of France while he was Secretary, and it is barely possible he might have entred into some deep Negotiation with the Pretender, though I could not believe him if he should have sworn it because he protested to me that he never saw him but once, and that was at a great distance in publick at an Opera. As to any others of the Ministry at that time, I am confident he cannot accuse them; and that they will appear as innocent with relation to the Pretender, as any who are now at the Helm; And as to my self, if I were of any Importance I should be very easy under such an Accusation, much easyer than I am to think Your Grace imagines me in any danger, or that Ld Bolingbroke should have any ill Story to tell of Me; He knows, and loves, and thinks too well of me, to be capable of such an Action. But I am surprised to think Your Grace could talk or act or correspond with me for some years past, while you must needs believe me a most false and vile man, declaring to you on all occasions my Abhorrence of the Pretender, and yet privately engaged with a Ministry to bring him in, and therefore warning me to look to my self and prepare my defence against a false Brother coming over to discover such Secrets as would hang me. Had there been ever the least Overture or Intent of bringing in the Pretender during my Acquaintance with the Ministry, I think I must have been very stupid not to have pickt out some discoveryes or Suspicions; and tho I am not sure I should have turned Informer, yet I am sure I should have dropt some generall Cautions, and immediately have retired. When People say things were not ripe at the Queen's death, they say they know not what Things were rotten, and had the Ministers any such Thoughts they should have begun 3 years before, and they who say otherwise understand nothing of the State of the Kingdom at that time. But whether I am mistaken or no in other Men, I beg Your Grace to believe, that I am not mistaken in my self; I always professed to be against the Pretender, and am so still; and

is only part of the letter of 22 Dec. Swift's autograph letter is, as above, continuous written on a folded sheet making four pages. The paragraph beginning 'I should be sorry' is a fresh paragraph on the second page of the letter, which continues on the third page, concluding with the formal ascription. The whole letter, as above, is covered by the one address. Editors, including Ball, misled by Faulkner, have divided the one letter into two.

this is not to make my Court, (which I know is in vain) for I own my self full of Doubts, Fears and Dissatisfactions, which I think of seldom as I can; Yet, if I were of any value, the Publick may safely rely on my Loyalty, because I look upon the coming of the Pretender as a greater Evil than any we are like to suffer under the worst Whig Ministry that can be found. I have not spoke nor thought much of Party these 2 years; nor could any thing have tempted me to it now, but the Grief I have for standing so ill in Your Grace's Opinion. I beg Your Grace's Blessing, and am with great Respect | My Lord | Your Grace's | Most dutifull and | most humble Serv^{nt} |

Jonath: Swift

Address: To His Grace, the Lord | Arch-Bishop of Dublin, at His | Lodgings in Suffolk-street | at Mrs Stoak's[1] near | St James's | London:

B.M. Add. MS. 39839

Swift to Miss Esther Vanhomrigh

[? December 1716]

I dined with the Provost[2] and told him I was coming here because I must be at Prayers at 6. He said you had been with him and would not be at home[3] this day, and went to Celbridge to morrow. I said, I would however go try: I fancy you told him so, that he might not come to night. If he comes, you must piece it up as you can, else he will think it was on purpose to meet me; and I hate any thing that looks like a Secret. I can not possibly call after Prayers, and therefore came here in the afternoon while People were at Church hoping certainly to find you. I am truly afflicted for poor Moll, who is a Girl of infinite value, and I am sure you will take all possible Care of her, and I hope to live to see the sincerest Friendship in the World long between you. I pray God of Heaven protect you both. and am entierement —— four a clock

Endorsed: 7th

[1] Ball has 'Stoat's'.
[2] Provost Pratt was appointed Dean of Down in June 1717. The date of this letter is uncertain; but it has here been conjecturally placed in Dec. 1716. This letter was not printed by Scott, 1814, either in vol. xvi or vol. xix.
[3] There is an obliteration before the words 'at home'.

Rothschild[1]

Swift to Archdeacon Walls

Trim. Dec[br] 23. 1716

I had all Your Dispatches by Will, and have thanks to give you upon a thousd Particulars;[2] *Pray ask Gilespy how* it comes to pass that the severall Articles of Summerstoun came this Year to not above 9[11]–6[s], and in the Year 1715 were near 17[11]—[3] Indeed I find he has sett every Article but scurvily; His Method was to ask how it sett last year, & then without further examining to ask the same Rate, and so fall lower as they could agree.

You are to know that when he came first to me he proposed to take a Farm on the Deanry from Whitshed the Judge,[4] and did so, as a thing of much Advantage to me; You know I lost 22[11] last year by it. Now he writes to Dr Raymd and me to know whether I would yet hold it, which I am against; unless I could *be sure of a Tenant*, and without Loss or Care; it would certainly be of use to have a few Acres there, but a Rent of above 40[11] p anñ is not to be thought on: However I desire you will *speak to Mr Gilespy to defer giving* up the Farmer till Monday or Tuesday sennight: At which time a Man will go from hence and meet Gillespy at Tallow[5] or Dublin, (but rather at the former) and view the Land and talk with him first, and afterwards with you, and advise whether it be proper & safe to hold the Land or no. Let Gillespy settle whether it can be Monday or Tuesday Sennight, or whether at Tallow or Dublin, that he can meet the Man, & *what Hour of the* Day, and Place, & the Man shall be exact. Rather I say again at Tallow, or if in Dublin at your House or the Deanry, just as he & you shall settle.

Pray let M[rs] *Brent buy a Hamper to hold* 2 dozen Bottles, and send by the first Conveniency a Dozen of gross Lee, and a Dozen of the

---

[1] Lord Rothschild's Library, No. 2281 (29).

[2] The reference is to a letter not forthcoming in reply to Swift's letter of 19 Dec.

[3] See Swift to Walls, 13 Dec.

[4] William Whitshed, who had been appointed Chief Justice of the King's Bench in Ireland upon the accession of George I. He was later, at the trial of Edward Waters, the printer, in 1720, to earn Swift's enmity, further intensified at the trial of John Harding, 1724. See *Poems*, p. 236; Ball, *Judges in Ireland*, ii. 80–81, 116–18, 186–7. His family appears to have been connected with the Clondalkin neighbourhood.

[5] Tallaght, written Tallow by Swift, is a village near Clondalkin.

last drawn wine *marking one dozen*[1]—Come down & see us if you can. Let the Wine be left at yr House. The Memorial is signed & shall be sent up. I cannot leave this place till I have divided my Ground & done some other things, and when I leave it, I believe it will be for Rochforts, for I cannot get to Dromore without another Horse, unless I walk it, which I will not promise to do. If you can govern yr Tongue say nothing of the Picture to Gossip Doll—

the Lettrs are just going & I believe I have forgot to say 20 things but I was so ill last night with a Head ake, I could not write a Line.

Address: To the Reverend Mr Archdeacon | Walls, at his House over against the
Blue-Coat Hospitall in Queen-street | Dublin
Postmark: Illegible.   *Stamp:* TRIM

Rothschild[2]

Swift to Archdeacon Walls

Trim Decbr 27. 1716

I had yrs this morning by yr Country Messenger, which put me out of pain, for I apprehended mine of last Sunday miscarryed.[3] I will contrive some way or other that a Messenger shall see you and Mr Gilespy either Saterday or Monday. Tis plain there is some great Mistake about the Tythes of Summerstown, which Percival and another Man have the Accounts of as sett for 20ll, and Gillespy's Bonds are but 4, which amount to under 10ll, pray let this matter be set right. It is thus in his Account

Part of Summerstown Michl Heaps & P. Connell - - -	1- 6-0
Part of Summerstn Jam. Murphy- - - - - - - - -	1- 6-0
Part of Summerstun Jon. Gray - - - - - - - - -	1-14-6
Part of Summerstn Jn. Greney - - - - - - - - -	5- 0-0
	9- 6-6

So that there wants 10ll 13s 6d to make up the Sum.

Pray mention to Gillespy as a piece of Favor that he hath had the setting money for all these bonds, which comes to near 4ll.

Mr Gillespy as Will tells me is every Saturday in Smithfield

[1] See Swift to Walls, 13 Dec.
[2] Lord Rothschild's Library, No. 2281 (30).
[3] The letter of 23 Dec. Swift was writing on Thursday.

Market or Corn market, if you will send Paddy to enquire for him, and fix him at Your House on Monday evening, where Mr Proudfoot (one whom I shall partly employ) will attend you. Pray let Paddy enquire diligently and ten to one but he will find him—Pray come down for 2 or 3 days; and have the Wine ready, at yr House & I will send for it.

Address: To the Reverend M^r | Archdeacon Walls, at his House | in Queen-street, over against the | Blue-coat Hospitall | Dublin
Postmark: ? DE   *Stamp:* TRIM
Later endorsement: Dr Swift | Decr 27th 1716

Rothschild[1]

Swift to Archdeacon Walls

Trim Dec^br 30th 1716

Last Post you sent me a Letter from our Friends at Dromore, full of Reproaches for my not writing to them or going down there: Pray in your next to Gossip Doll or the *Bishop let them tell* the two Ladyes, that I will write to them in a Post or two, but for coming down, tis impossible for me unless I gett a Horse; which I am laying out for on all Sides in vain. Neither can I stir till I have settled the Business of the Land with Mr Percivall, who lyes sick and is slowly recovering. We have I know not how, let slip the Opportunity of sending a Messenger to meet you and Gillespy on Saturday.[2] We expect a Lett^r from you, this Post, but I shall be at Laracor before it comes, and I will leave this for Dr Raymond to finish. We have found out the Secret of Summerstown, for examining a Farmer we found he had not given a Bond, which yesterday we took from him for *11^ll*. It was careless in Mr Gillespy to omitt this, and yet make no mention of it to us.

On second thoughts I stayd at home, and receivd y^rs; and Mr *Proudfoot will* be with You to morrow night. Gillespy's Excuse about Summerstown is a very sorry one; for he never said a word of it to You or me. You now have to adjust the matter about the Farm, or whether you would take it if you were as I. I cannot bear the thought[3]

---

[1] Lord Rothschild's Library, No. 2281 (31).
[2] Swift's letter to Walls 23 Dec., which was written on Sunday.
[3] thought] thoughts *Ball.*

of a heavy Rent without I am secure of some und^r Tenant to pay it. In that case, it will be useful no doubt to have a bit of Land to dray my Tythes to on Occasion.

You will direct and send away the inclosed.

Address: To the Reverend M^r | Archdeacon Walls | Dublin
Later endorsement: Dr Swift | Decr 30th 1716

Rothschild[1]

Swift to Archdeacon Walls

Trim Janry. 3^d. 17$\frac{17}{16}$

I had yrs of the 1st which makes me remember to write You a happy new Year. One passage in y^r Lettr is odd; You say *if* I write to the Ladyes it will be too late; Did not Proudfoot give you a Lett^r with one inclosed to Mrs Dingley, and I hope You have sent it to save my Credit. I approve all You say about the Farm. I cannot think of medling with paying Rent. I wish you would send us our Wine, and come down and drink part of it. I am heartily sorry for poor little Dolly.

I will come to Toun as soon as I can settle the Affair of the Lease with Mr Percivall, and have the Lines of Division &c, drawn upon the Land, which meets with a hundred Delays.[2] This would be a very good Place for you to keep y^r Christmas in, for there are no Cards nor Diversions, onely you cannot smoak or drink Ale. If the Bp of Down be in Toun, I would draw on him for 60^ll, which he was to pay me at Christmas, for which I hold his Bond in my *Cabinet, and can direct* You to it,[3] If he be in Toun I wish you would be so kind to tell him so, and see whether he be ready to pay the Money, and I would return it to pay a Debt in Eng^d.

The Silly Toryes here are just as you describe those in Dublin, very sanguine, and feeding themselves with foolish Imaginations.[4]

Since you complain of spending y^r Rheam of Paper, I wish you were Arch-Bishop of Rheimes to Re'mburse you.

[1] Lord Rothschild's Library, No. 2281 (34).
[2] See Swift's letter to Archbishop King, 22 Dec. 1716.
[3] Edward Smith, Bishop of Down, was a former Dean of St. Patrick's. This money transaction related to the Dean's lands at Kilberry. See Swift to Walls, 28 Mar. 1717.
[4] On the ministerial crisis caused by the removal of Lord Townshend.

I wonder how Gillespy's Northern Modesty became him when you charged him about the Summerstown bond.

I despair of getting any odd Acres from Gillespy or the Judge,[1] & I am sure the former will get rid of it as soon as he can—Y^{rs}—

Address: To the Reverend M^r | Archdeacon Walls, at his House | over against the Blue-coat | Hospitall in Queen-street | Dublin
Postmark: ? IA   *Stamp:* TRIM
Later endorsement: Dr Swift | Jan. 3^d 17$\frac{16}{17}$

Rothschild[2]
Swift to Archdeacon Walls

[? January 1716–17]

This Letter is to go to the Bp of Clogher on Saturday and should have gone last Night, if I had not thought you might be such a Fool as to copy it to day, and send it to the Bp of Dromore on Saturday likewise—If you will come this morning and do it here, we will dine together and get the Provast or Worrall—I send you the Print also, which may go with y^r Copy to Dromore, and because you will not understand some things in the Letter (that are known well enough in London) I will explain them to You, & to send the Notes with it to Dromore—If there be a greater fool than I who took Pains to write it, it must be he that Copyes it out. Adieu.
Thursday morn
8 a clock.

Addressed: To the Reverend | Mr Archdeacon Walls
Later endorsed: Dr Swift | 1716

Rothschild[3]
Swift to Archdeacon Walls

[? January 1716–17]

Your Acquaintance may possibly be a very honest man and a good Preacher, but he seems to have the least Wit, Manners or Discretion

---

[1] Whitshed.
[2] Lord Rothschild's Library, No. 2281 (34).
[3] Lord Rothschild's Library, No. 2281 (33).

in his Jesting, of any Pretender to it I ever knew, I mean except he were drunk when he writt the inclosed, as in charity to his understanding I would willingly believe. All I can further pick out of his Note is that he does not intend to preach for me to morrow, therefore I must beg you to provide somebody; for I have got so terrible a Cold that I shall not be able I fear so much as to read at the Altar. Adieu—. I dine with you to day, you know.

Saturday morn.

8 a clock.

Pray shew the inclosed to Mrs Johnson, to see if she be of my Opinion.

No address: later endorsement: | 1716.

4805

Erasmus Lewis to Swift

London Jan^{ry} 12. 171⅞

About two months ago I sent you a very long Epistle, & was in hopes, you wou'd either have made us a Visit or have let us heard from you, since you have done neither we must flatter our Selves that you'l be better the New year than the former.

Our friend Prior having not had the vicissitude of humane things before his Eyes is likely to end his dayes in as forlorn a State as any other Poet has done before him, if his friends doe not take more care of him, than he has done of himself, therefore to prevent the evil wch we see is coming on very fast, we have a project of printing his Solomon & other Poetical works by Subscribtion, one Guinea to be paid in hand, & the other at the delivery of the Books;[1] he, Arbuthnot, Pope, & Gay, are now with me & remember you, it is our joynt request that you will endeavour to procure some Subscriptions, you will give your Receipts for the money you receive, & when you return it hither you shall have others in lieu, there are no papers

---

[1] On his return from Paris, Mar. 1715, Prior was impeached and ordered into confinement. In 1717 he was exempted from the act of grace; but was, nevertheless, soon set at liberty. He was in sore financial difficulties, and his friends busied themselves in promoting the publication of his poems by subscription. As subsequent letters show Swift engaged himself in collecting subscribers. Ball reads 'book'.

printed here, nor are[1] any Advertisemts to be publish'd, for the whole matter is to be manag'd by friends in such a manner as shall be least shocking to the dignity of a Plenip^ry.

I am told the ArchBp of Dublin shews a Letter of your's reflecting on the high flying Clergy,[2] I fancy you have writ to him in an ironical Stile, & that he wou'd have it otherwise understood, this will bring to your mind what I have formerly said to you on that figure, pray condescend to explain this matter to me.

The removal of my Ld Townshend[3] has given a little Spirit, but that will soon flag if the King, at his return does not make further changes, what Measures his Ma^ty will take is uncertain; but this we are very sure of, that the division of the Whigs is so great, that, morally speaking, nothing but another Rebellion can unite 'em. Sunderland, Stanhope, & Cadogan are of one side; Townsend, Walpole, Orford, Devonshire, & the Chancellor,[4] on the other, the latter seem at present to be strongest, but when the former appear with a German reinforcem^t they will undoubtedly turn the balance.[5] they are both making their Court to the Tory's, who I hope will be a body by themselves, & not serve as recruits to either of the other two. Ld Townsend's friends give out that his disgrace is owing to his refusing four things, vizt, to keep up the Army, Repeal the Limitations of the Succession Act, to send money to Germany for carrying on a war against Sweden, & to attaint Ld Oxford. When Ld Sunderland comes over he will probably cry whore again & endeavour to Saddle Ld Townsend in his turn, for these reproaches now are like that of Jacobitism in former reigns. We are told that Ld Bolingbroke has permission to stay in France, notwithstanding the late Treaty, provided he retires from Paris.[6]

Address: To The Rev. Dr. Swift | Dean of St. Patrick's | Dublin | Ireland
Endorsed by Swift above the address: Jan. 12—1716[17] M^r L—

(*and*): Mr Lewis Jan^r | 12th—1716

[1] 'are' omitted by Ball.

[2] His letter of 13 Nov. 1716.

[3] Charles, second Viscount Townshend, was, on the accession of George I, appointed Secretary of State for the northern department. He was dismissed from this office on 15 Dec. 1716, and offered the viceroyalty of Ireland. See Mahon's *Hist. of England*, 1853, i. 232–53.

[4] Earl Cowper.

[5] On 15 Apr. 1717 Stanhope was promoted First Lord of the Treasury and Chancellor of the Exchequer.

[6] Bolingbroke received no comforting assurances, remaining for some time in a state of uncertainty.

Archbishop King to Swift

Suffolk street London Jany 12ᵗʰ 1716[–17]

Revᵈ Sir

I have yours of the 22ᵈ of December last, but have been so much out of order by a most violent Cough and Cold that I could not sooner acknowledge your Kindness. I do not clearly apprehend your purchase of the Glebe for the country benefice, it seems to me, that you have given 200ˡˡ for 20 Acres, and have laid out that 200ˡˡ in building on another 20 Acres, or are obliged to lay it out, and besides this it will cost you 250ˡˡ and after all you must pay 14ˡˡ per annum for the last 20 Acres of land, and yet pay 14ˢ per acre, tho' the other 20 Acres are free to the Church, if I take the case right, the gentleman has indeed played the Jew, the Church is a Gainer, but you have certainly had hard measure, but the gentlemen of Ireland are so deadly fond of land and love so extremely to live alone on the earth, that whoever would get a scrap for a Clergyman must go into their own terms, tho' never so unreasonable. If some of your Successors should be of the humour of some that I have known, they will let your house go out of repair, the rent run on 10 or 12 years, and then the landlord will re-enter for want of distress. Pray take some care, if possible, to prevent such an accident.

As to the part of my letter that related to my Lord Bolingbroke,[1] you took it too seriously; for I assure you, when I wrote that letter, I neither believed that Lord Bolingbroke would return, or that he would tell any ill story of you. I was of opinion, and advised by several of my friends that were in a Contrary party, to be quiet, give no disturbance, but to wait *reversum fortunae*—and if they had done so, they would soon have found that it was not in the nature of that Gentleman to be Constant in any one way, but many of them took all possible ways to fix her, and if she be long of coming about, let them remember tis their own fault. If I can't be of the same opinion with my friends, I can easily bear their dissenting.

There is one thing I heard often whilst it was practised, but suspended my belief till I have had it confirmed by above ½ a Dozⁿ concernd in it, and it is that the Duke of Ormond, and severall of the

[1] In this letter King is clearly answering one letter received from Swift, that of 22 Dec., dealing firstly with the purchase of glebe, and secondly with the unkindly observation upon Bolingbroke. Ball's footnote, ii. 362, is mistaken.

late Ministry used to closet gentlemen of Interest and posts, and Quare was will you come into the Quare measures, if they desired to know what those measures were, no answer was given, but the Question repeated, with a stern accent, and if they did not engage had no farther countenance but were turned out, I have a value for the Queens Memory on which this seems to reflect, and wish some-body would explain the meaning of it to me, for the matter of fact is not to be doubted. I never believed you for the Pretender, but remember that when the surmises of that matter run high, you re-tired, which agrees with what you say you ought to have done in that case.

The absence of his Majestie, and the unsettlement of the Govern-ment of Ireland,[1] has kept me here longer than I designed and I am afraid to very little purpose. If I had thought his Majestie would have stayed so long, I would have immediately gone to Ireland. I recommend you to Gods good care and am | Rev⁰ Sir | &c &c |

W. D.

There is a foolish profane letter here in yʳ name but you may be easy under it. It is universally condemned, and thought to be writ by a Jacobite and Deist.

Dr. Swift

Rothschild[2]

Swift to Archdeacon Walls

Trim. Janʳʸ. 13ᵗʰ 1716–17

I am glad Yr People came home safe; I suppose they have nothing in their Mouth but Maghherlin.[3] It was Doll's doings coming home so soon; How did the Adventure of the Picture pass;[4] I suppose You spoilt it by some Circumstance or other, or was Gossip Doll

---

[1] Lord Sunderland had accompanied the King to Hanover. The remark about the 'unsettlement of the Government of Ireland' relates to the appointment of Townshend as Lord Lieutenant. Townshend, however, never went to the country.

[2] Lord Rothschild's Library, No. 2281 (35).

[3] The episcopal house of Dromore (see i. 148) was situated in the parish of Magheralin.

[4] See p. 228, n. 6.

not so pleased as You expected; my service to them all; and I hope to see them in a few days; Pray stop Mrs Johnson's mouth with 14^{ll}: and if she or Mis^{trs} Dingley want as much more let them have it if they will give a Receit. You are but a scurvy Receiver with y^r 10^{ll}: talk to me of hundreds.

I have heard of Woodward; & wondred he never applyed before. I shall this Year follow Dr Raymonds Directions at a venture, whose strong side is employing able fellows to sett his Tythes. I should be heartily glad of the Provost's Success;[1] We were positively told that the Bp of Derry is dead;[2] but you say nothing of it, any more than of my Aunts death, which is certain.[3] I wonder what sort of Will she hath made: we think she hath left all in her Power to the Fosters. Dr Raymond desires to know something of the Bp of Killalla's will, if you can tell him any thing about it. He had some hopes that his Daughter was not forgot.[4] I suppose it will come to nothing. I read to the D^r what you say about the Bp of Clogher; and he must wait; I saw a printed Libel against my self call^d a Circular Letter &c;[5] It seems to be good for nothing, was it writ in England or here? Mr Percivall still keeps his Bed,[6] and I wait to finish with him, after which I will come to Toun.

I hope my Visitation will pass to morrow in form; Or was it last Monday? I have forgot.

I was at Mr Ludlow's[7] almost a Week, and stayd 3 days longer than I intended, by means of a broken Shin, which is now well; I returned thence last Thursday,[8]

---

[1] See p. 237.

[2] Bishop Hartstonge died on 30 Jan.

[3] Swift's uncle William married four times, and it is to his fourth wife (Elizabeth Naylor) that he refers. Her will was dated 21 Nov. 1716, and was proved on 18 Jan. following. Some of the legatees were close relatives of John Forster, Recorder of Dublin, a prominent Whig, who, on the accession of George I, was appointed Chief Justice of the Common Pleas. Politics seem, to some extent, to have governed the division of the aunt's property.

[4] Bishop Lloyd made no mention of Raymond or his family in his will.

[5] See the postscript to King's letter to Swift of 12 Jan.

[6] Swift to Walls, 30 Dec. 1716.

[7] Peter Ludlow, a collateral descendant of the regicide, and grandfather of the first Earl Ludlow, was then residing at Ardsallagh, between Trim and Navan, to which he had succeeded through his wife, a member of Viscount Gormanston's family. He had sat for Dunleer in Queen Anne's last Parliament, and was returned some years later as one of the representatives for the county of Meath.

[8] The 8th.

We have the Wine, and find it marked, I imagine the Mark is upon the New—Y^r Lemmons they say are good; but I have seen none of them. I believe the pun of the Northern Shoemaker is yr own; and that you are grown a profligate Punner, for it is our Custom to invent Storyes for the sake of a Pun.

I know not whether to be glad or sorry that Jack Grattan has or has not the Gout. Did Gossip Doll play at Ombre the first night of her Return, or did she s[t]ay for the Second? Poor Mrs Dingley was like to be robbed and overturnd[1] seven times. And so I take my leave.

Is Gillespy's Horse gone from my Stable; and have I done with him for ever?

I had a Lett^r from Ned Synge[2] this Post inclosed in Yours, in a most silly starched affected Style Somebody should go upon the Leads of the Deanry House and see whether all be right there.

Address: To the reverend Mr Archdeacon | Walls at his House over against | the Blue-coat Hospitall in | Queenstreet | Dublin
Postmark: 14 IA   *Stamp:* TRIM
Later endorsement: Dr Swift | Jan 13th 1716

Rothschild[3]

Swift to Archdeacon Walls

Jan^ry. 24th 1716–17

I am not assured wheth^r I can be with You before the beginning of next Week; My Friend Charleton[4] is still with us by our Persuasion. We heard yesterday[5] from Warburton, who appears to be very happy with his new Wife; and finds her Portion will be still greater than he expected; and that upon the Death of an old Uncle, one Jinny, there will be hopes of some new Addition. I am very sorry Mrs Johnson had preintelligence of it, The Jest was quite

---

[1] overturnd] murdered *Ball.*

[2] Edward Synge, son of Edward Synge, who had been enthroned Archbishop of Tuam on 7 Nov. 1716. The son, a prebendary of St. Patrick's, and Chancellor, became in time, through Whig interests, Bishop of Ferns and Leighlin.

[3] Lord Rothschild's Library, No. 2281 (36).

[4] Chaplain to the Duchess of Ormonde (see p. 166, n. 1). He is thus recorded in *Alum. Dubl.* 'Charleton, Arthur, Pen. (Mr Harvey, Lisburn), June 13, 1700, aged 15; s. of Andrew Clericus; b. Mallagh. Sch. 1702. B.A. Vern. 1704. M.A. Aest. 1707.' His relation, Chiverton Charleton, had died in 1716.

[5] 'yesterday' is written above 'last night', which has been scored through.

spoiled. We hear the Toun of Magherafelt is a very good one in a fine Country[1]—I hope they will take care *to air my* Room and bed: I intend to make 2 days Journy of it. I will provide *somebody to preach* here next Sunday, if I come home my self; so that Mr Warburton need be in no pain. And now I think you must look out for a *good Curate*, and he must preach well, or else it will not do after such a Predecessr. I suppose I shall have offers enough, but I shall be hard to please: My Service to the Ladyes, & Gossip Doll | Adieu

[*Postscript in another hand*]: The Dr[2] writes to Mr Warburton at yr House, & desires it may be sent to him as soon as possible & he must buy a pair of *black Shirt* sleeve buttons for the Doctr.

Address: To the Reverend Mr Archdeacon | Walls at his House over against | the Blue-coat Hospitall in | Queen-street | Dublin
Postmark: Illegible.   *Stamp:* TRIM
Later endorsement: Dr Swift | Jan 24th 17$\frac{16}{17}$

Rothschild[3]

Swift to Archdeacon Walls

Trim. Janry. 27. 1716–17

I had both yrs relating to poor Jo.[4] and Care was taken to send His Brother in law to Toun last night which is all we could do. I have hardly time to say a word to you, because I am just come from Laracor, and all are at Dinner here but I. You may expect me I dont know what day, for Warburton coming down I shall have a mind to stay with Him. I wish you would step down here and be merry 3 or 4 days, & we will all come back Monday sennight, & Dr Raymd with us My service to Gossip & the Ladyes

Pray enquire for a Curate, & get me a large Choice, I must have

---

[1] Swift's curate at Laracor, Thomas Warburton, had been appointed to the rectory of Magherafelt, in the diocese of Armagh, possibly through Swift's influence with Primate Lindsay. He held the living until his death in 1736. See Leslie, *Armagh Clergy and Parishes*, p. 364; and Landa, *Swift and the Church of Ireland*, pp. 38–39.

[2] Raymond.

[3] Lord Rothschild's Library, No. 2281 (37).

[4] Researches into the problem of the longitude were beginning to derange Joseph Beaumont's mind. In 1722, after a temporary recovery, he became hopelessly mad.

a good one, & soon, or I must return my self on Saturday sennight, for we are much out of Parsons here

Address: To the reverend M^r | Archdeacon Walls, at his House | over against the Blue-coat | Hospitall in Queen Street | Dublin
Postmark: Illegible.   *Stamp:* TRIM
Later endorsement: Dr Swift | Jan. 27th | 17$\frac{16}{17}$

Rothschild[1]

Swift to Archdeacon Walls

Trim. Janry. 28th 17$\frac{17}{16}$

Parvisol's Son the Collegian goes up to Town, and a Fellow follows him on Foot to bring back the horse. Parvisol desires you would give that Fellow the Bills of Rathbeggan for 1716, and the Arrears of the last or any other year for Rathbeggan: Safely sealed and bound up; provided you think the Fellow looks like one that will be carefull of them; For Parvisol goes up to Dublin in 2 or 3 days, and as he goes he will receive what money he can get there & pay it to You—

Jo. is come home, and protests to me he is not mad, and appeals to you; but we happen to be all against him. He talked to me a good while.

a Gentleman here shewd us the Finest large Oranges with Teats (the Ladyes know what I mean) that ever I saw, for 12 pence a dozen; I wish you would send us a Dozen such by the Fellow—

Address: To the Reverend Mr Archdeacon | Walls | Dublin
Later endorsement: Dr Swift | Jan 28th 17$\frac{16}{17}$

Rothschild[2]

Swift to Archdeacon Walls

Trim. Janry. 31st. 1716–17

I had yr last I am surprised to think Curates should be so hard to get. Mr Warburtons sudden going is very inconvenient to me.[3]

---

[1] Lord Rothschild's Library, No. 2281 (38).
[2] Lord Rothschild's Library, No. 2281 (39).
[3] His departure to take over his new living at Magherafelt.

I shall be able to get a Preacher for Sunday sennight, but then I must come down if I cannot provide my self in the intermediate twelve days—Parvisol s^d there was a Case on purpose for the Papers;[1] however you were on the secureer side tho the Fellow s^d Mrs Johnson would be engaged for him. Mr Charlton stays here with me till Monday & then we all part & the D^r[2] designs to go with me; but I will make it 2 days. You must be taking y^r own Methods about Tobacco, instead of sending Mrs Brent to the old place & so the D^r will not take a whif of it. I am glad You sent me the Letters one was from the A. Bp. tothr from Mr Lewis.[3] I am endeavoring to persuade Jo that he is mad. I have given him 20^shill. to buy a Perewig. If you can get a Coach to come six mile as far as Clonee[4] to fetch us for a Crown or thereabouts we will be there by one or 2 a Clock, the Coach may be there as soon as it please; if you cannot, send us word by Saturdays post. My Horses are the D^rs. If you take a Fancy to come you may, & if the Coach could come to Forbes[5] we would then dine with him. My service to Gossip & the Ladyes: all services here to you & them   turn over

[*Postscript in another hand*] the Dean is obliged to stay here a monday so the coach must come a Tuesday this I tell you by order . . . | yrs |

                                        A: Raymond.

Address: To the Rever^d | Mr Archdeacon Walls
Later endorsement: Dr Swift | Jan. 31st 17$\frac{16}{17}$

Rothschild[6]

Swift to Archdeacon Walls

Trim. Febr. 3^d 17$\frac{17}{16}$

There might be some little difficulty in explaining our last Letter, but I thought such wise Persons as you and y^r Coinspectors might easily get over it. The Matter is onely thus that a Coach and one pair of Horses be sent to Clonee (but six miles) on Tuesday next to be

---

[1] See previous letter.   [2] Raymond.
[3] Both dated 12 Jan.
[4] A village lying between Trim and Dublin.
[5] Forbes's rectory of Dunboyne was a little nearer Trim than Clonee.
[6] Lord Rothschild's Library, No. 2281 (40).

there by twelve a clock at noon (and not at midnight to avoyd mistake) and therefore keep yr four Horses, and yr *All the way to Trim* for yr Maherlin Folks, they are above our Reach.

The Doctors Horse[1] will go back from Clonee, and if you could get some hedge interim intermediate temporary Curate to trip down on Tuesday for a few weeks till I were better provided for, it would be very convenient both for the Doct[r] and me; but it must be such a one as we may cast off without any Consequence.

M[r] Lightburne[2] writt to me a very foolish Letter to be my Curate, but I do not intend it. He will not answer my Ends & I had rather serve him anothr way. The Doctor will provide a place for whoever comes down, if any little Parson desires onely to take the Air for a fortnight till the Doctor returns here, it would be a Help.

You tell us nothing of yr new L[ds] Justices, Conolly and others.[3] Turn over

P.S. We have been considering the Matter, and broke open the Letter, and upon second Thoughts we conceive it will be more convenient not to stay till Wednesday but to come on Tuesday, as we at first intended. (Vide the beginning of this Letter) M[r] Warburton leaves us to day & M[r] Charleton and I are just walking to Laracor, so that if I have a Letter from you I shall not answer it.

[*A second postscript—in Raymond's hand*] I wish you may get one to come down a Tuesday tho it be but for ten days, or a fortnight for fear we may be called upon to do occasionall services &c | y[rs]

A. Raymond.

Address: To the Reverend M[r] Archdeacon | Walls, at his House over against | the Blue-coat Hospitall in | Queen-street | Dublin
Postmark: Illegible.   *Stamp:* TRIM
Later endorsement: D[r] Swift | Feb 3[d] 17$\frac{16}{17}$

[1] i.e. Raymond's.
[2] Stafford Lightburne had married a relative, Hannah Swift. Nevertheless, Swift held him in no fond regard. Later, however, Lightburne served him as a curate from 1722 to 1733. See Leslie, *Biographical Succession Lists of the Clergy of the Meath Diocese*, ii. 446; and Landa, *Swift and the Church of Ireland*, pp. 38–39.
[3] On the appointment of Lord Townshend as Lord Lieutenant, in addition to Archbishop King, the Speaker, William Conolly, and the Lord Chancellor, Alan Brodrick, who had been raised to the peerage as Lord Midleton, were appointed Lords Justices.

Swift to Archbishop King

Dublin, March 2, 1716–17.[1]

My Lord,

Your Grace's Letter[2] was a long Time before it reached me; for I was several Weeks in the Country, dispatching the Affair of the Glebe, which, however, is not yet quite finished. Your Grace doth rightly conceive the Nature of my Purchase, and that I am likely to be 200*l*. poorer for it, only I shall endeavour to lose by Degrees, which is all I have for it. I shall endeavour, as much as I can, to prevent the Evil you foresee, of my Successors neglecting my Improvements, and letting them all go to Ruin. I shall take the best Advice I can, and leave them to be Fools as well as Knaves if they do so; for, I shall make so many Plantations and Hedges, that the Land will let for double the Value; and, after all, I must leave something to Fortune.

As to what your Grace mentions of a Practice in the late Reign, of engaging People to come into the Queen's Measures, I have a great deal to say on that Subject, not worth troubling you with at present, further than that I am confident those who pretend to say most of it, are conscious their Accusation is wrong: But, I never love myself so little as when I differ from your Grace; nor, do I believe I ever shall do it, but where I am Master of the Fact, and your Grace hath it only by Report.

I have been speaking much to the Provost about the Deanery of *Derry*,[3] or whatever other Employment under a Bishoprick may be designed him upon these Promotions.[4] I find Dr. *Coghill* hath been upon the same Subject with him, but he is absolutely positive to take nothing less at present; and his Argument is, that whatever shall be given him now, beneath the Station his Predecessors were called to, will be a Mark of his lying under the Displeasure of the Court, and that he is not to be trusted; whereas, he looketh upon himself to have acted with Principles as loyal to the present Government, as any the

---

[1] Faulkner (1762) and subsequent editors, previous to Ball, date this letter 22 Mar. The content of the letter and King's acknowledgement of the 12th show that the true date was 2 Mar.

[2] King's letter of 12 Jan.

[3] Swift's letter to King of 22 Dec. 1716.

[4] St. George Ashe had just been translated from Clogher to Derry.

King employs. He doth not seem to dislike either the Deaneries of *Derry* or *Down*,[1] but is persuaded it will reflect upon his Reputation; and, unless it could be contrived that he might have some Mark of Favour and Approbation along with such a Preferment, I believe your Grace may be assured he will not accept it. I only repeat what he says to me, and what I believe he will adhere to.

For my own Part, who am not so refined, I gave my Opinion, that he should take what was given him; but, his other Friends differ from me, and for aught I know, they may be in the Right; and, if the Court thinketh it of Consequence, that the present Provost should be removed, I am not sure but a Way may be found out of saving his Credit, which is all he seemeth to require; altho' I am confident, that if he were a Bishop, the Government might be very secure of him, since he seemeth wholly fallen out with the *Tories*, and the *Tories* with him; and I do not know any Man, who, in common Conversation, talketh with more Zeal for the present Establishment, and against all Opposers than he. The only Thing he desireth at present in his discoursing with me is, that no Proposal of a Deanery should be at all made to him, but that he may go on as he is until further Judgement shall be made of him by his future Conduct.

I thought proper to say thus much to your Grace, because I did not know whether you and he perfectly understood each other.

I hear your Grace intends, this Spring, for the *Bath*. I shall pray for the Good of the Church, that you may then establish your Health. | I am, with the greatest Respect, | Your Grace's most dutiful, | And most humble Servant, |

J. Swift.

Among other Things the Provost argued, that Dr. Forster[2] was promoted to a Bishoprick from being a Fellow; and therefore he must conclude, that offering him a less Preferment, is a Mark of Displeasure, with which Circumstance he is determined not to leave his present Station.

---

[1] Respectively held by John Bolton and Ralph Lambert.

[2] Nicholas Forster, brother of John Forster, Chief Justice of the Common Pleas. He was elected a fellow of Trinity, 1694; became a D.D. in 1707; and, after the Hanoverian accession, was successively appointed to the bishoprics of Killaloe and Raphoe.

Archbishop King to Swift

London March 2^d 1716[-17]

Revd Sir

I have been informed that Mr. Duncan by a fall off his horse is like to make a vacancy in St. Bride's,[1] I know not how that may be, but I am told there will be 3 competitors for it, Doctor Howard, Mr. Dopping[2] and Dr. Drury. As to the last I consider that he has the prebend of Tassagard, and if he should be removed to St. Bride's, he would carry that prebend with him, which would leave the cures of Rathcoole and Kilteel[3] naked and without support, and therefore I hope you and the Chapter will not think it convenient to elect him, as to the other two, Dr. Howard and Mr. Dopping they are Brothers[4] and I will not interpose between them, either of them will be very grateful to me, if you and the Chapter be of the same opinion.

In yours of the 13th of Novr last, you gave me your opinion of the Provost very justly in my Judgment, and intimated that you thought it would be much to his own ease, and theirs who dislike him, if he were put into another station, and if the government would not afford him a Bishoprick that they wou'd let him Succeed some Rich Country Dean, I have laboured that point, and brought it to bear as I hope, and I had this further reason to proceed in it, that he had signified to me that he was ready to come into my Scheme, he now may I believe have an offer of Derry or Down, but I hear he is fallen off, and scruples to take any thing but a Bishoprick to which with my good will, I would never promote any man that had not gone through the degrees and served in proper stations in the Church.

I may trust you with it as a secret, that neither of these Deans had been removed at this time, if it were not to make room for him, and if he refuse the offer, he may assure himself, he will have Cause to repent it, I think it is Tacitus who observed of Governments, *si non*

---

[1] The church of St. Bride lay a little to the north-east of St. Patrick's Cathedral, and the incumbency was in the gift of the Dean and Chapter. The Rev. James Duncan, to whom the Archbishop refers, had held the living for more than twenty years. He baptized Swift's biographer and cousin, Deane Swift (Carroll, *Clergy of St. Bride*, p. 16).

[2] See p. 202.

[3] A parish in the county of Kildare, not far from Rathcoole.

[4] Dopping married a sister of Howard.

vis ut bene tibi sit per eos facient ut male sit. I hope you will give him better advice, and contribute to the execution of your own Scheme, which as it will be a kindness to him and a benefit to the Society for which I can expect nothing from the Government or Parliament whilst he is at the head of it, so it will be a great ease to, | Reverend Sir, | &c &c

W. D.

Dean Swift

Faulkner 1762

Swift to Archbishop King

[Dublin] March 9, 1716–17

My Lord,

I had Yesterday the Honour of a Letter from your Grace,[1] wherein you first mention Mr. *Duncan*'s Accident, who, as it falls out, is quite recovered, and they say is since better of his *Asthma*: I believe, whenever he dieth, I shall be in some Difficulties, although I am wholely indifferent who may succeed him, provided he may be a deserving Person; unless I might say, that my Inclinations are a little turned to oblige Mr. *Dopping*, on Account of his Brother, for whom I have always had a very great Esteem. It will be impossible for me to carry any Point against that great Majority of the Chapter, who are sure to oppose me whenever Party interferes; and, in those Cases I shall be very ready to change my Nomination, only chusing those I least dislike among such as they will consent to; wherein, I hope, I shall have your Grace's Approbation.

About a Week ago, I wrote to your Grace in Relation to the Provost. My Lord Bishop of *Dromore*, Dr. *Coghill*, and I were yesterday using our Rhetorick to no Purpose.—The Topick he perpetually adheres to is, that the Court offers him a Deanery; because, they look upon him as a Man, they cannot trust, which, he says, affecteth his Reputation. That he professeth to be as true to the present King, as any Person in Employment: That he hath always shewn himself so: That he was sacrificed by the Tories in the late Reign, on Account of the Dispute in the *College*, and other Matters: That he publickly argues and appears against the same Party now, upon all Occasions, and expecteth as little Favour from them, if ever they should come

[1] 2 Mar.

into Power, as any man now in Employment. As to any Hints dropped to him of any Danger or Uneasiness from Parliament or Visitation, he declareth himself perfectly safe and easy; and if it might not affect the Society, he should be glad of such Enquiries, in order to vindicate himself: That he should like the Deanery of *Down* full as well, and perhaps better, than the Bishoprick of *Dromore*[1] provided the Deanery was given him in such a Manner, and with some Mark of Favour and Approbation, that the World would not think he was driven into it as a Man whom the King could not trust; and if any such Method could be thought on, he would readily accept it: That he is very sensible he should be much happier in the other Station, and much richer, and which weighs with him more, that it would be much for the present Interest of the *College* to be under another Head: But, that the Sense of his own Loss of Credit prevails with him above all Considerations; and, that he hopes in some Time to convince the World, and the Court too, that he has been altogether misrepresented.

This is the Sum of his Reasoning, by all I could gather after several Conversations with him, both alone and with some of his best Friends, who all differ from him, as, he allows, most of his Acquaintance do. I am no Judge of what Consequence his Removal may be to the Service of the *College*, or of any Favours to be shown it. But, I believe, it would be no difficult Matter to find a Temper in this affair: For instance (I speak purely my own Thoughts) if the Prince[2] would graciously please to send a favourable Message by his Secretary, to offer him the Deanery, in such a Manner as might answer the Provost's Difficulty. I cannot but think your Grace might bring such a Thing about: But that I humbly leave to your Grace.

My Lord Bishop of *Dromore* received Letters Yesterday from your Grace, and the Bishop of *Derry*,[3] with an Account of his succeeding to *Clogher*, of which I am sure all Parties will be exceeding glad. I wish your Grace a good Journey to the *Bath*, and a firm Establishment of your Health there. I am, with the greatest Respect, | My Lord, |

Your Grace's | Most dutiful, and | Most humble Servant,

J. Swift.

Not knowing but your Grace might be gone to the *Bath*, I have

---

[1] Bishop Stearne had been translated to Clogher in the room of St. George Ashe.

[2] The Prince of Wales, Chancellor of the University.   [3] Ashe.

mentioned something of the Provost's Affairs in a letter this Post, to my Lord Bishop of *Derry*.

King's Letter-book

Archbishop King to Swift

London March 12, 1716[–17]

Revd Sir

Yours of the 2^d inst gave some trouble to me to find that after I had a prospect of bringing to perfection that Scheme which all his friends came readily into and advised, and to which as I understand he himself Consented, he should now go about to make objections to it, and to mar it. I ought to deal ingenuously with you, and tell you my mind honestly, I believe the Provost to be a good man, and to mean well, and that he may be of good use in the Church, but withal it does not appear to me that either his Heart or his Talent lies in governing a College, if so, then why should he force his genius, and obstinately refuse what will certainly better suit that genius? as for his interpreting it a slight to take any thing less than what was offered his predecessors, I answered that Dr. Huntington, after he became Provost, took a plain rectory and left the College, and though 4 Bps were then vacant none of them were offered him.[1] But suppose the Court be jealous of him and therefore will not give a Bishoprick, will his refusing a deanery two or three hundred pounds better than the provostship contribute to remove that jealousy? Will it be either for his interest, or reputation, to be continually watched in a post, that exposed him more to the view and observation of his enemies than any other in the Kingdom? You know he has many enemies, and that the Gentlemen of the Kingdom have great resentments against him, and will not easily be prevailed on to lay them aside. In what position then must he and the Society be, if he provoke the Court and Government by refusing what they believe a favour? In the Canon law *malitia plebis* is one Reason of removing

[1] Robert Huntington, 1637–1701, fellow of Merton College, Oxford, spent over ten years in the Near East acquiring a large collection of oriental manuscripts. In 1683 he accepted the provostship of Trinity College, Dublin. He resigned in 1692, retiring to a country living in Essex. On 20 July 1701 he was consecrated Bishop of Raphoe (*Fasti Eccl. Hib.* iii. 353); but died within a few weeks. *D.N.B.*

an incumbent, and for my own part I must own it to be a most uncomfortable thing for a man to be in a Station where he is generally disliked, whether there be a reason for it or no. This is certainly the Provost's case, and what good can he expect to do in such circumstances?

If it be asked why do not they then make him a Bishop? I answer for my own part, that I would never consent to make any head of a house a Bishop without passing through other degrees, I think he is in a fair way to be one, when he has a deanery of a Thousand pounds, but if he think to force himself into a Bishoprick by obstinately sticking to a post that is not thought proper for him, he may perhaps find himself mistaken, for which I should be very sorry. As to reputation, I will engage he will lose none by it, perhaps he doth not know what his circumstances as to that matter are at present. I believe you remember your former Letter to me, but these things ought to be handled tenderly. I think it will be much for his Reputation to do a thing, though cross to his humour, which will Certainly be for his ease, and the Generality believe for the good of the Society of which he has been so long head, he that humbles himself shall be exalted, and I am persuaded he will find his account in this conduct with all good men, and others are not valuable. If I did not think this of moment, I would not have troubled you with so long a letter, and I assure you it is with regard to the Provost, as well as to the Society, that I write this. I do not love to be trifled with, and if the Provost break his word with me after signifying himself satisfied with this scheme, it will lessen, to be sure, my opinion of him.

I have done what business I had to do in London, and nothing keeps me from the Bath but the very ill weather, if that mend, God willing, I shall go on Friday. In the mean time I am, Revd Sir, | Yrs &c |

W. D.

Dean Swift

King's Letter-book

Archbishop King to Swift

London March 21st 1716[-17]

Revd Sir

I Rec^d y^rs of the 9 inst., and find by Mr. Duncan's Recovery that we shall have time enuff to adjust the affaire of St. Bridgets. I think his life is entirely to be ascribed to providence for I am assured none else is, or would be, concern'd to preserve it, I hope if God grant me life I shall be able to provide for one of the Candidates before the vacancy happen and that will take away all competition, I assure you I am as well inclined to take care of Mr. Dopping as you can desire me to be.

As to the Provost he is very much mistaken if he think it on account of party, that his friends desire to remove him, No 'Tis with a view to make him easy and put him in a post in the Church that I take to be more honourable than the Provostship, which gives no place at all, is more profitable & may fitt him for better preferment in the Church, for which in my opinion the College government rather disqualifys a man, and let me assure you that he has no other way to secure the favour of the Court or to give satisfaction to the Kingdom, than by accepting a better post when offered and more suitable to his Tallent, we have had a Specimen of his conduct in Governing the College for about seven years, & I think it now full time to try him in another post, sure he can't be so partiall as to think he has governed well, and I declare for my own part that without regard to any principle or party I should be for wishing him another post, and all that I am acquainted with, whether friends or enemys to him or indifferent are of the same opinion, and he ought to be thankfull to them that have so effectually recommended to the Court, as to obtain this favourable remove for him, it is intended and meant as a favour and if he will not take it as such, he will, if I be not mistaken, [have] reason to repent it, it was a thing proposed to me by his best friends, and he promised me under his hand to come into it, and if he deceives me and them, I shall know what to think of him. Mr. Molyneux[1] has writ to him in stronger terms than you propose, what effect it will have I can't tell, but assure yourself the deanery of Down will not go abegging.

The weather promises at last to be some what favourable, which will put me on my Journey to the Bath (God willing) to morrow, I hope I shall hear from you and that you will tell me something of what passes on your side to | Revd. S^r | Y^r &c

                                   W. D.

Dean Swift

[1] See p. 227, n. 2.

Swift to Archdeacon Walls

28 March 1717

Pray if Mrs Brent has sent my Stockins, send them by the Bearer,[2] or if not, and if the bearer will call again, send to Mrs Brent for them. I writt this day to the Bishop—The bearer gives you this to morrow night, and returns on Saterday. I had a Letter which I suppose you sent me, from Mr Deacon the Tenant of Kilberry who tells me, the Bp of Down had ordered him to pay me last Michaelmas Rent, which is 60ll for which you know I have his Lordships Bond.[3] Deacon desires further time till his Garrons[4] get flesh. I suppose the Bp has pd his own Rent and puts the Leavings upon me. I shall write to Deacon, & let him know I will not be so used. Tell the Bp of Clogher,[5] that Dilly Ash[6] had a slovenly way of urining as he lay in bed; I desire to know what sort of stone that was; make him guess; but I will tell you; It is Lay-pis Lazily Lapis lazuli:—

My service to Gossip & the Ladyes & Duty to the Bishop I am yr | &c

Thursday night

Mar. 28. 1717

Jo is as fain to know how le Mannian & Simmerian received you, and your Excuses for him.[7]

Address: To the Reverend Mr | Archdeacon Walls at his | House in Queen-street | Dublin

Later endorsement, in another hand to that of earlier letters: March. 28. 1717

---

[1] Lord Rothschild's Library, No. 2281 (41).

[2] Swift was again staying at Trim.

[3] See Swift to Walls, 3 Jan. 1716–17.

[4] A small type of horse. The word is of Gaelic derivation.

[5] Stearne.

[6] Dillon Ashe had died in May 1716. He was buried at Finglas on the 18th of that month.

[7] The allusion is apparently to some instance of Beaumont's derangement of mind.

Swift to Archdeacon Walls

Trim. Mar. 30th. 1717.

I shall not have a Stocking to my Foot, unless Mrs Brent sends them to you to morrow, and you put them in the Bishop's Bag on Tuesday,[2] I write early, because I go to Laracor, (make April Fools of the Ladyes to morrow). I have been three Times with Jo upon my new Estate, and three times I could not fix on the Spot where the House is to be.[3] Tantae molis erat &c. Mr Burn will be in Toun next Term to receive my Money and give you Ease. I had yours last night. One of the inclosed was from A. Bp. Dubl. all about the Provost and his taking the Deanry.[4] (Pay Sweetheart[5] her board-wages) Pray desire Clem Barry[6] to negotiate by all means & Methods for poor Prior's Subscriptions, a Guinea subscribed, and another Guinea on delivering the Book.[7] Let him get others to take Subscriptions as well as himself. I have had fresh Entreatyes from Engld about it just before I left you. Remember my Turns at St Patricks. Let the Bp[8] tell the Arch. Bp Tuam[9] that he takes me down with him, and hinders me from appearing at the Arch Bp of Dublin's Visitation, which holds. Or rather I think he need not, it is a sort of Condescension I am not obliged to, but it might be done occasionally, or let alone. When the Post comes in I will add a Postscript. Last night about 10 we were called out to see an Appearance in the Sky like what was last Summer, Streams shooting from the North, and the Night very light as at Full moon, but it differed from that of last year in this, that the rays which shot flew like lightening and flasht all over the Sky and darted as we agreed, like the Rays from a Looking glass when you turn it against the sun, as Boys do out of a Window with a sudden quivering motion, it was very amusing for about half an Hour. The Rays that flew about were distinguishable

[1] Lord Rothschild's Library, No. 2281 (42).

[2] Stearne was going to Clogher, and Swift was to accompany him.

[3] Swift's intention was to extend and improve the glebe at Laracor. The house which he built was referred to in a visitation report of 1723 as 'a neat cabin'. See further Landa, *Swift and the Church of Ireland*, pp. 37, 40, and notes.

[4] See p. 260, King to Swift, 12 Mar.

[5] Swift's cook. [6] See p. 171, n. 1.

[7] The volume in which Swift was taking so much interest finally appeared as a large folio *Poems on Several Occasions*, 1718.

[8] i.e. Stearne. [9] i.e. Synge.

like a white thin Cloud, and spent themselves soon, sometimes they ran in a circular motion, Dr Raymond says, it was like the Quivering of the Flame over burned Brandy when that Flame is just going out. This Appearance is for Sweden as Mrs Peggy says, as that of last year was for the Pretend^r.[1] Was this Appearance observed in Dublin?

I received the Bps Lett^r as I was going to Church: I find he does not think of going till Thursday,[2] I expect next Post to know from him what Road he is to take.

As to the Gown, it was never intended for you, but however I believe it will not fit me; pray pay Mr Craven what Charge he is been at; he says it is onely 2^s 2^d and the Porter that brought the Box. Young Man, the Gown & Cassock will smooth of themselves: You must pay what they cost in London, & then you will save Carriage & Custom, for Craven passed them as old Goods. I believe 6^11 English will be the Price.

My humble Service to Gossip Doll & the Ldyes Dr Raymd & she give you all theirs, & Jo his Respects.

Address: To the Reverend M^r | Archdeacon Walls, at his House over | against
the Blue-coat Hospitall | in Queen-street | Dublin
Postmark: ? AP   *Stamp:* TRIM
Later endorsement: Dr Swift | May 30th 1717[3]

Faulkner 1762

Swift to Archbishop King

Magherlyn,[4] *May* 1, 1717.

My Lord,

Your Grace's Letter of *March* 23d was brought to me at *Trim*, where I went a Month ago, to finish my Lease, and Purchase for my Country Parish. In some Days after, I met my Lord Bishop of *Clogher* at *Drogheda*, by Appointment; we went together to *Clogher*, where he was enthroned, and after three Days came to this Place, where his Lordship is settling every Thing against the coming of the new Bishop,[5] who is expected here next Week. My great

---

[1] Charles XII attacked Norway in 1716. The second allusion is to the Jacobite rising of 1715.

[2] This letter was written on Sunday.

[3] The endorsement dates the letter incorrectly.

[4] Cf. Swift to Walls, 13 Jan. 1716–17.

[5] Dean Lambert who had been appointed Stearne's successor at Dromore.

Business at *Clogher*, was to seduce his Lordship to lay out 2000*l.* in a new House, and, for that End, we rode about to find a Situation. I know not whether I shall prevail, for he hath a Hankereing after making Additions to the old one, which I will never consent to, and would rather he would leave all to the Generosity of a Successor.[1] My Notion is, that when a Bishop with good dispositions happens to arrive, it should be every Man's Business to cultivate them. It is no ill Age that produceth two such; and, therefore, if I had Credit with your Grace, and his Lordship, it should be all employed in pushing you both upon Works of Publick Good, without the least Mercy to your Pains or Purses. An expert Tradesman makes a few of his best Customers answer not only for those whom he gets little or nothing by, but for all who die in his Debt.

I will suppose your Grace hath heard of Mr. *Duncan*'s Death. I am sure I have heard enough of it, by a great Encrease of disinterested Correspondents ever since. It is well I am at free Cost for Board and Lodging, else Postage would have undone me. I have returned no Answer to any, and shall be glad to proceed with your Grace's Approbation, which is less a Compliment, because I believe my Chapter are of Opinion, I can hardly proceed without it. I desire only two Things; first, that those who call themselves my Friends may have no reason to reproach me; and, the second, that, in the Course of this Matter, I may have something to dispose of to some one I wish well to.

Some Weeks before Mr. *Duncan*'s Death, his Brother-in-Law, Mr. *Lawson*, Minister of *Galtrim*,[2] went for *England*, by Mr. *Duncan*'s Consent to apply for an adjoining Living, called *Kilmore*,[3] in *Duncan*'s Possession, and now in the Crown by his Death, I know not his Success, but heartily wish, if it be intended for him, that the Matter might take another Turn. That Mr. *Warren*, who is Landlord of *Galtrim*, might have that Living, and *Kilmore* adjoining,[4] both not 150*l.* and Mr. *Lawson* to go down to Mr. *Warren*'s Living in *Clogher* Diocese, worth above 200*l.* But this is all at Random,

----

[1] Stearne is said to have rebuilt the palace.

[2] The Rev. Wilfred Lawson was incumbent of Galtrim near Trim for sixteen years.

[3] Duncan appears to have been a clergyman of some substance. His wife was a daughter of Sir Henry Echlin, Bt. See *Genealogical Memoirs of the Echlin Family*, by J. R. Echlin.

[4] Warren does not appear to have received either Galtrim or Kilmore.

because I know not whether *Kilmore* may not be already disposed of, for I heard it is in your Grace's Turn.

I heard lately from the Provost, who talked of being in the *North* in a Month; but, our *Dublin* Account is, that they know not when the Deanry is to be given him.[1] I do not find any great Joy in either Party, on account of the Person who, it is supposed, will succeed him.[2] The wrong Custom of making that Post the next Step to a Bishoprick, hath been, as your Grace says, of ill Consequence; yet they think fit to take it, and make no Scruple of preceding on all Occasions, the best private Clergyman in the Kingdom, which is a Trifle of great Consequence when a Man's Head is possessed with it.

I pray God preserve your Grace for the Good of the Church, and the learned World; and, for the Happiness of those whom you are pleased to honour with your Friendship, Favour or Protection. I beg your Grace's Blessing, and remain with the greatest Truth and Respect, | My Lord, | Your Grace's most dutiful, | and most humble Servant, |

Jon. Swift.

Trinity College, Dublin, N.3.11.[3]

Archbishop King to Swift

Bath May 13th 1717

Revd Sir

I was favoured with yours of the 1st inst. which I perused with great pleasure, though I can claim but a little share in the good dispositions you are pleased to ascribe to me. As to Mr. Warren, if it be he that served the cure of St. Mary's, I take him to be a good man, and shall be ready to serve him; as to Mr. Lawson I know him not, and to be sure, shall not be very forward to assist any man that leaves Ireland in order to solicit at Court here. As to the benefice you mention in the diocese of Clogher, it cannot be expected that I should concern myself in the disposal of it, without the Bishop's desiring it

---

[1] Pratt was presented to the deanery of Down on 17 June.

[2] Richard Baldwin, a college contemporary of Swift, was elected a fellow of Trinity in 1693. He was appointed provost 24 June 1717. On his death, 30 Sept. 1758, he bequeathed his fortune of £80,000 to the college. The will was disputed; but in 1820 finally decided in favour of the college. *D.N.B.*

[3] This letter is now largely illegible.

of me. I should be glad, and thank God, if all your friends and mine were common to us both, and will endeavour to make them so; in the mean time I promise you that no person shall fare the worse on the account of their reckoning themselves here your friend, but the better.

I am now in a fit of the gout and I hope that will excuse the shortness of this answer. I hope to see you in the beginning of the next month, and will endeavour so to settle a good understanding between you, your Chapter and me, that we may have but one common interest. I heartily recommend you to God's good care, and am, Rev^d S^r | Y^{rs} &c |

W. D.

Dean Swift

Rothschild[1]

Swift to Archdeacon Walls

Magherlin. May. 19th 1717

To morrow morning My Lord[2] and I set out towards Dublin. I leave My Lord at Ardee or Droghedah,[3] and turn off to Trim for a few days to settle some things at Laracor, and then hope to see You in Dublin. I have had abundance of Letters about St Brides; and now Dr Howard gravely writes to me that the A. Bp Dublin has declared for him, and hopes I will consent; Nothing could put me more against him than the A. B's declaring, and I am resolved to oppose it, as long as I can. Not but that next to a Friend it is most to my Interest that Howard[4] should have it, because he hath something to give up which I may bestow a Friend: I mean the Advowson of a Toun Living which now will be worth something, and more in time; but there again I am at a Loss who to give it to: for I had Thoughts of a Scheam with the Grattans, and of Sam Holt, and the Provost writes to me about Forbes: and I know not what to think or say: but I will take Time like my Friend Ld Oxford:

[1] Lord Rothschild's Library, No. 2281 (43).

[2] i.e. Stearne.

[3] Ardee and Drogheda are on the main road from Dublin to the north. A cross-road from Ardee, as well as one from Drogheda, would have brought Swift to Trim.

[4] The Rev. Robert Howard was appointed to the benefice of St. Bride.

I wonder at the Provost's formality about the Deanry: They say here that the Governmt will not give it till he asks them, and he writes me word, that they expect Sollicitation; If so, I think he acts right I hope you have got money for me; and when I get to Trim I shall know how Davy Burn has performed. I writ to you about buying me some Wine. I know not what you have done in it. I would have none unless it be extreamily good, and that last Vintage was a very good one in the Opinion of the wise.

I design to write to Deacon the Bp of Down's Tenant as soon as I[1] get to Toun, and swinge him off if he does not pay me my Money. Tis pleasant to see My Lord mustring up his Goods upon leaving this Place, and missing Sheets, Table Cloaths, Napkins Candlesticks, by the dozen, and Bottles by the Hundred, and all within half a year past. He is now persuaded to take a Houskep[r] if he can get a good one.

Later endorsement: D[r] Swift | May 19th 1717

Rothschild[2]

Swift to Archdeacon Walls

Trim. May 23[d]. 1717

When I left my Lord Bishop[3] at Droghedagh as he tells you, I rode ten miles to Navan and there lay, and came here yesterday. My L[d] intended to ly at Droghedagh, and there I designed to finish my Lett[r] to you and Mrs Dingley but stopping at the gate,[4] I was forced to seal them, unfinished in a Cabbin. There has not been one thing done to my Rooms at Laracor since I went: as I hear, it was by the Perverseness of that Puppy Parvisol. I am going there this morning about it. I hope My Lord Bp got home safe, and desire my duty to him. We expected M[r] Warburton would have taken this Toun in his way home,[5] but we reckon he is gone a shorter road. I should have

---

[1] Ball introduces the word 'can' after 'I'. This is not in the manuscript.

[2] Lord Rothschild's Library, No. 2281 (44).

[3] i.e. Stearne.

[4] The gate of St. Lawrence, through which this historic town is still entered.—Ball.

[5] To Magherafelt.

been very glad to see him. I have read Hoadly's Sermon,[1] and the
Bp will tell you my Thoughts of it. I wonder whether his will be the
same, and what are yours, and whether the Whigs justify it. If
Exchange be low, I must return 100ll to Engld towards paying a
Debt there. I hope to get the Money from the Lands in Kildare. I
wish Mr Burn (who is in Toun) would write to Mr Deacon near
Athy, about it. There is 60ll due for half year Michalms, and 75ll (by
the advanced rent) due the 25th of March last: to let him know that
I expect to receive both immediatly, in all 135ll. This sum with
40 or 50ll if I can get it, will I hope clear my Grand English debt.
Returns and all. Tho I fear it hath increasd by Money pd to Mrs
Fenton[2] and others. However it will make it pretty light. Pray let me
know whether Mr Burn designs soon to leave Dublin. My humble
Service to my Gossip and the Ladyes. We expect Dr Raymd here
to morrow——

Address: To the Reverend Mr Archdeacon | Walls, at his House over against |
        the Blue-coat hospitall in Queen-street | Dublin
Postmark: Illegible   *Stamp:* TRIM
Later endorsement: Dr Swift | May 23d 1717

4805

Erasmus Lewis to Swift

London June 15, 1717.

Last night I recd your's of the 5th Inst and since you tell me I am
your onely Correspondent, I think I ought to be the more punctual
in my returns, & the more full in what relates to our friends here.
You'l see by the publick prints that Munday next come Senight[3] is
appointed for the tryall of my Ld Oxford, & that no less than Six &
twenty doughty Members are appointed to manage it,[4] the Lords

---

[1] On 31 Mar. 1716 Hoadly, Bishop of Bangor, preached before the King his
famous sermon on the 'Nature of the Kingdom or Church of Christ', in which he
denied that there was such a thing as a visible Church of Christ. The sermon was
printed by the King's command. Hoadly's challenge was accepted by high
churchmen. The Bangorian controversy aroused numerous pamphleteers animated by a rising spirit of bitterness. The ablest of Hoadly's critics was William Law.

[2] Swift's sister Jane. See *Journal*, p. 101 n.

[3] The 24th.

[4] In May Oxford, being still confined in the Tower, petitioned that his case

have likewise settled the whole forms of the proceedings. my L^d has ask'd that two Lawyers more might be added to his Council, yet is all this but a farce, for there is not a Creature living who thinks he will ever be try'd, for they publickly own that they neither have, nor ever had any Evidence, & laugh at Impeachm^{ts} & attainders, & party gambolls, and that all people deserve to be so punish'd who presume to dispossess the Whigs of their indefeasible right to the administration, but since he is not to be try'd, the next question is in what manner is he to be brôt off, so as to save the honour of his prosecutors, I think it will be by an Act of Grace, others say, it will be by the Com̄ons asking more time & the Lords of their party agreeing to refuse it, but as we are wholly ignorant of their intentions, it is possible neither of these guesses may be right & that they may keep him yet another year in Prison wch my Ld Marlborô seems passionately to desire.

We labour under all the disadvantages in the World in every respect for the Tide of party runs still very strong every where, but in no place more than in Westminster hall, those in this side whose honour & Interest both require that all people who pay Obedience shou'd be protected seem to want a capacity to govern, & the similitude of circumstances between the — and the Regent[1] render the latter a firm Ally, contrary to the natural interest of France, thus we are secure from any Foreign Enemy.

I agree with you that Snape's Letter is really but a Letter, and that it is much too short and too slight for such a Subject,[2] however his merit was great in being the first to give the alarm to his Brethren, & setting himself in the front of the battle against his adversary, in those respects his Letter has had it's full effect.

I desire you will be as quick as you can in the assistance you intend Prior, for those who have subscrib'd here are impatient to have their Books, and we can't keep it off much longer without passing for comᄆon cheats.

Dr Arbuthnot, & Mr Charleton,[3] & I remember you often. Ly M[4]

should be taken into consideration. The Lords decided that the trial should begin 13 June. The date was subsequently postponed to the 24th, Lord Cowper presiding.   [1] The King and Philip Duke of Orleans.

[2] Andrew Snape, 1675-1742, headmaster of Eton 1711; provost of King's College, Cambridge, 1719. He was one of the principal opponents of Hoadly in the Bangorian controversy. His first letter pressing the attack passed through seventeen editions in the year of its publication, 1717.

[3] The Duchess of Ormonde's chaplain.   [4] Lady Masham.

always asks for you very affectionately, by the way, I am perfectly restor'd to grace there, & am invited to their house in the Countrey. as soon as Ld Oxford's affair is over I intend to go amongst my friends in the Country not to return hither till about Michs: but if you'l direct to me at my house in Town your Letters will be convey'd to me where ever I am Mr Rochfort[1] seems to have a great many good quality's, & I am heartily glad he has met with Success. adieu.

Address: To the Revd Dr Swift | Dean of St Patricks | in Dublin | Ireland
Endorsed by Swift: (*a*) June 15. 1717 | Mr Lewis.
               (*b*) Mr Lewis June 15. 1717
Postmark: 15 IV

4805

Erasmus Lewis to Swift

London June 18. 1717

Having acquainted you in my Letter of Last post,[2] that it was the universal opinion the Com̃ons wou'd not proceed to the trial of my Ld Oxford, I think myself oblig'd to tell you, that we begin now to be something doubtfull, for the managers who are seven & twenty in number, strenuously give out, that they shall be ready to proceed on Munday next, therefore if you have any thoughts of coming over, let not any thing, which I have said in my last, have any wait with you to alter that resolution, I am wholly taken up with the men of the Law, & therefore have nothing to say to you at present upon any publick matters. I shall only just trouble you with one word relating to a private affair, my brother is Chaplain to Sr Charles Hotham's Regim^t wch is now order'd to Ireland,[3] if you cou'd find any young fellow, who wou'd buy that Com^n my Brother thinks his Patron (my Ld Carlile)[4] will easily prevaile wth my Ld Duke of Bolton[5] for leave

[1] Robert Rochfort, Chief Baron of the Irish Exchequer, had legal business in England which engaged him. See Swift to Walls, 18 June 1716.

[2] The previous letter.

[3] The regiment had seen much service during the rebellion. On being ordered to Ireland Sir Charles Hotham resigned. In the following year the regiment was disbanded (Dalton, *George the I's Army*, p. 172).

[4] Charles Howard, third Earl of Carlisle, was appointed one of the Lords Justices until the arrival of George I. He acted as First Lord of the Treasury from 23 May until 11 Oct. 1715.

[5] On 16 Apr. of this year Charles Paulet, second Duke of Bolton, was appointed Lord Lieutenant of Ireland.

to dispose of it. I shou'd be very glad you could find him a chapman.[1]

Address: To The Rev^d Dr Swift | Dean of St. Patrick's | in Dublin | Ireland.
Postmark: 18 IV
Frank: Mansel
Endorsed by Swift: Mr Lewis | Jun. 18—1717

4805

Erasmus Lewis to Swift

London Jul: 2. 1717.

I have the pleasure to acquaint[2] you that my Lord Oxford's Impeachm^t was discharg'd last night, by the unanimous consent of all the Lords present, & as nearly as I cou'd count their Number was an hundred & Six, the D. of Marlborô, my Lord Sunderland, my Lord Cadogan,[3] my Ld Coningsby,[4] & a few others of the most violent having withdrawn themselves before the Lords came into Westminster Hall; the acclamations were as great as upon any occasion, and our friend who seems more form'd for adversity, than prosperity, has at present more friends than ever he had before in any part of his life. I believe he will not have the fewer from a Message he receiv'd this morning from the King by my Ld Chamberlain to forbid him the Court.[5] you know the prosecution was at first the resentment of a Party, but it became at last, a ridiculous business weakly carry'd on, by the impotent rage of a woman (I mean of my Lady Marlborô) who is almost distracted that she cou'd not obtain her revenge.

---

[1] A dealer, customer. See Eric Partridge's edition of Grose's *Classical Dictionary of the Vulgar Tongue.*

[2] acquaint] inform *Ball.*

[3] Cadogan was quartermaster-general to Marlborough and was present at all his great battles. He naturally supported Marlborough. He had been raised to the peerage as Baron Cadogan of Reading on 30 June of the previous year.

[4] Thomas Coningsby, a strong Whig and a member of the Secret Committee, had also been rewarded with a barony in 1716. It was he who moved the impeachment of Oxford.

[5] For the Lord Chamberlain's message and Oxford's reply on the same day, 2 July, see *Bath MSS.* i. 249. The Duke of Newcastle, who then held the office of Chamberlain, emphasized the fact that he had a great respect for Oxford and was only acting under orders.

I am now going out of town with an intention to row¹ about from place to place, till about Mich: next, if you write to me direct to me as usual, & your Letter will be convey'd to me where I am.

Dʳ Arbuthnot, Mʳ Charleton, & Mʳ Currey have din'd with me to day, and you have not been forgot. I was in hopes we shou'd have seen you ere this, the Dʳ says you wait for the Act of Grace, if so, I hope to see you here¹ by next winter

Address: To the Revᵈ Dʳ Swift | Dean of Sᵗ Patricks | in Dublin | Ireland
Postmark: 2
Frank: Dupplin
Endorsed by Swift: Mʳ Lewis | July 2ᵈ 1717 | Lᵈ Oxfords Acquittal

Nichols 1779

Swift to Robert Cope

Dublin, July 9, 1717.

Sir,²

I received the favour of your letter before I came to town; for I stayed three weeks at *Trim* after I left you, out of perfect hatred to this place, where at length business dragged me against my will. The Archdeacon, who delivers you this, will let you know I am but an ill solicitor for him.³ The thing is indeed a little difficult and perplexed, yet a willing mind would make it easy, but that is wanted, and I cannot work it up. However, it shall not be my fault, if something be not made of it one time or other; but some people give their best friends reason to complain. I have at a venture put you down among

¹ Ball omits the word 'here'.
² Swift met Robert Cope of Loughgall, co. Armagh, for the first time in London. On 11 Feb. 1710–11 he wrote to Stella (*Journal*, p. 189): 'I dined with three Irishmen, at one Mr. Cope's lodgings; the other two were one Morris an archdeacon, and Mr. Ford.' A strong Tory, Cope sat for his county in Queen Anne's last Irish Parliament. Swift paid summer visits to Loughall on this occasion, probably in 1720, in 1722, and almost certainly on other occasions (see *Letters of Swift to Ford*, ed. Nichol Smith, p. 95; Sheridan's *Life of Swift*, 1784, pp. 217 n., 431). For verses addressed to Cope's second wife see *Poems*, pp. 320–2.
³ The Archdeacon, probably the same as the dinner-guest at 'Copes lodgings', would be Theodore Morris, or Maurice, who took his M.A. at Trinity College, Dublin, in 1692, and became rector of Desertcreat in 1708. He was Archdeacon of Tuam from 1706 till his death in 1731 (Leslie, *Armagh Clergy*, p. 219).

poor Mr. *Prior*'s benefactors,[1] and I wonder what exemption you pretend to as appears by your letter to Mr. *Stewart*. It seems you took the thousand pounds a year in a literal sense, and even at that rate I hope you would not be excused. I hope your sheep-shearing in the county of *Louth* hath established your health; and that Dr. *Tisdall*,[2] your brother of the spleen, comes sometimes, and makes you laugh at a pun or a blunder. I made a good many advances to your friend *Bolton*[3] since I came to town, and talked of you; but all signified nothing; for he has taken every opportunity of opposing me, in the most unkind and unnecessary manner; and I have done with him. I could with great satisfaction pass a month or two among you, if things would permit. The Archdeacon carries you all the news, and I need say nothing. We grow mighty sanguine, but my temper has not fire enough in it. They assure me that Lord *Bolingbroke* will be included in the Act of Grace; which, if it be true, is a mystery to me.

You must learn to winter in town, or you will turn a monk, and *Mrs. Cope* a nun; I am extremely her humble servant.

I have ventured to subscribe a guinea for Mr. *Brownlow*,[4] because I would think it a shame not to have his name in the list. Pray tell him so.

I doubt whether Mrs. *Cope* will be pleased with the taste of snuff I sent her.

Present my humble service to your mother and brother; and believe me to be, with great truth and esteem, Sir, | Your most obedient | humble servant, |

J. Swift

[1] As a subscriber to Prior's forthcoming volume of poems.
[2] William Tisdall, Stella's old admirer, who held the vicarage of Belfast and a rectory in the county of Armagh, was intimate with the Cope family.
[3] i.e. Theophilus Bolton.
[4] An ancestor of the Earl of Lurgan. He represented the county of Armagh. Cope married, as his first wife, one of the family.

Longleat XIII[1]

Swift to the Earl of Oxford

Dublin. Jul. 9th 1717

Since I am sure no Event[2] can have any Power upon Your Mind, I cannot help believing that during this glorious scene of your Life (I do not mean your Discharge but your two years Imprisonment) you have sometimes found a Minute to remember an inconsiderable Man who ever loved you above all things. I write to you from an Imagination I have allways had, that as soon as you were freed from your Jaylers, you would retire for some Months to Herefordshire, and that I should be a Companion in your Retirement. Therefore if you have any such Thoughts, I beg you will commend[3] me to attend, For I have many things to say to you, and to enquire of you, as you may easily imagine. You will forgive me if I talk ignorantly, For perhaps you intend to live in Toun, or pass the Summer with my Lord Harley, or perhaps (as some Refiners say) you are again to be a Minister; In any of these Cases, all I have said, I desire may go for nothing, and I will wait Your Leisure. However, pray let me know as soon as you can by a Line from yourself.

I will trouble you no more at present.[4]

Address: To the Earl of Oxford.

Berg Collection
New York Public Library

Swift to Joseph Addison

Dublin. July 9th 1717.

S[rs]

I should be much concerned if I did not think you were a little angry with me for not congratulating you upon being Secretary.[6]

---

[1] Swift's autograph of this letter is preserved in Longleat, xiii, ff. 49–50.

[2] After 'Event' the words 'of Life' are crossed out.

[3] 'command' written above the line.

[4] The letter is unsigned and the seal undamaged. Probably the letter was carried secretly by private hand. Apparently it never reached Oxford. Cf. his letter of the 16th.

[For notes 5 and 6 see opposite.

but I chuse my Time as I would to visit you when all your company
is gone. I am confident you have given Ease of Mind to many thousand People, who will never believe any ill can be intended to the
Constitution in Church and State while you are in so high a Trust,
and I should have been of the same Opinion thô I had not the
Happyness to know you.

I am extremely obliged for your kind Remembrance[1] some months
ago by the Bp. of Derry,[2] and for your generous Intentions if you
had come to Ireland, to have made Party give way to Freindship by
continuing your Acquaintance.

I examine my Heart, and can find no other Reason why I write to
you now, beside that great Love and Esteem I have always had for
you. I have nothing to ask you either for any Friend, or for my self.
When I conversed among Ministers I boasted of your Acquaintance,
but I feel no Vanity from being known to a Secretary of State. I am
only a little concerned to see you stand single, for it is a prodigious
singularity in any Court to owe ones Rise entirely to Merit. I will
venture to tell you a Secret, that three or four such Choices would
gain more hearts in three weeks than all the methods hitherto prac-
ticed, have been able to do in as many years.

It is now time for me to recollect that I am writing to a Secretary
of State, who has little time allowed him for Trifles, I therefore take
my Leave with Assurances of my being ever with the Truest
Respect | Sr Your most obedient | and most | humble Servt |

Jonath: Swift.

---

[1] 'of', following 'Remembrance', is deleted with a volute.
[2] St. George Ashe.

---

[5] This 'curious and valuable' letter was first printed by Scott, 1814, xix.
349–50, who acknowledged the communication of a group of letters, of which
this was one, from 'Major Tickell, the descendant of the poet'. Ball, ii. 394–5,
and Graham, *Letters of Addison*, pp. 503–4, followed Scott's text. The original,
from which, by kind permission, the present text is taken, is now in the Berg
Collection, New York Public Library. It was sold by E. J. Tickell, 16 July 1928.

[6] After the death of Queen Anne Addison was appointed secretary to the
Lords Justices. Upon the termination of the regency he was appointed secretary
to Lord Sunderland as Lord Lieutenant of Ireland. The latter resigned his
office in ten months. Neither he, nor Addison on this occasion, visited the country.
By warrant dated 12 Apr. 1717 Addison was honoured with the high administra-
tive office of Secretary of State for the Southern Department.

Swift to the Earl of Oxford

Dublin. July 16th 1717

My Lord

I wrote to you some days ago,[1] and enclosed the Letter in a Cover directed to Your Brother in Lincoln's-inn Fields; I need not repeat what I there said, but beg Your Lordship will answer my Letter as soon as you have an Hour of Leisure, and do not let Civility force you to say anything against your mind, for if it doth not consist with your Conveniency, the Matter is at an End. But I imagine, if you have any Thoughts of retiring for some time to Herefordshire, I ought to see you and ask you some Questions, and receive your Instructions, concerning some Things I have often spoke to you about, that might employ my Leisure in the present Situation of Affairs, which we then easily foresaw &c. I will now give you no further Trouble but remain &c.

Address: To the Right Honourable the | Earl of Oxford, at His | House at S[t] James's | London

Nichols 1801

Swift to Bishop Atterbury

Dublin, July 18, 1717.

My Lord,

Some persons of distinction, lately come from England, and not unknown to your Lordship, have made me extremely pleased and proud, by telling me that your Lordship was so generous as to defend me against an idle story that passed in relation to a letter of mine to the Archbishop of Dublin.[2] I have corresponded for many years with his Grace, though we generally differed in politicks, and therefore our letters had often a good mixture of controversy. I confess likewise that I have been his Grace's advocate, where he had not many others. About nine months ago I writ a letter to him in London (for in my little station it is convenient there should be some commerce between us); and in a short time after I had notice from several

---

[1] On the 9th. Apparently a letter which never reached Oxford.
[2] See 13 Nov. 1716; and Erasmus Lewis to Swift, 12 Jan. 1716–17.

friends, that a passage in my letter was shown to several persons, and a consequence drawn from thence, that I was wholly gone over to other principles more in fashion, and wherein I might better find my account. I neglected this report, as thinking it might soon die; but found it gathered strength, and spread to Oxford and this kingdom, and some gentlemen, who lately arrived here, assured me they had met it a hundred times, with all the circumstances of disadvantage that are usually tacked to such stories by the great candour of mankind. It should seem as if I were somebody of importance, and if so, I should think the wishes not only of my friends, but of my party, might dispose them rather to believe me innocent, than condemn me unheard. Upon the first intelligence I had of this affair, I made a shift to recollect the only passage in that letter which could be any way liable to misinterpretation.

I told the Archbishop—'we had an account of a set of people in London, who were erecting a new church, upon the maxim that everything was void, since the Revolution, in the Church as well as the State, that all priests must be re-ordained, Bishops again consecrated, and in like manner of the rest, that I knew not what there was in it of truth. that it was impossible such a scheme should ever pass, and that I believed if the Court, upon this occasion, would show some good-will to the Church, discourage those who ill treated the clergy, &c., it would be the most popular thing they could think of.'

I keep no copies of letters; but this, I am confident, was the substance of what I wrote, and that every other line in the letter which mentioned public affairs, would have atoned for this, if it had been a crime, as I think it was not in that juncture, whatever may be my opinion at present; for, I confess, my thoughts change every week, like those of a man in an incurable consumption, who daily finds himself more and more decay.

The trouble I now give your Lordship is an ill return to your goodness in defending me; but it is the usual reward of goodness, and therefore you must be content. In the mean time, I am in a hopeful situation, torn to pieces by pamphleteers and libellers on that side the water, and by the whole body of the ruling party on this; against which all the obscurity I live in will not defend me. Since I came first to this kingdom, it has been the constant advice of all my Church friends, that I should be more cautious. To oppose me in everything relating to my station, is made a merit in my Chapter, and I shall probably live to make some Bishops as poor, as Luther made many rich.

I profess to your Lordship, that what I have been writing is only with regard to the good opinion of your Lordship, and of a very few others with whom you will think it of any consequence to an honest man that he should be set right. I am sorry that those who call themselves churchmen should be industrious to have it thought that their number is lessened, even by so inconsiderable a one as myself. But I am sufficiently recompensed, that your Lordship knows me best, to whom I am so ambitious to be best known. God be thanked, I have but a few to satisfy. The bulk of my censurers are strangers, or ill judges, or worse than either, and if they will not obey your orders to correct their sentiments of me, they will meet their punishment in your Lordship's disapprobation, which I would not incur for all their good words put together, and printed in twelve volumes folio. | I am, with great respect, my Lord, | your Lordship's most dutiful | and most humble servant, |

Jon. Swift.

4805

Matthew Prior to Swift

Duke Street, Westminster
30 July 1717.

Dear Sir,[1]

I have the favour of four Letters from You of the 9th 13th 16th and 20th Inst[2] They all came safe to me, however variously directed but the last to me at my House in Duke Street is the rightest. I find my self equally Comforted by Your Philosophy and assisted by your Friendship. You will easily imagine that I have a hundred things to say to You which for as many reasons I omit, and only touch upon that Business to which in the Pride of your heart You give the Epithet of *Sorry*. I return You the Names of those who have been kind enough to subscribe that You may see if they are rightly spelt, and the just Titles put to them, as likewise if it has happened that

---

[1] This letter is in a clerical hand. It is doubtful whether the signature was written by Prior.

[2] Not one of these four letters can be traced.

any has Subscribed for more than one Volume[1] You will please to look over the Catalogue & return it to me at Your Leisure. You see that our Calculation comes even, the Gentlemans Name that desired it being omitted. I am sensible that this has given you too much trouble, but it is too late now to make an Apology Let Mr Lewis who is now with me do it for me at what time and in what manner he pleases. I take it for granted that what ever I write as what ever is writ to me will be broke open, So you'l expect nothing from me but what you may have as particularly from the Post-boy. We are all pritty well in health. I have my old whoreson Cough, and I think I may call it mine for Life. The Earl is Semper Idem.[2] Lord Harley in the Country, our Brotherhood[3] extreamly dispersed, but so as that we have been three or four times able to get as many of the Society together, and drink to our absent Friends. I have been made to believe that we may see your Reverend Person this Summer in England, if so, I shal be glad to meet You at any place, but when you come to London do not go to the Coco-tree (as you sent your Letter)[4] but come imediately to Duke Street where you shal find a Bed, a Book & a Candle So pray think of Sojourning no where else. Pray give my Service to all Friends in general; I think as you have ordered the matter you have made the greater part of Ireland list themselves of that number, I do not know how you can Recompence them, but by coming over to help me to Correct the Book, which I promise them you will pardon my having used an other hand, since it is so^e much better than my own, and believe Me ever with the greatest truth D^r S^r | yours |

M Prior

Duke Street West^r
July the 30th 1717.

Endorsed by Swift: Rx Aug. 6th 1717 | Answered the same day[4] | Mr Prior.

¹ The list of subscribers for the projected *Poems*.
² i.e. Oxford.
³ The Brothers' Club of which Prior was a member.
⁴ This letter also is not forthcoming. Only four letters from Swift to Prior have survived: 1 Mar. 1714–15 (Rothschild); 28 Apr. 1719, 25 Jan. 1719–20, 24 Mar. 1719–20, these latter three at Longleat.

The Earl of Oxford to Swift

Augu: 6: 1717

Two years retreat has made me taste the conversation of my Dearest Friend with a greater relish, than even at the time of my being charm'd with it in our frequent journeys to Windsor: Three of your Letters have come safe to my hands, the first about two years since,[1] that My Son keeps as a Family monument: The other two arriv'd since the first of July;[2] my Heart is often with you, but I delayd writing in expectation of giving a perfect Answer about my going to Bramton: But the truth is this, The warmth of rejoycing in those Parts is so far from abating that I am persuaded by my friends to go into Cambridge shire;[3] where you are too just not to believe you wil be welcome before any one in the world: the longing your Friends have to see you must be submitted to the judgment your self makes of all circumstances; at present this seems to be a cooler climate than your island is like to be when they Assemble[4] &c: our Impatience to see you, should not draw you into un Easyness; we long to embrace you—if you find it may be no inconvenience to your self.

Endorsed by Swift: Robt E. of Oxford | Aug. 6th 1717

Rothschild[5]

Swift to Archdeacon Walls

Ardsallagh. Augst 19th 1717

Sr

I am now with Mr Ludlow,[6] and Mr Gillespy is come hither to me, I have told him that there are sevrll Tenants in the Deanry, who affirm they have paid him certain Sums of money which he hath not accounted for; He can call nothing more to account then one or two odd Sums all under twenty Shill and ten Loads of Hay to be substracted from one Murphy's Bill at 4s 6d pr Load. He says he is ready

---

[1] 19 July 1715.   [2] 9 July 1717, 16 July 1717.
[3] To Wimpole.
[4] The Irish Parliament met on 27 Aug.
[5] Lord Rothschild's library, No. 2281 (45).   [6] See p. 249.

to answer for every thing, and desires I would advance the May rent
for the Farm from Judge Whitshed, which he was to pay; because
I ow Mr Gillespy near the sd Sum.[1] I know not well what to say in
this Matter; I would not use him hardly, & yet would be safe my
self: Mr Proudfoot can soon tell what People pretend to have pd
Mr Gillespy. He declares he received not one farthing of last years
Tythes, so that the odd sums above mentioned are for the year before
which was 1715. And then if the Tenants say they pd Mr Gillespy
one Penny for 1716, he insists they wrong him; pray settle this
matter as well as You can with Mr Gillespy, which may be done by
sending to Proudfoot. I know you have no Accounts by you of mine,
however Mr Gillespy insisting that he never received one single
Penny for 1716, I believe it may be made easy: I am | y^r most obd |
Servant |

J: Swift

Mr Proudfoot may tell L^d C^h. Justice Whitshed, that I have some
Accounts still with Mr Gillespy, and that Care shall be taken to pay
His L^dships Rent, so that he need not be uneasy.

If Mr Proudfoot has not got me any Hay, Mr Gillespy says he has
good & will sell it at Market Rate, & I would rather he should have
my money then another, as far as 30 Loads

Desire Mr Proudfoot to be easy with Mr Gillespy about the Tyths
of 4 Acres of Wheat he has upon the Farm of New-hall—

Address: To the Reverend | Mr Archdeacon Walls
Later endorsement, not in the usual hand: Aug. 19. 1717

4805

Matthew Prior to Swift

24 August 1717.

Yours,[2] my good friend of the 6th[3] finds Me [in] Oxfordshire with
the D: of Shrewsbury, which would sooner have been acknowledged
had I stayed in London: Before I left that pious city, I made due
enquiry, into the Methods and regularity of your correspondence

---

[1] See Swift to Walls, 30 Dec. 1716.
[2] A margin of this letter is soiled, injured, and illegible in places. The earlier
transcripts seem to be verbally correct.
[3] Presumably a reply to Prior's letter of 30 July.

with the Earl; He has received your letters, he will answer them—but not to day, sicut olim: nothing can change Him; I can get no positive answer from him, nor can any Man else; so trouble your self no more on that head than He does, He is still in London; and possibly has answered you while I am a little arraigning his Neglect: but in all cases liberavi animam meam: I wish you were in England, that you might a little look over the strange stuff that I am to give your friends for their Money, I shall be angry with you, if you are near and not with Me; but when I see you that mighty question may easily be decided: in the mean time I am taking your good counsel, and will be in the Country as much as I can. You have found two mistakes in the list, but I have not corrected them, I presume we shall have it of the best Edition when you send the list back again, of which, I say, no hast is required: give my service and thanks to all friends, reserve only to your self the assurance of my being beyond Expression My friend | Yours &c.

Heathrop[1] in Oxford shire | 24th Aug. 1717.

Endorsed by Swift: Mr Prior[2]

Forster Copy

Swift to Knightley Chetwode

Friday [Summer 1717?]

I look[ed] over the enclosed some time ago, and again just now; it contains many good things, and wants many alterations. I have made one or two, and pointed at others, but an author can only set his own things right.

Endorsed by Swift: This was my advice to a young lady.[3]

---

[1] Heythrop was a residence of the Duke of Shrewsbury. His health was declining at this time, and he succumbed at his seat Isleworth, in Middlesex, on 1 Feb. 1717–18.

[2] A second endorsement is illegible.

[3] The date of this letter is problematical. It may have been written during the summer of 1717. Some verses with a few words altered by Swift are said to have been enclosed.

The Marquess of Wharton to Swift

Monday morning [7 January 1717–18]

Dear Dean

I shall imbarque for England tomorrow.[1] It would be necessary for me to take leave of Ld Molesworth[2] on many accounts & as Young[3] is ingag'd in town I must infallibly go alone unless y^r charity extends it self to favour me wth y^r company there this morning I beg you would send me y^r answer & beleive me | Sincerely y^r faithful frid | & Servant. | Wharton.

p.s. If you condescend so far come to me about Eleven of the clock[4]

Monday Morning

Address: To | The Reverend Dr Swift | Dean of S^nt Patricks
Endorsed by Swift: D. Whar

---

[1] Philip, Marquis of Wharton, only son and heir of the subject of Swift's *Short Character*. He succeeded his father in April 1715, inheriting a large estate and both an English and Irish marquisate. Although only nineteen years of age he had been allowed to take his seat in the Irish House of Lords. He was now on his way to England in company with the Duke of Bolton, Lord Lieutenant. In 1716 he had visited the Old Pretender at Avignon, and Marie Beatrix, widow of James II at St. Germain. Despite these vagaries he was created Duke of Wharton in 1718 to retain him in the Whig interest. Nevertheless, leaving England, he openly espoused the cause of 'James III' in 1726; urged a Spanish invasion of England; served against Gibraltar in 1727; ending in destitution a reckless and dissolute life. See Pope, *Epistle to Cobham*, ll. 180–207.

[2] Robert Molesworth, 1656–1725, of Brackanstown, co. Dublin, the first of the title, was raised to the peerage as Viscount Molesworth in 1716 for his support of the Hanoverian succession (Lodge, *Peerage of Ireland*, v. 135).

[3] Wharton, strange as it may seem, was accompanied to Ireland by Edward Young, author of the *Night Thoughts*, to whom he was a generous patron.

[4] As Swift had gone to the country on 27 Dec. and did not return to Dublin till 10 Jan. (Forster Collection, No. 510) they could not have met on this occasion.

Joseph Addison to Swift

20 March 1717–18.

Dear Sir

Multiplicity of Businesse and a long dangerous fit of sicknesse have prevented me from answering the obliging letter[1] you honourd me with some time since, but God be thanked I can not make use of either of these Excuses at present being entirely free both of my office[2] and my Asthma. I dare not however venture my self abroad yet but have sent[3] the Contents of your last to a friend of mine (for he is very much so tho he is my successor) who I hope will turn it to the advantage of the Gentleman whom you mention. I know you have so much zeal and pleasure in doing kind offices for those you wish well to, that I hope you represent the Hardship of the case in the Strongest Colours that it can possibly bear. However as I always honoured you for your Good Nature, which is a very odd Quality to celebrate in a man who has talents so much more shining in the Eye of the world, I shoud be glad if I coud any way concurre with you in putting a stop to what you say is now in agitation. I must here condole with you upon the Losse of that Excellent man the Bp of Derry[4] who has scarce left behind him his equal in Humanity, agreeable conversation, and all kinds of Learning. We have often talked of you with great pleasure, and upon this Occasion I cannot but reflect upon my self who, at the same time that I omitt no opportunity of expressing my esteem for you to others have bin so negligent in doing it to Your-self. I have several times taken up my pen to write to you but have bin always interrupted by some impertinence or other and to tell you unreservedly I have been unwilling to answer so agreeable a Letter as that I received from you with one written in form only, but I must still have continued silent, had I defer'd writing till I coud have made a suitable Return. Shall we never again talk together in Laconick? Whenever you see

[1] 9 July 1717.

[2] Addison, never physically strong, was rapidly failing in health. In Mar. 1718 he retired with a pension of £1,600 charged on the Irish establishment (Smithers, *Addison*, p. 416). He was succeeded in office, 16 Mar., by James Craggs.

[3] 'sent' written above 'communicated' which is struck through.

[4] Addison had formed a friendship with St. George Ashe from the days when he crossed to Ireland as secretary to Lord Wharton. Ashe had died on 27 Feb.

England your Company will be the most acceptable in the world at Holland house¹ where you are highly esteemed by Lady Warwick and the young Lord, tho by none any where more than by Sir | Your most Faithfull and | most Obedient Humble Servant | J. Addison.

Mar. 20: | 1717/8

Endorsed by Swift: Mʳ Addison just | after resigning the | Secretary of State Office | Mar. 26ᵗʰ 1717–18

Hawkesworth 1766

Lord Harley to Swift

[24] April 1718²

His Lordship writes to the Dean, that he hopes to see him at *Wimple* this year: that Lord Oxford was well, and talked of going into *Herefordshire*. He adds, your sister³ is obliged to go to *Bath*, presents her humble service, and desires you to accept of a little etuy. I beg you will not deny me the favour to take the snuff-box, which comes along with it, to supply the place of that, which was broke by accident some time ago.⁴ I am, with true respect, your most humble servant, and brother, | Harley.

¹ Which had become Addison's London residence on his marriage, 3 Aug. 1716, to the Countess of Warwick.
² This is only an epitome of Lord Harley's letter, thus printed by Hawkesworth, 1766, who assigned to it the date 'April 12', which was followed by all editors prior to Ball. Swift's reply, however, of which we have the original, *Portland MSS.*, refers to it as '24ᵗʰ of April'. Harley's letter is a long-delayed reply to Swift's of 8 Mar. 1714–15.
³ Lord Harley was a member of the Brothers' Club, and therefore refers to his wife as 'your sister'.
⁴ In his letter to Harley of 8 Mar. 1714–15 Swift tells how he broke the snuff-box which Lady Harley had given him. Harley had not forgotten, or had come upon the mislaid letter, and sends him a replacement. This 'square tortoise-shell snuff-box, richly lined and inlaid with gold' was left in Swift's will to 'Mrs. Mary Swift, alias Harrison', Martha Whiteway's daughter (*Prose Works*, ed. Temple Scott, xi. 411).

Matthew Prior to Swift

1 May 1718.

Dear Sir,[1]

A pretty kind of Amusement. I have been engaged in Comma's, Semicolons, Italic and Capital, to make Nonsense more pompous and Fabbelow[2] bad Poetry, with good Printing.[3] My Friends Letters in the mean time have lain unanswered, and the Obligations I have to them on Account of the very Book it self are unacknowledged. This is not all I must beg You once more to transfer to Us an intire List of my Subscribers with their Distinct Titles that They may for my Honour be printed at the beginning of my Book.[4] This will easily be done by revising the list which we sent to You, I must pray You that it may be Exact. The Money I receive of Mitford[5] as I intimated in You last.

E.O.[6] has not at all Disappointed my Speculations.[7] He is *Semper idem* and has as much Business to do now as when he was Governing England or Impeached for Treason. He is stil in Town but going in a Week or ten Days into Hereford shire. Lord and Lady Harley are at the Bath and as soon as I shal have settled my Affairs of the Printing Press, sad Business as you very well call it, I shall go into the Country to them.

My health I thank you is pretty good, My Courage better. I drink very often to Your health with some of our Friends here and am always with the greatest Truth and Affection | Dear S[r] | Your obliged and | most obedient Ser[t] | M Prior

May 1st 1718.

Address: To | The Reverend D[r] Swift | Dean of S[t] Patrick at | Dublin | Ireland.
Postmark: Illegible.   *Endorsed by Swift:* Mr Prior

[1] This letter is in the hand of a scribe.   [2] i.e. Furbelow.

[3] The great folio edition of Prior's *Poems on Several Occasions*, published by Jacob Tonson and Barber, extended to over 500 pages. The frontispiece and vignettes were designed by Louis Chéron, who was at his best in work of this nature.

[4] The subscribers' names cover twenty pages. Prior is stated to have realized 4,000 guineas by the publication of the work. Swift subscribed for five copies.

[5] Probably Samuel Mitford of the county of Dublin, who describes himself in his will as the son of a merchant and citizen of London.

[6] i.e. Earl of Oxford.

[7] Hawkesworth, followed by other editors, including Ball, printed 'expectations'. Possibly the scribe, writing from dictation, mistook Prior's word.

B.M. Portland MSS.

Swift to Lord Harley

Dublin. May 17th 1718.

Dear Sir

I had the Honor and Favor of a very kind Letter from Your Lordship of the 24th of April, which has given me the only Pleasure I ever received since I left you in Oxford.[1] To be remembered in so friendly a manner, and after so long an Absence, by that Person of the World for whom I have the greatest Love and Esteem, is a Happyness which no Mortification of Life can hinder me from relishing. Yet perhaps it is but Justice, that Persons like you, who are in the Years of good Nature, should now and then condescend to comfort us, who are arriving to the Age of Sourness and Morosity; Not that I would have Your Lordship think this any way concerns me, for my Servants tell all our Neighbourhood, that I grow gentler every day, and am content only to call my Footman a Fool, for that which, when you knew me first I would have broke his Head. But this is to be able to give a good Answer to Horace's Question: Levior ac melior fis accedente senectâ?[2]

Your Lordship and my Lady Harriette[3] have given me more disquiet for some days past, than I care to reproach You with. I have sent five or six Orders and Counter orders about a safe conveyance for my Etuy and Snuff-box, and shall have no Peace of Mind till I feel them in my Pockets, and I think in Conscience your Family ought to give me some Annuity for repairing my Pockets worn out in carrying Your Presents. There is my Lord Oxford's Table-book,[4] my Lady Harriette's former Snuff-box (of melancholy Memory)[5] besides these new Acquisitions. I say nothing of two Drawings, one of them Lady Dupplins[6] handiwork, which I am assured will in some years put me to the Charge of new painting the Panel against which they hang.

I was told that my Lord Oxford intended to write to me before he

---

[1] See Swift to Arbuthnot, 22 July 1714.

[2] Horace, *Ep.* II. ii. 211.

[3] Her true name was Henriette.

[4] See Appendix for a humorous bill presented by Swift to Lord Oxford including £5 for 'A Table Book like Your Ldships'.

[5] Cf. Harley to Swift, 24 Apr. 1718, and note.

[6] Abigail Harley, Oxford's second daughter, who was married to Lord Dupplin in 1709.

went to Hereford shire; I always thought I had some Business with him if he got there, and resolved to pay him a Visit, but he has delayd or forgot it, or altered his Resolutions of going.

I have sent Mr Prior all the Money which this hedge Country would afford, which for want of a better Sollicitor is under 200 pounds. I believe he is the first Person in any Christian Country that ever was suffered to starve after having been in so many great Employ^ts. But among the Turks and Chineses it is a very frequent Case, and those are the properest Precedents for us at this time.

My Lord Primate of Ireland[1] is with you at the Bath, he is a very worthy Gentleman, hath great Obligations to my Lord Oxford and I hope your Lordship lets him visit You.

I desire you will present my most humble Respects to my Sister Henrietta, and tell her I have something by me that I value more than a thousand of her Etuyes, but which I dare not trust to my Pocket. It is a Letter directed to Brother Swift after which I could do no less than own her for a Sister, and as Capt Fluellin told Harry the Fifth,[2] I am not ashamed of her, since she is an honest Woman.

I pray God continue Health and Happyness to you both, for the sake of your Friends and Country, as well as Your own, and in the mean time I expect the Justice to be ever believed Your Lordships | most obedient and | most obliged humble | Servt and | Brother, | J: Swift

Address: To the Right Honorable | the Lord Harley at his | Lodgings at Bath, | England

4805

Matthew Prior to Swift

[29 May 1718]

Dear Sir,[3]

I have received Yours of the 6th with the List corrected. I have two Colon and Comma Men. We correct and design to publish as

---

[1] Thomas Lindsay, Archbishop of Armagh, was held in esteem by Swift. His political sympathies were Tory.

[2] 'I need not be ashamed of your Majesty, praised be God, so long as your Majesty is an honest man' (*Hen. V.* iv. 7).

[3] This letter is written in the hand of a scribe except for the sentence at the end enclosed in half-brackets, which is in Prior's hand.

fast as the nature of this great, or sorry work, as You call it, will bear, but we shal not be out before Christmas, so that our Friends abroad may compleat their Collection till Michaelmas and be returned soon enough to have their names printed, and their Books got ready for them. I thank you most heartily for what You have been pleased to do in this kind. Give your self no further trouble but if any Gent: between this and Michael: desires to Subscribe do not refuse it.

I have received the Money of Mʳ Mitford. I am going to morrow Morning to the Bath to meet Lord Harley there. I shal be back in a Month. The Earl of Oxford is stil here: He will go into Hereford shire some time in June, he says he will write to You himself. am I particular enough? is this prose? and do I distinguish Tenses? I have nothing more to tell You but that You are the happyest Man in the World, and if You are once got into *la bagatelle*, You may despise the World. Besides contriving Emblems such as Cupids, Torches and Hearts for great Letters,[1] I am now unbinding two Volˢ of printed Heads to have 'em bound together in better order than they were before; dont you envy me? for the rest matters continue Sicut olim.[2] I will not tell You how much I want You, and I cannot tell You how well I love You. ⌐write to Me, my Dear Dean, and give my Service to all our Friends. | yours Ever | M Prior.¬

May 29ᵗʰ 1718.

Address: To | The Reverend Dʳ Swift | Dean of Sᵗ Patricks | Dublin | Ireland
Postmark: 30 or 31 MA
Endorsed by Swift: Mʳ Prior May 29|1718 (*and twice again*).

Rothschild

Swift to Charles Ford

Laracor. or Trim. Aug. 20ᵗʰ 1718

I met your Letter at Gallstoun,[3] but intending to leave it before next Post, I could not write till now. I am here upon a Clergy

---

[1] There are fourteen large historiated initial letters used in the volume. Only in a single instance is the same design repeated. In the case in which the design is used more than once the figure is that of a cupid with a torch.

[2] The folio volume consisted for the most part of poems which had previously appeared in the authorized octavo of 1709. The earlier volume opened with a lengthy 'Dedication' to Lionel Cranfield Sackville, seventh Earl of Dorset and Earl of Middlesex. His father, himself a poet and man of wit, had early befriended Prior.   [*For note 3 see overleaf.*

business called a Trienniall Visitation, which begins to morrow. I
intend to be in Town next week, and shall see you the morning after
I come, thô I expect you will give me more Spleen than ever. But
every body now is as desponding as I have been always. The
Toryes have lived all this while on whipt Cream, and now they have
even lost that. I find you intend onely a Visit, and a short one too.[1]
I keep much in the Country because it is more unlike Dublin than
any thing I can find on this side the Water. I can give you no
Arguments to live in Ireland, but what the Fox gave about his Tail.
Mr Rochfort[2] has a mind that you and I should pass a fortnight with
him between this and Michaelmas, I know not how that will fall in
with your Methods.

I send this by a Gentleman who is just going, so adieu.

Address: To Charles Ford Esqr, at his | Lodgings at Mr Shaw's house on Or-
monde key | Dublin.

Forster Copy

Swift to Knightley Chetwode

Dublin, 2 September, 1718.

I received your first of August 13th when I was just leaving Gaulstown;[3] from whence I went to a visitation at Trim.[4] I saw Dame

---

[1] Ford had returned from the Continent after the middle of July, and was
still in Dublin at the middle of October.

[2] George Rochfort.

[3] In 1718 Swift stayed with the Rochforts at Gaulstown from 19 July to 16
Aug. (Forster Collection, No. 510). The date on which Swift received Chetwode's
letter leaves it in no doubt that Chetwode was writing from France where he had
gone to join Ormonde, and that he was dating new style.

[4] In a footnote to this letter Ball attributes an altercation between Swift and
Bishop Evans of Meath to the occasion of a visitation held by the Bishop at
Trim in Aug. 1718. Evans, however, writing to Wake, Archbishop of Canterbury, 20 June 1718, then refers to the 'insolent rudeness' with which Swift had
arraigned him (*Wake Correspondence*, Christ Church, Oxford, vol. xii); and
another Whig bishop, Nicolson of Derry, refers to the incident on 8 July (ibid.,
vol. xii). Ball was unaware that Swift had attended two visitations within a period
of less than three months, that held by Evans in June and the Primate's visitation
of Meath held in the third week of August. It was at the former that Swift took

---

[3] For Gallstown, or Gaulstown, the seat of the Rochfort family, situated in
Westmeath, see p. 170, n. 4.

Plyant.[1] I stayed two days at Laracor,[2] then five more at a friend's, and came thence to this Town, and was going to answer your letter when I received the second of August 23rd.[3] I find it is the opinion of your friends that you should let it be known as publicly here as can be done, without overacting, that you are come to London, and intend soon for Ireland, and since you have set[4] Woodbrooke, I am clearly of opinion that you should linger out some time at Trim, under the notion of staying some time in order to settle.[5] You can be conveniently enough lodged there for a time, and live agreeably and cheap enough, and pick up rent as you are able; but I am utterly opposite to your getting into a Figure all on a sudden, because every body must needs know that travelling would not but be very expensive to you, together with a scattered family, and such conduct will be reckoned prudent and discreet, especially in you whose mind is not altogether suited to your fortune. And therefore though I have room enough in an empty Coach-house which is at your service, yet I wish you would spare the expenses, and in return you shall fill the Coach-house with anything else you please.

I fear you will return with great contempt for Ireland, where yet we live tolerably quiet, and our enemies seem to let us alone merely out of weariness. It was not my fault that I was not in England last June. I doubt you will make a very uneasy change from Dukes to Irish Squires and Parsons, wherein you are less happy than I, who never loved great company, when it was most in my power, and now I hate everything with a title except my books, and even in those the shorter the title the better; and—you must begin on the other side for I began this letter the wrong way—whenever you talk to me of

the Bishop to task for rough treatment of one of his clergy; although, according to Delany, 'in the most gentle and respectful manner' (*Observations*, pp. 216–17). See further a full note upon the whole incident by Louis A. Landa, 'The Insolent Rudeness of Dr. Swift', *Mod. Language Review* (Apr. 1953), lxviii. 223–6; and Nichols's *Supplement*, 1779, xxvi. 158–9.

[1] Mrs. Chetwode.

[2] Swift had been staying at Laracor at the beginning of the preceding January and again in April and in June (Forster No. 510).

[3] Probably written from London and dated old style.

[4] In local sense—to let on lease.

[5] Chetwode had, endangering his own interests and personal safety, associated himself with Ormonde and the Pretender. As subsequent letters show he narrowly escaped prosecution. During his absence Mrs. Chetwode had apparently been living at Trim; and Martry, as well as Woodbroke, was in other hands.

Regents or grandees, I will repay you with passages of Jack Grattan and Dan Jackson.[1] I am the only man in this kingdom who is not a politician, and therefore I only keep such company as will suffer me to suspend their politics, and this brings my conversation into very narrow bounds. Joe Beaumont is my oracle for public affairs in the country,[2] and an old Presbyterian woman in town.[3] I am quite a stranger to all schemes and have almost forgot the difference between Whig and Tory, and thus you will find me when you come over. Adieu. My true love to Ben[4]—

Address: To Knightley Chetwode, Esq., at Mr. Tooke's shop | at the Middle-Temple Gate, in Fleet Street. London.

Deane Swift 1768

Peter Ludlow to Swift

September 10, 1718.

I send you the inclosed pamphlet by a private hand, not daring to venture it by the common post; for it is a melancholy circumstance we are now in, that friends are afraid to carry on even a bare correspondence, much more to write news, or send papers of consequence (as I take the inclosed to be) that way.[5] But I suppose I need make no apology for not sending it by post, for you must know, and own too, that my fears are by no means groundless. For your friend, Mr. *Manley*,[6] has been guilty of opening letters that were

---

[1] The Rev. Daniel Jackson was a cousin-german of the Grattans. His brother, the Rev. John Jackson, held the living of Santry, within a few miles of Dublin, where his grandfather and father before him had been vicars. Daniel Jackson's large nose was a subject of jest in the circle of Swift's friends. See *Poems, passim.*

[2] Apparently Beaumont was once again in his right mind.

[3] i.e. Mrs. Brent.

[4] i.e. Ben Tooke.

[5] The first intimation of friendly relations between Swift and Peter Ludlow, for whom see Swift to Walls, 13 Jan. 1716–17 *ad fin.*, carries us back less than two years. He had stayed with Ludlow at Ardsallagh for six days in Jan. 1717, for four days in April, for three weeks in June and July, and for five days in August (Forster Collection, No. 510). Delany (*Observations*, p. 96) counts Ludlow among Swift's Irish friends 'who were men of fortune, scholars, men of parts, men of humour, men of wit, and men of virtue'. Mrs. Ludlow was a great admirer of Swift.

[6] Isaac Manley, Postmaster in Ireland.

not directed to him, nor his wife, nor really to one of his acquaintance. Indeed I own it so happened, that they were of no consequence, but secrets of state, secrets of families, and other secrets (that one would by no means let Mr. *Manley* know) might have been discovered; besides a thousand, nay, for ought I know, more than a thousand calamities might have ensued; I need not (I believe) enumerate them to you; but to be plain with you, no man nor woman would (with their eyes open) be obliged to show all they had to Mr. *Manley*. These I think sufficient reasons for sending it in the manner I do; but submit them and myself to your candour and censure.

The paper, I believe, you'll find very artfully written, and a great deal couched under the appearance (I own at first) of blunders and a silly Tale. For who, with half an eye, may not perceive, that by the old woman's being drowned at *Ratcliff-highway*, and not dead yet, is meant the Church, which may be sunk or drowned, but, in all probability, will rise again. Then the man, who was followed, and overtaken, is easily guessed at. He could not tell (the ingenious author says) whether she was dead: true, but may be he will tell soon. But then the author goes on (who must be supposed a high-church-man) and inquires of a man riding a horseback upon a mare. That's preposterous, and must allude to a great man who has been guilty (or he is foully belied) of very preposterous actions; when the author comes up to him, the man takes him for a Robber, or *Tory*, and ran from him, but you find he pursued him furiously. Mark that: and *The Horse.*—This is indeed carrying a figure farther than *Homer* does: he makes the shield or its device an epithet sometimes to his warrior, but never, as I remember, puts it in place of the person; but there is a figure for this in rhetorick, which I own I don't remember, by which we often say, He is a good fiddle, or rather as by the Gown is often meant particular Parsons. Well then, you find the Horse, seeing himself dead, or undone, ran away as fast as he could, and left the preposterous fellow to go afoot. During this their misfortune, the candid author (whom I cannot mention without a profound respect) calls them friends, and means to do them no harm; only enquires after the welfare of the church.—Ah! Dear Sir, this is the true character of the *Tories*. And here I cannot but compare the generosity and good-nature of the one, with the sullen ingratitude of the other; we find the horse gone, and they footing it give a surly answer, while the other (though a conqueror) offers his friendship, and asks the question with a *Pray inform me*.

I have gone, my dear friend, thus far with the paper, to shew you how excellent a piece I take it to be, and must beg the favour of you to give me your opinion of it, and send me your animadversions upon the whole, which I am confident you won't refuse me, when you consider of how great anadvantage they will be to the whole earth, who, maybe, to this day, have read over these sheets with too superficial an understanding; and especially since it is the request of, learned Sir, | your most dutiful and obedient humble servant, |

SIR POLITICK WOULD-BE.

I submit it to your better judgement (when you make a more curious enquiry into the arcana of this piece) to consider whether, by Sir *John Vangs* (who you find lives by the water-side) must not be meant the *Dutch*; since you find too, that he eats bag-pudding freezing hot; this may seem a paradox, but I have been assured by a curious friend of mine of great veracity, who had lived many *Winters* in *Holland*, that nothing is more common than for hot pudding to freeze in that cold country: but then what convinces me that by Sir *John* the *Dutch* must be meant, is, that you find he creeps out of a stopper-hole, which alludes to their mean origin. I must observe too, that gammer *Vangs* had an old woman to her son. That's a bob for Glorious.[1]—But I am under great concern to find so hard a sentence passed upon poor *Swift*, because *he's* little. I think him better than any of them, and hope to see him greater.

B.M. Add. 38671

Swift to Mrs. Robert Rochfort

Dublin. Sep. 22ᵈ 1718

Madam

Mʳ Rochfort[2] tells me that he apprehends My Lord and you will hardly come over this Winter,[3] and at the same time I must tell you that I am mighty desirous to have My Lord Harley's and His Lady's

[1] i.e. William III.

[2] George Rochfort.

[3] During July and Aug. 1718, as noted before, Swift had been staying with the Rochforts at Gaulstown. Chief Baron Rochfort was still, with his wife, to whom this letter is addressed, in England on his law business, see p. 207.

Presents,[1] and have desired Mr Nedley when he waits on you, that he will take the Custody of them. I humbly thank you for the Care you have been at, but am extreamly angry at My Lords and your long Absence. I desire you will present my most humble service to His Lordship | I am | Madam | Your most obedient | and most humble Servant | J: Swift

Address: To Mrs Rochfort

4805

Matthew Prior to Swift

London. Sepr the 25th 1718

My Dear Dean.[2]

I have now made an end of what You in Your Naughty manner have called wretched work:[3] My Book is quite printed off, and if You are as much up on the Bagatelle as You pretend to be You will find more pleasure in it than You imagine. We are going to print the Subscribers Names,[4] If therefore You have any by You which are not yet remitted, pray send them over by the next Post: If You have not, pray send me word of that too, that in all cases I may at least hear from You. E. of O.[5] has been in Town all this Summer, is now going into Hereford-shire, and says I shal see You very soon in England. I would tell You with what pleasure this would be, if I knew upon what certainty the Hopes of it were founded. Write me a word of this too, for upon it I would order my matters so that I may be as much with You as I can, And this You will find no little favor, for I assure You we are all so changed that there is very little choice of such Comp^a[6] as You would like, and except about Eighteen hundred that have Subscribed to my Book I do not hear of as many more in this Nation that have common Sense. My Cousen Penny-father[7] and Will: Philips,[8] Drink Your health, I Cough but am

---

[1] The allusion is to the étui and snuff-box Swift was expecting from Lord and Lady Harley. See p. 287, n. 4. These had been promised in April, and Swift was at pains to find some reliable person to bring them over.

[2] In the hand of a scribe.

[3] 'great, or sorry work', 29 May 1718.

[4] Ball inaccurately, 'subscriber's name'.

[5] Earl of Oxford.   [6] Company.

[7] Probably Colonel Matthew Pennefather, see i. 381, n. 8.

[8] Probably the attaché of Sir Thomas Hanmer mentioned by Sir Gilbert Dolben, 22 Dec. 1713.

otherwise well, and till I cease to Cough i.e. to Live, I am with entire Friendship and Affection | Dear Sʳ | Your most Obᵗ and | humble Serᵗ | M Prior.

Address: To | The Reverend Dʳ Swift | Dean of Sᵗ Patricks at | Dublin | Ireland
Endorsed by Swift twice with name and date; & also:
  Levanda est enim paupertas eorum | Hominum qui diu reipublicae viventes |
  pauperes sunt, et nullorum magis

4805

Joseph Addison to Swift

[1 October 1718]
Bristol 8ᵇʳ 1ˢᵗ

Dear Sir

I have just received the honour of your Letter[1] at Bristol where I have just finish'd a Course of Water-drinking which I hope has pretty well recovered me from the Leavings of my last Winter's Sicknesse. As for the subject of your Letter, tho you know an affaire of that nature can not well nor safely be Treated in Writing, I desired a friend of mine to acquaint Sʳ Ralph Gore[2] that I was under a praeengagement and not at my own choice to act in it and have since troubled my Lady Ash[3] with a Letter to the same Effect which I hope has not miscarried. However upon my return to London I will further enquire into that matter and see if there is any Room left for me to negociate as you propose. I live still in hopes of seeing you in England and if you woud take my House at Bilton[4] in your way which lies upon the Road within a Mile of Rugby I woud strain hard to meet you there provided you woud make me happy in your Company for some Days. The greatest pleasure I have met with for some months is in the conversaon of my old friend

---

[1] This letter evidently concerned the friend for whom Swift sought Addison's assistance. Bishop Ashe's family were also, apparently, interested in soliciting Addison's influence to the same purpose.

[2] Gore, who was then Chancellor of the Exchequer in Ireland and became Speaker of the Irish House of Commons, married Bishop Ashe's only daughter.

[3] Bishop Ashe's widow.

[4] In 1713 Addison purchased Bilton, near Rugby, an estate of 1,000 acres, together with a mansion which he enlarged. See Graham, *Letters of Addison*, p. 459, n. 3; and Smithers, *Addison*, pp. 247-8, 308-12.

Dr Smalridge[1] who since the Death of the Excellent man you mention is to me the most candid and agreeable of all Bishops, I woud say clergymen, were not Deans comprehended under that Title. We have often talkd of you and when I assure you he has an Exquisite taste of writing I need not tell you how he talks on such a Subject. I look upon it as my good fortune that I can expresse my Esteem of You even to those who are not of the Bishop's party without giving Offence. When a man has so much Compass in his character he affords his friends topicks enough to enlarge upon that all sides admire. I am sure a sincere and zealous friendly Behavior distinguishes you as much as your many more shining talents, and as I have received particular Instances of it you must have a very bad opinion of me if you do not think I heartily Love and respect you and that I am Ever, Dear Sir | Your most Obedient | and most Humble Servant | J. Addison

Endorsed by Swift: Mr Secretary Addison | Octb 18t 1718.

4805

John Arbuthnot to Swift

London. Octobr 14/1718

Dear Sir

This serves for an envelope for[2] the enclosed, for I cannot tell whither yow care to hear from any of your freinds on this side. in your last I think yow desird me to lett yow alone to enjoy your own Spleen.[3] can yow purchase your fifty pound a year in Wales, as yet. I can tell yow befor hand Lewis scorns to live with yow ther. he keeps company with the greatest, and is princ-Governour in many familys.[4] I have been in France six weeks at Paris and as much at Rowen[5] where I can assure yow I hardly heard a word of newes or

---

[1] Since their schooldays Smalridge and Addison had been friends. The former was consecrated Bishop of Bristol on 4 Apr. 1714. The 'Excellent man' mentioned would be Ashe.

[2] for] to *Hawkesworth, Ball.*

[3] Swift's last letter to Arbuthnot appears to be that of 25 July 1714.

[4] Aitken in the *D.N.B.* states that, 'After Oxford's fall Lewis served him as a kind of steward'. The evidence for this is doubtful, though Lewis was himself a substantial and experienced landowner in Wales.

[5] Two brothers of Arbuthnot, Robert born 1699, and George born 1688,

politicks except a little clutter about sending some impertinent presidents du parlement to prison that had the impudence to talk for the lawes and Libertys of their Country. I was askd for Mon[sr] Swift by many people I can assure yow, and particularly by the Duke D'aumont.[1] I was respectfully & kindly treated by many folks & ev'n by the great M[r] Lawes:[2] amongst other things I had the Honour to carry an Irish Lady to Court that was admired beyond all the Lady's in France for her Beauty.[3] She had great Honours done her The Hussar himself was orderd to bring her the King's Catt to Kiss, her name is Bennet. amongst other folks I saw your old freind L[d] Bolingbroke, who asked for yow he looks just as he did, your freinds here are in good health, not changd in their sentiments towards yow. I left my two Girls[4] in France with their uncle which was my chief business. I don't know that I have any freinds on your side besides M[r] Foord[5] to whom give my service & to D[r] Parnell[6] [and] M[r] Jervas.[7] If it be possible for you obey the contents of the enclosd which I suppose is a kind invitation The Dragon is just

---

found it advisable on political grounds to live abroad, Paris and Rouen, engaging themselves in banking. George had served in the English army (*Journal*, p. 370 and note); but he appears to have taken part in the rising of 1715.

[1] Louis, Duc d'Aumont, was sent to England as French Ambassador as soon as the Treaty of Utrecht was concluded. On the death of Queen Anne he busied himself in working secretly for a Jacobite restoration.

[2] John Law, 1671–1729, financial adviser in France; projector of the 'Mississippi' and other schemes.

[3] This famous beauty, Miss Nelly Bennet, was celebrated by Arbuthnot in the 'Ballad', printed in the Pope and Swift *Miscellanies. The Last Volume.* 1727, pp. 168–71.

> For when as *Nelly* came to *France*
> (Invited by her Cosins)
> Across the *Tuilleries* each Glance
> Kill'd *Frenchmen* by whole Dozens.
> The King as he at Dinner sate,
> Did beckon to his *Hussar*,
> And bid him bring his Tabby Cat,
> For charming *Nell* to buss her.

[4] Arbuthnot was survived by two sons and two daughters.

[5] Ford was still in Ireland at this time.

[6] In the summer of 1718 Parnell was in London. In October he left for Ireland; but was taken ill at Chester, where he died 24 Oct. and was buried in the graveyard of Holy Trinity Church.

[7] Jervas returned to Ireland in the summer of 1717; and in the following years continued to paint in his native country with approbation and success.

as he was, only all his old habits ten times stronger upon him than ever. let me beg of yow not to forgett me, for I can never cease to love & esteem you. being ever | Your most affectionat & obliged humble | servant | Jo: Arbuthnott.

Address: For | The Reverend | Doctor Swift. Dean | of S^t patricks | Dublin
Endorsed by Swift: Dr Arbut | Rx Octr 25th 1718 (*and twice again with name and date of letter*).

Forster 541

Swift to the Rev. Patrick Delany

10 November 1718.

S^r

 I allow in all justice you ought to be ten times more a friend to Mr Sheridan[1] than to me; and yet I can demand of you to keep a secret of a lesser Friend from a greater.[2] Therefore I expect you will not tell Mr Sheridan one word of the inclosed, nor shew it him thô in Confidence. But you are to know that I have long thought severall of his Papers, and particularly that of the Funerall, to be out of all the Rules of Raillery, I ever understood, and if you think the same you ought to tell him so in the manner you like best, without bringing me into the Question, else I may be thought a Man who will not take a Jest; to avoid which Censure with you, I have sent you my thoughts on that Subject in Rime; but why in Rime, I know not, unless because it gives me an Opportunity of expressing my Esteem

[1] In the Forster Collection (541) this letter, covering four pages of verses, is preserved (*Poems*, pp. 214–19). Thomas Sheridan, born in 1687, came of an Irish family of some distinction (see Sichel's *Sheridan*, i. 215–17). He was educated at Trinity College, Dublin, proceeding M.A. in 1714, and soon won fame as a schoolmaster. He was the father of Swift's biographer and grandfather of Richard Brinsley Sheridan. For many years an intimate friendship subsisted between Sheridan and Swift, strings of verse trifles passing between them. Their acquaintance at this time was of short standing; and the verses to which the letter alludes clearly rankled with Swift.

[2] Swift's acquaintance with Delany appears to have begun no earlier than the year in which this letter was written. Patrick Delany was at the time a Junior Fellow of Trinity College, Dublin. He enjoyed a reputation both as a scholar and preacher. His *Observations upon Lord Orrery's Remarks*, 1754, was a defence of Swift. He died in 1768.

for you—which is greater than I care to tell you whatever I may do to others. | I am S^r | Y^r most obed^t | St. | J.S.

Deanry-house | Novr 10th 1718 | 9 in the morning.

Address: To the Reverend | Mr Delany, at his | Chambers in the College

Forster copy

Swift to Knightley Chetwode

Dublin, 25 November, 1718.

I have had your letters, but have been hindered from writing by the illness of my head and eyes, which still afflict me.[1] I have not been these five[2] months in the country, but the people from Trim tell me that yours are all well.

I do not apprehend much consequence from what you mention about informations, etc. I suppose it will fall to nothing by time. You have been so long in the grand monde that you find it difficult to get out. I fear you mistook it for a compliment, when you interpret something that I said as if you had a spirit above your fortune. I hardly know anybody but what has the same, and it is a more difficult virtue to have a spirit below our fortune, which I am endeavouring as much as I can, and differ so far from you, that instead of conversing with Lords, if any Lord here would descend to converse with me, that I wholly shun them for people of my own level, or below it, and I find life much easier by doing so; but you are younger and see with other eyes. The epigram you mention is but of two lines. I have done with those things. I desired a young gentleman to paraphrase it, and I do not much like his performance, but if he mends it I will send it to Ben,[3] not to you.

I think to go soon into the Country for some weeks for my health, but not towards Trim, I believe. Mr. Percivall is dead,[4] and so is poor Parvisol. This is a bad country to write news from. Lord Archibald Hamilton is going to be married to one Lady Hamilton

---

[1] During that year Swift appears to have suffered acutely from vertigo. In his account-book (Forster, No. 510), under 3 May, the following note appears: 'Terrible fall; God knows what may be the event; better towards the end.'

[2] *Recte* three. For this and for Chetwode's evident unwillingness to accept Swift's advice see Swift to Chetwode, 2 Sept. 1718.   [3] i.e. Tooke.

[4] Percival's will was proved a few days later. He had retained his seat as a member for Trim until his death.

the best match in this kingdom.¹ Remember me to Ben and John²
when you see them. Neither my head nor eyes will suffer me to write
more, nor if they did, have I anything materiall to add but that I am, |
Yours &c.

Address: To Knightley Chetwode, Esqr to be left at Mr. | Tooke's shop at the
middle Temple gate, in Fleet | street, London.

4805

John Arbuthnot to Swift

London Der. 11ᵗʰ 1718

Dear Brother,

for so I had call'd yow before were it not for a certain Reverence
I pay to Deans, I find yow wish both me & your self to be old &
rich.³ the second gos in course along with the first; but yow cannot
give 7 (that is the tith of 70) good reasons for either glad at my heart
should I be if Dr Helsham⁴ or I could do yow any good. My service
to Dr Helsham, he dos not want my advice in the Case. I have done
good lately to a patient & a freind in that Complaint of a Vertigo by
Cinnabar of Antimony & Castor, made up into Boluss with Confect
of Alkermes. I had no great opinion of the Cinnabar, but trying it
amongst other things, my freind found good of this prescription;
I had tryd the Castor alone before; not with so much success. Small
quantitys of Tinctur Sacr: now & then will do yow good. Ther is
20 Lords I believe, would send yow horses, if they knew how. one or
two have offerd to me, who, I beleive, would be as good as their
word. Mr Rowe the Poet Laureat⁵ is dead and has left a Damn'd

---

¹ Lord Archibald Hamilton, seventh son of William, first Duke of Hamilton,
married then, as his second wife, the widow of Sir Francis Hamilton of Kil-
laugh, baronet. She had a great jointure, 'a part whereof for perpetuity upon
condition of not marrying except one of the name of Hamilton' (*Portland MSS.*
v. 572).—Ball.

² i.e. Tooke and Barber.

³ Swift had evidently sent a reply to Arbuthnot's letter of 14 Oct.

⁴ Dr. Richard Helsham, senior Fellow of Trinity College, Dublin, where also
he was professor of medicine and moral philosophy. It was probably through
Delany and Sheridan that he became acquainted with Swift.

⁵ Nicholas Rowe, 1674–1718, succeeded Nahum Tate as Poet Laureate 1 Aug.
1715. His death took place five days before Arbuthnot wrote this letter.

jade of a pegasus.¹ Ile answer for it he wont do as your Mare did having more need of Lucan's present² than Sir Richard Blackmore. I would fain have Pope gett a patent for life for the place with a power of putting in Durfy³ his deputy. I sent for the two Roseingraves⁴ & examin'd the matter of fact. The younger had no Concern in this note of 20ˡˡ. The Elder sayes that he thought the 20ˡˡ due to him for the pains & some expenses he had been at about the young fellow & his Master Bethel⁵ who had given Mr Roseingrave the Elder 10 guineas befor thought the same reasonable. he sayes he did not take it by way of a Bribe but as his due & did never intend to make use of it but when the young fellow was in circumstances to pay him. the yo[unge]r Roseingrave was begg'd & entreated both by Bethel & the young fellow (who would not go without him) to accompany him to Ireland & did believe that Bearing his expenses, which was done by Bethel was the least he could take. Ther is one thing in the fellows paper that I know to be a lye his being used by Roseingrave at Lᵈ Carnavons⁶ he sung there I believe once or twice for his own instruction or tryal & Lord Carnavon gave him a guinea: he went sometimes to hear the musick for his improvement. This is what they told me, however I have Reprimanded The Elder Roseingrave for taking the note. when this fellow came first to town I thought his Voice might do but found it did not improve.

¹ The allusion is presumably to Laurence Eusden, who, however, did not officially succeed to the post of Poet Laureate till 24 Dec. He was satirized by Swift in 'Directions for a Birth-day Song', *Poems*, pp. 459–69.

² In *The Battle of the Books* Lucan bestowed on Blackmore a pair of spurs (ed. Guthkelch and Nichol Smith, p. 248).

³ Tom Durfey, prolific writer of burlesque songs, was at this time sixty-five years of age.

⁴ The organist of St. Patrick's Cathedral and his son. Arbuthnot himself was fond of music, and composed an anthem, 'As pants the heart', &c. See Aitken's *Arbuthnot*, p. 113. The passage about the Roseingraves from 'I sent for' to 'Maturely consider'd this matter' was omitted by Hawkesworth. Aitken only printed part of the letter.

⁵ The reference is probably to Hugh Bethel, sometime member for Pontefract, friend and correspondent of Pope. See Pope's *Works*, Elwin and Courthope, ix. 147–68; *Imitations of Horace*, ed. John Butt, pp. 344–5; Pope's *Correspondence*, ed. Sherburn, *passim*.

⁶ On 19 Oct. 1714 James Brydges was created Viscount Wilton and Earl of Carnarvon. He built at Canons a magnificent chapel, maintaining a full choir. Handel spent two years there. In 1719 Brydges was created Marquis of Carnarvon and Duke of Chandos. Ball omits the words 'he sung there I believe once or twice'.

It is mighty hard to gett such a sort of Voice. Ther is an excellent one in the Kings chappell but he will not go. The top one of the world is in Bristol Quire & I beleive might be manag'd tho your Roseingrave is really much improvd so do not totally exclude the young fellow till yow have more Maturely consider'd this matter. The Dragon is come to town, & was entering upon the detail of the Reasons of State that kept him from appearing at the beginning, &c. when I did beleive at the same time, it was only a Law of Nature to which the Dragon is most subject Remanere in statu in quo est nisi deturbetur ab extrinseco. Ld Harley & Lady Harley give yow their service. Lewis is in the country with Lord Bathurst[1] & has wrote me a most dreadfull story of a Mad Dog that bit their Huntsmen since which accident I am told he has shortened his stirrups three Bores, they were not long befor. Ld Oxford presented him with two Horses he has sold one & sent the other to Grass avec Beaucoup de sagesse. I don't beleive the story of Ld Bolingbrokes Marriage;[2] for I have been consulted about the lady, & by some defects in her constitution, I should not think her appetite lay much toward Matrimony. There is some talk about reversing his attainder, but I wish he may not be disappointed. I am all for presidents of that kind. They say the pretender is like to have his chief minister impeached too.[3] he has his wife prisoner. The footmen of the House of Commons choose their Speaker and impeach &c. I think it were proper that all monarchs should serve their apprenticeships as pretenders, that we might discover their defects. Did yow ever expect to see the Duke of Ormond fighting against the protestant succession & the Duke of Berwick fighting for it; [and] France in confederacy with England, to reduce the exorbitant power of Spain. I really think there is no such good reason for living till 70 as curiosity. Yow say yow are ready to Resent it as an affront if I thought a Beautiful Lady a curiosity in Ireland,[4] but pray is it an affront to say that a Lady hardly known or observed for her beauty in Ireland, is a curiosity in

---

[1] Allen Bathurst, 1685–1775, Tory M.P. for Cirencester from 1705 till he was raised to the peerage as Baron Bathurst, 1 Jan. 1712. In 1772 he was created an Earl. He was a lifelong friend of Swift and Pope.

[2] Bolingbroke had formed an intimacy with the Marquise de Villette; but their marriage did not take place till May 1720. Lady Bolingbroke had died in Nov. 1718.

[3] The Earl of Mar, declaring that the Pretender's affairs were 'desperate', had by this time retired to Italy.

[4] See Arbuthnot to Swift, 14 Oct.

France. all Deans naturally fall into paralogysms. my wife gives yow her kind love & service, & which is the first thing to occur to all wives wishes yow well married. I have not clean paper more than to bid you adieu.

Address: For | The Reverend Doctor Swift | Dean of S^t patricks | Dublin
Endorsed by Swift: Dr Arbuthnott | Directions to me | About my Disease

Rothschild

Swift to Charles Ford

Dublin.   Dec^{br} 20th 1718

I have but just received Yours of Nov^{br} 13th for we had 11 Packets together. I desire I may never hear more from you of the Person you reproach me with.[1] Since his coming from abroad I have had 20 Letters from him, teazing me to death to write to him about an Information he apprehends against him, and about his Family. I had a great Respect and Friendship for his Wives Mother, and at last I was forced to let him know that my Head and Eyes were so bad I could not write, nor could tell him any thing of his Affairs, and desired to be excused. He came to know me inspight of my Teeth, and writes to me inspight of my Teeth, and there's an end.

I stayd to hear from You, that I might know you were in Town but what can you expect from hence, from a Place every way contemptible in it self, and yet more so in your Esteem. What have I to say unless I should transcribe a Sermon or a Pamphlet. It is a just Tax upon you in great Scenes to entertain us who are out of the World, but it is a cruell Tyranny to expect Returns. We had been undone for Talk during the Northwest Winds if two Ladyes had not been carryed off and ravished in the Country. Mrs Ford[2] is so great a Rambler since your Absence, that in ten Attempts I have seen her but thrice, and once more in a third Place, where she tells me of an Account from you that a certain Friend of ours[3] complains of my Silence. I suppose it is the Friend that saw me coming in the Cloud. I wrote him a long Romantick Letter, and desired a Correspondence; perhaps it miscarryed; I have his Address and will write again, and so I will to my Sister O—[4] in a day or two, but she must

---

[1] Knightley Chetwode, now in London.   [2] Ford's mother.
[3] Unidentified.   [4] The Duchess of Ormonde.

stay till I have done my Christmas Sermon. It seems the Politicians are so busy in Parliament matters, that I cannot yet get a Successor to Dr Parnel in Finglas, where I have prevailed to place one of my Grattans,[1] as soon as our great Viceroy[2] will have Leisure from the weighty Affairs of Europe to remove an Impediment.

Monsr Charelot[3] is in debt to me not I to him: I wish he would mind his Interest upon the Death of an old Dean, now that the Person who can make him easy is on the Spot.

If my Spirit of repining were at Leisure, I could use it much upon the Subject of your Parliamentary Debates. Perhaps the Toryes had a Mind it should go for the Court upon Sr James Forbes's[4] Reasons. For I have been told, that for two Years past it hath been the Politicks of that Party to let every thing go as it would, without interposing. But I am more concerned about Sheridan the Schoolmaster[5] plaguing me with bad Verses during his Christmas Leisure; and about contriving how to hinder an old Knave of an Alderman from cheating me in a Lease, and where to find a proper Successor for Parvisol,[6] who dyed last Month without any Notice taken of it either in Court or Parliament. But I am at present casting about how to get Acquaintance with one Boswell a Prentice boy,[7] who acts Punch to Admiration, and besides I am under great Difficultyes how to entertain seven Butchers and Grocers with their Wives and Familyes at a Christmas Dinner. I am afraid all these Momentous matters are as indifferent to you as the Sliding of a Duck. I am concerned for my Friend Hatton,[8] but not disappointed, because it was what I ex-

---

[1] John Grattan, Vicar of Finglas, 1719–20.

[2] The Duke of Bolton. War was declared against Spain on 17 Dec.

[3] Under this name Bolingbroke had asked Swift to address him in Paris, 'chez Monsieur Cantillon, banquier'. Cf. 23 Oct. 1716. Bolingbroke was reported to have supped with Stanhope in Paris during July (*Stuart Papers*, vii. 48).

[4] Clerk of the Green Cloth in 1689, when he was knighted; mentioned in letters by, or to, Prior (*Longleat MSS*. iii. 281, 283, 304). The debates were on the war with Spain, which was opposed by Walpole.

[5] See Swift to Delany, 10 Nov. 1718.

[6] Writing to Chetwode, 25 Nov., Swift refers to Parvisol.

[7] Apparently Swift's only mention of him.

[8] William, second Viscount Hatton, 1690?–1760, mentioned as dining with Swift, *Journal*, 29 Oct. 1711. His half sister, Anne, married in 1685, as his second wife, Daniel Finch, second Earl of Nottingham. The Hatton, mentioned by Miss Long, 18 Nov. 1711, in connexion with Vanessa, may have been the same person or a relation.

pected, and said something to you that way when you were here. He and Carteret[1] were the onely two young Lords that I threw away some Esteem on, and I heartily repent it.

The Grattans and Jacksons would not believe that you remembred them but I assured them I gave you a Copy of their Names and Callings. Your other Friends are well, and Peter Ludlow[2] came to Town with his Lady who is soon to be brought to bed of another Son. Jervas must positively be in London before Christmas day but is not yet preparing his Equipage. Remember me to John and Ben[3] when you see them.

Did I tell you that Octr 28th I received a Letter from the Dragon.[4] Octr 28th it came to my hands, and Nov^br 15th he was to be back in Town, and I must visit him for 3 days, and take a good Winter Journey Ætat. suae[5] 51. I wrote him such an Answer as he deserved, and stayd here, and saved 50^ll—I have been just dining in my Closet alone on a Bief Stake and Pint of wine, in 7 Minutes by my Watch; and this is what I often do, to encourage Cheerfullness. I am heartily concerned for Lady Boling—but we have a story, that some Proceeding in my L^d had provoked her.[6]

On second thoughts I write this Post to my sister O—[7]

Address: To Charles Ford Esqr, at | his Lodgings at the Golden | Perewig in Pell-mell | London[8]
Postmarks: D *and* 29 DE

Swift to Charles Ford

Dublin. Jany 6th 1718–19.

I answered your Former letter as I remember, the very Post after I received it. But there was at that time a great delay for want of Packets on each side, and so probably mine had not reached you.

[1] John, second Baron Carteret, 1690–1763, had joined the Whig party since Swift's London days, and was now steadily rising to power.
[2] See p. 249.
[3] John Barber and Benjamin Tooke.
[4] Oxford's letter and Swift's reply have both disappeared.
[5] A slip for 'meae'?
[6] His association with the Marquise de Villette.
[7] Duchess of Ormonde.
[8] Added in another hand—'Gold perreywig over gain Rochd's'.

After all I am not satisfied, that it hath been my old Custom not to write to you; while you were abroad you could not easily be come at, and except that Period, I deny that we were long asunder. It is really a difficult matter to be a good Correspondent from hence, where their is nothing materiall to say, where you know very few, and care for nothing that can pass in such a Scene as this, not I neither if I could help it. You know I chuse all the sillyest Things in the world to amuse my self, in an evil age, and a late time of life, ad fallendam canitiem quæ indies obrepit. Little trifling Businesses take up so much of my time, that I have little left for speculation, [in] which I could gladly employ my self, for my Eyes begin to grudge (that I may speak in Royall Style) me reading, and the Pen is not half so troublesom. But instead of that, I do every thing to make me forget my self and the World as much as I can; and this is a full and true Account of your Correspondent. Here is a Pamphlet come over, and they say privatly reprinted here, called an Apology for Alberoni,[1] they say 6 Editions are already printed in England, and that it is a wonderfull Piece of wit and Satyr. I have read it, and lament the Tast of the Age, as well as the Malice, for except the latter, I can impartially find nothing in it but great Impudence, Wickedness and wrong Representation. I wonder when men sit down with a Resolution to stick at nothing how they contrive to be so very dull and unentertaining, but de his satis. Mrs Ford told me what you desired her about our absent returning Friend. I am glad he received my last Letter.[2] I never had his Answer, but that shall not hinder me from writing again.

Pray tell Mr Pope that I will never be angry with him for any Mark of his Kindness, and will therefore pardon his Concern, or rather thank him for it. I hope this is enough, and that he will not require me to assure him he is misinformed, honest men know each other better: and I believe you have heard me say that Lord Oxford took it as the greatest Compliment ever made, when I told him on Occasion that I never regarded what I said to him, nor what I said of him.[3]

I have as great a desire as my Nonchalance will permit me to pass

---

[1] *A Modest Apology for Parson Alberoni . . . The Whole being a short, but unanswerable Defence of Priestcraft, and a New Confutation of the Bishop of Bangor*, dated 1719, but published Dec. 1718. See *Post Boy*, 9–11 Dec. The author was Thomas Gordon.   [2] The previous letter.

[3] See Swift to Oxford, 3 July 1714 *ad fin.*

some Months in England, but not in London; and if I can adjust matters to bear, I have had some Intentions that it might be this Summer. But my Resolutions are like the Scheams of a Man in a Consumption which every returning fit of Weakness brings to nothing.

Tell Dr Arbuthnot, that I received his last Letter,[1] and will write to him when he has recovered Breath to read another of mine.

I am extremely sorry that the Clause to make voyd the Test by a Certificate, &c. did not pass,[2] and I have a true Veneration for those Prelates who stood for it; The first part of this Assertion is actually true.—I writt to my sister O— the same Post that I did to you, I hope my Letter did not miscarry.[3]

I hope you have found your English Climate since you left us, as bad as ours. Jervas happened to read the Story of Belphigor in an Italian Machiavel, and not knowing it was already in English, very gravely translated and published it here,[4] so that I assure you he is an Author. I was not let into the Secret till lately, so this is entre nous, but it may serve for Pope to laugh at, if he can pretend to come by it any where else. Has Gay done nothing of late? He is too idle for a young Fellow, pray tell him so: And I think Pope should bestow a few Verses on his friend Parnels memory,[5] especially if it is

---

[1] 11 Dec. 1718.

[2] The 'Act for strengthening the Protestant Interest in these Kingdoms' had been introduced by Stanhope in December, but reasons offered by Cowper and other peers 'had so much weight, that some clauses derogatory to the Test and Corporation Acts were agreed to be left out'. The Prelates who spoke in favour of the Bill were the Bishops of Bangor (Hoadly), Gloucester (Willis), Lincoln (Gibson), and Peterborough (White Kennett). See *Political State*, Dec. 1718, pp. 613–26.

[3] This letter to the Duchess of Ormonde is missing.

[4] 'The Marriage of Belphegor, An Italian Novel, Translated from Machiavel' had been added to *The Novels of Quevedo, Faithfully Englished*, 1671, and reprinted in *The Works of the Famous Nicolas Machiavel*, translated by Henry Nevile, 1675, pp. 524–9. Another version is given in Samuel Croxall's *Select Collection of Novels in Four Volumes . . . all new translated from the Originals, By Several Eminent Hands*, 1720, vol. i, pp. 265–79; and perhaps this version is by Jervas. The separate Dublin issue of 1718 has not been traced. Jervas became a substantial author when he translated *Don Quixote*.

[5] At the conclusion of his notes to *The Iliad*, 1720, Pope says that Parnell entrusted him with the publication of his poems 'almost with his dying breath'. *Poems on Several Occasions. Written by Dr. Thomas Parnell, Late Arch-Deacon of Clogher: and published by Mr. Pope* appeared in Dce. 1721, though dated 1722. The verses which Pope there bestowed on Parnell's memory took the form of the

intended (as I think I have heard,) that some of Parnels scattered Things are to be published together. Who is that same Eusden, they have made Laureat? is he a Poet?[1]

I am personally concerned for the Death of the K of Sweden,[2] because I intended to have beggd my Bread at His Court, whenever our good Friends in Power thought fit to put me and my Brethren under the necessity of begging. Besides I intended him an honor and a Compliment, which I never yet thought a Crownd head worth, I mean, dedicating a Book to him.[3] Pray can you let me know how I could write to the Count of Gillenburg.

This is enough at present so adieu.

Address: To Charles Ford Esqr, at | his Lodgings at the blue | Perewig in Pell-mell | London
Postmarks: D *and* 12 IA

Rothschild

Swift to Charles Ford

Dublin. Feb. 16th 1718-19.

I continue in an ugly State of Health by the disorder in my Head, which Blister upon Blister and Pills upon Pills will not remove, and this whole Kingdom will not afford me the medicine of an unfoundred trotting Horse. I have yours of Jan^ry 13th and ought to have answered

famous dedication to the Earl of Oxford, which says more about Oxford than Parnell.   [1] See p. 304, n. 1.

[2] Charles XII of Sweden was killed at Fredrikshald on 11 Dec. (N.S.) 1718. Swift had been invited to the Swedish court before 1710. Pope in his letter to Arbuthnot of 11 July 1714 records a talk with Swift, who 'gave us a Hint as if he had a Correspondence with the King of Sueden' (Sherburn, i. 234).

[3] The work survives in a fragment called *An Abstract of the History of England*, first printed by Deane Swift in 1765, 1768, quarto edn., vols. viii and xiii. The *Abstract* consists of three parts: (*a*) A dedication, 1719, which has distinct political implications; (*b*) facts based on Sir William Temple's *Introduction to the History of England*, completed 1693-4. This part was probably done by Swift before Temple's death in 1699; (*c*) reigns of four English Kings, probably written 1700 to 1702. The parallel on 'mixed governments' with *Contests and Dissensions* is very marked. The three fragments extend in composition over twenty years. Gyllenborg had been Swedish ambassador in London from 1710 to 1717 when, on 30 Jan., he was arrested for complicity in the plot to support a new Jacobite rising with 12,000 Swedish troops. See *The English Historical Review*, 1903, xviii. 81-106.

it immediately if I intended to talk to the purpose, for there are such
sudden whirles in your Court and Parliament, that Affairs are at an
Issue before one can have time to reason on them. It would be an
admirable Scituation to be neither Whig nor Tory. For a Man without Passions might find very strong Amusements. But I find the
turn of Blood at 50 disposes me strongly to Fears, and therefore I
think as little of Publick Affairs as I can, because they concern me as
one of the Multitude; and for the same Reason I dare not venture to
play at threepeny Basset, because it is a Game where Conduct is of no
use, and I dare not trust to Fortune as the younger Folks do, and
therefore I divert my self with looking upon others at Play mea sine
parte pericli,¹ which if a Man could do in what concerns the Publick,
it would be no ill Entertainment. But when the Diversion grows to
throw Fire-balls at Random, how can I be certain that Ucalegon may
not live at the Deanry-house.²—There is a Proverb that shews what
is the Time when honest People come by their own. I wonder
whether that Proverb hath a Reverse. A Friend of ours³ proposeth
to set up a School of Strong Believers, and desires that his own
Father now in London may be at the Head of it. I just now think of
carrying this Proposal further, and there may be a Whig and Tory
side of the School. The Test of the latter was the K. of Sweden's
Death, which the best Scholars would not allow till Friday last at
seven Minutes past eleven. The Whig Test shall be that no Further
Attempts shall be made against the Church.

I was so unfortunate to lose your note about the Chaise by an
Excess of Care; for I had mislayd it before, and keeping it in my
Pocket to shew a Merchant, it is irrecoverably gone, which I forgot
to tell you in my last. Jam quoque Mœrim vox fugit ipsa, lupi
Mœrim videre priores;⁴ and my onely Merchant Friend Samson⁵
I fear is dying of a Consumption. But I shall endeavor to patch up
the Matter with somebody else.—Ask your sanguine black Friend
at My Sister O's⁶ how his match goes on, and tell him the Story of
Picrochole out of Rablais,⁷ which I think I mentioned in my last. I

¹ Lucretius, ii. 6.
² *Aeneid*, ii. 311-12.
³ Probably George Rochfort. His father was at this time in London.
⁴ Virgil, *Eclogues*, ix. 53-54.
⁵ Probably the Michael Sampson, M.P. for Lifford, who died in 1719.
⁶ Unidentified.
⁷ *Gargantua*, xlix. Swift referred to the story in a letter written on the same
day to Bolingbroke, now lost. See Bolingbroke's reply, 17 Mar. [o.s.] 1718-19.

had lately a Letter from an Inmate of John's,[1] who tells me that poor Ben Took grows ill an[d] spleenatick, and talks of selling his share in the Patent &c. It seems that Inmate and Ben have referred a Case to me, which I entirely give against Ben; for I am Party to the Bargain made by Ld B.'s order when that Patent was granted; and pray signify to that Person that I would write if I knew some Name to direct to. I do not find among those that talk news, any discourse of Ld Bolingbroke's Return, therefore I suppose that Matter is dropt. If his Lordship expects Mercy he must get ready a Sacrifice, wherein the Princes of the Earth seem to differ a little from God Almighty, who says, he will have Mercy and not Sacrifice.—This is all I can work out of an ill Head at present: I have a mind to drink the Waters of Aix la Chappelle[2] this Summer. Pray tell me the proper time to take them and my Journy. I will once desire you to present my humble Service to severall Persons by name, My Ld Kinoul, Dartmouth, Harly, Masham, Bingly, Arran, Mr Bromly, S^r Th. Hanmer, Dr Arbuthnot, Mr Pope, Gay, &c, but especially friend Lewis; not forgetting Ld Bathurst. I can recollect no more at present, but I am in a humor of Civility; and my humble Respects to Sister O—.

My humble Service to Mr Prior. I expect his Works[3] daily, I think the Method must be to consign them to a Bookseller here, and I am sending for one Hide,[4] who has dealt that Way already and is recommended to me as an honest man.

We have found out the Fellow that killd[5] Harry Lutterel,[6] but cannot hang him. No doubt you know the Story, but it is very odd that he who hired the murderer should confess in hope of the Reward,

---

[1] John Barber's. In 1711 Swift had procured for Barber and Tooke the printing of the *Gazette*; and in 1713 they were made Queen's Printers, their term to begin after Baskett's had expired. But Baskett bought back the reversion. See *Life of Barber*, Curll, 1741, p. 7.

[2] Writing to Prior on 28 Apr. Swift states that he could not be at Aix-la-Chapelle in May. He would have met Bolingbroke.

[3] The folio edition of his *Poems on Several Occasions*.

[4] John Hyde, who brought out the Dublin edition of *The Conduct of the Allies*. In 1726 he published the first Dublin edition of *Gulliver's Travels*. In the following year he died.

[5] 'that killd' is repeated in the manuscript.

[6] Col. Henry Luttrell was shot dead before his house in Stafford Street, Dublin. See Ball, *History of County Dublin*, iv, pp. 14-16, and Macaulay's *History*, ch. xvii. Prior to this statement by Swift it has been understood that the assassin was not discovered.

which however he must have had by the Letter of the Proclamation, if it were not for his Perjury in swearing before against Lutterell's widow.

Address: To Charles Ford Esqr, at his | Lodgings at the blue Perewig | in the Pell-mell | London
Postmarks: D *and* 23 FE

4805

Viscount Bolingbroke to Swift

17 March [o.s. 6] 1718-19.

I have not these several years tasted so sensible a pleasure as yr letter of the 6th of Jan: & 16th of feb. gave me;[1] and I know enough of the tenderness of your heart to be assured that the letter I am writing will produce much the same effect on you. I feel my own pleasure, and I feel yours. the truest reflexion, and at the same time, the bitterest satyr which can be made on the present age, is this, that to think as you think, will make a man pass for Romantick. Sincerity, constancy, tenderness are rarely to be found. they are so much out of use, that the man of mode imagines them to be out of nature. we meet with few friends. the greatest part of those who pass for such, are properly speaking nothing more than acquaintance, and no wonder, since Tullys maxim is certainly true, that friendship can subsist non nisi inter bonos. att that age of life when there is balm in the blood, and that confidence in the mind which the innocency of our own heart inspires, and the experience of other men's destroys, I was apt to confound my acquaintance & my friends together. I never doubted but that I had a numerous cohorte of the latter. I expected if ever I fell into misfortune to have as many & as remarkable instances of friendship to produce, as the Scythian in one of Lucians Dialogues[2] draws from his nation. into these misfortunes I have fallen. thus far my propitious stars have not disappointed my

---

[1] Swift had begun his letter to Bolingbroke on 16 Jan., but, as appears from the postscript, had been unable to finish it for a month. The idea of writing to Bolingbroke was perhaps prompted by the rumour that his friend's attainder was to be reversed. These letters were probably the first that passed between them since the autumn of 1716.

[2] *Τάραξις ἤ φιλία*.

expectations. the rest has almost entirely fail'd me. the fire of my adversity has purg'd the mass of my acquaintance; and the separation made, I discover on one side, an handfull of friends, but on the other, a legion of Enemys, at least of strangers. happily this fiery tryal has had one effect on me wch makes me some amends. I have found less resource in other people & more in myself than I expected. I make good att this hour the motto[1] wch I took nine years ago, when I was weak enough to list again under the conduct of a man,[2] of whom nature meant to make a spy, or, att most a Captain of Miners, and whom fortune in one of her whimsical moods made a general. I enjoy att this hour with very tolerable health, great tranquillity of mind. You will, I am sure, hear this with satisfaction; and sure it is that I tell it you without the least affectation. I live, my friend, in a narrower circle than ever, but I think in a larger. when I look back on what is past, I observe a multitude of errors, but no crimes. I have been far from following the advice wch Caelius gave to Cicero, id melius statuere quod tutius sit.[3] and I think I may say to myself what Dolabella says in one of his letters to the same Cicero: Satisfactum est jam a te, vel officio, vel familiaritati: satisfactum etiam partibus, et ei reipublicae, quam tu probabas. Reliquum est, ubi nunc est respublica: ibi simus potius, quam, dum illam veterem sequamur, simus in nullâ.[4] what my memory has furnish'd on this head, for I have neither books nor papers here concerning home affairs, is writ with great truth, and with as much clearness as I could give it. if ever we meet, you will, perhaps, not think two or three hours absolutely thrown away in reading it. one thing I will venture to assure you of beforehand, which is that you will think I never deserv'd more to be commended than whilst I was the most blam'd, and, that you will pronounce the brightest part of my character to be that which has been disguised by the nature of things, misrepresented by the malice of men, & which is still behind a cloud. in what is past therefore I find no great source of uneasiness. as to the present, my fortune is extreamly reduced, but my desires are still more so. nothing is more certain than this truth, that all our wants beyond those which a very moderate income will supply, are purely imaginary, and that his happyness is greater & better assur'd who brings his mind up to a temper of not feeling them, than his, who feels them, & has wherewithall to supply them. Hor: Ep: i. Lib: i:

---

[1] 'Nec quaerere, nec spernere, honorem.'
[2] i.e. Oxford.   [3] *Epp.* viii. 14.   [4] *Epp.* ix. 9.

        vides, quae maxima credis
    esse mala, exiguum censum, turpemque repulsam,
    Quanto devites &c.

which I paraphrased thus not long ago, in my post-chaise:

    Survey mankind, observe what risks they run,
    What fancy'd ills, thro' real dangers, shun,
    Those fancy'd ills, so dreadful to the great,
    A lost election, or impair'd Estate.
    Observe the merchant, who, intent on gain
    Affronts the terrors of the Indian main,
    Tho' storms arise, & broken Rocks appear,
    He flys from poverty, & knows no other fear.
    Vain Men! who might arrive, with toil far less,
    By smoother paths, att greater happiness;
    For 'tis superior bliss not to desire
    That trifling good, which fondly you admire,
    Possess precarious, & too dear acquire.
    What hackney gladiator can you find,
    By whom th' olympick crown wou'd be declin'd,
    Who rather than that glorious Palm to seize,
    With safety combat, & prevail with ease,
    Would choose on some inglorious stage to tread,
    And, fighting strole from wake to wake for bread?

as to what is to happen, I am not anxious about it. on which subject I have twenty fine quotations att the end of my pen, but I think it better to own frankly to you, that upon a principle which I have long establish'd, that we are a great deal more mechanical than our vanity will give us leave to allow. I have familiaris'd the worst prospects to my sight, and that by staring want, solitude, neglect, & the rest of that train in the face, I have disarmed them of their terrors. I have heard of some body, who while he was in the Tower, used every morning to lie down on the block, and so act over his last scene. nothing disturbs me, but the uncertainty of my situation, which the zeal of a few friends, and the inveteracy of a great many Enemys entertain. the more prepared I am to pass the remainder of my life in exile, the more sensibly shall I feel the pleasure of returning to you, if his Mty's unconditional favour, the offers of which prevented even my wishes, proves att last effectual.[1] I cannot apply

---

[1] In Mar. 1716 Stanhope authorized Lord Stair to place himself in touch with

to myself, as you bid me do, *non tibi parvum ingenium, non inulctum est*, & what follows;[1] and, if ever we live in the same country together, you shall not apply to me—*quod si frigida curarum fomenta relinquere posses*.[2] I have writ you before I was aware of it a long letter. The pleasure of breaking so long a silence transports me, & your sentiment is a sufficient excuse. It is not so easy to find one for talking so much about myself, but I shall want none with you upon this score. Adieu. this letter will get safe to London, and from thence, I hope, the friend, to whom I recommend it, will find means of conveying it to you. For Gods sake no more apologys for your quotations, unless you mean, by accusing yourself, to correct me. there never was a better application than yours of the story of Picrochole.[3] the storks will never come, & they must be Porters all their lives. they are something worse, for I had rather be a porter, than a tool, & would sooner lend out my back to hire than my name. they are at this time the instruments of a sawcy gardener, who has got a gold cross on his stomach, and a red cap on his head.[4] a poor gentleman[5] who puts me often in mind of one of Scandals pictures in Congreve's play of Love for Love, where a soldier is represented

Bolingbroke. In September of that year Bolingbroke wrote his private letter to Sir William Wyndham exhorting him to abandon the Jacobites. This letter was not published till 1753. Whig opposition to the reversion of the attainder was strong, and it was not till May 1723 that the pardon of Bolingbroke passed the Great Seal.

[1] Horace, *Ep.* I. iii. 22.

[2] Ibid. 26.

[3] Writing to Ford, 16 Feb. 1718–19, Swift had alluded to the story of Picrochole. In his letter written to Bolingbroke on the same day, now lost, he had evidently applied to the Pretender and his party the following passage in Rabelais, *Gargantua*, xlix: 'Ainsi s'en alla le pauvre cholerique; puis, passant l'eau au Port Huaulx, et racontant ses males fortunes, fut advisé par un vieille lourpidon que son royaume luy seroit rendu à la venue des cocquecigrues: depuis ne sçait on qu'il est devenu. Toutefois, l'on m'a dict qu'il est de present pauvre gaigne denier a Lyon, cholere comme devant. Et tousjours se guemente à tons estrangiers de la venue des cocquecigrues, esperant certainement, selon la prophetie de la vieille, estre à leur venue réintigré en son royaume.'

[4] The allusion is to the Prime Minister of Spain, Cardinal Alberoni, who was the son of a gardener.

[5] Dissensions which arose between Ormonde, who is the subject of this reference, and Bolingbroke were made the ostensible reason for the dismissal of the latter from the Pretender's service. Their relations were not improved by the fact that Ormonde was deputed by the Pretender to demand from Bolingbroke his papers and seals.—Ball.

with his Heart where his head should be, & no head att all,[1] is the
conductor of this doughty enterprise wch will end in making their
cause a little more desperate than it is. Again, adieu.

March the 17th 1719

Let me hear from you by the same conveyance as brings you this.
I am in pain about your health. from the 6th of Jan: to the 16th of
feb: is a long course of illness.

Endorsed by Swift: Mar. 17th 1718 N.S. | Ld Bol—

Longleat vii[2]

Swift to Matthew Prior

Dublin. Apr. 28th 1719

Sr

I thought to have had the Happyness of seeing you before this
Time because my Health required a Journey. But whether I fancy
my Head is some thing better, or that little paultry Impediments
stop me, or the sang froid of fifty, I cannot tell, but so it is, that I
have past the Time and cannot be at Aix le Chapelle in May as
I intended, and writt to my Friends in London that I would. But I
am going[3] to try a more lazy Remedy of Irish Country Air, and as
my Return is uncertain I thought fit to let you know that your Subscribers want their Books,[4] and that your Bookseller is a Blockhead
for not sending them.[5] I spoke to one Mr Hyde a Bookseller here,
who has been employd that way; And they must be sent in Quires
consigned to Mr Hyde Bookseller at his Shop in Dames street[6]—
Dublin. Pray order that they may be sent as soon as possible, and
care shall be taken to have them delivered to the Subscribers,
and receive the second Guinea. I am just getting on Horseback, and

---

[1] '*Scan.* I have some hieroglyphics too; I have a lawyer with a hundred hands,
two heads, and but one face; a divine with two faces, and one head; and I have a
soldier with his brains in his belly, and his heart where his head should be.
Mrs. Frail. And no head? *Scan.* No head.'—Act I, sc. 2.

[2] The original of this letter is in the volume of *Prior Papers, 1701–1721*,
Longleat, vii. 101.

[3] 'going' above the line in manuscript.

[4] See p. 281.

[5] Words struck out after 'them'. 'in Quires to us' (?).

[6] Dame Street, a business thoroughfare largely occupied by booksellers.

have only time to desire you will please to present my humble service to the Earl of Oxford S^r | Your most obedient | and most humble Servt | J: Swift.

Your Letters will be sent me
thô I should continue in the
Country.

Address: To Matthew Prior Esqr | at His House in Duke- | street   Westminster
Postmarks: D *and* 4 MA

Deane Swift 1765
Swift to Viscount Bolingbroke

May, 1719
My Lord,[1]
    I forget whether I formerly mentioned to you what I have observed in Cicero; that, in some of his letters, while he was in exile, there is a sort of melancholy pleasure, which is wonderfully affecting. I believe the reason must be, that, in those circumstances of life, there is more leisure for friendship to operate, without any mixture of envy, interest, or ambition. But, I am afraid, this was chiefly when Cicero writ to his brethren in exile, or they to him; because common distress is a great promoter both of friendship and speculation. For, I doubt, prosperity and adversity are too much at variance, ever to suffer a near alliance between their owners.
    Friendship, we say, is created by a resemblance of humours. You allow that adversity both taught you to think and reason much otherwise than you did; whereas, I can assure you, that those who contrived to stay at home, and keep what they had, are not changed at all; and, if they sometimes drink an absent friend's health, they have fully discharged their duty. I have been, for some time, nursing up an observation, which, perhaps may be a just one: That no men are used so ill, upon a change of times, as those who acted upon a public view, without regard to themselves. I do not mean from the circumstance of saving more or less money, but because I take it, that the same grain of caution, which disposeth a man to fill

----

    [1] In his letter to Bolingbroke, 19 Dec. 1719 *ad fin.*, Swift writes in the belief that this letter miscarried. It came into the hands of Deane Swift by whom it was first printed in 1765.

his coffers, will teach him how to preserve them upon all events. And I dare hold a wager, that the Duke of Marlborough, in all his campaigns, was never known to lose his baggage. I am heartily glad to hear of that unconditional offer you mention; because I have been taught to believe there is little good-nature to be had from that quarter: And, if the offer were sincere I know not why it has not succeeded, since every thing is granted that can be asked for, unless there be an exception only for generous and good-natured actions. When I think of you with a relation to Sir Roger,[1] I imagine a youth of sixteen marrying a woman of thirty for love; she decays every year, while he grows up to his prime; and, when it is too late, he wonders how he could think of so unequal a match, or what is become of the beauty he was so fond of.—I am told he outdoes himself in every quality for which we used to quarrel with him. I do not think, that leisure of life, and tranquillity of mind, which fortune and your own wisdom hath given you, could be better employed than in drawing up very exact memoirs of those affairs, wherein, to my knowledge, you had the most difficult and weighty part: And I have often thought, in comparing periods of time, there never was a more important one in England than that which made up the four last years of the late Queen. Neither do I think any thing could be more entertaining, or useful, than the story of it fully and exactly told, with such observations, in such a spirit, style, and method, as you alone are capable of performing it. One reason why we have so few memoirs written by principal actors, is because much familiarity with great affairs makes men value them too little; yet such persons will read Tacitus and Commines[2] with wonderful delight. Therefore I must beg two things; first, that you will not omit any passage because you think it of little moment; and, secondly, that you will write to an ignorant world, and not suppose your reader to be only of the present age, or to live within ten miles of London. There is nothing more vexes me in old historians, than when they leave me in the dark in some passages which they suppose every one to know. It is this laziness, pride, or incapacity of great men, that has given way to the impertinents of the nation where you are, to pester us with memoirs full of trifling and romance. Let a Frenchman talk twice with a minister of state, he desires no more to furnish out a

[1] i.e. Oxford.
[2] Philippe de Commynes, 1447-1511. His *Mémoires* present an authentic portraiture of the court of Louis XI and the character of the age in which he lived.

volume; and I, who am no Frenchman, despairing ever to see any thing of what you tell me, have been some time providing materials for such a work, only upon the strength of having been always amongst you, and used with more kindness and confidence, that it often happens to men of my trade and level. But I am heartily glad of so good a reason to think no farther that way, although I could say many things which you would never allow yourself to write. I have already drawn your character at length in one tract,[1] and a sketch of it in another.[2] But I am sensible that when Caesar describes one of his own battles we conceive a greater idea of him from thence, than from all the praises any other writer can give him.

I read your Paraphrase with great pleasure, and the goodness of the poetry convinces me of the truth of your philosophy. I agree, that a great part of our wants is imaginary, yet there is a different proportion, even in real want, between one man and another. A King, deprived of his kingdom, would be allowed to live in real want, although he had ten thousand a year; and the case is parallel in every degree of life. When I reason thus on the case of some absent friends, it frequently takes away all the quiet of my mind. I think it indecent to be merry, or take satisfaction in any thing, while those who presided in councils, or armies, and by whom I had the honour to be beloved, are either in humble solitude, or attending, like Hannibal, in foreign courts, *donec Bithyno libeat vigilare tyranno.*[3] My health (a thing of no moment) is somewhat mended; but, at best, I have an ill head and an aching heart. Pray God send you soon back to your country in peace and honour, that I may once more see him *cum quo morantem saepe diem fregi*, &c.

Swift to Charles Ford

Laracor. May. 3ᵈ 1719. Ireld.

I here send you inclosed an Answer to the Letter you sent me, which you will please to conveigh.[4] You see what a Master a man is

---

[1] In *An Enquiry into the Behaviour of the Queen's Last Ministry*, ed. Davis, vol. viii. See also the edition of this pamphlet by Ehrenpreis, xxix and n., 8-9 and n.; also *Journal*, 3 Nov. 1711.
[2] See 17 Mar. N.S.   [3] Juv. 10, 162.
[4] The answer was to Bolingbroke's letter of 17 Mar. N S.

of his Resolutions after 50. But I am absolutely ordered to ride, and my Health having grown somewhat better, I have bought a Horse at a great Price, and am resolved to ramble about this Scurvy Country this Summer, and take the Shame to my self of being lazy and irresolute. One thing shook my Measures, that Mr Dopping[1] who was to have been my Companion is not thought strong enough by his Physicians to undertake so long a Journey. I go soon from hence to Mr Rochforts,[2] so to Ld Anglesey's[3] &c. I made twenty other Difficultyes not worth troubling you with. But I hope we shall see a quiet World, and then I will rouze up my self, if Health and Humor will permit me. I wrote last week to Mr Prior[4] to send over His Suscribed Books, which has been a great Neglect in his Bookseller to omit: There is one Hyde a Bookseller in Damas-street[5] Dublin, who has a good Repute, and is used to that Business, and is content to undertake delivering them, and receiving the other Guinea from the Subscribers. Pray speak to Mr Prior—

You will not let us be quiet here one Moment with Your confounded Invasions. A great Whig Prelate[6] says, this is the Invisible, as tother was called the Invincible Armada. There is such Doubling and trebling of militia Guards, and such a Dread of the Ld Lucan's Ghost,[7] and of the D. of O.[8] who is likewise reported dead, that we cannot sleep in our Beds for them.—Mr Charlot[9] still passes very ill among our comers from England.

Pray tell Ben Took if you see him, that I shall obey the Commands

---

[1] Samuel Dopping, eldest son of Anthony Dopping, Bishop of Meath. See p. 327. He is mentioned several times in the *Journal*. From 1715 till his death in 1721 he was member for Dublin University. The long journey was to have been to Aix-la-Chapelle.   [2] At Gaulstown.

[3] At Camolin Park, co. Wexford.   [4] On 28 Apr.

[5] Dame Street, the book-selling centre in the eighteenth century; see Gilbert's *Hist. of the City of Dublin*, ii. 263.

[6] Archbishop King.

[7] Patrick Sarsfield, created Earl of Lucan by James II in 1691 for his brilliant services in Ireland, and mortally wounded at Landen in 1693, left a son who was popularly known by his father's title. He had come to Ireland in 1715. Boyer's *Political State* for Apr. 1719, p. 408, reports that 'About this Time the Lord Lieutenant of *Ireland* received Letters from General Wynne at *Galway*, who by his Grace's Order had made search in those Parts for *Sarsfield*, commonly called Lord *Lucan*, that Information had been given him, that the said Lord had made his Escape out of the Kingdom, taking Shipping at *Killicolgan*, a Creek within 6 miles of *Galway*.'

[8] Duke of Ormonde.   [9] Bolingbroke.

in his this days Letter, and I shall write to him soon; His Friend
Capt Cock never called on me but just when he was going to sea, and
I searched for him in vain at his old Lodgings.

If you visit L^d Ch. Baron Rochford, and he has not left London,
it would be kind in you to desire he would order to buy and bring
me over a good Beaver,¹ I have a tolerable large head, thô it be not
a very good one at present; and that Beaver will be a good riding one
when I ride next year to see You. Where is Friend L—,² I suppose
diverting himself with Ld Lexinton³ or Mansel,⁴ or Dartmouth, in
the Country, and I conceive you will pass this Summer in the same
Manner. Adieu—

Address: To Charles Ford Esqr, at | His Lodgings at the blue | Perewig in
Pel-mel | London
Postmarks: D *and* 12 MA

4805

Matthew Prior to Swift

5 May 1719.

Dear S^{rs}

Since I love You with all the Tyes of Inclination and Friendship,
and wish You all the happiness of Life, Health especially the
Chiefest: you will pardon me⁶ being a little peevish, when I received
yo^{rs} of the 28th past, which told Me I must not expect to see You
here, and that You were not perfectly well at Dublin. I hope there is
a little Spleen mixt with yor Distemper, in wch case y^{or} Horse may
be your Physician, and your Physician may have the happiness of
being your Companion (an honor wch Many here would envy him)
as to the Sang froid of fifty who has it not that is worth conversing

---

¹ Swift's 'best', 'second best', and 'third best' beaver hats are mentioned in
his will.   ² Erasmus Lewis.

³ Robert Sutton, second Baron Lexington, ambassador to Madrid for the
Treaty of Utrecht. In his remarks on Macky's *Characters* Swift credits him with
'a very moderat degree of Understanding'.

⁴ Sir Thomas Mansell, 1668?–1723, succeeded as sixth Baronet in 1706. From
1712 to 1714 he was one of the Tellers of the Exchequer. On 1 Jan. 1712 he was
created Baron Mansell of Margam. In his note in Macky's *Characters* Swift
described him as possessed of 'Good nature but a very moderate capacity'.

⁵ This letter is written in a clerical hand.

⁶ Ball prints 'my'. Hawkesworth correctly printed 'me'.

with except Harley and Bathurst?[1] at least make no more than Sort
of complaint to Me—isthaec commemoratio est quasi exprobatio[2]—
for fifty (as Mr Locke observes) is equal to Fifty, and a Cough[3] is
worse than the Spleen my bookseller is a blockhead, so have they all
been or worse from Chaucer's Scrivener down to John and Jacob:[4]
Mr Hyde[5] only excepted to whom my books in Quires are consigned
and the greatest care taken that they are rightly put up: several of
the Subscribers to you[6] requiring their books here have had them I
need not repeat my thanks to you for the trouble this matter has
given You; or intreat your favor for Alma and Solomon[7] I shall
perform your Commands to the Earl of Oxford Semper Idem and
drink your health with our friends wch is all that I can do at this
distance, till your particular order enjoyns Me any thing by w^ch
I may show you that I am and desire always to continue with the
greatest truth and regard S^r | Your most ob^t and | most humble
Ser^t | M Prior.

May. 5th

Address: To Gallstowne | The Reverend Dr Swift | Dean of St Patrick in
Trim[8] | Ireland
Endorsed by Swift: May 5. 1719 | Mr Prior.

B.M. Add. MS. 39839

Swift to Miss Esther Vanhomrigh

May. 12me 1719

On vous a trompè en vous disant que je suis party pour trois mois.
des Affaires assez impertinentes m'ont tiree si tost,[9] et je viens de

---

[1] Prior, born on 21 July 1664, was now nearly fifty-five. Harley was twenty
nine, and Bathurst five years older.   [2] Terence, *And.* 43.

[3] Prior suffered from severe fits of coughing. The paper is here frayed.

[4] i.e. Barber and Tonson, Swift's publishers.

[5] John Hyde was in business in Dame Street from 1709 to 1728. His will was
proved in the Prerogative Court at Dublin in 1728 (*Dict. of Booksellers and
Printers, 1726–1775*, p. 390).   [6] 'to you' written above the line.

[7] *Alma*, written on the model of *Hudibras*, was described by Pope as 'a
master-piece', by Prior himself as a 'loose and hasty scribble'. *Solomon*, which
Prior, in Johnson's words, 'expected succeeding ages to regard with veneration',
is a monument of tediousness.

[8] The word 'Dublin' has been struck through. The form of the address was
intended to simplify forwarding the letter to follow Swift's movements.

[9] i.e. to Trim.

quitter cette place pour aller voir quelques amis plus loin, purement pour le retablissement de ma santè,[1] Croyez moy s'il y a chose croyable au monde que je pense tout ce que pouvez souhaiter de moy, et que tous vos desires seront toujours obèi, comme de commandemens quil sera impossible de violer. Je pretends de mettre cette Lettre dans une ville de Poste ou je passeray. J'iray en peu de tems visiter un Seigneur, mais je ne scay encore le nom de sa Maison ni du pais ou il demeure.[2] Je vous comjure de prendre guarde de votre santè, J'espere que vous passerèz quelque part de cet etè dans votre maison de campagne, et que vous vous promeneray a cheval autant que vous pouvez.[3] Vous aurez vos vers à revoir, quand j'auray mes pensees et mon tems libre, la Muse viendra,[4] faites mes complimens a la mechante votre compagnone,[5] qui aime les contes et le Latin. J'espere que vos affaires de chicane sont en un bon train,[6] je vous fais des complimens sur votre perfection dans le langue Françoise. il faut vous connoitre long temps de connoitre toutes vos perfections, toujours en vous voyant et entendant il en paroissent des nouvelles qui estoient auparavant cacheès. Il est honteux pour moy de ne savoir que le Gascon, et le patois au prix de vous. Il n'y a rien a redire dans l'orthographie, la proprietè, l'elegance, le douceur et l'esprit, et que je suis sot moy, de vous repondre en meme langage; vous qui estes incapable d'aucune sottise si ce n'est l'estime qu'il vous plaist d'avoir pour moy, car il n'y a point de merite, ni aucune preuve de mon bon goût de trouver en vous tout ce que la Nature a donnee à un mortel, je veux dire l'honneur, la vertue, le bon sens, l'esprit, la douceur, l'agrement, et la firmitè d'ame, mais en vous cachant commes vous faites, le monde ne vous connoit pas, et vous

[1] The relations between Vanessa and Swift during the four years which had passed since she came to Ireland are by no means easy to follow. How much they saw of each other is very uncertain.

[2] Ball suggests that this was the visit said by Sheridan (*Life*, pp. 419–22) to have been paid by Swift to the home of a wealthy gentleman of the name of Mathew, proprietor of a large estate and mansion in co. Tipperary, who entertained as many as forty guests at a time without charge.

[3] It is probable that Vanessa lived chiefly in Dublin. From subsequent letters it will be seen that he had never visited her in Celbridge.

[4] The improbable suggestion has been made that the allusion is to *Cadenus and Vanessa*; but Vanessa is believed to have turned verses, and the reference may be to the revision of lines submitted by her (*Poems*, p. 685).

[5] i.e. her sister Moll.

[6] A reference to the difficulty of clearing up the trust executed by Vanessa's father.

perdez l'eloge des millions de gens. Depuis que j'avois l'honneur de vous connoitre j'ay toujours remarquè que ni en conversation particuliere, ni general aucun mot a echappè de votre bouche, qui pouvoit etre mieux exprimè; et je vous jure qu'en faisant souvent la plus severe Critique, je ne pouvois jamais trouver aucun defaut ni en vos Actions ni en vos parolles. la Coquetrie, l'affectation, la pruderie, sont des imperfections que vous n'avois jamais connu. Et avec tout cela, croyez vous qu'il est possible de ne vous estimer au dessus du reste du genre humain. Quelles bestes en juppes sont les plus excellentes de celles que je vois semeès dans le monde au prix de vous; en les voyant, en les entendant je dis cent fois le jour—ne parle, ne regarde, ne pense, ne fait rien comme ces miserables, sont ce du meme Sexe—du meme espece de Creatures? quel cruautè de faire mepriser autant de gens qui sans songer de vous, seroient assès supportable.—Mais il est tems de vous delasser, et dire adieu avec tous le respecte, la sincerite et l'estime du monde. Je suis et seray toujours——

Address: For Madam Hester | Vanhumri.
                        This
Endorsed: 8th.

Nichols 1801
Swift to Bishop Evans

May 22, 1719.[1]

I had an express sent to me yesterday by some friends, to let me know that you refused to accept my proxy, which I think was in legal form, and with all the circumstances it ought to have.[2] I was likewise informed of some other particulars, relating to your displeasure

[1] 'The two following unprinted Letters of the Dean were communicated to the Editor, by the Rev. John Williams of Llanrwst, while the present Sheet was actually in the Press.'—Nichols. The second letter was that addressed to the Rev. Daniel Jackson, 6 Oct. 1721.

[2] Bishop Evans was holding his diocesan visitation at about the same date as in 1718 (see p. 292), when Swift had risen in defence of three clergymen whom Evans had censured. Now Evans refused to accept Swift's proxy. It can only have been a day or two before the visitation took place that Swift left Trim for Gaulstown, whence, presumably, he was writing. Evans, a violent Whig (*Wake Corresp.* xiii), regarded Swift as a treasonable character, and the enmity between them ceased only with the Bishop's death in 1724. See further Landa, *Swift and the Church of Ireland*, pp. 181–4.

for my not appearing. You may remember if you please, that I promised last year never to appear again at your visitations; and I will most certainly keep my word, if the law will permit me: not from any contempt of your Lordship's jurisdictions, but that I would not put you under the temptation of giving me injurious treatment, which no wise man, if he can avoid it, will receive above once from the same person.

I had the less apprehension of any hard dealing from your Lordship, because I had been more than ordinary officious in my respects to you from your first coming over.[1] I waited on you as soon as I knew of your landing. I attended on you in your first journey to Trim. I lent you a useful book relating to your diocese;[2] and repeated my visits, till I saw you never intended to return them. And I could have no design to serve myself, having nothing to hope or fear from you. I cannot help it, if I am called of a different party from your Lordship: but that circumstance is of no consequence with me, who respect good men of all parties alike.

I have already nominated a person to be my curate, and did humbly recommend him to your Lordship to be ordained, which must be done by some other bishop, since you were pleased (as I am told) to refuse it:[3] and I am apt to think you will be of opinion, that when I have a lawful curate, I shall not be under the necessity of a personal appearance, from which I hold myself excused by another station. If I shall prove to be mistaken, I declare my appearance will be extremely against my inclinations. However I hope that in such a case your Lordship will please to remember in the midst of your resentments that you are to speak to a clergyman, and not to a footman. I am, your Lordship's most obedient, | humble servant, | Jonathan Swift.

[1] Bishop Evans was translated from Bangor to Meath by letters dated 19 Jan. 1715–16.

[2] Accounts of the diocese had been compiled by two of Evans's predecessors, James Ussher and Anthony Dopping. Possibly it was a copy of one of these which Swift lent him.—Ball.

[3] This was not the first person whom Swift had nominated in place of Warburton. Evans declared that Swift wanted, after the Primate had already preferred one of his curates, to put upon him another curate, who was already licensed in the diocese of Clogher. This he refused to do (*Wake Correspondence*).

Matthew Prior to Swift

West^r Dec: 8. 1719

S^rI

Having spent part of the Summer very agreably in Cambridge-shire[2] with Dear Lord Harley, I am returned without Him to my own Palace in Duke street whence I endeavour to exclude all the tumult and Noise of the neighbouring Court of requests,[3] and to live aut nihil agendo aut aliud agendo till He comes to Town: but there is worse than this yet, I have treated Lady Harriot at Cambridge Good God! a fellow of a college treat! and spoke verses to Her[4] in a gown and Cap: what! the Plenipotentiary so far concerned in the damned peace at Utrecht, the man that makes up half the Volume of terse Prose that makes up the report of the Committee,[5] speaking Verses: Sic est, homo sum, and am not ashamed to send those very Verses to One who can make much better. and now lett Me ask You how you do and what you do, how your Irish Country Air agreed with you, and when you intend to take any English Country Air [In][6] the spring I will meet you where you will, and go with you where you will: but I believe the best rendevous will be Duke streett and the fairest feild for Action Wimpole: the Lords of both those seats agreing that no Man shall be more welcome to either than your self. it is many Months since the Complaints of my

---

[1] This letter is written in a clerical hand.

[2] At Wimpole.

[3] A court of equity, inferior to the court of Chancery. Abolished in 1641. The room at Whitehall in which the court used to be held seems to have retained the name long after the extinction of the court. Frequently mentioned in the *Journal to Stella*.

[4] Prior retained his fellowship till his death on the ground that 'when all failed that would be bread and cheese at the last'. He invited Lord Harley's wife to visit the college, St. John's, Cambridge, where, on 9 Nov. 1719, he welcomed her in the library with the verses beginning:

> 'Since Anna visited the Muses' seat
> (Around her tomb let weeping angels wait!)
> Hail thou, the brightest of thy sex, and best,
> Most gracious neighbour, and most welcome guest.'

Hawkesworth, in his footnote, mistakenly presumes the verses to be addressed to Harley's only daughter, afterwards Duchess of Portland.

[5] The Committee of Secrecy, see p. 175.

[6] Paper injured.

Subscribers are redres'd, and that they have ceased to call the Book-seller a blockhead,[1] by transferring that title to the Author, We have not heard from Mr Hyde, but expect that at his Leisure He will signify to Tonson what may relate to that whole matter, as to the second Subscriptions:[2] in the mean Time I hope the Books have been delivered without any mistake, and shall only repeat to You that I am sensible of the trouble my Poetry has given you, and return you my thanks in plain Prose. [Earl[3] of] Oxford pro more suo went late into the Country, and continues there still, our friends are all well, so am I nisi cum pituita molesta est, which is at this present writing and will continue so all the winter: so with weak lungs and a very good heart I remain always | S^r | Your most ob^t | humble ser^t | M Prior

Service to Matthew Pennyfather[4] and all friends. Adieu

Three endorsements by Swift: Mr Prior Dec^br 8th 1719
Mr Prior with Verses | Decr 8th 1719
Dec. 8 | Mr Prior's own Verses | on Ldy Harriett | Harley

Pierpont Morgan Library

Swift to Charles Ford

Dublin. Dec^br. 8th. 1719

I had yours of above six weeks ago, and your last yesterday.[5] I do not think that Men who want their Health, are answerable for Lazyness and Indolence. If they keep the same Affection for their Friends, no more in justice ought to be required. Indeed I fear, when Life grows indifferent every Thing grows so too. I was some-what recovered from a long Disorder when a pitifull broken shin, which I skillfully cookt up into a sore of Importance, confined me above a Month, and is not yet well, and my want of Exercise under it, has been of ill use to my Head; Thus in Excuse for my Silence, I am forced to entertain you like an old Woman with my Aylments. But your Complaint is not dans les formes. You live in the midst of the

---

[1] See Prior's letter of 5 May.
[2] Of the subscriptions one guinea was to be paid 'in hand', the other on delivery of the work.   [3] Paper injured.
[4] See i. 381.   [5] Missing.

World, I wholly out of it, and therefore ought to be the Writer and complain of you. I am very confident, that in the whole year I do not speak to above a dozen Persons, and make choice onely of such with whom it is of no manner of Consequence what I say to them, or what they say to me. When it happens otherwise I am not at my Ease, and that is the true Reason why I cannot think of a Journy to England till I get more Health and Spirits. I will tell you a grievous unhappyness under the Sun, that when Time brings a man to be hard to please, he finds the World less carefull to please him. Which however is less to be wondred at, because it is what every man finds in himself. When his Invention decays, his Judgment grows nicer, and thus he is left in the state of those who ruin their Fortunes, and enlarge their Appetites. Take this Philosophy in return of your Apology for writing a word of Politicks. But as the World is now turned, no Cloyster is retired enough to keep Politicks out, and I will own they raise my Passions whenever they come in my way, perhaps more than yours who live amongst them, as a great noise is likelyer to disturb a Hermit than a Citizen.

I began this a week ago,[1] and between disorder and Interruption was not able to finish it. I am heartily glad Mr Dopping[2] has found Benefit by his Journy. It is impossible to describe to you how I have been hindred from accompanying or following him. This silly station I am in engages me in more trifling Business than a high Treasurer, and besides the publick wind is full in my Teeth. But however I will try next Spring what can be done, thô I foresee a foolish Impediment already: But the Truth is, the fear of returning in ten times worse humor than I should go, has been my strongest discouragement, as a prudent Prisoner would not chuse to be a day out of Jayl, if he must certainly go back at night. I here inclose a Letter to Monsr [   ]—[3] and hope it will not miscarry like the former. I saw a very foolish Pamphlet of Steele's to Lord Oxford without Method Argument or Style,[4] for my own Part I wish the Bill had passt upon

---

[1] The second paragraph cannot be earlier than 19 Dec., the date of Swift's letter, next following, to Bolingbroke, see p. 331, n. 8. Furthermore, the London postmark is 1 Jan.   [2] Cf. Swift's letter to Ford of 3 May 1719.

[3] 'Char' obliterated followed by a dash, i.e. Charlot, or Bolingbroke.

[4] *A Letter to the Earl of O——d, concerning the Bill of Peerage*, published on 7 Dec., the day before the Bill, after having passed the Lords, was rejected by the Commons. It provided that no more than six English peerages should be added to the existing number of 178, and that the 16 Scottish representative peers be replaced by 25 hereditary peers.

Sr James Forbes's[1] Reason: And I remember to have agreed many years ago with some very great men, who thought a Bill for limiting the Prerogative in making Peers would mend the Constitution, but as much as I know of this it was wholly naught, and there is one invincible obvious Argument which Steel lightly touches; That the Lords degenerate by Luxury Idleness &c and the Crown is always forced to govern by new Men. I think Titles should fall with Estates. The ABD[2] (who is half a Tory) seems to be at a Loss what the Bill was intended for, and will not allow the common Reason. I should not be sorry to know what is said on that Subject. If you see Mr. Charleton[3] pray tell him I had his Letter, but have not seen the Doctor he mentions. I hear My Sister O—[4] has very ill Health, which is an Affliction she does not want. I desire you will present my most humble Service to her and L^d A—[5] when you see them, and particularly to Mr. L— D^r. A—[6] &c, and to M^r. Pope and Gay.—I write nothing but Verses of late, and they are all Panegyricks.[7]—I like Mr. L—s manner of Life, strolling thro the Kingdom, better than any amongst you.

Address: To Charles Ford Esqr, | at his Lodgings at the blue Perewig in the Pell-mell | London
Postmarks: D *and* I IA

Deane Swift 1765

Swift to Viscount Bolingbroke

December 19, 1719.

My Lord,[8]
I first congratulate with you upon growing rich; for I hope our friend's information is true, *Omne solum diti patria.* Euripides makes

---

[1] See p. 307, n. 4.
[2] Archbishop of Dublin. King, who was a Whig, was imbued also with strong Church of England principles, and in consequence with Tory leanings. Cf. *Cambridge Modern History*, vi. 482.
[3] Bolingbroke.   [4] Duchess of Ormonde.
[5] The Earl of Arran.
[6] Erasmus Lewis, Dr. Arbuthnot.
[7] See *Poems*, pp. 204–25. But no surviving poem of the years 1715–19 can well be described as a 'Panegyrick'.
[8] This letter is a reply to Bolingbroke's letter of 17 Mar.

the Queen Jocasta ask her exiled son, how he got his victuals?[1]
But, who ever expected to see you a trader or dealer in stocks?[2] I
thought to have seen you where you are, or perhaps nearer: But
diis aliter visum. It may be with one's country as with a lady: If she
be cruel and ill-natured, and will not receive us, we ought to consider that we are better without her. But, in this case, we may add,
she has neither virtue, honour, nor justice. I have gotten a mezzo-
tinto (for want of a better) of Aristippus, in my drawing-room:
The motto at the top is, *Omnis Aristippum, &c.* and at the bottom,
Tant^ foedus cum gente ferire, commissum juveni. But, since what I
heard of Mississippi, I am grown fonder of the former motto. You
have heard that Plato followed merchandize three years, to shew he
knew how to grow rich, as well as to be a philosopher: And, I guess,
Plato was then about forty, the period which the Italians prescribe
for being wise, in order to be rich at fifty. *Senes ut in otia tuta
recedant.* I have known something of Courts and Ministers longer
than you, who knew them so many thousand times better; but I
do not remember to have ever heard of, or seen, one great genius,
who had long success in the Ministry: And, recollecting a great
many, in my memory and acquaintance, those who had the smooth-
est time were, at best, men of middling degree in understanding. But,
if I were to frame a romance of a great minister's life, he should
begin it as Aristippus has done; then be sent into exile, and employ
his leisure in writing the memoirs of his own administration; then
be recalled, invited to resume his share of power, act as far as was
decent; at last, retire to the country, and be a pattern of hospitality,
politeness, wisdom, and virtue. Have you not observed, that there
is a lower kind of discretion and regularity, which seldom fails of
raising men to the highest stations, in the court, the church, and the
law? It must be so: For Providence, which designed the world
should be governed by many heads, made it a business within the
reach of common understandings; while one great genius is hardly
found among ten millions. Did you never observe one of your clerks

---

[1] Phoenissae, l. 400: πόθεν δ' ἐβόσκου πρὶν γάμοις εὑρεῖν βίον;—'Whence
wast thou fed, ere marriage brought thee substance?' Arthur S. Way's translation.

[2] John Law had expanded his Mississippi Scheme to embrace East India and
the whole of the non-European trade of France. In the winter of 1719–20 his
system reached its acme. The market price of shares issued at 500 livres reached
18,000 livres and speculators made enormous fortunes. In May 1720 his system
toppled to a financial crash.

cutting his paper with a blunt ivory knife? Did you ever know the knife to fail going the true way? Whereas, if he had used a razor, or a penknife, he had odds against him of spoiling a whole sheet. I have twenty times compared the motion of that ivory implement to those talents that thrive best at court. Think upon Lord Bacon, Williams,[1] Strafford, Laud, Clarendon, Shaftesbury, the last Duke of Buckingham; and of my own acquaintance, the Earl of Oxford and yourself: All great geniuses in their several ways; and, if they had not been so great, would have been less unfortunate. I remember but one exception, and that was Lord Somers, whose timorous nature, joined with the trade of a common lawyer, and the consciousness of a mean extraction,[2] had taught him the regularity of an alderman, or a gentleman-usher. But, of late years, I have been refining upon this thought: For I plainly see, that fellows of low intellectuals, when they are gotten at the head of affairs, can sally into the highest exorbitances, with much more safety, than a man of great talents can make the least step out of the way. Perhaps it is for the same reason, that men are more afraid of attacking a vicious than a mettlesome horse: But I rather think it owing to that incessant envy, wherewith the common rate of mankind pursues all superior natures to their own. And, I conceive, if it were left to the choice of an ass, he would rather be kicked by one of his own species, than a better. If you will recollect that I am towards six years older than when I saw you last, and twenty years duller, you will not wonder to find me abound in empty speculations: I can now express in a hundred words what would formerly have cost me ten. I can write epigrams of fifty distichs, which might be squeezed into one. I have gone the round of all my stories three or four times with the younger people, and begin them again. I give hints how significant a person I have been, and no body believes me: I pretend to pity them, but am inwardly angry. I lay traps for people to desire I would shew them some things I have written, but cannot succeed; and wreak my spight, in condemning the taste of the people and company where I am. But it is with place, as it is with time. If I boast of having been valued three

[1] John Williams, 1582–1650, ordained 1605. In 1621 he succeeded Bacon as Lord Keeper, and in the same year he was appointed Bishop of Lincoln. In 1641 he was promoted to the Archbishopric of York.

[2] Swift refers more than once to Lord Somers as a man of humble birth. He came of a family of small landed gentry. His father was an attorney who fought on the parliamentary side during the civil war, and later acquitted himself with success in his profession.

hundred miles off, it is of no more use than if I told how handsome I was when I was young. The worst of it is, that lying is of no use; for the people here will not believe one half of what is true. If I can prevail on any one to personate a hearer and admirer, you would wonder what a favourite he grows. He is sure to have the first glass out of the bottle, and the best bit I can carve.—Nothing has convinced me so much that I am of a little subaltern spirit, *inopis atque pusilli animi*, as to reflect how I am forced into the most trifling amusements, to divert the vexation of former thoughts, and present objects.—Why cannot you lend me a shred of your mantle, or why did not you leave a shred of it with me when you were snatched from me?—You see I speak in my trade, although it is growing fast a trade to be ashamed of.

I cannot but wish that you would make it possible for me to see a copy of the papers you are about; and I do protest it necessary that such a thing should be in some person's hands besides your own, and I scorn to say how safe they would be in mine. Neither would you dislike my censures, as far as they might relate to circumstantials. I tax you with two minutes a day, until you have read this letter, although I am sensible you have not half so much from business more useful and entertaining.

My letter which miscarried[1] was, I believe, much as edifying as this, only thanking and congratulating with you for the delightful verses you sent me. And I ought to have expressed my vexation, at seeing you so much better a philosopher than myself; a trade you were neither born nor bred to: But I think it is observed that gentlemen often dance better than those that live by the art. You may thank Fortune that my paper is no longer, *&c.*

B.M. Add. MS. 39839

Miss Esther Vanhomrigh to Swift

[? 1719–20][2]

Is it possible that again, you will do, the very same thing I warned you of so lately. I believe you thought I only rallied when I told

---

[1] Swift's letter to Bolingbroke of May 1719. See p. 319.
[2] It is difficult to assign reliable dates to this or the following letter, evidently an answer. Hawkesworth introduces this letter with the note: 'Part of a Letter

you the other night that I wou'd pester you with letters. ⟨did not I know you very well I should think you knew little of the world, to imagine that a woman would not keep her word when ever she promised any thing that was malicious. had not you better a thousand times, throw away one hour, at some time or other of the day. then to be interrupted in your business at this rate for I know tis as impossible for you to burn my letters, without reading them. as tis for me to avoid reproving you when you behave yourself so wrong.⟩ once more I advise you if you have any regard for your quiete to allter your behaviour quickly for I do assure you I have too much spirrite to sitt down contented with this treatment now because I love frankness extreamly I here tell you that I have determined to try all manner of humain artes to reclaim you and if all those fail I am resolved to have recourse to the black one which [it]¹ is said never dos now see what inconveainences you will bring both me and your self into. pray think calmely of it is it not much better to come of your self than to be brought by force & that perhaps when you have the most agreaible ingagement in the world for when I under take any thing I don't love to do it be halves ⟨but there is one thing falls out very ruckiley² to you which is that of all the pasions revenge hurryes me least so that you have it yet in your power to turne all this furry³ in to good humer, and depend upon it and more I assure you come at what time you pleas you can never fail of being very well received⟩

B.M. Add. MS. 39839

Swift to Miss Esther Vanhomrigh

[1720?]

If you write as you do, I shall come the seldomer on purpose to be pleased with your Letters, which I never look into without

written in the year 1720.' He omits those portions here enclosed within angular brackets. If the endorsement is '3', though the paper is torn and this is uncertain, the letter can hardly belong to the latter part of 1720. The letter, a draft or hurried copy, is written on a long slip.

¹ 'the say', i.e. 'they say', is cancelled and 'is said' written above. In changing the construction Vanessa forgot to write 'it'. The many erasures and scratchings out would be difficult and purposeless to indicate.

² i.e. 'luckily'.   ³ i.e. 'fury'.

wondring how a Brat who cannot read, can possibly write so well. You are mistaken; send me a Letter without your Hand on the outside, and I hold you a Crown, I shall not read it. But raillery a Part, I think it inconvenient for a hundred Reasons that I should make your House a sort of constant dwelling place.¹ I will certainly come as often as I conveniently can, but my Health and the perpetuall run of ill Weather hinders me from going out in the morning, and my afternoons are taken up I know not how, that I am in rebellion with a dozen People beside your self, for not seeing them. For the rest, you need make use of no other Black Art besides your Ink, 'tis a pity your Eyes are not black, or I would have said the same of them : but you are a white Witch, and can do no Mischief. If you have employd any of your Art on the Black Scarf, I defy it, for one reason; guess.

adieu for Dʳ P—² is come in to see me.

Address: To Miss Hessy Vanhom[r]i
Endorsed: 3rd (?).

Longleat vii

Swift to Matthew Prior

Dublin. Janʳʸ 1719-20³

Sʳ

I have been long pursued with one or two Disorders, which though not very painfull, are so incommodious, that they quite disconcert me, and among other Effects make me so Lazy and listless, that I can hardly mind the Affairs of my Friends much less my own.——

Since I begun this Letter I have been so pursued with a giddy Head that I could not finish it. I had yours of the 10ᵗʰ of last Month, with your Verses on my Sister Harriet enclosed;⁴ I have more Obligations to than You, and yet never gave her any Verses; because it is not in my Power to say as you Carmina possumus donare. I

---

¹ Vanessa was evidently living in Dublin; and the visits to Celbridge had not begun.

² Benjamin Pratt. The style of reference suggests that he was no longer Provost of Trinity. He was presented to the deanery of Down on 17 June 1717.

³ Endorsed below the date: 'Recd: Februʸ $\frac{9\text{th}}{14}$ days'. This would imply a date for the letter of 26 January.

⁴ See p. 328. Prior to Swift, 8 Dec. 1719, and footnote.

begun some when I was in England; but it being not quite six years, I could never finish them since. No thanks to you for your Good Verses with such an Advantage, when Your Muse was your Subject, and was present, Send her over here to St Patrick's and you shall see, me quoque vatem. What do you tell me of a Plenipotentiary? all that is a Parenthesis.[1] The Muses found you at St John's, and there they meet you again: If you writt no better Verses than your Enemyes do prose; tis a Pity but you were a Plenipotentiary again.—I wish your Subscribers in this Kingdom could as well answer your Complaints as you have done theirs, but I find them much backwarder in acquitting themselves of their second Paymt than their first; But it is the disease of the Country; first they shew Vanity and good Will, and secondly Poverty; Ut Gallorum subita sunt ingenia;[2] But my ill health is a good deal in fault: Thô all Methods of Advertisements and Sollicitations of Friends have been employd. Two Remedyes I shall apply; One is a little more time, and t'other, that if they will not pay their second Subscription, their first shall be disposed of to others who come at the tenth, hour of the Day. And in the mean time I will take Care of the most convenient Season to return you what we have already mustred up.— As to my self I have not yet Health enough to go to Engld for more; I have been a Month subject to a Deafness; And it is with Hearing as it is with Riches; And a Philosoph^r would have it thô he despises it, onely to have it in his Power to make use of it when he pleases. I extremely long for Lord Oxford's Picture which he promised me a hundred times. His Lordship is poor, but has rich Friends and may give me his, if ever he performed one Promise he made in his Life. I beg you will no further sollicite him than by reading this to him, and desire his Answer; but Kneller or Dahl[3] shall be the Painters.

You are to understand that the French Pistol you sent me from Paris above six years ago to drink with your Cousin[4] is now safe in my Cabinet with my other Rarityes; and that I never spoke to him in my Life but once, in the Castle of Dublin, I have upon

---

[1] After 'Parenthesis' the words 'the Muses' scrawled out in manuscript.

[2] Caes. *Bell. Gall.* iii. 8.

[3] Michael Dahl, 1656–1743, born at Stockholm, settled as a portrait-painter in London in 1688, and soon secured an extensive patronage. Both Kneller and Dahl painted Prior's portrait.

[4] Matthew Pennefather. He is mentioned by Prior in his letter of 16 Aug. 1713, as is also the dispatch of the 'Louis'. Two words are obliterated after 'Cousin'.

second thoughts blotted out his name as you see; Because he is a Person in Office, but very obnoxious, I suppose chiefly for being related to you, and durst never drink a Bottle of Wine with me; and so that Pistol and meeting are reserved to other Junctures; I hear he is well, and is a very honest Gentleman.

I had a Letter tother day from Mr Auditor Harley[1] upon a most important Affair of recommending a Singing Man to my Cathedrall, which (if you see him) you will please to say, I will answer soon; I wish he had spent a line or two to tell me of the Health of the Family, it would have been more like a Nathaneel[2] | I am ever | Your most obedient | &c

You are bound to present my most humble service particularly to your two Favorites, and my two Brothers My Lord Harley and Lord Bathurst.

Address: To Matthew Prior Esqr | at his House in Duke-street | Westminster *Three Postmarks. One:* Dublin. Others imperfect.

Brotherton Collection[3]
Univ. of Leeds

Swift to Edward Harley

Dublin, Febr. 9th 17$\frac{20}{19}$

S^r

I was twice disappointed with Your Letter;[4] when I saw your Name on the out side I thought it had been a Civility you had done to some Friend, to save me Postage; when I saw the same Name after opening I was in hopes to hear something of you and Family, My Lord Oxford, Lord Harley, and Your Son,[5] and I wish you had

---

[1] Oxford's brother Edward Harley.

[2] Oxford had another brother called Nathaniel, who for more than thirty years had been established as a merchant at Aleppo. In the Welbeck correspondence many letters from him are preserved.

[3] The original was formerly among the manuscripts of Captain Loder-Symonds.—H.M.C. Rept. 13, App., pt. iv, p. 404. Now in the Brotherton Collection, University of Leeds.

[4] This letter from Edward Harley, Oxford's brother, referred to in Swift's letter to Prior, Jan. 1719-20, is missing. The only letter passing between Swift and Edward Harley which has survived is that above.

[5] Edward, eldest son, who succeeded his cousin Edward as third Earl of Oxford, 1741.

said something on that Head by way of Postscript. I desire you will ask My Lord Oxford whether his Brother Nathaniel[1] understands Musick; if he does, and recommends Mr Lovelace[2] particularly from his own knowledge, something may be said. I have the honour to be Captain of a Band of Nineteen Musicians (including boys) which are I hear about five Less than my Friend the D. of Chandois[3] and I understand Musick like a Muscovite; but my Quire is so degenerate under the Reigns of former Deans of famous Memory, that the Race of People called Gentlemen Lovers of Musick, tell me I must be very careful in supplying two Vacancyes, which I have been two Years endeavoring to do. For you are to understand that in disposing of these Musical Employmts I determine to act directly contrary to Ministers of State, by giving them to those who best deserve. If you had recommended a Person to me for a Church-Living in my Gift, I would be less curious; because an indifferent Parson may do well enough, if he be honest, but Singers like their brothers the Poets must be very good, or they are good for Nothing. I wish My Lord Oxford had writ to me on this Subject that I might have had the Pleasure of refusing him in direct Terms.

If you will order Mr Lovelace to enquire for one Roseingrave my organist now in London,[4] and approve his Skill to him; on his Report I shall be ready to accept Lovelace, which is the short of the Matter that I have made so many words of, in revenge for your saying nothing of what I would desire to know; and I must desire you to put my Lord Oxford in mind of sending me his Picture, for it is just eight Years last Tuesday since he promised me.[5] If you had but said but one Syllable of my sister Hariette,[6] I could have pardoned you.

Pray believe that there is no man who can possibly have a greater

[1] Apparently Nathaniel, who died a few months later, had some interest in recommending a candidate for Swift's choir.

[2] Lovelace does not appear among the Vicars Choral of St. Patrick's Cathedral.—Ball.

[3] See p. 304, n. 6. The Duke of Chandos maintained a musical establishment at Canons.

[4] See i. 380, n. 3.

[5] Swift was anxious to secure portraits of all 'those I really love'; but he despaired of Oxford, 'onely I hope he will give me a Copy' (*Journal*, 27 Feb. 1712-13). In his will Swift bequeathed 'to my dearest Friend Alexander Pope, of Twittenham, Esq; my Picture in Miniature, drawn by Zinck[e], of Robert, Late Earl of Oxford'. For Zincke see *D.N.B.*

[6] i.e. Lady Harley.

Respect for you and your Family than My self, nothing but a
scurvy State of Health could have hindered me from the happiness
of once more seeing you all. | I am | with great Respect | Sr Your
most obedient | and most humble serv^t | J: Swift.

Endorsed: Dr Swift Feb: 9th 1720.

Portland Papers
Swift to the Earl of Oxford

Dublin. Feb. 16th 1719[-20].

I was surprised to hear of a Domestick of Your Lordship's in this
Country, who was so kind to call upon me, and give me an Account
of Your health But I could not gather from him that he had any
Orders to do so, and therefore his Kindness is the greater; I live
such a Stranger to Intelligence, that I had not heard of Your passing
so long a time in the Country; otherwise it would have been a great
Temptation for me to have been one of Your Family for some
Months . . I think this is the first Letter of Form that ever I writt to
Your Lordship, and consequently will be the worst. I was so well-
pleased with Mr Minheed's[1] Company, and the Informations he gave
me, that I did not remember my ill Health while he was with me,
he assures me that Yours is in very good Order, for which no Man
can be gladder than my self. I never complained of Your Neglect
when you were the greatiest and busiest Minister in Europe; but I
am afraid Your Sufferings have made you proud and forgetfull of
your Friends. I have long begged Your Picture, and continue to do
so, and it is the only Thing I ever begged of you for my self.[2] But I
shall order my Brother Harley and Sister Harriette to be my Solicitors, who have shewn their Remembrance of me in so obliging a
Manner, as I never can express my Acknowledgements for it. Your
Servant the Bearer has so little Relish for this fine Country that I
could hardly get time to write this. Your Lordship and Family have
my constant Prayers, and I shall ever remain with the greatest
Respect and Truth, | Your most obedient | and most humble Servt |
J: Swift

[1] Minet's name appears frequently in the Portland papers. He was for many
years a member of Oxford's household.
[2] See previous letter.

Longleat vii[1]

Swift to Matthew Prior

Dublin. Mar. 24th 1719[-20.]

S[r]

The Person who delivers you this, is the son of S[r] Theobald Butler;[2] The Father is one of the most eminent Lawyers among us, and hath an Appeal before the House of Lords to be heard on the 6th of April His Adversary is one Lady Prendergrass, Sister of Cadogan,[3] and the greatest Widow Blacacre[4] now in Christendom. I desire the Favor of you to speak to some Lords of Your Acquaintance to attend the Hearing because it is of very great Consequence to S[r] Theobald's Fortune, and he is very confident of the Justice of His Cause. He is one of my Flock upon the Deanry,[5] a Gentleman universally beloved, and therefore I could not refuse him this good Office: | I am | S[r] | Your most obedient | humble Ser[vt] | Jonath: Swift

Address: The covering leaf is torn across below the words: 'To Matthew Prior Esq[r]' and above is written in another hand, 'Lansdon| Barkley of Stratton | Dorsett.'

Rothschild

Swift to Charles Ford

Dublin Apr. 4th 1720.

I had your former Letter with the inclosed from our Mississipi Friend,[6] I can make no excuse for my not acknowledging it than my perpetuall ill Health. I should not scruple going abroad to

[1] Swift's autograph.

[2] A Roman Catholic, who had been Solicitor-General for Ireland under James II, he generally went by the name of Sir Toby. He was, however, a man of liberal mind, and was largely instrumental in negotiating the Treaty of Limerick. His son became a Protestant.

[3] The mother of Sir Thomas Prendergast, second baronet, lampooned by Swift in 'On Noisy Tom' (*Poems*, pp. 824-6). He and his father were both attacked in 'The Legion Club'.

[4] The 'petulant, litigious Widow, always in law' of Wycherley's *Plain Dealer*.

[5] Sir Toby occupied a house in the parish of Clondalkin called Ballymount, which had been in the seventeenth century a residence of the ancestors of the Earls of Rosse.—Ball.

[6] Bolingbroke, on the advice of Law himself, as he wrote to inform Ford,

mend it, if it were not for a foolish importunate Ailment that quite disspirits me; I am hardly a Month free from a Deafness which continues another month on me, and dejects me so, that I can not bear the thoughts of stirring out, or suffering any one to see me, and this is the most mortal Impediment to all Thoughts of travelling, and I should dy with Spleen to be in such a Condition in strange Places; so that I must wait till I grow better, or sink under it if I am worse. You healthy People cannot judge of the sickly. Since I had your last of Mar. 10th I have not been able to write; and three Days ago having invited severall Gentlemen to dinner, I was so attacked with a fitt of Giddyness for 5 Hours, that I was forced to constitute a Grattan to be my Deputy and do the Honors of the House while I lay miserable on my Bed. Your friendly Expostulations force me[1] upon this old Woman's Talk, but I can bring all my few Friends to witness that you have heard more of it, than ever I troubled them with. I cannot understand the South-Sea Mystery, perhaps the Frolick may go round, and every Nation (except this which is no Nation) have it's Missisippi. I believe my self not guilty of too much veneration for the Irish H. of Lds, but I differ from you in Politicks, the Question is whether People ought to be Slaves or no.[2] It is like the Quarrell against Convocations; they meet but seldom, have no Power, and for want of those Advantages, cannot make any Figure when they are suffered to assemble. You fetter a Man seven years, then let him loose to shew his Skill in dancing, and because he does it awkwardly, you say he ought to be fetterd for Life. Scotland is poorer and more Northward than this Island, yet were satisfied with their own Legislature till they were united on their Conditions, which though I think too good for them, yet they are proud enough to be ashamed of. I do assure you I never saw so universall a Discontent as there is among the highest most virulent and antichurch

subscribed to the 'new Stocks'. See *Letters of Swift to Ford*, pp. 233–5. The rise in these stocks had, so Bolingbroke averred, procured him 'att least as much as I have been hitherto robbed of'. In May 1720 he acquired La Source, near Orleans, as a retreat. His letter to Swift of 29 Jan. 1720, and Ford's letter on forwarding it, are both lost.

    [1] 'force me' repeated in the manuscript.

    [2] In 1720 an Act passed through the English Parliament asserting the subjection of the Parliament of Ireland; and, further, depriving the Irish House of Lords of all power of appellate jurisdiction. See *Political State*, Mar. 1720, pp. 258–96; and Lecky, *Hist. of England in the Eighteenth Century*, edn. 1879, ii, pp. 419–20.

Whigs against that Bill and every Author or Abetter of it without Exception. They say publickly that having been the most loyall submissive complying Subjects that ever Prince had, no Subjects were ever so ill treated. They tell many aggravating Circumstances relating to the manner of rejecting their Addresses &c. I who am to the last degree ignorant, was some time at a Loss how the Commons at this Juncture when the H. of L^{ds} are not very gracious with them, and at all times think not very well of their Jurisdiction, should agree to extend it. But it is easy to see why the Ministry presst it, and as easy to guess what methods a Ministry uses to succeed.

I cannot help the usage which honest Mr Curl gives me.[1] I watched for his Ears in the Queens time, and was I think once within an Inch of them.[2] There is an honest humersom Gentleman here[3] who amuses this Town sometimes with Trifles and some Knave or Fool transmitts them to Curl with a Hint that they are mine. There is one about Precedence of Doctors,[4] we do not know who writt it; It is a very crude Piece, tho not quite so low as some others; This I hear is likewise a Present of Curl to me. I would go into any Scheam you please with Mr Congreve and Mr Pope and the rest, but cannot imagine a Remedy unless he be sent to Bridewell for Life.—You will present my humble service to My Ld Arran and Ld Harley and L^{dy} Harriette, and Friend L— and the rest.—I can write no more for my Head, and so much the better for you.

Address: To Charles Ford Esqr, | at his Lodgings at the blue | Perewig in Pell-mell | London
Postmark: 11 AP

[1] The reason for this allusion to Curll is not clear. On 23 July 1720 J. Roberts, under whose name Curll printed many of his ventures, 'Reprinted at London' *A Defence of English Commodities . . . Written by Dean Swift*, as a professed answer to the *Proposal for the universal Use of Irish Manufacture*. The *Defence of English Commodities* (*Prose Works*, ed. Davis, ix. 265) is not by Swift, nor *The Art of Punning* (Aug. 1719) nor *The Right of Precedence* (12 Feb. 1720), also attributed to Swift.

[2] Cf. Swift's letter to Pope, 30 Aug. 1716: 'I had long a design upon the ears of that Curll, when I was in credit; but the rogue would never allow me a fair stroke at them.'

[3] Perhaps Sheridan.

[4] *The Right of Precedence between Phisicians and Civilians Enquir'd into*, 'Dublin: Printed by John Hyde in Dame's-Street, and Robert Owen in Skinner-Row', and thrice 'Reprinted at London for J. Roberts', 1720. This tract, which is not by Swift, has been wrongly included in his *Works* since Nichols's *Supplement*, 1779.

The Duchess of Ormonde to Swift

Ap: the 18th 1720

Sir

you'd have great reason to be angry with me, if my long silence had bin occasioned by any thing, but my care of you, for having no safe hand to send by, till now, I wou'd not write, for fear it might be construed a sort of Treason, (Misprision at least) for you to receive a letter from one half of a proscribed man,[1] I inquire of every body I see, that I imagine has either seen you, or heard from you, how you have yr health, for wealth & happiness I don't suppose you abound in, for tis hard to meet wth either in the country you are in, & be honest as you are, I thank God our Parliament has taken them to task, & finding how ill a use they made of their judicature when they had it, have thought it not fit to trust them with it any longer.[2] I hope the next thing will be to tax Ireland from hence & then no more opertunityes for Bills of Attainder wch is very happy, for else young hopefull[3] might have bin in danger, they were so good & obedient to the powers above, that whether there were reason or not, or as Prince Buttler[4] said Crime or no Crime, the man was condemned, & a Price set upon his head,

I want much to hear what you think of Great Brittain, for all your Relations[5] here want much to see you, where are strange changes every day, you remember & so do I, wⁿ the S: Sea was said to be my Lord Ox—ds brat,[6] & must be starved at Nurse, now the King has adopted it, & calls it his beloved Child, tho perhaps you may say, if he loves it but better then his son it may not be saying much, but he loves it as much as he dos the Dut: of K:[7] & that is saying a

---

[1] It is probable that the last letter of the Duchess addressed to Swift was that of 14 Sept. 1716.

[2] See p. 342, n. 2   [3] The Prince of Wales.

[4] Brinsley Butler, later first Viscount Lanesborough.

[5] i.e. Members of the Brothers' Club.

[6] The South Sea Company was Harley's famous scheme, 1711, for consolidating the national debt. It was not at first the wild-cat scheme it became in 1720, when the bubble burst. See Lecky's *Hist. of England in the Eighteenth Century*, edn. 1879, i. 321–3; Trevelyan, *England under Queen Anne*, iii. 123–4; *The South Sea Bubble*, by Lord Erleigh, 1933; and *The Bubble*, *Poems*, pp. 248-59.

[7] Melusina von der Schulenburg, 1667–1743, mistress of George I over whom she exercised great influence. She was created Duchess of Kendal in 1719.

good deal, I wish it may thrive for many of my friends are deep in it, I wish you were so too, I believe you are by this time very sorry I have met with an opertunity of troubling you wth this scrall, but the strong must bear wth the infirmitys of the weak, & therefore Brother I hope you will pardon the impertinency of yr poor sister, whose brain may be reasonably thought turned, wth all she has met w^th,[1] but nothing will hinder from being as long as she lives, most sincerely | yr very humble | servant & | faithfull | freind

Endorsed by Swift: Apr. 18. 1720 | Dutess Ormonde

4805

Matthew Prior to Swift

West: May 4 1720

S^r,

From my good friend the Dean I have Two Letters before Me,[2] of what Date I will not say and I hope you have forgott, that call out for Vengeance or as other readings have it, for an Answer. You told Me in one of them that you had been pursued with a giddy head and I presume you judge by my silence that I have laboured under the same Distemper; I don't know why you have not buried Me as you did Partridge, and given the Witts of the Age the Steels and Addisons a new Occasion of living seven years upon One of yr: thoughts;[3] when you have finished the Copy of Verses which you began in England, our writers may have an other Hint upon wch they may dwell seven years longer. are you French Man enough to know how a Gascon sustains his Family for a Week,

[1] It was more than once reported that Ormonde had returned to the British Dominions. Rewards for his apprehension were proclaimed in England and Ireland. He was supposed to be concealed in Ireland by the aid of ex-Judge Nutley and others (Primate Lindsay to Dr. Charlett, 31 Jan. 1718-19, Bodleian MS. 10,794, f. 113). But as far as is known he never left foreign territory nor saw his wife again. Not only did she suffer separation from her husband, but, as her letters show, want of the necessaries of life.—Ball.

[2] 25 Jan. and 24 Mar. 1719-20.

[3] The suggestion is that not only the *Tatler*, but all the serials for which Steele and Addison were responsible owed their origin to the Bickerstaff pamphlets.—Ball.

Dimanche, une Esclanche,
Lundi, froide et Salade
Mardi, j'aime la Grillade
Mercredi, Hachée
Jeudi, bon pour la Capillotade
Vendredi, point de Gras
Samedi, qu'on me casse les os, et les chiens se creveront des
restes de mon mouton

We can provide such sort of Cookery if you will but send us the Esclanche but rather bring it with you, for it will eat much better when you are in the Company.

Lord Oxford has been a twelvemonth in Herefordshire, as far from us, literally tho' not geographically as if he had been with you in Ireland; He has writt no more to Us than if we were still Ministers of State; but in the balance of acc^t per contra I have Lord Harley at London, and have either lived with Him at Wimpole or upon Him here ever since his Father left Us: I know no reason why you should not expect his Picture but that He promised it to you so often, I wrote to him six months since, and in stead of acknowledging my Letter, He took a more compendious way of sending a Gentleman to Lady Harriette in Dover Streett, and bid him call in at Westm^r to know if I had any thing to say to his Lord. He was here to a Day when he was sure the Scaffold was ready and the Axe whetted and is in Herefordshire when the consent of all Mankind either justifies his Ministry or follows the plan of it, the South Sea company have raised their stock to 350, and he has not Sixpence in it: Thou art a Stranger in Israel my good Friend, and seemest to know no more of this Lord than Thou didst of the Condé de P—[1] when first I construed Him to Thee at the Coffee house.

I labour under the distemper you complaine of, Deafness: especially upon the least Cold, I did not take care of my Ears till I knew if my head were my own or no,[2] but am now syringing, and hope to profit by it.

My Cousin is here,[3] and well, I see him some times, but I find he has had a Caution wch depended upon his expecting more from Court, and is justifiable in a Man who like him has a great family.

---

[1] Arbuthnot uses this appellation for Peterborough in his letter to Swift of 19 Oct. 1714.
[2] Whether he would be brought to the block for his part in the peace.
[3] i.e. Matthew Pennefather.

I have given your Complem^t: to my 2 favourites, we never forget your health.

I have seen Mr Butler[1] and served him to the utmost of my power with my Amici potentiores: tho' he had a good Cause, and a strong recommendation He trusted wholy to neither of them but added the greatest Diligence in his sollicitations.

Auditor Harley thanks you for remembering him and his Singing-man.[2]

As to the affair of subscriptions do all at your Leisure and in the manner you judge most proper, and so I bid you heartily farewell, assuring you that I am ever most truly Yours MP

Friend Ford salutes you adieu.

Richardson[3] whom I take to be a better painter than any named in your letter has made an excell^t picture of me, from whence Lord Harley, (whose it is) has a Stampe taken by Vertue:[4] he has given Me some of them for you to give to our friends at or about Dublin I will send them by Tonson's Canal[5] to Hyde at Dublin in such a manner as that I hope they may come safe to You.

Endorsed by Swift: May 4th 1720 | Mr Prior.

Nichols 1779

Swift to Robert Cope

Dublin, May 26, 1720.

If all the world would not be ready to knock me down for dis-puting the good-nature and generosity of you and Mrs. *Cope*, I should swear you invited me out of malice:[6] some spightful people have told you I am grown sickly and splenetic; and, having been formerly so yourself, you want to triumph over me with your health

[1] The son of Sir Theobald Butler.

[2] See p. 339.

[3] Jonathan Richardson, 1665–1745, portrait-painter and author of works treating of the art of painting.

[4] George Vertue, 1684–1756, engraver. *D.N.B.*

[5] By means of Tonson.

[6] Cope had evidently invited Swift to visit him again at Loughall. Sheridan (*Life of Swift*, 1784, p. 341) says: '[Swift] spent a good deal of time in the north at Mr. Robert Cope's.' He was certainly there in 1717, probably in 1720, and again in 1722. See *Poems*, p. 320.

and good humour; and she is your accomplice. You have made so particular a muster of my wants, and humours, and demands, and singularities, and they look so formidable, that I wonder how you have the courage to be such an undertaker. What if I should add, that once in five or six weeks I am deaf for three or four days together;[1] will you and Mrs. *Cope* undertake to bawl to me, or let me mope in my chamber till I grow better? *Singula de nobis anni praedantur euntes.*[2] I hunted four years for horses, gave twenty six pounds for one of three years and a half odd, have been eighteen months training him, and when he grew fit to ride, behold my groom gives him a strain in the shoulder, he is roweled, and gone to grass. Shew me a misfortune greater in its kind. Mr. *Charleton* has refused *Wadman*'s living; why, God knows; and got the Dutchess to recommend his brother to it; the most unreasonable thing in the world. The day before I had your letter, I was working with Mr. *Nutley* and Mr. *Whaley*, to see what could be done for your lad, in case *Caulfield* should get the living which Mr. *Whaley* (the Primate's chaplain) is to leave for *Wadman*'s. Because, to say the truth, I have no concern at all for *Charleton*'s brother, whom I never saw but once. We know not yet whether *Whaley*'s present living will not be given to Dr. *Kearney*; and I cannot learn the scheme yet, nor have been able to see Dr. *Stone*. The Primate is the hardest to be seen or dealt with in the world. *Whaley* seems to think the Primate will offer *Caulfield*'s living to young *Charleton*. I know not what will come of it.[3]

[1] The attacks of deafness and giddiness from which Swift suffered throughout a large part of his life, to which there are frequent references in the *Journal* and in his letters, were symptoms of the *labyrinthine vertigo*, or Ménière's disease, possibly the cause of a final paralysis of the brain. See J. C. Bucknill, 'Dean Swift's Disease', in *Brain*, 1882, iv. 493–506; T. G. Wilson, 'Swift's Deafness and his Last Illness', in the *Irish Journal of Medical Science*, June 1939; and op. cit., Aug. 1952, 'The Illness of Dean Swift', by Sir Russell Brain.

[2] Hor. *Ep.* ii. 2, 55.

[3] Donoughmore, a living in co. Tyrone, held by a former headmaster of Armagh Royal School, Thomas Wadman, became vacant. Apparently Cope had urged Swift to use his influence with Primate Lindsay, in whose diocese the benefice lay, on behalf of a young clergyman of the name of Barclay. It had been offered to Arthur Charleton, the Duchess of Ormonde's chaplain, who, declining it, endeavoured to secure it for his younger brother. The living had been given to the Primate's chaplain, Nathaniel Whaley. Whaley's promotion rendered vacant another good benefice, Loughilly, in co. Armagh. Finally Loughilly was given to an ex-Fellow of Trinity College, Dublin, John Kearney. Cf. Leslie's *Armagh Clergy, passim*. These transactions reveal that the Primate's diocese was a close borough for Tories, as was King's for Whigs.

I called at Sir William *Fownes*'s;[1] but he is in the county of *Wicklow*.
—If we could have notice of any thing, in good time, I cannot but
think that, mustering up friends, something could be done for
Barclay; but really the Primate's life is not upon a very good foot,
though I see no sudden apprehensions.[2] I could upon any occasion
write to him very freely. and I believe my writing would be of some
weight, for they say he is not wholly governed by *Crosse*.[3] All this
may be vision; however you will forgive it. I do not care to put my
name to a letter; you must know my hand. I present my humble
service to Mrs. *Cope*; and wonder if she can be so good to remember an absent man, of whom she has no manner of knowledge,
but what she got by his troubling her. I wish you success in what
you hint to me; and that you may have enough of this world's
wisdom to manage it! Are none of them yet in your lady's opinion
ripe for *Sheridan*?[4] I am still under the discipline of the bark, to
prevent relapses. *Charles Ford* comes this summer to *Ireland*.
Adieu.

B.M. Add. MS. 39839

Swift to Miss Esther Vanhomrigh

[? 13 or 20 July 1720[5]]

    I am now writing on Wednesday night, when you are hardly
settled at home,[6] and it is the first hour of Leisure I have had, and it
may be Saterday before you have it, and then there will be Govern^r

---

[1] Cope's second wife was a daughter of Sir Williams Fownes.

[2] Lindsay survived for over four years. See Swift to King, 14 July 1724.

[3] Nichols, *Works*, 1801, xii. 39, has an exceptionally lengthy note on this
name. Faulkner stated that the reference was to the rector of St. Mary's,
Dublin. Deane Swift pointed out that Crosse, 'who had been chaplain to the
Smyrna company', did not become rector of St. Mary's till later. Further, that
he was scarcely known in Ireland, save as an object of detestation. 'My real
opinion is', he continues, 'that Crosse, in that passage, is no more than a pun.'
Ball believes the allusion to be to Silvester Crosse, a graduate of Oxford, 'who was
a native of the county of Cork but resided in Dublin'. The identification remains
in doubt.   [4] i.e. for his school.

[5] Scott, xix. 245, leaves this letter undated; Ball conjectures 'July 22, 1720';
and Freeman assigns it vaguely to the month of July in the same year.

[6] At Celbridge. These words, denoting a move from Dublin, give some
indication of the date.

Huff,[1] and to make you more so, I here inclose a Letter to poor Molkin,[2] which I will command her not to shew you, because it is a Love-Letter. I reckon by this time the Groves and Fields and purling Streams have made Vanessa Romantick, provided poor Molkin be well: Your Friend sent me the verses he promised, wch I here transcribe.

> Nymph, would you learn the onely Art
> To keep a worthy Lover's heart
> First, to adorn your Person well,
> In utmost Cleanlyness excell
> And thô you must the Fashions take,
> Observe them but for fashion sake.
> The strongest Reason will submit
> To Virtue, Honor, Sense and Wit.
> To such a Nymph the Wise and Good
> Cannot be faithless if they wou'd:
> For Vices all have diff'rent Ends,
> But Virtue still to Virtue tends
> And when your Lover is not true,
> Tis Virtue fails in Him or You:
> And either he deserves Disdain,
> Or you without a Cause complain.
> But—here Vanessa cannot err,
> Nor are these Rules applyd to Her:
> For who could such a Nymph forsake
> Except a Blockhead or a Rake
> Or how could she her Heart bestow
> Except where Wit and Virtue grew

In my Opinion these Lines are too grave, and therefore may fit you who I fear are[3] in the Spleen, but that is not fit either for your self or the Person you tend,[4] to whom you ought to read diverting Things. Here is an Epigram that concerns you not

> Dorinda dreams of dress a bed
> 'Tis all her Thought and Art.
> Her Lace hath got within her Head
> Her Stays stick to her Heart.

[1] Swift's nickname for Vanessa in a temper when she considered herself neglected.
[2] The health of Vanessa's sister was deteriorating. She died in the following year.   [3] Written above the line.   [4] Vanessa's sister.

If you do not like these Things, what must I say: This Toun yields no better. The Questions wch you were used to ask me, you may suppose to be all answered; just as they used to be after half an hour Debate, entendez vous cela: You are to hear a number of Persons in your Nighbourhood, but not one that You love: for your Age of loving Parsons is not yet arrived.[1] What This Letter wants in length it will have in difficulty; for I believe you cannot read it, I will write plainer to Molkin, because she is not so much used to my Hand:[2] I hold a wager there are some Lines in this Letter you will not understand thô you can read them. So drink your Coffee,[3] and remember you are a desperate Chip; and that the Lady who calls you bastard, will be ready to answer all your Questions.

Tis now Sunday night before I could finish this.

Address: To Missessy
Endorsed: 2nd

---

[1] Ball suggests, rather improbably, that there may be here a covert allusion to Vanessa's rejection of offers of marriage from clerical quarters. According to Deane Swift, *Essay*, pp. 263–4, Swift paid her a visit in 1716 in company with 'Dean Winter, who was her professed admirer'. Deane Swift also avers that she was 'frequently solicited' by 'Dr. Price, who lived at *Celbridge*', in spite of her constant refusal to receive his addresses. The Rev. Sankey Winter, then Archdeacon of Killala, afterwards became Dean of Kildare. Dr. Price became Bishop of Meath, and later Archbishop of Cashel. In the Wake Correspondence, Christ Church, Oxford, there is a letter from Evans, Bishop of Meath, addressed to the Archbishop, 27 July 1723, who says of Vanessa: 'Tis generally believed she lived without God in the world. When Dean Price (the Minister of her Parish) offered her his services in her last minutes: she sent him word no Price no Prayers with a scrap out of the Tale in (*sic*) a Tub . . . and so she dyed.' See, further, *Prose Works*, ed. Temple Scott, xii. 94–95. The inveterate enmity displayed by Evans to Swift discredits the story.

[2] A word following 'Hand' has been obliterated.

[3] Coffee is a topic which frequently recurs in letters from Swift to Vanessa. Horace Walpole was the first to lend it a sinister interpretation. In a letter to Montagu, 20 June 1766, Yale edition of the *Correspondence*, x. 218–19, misreading Swift's allusion to coffee in his letter to Vanessa of 13 July 1722, he says: 'I think it plain he lay with her . . . you will see very plainly what he meant by coffee.' Walpole's interpretation of its meaning was upheld by Stanley Lane-Poole in the *Fortnightly Review*, Feb. 1910, and by Stephen Gwynn, *Life and Friendships of Dean Swift*, 1933. This interpretation has been ably contested by Archbishop Bernard in his introduction to Ball's edition of the *Correspondence*, p. xxv.

B.M. Add. MS. 39839

Miss Esther Vanhomrigh to Swift

Cellbridg 1720 [27 or 28 July][1]

I thought I should have heard from you[2] in a week according to your promise but that week consisted of fourteen days which were to me after the first seven very long long ones I owne I never expected to have another letter from you for two reasons first because I thought you had quite forgott me and because I was so very ill that I thought I should have died.[3] but ever since I received your letter which was last Friday I have been pretty well[4] . . .[5] just that day fortnight I saw you I have done all that lay in my Power to follow your example for fear of teasing you but find I cannot deffer writeing to you any longer when I opened your letter I thought you had wrote to me two as you said perhaps you might but instead of that to find 'twas a letter to another and that a love letter how do you think I could support it but upon my word when I see you I have a vast deall to say to you about that letter I have asked you[6] all the questions I used ten thousand times and don't find them answered at all to my satisfaction

B.M. Add. MS. 39839

Swift to Miss Esther Vanhomrigh

[4 August 1720]

If you knew how many difficultyes there are in sending Letters to you, it would remove five Parts in six of your Quarrell;[7] but since you lay hold of my Promises, and are so exact to the day, I shall

---

[1] See note to the following letter.

[2] This draft, written on two small octavo pages, with words above the line, close compressions at the end of lines, and scorings through, is unusually difficult to read.

[3] After 'died' the words 'which if I had it would have maid both you and I easy' have been struck through.   [4] 'except' struck through.

[5] The bottom of the leaf has been torn away.

[6] The word 'you' may not have appeared in the copy sent to Swift. See the next letter but one.

[7] In her previous letter Vanessa had taken Swift to task for not writing sooner. His difficulty lay in transmitting letters to her by safe means.

promise you no more, and rather chuse to be better than my Word than worse. I am confident you came chaiding into the World, and will continue so while you are in it. I was in great Apprehension that poor Molkin was worse, and till I could be satisfied in that particular, I would not write again but I little expected to have heard of Your own ill Health, and those who saw you since, made no mention to me of it: I wonder what Molkin meant by shewing you my Letter, I will write to her no more, since she can keep secrets no better. It was the first Love-Letter I have writ these dozen years, and since I have so ill Success, I will write no more, never was a belle passion so defeated but the Govern^r I hear is jealous, and upon your word you have a vast deal to say to me about it. Mind your nurse keeping; do your duty and leave off your huffing. One would imagine you were in love by dating your Lett^r Aug. 29th[1] by which means I received it just a month before it was written. You do not find I answer your Questions to your Satisfaction, prove to me first that it was possible to answer any thing to your satisfaction so as that you would not grumble in half an hour. I am glad my writing puzzles you, for then your time will be employd in finding it out: And I am sure it costs me a great many thoughts to make my Letters difficult. Sure Glass heel[2] is come over, and gave me a message from J. B—[3] about the Money on the Jewels wch I will answer. Molkin will be so glad to see Glass heel. Ay Molkin. Yesterday I was half way towards you; where I dined, and returned weary enough. I ask where that Road to the left led, and they named the Place—[4] I wish your Letters were as difficult as mine; for then they would be of no consequence if they were dropt by careless messengers—a Stroak thus—— signifies every thing that may be said to Cad—at the beginning or Conclusion. It is I who ought to be in a huff that anything written by

[1] 4 Aug. 1720 was a Thursday, so the Friday mentioned by Vanessa in her previous letter would be 22 July.

[2] Ford knew well both Vanessa and Stella. Vanessa used to call him 'Glassheel' and Stella called him 'Don Carlos'.

[3] John Barber. According to Lord Orrery (*Remarks*, pp. 106-7) Mrs. Vanhomrigh and her daughters lived 'far beyond the limits of their income' in London; and after the mother's death the two sisters 'hastened in all secrecy to *Ireland*', beginning their journey on a Sunday to avoid interruption by bailiffs. On the advice of Swift they had evidently deposited jewellery with Barber as security for money borrowed from him. See Swift to Vanessa, 8 July 1714.

[4] As will be seen subsequently it was not till after that time that Swift visited Vanessa at Celbridge.

Cad—should be difficult to Skinage.[1]—I must now leave off abruptly, for I intend to send this Lett to-day—Aug. 4—

Address: To Missess
Endorsed: 3rd

B.M. Add. MS. 39839

Miss Esther Vanhomrigh to Swift

CellBridg 1720[2]

——Cad—you are good beyond expression and I will never quarrell again if I can help it but with submition tis you that are so hard to be pleased thô you complain of me I thought the last letter I wrote you was obscure and constrained enough I took pains too write it after that manner it would have bin much easier for me to have wrote otherwise I am not so unreasonable as to expect you should keep your word to a day but six or seven days are great odes why should your apprehensions for Molkin hinder you from writing to me I think you ought to have wrote the sooner to have comforted me molkin is better but in a very weak way thô those that saw me told you nothing of my illness I do assure you that I was for 24 hours as ill as twas possible to be and live, you wrong me when I say I did not find that you answered my questions to my satisfaction what I sayd was that I had asked those questions as you bid[3] but could not find them answered to my satisfaction how could they be answered[4] in absence since Somnus is not my friend we have had a vast deal of thunder and lightning where do you think I wished to be then and do you think that was the only time I wished so since I saw you I am sorry my jealously should hinder you from writing more love letters for I must chide some times and I wish I could gain by it at this instant[5] as I have done and hope to do is my dateing my letters wrong the only signe of my being in love pray tell me did not you wish to come where that Roade to the left would have led you I am mightily pleased to hear you talke of being in a huff t'is the first time you ever told me so I wish I could see you in one. I am

---

[1] 'Skinage', or 'Heskinage', were names applied to Vanessa.
[2] The day of the month is doubtful—perhaps Monday, 8 Aug.
[3] 'as you bid' written above the line.
[4] 'be answered' above the line.
[5] 'at this instant' above the line.

Vanessa's letter to Swift (1720)

Vanessa's letter to Swift (1720)

now as happy as I can be without seeing——Cad I beg you'd continue happyness to your owne Skinage

B.M. Add. MS. 39839

Swift to Miss Esther Vanhomrigh

Aug. 12th1 1720

I apprehended on the Return of the Porter I sent with my last Lett^r,² that it would miscarry, because I saw the Rogue was drunk but yours³ made me easy. I must neith^r write to Molkin, nor not write to her, you are like Ld Pembroke who would neither go nor stay.⁴ Glass heel talks of going to see you and taking me with him as he goes to his Country house.⁵ I find you have Company with you these 2 or 3 days; I hope they are diverting, at least to poor Molkin. Why should Cad's Letters be difficult, I assure you —'s⁶ are not at all.—I am vexed that the weather hinders you from any Pleasure in the Country because walking I believe would be of good use to You and Molkin. I reckon you will return a most prodigious Scholar, a most admirable House keeper, a perfect Huswife, and a great drinker of Coffee I have asked and am assured there is not one Beech in all your Groves to carve a name on, nor a purling Stream for love or money, except a great River,⁷ which sometimes roars, but never murmurs; just like Governor Huff. We live here in a very dull Toun, every valuable Creature absent, and Cad—says he is weary of it, and would rath^r drink his Coffee on the barrenest highest⁸ mountain in Wales, than be King here

> A Fig for Partridges and Quails
> Ye Daintyes, I know nothing of ye,
> But on the highest mount in Wales
> Would chuse in Peace to drink my Coffee.

¹ Swift dates this letter '12ᵗʰ' quite clearly. Ball dates '13', Swift's date at the end.   ² [4 Aug. 1720]
³ The letter probably written on 8 Aug.
⁴ Pembroke had served a distinguished term of office as Lord Lieutenant of Ireland 1707–9. A man of culture and learning he preferred after the death of Queen Anne to live a retired life.
⁵ The estate of Wood Park, Ford's residence, was purchased by his father in 1698. It lay about eleven miles from Dublin, in co. Meath, on the way to Trim. Although not on the direct road from Dublin, Celbridge lay in the same direction.
⁶ Vanessa.   ⁷ The Liffey.   ⁸ Scott and Ball omit 'highest'.

And you know very well that Coffee makes us severe and grave and philosophicall, What would you give to have the History of Cad— and ——[1] exactly written through all its steps from the beginning to this time. I believe it would do well in Verse, and be as long as the other. I hope it will be done. It ought to be an exact Chronicle of 12 Years; from the Time of spilling the Coffee to drinking of Coffee, from Dunstable[2] to Dublin with every single passage since. There would be the Chapter of the Blister, the Chaptr of Mad[m] going to Kensington[3] the Chaptr of the Colonells going to Franc[e][4] the Chaptr of the Wedding with the Adventure of the lost Key. Of the Strain,[5] of the joyfull Return two hundred Chapters of madness. The Chaptr of long walks. The Berkshire Surprise.[6] fifty Chapters of little Times: The Chaptr of Chelsea:[7] The Chapter of Swallow, and Cluster: A hundred whole Books of my self and so low. The Chaptr of hide, and whisper. The Chapter of who made it so. My Sisters money. Cad-bids me tell you, that if you complain of his puzzling you with difficult writing he will give you enough of it.— See how much I have written without saying one word of Molkin, and you will be whipt before you will deliver her a Message with Honor. I shall write to J. Barber next Post, and desire him to be in no pain about his money,[8] and I will take not one word of Notice of his Riches, on purpose to vex him. If Heaven had lookt upon riches to be a valuable Thing, it would not have given them to such a Scoundrell.[9] I delivered your inclosed Letter to our Friend,[10] who happened to be with me when I received it: I find you are very much in his good Graces: for he said a million of fine things, upon it thô

---

[1] Vanessa.

[2] Writing to Vanessa from Chester, 6 June 1713, Swift refers to coffee spilt by 'Hessy' at Dunstable, for traces of which he sought in vain.

[3] Scott and Ball incorrectly place the Chapter of the Blister after the Kensington chapter. The latter may refer to the visit which Vanessa paid to Swift while he was at Kensington in the summer of 1712.

[4] The visit of Bartholomew, Vanessa's brother, to France.

[5] The word written by Swift. Scott and Ball incorrectly read 'sham'.

[6] Vanessa's expedition to Letcombe. See Swift to Vanessa, 12 Aug. 1714.

[7] Possibly a reference to Swift's sojourn in Chelsea during the summer of 1711; but the allusion may have had another meaning for Swift and Vanessa.

[8] His loan to Vanessa.

[9] The thought is introduced into Arbuthnot's epitaph on Charteris, Pope, and Swift, *Miscellanies. The Third Volume*, 1732, p. 63. It has been used by Luther and others.

[10] Charles Ford.

he would let nobody read a word of it but himself, thô I was so kind to shew him yours to me, as well as this, which he has layd a Crown with me, you will not understand, which is pretty odd. for one that setts up for so high an Opinion of yr good Sense.—I am ever with the greatest Truth, Yr &c.

Aug. 13.

Address: To Miste.
Endorsed: 4th.

B.M. Add. MS. 39839

Miss Esther Vanhomrigh to Swift

CellBridg 1720[1]

——, ——, ——, Cad. is it possible that you will come and see me, I beg for god sake you will I would give the world to see you here (and Molkin would be extreamly happy). do you think the time long since I saw you I did designe seeing you this weeke but will not stir in hopes of your coming here[2] I beg you'l write two or three words by the bearer to let me know if you think you'l come this weeke I shall have the Note to night you make me happy beyond expression by your goodness it would be to much once to hope for such a history if you had laid a thousand pound that I should not understand your letter you had lost it tell me sincerely did those curcumstances crowd on you or did you recolect them only to make me happy

Rothschild[3]

Swift to Sir Thomas Hanmer

Dublin. Oc^{tbr} 1st 1720

S^{r4}

There is a little Affair that I engaged some Friends of mine to trouble You about, but am not perfectly informed what Progress

[1] Evidently this hurried note was written immediately upon receipt of the preceding letter. Vanessa asks for a few words in return by the bearer.

[2] It is evident by this sentence that Vanessa used to come to Dublin on purpose to see Swift.

[For notes 3 and 4 see overleaf.

they have made. Last Term one Waters a Printer was accused and tryed for printing a Pamphlet persuading the People here to wear their own Manufactures exclusive of any from Engld with some Complaints of the Hardships they lye under.[1] There was nothing in the Pamphlet either of Whig or Tory or reflecting upon any Person whatever. But the Chanceller[2] afraid of losing his Office, and the Chief Justice[3] desirous to come into it, were both vying who should shew their Zeal most to discountenance the Pamphlet; the Printer was tryed with a Jury of the most Violent Party men, who yet brought him in not guilty, but were sent back nine times, and at last brought in a Speciall Verdict, so that the Man is to be tryed again next Term. The Whigs in generall were for the Pamphlet tho it be a weak hasty Scribble, and generally abominated the Proceeding of the Justice, particularly all the Bishops except the late ones

---

[1] Swift's pamphlet *A Proposal for the Universal Use of Irish Manufacture* (*Prose Works*, Davis, ix, pp. xv–xvi, 13–22) was the first of a long series which gained for him fame as an Irish patriot. Publication had been timed for its appearance shortly before the sixtieth birthday of George I on 28 May 1720— 'nothing could please his Majesty better than to hear that his loyal Subjects, of both Sexes, in this Kingdom, celebrated his *Birth-Day* (now approaching) *universally* clad in their own Manufacture'. In this pamphlet Swift came out into the open against the misguided and unjust restrictions which England imposed on Irish trade. The pamphlet was characterized as seditious. Edward Waters, the printer, was brought to trial. The jury returned a verdict of not guilty. Lord Chief Justice Whitshed refused to accept this verdict, sent the jury back nine times, and kept them eleven hours. In Aug. 1721 the Duke of Grafton arrived in Dublin as Lord Lieutenant, and the matter ended in the grant of a *noli prosequi*.

[2] Lord Midleton, who was imbued with Whig opinions, was also a man of wisdom and moderation which led to his offending, from time to time, one party or the other. He was also in the difficult position of being a member of the English House of Commons as well as Chancellor of Ireland.

[3] William Whitshed, Chief Justice of the King's Bench in Ireland, despite his unhappy relations with Swift, was regarded with favour by many both in civil and ecclesiastical affairs.

---

[3] Original sold at Sotheby's, 22 July 1929, Lot 214. Now Lord Rothschild's Library 2289. The letter was previously printed in *The Correspondence of Sir Thomas Hanmer*, edited by Sir Henry Bunbury, 1838, p. 190.

[4] Sir Thomas Hanmer had succeeded William Bromley as Speaker of the House of Commons in 1714; but the accession of George I soon terminated his occupancy of the chair. Although he remained in Parliament till 1727 he gradually became a less and less important figure.

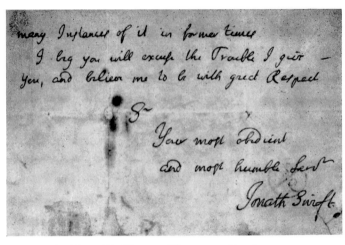

many Instances of it in former times.
I beg you will excuse the Trouble I give
you, and believe me to be with great Respect

                        Sr

                    Your most obedient

                    and most humble Servt

                            Jonath Swift.

Swift to Sir Thomas Hanmer. 1 October 1720

Trustees. Executors or Governors. according as You shall
please to advise And out of these, Committees may be
appointed to meet at proper times — My thought is that
the City will be carefull in an Affair calculated wholly
for the City's advantage. If you would favor me so much
to fix any Day during this Vacation, to dine at the
Deanry, I shall be extremely obliged to You; and give you
my very crude notions of my Intentions.
        I am with very great Esteem, Sr

Deanry-house.   Your most obedient and
Apr. 11th 1735.   obliged Servant

                            Jonath: Swift.

Swift to Eaton Stannard. 11 April 1735

from Engld,[1] the Duke of Wharton[2] Lord Molesworth and many others. Now if the Chief Justice continues his Keeness, the Man may be severely punished: but the Business may be inconvenient, because I am looked on as the Author. And my Desire to you is that you would please to prevayl on the Duke of Grafton to write to the Chief Justice to let the Matter drop, which I believe his Grace would easily do on Your Application if he knew that I truly representd the Matter, for which I appeal both to the Duke of Wharton and Lord Molesworth . . . I have the Honor to be many Years known to his Grace, and I believe him ready to do a Thing of good Nature as well as Justice, and for Your self I am confident that you will be ready to give me this Mark of Your Favor . . . having received so many Instances of it in former times.

I beg you will excuse the Trouble I give you, and believe me to be with great Respect | S^r | Your most obedient | and most humble Servt | Jonath Swift.

Address: To the Honorable | Sr Thomas Hanmer Bart. | at his House in the Pell-mell | London
Stamp: DUBLIN   *London postmark:* 6 OC
Later endorsement: Oct. 1 1720 | Dr Swift

B.M. Add. MS. 39839

Swift to Miss Esther Vanhomrigh

Octr 15th 1720

I sit down with the first Opportunity I have to write to you,[3] and the Ld knows when I can find conveniency to send this Lettr; for all

---

[1] Since the accession of George I, in addition to Bishop Evans, Timothy Godwin, William Nicolson, and Henry Downes had been appointed to the Irish episcopal bench, as bishops respectively of Kilmore, Derry, and Killala, direct from the English Church, and were unceasing in their efforts to promote the English interest.—Ball.

[2] The Duke of Wharton had again visited Ireland that summer for the purpose of selling his Irish estate, which he had derived through his mother, who was a Loftus. It was reported that he had in two days sold the entire estate for a hundred and thirty thousand pounds which was calculated to be nearly forty years' purchase (Bishop Nicolson's *Letters,* ii. 528).—Ball.

[3] As a subsequent paragraph shows Swift had evidently visited Vanessa at Celbridge since his last letter was written.

the morning I am plagued with impertinent Visits, or impertinent Business below any man of Sense or honor to endure, if it were any way avoydable. Dinners and afternoons and Evenings are spent abroad and in walking, to help and avoyd Spleen as far as I can so that when I am not so good a Correspondent as I could wish, you are not to quarrell and be Governr, but to impute it to my Scituation, and to conclude infallibly that I have the same Respect esteem and Kindness for you I ever professed to have and shall ever preserve, because you will always merit the utmost that can be given you especially if you go on to read and still further improve Your Mind and the Talents that Nature have (*sic*) given you I had a Lettr from Your Friend JB—[1] in London in answer to what I told you that Glass[2] sayd about the Money. JB's answer is that you are a Person of Honr, that you need give your self no Trouble about it, that you will pay when you are able, and he shall be content till then[3]—Those are his very words, and you see he talks in the Style of a rich Man, which he says he yet is, though terribly pulled down by the Fall of Stocks.[4] I am glad you did not sell your Annuityes unless somebody were to manage and transfer them while Stocks were high. I am in much concern for poor Malkin, and the more because I am sure you are so too, you ought to be as chearfull as you can for both your Sakes, and read pleasant things that will make you laugh, and not sit moping with your Elbows on your knees on a little Stool by the Fire. It is most infallible that riding would do Malkin more good than any other Thing, provided fair days and warm Cloaths be provided; and so it would to you, and if you lose any Skin, you know, Job says Skin for Skin will a Man give for his Life.[5] it is either Job or Satan says so, for ought you know.—Octbr. 17th—I had not a moment to finish this since I sate down to it. A Person was with me just now and interrupted me as I was going on, with telling me of great People here losing their Places[6]—and now some more are coming

[1] John Barber.   [2] Ford.

[3] Barber still held the jewels. These he sold nearly three years after Vanessa's death.

[4] Barber was involved in business with promoters of the South Sea scheme. In three months the value of the stock had fallen from £1,000 to £150.

[5] 'And Satan answered the Lord, and said, Skin for skin, yea, all that a man hath will he give for his life' (Job ii. 4).

[6] The allusion is probably to a rumour of the removal of Lord Midleton, who had opposed the English Government in regard to the Peerage Bill, and expected himself to be dismissed.—Ball.

about Business, so adieu till by and by or to morrow.—Octr. 18. I am getting an ill Head in this cursed Toun for want of Exercise I wish I were to walk with you fifty times about yr Garden, and then —drink your Coffee I was sitting last night with half a score of both Sexes for an hour and grew as weary as a Dog.—Glass heel takes up abundance of my time in Spight of my Teeth, Every body grows silly and disagreable or I grow monkish and Spleenatick; which is the same Thing. Conversation is full of nothing but South-sea, and the Ruin of the Kingdom, and scarcity of money; I had a thousand times hear the Governor chide two hours without Reason.—

Octr. 20. The Governr was with me at six a Clock this morning but did not stay two minutes, and deserves a chiding wch you must give when you drink yr Coffee next—I hope to send this Letter to morrow,—I am a good deal out of order in my Head after a little Journy I made, and eat too much, I suppose, travailing in a Coach after it. I am now sitting at home alone, and will go write to Molkin — — so adieu — — — — —

Address: To Misessy
Endorsed: 5th

4805

Sir Thomas Hanmer to Swift

Mildenhall near Newmarket in
Suffolk Oct. 22 1720[1]

Sr

I received the favour of a letter from you about ten days[2] since at which time the Duke of Grafton was at London, but as he was soon expected in the Countrey and is now actually returned, I thought it best rather than write to wait for an oportunity of speaking to him and yesterday I went over to his house[3] on purpose to obey your Comands. I found he was not a Stranger to the subject of my Errand for he had all the particulars of the Story perfect and told me my

---

[1] After the death of Queen Anne Hanmer attached himself strongly to the Tory opposition. Gradually, however, he took less and less interest in parliamentary affairs, devoting himself to literature and his garden at Mildenhall. In 1727 he retired from Parliament, and died in 1746.

[2] Three weeks, 1 Oct. 1720.

[3] Euston Park.

Lord Arran[1] had spoken to him concerning it: I added my sollicitations backed with the reasons with which you had furnish'd me and he was so kind to promise he would by this Post write to the chief Justice, how explicitly or how pressingly I cannot say because Men in high Posts are afraid of being positive in their answers but I hope it will be in such a manner as will be effectual. If the thing is done it will be best that the means should be a secret by which it is brought about and for this reason you will excuse me, if I avoid putting my name to the outside of my letter, lest it should excite the curiosity of the Post-Office. If this Affair ends to your satisfaction I am glad it has proved to me a cause of hearing from you and an occasion of assuring you that I am | S^r | Your very humble servant | Tho: Hanmer

Endorsed by Swift: S^r Th— Hanmer | Octr 22^d 1720.

B.M. Add. MS. 39839

Miss Esther Vanhomrigh to Swift

[CellBridg 1720]

You had heard from me before but that my messenger was not to be had till to day and now I have only time to thank you for yours because he is going about his business this moment which is very happy for you or you would have had a long letter full of Spleen never was humain creature more distressed than I have been since I came poor Molkin has had two or three relapses and is in so bad a way that I fear she will never recover Judge now what a way I am in absent from you and loaded with melancholy on her score I have been very ill with a stich in my side which is not very well yett

Endorsed: 1st.

B.M. Add. MS. 39839

Miss Esther Vanhomrigh to Swift

[CellBridg 1720][2]

Believe me it is with the utmost regret that I now complain to you because I know your good nature such that you cannot see any

---

[1] Charles Butler, second son of Thomas, Earl of Ossory, eldest son of the first Duke of Ormonde, a Jacobite in sympathy. In the following year he obtained possession of his brother's estate.   [*For note 2 see opposite.*]

humaine creature miserable without being sensibly touched yett what can I do I must either unload my heart and tell you all its griefs or sink under the unexpressable distress I now suffer by your prodigious neglect of me Tis now ten long long weeks since I saw you and in all that time I have never received but one lettr from you and a little note with an excuse O — — — how have you forgott me you indeavour by severities to force me from you nor can I blame you for with the utmost distress and confusion I behold my self the cause of uneasie reflections to you yet I can not comfort you but here declair that tis not in the power of arte time or accident to lessen the unexpressible passion which I have for — — — put my passion under the utmost restraint send me as distant from you as the earth will alow yet you can not banish those charming Idaea's which will ever stick by me whilst I have the use of memory nor is the love I beare you only seated in my soul for there is not a single atome of my frame that is not blended with it therefor don't flatter your self that separation will ever change my sentiments for I find myself unquiet in the midst of silence and my heart is at once pierced with sorrow and love for heavens sake tell me what has caused this prodigious change in you which I have found of late If you have the least remains of pitty for me left tell me tenderly No don't tell it so that it may cause my present Death and don't suffer me to live a life like a languishing Death which is the only life I can leade if you have lost any of your tenderness for me

B.M. Add. MS. 39839

Miss Esther Vanhomrigh to Swift

[CellBridg 1720]

Tell me sincerely if you have once wished with earnestness to see me since I wrote to you No so far from that you have not once pity'd me though I told you how I was distressed solitude is insupportable to a mind which is not easie I have worn out my days in sighing and my nights with watching and thinking of —, —, —, — — —, who thinks not of me how many letters must I send you before I shall receive an

---

[2] The previous letter, this, and the next following can only be dated conjecturally, but by their content they appear to belong to the latter part of 1720, perhaps November or early in December.

answer can you deny me in my misery the only comfort which I can
expect at present oh that I could hope to see you here or that I could
go to you[1] I was born with violent passions which terminate all in
one that unexpressible passion I have for you consider the killing[2]
emotions which I feel from your neglect of me and shew some
tenderness for me or I shall lose my senses sure you can not possibly
be so much taken up but you might command a moment to write
to me and force your inclynations to do so great a charity

I firmly believe could I know your thoughts (which no humane
creature is capable of geussing at because never any one liveing
thought like you) I should find you have often in a rage wished me
religious hopeing then I should have paid my devotions to heaven
but that would not spair you for was I an Enthusiast still you'd be
the Deity I should worship what markes are there of a Deity but
what you are to be known by you are present every where your
D[r] Image is before my eyes some times you strike me with that
prodigious awe I tremble with fear at other times a charming compassion shines through your countynance. which revives my soul
is it not more reasonable to adore a radiant forme one has seen than
one only described[3]

Rothschild

Swift to Charles Ford

[15 December 1720]

We were for some days in a good deal of pain about [you], but
at last were assured you were safe in London.[4] I have been for some
d[ays] out of Order with my old Deafness, which hath hindred
me from going to [Da]wson-street.[5] I here send you the Thing I

[1] 'or that I could go to you' is written above the line.
[2] 'violent' is scored through and 'killing' written above. 'violent passions'
appears in close proximity.
[3] No address. The letter did not pass through the post.
[4] Ford had been in Ireland from July or August of this year, and returned to
England some time after 18 Oct. (see Swift to Vanessa 15–20 Oct.), probably
about the middle of November. The London newspapers report a great storm
on 19 and 20 Nov.
[5] The residence of Ford's mother.

promised,¹ as correct as I can [ma]ke it, and it cost me Pains enough, whether it be good or no. The way to pub[lish] it will be to send it by the peny Post or an unknown Hand to some [. . .]er Printer, and so let him do what he pleases: only tear out this prose P[art an]d blot out the Subscription; and then there can be no other Inconvenience than the Loss of the Copy. When it comes out, buy one and send it franked and inclosed, immediatly, and I will send it to the Printer here.

You will let me know that   Dec^br. 15th. 1720.
You have received this.

Address: To Charles Ford Esqr, | at His Lodgings at the | blue Perewig in Pell-Mell | London
Postmarks: Dublin *and* 26 DE

H. MSS. Commission

Swift to Viscount Molesworth

[? December 1720.]

Historical MSS. Commission. Various Collections. viii. 291. Allusion is made to a letter from Viscount Molesworth to his wife, written from London, 27 Dec. 1720. He asks her to send his compliments to 'Mr. Dean of St. Patrick's' from whom he has received 'a very kind and civil letter', which he intends to answer 'speedily'. No letter addressed by Swift to Molesworth, or received from him has been traced.

Robert Molesworth, 1656–1725, was created first Viscount Molesworth in 1719. The fifth (sixth) *Drapier's Letter* was addressed to him.

Faulkner 1741²

Swift to Alexander Pope

Dublin, Jan. 10, 1721.

A Thousand things have vex'd me of late years, upon which I am determined to lay open my mind to you. I had rather chuse to appeal

¹ This letter is written at the end of Swift's original manuscript of his poem on 'The Bubble' (*Poems*, pp. 248–59). Swift directed Ford to send the manuscript to the printer without revealing the authorship of the poem. As the original survives with other Ford letters and manuscripts it is clear that he sent the printer a transcript, and that the poem was printed (by Roberts) in seven or eight days. The textual history is complicated and is fully discussed in *Poems*.

[For note 2 see overleaf.]

to you than to my Lord Chief Justice Whitshed,[1] under the situation I am in. For I take this cause properly to lie before you: You are a much fitter Judge of what concerns the credit of a Writer, the injuries that are done him, and the reparations he ought to receive. Besides I doubt, whether the Arguments I could suggest to prove my own innocence would be of much weight from the gentlemen of the Long-robe to those in Furs,[2] upon whose decision about the difference of Style or Sentiments, I should be very unwilling to leave the merits of my Cause.

Give me leave then to put you in mind, (although you cannot easily forget it) that about ten weeks before the Queen's death, I left the town, upon occasion of that incurable breach among the great men at Court, and went down to Berkshire,[3] where you may remember that you gave me the favour of a visit. While I was in that retirement, I writ a Discourse[4] which I thought might be useful in such a juncture of affairs, and sent it up to London; but upon some difference in opinion between me and a certain great Minister now abroad,[5] the publishing of it was deferred so long that the Queen died, and I recalled my copy, which hath been ever since in safe hands. In a few weeks after the loss of that excellent Princess, I came to my

---

[1] Faulkner has a needless footnote: 'A Judge in Ireland.'

[2] Lawyers and judges.   [3] Letcombe.

[4] *Some Free Thoughts* . . . , as noted above, first printed in 1741 in Faulkner's volume.

[5] Bolingbroke; and for the volume see Ford's letter to Swift, 17 July 1714, and notes.

---

[2] This letter, not a 'letter' in the ordinary sense, has a curious and complicated history. It seems not to have been in Pope's volume of 1740. It was, at the prompting of Swift, printed in Faulkner's volume of 1741, vii. 12–27. To the caption of the letter Pope added a footnote: 'This letter Mr. Pope never received.' This statement may be accepted confidently. It was written by Swift, dated 'Jan. 10, 1721', to explain his position in retirement to Ireland during early years after the death of Queen Anne. It is a pamphlet, not a letter intended for dispatch to Pope. Nevertheless it has the form of a lengthy letter and was so introduced, evidently at Swift's instance, in Faulkner's 1741 volume. It is noteworthy also that at the end of the 1741 volume *Some Free Thoughts upon the Present State of Affairs*, written in 1714, is introduced, and to that pamphlet the 'letter' makes reference.

Ball (iii. 113), persuaded by Sir Henry Craik (*Life*, ii. 60), assigns the letter to 1721–2; but as Herbert Davis shows (*Prose Works*, xii. 12 n.), 'the main contents imply the earlier date'. For a note on textual variants, 1741 to 1746 printings, see Herbert Davis's volume, pp. 370–1.

station here; where I have continued ever since in the greatest privacy, and utter ignorance of those events which are most commonly talked of in the world; I neither know the Names nor Number of the Family which now reigns, further than the Prayer-book informs me. I cannot tell who is Chancellor, who are Secretaries, nor with what Nations we are in peace or war. And this manner of life was not taken up out of any sort of Affectation, but meerly to avoid giving offence, and for fear of provoking Party-zeal.

I had indeed written some Memorials of the four last years of the Queen's reign,[1] with some other informations which I receiv'd, as necessary materials to qualify me for doing something in an employment then design'd me:[2] But as it was at the disposal of a person,[3] who had not the smallest share of steddiness or sincerity, I disdained to accept it.

These papers, at my few hours of health and leisure, I have been digesting into order by one sheet at a time, for I dare not venture any further, lest the humour of searching and seizing papers should revive; not that I am in pain of any danger to my self, (for they contain nothing of present times or persons, upon which I shall never lose a thought while there is a Cat or a Spaniel in the house) but to preserve them from being lost among Messengers and Clerks.

I have written in this kingdom, a discourse[4] to persuade the wretched people to wear their own Manufactures instead of those from England: This Treatise soon spread very fast, being agreeable to the sentiments of the whole nation, except of those gentlemen who had Employments, or were Expectants. Upon which a person in great office here[5] immediately took the alarm; he sent in hast for the Chief Justice, and inform'd him of a seditious, factious and virulent Pamphlet, lately publish'd with a design of setting the two kingdoms at variance, directing at the same time that the printer should be prosecuted with the utmost rigour of Law. The Chief Justice had so quick an understanding, that he resolved if possible to out-do his orders. The Grand-Juries of the county and city were practised effectually with to represent the said Pamphlet with all

[1] The compilation of a history of contemporary affairs was in contemplation by Swift as early as Aug. 1712, and from Sept. 1713 he devoted himself to the work.

[2] The office of Historiographer.

[3] The Duke of Shrewsbury, Lord Chamberlain, 1710–14.

[4] *A Proposal for the Universal Use of Irish Manufactures.*

[5] The Chancellor, Lord Midleton.

aggravating Epithets, for which they had thanks sent them from England, and their Presentments publish'd for several weeks in all the news-papers. The Printer was seized, and forced to give great bail: After his tryal the Jury brought him in Not Guilty, although they had been culled with the utmost industry; the Chief Justice sent them back nine times, and kept them eleven hours, until being perfectly tired out, they were forced to leave the matter to the mercy of the Judge, by what they call a special Verdict. During the tryal, the Chief Justice among other singularities, laid his hand on his breast, and protested solemnly that the Author's design was to bring in the Pretender; although there was not a single syllable of party in the whole Treatise, and although it was known that the most eminent of those who professed his own principles, publickly disallowed his proceedings. But the cause being so very odious and impopular, the tryal of the Verdict was deferred from one Term to another, until upon the Duke of G-ft-n the Lord Lieutenant's arrival[1] his Grace after mature advice, and permission from England, was pleased to grant a *noli prosequi*.

This is the more remarkable, because it is said that the man is no ill decider in common cases of property, where Party is out of the question; but when that intervenes, with ambition at heels to push it forward, it must needs confound any man of little spirit, and low birth, who hath no other endowment than that sort of Knowledge, which, however possessed in the highest degree, can possibly give no one good quality to the mind.

It is true, I have been much concerned for several years past, upon account of the publick as well as of myself, to see how ill a taste for wit and sense prevails in the world, which politicks and South-sea, and Party, and Opera's and Masquerades have introduced. For, besides many insipid papers which the malice of some hath entitled me to, there are many persons appearing to wish me well, and pretending to be judges of my style and manner, who have yet ascribed some writings to me, of which any man of common sense and literature would be heartily ashamed. I cannot forbear instancing a Treatise called a Dedication upon Dedications,[2] which many would have to be mine, although it be as empty, dry, and servile a

---

[1] The Duke of Grafton landed in Ireland on 28 Aug. 1721.

[2] *A Dedication to a Great Man, Concerning Dedications*, which has been attributed to Thomas Gordon, the Whig pamphleteer. For an account of him see Nichols, *Lit. Anec.* i. 709-10, and *D.N.B.*

composition, as I remember at any time to have read. But above all, there is one Circumstance which maketh it impossible for me to have been Author of a Treatise, wherein there are several pages containing a Panegyrick on King George, of whose character and person I am utterly ignorant, nor ever had once the curiosity to enquire into either, living at so great a distance as I do, and having long done with whatever can relate to publick matters.

Indeed I have formerly delivered my thoughts very freely, whether I were asked or no, but never affected to be a Councellor, to which I had no manner of call. I was humbled enough to see myself so far out-done by the E. of Oxford in my own trade as a Scholar, and too good a Courtier not to discover his contempt of those who would be men of importance out of their sphere. Besides, to say the truth, although I have known many great Ministers ready enough to hear Opinions, yet I have hardly seen one that would ever descend to take Advice; and this pedantry ariseth from a maxim themselves do not believe at the same time they practice by it, that there is something profound in Politicks, which men of plain honest sense cannot arrive to.

I only wish my endeavours had succeeded better in the great point I had at heart, which was that of reconciling the Ministers to each other. This might have been done, if others who had more concern and more influence would have acted their parts; and if this had succeeded, the publick interest both of Church and State would not have been the worse, nor the Protestant Succession endangered.

But, whatever opportunities a constant attendance of four years might have given me for endeavouring to do good offices to particular persons, I deserve at least to find tolerable quarter from those of the other Party; for many of which I was a constant advocate with the Earl of Oxford, and for this I appeal to his Lordship: He knows how often I press'd him in favour of Mr. Addison, Mr. Congreve, Mr. Row, and Mr. Steel,[1] although I freely confess that his Lordship's kindness to them was altogether owing to his generous notions, and the esteem he had for their wit and parts, of which I could only pretend to be a remembrancer. For I can never forget the answer he gave to the late Lord Hallifax, who upon the first change of the Ministry interceded with him to spare Mr. Congreve: It was by repeating these two lines of Virgil,

[1] About the time of Swift's correspondence with Steele Oxford was receiving letters from the latter without Swift's knowledge (*Portland Manuscripts*, v. 211).

Non abtusa adeo gestamus pectora Pœni,
Nec tam aversus equos Tyria Sol jungit ab urbe.[1]

Pursuant to which, he always treated Mr. Congreve with the greatest personal civilities, assured him of his constant favour and protection, adding that he would study to do something better for him.

I remember it was in those times a usual subject of raillery towards me among the Ministers, that I never came to them without a Whig in my sleeve; which I do not say with any view towards making my Court: For, the new Principles fixed to those of that denomination, I did then, and do now from my heart abhor, detest and abjure, as wholly degenerate from their predecessors. I have conversed in some freedom with more Ministers of State of all Parties than usually happens to men of my level, and I confess, in their capacity as Ministers, I look upon them as a race of people whose acquaintance no man would court, otherwise than upon the score of Vanity or Ambition. The first quickly wears off (and is the Vice of low minds, for a man of spirit is too proud to be vain) and the other was not my case. Besides, having never receiv'd more than ne small favour, I was under no necessity of being a slave to men in power, but chose my friends by their personal merit, without examining how far their notions agreed with the politicks then in vogue.[2] I frequently conversed with Mr. Addison, and the others I named (except Mr. Steel) during all my Lord Oxford's Ministry, and Mr. Addison's friendship to me continued inviolable, with as much kindness as when we used to meet at my Lord Sommers or Hallifax, who were leaders of the opposite Party.

I would infer from all this, that it is with great injustice I have these many years been pelted by your Pamphleteers, merely upon account of some regard which the Queen's last Ministers were pleased to have for me: and yet in my conscience I think I am a partaker in every ill design they had against the Protestant Succession, or the Liberties and Religion of their Country; and can say with Cicero, that I should be proud to be included with them in all their actions *tanquam in equo Trojano*.[3] But, if I have never discovered

---

[1] *Aen.* i. 567–8. Faulkner, in a footnote, gives Dunkin's translation:
'Our Hearts are not so cold, nor flames the Fire
Of Sol so different from the Race of Tyre.'

[2] See Swift to Archbishop King, 8 Jan. 1712–13.

[3] 'As if in the Trojan Horse'—Faulkner's footnote. Cicero, *Phillipic*, ii. 13.

by my words, writings, or actions, any Party virulence, or dangerous designs against the present powers; if my friendship and conversation were equally shewn among those who liked or disapproved the proceedings then at Court, and that I was known to be a common friend of all deserving persons of the latter sort when they were in distress; I cannot but think it hard that I am not suffer'd to run quietly among the common herd of people, whose opinions unfortunately differ from those which lead to Favour and Preferment.

I ought to let you know, that the Thing we called a Whig in England is a creature altogether different from those of the same denomination here, at least it was so during the reign of Her late Majesty. Whether those on your side have changed or no, it hath not been my business to inquire. I remember my excellent friend Mr. Addison, when he first came over hither Secretary to the Earl of Wharton, then Lord Lieutenant,[1] was extremely offended at the conduct and discourse of the Chief Managers here: He told me they were a sort of people who seemed to think, that the principles of a Whig consisted in nothing else but damning the Church, reviling the Clergy, abetting Dissenters, and speaking contemptibly of revealed Religion.

I was discoursing some years ago with a certain Minister about that whiggish or fanatical Genius so prevalent among the English of this kingdom: his Lordship accounted for it by that number of Cromwell's soldiers, adventurers establish'd here, who were all of the sourest Leven, and the meanest birth, and whose posterity are now in possession of their lands and their principles. However, it must be confessed that of late, some people in this country are grown weary of quarrelling, because interest, the great motive of quarrelling is at an end, for it is hardly worth contending who shall be an Excise-man, a Country-Vicar, a Cryer in the Courts, or an Under-Clerk.[2]

You will perhaps be inclined to think, that a person so ill treated as I have been, must at some time or other have discovered very dangerous opinions in government; in answer to which, I will tell you what my Political principles were in the time of her late glorious

---

[1] 21 Apr. 1709.
[2] The only offices open to men of Irish birth, as the patriotic party alleged, were of a subordinate character; the chief appointments were all conferred on English partisans. This was hardly the case at that moment but became so not many years later.—Ball.

Majesty, which I never contradicted by any action, writing, or discourse.

First, I always declared my self against a Popish Successor to the Crown, whatever Title he might have by the proximity of blood: Neither did I ever regard the right line except upon two accounts, first as it was establish'd by law; and secondly, as it hath much weight in the opinions of the people. For necessity may abolish any Law, but cannot alter the sentiments of the vulgar; Right of inheritance being perhaps the most popular of all topicks; and therefore in great Changes, when that is broke, there will remain much heart burning and discontent among the meaner people; which (under a weak Prince and corrupt Administration) may have the worst consequences upon the peace of any state.

As to what is called a Revolution-principle, my opinion was this; That whenever those evils which usually attend and follow a violent change of government, were not in probability so pernicious as the grievances we suffer under a present power, then the publick good will justify such a Revolution; and this I took to have been the Case in the Prince of Orange's expedition, although in the consequences it produced some very bad effects, which are likely to stick long enough by us.

I had likewise in those days a mortal antipathy against Standing Armies in times of Peace. Because I always took Standing Armies to be only servants hired by the master of the family, for keeping his own children in slavery: And because, I conceived that a Prince who could not think himself secure without Mercenary Troops, must needs have a separate interest from that of his subjects. Although I am not ignorant of those artificial Necessities which a corrupted Ministry can create, for keeping up forces to support a Faction against the publick Interest.

As to Parliaments, I adored the wisdom of that Gothic Institution, which made them Annual: and I was confident our Liberty could never be placed upon a firm foundation till that ancient law were restored among us. For, who sees not, that while such assemblies are permitted to have a longer duration, there grows up a commerce of corruption between the Ministry and the Deputies, wherein they both find their accounts to the manifest danger of Liberty, which traffick would neither answer the design nor expence, if Parliaments met once a year.

I ever abominated that scheme of politicks, (now about thirty

372

years old) of setting up a mony'd Interest in opposition to the landed. For I conceived there could not be a truer maxim in our government than this, That the possessors of the soil are the best judges of what is for the advantage of the kingdom: If others had thought the same way, Funds of Credit and South-sea Projects would neither have been felt nor heard of.[1]

I could never discover the necessity of suspending any Law upon which the Liberty of the most innocent persons depended: neither do I think this practice hath made the taste of arbitrary power so agreeable as that we should desire to see it repeated.[2] Every Rebellion subdued and Plot discovered, contributes to the firmer establishment of the Prince. In the latter case, the knot of Conspirators is entirely broke, and they are to begin their work anew under a thousand disadvantages; so that those diligent enquiries into remote and problematical guilt, with a new power of enforcing them by chains and dungeons to every person whose face a Minister thinks fit to dislike, are not only opposite to that maxim, which declares it better that ten guilty men should escape, than one innocent suffer, but likewise leave a gate wide open to the whole Tribe of Informers, the most accursed, and prostitute, and abandoned race, that God ever permitted to plague mankind.

It is true, the Romans had a custom of chusing a Dictator, during whose administration, the Power of other Magistrates was suspended; but this was done upon the greatest emergencies; a War near their doors, or some civil Dissention, for Armies must be governed by arbitrary power. But when the Virtue of that Commonwealth gave place to luxury and ambition, this very office of Dictator became perpetual in the persons of the Caesars and their Successors, the most infamous tyrants that have any where appeared in story.

These are some of the sentiments I had relating to public affairs while I was in the world; what they are at present, is of little importance either to that or my self; neither can I truly say I have any at all, or if I had, I dare not venture to publish them: For however orthodox they may be while I am now writing, they may become

---

[1] Swift's constant opinion. See his letter to Bolingbroke, 14 Sept. 1714. He had stated it emphatically in *The Examiner*, no. 35, 5 Apr. 1711: 'One Thing I might add, as another acknowledged Maxim in that Party [the Whig], and in my Opinion as dangerous to the Constitution as any I have mentioned; I mean, That of preferring on all Occasions, the *Moneyed* Interest before the *Landed*' (*Prose Works*, ed. Davis, iii. 124).

[2] The suspension of the Habeas Corpus Act.

criminal enough to bring me into trouble before midsummer. And indeed I have often wish'd for some time past, that a Political Catechism might be published by authority four times a year, in order to instruct us how we are to speak and write, and act during the current quarter. I have by experience felt the want of such an instructor: For intending to make my court to some people on the prevailing side, by advancing certain old whiggish principles, which it seems had been exploded about a month before, I have passed for a disaffected person. I am not ignorant how idle a thing it is for a man in obscurity to attempt defending his reputation as a writer, while the spirit of Faction hath so universally possessed the minds of men, that they are not at leisure to attend to any thing else. They will just give themselves time to libel and accuse me, but cannot spare a minute to hear my defence. So in a plot-discovering age, I have known an innocent man seized and imprisoned, and forced to lie several months in chains, while the Ministers were not at leisure to hear his petition, till they had prosecuted and hanged the number they proposed.[1]

All I can reasonably hope for by this letter, is to convince my friends and others who are pleased to wish me well, that I have neither been so ill a Subject nor so stupid an Author, as I have been represented by the virulence of Libellers, whose malice hath taken the same train in both, by fathering dangerous principles in government upon me which I never maintained, and insipid productions which I am not capacle of writing. For, however I may have been sowred by personal ill treatment, or by melancholy prospects for the publick, I am too much a politician to expose my own safety by offensive words; and if my genius and spirit be sunk by encreasing years, I have at least enough discretion left, not to mistake the measure of my own abilities, by attempting subjects where those talents are necessary, which perhaps I may have lost with my youth.

[1] The reference is to the imprisonment of the Earl of Oxford.

Sir Constantine Phipps to Swift

S^{r1}

Ormond Street Janry 14. 1720[21]

Having been a little indisposed I went at X^tmas into the Country wch p^rvented me from sooner acknowledging the favour of yor Lr̃e² As to Waters's Case I was inform'd of it & the last Term I spoke to Mr Attorney General about it³ but he told me he could not grant a Writ of Error in a criminal Case without direction from the King so that Waters is not like to have much relief from hence & therefore I am glad you have some hopes it will drop in Ireland I think the Chief Justice should have that regard to his own reputation to let it go off so for I believe the Oldest man alive or any Law Book cannot give an instance of such a proceeding I was inform'd who was aim'd at by the prosecution wch made me very zealous in it wch I shall be in every thing wherein I can be serviceable to that Gentleman for whom nobody has a greater esteem then | your most faithfull | humble serv^t | Coñ Phipps

Address: For | The Reverend Dr Swift | Dean of St Patrick's | in | Dublin | Ireland
Frank: Sr C. | Phipps
Postmark: 14?
Endorsed by Swift: Sr C. Phipps | Jany 14th 1720

¹ Phipps's extreme Tory and High Church principles excited opposition almost as soon as he arrived in Ireland as Lord Chancellor. When removed from office in Sept. 1714 he was compelled to take refuge in the Castle from an infuriated mob. He returned to England (*Political State*, viii. 246, 340). After receiving an honorary degree from the University of Oxford he resumed practice at the English bar.
² i.e. letter.
³ Evidently Swift had asked Phipps to induce Sir Robert Raymond, who had been appointed Attorney-General in England, to intervene on behalf of Waters, the printer. Raymond was well known to Swift as a member of the Brothers' Club.

Historical Society of Pennsylvania[1]

Swift to Dean Mossom

Dublin. Feb. 14th 1720–21

S^{r2}

When I had the Favor of yours of the 8th instant, I was in very ill health, and am since but slowly recovering. About five years ago I had some disputes with my Chapt^r upon the Occasion of my Negatives[3] which was never contradicted before, nor did the Members directly do it then, but by some side ways of arguing the ill Consequences which might follow if it had no exceptions; This they were spirited to by the Ar Bp of Tuam,[4] who visited for[5] the A.B. of Dublin, and who sd he had long entertained an Opinion agst my Negative. Since that, they never contended[6] it; and the point is as you say, perfectly absurd. I then writt to the Bishop of Rochester and Dean of Sarum; who had been my old Friends. The former distinguished between Deanery's of the old and the new Establishment, and both of them advised me to make as little Stir as I could, the Dean of Sarum sd positively that he had no more Power in the Chap^{tr} than as Senr Prebend^{ry}, that when he was absent the next Senr presided of course, and had onely a Vote: In this Case without doubt Custom[7] hath made it, that Things may be [done] by the Dean and Chap^{tr} whether the former consents or no. But you are to understand that the Priviledges and Powers of the Dean of St Patricks upon subsequent grants and Confirmations of Popes, Parlmts, Kings, and Arch-Bishops. Now if Your Charter be much older than Edward 4^{ths} time, for ought I know, you may be on the Foot of St Patricks, as that was upon the foot of Sarum, before

---

[1] This letter was first printed by Scott, xix. 351, from the original which was then in the possession of Leonard MacNally, a Dublin barrister, who endorsed it as given to him by Mr. Elom Mossom. The original is now in the keeping of the Historical Society of Pennsylvania, Philadelphia. Scott's deciphering, followed in the main by Ball, is occasionally at fault.

[2] Robert Mossom, born about 1666, became a Fellow of Trinity College, Dublin, in 1692. He was at this time Dean of Ossory. He had evidently been involved in disputes with his chapter, and had written to Swift for advice.

[3] See Swift's correspondence with Atterbury, 24 Mar., 6 and 18 Apr. 1716.

[4] Edward Synge, who was a great friend of Archbishop King.

[5] visited for] incited *Scott, Ball.*

[6] contended] contradicted *Scott, Ball.*

[7] Custom] time *Scott, Ball.*

the subsequent Immunity's;[1] There is a French Act of Parlmt—Edw. 4th where it is recited that whereas the Dean of St Pat is ordinary &c, and has such and such Priviledges, &c so that they were known. This Deanry is just 503 years old, and severall of the Dean's Powers were granted in the first second and 3d Century after, and the Error of my Opponents lay in thinking that this Deanry was like that of Sarum, without considering what came after. I believe your best Argument will be to insist in generall that you copy after St Patrick's, and if they allow that; I will provide you with Powers and Priviledges enough. It is an infallible Maxim that not one thing here is done without the Dean's Consent; if he proposeth, it is then left to the Majority, because his Proposall is his Consent. This is as much as I can send you from a giddy aking Head; If you command any further Particulars from me of my Practice here, or any other point wherein I can do you Service, You shall find me ready to obey; For I think there are few older Acquaintance than you and I;[2] . . . believe me with great Truth, | Sr Your most obedient | humble Servt | Jonath Swift

Address: To the Reverend Doctor | Robert Mossom, Dean of | Ossory, at | Kilkenny

Endorsed: Given to me by Mr Elom[3] Mossom, at Dublin July 3. 1814 Harcourt Street   Leo: MacNally

B.M. Add. MS. 39839

Swift to Miss Esther Vanhomrigh

[? 27 February 1721]

I am surprised and grieved beyond what I can express, I read yr Lettr twice before I knew what it meant[4] nor can I yet well believe

---

[1] Immunitys] Scott finds 'some words illegible'. Ball conjectures 'grants etc'.

[2] Mossom, who had been Professor of Divinity in Dublin University, was a contemporary of Swift. He held the deanery of Ossory from 1703 until his death in 1747.

[3] Should be Eland.

[4] It is probable that Vanessa's sister died at their Dublin home on the day this letter was written. From the register of St. Andrew's Church in that city it appears that on the following Friday, 3 Mar., she was buried with her father in the churchyard. Her will, by which she bequeathed all her property to her sister, is not dated or witnessed, but was proved on 11 May following.—Ball.

my Eyes, Is that poor good Creature dead; I observed she lookt a little ghastly on Satrday but it is against the usuall way for one in her Case to dye so sudden; For Gods sake get your Friends about you to advise and to order every thing in the Formes. It is all you have to do, I want comfort my self in this case, and I can give little, Time alone must give it to you, nothing now is your Part but Decency; I was wholly unprepared against so sudden an Event, and pity you most of all Creatures at present Monday

Address: To Mrs. Esthr. Van

4805

Matthew Prior to Swift

[Westminster, 28 February 1721]

If I am to chide you for not writing to Me or beg your pardon that I have not writ to you is a question,[1] for our Correspondence has been so long interrupted, that I swear I don't know wch of Us wrote last! In all cases I assure You of my continual friendship and kindest remembrance of You, and with great pleasure, expect the same from you: I have been ill this Winter, Age I find comes on, and the Cough does not diminish:

> Non sum qualis eram bonae
> Sub regno Cynerae.[2]

pass for that,

I am tired with politics and lost in the South Sea: the roaring of the Waves and the madness of the people were justly putt together:[3] I can send you no sort of News that holds either Connexion or sense, 'tis all wilder than St Anthony's dream, and the Bagatelle is more solid than any thing that has been endeavoured here this Year: our old friend Ox:[4] is not well, and continues in Herefordshire, John of Bucks[5] dyed last week, and Coningsby[6] was sent last Night to the Tower; I frequently drink Your Health with Lord Harley

---

[1] Presumably it was Prior, 4 May 1720.
[2] Hor. *Odes*, IV. i. 3.
[3] Before this time the Bubble had burst completely; and the unhappy victims were crying for vengeance on the promoters of the scheme.
[4] Oxford.

[*For notes 5 and 6 see opposite.*

who is always the same good Man, and grows dayly more beloved and more universally known I do so too with our honest and good natured friend Ford, whom I love for many good reasons, and particularly for that He loves you.

As to the Subscriptions in wch I have given You a great deal of trouble already, to make the rest of that trouble less I desire you to send the inclosed letter to Mr: Hyde, that he may raze out the Names of those Gentlemen who have taken out their books, and take w^t Convenient care He can of the remaining Books: and as to the pecuniary part, I find no better way than that you will remit it as you did the former Summ by bill of Exchange: m^r Ford likewise judges this the best and securest Method.

How do you do as to your health? are we to see you this Summer? answer me these questions, give my service to all friends, and believe Me to be ever with great truth and esteem | D^r S^r | Yours | M Prior

West^r ffeb: 28th 172$\frac{0}{1}$

Rothschild

Swift to Charles Ford

Dublin. Apr. 15th 1721

You and I do not correspond upon equall Terms, for your Letters are usefull and entertaining, and often cost me nothing; whereas you are sure to pay for mine, which from such a Scene as this must be wholly useless and insipid. I dined a few days ago with your People, who were in good Health, and assured me of Yours, and I believe you are now thorowly amused in the height of all these present Combustions; and I find the People here of each Party are as fully taken up as if it were there own Affair, and so far it is, that they are equally ruined with you, and at least as much and universally

[5] John Sheffield, first Duke of Buckingham, appointed Lord President of the Council in 1711. He was Dryden's patron, and his writings, especially the *Essay on Poetry*, won the praise of Pope, who in 1722 edited a collection of his works at the request of his widow. Swift never liked Buckingham and endorsed Macky's harsh verdict on his character (*Prose Works*, ed. Temple Scott, x. 273).

[6] Thomas Coningsby, created Earl 30 Apr. 1719, had taken a prominent part in the impeachment of Lord Oxford. It was with satisfaction therefore that Oxford's friends, and Tories in general, greeted his commitment to the Tower, 27 Feb. 1720–1, in consequence of his publishing a pamphlet libelling Lord Macclesfield, the Lord Chancellor.

discontented. Upon a Charitable Collection some days ago for the Poor Weavers, the Return of those who are starving for want of Work amounts to above 1600, which is pretty fair for this Town,[1] and one Trade, after such Numbers as have gone to other Countryes to seek a Livelyhood.—I sent Mr Prior a Bill of 80^{ll} above a Month ago, and desired he would let me know he had received it; pray ask him the Question, and return the Answer your self. Somebody or other told me that the Gentlewoman whose Bond I gave you was in prison for other Debts, and Mr Charleton writt to me in her Favor; I am sure she is an old Knave; but if you please to send the Bond back by the first safe hand, I will use it against the principall Rascall, who I find sculks about this Town.—I have been employing my Credit by Ld Arran and other Means to get the D. of Gr—[2] to order putting off the Affair of the Printer[3] till He comes over, but my Sollicitor Mr Charleton[4] meets no Success; Surely tis a small Favor, and I desired S^r Th. Hanmer might use his Credit the same way: But I find there is less trusting in Friends than ever our Grandmothers warn us again[st]; and the Term begins in ten days, and the Matter will be resumed afresh, to great Expence and more Vexation neither of which I am well capable of bearing either by my Health or Fortune, and this hinders me from going to England as I intended.—The letter of Brutus to Cicero[5] should have been better translated; Your Ministry seems to me to want Credit in suffering so many Libells published against them; and here there is a worse Matter; for many of the violent Whigs profess themselves perfect Jacobites, and plead for it the Miseryes and Contempt they suffer by the Treatment of England. We abound in Papers[6] as

---

[1] The weaving industry in Ireland had been severely crippled by English legislation; and in the earlier part of 1721 unemployment, poverty, and suffering became acute. In a letter of 8 Apr. Archbishop King calculated the number of the families belonging to the weaving trade in distress at 1,700 and the persons at near 6,000. The Government ordered £100 for relief purposes; and collections were made in the churches. See *Poems*, pp. 273–6.

[2] The Duke of Grafton, Lord Lieutenant, came over on 28 Aug.

[3] The prosecution of Waters for printing Swift's pamphlet, *A Proposal For the Universal Use of Irish Manufacture*.

[4] Chaplain to the Duchess of Ormonde.

[5] Printed in the *London Journal* for 1 Apr. 1721 as the main portion of one of 'Cato's Letters'; reprinted in the *Political State* for April, and in *The Fourth Collection of Cato's Political Letters*, 1721, pp. 3–12. 'Cato' was John Trenchard and Thomas Gordon.

[6] The chief Dublin periodicals of the time were the *Dublin Gazette*, the

well as you, and I have observed it to be one of the Consequences of wretched Times, and it seems naturall enough, that when People[1] are reduced to Rags they should turn them to the onely Use that Rags are proper for.—The sanguine Stile begins to revive, the D. of Ormonde and his naturall Son were last week in Ireland, and went over to the West, with the like Trumpery. Sheridan put the Players upon acting a Puppet shew, but his Subject was ill chosen, and his Performance worse, and it succeeded accordingly; yet gave Occasion to a very pretty Copy of Verses on Puppet shews[2] printed here but not published, yet I shall soon get one, and would send it to you if I could Frank it; We cannot find the Author, and it is not Delany. —Are not these fine materialls for a Letter; but I have no others.— I am now writing a History of my Travells, which will be a large Volume, and gives Account of Countryes hitherto unknown; but they go on slowly for want of Health and Humor.[3] I condole with you for the Death of Lady Newtoun.[4] They are bringing over her Body as I am told. Remember me to Mr Lewis and Pope and Gay. Some people complain for want of Mr Pope's 2 last Volumes of Homer[5]—and my remembrance to Dr Arbuthnot.

Address: To Charles Ford Esqr, at | his Lodgings at the blue | Perewig in Pel-mel | London
Postmark: 21 AP

Dublin Courant, the *Post-Man*, *Whalley's News-Letter*, *Harding's Weekly News-Letter*, *Pue's Occurrences*, and *Dublin Intelligence*.

[1] 'kingdoms' obliterated before 'People'.

[2] *The Puppet-Show* was first included in Swift's *Works* by Faulkner in 1762, and reprinted in the London trade edition of the *Works* in the same year (xiv. 148), and thence, accepted as Swift's, passed into later editions. The comment by Swift in this letter, however, makes his authorship very questionable. For a full discussion of the authorship and a reprint of the text from Faulkner's edition see *Poems*, pp. 1102–5.

[3] This is the first reference to *Gulliver's Travels*, disposing of the belief expressed by Deane Swift (*Essay*, 1755, pp. 278–81) and Orrery (*Remarks*, 1752, p. 196) that the book was finished about this time.

[4] Emily, wife of Theophilus Butler, first Lord Newtown-Butler. She was the daughter of Ford's aunt, Mary Ford, who married James Stopford, of New Hall, co. Meath. Lodge's *Peerage of Ireland* (1754), ii. 339, says that she died 13 June 1722, and was buried on the 15th in the family vault under St. Ann's Church, Dublin, and that her only son died 10 Jan. 1721, and was also buried there. These dates cannot be reconciled by what we are told by Swift. The burial records of St. Ann's have perished and the existing extracts from them are said to leave the problem unsolved.

[5] Vols. v and vi of *The Iliad* were published as far back as May 1720.

Matthew Prior to Swift

Westminster, April 25, 1721.

Dear Sir,

I know very well, that you can write a good letter, if you have a mind to it; but that is not the question.[1] A letter from you sometimes is what I desire. Reserve your tropes and periods for those you love less; and let me hear how you do, in whatever humour you are; whether lending your money to the butchers, protecting the weavers, treating the women,[2] or construing *propria quae maribus* to the country curate.[3] You and I are so established authors, that we may write what we will, without fear of censure: and if we have not lived long enough to prefer the *bagatelle* to any thing else, we deserved to have had our brains knocked out ten years ago.

I have received the money punctually of Mr. *Dan. Hayes*, have his receipt, and hereby return you all the thanks, that your friendship in that affair ought to claim, and your generosity does contemn. There's one turn for you: good.

The man you mentioned in your last[4] has been in the country these two years, very ill in his health, and has not for many months been out of his chamber; yet what you observe of him is so true, that his sickness is all counted for policy, that he will not come up, till the public distractions force somebody or other (whom God knows) who will oblige somebody else to send for him in open triumph, and set him in *statu quo prius*. That, in the mean time, he has foreseen all that has happened; checkmated all the Ministry; and to divert himself at his leisure hours, he has laid all those

---

[1] Evidently Swift had replied to Prior's letter of 28 Feb. excusing himself for not having written earlier on the ground of wanting congenial matter.

[2] See Swift's letter to Ford of 15 Apr. 1721 and the note on the distress of those employed in the Irish weaving trade.

[3] For six years after taking possession of the deanery of St. Patrick's Swift led a secluded life. In 1720 he came out into the open with his *Proposal for the Universal Use of Irish Manufacture*—a return to political pamphleteering; and in the same year appeared *A Letter from a Lay-Patron to a Gentleman Designing for Holy Orders*, published in Dublin, and reprinted in London, 1721, under the title *A Letter to a Young Gentleman, Lately enter'd into Holy Orders*—the pamphlet which explains Prior's allusion to the 'country curate'. Further to these two pamphlets see *Prose Works*, ed. Davis, vol. ix.

[4] i.e. Oxford.

lime-twigs for his neighbour *Coningsby*,¹ that keep that precious bird in the cage, out of which himself slippt so cunningly and easily.

Things, and the way of mens judging them, vary so much here, that it is impossible to give you any just account of some of our friends' actions. *Roffen*² is more than suspected to have given up his party, as *Sancho* did his subjects, for so much a head, *l'un portant l'autre*.³ His cause, therefore, which is something originally like that of [*le*] *Lutrin*,⁴ is opposed or neglected by his ancient friends, and openly sustained by the Ministry. He cannot be lower in the opinion of most men than he is; and I wish our friend *Har*[*court*] were higher than he is.⁵

Our young *Harley*'s vice is no more covetousness,⁶ than plainness of speech is that of his cousin *Tom*. His lordship is really *amabilis*; and Lady *Harriette*, *adoranda*.

I tell you no news, but that the whole is a complication of mistakes in policy, and of knavery in the execution of it: of the Ministers I speak, for the most part as well ecclesiastical as civil. This is all the truth I can tell you, except one, which I am sure you receive very kindly, that I am ever,

Your friend and your servant,

M. Prior.

Friend *Shelton*, commonly called *Dear Dick*,⁷ is with me. We drink your health. Adieu.

¹ Coningsby, to whom reference was made in Prior's letter to Swift 28 Feb., came of a family connected with Herefordshire, of which county he was at this time Lord-Lieutenant. He was also Lord-Lieutenant of Radnorshire. The pamphlet in which he reflected on Lord Macclesfield concerned the presentation to the vicarage of Leominster. This involved him in resignation of his two lord-lieutenancies; and in Nov. 1724 he was dismissed from the Privy Council.

² i.e. Bishop Atterbury.

³ Writing to Atterbury, 3 Aug. 1713, Swift observed: 'I envy Dr. Freind that he has you for his inspector.' Events belied the expectation that Atterbury and the headmaster of Westminster School would remain on friendly terms. The two were at this time at law with each other (*Portland MSS.* vii. 290–4).

⁴ The title of Boileau Despréaux's poem.

⁵ Within three months, 24 July, Harcourt was created a Viscount; and in Aug. 1722 he was readmitted to the Privy Council.

⁶ Edward Harley, second Lord Oxford, was the reverse of covetous. He was generous to those in need; and his passion for collecting books, manuscripts, pictures, and miscellaneous curiosities brought him into severe financial embarrassment.

⁷ The friend immortalized in Prior's *Alma*.

Swift to Knightley Chetwode

Dublin, 29 April, 1721.

Sir,

Your servant brought your letter when I was abroad, and promised to come next morning at 8 but never called; so I answer it by Post; you have been horribly treated, but it is a common calamity.[1] Do you remember a passage in a play of Molière's, *Mais que Diable avait il à faire dans cette galere?*[2] What had you to do among such company? I showed your letter yesterday to the A.Bp.[3] as you desire; I mean I read the greatest part to him. He is of opinion you should take the oaths;[4] and then complain to the government if you thought fit. But I believe neither; nor any body can expect you would have much satisfaction, considering how such complaints are usually received.

For my own part I do not see any law of God or man forbidding us to give security to the powers that be; and private men are not [to] trouble themselves about titles to crowns, whatever may be their particular opinions. The abjuration is understood as the law stands; and as the law stands, none has title to the crown but the present possessor. By this argument more at length, I convinced a young gentleman of great parts and virtue; and I think I could defend myself by all the duty of a Christian to take oath to any prince in possession. For the word lawfull, means according to present law in force; and let the law change ever so often, I am to act according to law, provided it neither offends faith nor morality.

You will find a sickly man when you come to town; and you will find all parties and persons out of humour. I envy your employments of improving bogs; and yet I envy few other employments at present. My humble service to Mrs. Chetwode and believe me to be, ever, |Sincerely yours, &c.

Address: To Knightley Chetwode, Esqr. at his House at | Woodbrooke near Portarlington.

[1] During the two years that had elapsed since Swift sent his last letter to him, 25 Nov. 1718, Chetwode had returned to Ireland and taken up his residence again at Woodbrooke. As appears from a subsequent letter, while attending the spring assizes he had come into conflict with his Whig neighbours and had been challenged to fight a duel.—Ball.

[2] The correct reading of the sentence in *Les Fourberies de Scapin*, II. xi, is 'Que diable allait-il faire dans cette galère?'

[3] i.e. Archbishop King.   [4] Of allegiance and abjuration.

Swift to Stella

[Deanery House, Sunday Morning, 30 April 1721.

Jack Grattan said nothing to me of it till last night; 'tis none of my fault: how did I know but you were to dine abroad? You should have sent your messenger sooner; yes, I think the dinner you provided for yourselves may do well enough here, but pray send it soon. I wish you would give a body more early warning; but you must blame yourselves. *Delany* says he will come in the evening; and for aught I know *Sheridan* may be here at dinner: which of you was it that undertook this frolick? Your letter hardly explained your meaning, but at last I found it. Pray don't serve me these tricks often. You may be sure, if there be a good bottle you shall have it. I am sure I never refused you, and therefore that reflection might have been spared. Pray be more positive in your answer to this.

Deanry-house
Sunday morning, April 30. 1721

Margoose, and not *Mergoose*;[2] it is spelt with an *a*, simpleton.

No, I am pretty well after my walk. I am glad the Archdeacon got home safe, and I hope you took care of him.[3] It was his own fault; how could I know where he was? and he could have easily overtaken me; for I walked softly on purpose, I told *Delany* I would.

Endorsed by Stella: An answer to no letter.

[1] This letter, with the exception of the letters of the *Journal to Stella*, perhaps the early letter of 1698, written from Moor Park (i, p. 23), and the fanciful 'Prince of Lilliput to Stella', 11 March 1726–7, remains the only surviving letter from Swift to Stella. It was in the possession of Deane Swift, and was printed by him in 1768. As Ball observes, the letter 'indicates that the shadow of Vanessa did not interrupt the intercourse' between Swift and Stella and shows, as we know from other sources, that she was intimate with Swift's inner circle of friends. The letter is, as Stella's endorsement shows, an answer to an imaginative one.

[2] A jest which may have some relation with Stella's pronunciation.

[3] This may be taken to imply that Stella and Rebecca Dingley were living with Archdeacon Walls and his wife, as some years before they undoubtedly were.

Forster copy

Swift to Knightley Chetwode

Dublin, 9 May, 1721.

Sir,

I did not answer your last[1] because I would take time to consider it. I told the Ar. Bp. what you had done, that you had taken the oaths, etc., and then I mentioned the fact about Wall who brought a challenge, etc., though you did not tell from whom,[2] and whether you should apply to have him put out of the commission.[3] The Archbishop said he thought you ought to let the matter rest a while, and when you have done so, and get your materials ready and that it appears not to be a sudden heat, he did hope the Chancellor would do you justice.

As to the business of Sandes[4] going about for hands I know not what to say. That was rather a scoundrel than an illegal thing, and probably will be thought merit and zeal rather than a fault. I take your part to be only despising it; as you ought to do the bravery of his brother, and his manner of celebrating it. For my own part, and I do not say it as a divine, there is nothing I have greater contempt for than what is usually styled bravery, which really consists in never giving just offence, and yet by a general demeanour make it appear that we do not want courage, though our hand is not every hour at our hilt. I believe your courage has never been suspected, and before I knew you I had heard you were rather much too warm, and

---

[1] A reply to Swift's letter of 29 Apr.

[2] The challenge to fight a duel was probably brought to Swift by William Wall of Maryborough, a gentleman who displays in his will a militant spirit against even those of his own household. The challenger, as appears from an endorsement, was Col. Robert Pigott, of Dysart, from whose family the Lords Dysart trace descent. In a curious and interesting autobiography of a contemporary Queen's county magnate, Pigott is described (*Journal of the County Kildare Archaeological Society*, v. 256) as 'a most violent man in his friendships and enmities, and also violent in his principles', who would brook no contradiction.—Ball.

[3] Of the peace.

[4] Lancelot Sandes, of Kilkevan, who married a sister of Col. Pigott. To him Pole Cosby, the author of the autobiography, thus refers (op. cit., p. 254): 'He was of no great parts or sense, . . . I know no perfections, only that he did provide and manage very well for his family, and did increase his fortune very considerably to what it was, and lived very plentifully and hospitably, and did entertain his friends heartily and cheerfully.'—Ball.

you may take what Sandes said as a compliment that his brother's bravery appeared by venturing to quarrel with you.

You are to know that few persons have less credit with the present powers than the Archbishop,[1] and therefore the redress you are to expect must be from the justice of those who have it in their way to do you right; I mean those at the helm, or rather who have their little finger at the helm, which however is enough for your use, if they will but apply it. But in great matters of government the Lord-Lieutenant[2] does all, and these folks[3] cannot make a vicar or an ensign. I am, | Your &c. | J.S.

My humble service to your Lady.

Address: To Knightley Chetwode, Esq., at his house at Woodbrooke, near Portarlington.

Endorsed by Chetwode: Upon the Subject of my quarrel with Coll. Pigott at Maryborough Assizes.

Duncombe[4]

Swift to the Rev. Thomas Wallis

13 May 1721[4]

Sir,[5]

I had your letter, and the copy of the bishop's circular enclosed,[6] for which I thank you; and yet I will not pretend to know any thing

---

[1] Archbishop King had been omitted from the number of the Lords Justices when the Duke of Bolton left Ireland after the last session of the Irish Parliament, and had received, as his correspondence shows, little attention from the Duke of Grafton since his appointment.—Ball.

[2] i.e. the Duke of Grafton.

[3] i.e. the Lords Justices, Lord Midleton and Speaker Conolly.

[4] For this and subsequent letters addressed by Swift to Wallis we are indebted to John Duncombe's *Letters by Several Eminent Persons Deceased*, 3 vols., 1772. This letter was dated 13 May by Duncombe. When reprinting it in his *Supplement*, 1779, and his edition of Swift's *Works*, 1801, Nichols assigned the date 18 May. Probably a printing error, for Nichols was extracting these letters from Duncombe.

[5] Thomas Wallis was a son of the Dean of Derry, who became vicar of Athboy, a benefice he held from 1713 to 1746. Subsequent references make it probable that Swift had been a guest of Wallis before the writing of this letter.

[6] John Evans, Bishop of Meath, with whom Swift was on no friendly terms, was holding another visitation.

of it, and hope you have not told any body what you did. I should be glad enough to be at the visitation, not out of any love to the business or the person, but to do my part in preventing any mischief. But in truth my health will not suffer it; and you, who are to be my proxy, may safely give it upon your veracity. I am confident the bishop would not be dissatisfied with wanting my company, and yet he may give himself airs when he finds I am not there. I now employ myself in getting you a companion to cure your spleen. I am | your faithful humble servant, | J.S.

B.M. Add. MS. 39839

Swift to Miss Esther Vanhomrigh

June. 1st. [1721 ?][1]

‒ ‒ ‒ ‒ ‒ ‒ ‒

I can not contrive to get this Catalogue copied out and therefore I have delivered it to Mr Worall for you and told him it was some Papers directed to me for you from Engld—Pray God protect you adieu—

Address: To Mrs. Esthr. Vanhomrigh

Deane Swift 1765

Swift to Bishop Evans

Dublin, June 5, 1721.

My Lord,
    I have received an account of your Lordship's refusing to admit my proxy at your visitation,[2] with several circumstances of personal

---

[1] The date of this letter is doubtful; but as Freeman notes: 'It belongs to the period of "strokes".' As will be seen by a subsequent letter on 1 June 1722 Swift was writing from Clogher. The endorsement to this present letter may be by Vanessa, but, if so, the writing is not characteristic.
[2] Previous editors, including Ball, date this letter 5 July. Deane Swift, who first printed the letter in 1765, dated it 'June 5'. As Bishop Evans's refusal to

reflexions on myself, although my proxy attested my want of health; to confirm which, and to lay before you the justice and Christianity of your proceeding, above a hundred persons of quality and distinction can witness, that since Friday the 26th of May, I have been tormented with an ague, in as violent a manner as possible, which still continues, and forces me to make use of another hand in writing to you. At the same time, I must be plain to tell you, that if this accident had not happened, I should have used all endeavours to avoid your visitation, upon the public promise I made you three years ago,[1] and the motives which occasioned it; because I was unwilling to hear any more very injurious treatment and appellations given to my brethren or myself; and by the grace of God, I am still determined to absent myself on the like occasions, as far as I can possibly be dispensed with by any law, while your Lordship is in that diocese and I a member of it. In which resolution I could not conceive but your Lordship would be easy: Because, although my presence might possibly contribute to your real (at least future) interest, I was sure it could not to your present satisfaction.

If I had had the happiness to have been acquainted with any one clergyman in the diocese, of your Lordship's principles, I should have desired him to represent me, with hopes of better success: But I wish you would sometimes think it convenient to distinguish men, as well as principles, and not to look upon every person, who happens to owe you canonical obedience, as if —[2]

I have the honour to be Ordinary over a considerable number of as eminent divines as any in this kingdom, who owe me the same obedience as I owe to your Lordship, and are equally bound to attend my visitation; yet neither I, nor any of my predecessors, to my knowledge, did ever refuse a regular proxy.

I am only sorry that you, who are of a country[3] famed for good-nature, have found a way to unite the hasty passion of your own countrymen, with the long, sedate resentment of a Spaniard: But

accept Swift's proxy was almost certainly communicated to him by Wallis, see his letter of 18 May 1721, it seems likely that Swift would have communicated with the bishop sooner than July.

[1] See p. 292, n. 4.
[2] It has been suggested that 'he was a footman' are the words to be supplied. Cf. Swift's letter to Evans, 22 May 1719, *ad fin.*
[3] i.e. Wales.

I have an honourable hope, that this proceeding has been more owing to party than complexion.[1] I am, | my Lord, | Your Lordship's | Most humble servant.

Forster copy

Swift to Knightley Chetwode

Dublin, 10 June, 1721.

Sir,

I received both your letters[2] and the reason why I did not answer the first was because I thought I had said all I had to say upon the occasion, both as to the A. Bp's opinion and my own. But if that reason had not been sufficient there was another, and a better, or rather a worse, for I have been this last fortnight as miserable as a man can possibly be with an ague, and after vomiting, sweating and Jesuit's bark,[3] I got out to-day, but have been since my beginning to recover, so right seized with a daily headache, that I am but a very scurvy recovered man. I suppose you may write to the Chancellor and tell him the full story, and leave the rest to him.

As to your building I can only advise you to ask advice, to go on slowly, and to have your house on paper before you put it into lime and stone.[4] I design in a very few days to go somewhere into the country, perhaps to Gaulstown. I have been 7 years getting a horse and have lost a 100[11] by buying without success. Sheridan has got his horses again, and I recovered one that my servant had lost. Everybody can get horses but I. There is a paper called Mist come out, just before May 29th, terribly severe.[5] It is not here to be had. The

---

[1] Not long after Evans attributed to Swift a letter sent from Dublin to the London Press under the pseudonym of Thomas Strangways. Swift was in no way responsible for it; and the bishop's attempts to discredit the letter only reveal his inability to understand Swift's true character (Archbishop Wake's *Correspondence*, 16 Sept. 1721).　　　　[2] In answer to Swift's letter of 9 May.

[3] Peruvian bark, or chinchona, usually spelled cinchona. Named after a Countess of Chinchón, wife of the Governor of Peru in 1638.

[4] Evidently Chetwode had embarked on further building work at Woodbrooke. Cf. Chetwode's letter to Swift of 5 Apr. 1715.

[5] The reference is to Nathaniel Mist's *Weekly Journal* in which Defoe had some share. This publication became the recognized organ of High-fliers and Jacobites; and Mist suffered frequent punishment for 'libels' which appeared in his paper. Swift's *Short View of the State of Ireland*, 1727–8, was in part reprinted by Mist in England and brought down a prosecution upon him.

printer was called before the Commons. It applies Cromwell and his son to the present Court.[1] White roses we have heard nothing of to-day.[2] | I am your most obedient, &c. | J.S.

My head is too ill to write or think.

Endorsed by Chetwode: Swift dated at Dublin June 10th, 1721; the Archbishop's and his own opinion of the prosecution[3] against me.

Rothschild

Swift to Charles Ford

Dublin. Jun. 19ᵗʰ 1721

I send you here a Letter inclosed to Friend Charlotte,[4] and wish I had health or humor to have it done sooner, nor can I brag of either now, being hardly got out of an Ague, and am to morrow morning going in a Stage Coach for want of Horses to George Rochfort,[5] not being able to stir further by reason of that Scoundrel Circumstance of the Printer. I am now in the midst of Packing, and am awkward as an Alderman by long confinement. Your People are well, and were so kind to send frequent Messages to me while I was Sick.—I hear you are grown weary of prosecuting the South Sea, and our News writers bawl about that Ld Mar and the D. of Ormond are to be restored, and folks tell me there is some Truth in it: I believe the Former but not the latter. I have finished that Tract you saw,[6] where you said I was mistaken about some Persons; I mean Ld Poulet &c and I have some thoughts of sending that and the other Thing which was sent to you before the Qu— died,[7] and have them both printed in a Volume by some Whig Bookseller, by sending it to him at a venture. Ld Anglesea is mortally fallen out with me

---

[1] The application was ambiguous; but no doubt intended.

[2] Swift was writing on the Pretender's birthday, when white roses were worn by the Jacobites.

[3] One was instituted in consequence of the challenge to a duel (Swift to Chetwode, 9 May).

[4] Swift's letter is not known, but we have Bolingbroke's reply of 28 [o.s. 17] July.

[5] At Gaulstown.

[6] *An Enquiry into the Behaviour of the Queen's Last Ministry.* The reference to Lord Poulett in the first draft was omitted from the second on the advice of Ford. See the edition by Ehrenpreis, pp. 50, 38 n., 69 n.

[7] *Some Free Thoughts upon the Present State of Affairs.*

about a passage in the Pamphlet of Irish Manufacture,[1] where he
was meant, but with no Reflection further than differing in Opinion,
he has not been to see me, and I him. He is for all the Hardships that
have been put on this Kingdom. He sent me a Message, and I have
returned him an Answer that will sting him.—Tis late, and I have
not packt up my Shirts and Jesuits Bark.

Address: To Charles Ford Esq[r], at | His Lodgings at the Blue | Perewig in Pell-
mell | London
Postmark: 26 IV

B.M. Add. MS. 39839

Swift to Miss Esther Vanhomrigh

Gallstoun near Kinnegad. July. 5th. 1721

It was not convenient, hardly possible to write to you before now,
though I had a more than ordinary desire to do it, considering the
Disposition I found you in last, though I hope I left you in a better.[2]
I must here beg you to take more Care of your Health, by Company
and Exercise or else the Spleen will get the better of you, than which
there is not a more foolish or troublesome Disease; and what you
have no Pretence in the World to, if all the Advantages of Life can
be any Defence against it . . Cad—assures me he continues to esteem
and love and value you above all things, and so will do to the End
of his Life; but at the same time entreats that you would not make
your self or him unhappy by Imaginations. The Wisest men of all
Ages have thought it the best Course to Seize the Minutes as they
fly, and to make every innocent action[3] an Amusement. If you knew
how I Struggle for a little Health, what uneasyness I am at in riding
and walking, and refraining from every thing agreeable to my Tast,
you would think it but a small thing to take a Coach now and then,
and to converse with Fools or impertinents to avoid Spleen and
Sickness—Without Health you will lose all desire of drinking your

---

[1] The passage beginning 'I was much delighted with a person who hath a
great estate in this kingdom', in *A Proposal for the Universal Use of Irish
Manufacture.*

[2] Swift may have seen Vanessa several times since her sister's death. The
allusions in this letter, as Ball points out, seem to have reference to a letter received from her since he had left town.

[3] Two words scribbled out before 'action'.

Coffee, and be *so low* as to have no Spirits—I answer all your Questions that you were used ask Cad—and he protests he answers them
in the Affirmative—How go your Law Affairs. You were once a
good Lawyer, but Cad—hath spoiled you—I had a weary Journy
in an Irish Stage Coach,[1] but am pretty well since—Pray write to
me cheerfully without Complaints or Expostulations or else Cad—
shall know it and punish you—What is this world without being as
easy in it as Prudence and Fortune can make it I find it every day
more silly and insignificant, and I conform my self to it for my own
Ease; I am here as deep employd in othr Folks Plantations and
Ditchings as if they were my own Concern. and think of my absent
Friends with delight, and hopes of seeing them happy, and of being
happy with them. Shall you who have so much Honor and good
Sense act otherwise to make Cad—and your self miserable.—Settle
your Affairs, and quit this scoundrel Island, and things will be as
you desire—I can say no more being called away, mais soyez
assurè que jamais personne du monde a etè aimèe honorèe estimeè
adoreè par votre amie [*sic*] que vous, I drank no Coffee since I left
you nor intend till I see you again,[2] there is none worth drinking but
yours, if my *self* may be the judge—adieu

Address: To Mʳˢ Vanhomrigh

B.M. Add. MS. 39839

Miss Esther Vanhomrigh to Swift

[July 1721][3]

—, —, —, Cad I am and cannot avoid being in the Spleen to the
last degree every thing combines to make me so is it not very hard to
have so good a fortune as I have if I had no Title to it one of The
D—rs[4] is—I don't know what to call him He behaved himself so

---

[1] It was probably of most primitive construction. The allusion is the earliest
which I know to the use in Ireland of a public conveyance by a man of Swift's
rank.—Ball.

[2] As Ball observes, 'These words can hardly have an ulterior meaning'.

[3] Freeman prints this as the last but one (no. xlvii, pp. 140-1) of the letters
included in his edition of the Vanessa–Swift correspondence; but it is obviously
an answer to the previous letter, that of 5 July, and presumably was written in
July 1721.

[4] Probably the Masters in Chancery are indicated.

abominably to me the other day that had I been a man he should
have heard more of it in short he does nothing but trifle and make
excuses I realy believe he heartily repents that ever he undertook it
since he heard the councell first plead finding his friend more in the
wrong than he imagined here am I obliged to stay in this odious
Town attending and losing my health and humore yet this and all
other disapointments in life I can bear with ease but that of being
neglected by —, —, —, Cad. he has often told me that the best
maxim in life and allwas [*sic*] held by the wisest in all ages is to
sease the moments as they fly but those happy moments allwas [*sic*]
fly out of the reach of the unfortunate pray tell — — — Cad. I
don't remember any angry passages in my letter and that I am very
sorry if [they] appeared so to¹ him Spleen I cannot help so you must
excuse it I do² I can to get the better of it and it is to strong for me
I have read more since I saw Cad than I did in a great while passed
and chose those books that required most attention on purpose to
engage my thoughts but I find the more I think the more unhappy
I am I had once a mind not to have wrote to you for feare of making
you uneassy to find me so dull but I could not keep to that resolution
for the pleasure of writing to you the satisfaction I have in you
remembring me when you read my letter and the delight I have in
expecting one from — — — Cad makes me rather chuse to give you
some uneasiness then to add to my owne

4805

Viscount Bolingbroke to Swift

[28 July [o.s. 17] 1721]³

I never was so angry in all my life, as I was with you last week, on
the receipt of yʳ letter of the 19ᵗʰ of June. the extream pleasure it
gave me takes away all the excuses which I had invented for your
long neglect.⁴ I design to return my humble thanks to those men of

¹ 'appeared so to' above 'the made' which is struck through.
² Presumably the word 'all' is omitted after 'I do'.
³ The original is dated 28 July. Subsequent editors follow, until Ball, presumably by a slip, dates this letter 21 July.
⁴ Apparently there had been no correspondence between them since Swift's
letter of 19 Dec. 1719 (which may have gone astray) till Swift's letter of 19 June
1721, which is missing.

eminent gratitude & integrity, the Weavers & the Judges, and earnestly to entreat them, instead of tossing you in the person of yr Proxy,[1] who had need to have iron ribs to endure all the drubbings you will procure him, to toss you in yr proper person, the next time you offend by going about to talk sense or to do good to the Rabble. is it possible that one of yr age & profession should be ignorant that this monstrous Beast has passions to be mov'd, but no reason to be appeal'd to, and that plain truth will influence half a score men att most in a Nation, or an age, while Mystery will lead millions by the nose? Dear Jon: since you cannot resolve to write as you preach, what publick authority allows, what councils & senates have decided to be orthodox, instead of what private opinion suggests, leave off instructing the Citizens of Dublin. believe me there is more pleasure, and more merit too, in cultivating friendship, than in taking care of the State. fools & knaves are generally best fitted for the last, & none but Men of Sense & virtue are capable of the other. how comes it then to pass that you, who have Sense tho' you have wit, and virtue tho' you have kept bad company in yr time, should be so surpriz'd that I continue to write to you, & expect to hear from you, after seven years absence? Anni praedantur euntes,[2] say you, & time will lop off my luxuriant branches. perhaps it will be so. but I have put the pruning hook into a hand which works hard to leave the other as little to do of that kind as may be. some superfluous twigs are every day cut, & as they lessen in number the bough wch bears the golden fruit of friendship, shoots, swells, & spreads.

our friend told you what he heard, & what was commonly said, when he told you that I had taken the fancy of growing rich. if I could have resolv'd to think two minutes a day about stocks, to flatter law[3] half an hour a week, or to have any obligation to people I neither lov'd nor valu'd, certain it is that I might have gained immensely. but not caring to follow the many bright examples of these kinds, which France furnish'd and which England sent us over, I turn'd the little money I had of my own, without being let into any Secret, very negligently, and if I have secur'd enough to content me it is because I was soon contented. I am sorry to hear you confess, that the love of money has got into yr head. take care, or it will ere long sink into yr heart, the proper seat of passions. Plato, whom you

---

[1] Swift's printer, Waters.   [2] Hor. *Ep.* ii. 2, 55.
[3] After months of wandering John Law took refuge from his creditors in Copenhagen.

cite, look'd upon riches, & the other advantages of fortune, to be desirable, but he declar'd, as you have read in Diog: Laertius, ea etsi non afuerint, nihilominus tamen beatum fore Sapientem.[1] you may think it, perhaps, hard to reconcile his two journeys into Sicily[2] wth this maxim, especially since he got fourscore talents of the tyrant. but I can assure you, that he went to the elder Dionysius only to buy books,[3] & to the younger only to borrow a piece of ground, & a number of men, women, & children, to try his Utopia.[4] Aristippus was in Sicily att the same time, & there pass'd some billingsgate between these reverend Persons. this Philosopher had a much stronger fancy to grow rich than Plato. he flatter'd, he crack'd jests, & danc'd over a stick, to get some of the Sicilian gold,[5] but still even he took care, sibi res, non se rebus submittere,[6] and I remember, with great edification how he reprov'd one of his Catechumens, who blush'd & shrunk back, when his Master shew'd him the way to the bawdy House. non ingredi turpe est, sed egredi non posse turpe est.[7] the conclusion of all is this un honnête homme ought to have cent mille livres de rente if you please, but a wise Man will be happy with the hundredth part. let us not refuse riches, when they offer themselves; but let us give them no room in our heads or our hearts. let us enjoy wealth, without suffering it to become necessary to us, and, to finish with one of Seneca's quaint Sentences, let us place it so, that Fortune may take it without tearing it from us.[8] the passage you mention does follow that which I quoted to you,[9] and the advice is good. Solon thought so, nay he went further, and you remember the reason he gave for sitting in the council of

[1] Diogenes Laertius, *De Vitis Clarorum Philosophorum*, ed. Amsterdam, 1692, p. 213.

[2] He made three. The allusion is to the first two.

[3] Diogenes, op. cit., p. 127.   [4] Ibid., p. 178.

[5] Ibid., p. 125.   [6] Hor. *Ep*. i. 1, 19.

[7] Diogenes, op. cit., p. 121.

[8] Bolingbroke is quoting from a passage in Sir Roger L'Estrange's version of 'Seneca's Morals' (Savoy, 1696, p. 175): 'True happiness is not to be found in the Excesses of Wine or of Women, nor in the Largest Prodigalities of Fortune. What she has given me, she may take away, but she shall not tear it from me; and so long as it does not grow to me, I can part with it without Pain'.

[9] Bolingbroke is referring to the quotation from Dolabella's letter to Cicero which he had sent to Swift two years before, 17 Mar. 1718–19. The passage which Swift had mentioned is the following: 'Quaecumque de tua dignitate ab imperatore erunt impetranda qua est humanitate Caesar, facillum erit ab eo tibi ipsi impetrare.'

Pisistratus,[1] whom he had done his uttmost to oppose, & who, by the way, prov'd a very good Prince. but the Epistle is not writ by Cicero, as you seem to think. it is, if I mistake not an Epistle of Dolabella's to him. Cato, you say, would not be of the same mind. Cato is a most venerable Name, & Dolabella was but a Scoundrel with wit & Valour, and yet there is better sense, nay there is more Virtue, in what Dolabella advises, than in the conduct of Cato. I must own my weakness to you. this Cato, so sung by Lucan in every page, & so much better sung by Virgil in half a line,[2] strikes me with no great respect. when I see him painted in all the glorious colours which eloquence furnishes, I call to mind that image of him wch Tully gives in one of his letters to Atticus, or to somebody else, where he says that having a mind to keep a debate from coming on in the Senate, they made Cato rise to speak, & that he talk'd till the hour of proposing matters was over.[3] Tully insinuates that they often made this use of him. does not the moving picture shift? do you not behold Clarke of Taunton Dean[4] in the gown of a Roman Senator, sending out the members to piss? the Censor us'd sharp medicines, but in his time the patient had strength to bear them. the second Cato inherited this receit, without his Skill, & like a true quack, he gave the remedy, because it was his only one, tho' it was too late he hasten'd the patient's death, he not only hasten'd it, he made it more convulsive and painful.

the condition of yr wretched country is worse than you represent it to be. the healthful Indian follows his master, who dy'd of sickness, to the grave, but I much doubt whether those charitable legislators exact the same, when the Master is a lunatick, & cuts his own throat. I mourn over Ireland with all my heart, but I pity you more. in reading yr letter I feel yr pulse, and I judg of yr distemper as surely by the figures into which you cast your ink, as the learned Doctor att the hand & urinal could do, if he por'd over yr water. you are really in a very bad way. you say yr memory declines. I believe it does since you forget your friends, & since repeated importunity can hardly

---

[1] Σὲ φημὶ πάντων τυράννων εἶναι βέλτιστον (Diogenes, op. cit., p. 41).

[2] *Aen.* viii. 670: 'Secretosque pios, his dantem iura Catonem.'

[3] 'Atque erat dicturus, ad quem propter diei brevitatem perventum non est, heros ille noster Cato. Sic ego conservans rationem institutionemque nostram tueor' (*Ad Atticum*, i. xvii, § 9).

[4] The borough of Taunton was represented by Edward Clarke from 1689 to 1710.

draw a token of remembrance from you. there are bad airs for the mind, as well as the body, and what do you imagine that Plato, since you have set me upon quoting him, who thank'd heaven that he was not a Boeotian, would have said of the ultima Thule?[1] Shake off yr lazyness, ramble over hither, & spend some months in a kinder climate. you will be in danger of meeting but one plague here, & you will leave many behind you. here you will come among people, who lead a life singular enough to hit yr humour, so near the world, as to have all its conveniences; so far from the world, as to be strangers to all its inconveniences, wanting nothing which goes to the ease & happiness of life, embarrass'd by nothing which is cumbersome. I dare almostt venture to say, that you will like us better than the persons you live with, & that we shall be able to make you retrograde, that I may use a canonical simily, as the sun did on the dial of Hezekiah, & begin anew the twelve years which you complain are gone. we will restore to you the nigros angusta fronte capillos; and with them, the dulce loqui, the ridere decorum, et inter vina fugam Cinarae moerere protervae.[2] Haec est vita solutorum miserâ ambitione gravique,[3] and not yours.

I was going to finish with my sheet of paper, but having bethought myself that you deserve some more punishment, & calling all my anger against you to my aid, I resolve, since I am this morning in the humour of scribbling, to make my letter at least as long as one of your sermons, and if you do not mend my next shall be as long as one of Dr Mantons,[4] who taught my youth to yawn, and prepar'd me to be an High church man, that I might never hear him read, nor read him more. You must know that I am as busy about my hermitage, which is between the château & the maison bourgeoise, as if I was to pass my life in it; and if I could see you now & then, I should be willing enough to do so. I have in my wood the biggest & clearest spring perhaps in Europe, which forms before it leaves the park a more beautiful River than any which flows in greek or latin verse. I have a thousand projects about this spring, and, among others one wch will employ some marble. now marble you know makes one

[1] Juv. xv. 112.   [2] Hor. *Ep.* i. 7, 26.
[3] Hor. *Sat.* i. 6, 129.
[4] Thomas Manton, a popular Presbyterian minister, born in 1620, died in 1677 the year before Bolingbroke was born. After his death six folio volumes were published containing 589 of his sermons. The recollection of these, which as a boy Bolingbroke may have been set to read, evidently remained an ineradicable memory.

think of inscriptions, and if you will correct this, which I have not yet committed to paper, it shall be grav'd, & help to fill the table books of Spons[1] and Missons[2] yet to come.

> Propter fidem adversus Reginam, et Partes,
> Intemeratè servatam,
> Propter operam, in pace generali conciliandâ
> Strenuè saltem navatam,
> Impotentiâ vesanae Factionis
> Solum vertere coactus,
> Hîc ad aquae lene caput sacrae,
> Injustè exulat,
> Dulcè vivit,
> H. De B. An. &c.[3]

Ob were better than propter, but ob operam would never please the ear. In a proper place, before the front of the house, which I have new built, I have a mind to inscribe this piece of patchwork.

> Si resipiscat Patria, in patriam rediturus,
> Si non resipiscat, ubivis melius quam inter tales Cives
> futurus,
> Hanc villam instauro, et exorno.
> Hinc, velut ex portu, alienos casus,
> Et fortunae ludum insolentem,
> Cernere suave est.
> Hic, mortem nec appetens nec timens,
> Innocuis deliciis,
> Doctâ quiete,
> et
> Felicis animi immotâ tranquillitate
> Fruniscor.
> Hic mihi vivam quod superest aut exilii, aut aevi!

---

[1] Jacques Spon, 1647–85, French antiquary and traveller. The author of important works on Greek monuments.

[2] Francis Maximilian Misson, ?1650–1722, French refugee and miscellaneous writer. His works received commendation from Addison, whose *Travels in Italy*, when translated into French, was published as a fourth volume to Misson's *Voyages*.

[3] As Ball remarks although Swift was widely read in the classics his powers of composition were not outstanding. In this respect Bolingbroke was appealing to a scholar less accomplished than himself.

if in a year's time you should find leisure to write to me, send me some mottos for groves, & streams, & fine prospects, & retreat, & contempt of grandeur &c. I have one for my green house, & one for an ally which leads to my apartment, which are happy enough. the first is hic ver assiduum, atque alienis mensibus aestas. The other is—fallentis semita vitae.[1]

you see I amuse myself *de la bagatelle* as much as you, but here lyes the difference, yr *bagatelle* leads to some thing better, as fiddlers flourish carelessly before they play a fine air, but mine begins, proceeds, and ends in *bagatelle*. Adieu: it is happy for you that my hand is tir'd.

Ile take care that you shall have my picture, & I am simple enough to be oblig'd to you for asking for it. if you do not write to me soon, I hope it will fall down as soon as you have it, & break your head.

July the 28th 1721.

4805

The Duchess of Ormonde to Swift

Sept: the 1st 1721

Sir

I don't know how to account for yr long silence,[2] unless yr time has bin taken up on making an interest wth those in power here, for one of the two Arch-Bishopricks, that we heard were void[3] (but I am very glad are not so) set yr heart at rest, for they are promis't, & therefore you may as well write to a sister, w[n] next you honour this kingdom wth any dispatches as to any greater people, tis a shame to think how you have neglected those of y[r] own house, I had once determined to write to you no more, since no answer was to be

---

[1] For these mottoes Bolingbroke was indebted to Virgil, *Georg.* ii. 149, and Horace, *Ep.* i. 18, 103.

[2] From a letter of two years later, 9 Dec. 1723, it seems probable that Swift's reply to the Duchess's last letter to him, 18 Apr. 1720, had miscarried.

[3] With the exception of Tuam (Synge) the Irish Archbishoprics were held by prelates who by infirmity or advanced age might naturally give rise to rumours of impending vacancies. Primate Lindsay was in dangerous ill health; Archbishop King was frequently incapacitated by severe attacks of gout; and Palliser, Archbishop of Cashel, was verging on eighty.

expected, but then revenge came in to my head, & I was resolved to tease you, till at last to be quiet, you'd send me some plausible excuse at least, for never inquiring after Brother or Sister, I wonder when you'l be good natured enough to come & see how we do, but Ireland has such powerfull charms, that I question whether you'd leave it, to be one of our Archbishops, I was at your Bro: Arrans[1] a good while this summer, & bin much upon the ramble, or else you had sooner had these just reproaches, from me, whom you have no way of appeazing, but by a Letter of at least four sides of paper, tho I am so good a Christian upon this occasion as to be notwithstanding all this ill treatment | Sir | y^r most sincere | freind & humble | servant | M Ormonde

Endorsed by Swift: Sep: 1. 1721

Forster copy

Swift to Knightley Chetwode

Gaulstown, 14 September, 1721.

Sir,

I have been here these three months, and I either answered your former letter,[2] or else it required no answer. I left the town on a sudden, and came here in a stage coach[3] merely for want of horses. I intend a short journey to Athlone,[4] and some parts about it, and then to return to Dublin by the end of this month, when the weather will please to grow tolerable; but it hath been so bad for these ten weeks past that I have been hindered from several rambles I intended. Yours of the 5th instant was sent here last post.[5] It was easy for you to conceive I was gone out of town considering my state of health, and it is not my talent to be unkind or forgetful, although it be my misfortune as the world runs, to be very little serviceable. I was in

---

[1] The Earl of Arran resided at Bagshot Park.

[2] Probably a reply to Swift's letter of 10 June.

[3] See p. 393.

[4] Athlone stands on both sides of the Shannon about eighty miles west of Dublin. It was unsuccessfully besieged by William III in person; but was afterwards taken by General Ginkel.

[5] Evidently Chetwode had written to Swift again nine days before the date of the present letter.

hopes that your affair[1] by this time had come to some issue, or at least, that you who are a warm gentleman, like others of your temper, might have cooled by degrees. For my own part, I have learned to bear everything, and not to sail with the wind in my teeth. I think the folk in power,[2] if they had any justice, might at least give you some honorary satisfaction, but I am a stranger to their justice and all their good qualities, having only received marks of their ill ones.

I had promised and intended a visit to Will Pole,[3] and from thence would have called at Woodbrooke, but there was not a single interval of weather for such an expedition. I hope you have good success with your drains and other improvements, and I think you will do well to imitate our landlord here, who talks much of building, but is as slow as possible in the execution. Mr. Jervas is gone to England, but when I go to town I shall enquire how to write to him, and do what you desire.[4] I know not a more vexatious dispute than that about meres and bounds, nor more vexatious disputants than those righteous. I suppose upon the strength of the text, that the righteous shall inherit the land. My humble service to your lady. I am, | Your most humble, &c. | J.S.

Address: To Knightley Chetwode, Esq., at his house at | Woodbrooke, near Portarlington.
Endorsed: a humorous pleasing Letter.

Hawkesworth 1766
Swift to the Rev. John Worrall

Gallstown, Sept. 14, 1721.

Dear Jack,[5]

I answered your letter long ago, and have little to say at present. I shall be in town by the beginning of next month, altho' a fit of good weather would tempt me a week longer; for I never saw or heard of

---

[1] His complaint against Col. Pigott.

[2] The Irish government.

[3] William Pole, related to the Devonshire baronets of that name, lived at Ballyfin about six Irish miles to the south of Woodbrooke. He enlarged his seat in an expensive style.

[4] Jervas, who had married a widow with a large fortune, was possessed of considerable property in Ireland, and stocked the lands himself. Swift appears to refer to his country interests.

[For note 5 see opposite.

so long a continuance of bad, which has hindered me from several
little rambles I intended; but I row or ride every day, in spite of the
rain, in spite of a broken shin, or falling into the lakes,[1] and several
other trifling accidents. Pray what have you done with the *Lichfield*
man? Hath he mended his voice, or is he content to sit down with
his *Christ Church* preferment?[2] I doubt Mrs. *Brent* will be at a loss
about her industry-books,[3] for want of a new leaf, with a list drawn
of the debtors. I know you are such a bungler you cannot do it, and
therefore I desire that you would, in a loose sheet of paper, make a
survey list in your bungling manner, as soon as she wants it, and let
that serve till I come. Present my service to Mrs. *Worrall.* I wonder
how you and she and your heir[4] have spent the summer, and how
often you have been at *Dunleary,*[5] and whether you have got her
another horse, and whether she hates dying and the country as much
as ever.—Desire Mrs. *Brent*, if a messenger goes from hence, to give
him my fustian waistcoat, because the mornings grow cold. I have
now and then some threatenings with my head; but have never been
absolutely giddy above a minute, and cannot complain of my health,
I thank God. Pray send them enclosed to the post-office. I hear you

---

[1] The 'lakes' at Gaulstown were artificial.

[2] The one choir served both St. Patrick's and Christ Church Cathedrals.
Presumably a singing-man from Lichfield was prepared to accept preferment to
one choir.

[3] Swift's custom of lending money to necessitous tradespeople began in the
early part of this year with the outbreak of distress among the weavers. The
accountant was Mrs. Brent, and the interest charged merely served to provide
her with a small gratuity.

[4] A young man called Fairbrother to whom Worrall did *not* leave his money.
Deane Swift claimed to be acquainted with Fairbrother (*Essay*, pp. 297–8).

[5] Seven miles to the south of Dublin. Renamed Kingstown on the visit of
George IV in 1821. The old name, Dunlaoghaire, has been restored.

---

[5] Stearne, on leaving St. Patrick's, recommended Swift to appoint John
Worrall to some office in the Cathedral. Swift gave him the post of Dean's Vicar.
This was the beginning of a long friendship, Swift constantly dining with Worrall
and his wife, using their home in Deane Swift's words 'as a tavern' until after
Mrs. Worrall's death, when the Dean shook him off 'as a man of little or no
consequence'. According to Delany (*Observations*, pp. 91–92), Worrall was the
'meanest man' socially with whom Swift had constant converse. Deane Swift
(*Essay*, pp. 293–300) spends pages in pouring obloquy on Worrall, confessing
this to be 'one of the most disagreeable parts in the whole subject I have undertaken to manage'. The chief recommendation of Worrall to Swift seems to have
been that he found him a good walking companion and his wife a good cook.

have let your house to Mrs. *Dopping*,[1] who will be a good tenant if she lives. I suppose your new house is finished, and if Mrs. *Worrall* does not air it well, it may get you a new wife, which I would not have you tell her, because it will do the business better then a boat at *Dalkey*.[2] I hope you have ordered an account of absent vicars, and that their behaviour has not been so bad as usual during my sickness in town; if so, I have but an ill sub-dean. | I am, Sir, Yours &c.

P.S. Tell Mrs *Brent*, that, if *Lloyd* agrees, I will but[3] be glad one of his hogsheads was left unrack'd.

Faulkner 1762

Swift to Archbishop King

Gallstown near Kinnegad, Sept. 28, 1721.

My Lord,

I had the Honour of your Grace's Letter the first instant;[4] and although, I thought it my Duty to be the last Writer, in corresponding with your Grace, yet I know you are so punctual, that if I should write sooner, it would only be the Occasion of giving you a new Trouble, before it ought, in Conscience to be put upon you. Besides, I was in some Pain that your Letter of *Sept.* 1, was not the first you had writ, because, about ten Days after, a Friend sent me Word, that your Grace said you had writ to me six Weeks before, and had no Answer; whereas, I can assure your Grace that I received but one from you, nor had I Reason to expect it, having not done myself the Honour to write to you before. I will tell you the Secret of dating my Letter, I was in Fear lest the Post should be gone, and so left a Blank, and wisely huddled it up, without thinking of the Date; but,

---

[1] The mother of Samuel Dopping. He died in 1720.

[2] Three miles south of Dunlaoghaire. The port of Dublin in medieval times.

[3] 'will but'. Subsequent editors substitute 'shall'.

[4] Evidently Swift had written to the Archbishop a letter not fully dated, and on 1 Sept. King had sent a reply. That reply, which Swift here acknowledges, is not forthcoming, for there is a gap in the Archbishop's letter-book. As Ball observes, the present letter exhibits a renewal of friendliness between the two correspondents which had not been in evidence since Swift joined the Tory party. The reason for this better feeling was their agreement on questions concerning Ireland, and Swift's activity in connexion with the distress among the weavers. Only three further letters from Swift to King have come down to us, and those in printed form, and none written from King to Swift.

we Country Gentlemen are frequently guilty of greater Blunders; and, in that Article, I grow more perfect every Day.

I believe you seriously that you will take Care of your Health, to prevent a Successor; that is to say, I believe you tell Truth in Jest; for, I know it is not the Value of Life, that makes you desire to live, and am afraid the World is much of your Mind; for it is out of Regard to the publick, or some of themselves, more than upon your own Account, that they wish your Continuance amongst us.

It seems you are a greater Favourite of the Lieutenant's than you care to own,[1] for we hear, that he killed but two bucks, and sent you a present of one.[2]

I hear you are likely to be the sole Opposer of the Bank, and you will certainly miscarry, because it would prove a most perfidious Thing.[3] Bankrupts are always for setting up Banks: How then can you think a Bank will fail of a Majority in both Houses?

You are very perverse, my Lord, in misinterpreting the Ladies Favour, as if you must die to obtain it; I assure you it is directly contrary, and if you die, you will lose their Favour for ever; I am commanded to tell you so; and therefore at the Peril of your Life, and of their good Graces, look to your Health.

I hear the Bishop of *Bangor*, despairing of doing any Good with you,[4] hath taken up with *Hereford*. I am a plain Man, and would be glad at any Time to see Fifty such Bishops hanged, if I could thereby have saved the Life of his Predecessor,[5] for whom I had a great

[1] The Duke of Grafton who had landed in Ireland on 28 Aug. opened the Irish Parliament on 12 Sept.

[2] It was the custom to send venison from the herd of deer in Phoenix Park to principal functionaries in Ireland.—Ball.

[3] A project for establishing a National Bank in Ireland was put forward in 1720. Swift associated the scheme with Whig interests and stock-jobbers, and there was general opposition to the plan. The scheme was approved by the King in July 1721, but rejected by both Houses of the Irish Parliament in December of the same year. See *Journals of the House of Commons of Ireland*, iii, pt. i, pp. 253, 256–7, 283, 289; *Journals of the House of Lords of Ireland*, ii. 711–13, 716, 720. Cf. also *Poems*, pp. 241–3, 286–8; *Prose Works*, ed. Davis, vol. ix.

[4] i.e. of succeeding to his see. Bishop Evans, writing to Archbishop Wake, 31 Jan. 1717–18, about the illness of Ashe, Bishop of Derry, says: 'I hear Jon. Swift &c. have given out that my successor [Hoadly, at Bangor] is to be there.' Hoadly, however, was successively translated from Bangor to Hereford, Salisbury, and Winchester.

[5] Philip Bisse, consecrated Bishop of St. David's 19 Nov. 1710, and translated to Hereford 16 Feb. 1712–13. He died 6 Sept. 1721. Boyer, *Political State*, xxii. 329, paid a generous tribute to his sanctity, integrity, and learning.

Esteem and Friendship. I do not much approve the Compliments made you by Comparisons drawn from good and bad Emperors, because the Interist falls short on both Sides. If *Julian* had immediately succeeded *Constantine*, it would have been more to the Purpose. Sir *James* of the *Peak* said to *Bouchier* the Gamester, 'Sirrah, I shall look better than you, when I have been a Month in my Grave.'[1] A great Man in *England* was blaming me for despising somebody or other; I assured him I did not at all despise the Man he mentioned, that I was not so liberal of my Contempt, nor would bestow it where there was not some Degree of Merit. Upon this Principle, I can see no proper Ground of Opposition between your Grace, and that Wretch of *Bangor*. I have read indeed, that a Dog was once made King of *Norway*, but I forget who was his Predecessor; and, therefore am at a Loss for the other Part of the Comparison.

I am afraid the Clatter of Ladies Tongues is no very good Cure for a Giddiness in the Head. When your Grace (as you say) was young, as I am not, the Ladies were better Company, or you more easily pleased. I am perpetually reproaching them for their Ignorance, Affectation, Impertinence (but my Paper will not hold all) except Lady *Betty Rochfort*, your old Acquaintance.

I own my Head and your Grace's Feet would be ill joined; but, give me your Head, and take my Feet, and match us in the Kingdom if you can.

My Lord, I row after Health like a Waterman, and ride after it like a Post boy, and find some little Success; but *subeunt morbi tristisque senectus*. I have a Receipt to which you are a Stranger; my Lord *Oxford* and Mr. *Prior* used to join with me in taking it, to whom I often said, when we were two Hours diverting ourselves with Trifles, *vive la bagatelle*. I am so deep among the Workmen at Mr. *Rochfort*'s Canals and Lakes, so dextrous at the Oar, such an Alderman after the Hare ——

I am just now told from some News Papers, that one of the King's Enemy's, and my excellent Friend, Mr. *Prior*, is dead,[2] I pray God deliver me from any such Trials. I am neither old nor Philosopher

---

[1] Sir James of the Peak is stated to have been sometimes called Sir James Baker. Swift's poem, 'The Journal', when printed in Smedley's *Gulliveriana*, 1728, p. 13, was introduced by a letter from 'Philoxenus' to 'Sir James Baker, Knight, Chief Journalist of Great Britain'. Bouchier was a notorious gambler.

[2] Prior died at Wimpole, Lord Harley's seat, on 18 Sept. in his fifty-eighth year.

enough to be indifferent at so great a Loss, and, therefore, I abruptly conclude, but with the greatest respect, | My Lord, | Your Grace's, Most dutiful, and | obedient Servant, | J. Swift.

Rothschild

Swift to Charles Ford

Sep^{br}. 30. 1721

I am forced to put you to double Charges by sending the inclosed to Monsr Charlotte:[1] this you might avoyd if you would let me know whom I could direct to that it might be francked, for I never pay for any of yours. I have been in the Country at Mr Rochforts above 3 Months, and from your Letter I conceived you would have been long before this in Dublin, and you left me so loose that I did not know how to send sooner to Mr Charlotte, though I resolved to answer him soon; I send this to Mrs Ford[2] in Dublin, who knows best what measures to take with you. I shall be in Dublin in a short time.[3] A Friend is just going to Dublin, who will take this with him, and the inclosed must make up for the shortness of this. | I am &c.

Address: To Charles Ford Esqr, at his | Lodgings at the blue Perewig in | Pell-mell | London

Nichols 1801

Swift to the Rev. Daniel Jackson

Dublin, Oct. 6, 1721

I had no mind to load you with the secret of my going, because you should bear none of the blame.[4] I talk upon a supposition, that

---

[1] Again, as in the case of the letter of 28 July 1721, only Bolingbroke's reply is known, 1 Jan. 1721–2 O.S. 21 Dec. 1721.

[2] Mother of Charles. The widow of Phineas Preston of Ardsallagh she married Edward Ford in 1676. See *Letters of Swift to Ford,* ed. D. Nichol Smith, pp. x–xi.

[3] Swift's long summer stay at Gaulstown was celebrated in 'The Journal', which in the Pope and Swift *Miscellanies* volume of 1732 appears under the title of 'The Country Life' (*Poems,* pp. 276–83). In the following letter addressed to Daniel Jackson the return journey from Gaulstown to Dublin is described.

[For note 4 see overleaf.

Mr. Rochfort had a mind to keep me longer, which I will allow in him and you, but not one of the family besides, who I confess had reason enough to be weary of a man, who entered into none of their tastes, nor pleasures, nor fancies, nor opinions, nor talk.[1] I baited at Cloncurry,[2] and got to Leixlip[3] between three and four, saw the curiosities there, and the next morning came to Dublin by eight o'clock, and was at prayers in my cathedral.[4] There's a traveller. I forgot a long treatise copied by my Irish secretary, which I lent Clem. Barry[5]—Pray get it from him, and seal it up, and keep it, till you get a convenience of sending it. Desire Lady Betty to give you the old silver box that I carried the comfits in; it belongs to poor Mrs. Brent, and she asked me for it with a sigh. You may trust it with Arthur, You are now happy, and have nobody to tease you to the oar or the saddle. You can sit in your nightgown till noon without any reproaches.

I left a note for you with James Doyl, with commissions which I hope you will fulfil, though you borow the money; I will certainly be out of your debt in all articles between us, when you come to town,

[1] Doubtless Swift became conscious, after a stay of three months at Gaulstown, that the family was beginning to weary of his visit. Over and above this awareness he may also, as Ball suggests, have become anxious 'to inspirit the opposition' directed against the establishment of a national bank. Archbishop King was a prominent adversary of the scheme, and for this reason and at this critical juncture Swift desired to lend him support. See his verses 'Part of the 9th Ode of the 4th Book of Horace, address'd to Doctor William King' (*Poems*, pp. 241–3). The close association between King and Swift is also evident from a letter written at this time by the Archbishop to Bishop Stearne: 'Dean Swift offered to lay me five guineas this morning the bill would pass, for a good natural reason to be sure, which was no other than that it was for private advantage and public mischief.'

[2] A village in co. Kildare about half-way between Gaulstown and Dublin.

[3] Leixlip is about twenty-six Irish miles from Gaulstown, and eight from Dublin. It is situated on the river Liffey, and 'the curiosities' to which Swift refers are a salmon leap and a castle said to date from the time of King John.

[4] A week-day service. Swift was writing on Friday.

[5] In 'The Journal' the arrival of Clem Barry and his wife is described as a 'Grand Event' which upset the measures of the household. Clement Barry, a distant cousin of Lord Sautry, lived near Dublin.

---

[4] Copied from the original in the possession of two Irish ladies of the name of Shenton (daughters of a late precentor of Christ Church, Dublin).—Nichols, xix. 236. According to Ball the two ladies were, more correctly, daughters of the Rev. Robert Staurton, a vicar-choral of the Dublin cathedrals in the latter part of the eighteenth century.

or before, if you draw a bill upon me, for now I have money, and value no man. I am told your tribe here is all well, though I have seen none but Jack Jackson.

Farewell, go to cards, and lose your money with great gravity.

My service to all your girls.

I gave James Doyl two crowns, and a strict order to take care of ^{my}/_{our} gray colt, which I desire you will second.

I had a perfect summer journey, and if I had stayed much longer, I should have certainly had a winter one, which, with weak horses and bad roads, would have been a very unpleasant thing.

Address: To the Rev. Mr. Jackson at Gallstown.

Duncombe

Swift to the Rev. Thomas Wallis

Dublin, Nov. 3, 1721.[1]

Sir,

You stole in and out of town without seeing either the ladies or[2] me, which was very ungratefully done, considering the obligations you have to us, for lodging and dieting with you so long.[3] Why did you not call in the morning at the deanry? Besides, we reckoned for certain that you came to stay a month or two, as you told us you intended. I hear you were so kind as to be at Laracor, where I hope you planted something, and I intend to be down after Christmas, when[4] you must continue a week. As for your plan, it is very pretty, too pretty for the use I intend to make of Laracor. All I would desire is, what I mention in the paper I left you, except a walk down to the canal. I suppose your project would cost me ten pounds, and a constant gardener. Pray come to town and stay some time, and repay yourself some of your dinners. I wonder how a mischief you came to miss us. why did you not set out a Monday,[5] like a true country parson? Besides, you lay a load on us, in saying one chief end of your journey was to see us; but I suppose there might be

---

[1] Duncombe dates this letter 1722, but this is evidently a mistake.

[2] Duncombe prints 'and', no doubt by mistake.

[3] The visit which Stella, Mrs. Dingley, and Swift paid to Wallis probably preceded the previous letter of 13 May 1721.

[4] Duncombe printed 'where', possibly a mistake by the transcriber, the printer, or by Swift himself.   [5] Swift was writing on Friday.

another motive, and you are like the man that died of love and the colic. Let us know whether you are more or less monkish, how long you found yourself better by our company, and how long before you recovered the charges we put you to. The ladies assure you of their hearty services, and I am with great truth and sincerity, | Your most faithful humble servant, | Jonath. Swift.

Forster copy

Swift to Knightley Chetwode

Dublin, November 11, 1721.

Sir,

I received yours yesterday. I writ to Mr. Jervas from the country,[1] but have yet received no answer, nor do find that any one of his friends hath yet heard from him, so that some of them are in a good deal of pain to know where he is, and whether he be alive. I intend, however, to write a second time, but I thought it needless to trouble you till I could say something to the purpose. But indeed I have had a much better or rather a much worse excuse, having been almost three weeks pursued with a noise in my ears and deafness that makes me an unsociable creature, hating to see others, or be seen by my best friends, and wholly confined to my chamber. I have been often troubled with it, but never so long as now, which wholly disconcerts and confounds me to a degree that I can neither think nor speak nor act as I used to do, nor mind the least business even of my own, which is an apology I should be glad to be without. I am ever, | Yours, &c. | J. S.

Address: To Knightley Chetwode Esq., at his house at Woodbroke, near Portarlington.

Forster copy

Swift to Knightley Chetwode

Dublin, 5 December, 1721.

Sir,

When I received your French letter[2] I was going to write you an English one. I forsook the world and French at the same time, and

[1] Gaulstown.   [2] Probably a reply to the preceding letter.

have nothing to do with the latter further than sometimes reading or gabbling with the French clergy who come to me about business of their church,[1] *car je parle à peindre, mais pour l'écrire je n'en songe guère depuis que j'ay quitté la politique.* I am but just recovered of my deafness, which put me out of all temper with myself and the rest of mankind. My health is not worth a rush, nor consequently the remaining part of my life.

I just now hear that Dr. Pratt, Dean of Down, my old acquaintance is dead,[2] and I must here break off to go to his relations.

[December] 9.

The poor Dean died on Tuesday, and was buried yesterday. He was one of the oldest acquaintance I had,[3] and the last that I expected to die. He has left a young widow,[4] in very good circumstances. He had schemes of long life, hiring a town-house, and building a country, preparing great equipages and furniture. What a ridiculous thing is man.[5] I am this moment inevitably stopped by company, and cannot send my letter till next post.

[*December*] 12.

I have writ twice to Mr. Jervas, and got no answer, nor do I hear that anyone has. I will write again when I can be informed where to reach him. You hear the bank was kicked out with ignomiy last Saturday.[6] This subject filled the town with pamphlets, and none writ so well as by Mr. Rowley[7] though he was not thought to have many talents for an author. As to my own part, I mind little what is

---

[1] From the Restoration to the beginning of the nineteenth century the French Protestant refugees in Dublin were allowed to use the Lady Chapel of St. Patrick's Cathedral as a place of worship.—Ball.

[2] Pratt died on the day on which Swift was writing—a Tuesday.

[3] Pratt and Swift were contemporaries at college. Pratt was a year or two Swift's junior.

[4] See *Poems*, pp. 289–95, 'The Progress of Marriage'. About a year before his death Pratt had married Philippa, daughter of the sixth Earl of Abercorn.

[5] In his will Pratt left £1,000 to Trinity College. He was succeeded as Provost by Dr. Richard Baldwin, who was to prove a generous benefactor of the University of Dublin.

[6] On 9 Dec. the House of Commons rejected the Bill for the establishment of a bank. See p. 408, n. 1.

[7] Hercules Rowley, M.P. for Londonderry.

doing out of my proper dominions, the Liberties of the Deanery;[1]
yet I thought a bank ought to be established and would be so
because it was the only ruinous thing wanting to the kingdom, and
therefore I had not the least doubt but that the Parliament would
pass it.

I hope you are grown regular in your plantations, and have got
some skill to know where and what trees to place, and how to make
them grow. For want of better I have been planting elms in the
Deanery garden, and what is worse, in the Cathedral churchyard
where I disturbed the dead, and angered the living, by removing
tombstones, that people will be at a loss how to rest with the bones
of their ancestors.

I envy all you that live retired out of a world where we expect
nothing but plague, poverty, and famine which are bad words to
end a letter with; therefore with wishing prosperity to you and your
family, I bid you adieu.

Address: To Knightley Chetwode, Esq., at his house at Woodbrooke, near
    Portarlington.

4805

Viscount Bolingbroke to Swift

1 January 1721-2 [O.S. 21 December 1721]

I receiv'd y^r letter of the 29th of Sep:[2] above a fortnight ago, and
should have set you an example by answering it imediately which I do
not remember that you ever set me, if I had not been oblig'd to
abandon the silence & quiet of this belov'd retreat,[3] & to thrust
myself into the hurry and babble of an impertinent town. In less
than ten days which I spent att Paris I was more than ten times on the
point of leaving my business there undone, and yet this business was

[1] This disclaimer must be accepted with some doubt. Swift probably did
play a part in the war of pamphlets against the bank; but the limits of that part
are questionable. *The Swearers Bank*, though generally accepted, was probably
not from his pen. *Subscribers to the Bank Plac'd according to Their Order and
Quality* and *A Letter to the King at Arms* may be his. See further, *Prose Works*,
ed. Davis, ix, pp. xviii–xxi, 288–321.

[2] Doubtless a reply to Bolingbroke's letter of 28 July.

[3] The family mansion of the Marquise de Villette at Marcilly, near Nogent-
sur-Seine. Her marriage to Bolingbroke had ultimately taken place in May 1720.
She joined the Church of England on that occasion.

to save four fifths of 400 M : livres, which I have on the town house,[1] restes miserables du naufrage de ma fortune. luckily I had the fear of you before my eyes, and tho' I cannot hope to deserve y^r esteem by growing rich, I have endeavour'd to avoid y^r contempt by growing poor. the expression is equivocal, a fault which our language often betrays those who scribble hastily into, but y^r own conscience will serve for a comment, & fix the Sence. Let me thank you for remembring me in y^r prayers, & for using y^r credit above so generously in my behalf. to despise riches with Seneca's purse,[2] is to have att once all the advantages of fortune & philosophy. Quid voveat dulci nutricula majus alumno ?[3] you are not like H: Guy,[4] who, among other peices of excellent advice, gave me this, when I first came to court; to be very moderate & modest in my applications for my friends, & very greedy & importunate when I ask'd for my self. you call Tully names to revenge Catos quarrel, and to revenge Tully's I am ready to fall foul on Seneca. you Church men have cry'd him up for a great Saint, and, as if you imagin'd that to have it beleiv'd that he had a months mind to be a christian would reflect some honour on christianity, you employ'd one of those pious frauds, so frequently practic'd in the days of primitive simplicity, to impose on the world a pretended correspondence between him & the great Apostle of the Gentiles.[5] yr partiallity in his favour, shall biass me no more, than the pique which Dion Cassius & others show against him. like an equitable judg I shall only tax him with avarice in his prosperity, adulation in his adversity, and affectation in every state of life. was I considerable enough to be banish'd from my country, methinks I would not purchase my restoration, att the expense of writing such a letter to the Prince himself, as y^r Christian Stoick wrote to the Emperors Slave, Polybius.[6] thus I think of the

---

[1] In the Rue St. Dominique, Faubourg St. Germain. This house was also the property of the Marquise.

[2] 'No Man shall ever be Poor, that goes to himself for what he wants: and that's the readiest way to Riches: Nature indeed will have her Due, but yet whatsoever is beyond Necessity is Precarious and not Necessary' (*Seneca's Morals*, L'Estrange's version, p. 337).

[3] Hor. *Ep.* i. 4, 8.

[4] Henry Guy, 1631–1710, an adept, from small beginnings, at making his way to fortune as a politician and courtier. *D.N.B.*

[5] Fourteen spurious epistles of St. Paul and Seneca were first cited by St. Jerome. They were a forgery of the fourth century.

[6] A freedman of Claudius, serving as his secretary. Seneca addressed to him a *Consolatio* for the death of one of his brothers.

man, and yet I read the author with pleasure, tho' I joyn in condemning those points which he introduc'd into the latin stile, those eternal witticisms strung like beads together,[1] & that impudent manner of talking to the passions, before he has gone about to convince the judgment, which Erasmus, if I remember right, objects to him. he is seldom instructive, but he is perpetually entertaining; & when he gives you no new idea, he reflects yr own back upon you with new luster. I have lately wrot an excellent treatise in praise of Exile.[2] many of the hints are taken from his Consol: ad Helviam & other parts of his works, the whole is turn'd in his stile & manner, & there is as much of the spirit of the portique as I could well infuse without running too far into the mirabilia, inopinata, & paradoxa, wch Tully,[3] & I think Seneca himself,[4] ridicules the School of Zeno for. that you may laugh at me in yr turn I own ingenuously, that I began in jest, grew serious att the third or fourth page, & convinc'd myself before I had done, of what perhaps I shall never convince any other; that a man of sense & virtue may be unfortunate but can never be unhappy. do not imagine however that I have a mind to quarrel with Aristippus. he is still my favourite among the philosophers; and if I find some faults in him, they are few and venial. You do me much honour in saying that I put you in mind of Ld Dig;[5] but say it to no one else, for fear of passing for partial in yr paralells, which has done Plutarch more hurt than it has done good to his grecian Heros. I had forgot, or I never knew, the very remarkable passage which you mention. great virtue unjustly persecuted may hold such language, & will be heard with applause, with general applause I mean, not universal. there was at Athens a wretch, who spit in the face of [Phocion][6] as he march'd firm, calm, and almost gay to execution. perhaps there was not another Man among the

---

[1] Cf. Caligula's criticism *arena sine calce* (Suet. *Caligula*, liii).

[2] Bolingbroke's 'Reflections upon Exile', dated 1716, was printed in Mallet's edition of the *Works*, 1754, i. 99–128. Passages in this treatise are borrowed from Seneca.   [3] Cicero, *Acad.* ii. 136.   [4] Cf. *Epist.* 81, 11.

[5] George Digby, 1612–77, second Earl of Bristol, a Royalist and for years an exile. Ball suggests that the passage to which Swift alluded may have been one which occurs in the concluding paragraphs of *The Lord George Digbies Apologie* of which there are two editions, 1642, Oxford and London: 'By the grace of God it shall never be said that either the Parliament hath brought me, or his Majesty exposed me to a trial, my own uprightness shall constantly solicit it, and without recourse in this to either of their favours, I will either stand a justified man to the world, or fall an innocent.'

[6] By a slip Bolingbroke wrote Aristides. See Plutarch's *Life of Phocion*, c. 36.

Athenians, capable of the same vile action; and for the honour of my country I will beleive that there are very few Men in England, besides Ld: Oxf:, capable of hearing that strain of Eloquence, without admiration. there is a sort of kindred in souls, and they are divided into more familys than we are apt to imagine. Digbys & Harl: are absolute strangers to one another. touch a unison, and all the unisons will give the same sound; but you may thrum a lute till y^r fingers are sore, and you will draw no sound out of a Jews Harp. I thank you for correcting my inscriptions,[1] & I thank you still more for promising to gather up mottos for me, & to write often to me. I am as little given to beg correspondents as you are to beg pictures, but since I cannot live with you, I would fain hear from you. to grow old with good sence, and a good friend, was the wish of Thales,[2] I add, with good health. to enjoy but one and an half of these three is hard. I have heard of Prior's death and of his Epitaph,[3] and have seen a strange book writ by a grave & Eloquent Doctor,[4] about the Duke of Buckinghamshire people, who talk much in that moment can have, as I beleive, but one of these two principles, fear, or vanity. it is therefore much better to hold one's tongue. I am sorry, that the first of these persons our old acquaintance Mat:, liv'd so poor as you represent him. I thought that a certain Lord[5] whose marriage with a certain Heiress was the ultimate end of a certain administration, had put him above want. Prior might justly enough have address'd himself to his young Patron, as our friend Aristippus did to Dionysius. you have money, which I want: I have wit and knowledg, which you want.[6] I long to see yr travels,[7] for take it as you will, I do not retract

---

[1] This terse acknowledgement suggests that Bolingbroke found little value in Swift's corrections.

[2] Bolingbroke appears to have had in mind a confused reading of the reply of Thales to the question τίς εὐδαίμων; and a sentence which follows: ὁ τὸ μὲν σῶμα ὑγιής, τὴν δὲ τύχην εὔπορος, τὴν δὲ ψυχὴν εὐπαίδευτος &c. Diogenes, op. cit., p. 22.

[3]   To Me 'twas giv'n to die: to Thee 'tis giv'n
       To live: Alas! one Moment sets us ev'n.
       Mark! how impartial is the Will of Heav'n?

[4] Richard Fiddes. His work to which Bolingbroke refers was *A Letter in Answer to a Freethinker, occasioned by the Late Duke of Buckingham's Epitaph*, published in 1721.

[5] The sarcastic allusion is to the marriage of Lord Harley to Lady Henrietta Cavendish Hollis, daughter of John, Duke of Newcastle, in 1713.

[6] Diogenes, op. cit., p. 125.

[7] This reference has been interpreted as evidence that *Gulliver's Travels* was

what I said, and will undertake to find, in two pages of yr Bagatelles, more good sence, useful knowledg, and true Religion, than you can shew me in the works of nineteen in twenty of the profound Divines & Philosophers of the age. I am oblig'd to return to Paris in a month or six week's time, and from thence will send you my picture. would to heaven I could send you as like a picture of my mind, you would find yr self, in that draught the object of the truest esteem, & the sincerest friendship.

Jan. ye 1st 1722.

Endorsed by Swift: Ld Bolingbrok | Jan. 1st 1722

Portland MSS.

Adrian Drift to Swift

Duke Street, Westminster, January 25, 1721–2

Sir,

    My Lord Harley who is principal executor to Mr. Prior,[1] my late dear master, deceased, being desirous to see a state of Mr. Hyde's account of the books which he has delivered out to the gentlemen in Ireland who were subscribers to Mr. Prior's Poems, occasions you this new trouble, Sir, on that head, and to pray that you will be pleased to direct Mr. Hyde to transmit to me to be laid before his Lordship such account, specifying what number of books he has delivered and to whom, including the eighty books already delivered by him, as mentioned in your letter of the 16th March last, and paid for by Mr. Daniel Hayes of London, merchant,[2] pursuant to your orders the 21st of April following; to which account Mr. Hyde will add his own charges on the delivery of the said books, which I

by this time completed. Whatever fragmentary passages of the work may have been written by 1720, the real composition began in 1721. In 1725 Swift spent the summer and autumn in transcribing his draft for the press; and about six months later he was in London carrying the manuscript with him. See *Gulliver's Travels*, ed. Harold Williams, pp. xvi–xxii.

  [1] This letter relates to the executorship of Matthew Prior who died in the previous September. Drift had acted as his secretary since Prior's first employment in the embassy to France at the close of the seventeenth century (*Bath MSS.* iii, *passim*).   [2] See p. 382.

humbly entreat you to desire him to do as soon as possible, to the end Mr. Hyde may be reimbursed his said charges, and the inventory of Mr. Prior's effects be perfected, and lodged, as usual, in Doctors' Commons. I shall, by the very first opportunity, in obedience to my Lord Harley's commands, convey to you under Mr. Hyde's cover a little box with three rings enclosed therein, one of which you will be pleased to accept and wear in memory of Mr. Prior, whom you so dearly loved, and present the other two to Colonel Pennefather and his lady, to whom I do not know how to address a letter, and pardon this trouble given you by him who has the honour to be, with great respect, Sir, |

Your most obedient and most humble servant, | Adrian Drift.

Forster copy

Swift to Knightley Chetwode

Dublin, January 30, 1721-22.

Sir,

I have been these five weeks, and still continue so disordered with a noise in my ears and deafness, that I am utterly unqualified for all conversation or thinking. I used to be free of these fits in a fortnight, but now the disease I fear is deeper rooted, and I never stir out, or suffer any to see me but trebles and counter-tenors, and those as seldom as possible.

I have often thought that a gentleman in the country is not a bit less happy for not having power in it,[1] and that an influence at Sizes and Sessions, and the like, is altogether below a wise man's regard, especially in such a dirty obscure nook of the world as this kingdom. If they break open your roads, they cannot hinder you from going through them. You are a King over your own district though the neighbouring Princes be your enemies; you can pound the cattle that trespass on your grounds, though the next justice replevins them. You are thought to be quarrelsome enough and therefore peaceful people will be less fond of provoking you. I do not value

[1] In a reply to Swift's letter of 5 Dec. Chetwode had evidently returned to the incident at the Assizes which led to the embroilment with Col. Pigott.

Bussy's maxim of life, without the circumstances of health and money.[1] Your horse is neither Whig nor Tory, but will carry you safe unless he stumbles or be foundered. By the way, I am as much at a loss for one as ever, and so I fear shall continue till my riding days are over. I should not much mislike a presentment against your going on with your house, because I am a mortal enemy to lime and stone, but I hope yours moves slowly upwards.

We are now preparing for the plague, which everybody expects before May;[2] I have bespoke two pairs of shoes extraordinary. Everybody else hoards up their money, and those who have none now, will have none. Our great tradesmen break, and go off by dozens, among the rest Archdeacon, Burgin's son.[3] Mr. Jervas writes me word, that Morris Dunn is a person he has turned off his lands, as one that has been his constant enemy, etc., and in short gives him such a character as none can be fond of, so that I believe you were not apprised on what foot that man stands with Mr. Jervas. I am quite weary of my own ears, so with prayers for you and your fire-side, I remain |

Yours &c.

Addressed: To Knightley Chetwode, Esq., at Woodbrooke, near Portarlington.
Endorsed: A very noble and pleasant letter.

---

[1] Birkbeck Hill (*Unpublished Letters*, p. 117) suggested that the maxim for which Roger de Rabutin, Comte de Bussy, was responsible was contained in his *Discours à ses enfants sur le bon usage des adversités et les divers événements de sa vie*, 1694.

[2] During the preceding autumn the presence of the plague in France had caused the greatest alarm in England. After consultation with the leading physicians, including Swift's friend Arbuthnot, the government, in order to prevent the introduction of the disease into England, had carried through the British Parliament measures of a most drastic kind, authorizing even the sinking of infected ships; and a general fast had been proclaimed.—Ball.

[3] Ball states that this need not indicate any Church dignitary or his connexion. There were none of the name in the Irish Church at the time. Members of the families of Archdeacon and Burgin were to be found among Dublin tradespeople.

Swift to Adrian Drift

Dublin, February 3, 1721-2.

Sir,

I had a letter from you this day, which I was very glad to receive, being altogether at a Loss with whom I should account for Mr. Prior's books sent into this kingdom, though I often writ to some friends in England to inform me. You will please to know that although I prevail to get more subscriptions than I could expect from this poor country, yet many gentlemen have been very backwards in taking out their books, and paying their second subscriptions. I have been for some weeks confined by a deafness and noise in my ears, which disorder my excellent friend was subject to. I sent this day to Mr. Hyde to come to me, but he is laid up with a rheumatism; however he hath sent an abstract of his account, of which I here send you a copy. We must pick the remaining money as we can. You have no such notion of beggary in England, but it cannot be helped. I am very much pleased that my Lord Harley has been pleased to act as one of Mr. Prior's executors. I beg you will present my most humble service to him.

I shall be sure to gather up the money as fast as I can, and have it sent in specie by some friend. I doubt you cannot very safely send so small a thing safely as the box you mention, but I shall consult Colonel Pennefather who belongs to the Custom House here, and then give you notice and be very thankful of a memorial of Mr. Prior, though I need nothing to make me remember him with all regard due to his merits, and whose friendship I so highly esteemed. I am with great truth, Sir,

Your most faithful humble servant,

Jonathan Swift.

You are to take notice that Mr. Hyde's account is Irish, where a guinea is one pound three shillings. If a good picture of Mr. Prior's could be sent to Mr. Jervas, I would write to Mr. Jervas to copy it for me. Mr. Hyde has not time or health at present to send me an account of what number of books he has remaining. I heard him once complain that one or two of them wanted odd sheets. I find by Mr. Prior's list returned, I believe in your hand, that the books sent over were a hundred and fifty-three. I cannot well understand his account, but I will place it fair to your view, he is a very honest man, and has not made any demand for his trouble, and when he does it shall be very reasonable. In the meantime the account stands thus; the account is all in Irish money:

A hundred and fifty-three guineas make of Irish money		£175 19 0
Returned to Mr. Prior eighty guineas, which with exchange makes of Irish money, exchange being then at thirteen per cent. £94 0 0		
For carriage to Chester, freight, and custom . . 8 2 10		
		102 2 10
So there remains due by Mr. Hyde to Mr. Prior, Irish money		73 16 2

Sixty-four guineas make Irish money £73 12*s*. 0*d*., so that Mr. Hyde hath sixty-four books to account for, and four shillings and two pence odd money.[1]

Portland MSS.

Adrian Drift to Swift

London, February 15, 1721–2.

Sir,

I have received the honour of your letter of the 3rd instant, for which I humbly thank you, as I do likewise for the stated account of the subscriptions therein contained, and hope that you will have the goodness to satisfy Mr. Hyde for his trouble and all other expenses out of the money which may arise on the disposition of the sixty-four books remaining, in the manner you judge best.

I am commanded by my Lord Harley, to whom I communicated your letter, to present his service to you, and to acquaint you that his Lordship is ready to send the picture of Mr. Prior painted by Monsieur Rigault[2] at Paris in 1699, to Mr. Jervas, to be by him copied for you, if you approve thereof, his Lordship taking it to be an admirable picture of Mr. Prior; and truly, Sir, if I may add my own sentiments,

[1] The following receipt is appended to this letter: 'April 28th 1726. Received of Dr. Swift by the hands of Erasmus Lewis Esq., two and twenty guineas remitted in specie from Ireland by the Doctor for twenty two books, subscription money to Mr. Prior's Works, second payment, £23. 2. 0.'

[2] Hyacinth Rigaud, 1659–1743. Engraved by J. Clark or Isaac Basire it serves as a frontispiece to several editions of Prior's poems.

I think the best. You will please to signify your pleasure on this head.

As to the little box, I hope it will come safe to you, the same having been sent the 5th instant, in a chest of books transmitted from hence by Mr. Taylor, bookseller, to Mr. Dobson, bookseller, at Dublin,[1] the said little box being directed to Mr. Hyde, to be by him forwarded to you, which may possibly reach your hand as soon as this letter, when you will be pleased with my great respects to present the two rings to Colonel Pennefather and his lady, and pardon all this trouble given you by him, who wishes you entirely freed from the indisposition you complain of, and that you may long enjoy a perfect state of health, as being, Sir, Your most obedient and most obliged humble servant, | Adrian Drift.

Forster copy

Swift to Knightley Chetwode

Dublin, March 13, 1721-22

Sir,

I had a letter from you some time ago,[2] when I was in no condition for any correspondence or conversation. But I thank God for some time past I am pretty well recovered, and am able to hear my friends without danger of putting them into consumptions. My remedy was given me by my tailor, who had been four years deaf, and cured himself as I have done, by a clove of garlic steeped in honey, and put into his ear, for which I gave him half a crown after it had cost me five or six pounds in drugs and doctors to no purpose.

Surely you in the country have got the London fancy, that I am author of all the scurvy things that come out here. The slovenly pages called the Benefit of ——— was writ by one Dobbs a surgeon. Mr. Sheridan's hand sometimes entertains the world,[3] and I pay for

---

[1] William Taylor, best known as the publisher of Defoe's *Robinson Crusoe*. E. Dobson worked in partnership with John Hyde in Dame Street, Dublin (*Dictionary of Booksellers and Printers 1726–1775*, p. 390).

[2] Presumably a reply to the letter of 30 Jan.

[3] About this time there appeared two pieces of a singularly unsavoury character, *The Wonderful Wonder of Wonders* and *The Wonder of all the Wonders*, which have been attributed to Swift. They were printed in the Pope and Swift *Miscellanies. The Third Volume*, 1732, and Professor Davis includes them in vol. ix of his edition of the *Prose Works* as 'probably' by the Dean. It may be,

all, so that they have a Miscellany of my works in England, whereof you and I are equally authors.[1] But I lay all those things at the back of my book, which swells so much, that I am hardly able to write anything on the forepart. I think we are got off the plague,[2] though I hear an Act of Parliament was read in churches, not in mine, concerning it and the wise say, we are in more danger than ever, because infected goods are more likely to be brought us. For my part, I have the courage of a coward, never to think of dangers till they arrive, and then I shall begin to squeak. The Whigs are grown such disaffected people that I dare not converse with them; and who your Brit[annus][3] Esq. is, I cannot tell. I hear there is an Irish paper called the Reformer. I saw part of one paper, but it did not encourage me to enquire after more. I keep the fewest company of any man in this town, and read nothing that hath been written on this side fifteen hundred years, so you may judge what an intelligencer I am like to be to a gentleman in the country, who wants to know how the world goes.

Thus much for your first letter, your last which came just now is a condolence on my deafness. Mr. Le Hunte[4] was right in my intentions, if it had continued, but the effect is removed with the cause. My friends shall see me while I am neither troublesome to them nor myself. I was less melancholy than I thought I should have been, and less curious to know what people said, when they talked before me: but I saw very few, and suffered hardly any to stay. People whisper here too, just as they have whispered these thirty years, and to as little purpose. I have the best servant in the world dying in the house, which quite disconcerts me.[5] He was the first good one I ever had, and I am sure will be the last. I know few greater losses in

however, that they should be assigned to 'Mr. Sheridan's hand'. About this time the latter wrote a prologue and Swift an epilogue for a play performed in Dublin on 1 April on behalf of the distressed weavers. They were almost immediately reprinted in several London newspapers. See *Poems*, pp. 273–6. The play realized £73.

[1] If Swift is referring to *Miscellaneous Works, Comical & Diverting . . . Printed by Order of the Society de propagando, &c.*, 1720 (Teerink 17), the volume contains much which came from his hand.   [2] See p. 418.

[3] One of the contributors to Mist's *Weekly Journal* wrote under that pseudonym.

[4] Possibly Richard Le Hunte, a member of a well-known Wexford family, who then represented Enniscorthy in the Irish Parliament.—Ball.

[5] A small tablet in the south transept of St. Patrick's Cathedral bears this inscription: 'Here lieth the Body of Alex^r McGee, servant to Dr. Swift, Dean

life. I know not how little you may make of stone walls; I am only going to dash one in the garden, and think I shall be undone. I hope your lady and fire-side are well. I am |

Ever &c.

Address: To Knightley Chetwode, Esq., at Woodbrooke, near Portarlington.
Endorsed: a very merry pleasant letter.

A. A. Houghton, Jr.
Swift to the Rev. Daniel Jackson

Dublin. Mar. 26th [28?] 1722[1]

Dear Dan

I spoke to George Rochforts Groom to bring up my Nag and I desire you will take Care to have him well shod some days before he begins his Journy, and that he may be led and not rode up for fear of spoiling him—pray undertake this matter, and do it as it ought to be done. Poor Saunders[2] dyed on Saturday last and was buryed on Easter Sunday, and in him I have lost one of my best Friends as well as the best Servant in the Kingdom. I suppose you are in a merry house, and as great Rakes as I can imagine you. I wish Nim[3] would appoint a Curate to bottle off my Hogshead of White wine this week, for it must be done, and I shall stop his wages

of St. Patrick's. His grateful Master caused this monument to be erected in Memory of his Discretion, Fidelity and Diligence in that humble Station. Ob. Mar. 24 1721/2. Aetat 29.' According to Delany (*Observations*, pp. 194–6) a gentleman more distinguished for vanity than wisdom induced Swift to substitute 'his grateful master' for 'his grateful friend and master', which were the words Swift originally designed.

   [1] The original of this letter is now in the possession of Mr. Arthur A. Houghton, Jr., of New York. There is a copy in the Forster Collection which was made when it was in the possession of Mr. Richard J. Greene. It had been given to him by his brother-in-law, Lord Rathmore, and had been in the possession of the first Lord Plunket's brother, an eminent Dublin physician. The contents of the letter show that it was written after the date heading the original, '26th', perhaps on the 28th. Easter Sunday fell on the 25th, and Jackson had evidently then gone down for a visit to Gaulstown.

   [2] The appellation used by Swift, and known to his friends, to denote his servant McGee.

   [3] Or 'Nimrod', a name given to Lord Chief Justice Rochfort's second son on account of his fondness for hunting. See 'The Journal' (*Poems*, pp. 278–83), ll. 73–74. He was M.P. for Ballyshannon.

for non attendance. . I called at Lady Betty's[1] twice last week but found she was abroad; I want you here for I lose all my Acquaintance by my quarrellsome Temper—In what Condition are your Gardens and Forest Trees?[2] have you beheaded any of the latter? is any new work to begin this Summer? My Service to your Company, who they are God knows I think John Walmsley[3] is one, Sheridan is daily Libelled in abominable Rimes but he is safe in the County of Cavan.[4] My Service to the Wests[5] but first to George and Nim. Pray desire George to bring or send my Livy;[6] for I want it much, and am going to re-read it on a particular Occasion. Parnell's Poems[7] are just published, but that inscribed to Ld Bolingbroke is omitted in this Irish Edition by the Zeal of his Booby Brother[8] who is endeavoring to be a Judge all your Friends are wickedly residing at this Season,[9] and I want you to preach for me on Sunday next.—

[1] George Rochfort's wife was evidently in Dublin.

[2] Jackson is commemorated in 'The Journal' as a horticulturist—l.32, 'Dan leaves the Earthly Spade and Rake'.

[3] John Walmsley became a fellow of T.C.D. in 1703, Senior Fellow in 1713. In 1723, on his marriage, he was presented to the living of Clonfeacle, co. Tyrone, where he often officiated though he did not reside. He died at Armagh, 12 Dec. 1737. Leslie, *Armagh Clergy*, p. 183.

[4] At Quilca where Swift visited him for the first time a few months later.

[5] The family of George West of Athlone, who had died some years before, and acknowledged in his will his indebtedness to chief Baron Rochfort.

[6] According to 'The Journal' Swift used to read the classics with the Rochforts. The edition of Livy which he had left at Gaulstown was probably the folio entered in the sale catalogue of his books as '384 Livii Hist. Romana. Paris. 1625', for this is marked with an asterisk as annotated by him. He also had an Elzevir edition of 1634, three volumes, small duodecimo, no. 157.

[7] In Dec. 1721 there appeared Pope's edition of *Poems on Several Occasions. Written by Dr. Thomas Parnell . . . Printed for B. Lintot, . . . 1722.* A Dublin edition was published about the same time. Swift was under a misapprehension in supposing that Parnell's *Essay on the Different Stiles of Poetry*, which contained elaborate compliments to Bolingbroke, appeared in the London volume and was deliberately omitted from the Dublin edition of *Poems on Several Occasions.* Pope did not print it. The *Essay* was printed as an octavo pamphlet on 23 or 24 Mar. 1712–13.

[8] John Parnell, the poet's brother, does not appear to have possessed remarkable gifts. He was entered at the Inner Temple in 1698, and called to the Irish bar in 1706. He was appointed a Justice of the King's Bench in 1722, and died in 1727. He had married Chief Justice Whitshed's sister which would not commend him to Swift. See, further, Ball, *Judges in Ireland*, ii. 196–7.

[9] Swift means that they were discharging their duties in their parishes and therefore unable to preach in his cathedral.

You have heard of the Rebellion in the Colledge, it hath encreased Delany's Spleen fifty per cent;[1] The Ladyes[2] are undone for want of you to keep up their practice of calling Names, and I believe you will be the onely plain Dan at the Japan board[3] when you return. Saunders's Successor is a Lad that understands Greek, but I wish he may understand English.—The black Wench rides the Slack[4] Rope better than the brown one, but it is thought does not dance so well.—Jo Beaumont is mad in London,[5] riding thro the Street on his Irish horse with all the Rabble after him and throwing his money among them; I have writ to the Secretary of the Governors of Bedlam to have him sent there, for you know I have the Honr to be a Governr there[6] | J. S.

Address: To the Reverend Mr Daniel | Jackson, at Gallstown | near Kinnigad
Endorsed: Doctor Swift

4805

The Rev. Andrew Snape to Swift

Windsor 23 Apr. 1722.

Revd Sr[7]

I take the Opportunity of two of our Choir going over to try their Fortune in your Country, at once to return my Thanks for a very obliging Letter you favour'd me with some years ago,[8] & your kind Interpretation of my Endeavours at that time to assert the Cause of our Establishmt against a Prelate who was undermining it, & also to recommend to your Favour the Bearer, Mr Elford, who, upon the

[1] Delany disapproved of the Whig Provost, Baldwin.
[2] i.e. Stella and Rebecca Dingley.
[3] The card table.
[4] Ball's footnote was written under the misapprehension that Swift had written 'stack'.
[5] The linendraper of Trim.
[6] On 26 Feb. 1714 Swift, together with Atterbury, was elected a governor of Bedlam. See *Journal*, p. 122, n. 27. Ball omits the final 'there'.
[7] Snape, who was one of Hoadly's chief antagonists, had been installed a Canon of Windsor in 1713, and was elected Provost of King's College, Cambridge, in 1722. Evidently he is writing as a Canon of Windsor. There is a good account of Snape in Clutterbuck's *Hist. of Hertfordshire*, ii. 380.
[8] Presumably Swift had written congratulating Snape in 1717 when he entered the field against the Bishop of Bangor.

encouraggem^t of your worthy Primate[1] is going to settle at Armagh. I cannot pretend to say he has the same Compass of Voice wich his late Brother, whom the good Queen so much admir'd, but I will venture to say he has a greater Compass of Understanding, & upon the whole that he is a good Choir-man. The other that bears him Company was a very usefull Chorister to us, his Voice since its breaking is somewhat harsh, but I believe will grow mellower. If you find either of them for your Purpose, especially the Bearer, when you have a Vacancy in your Church, I shall be much oblig'd to you for any Favour you are pleas'd to shew, & be ready to approve my self on any Occasion, | Rev^d S^r | Yo^r most oblig'd & affectionate | Servt | A: Snape

Endorsed by Swift: Dr Snape's | Apr. 23^d 1722

B.M. Add. MS. 39839

Swift to Miss Esther Vanhomrigh

Cloghr Jun. 1st 1722

This is the first time I have set pen to paper since I left Dublin; having not been in any settld place till ten days ago, and I missed one Post by Ignorance, and that has stopt me 5 days;[2] before that time I was much out of order by usuall Consequences of wet weathr and change of Drink, neither am I yet established, tho much bettr than I was, The weathr has been so constantly bad, that I have wanted all the healthy advantages of the Country, and seems likely to continue so; It would have been infinitly better once a week to have met Kendall,[3] and so forth, where one might pass 3 or 4 hours

[1] Primate Lindsay was a generous benefactor of the choral establishment of Armagh Cathedral.

[2] Vanessa's reply to this letter shows that Swift had left Dublin five weeks before; and as subsequently appears he did not return to Dublin till the beginning of October. He filled in his time by travelling in the north of Ireland. He visited Bishop Stearne at Clogher, Robert Cope at Loughgall, and Sheridan at Quilca. Otherwise we have no clue to the places he saw. He speaks of travelling 400 miles and sleeping in thirty different beds, which would have enabled him to cover a large part of the province of Ulster.

[3] In the earlier half of the eighteenth century a family of the name of Kendall carried on the trade of bookbinding in the parish in which Vanessa lived in Dublin. Ball conjectures that a member of the family may have afforded facilities for private meetings between her and Swift.

in drinking Coffee in the morning, or dining tête à tête, and drinking Coffee again till 7. I answer all the Questions you can answer[1] me in the affirmative; I remember your detesting and despising the Conversations of the World; I have been so mortifyed with a Man and his Lady here 2 days, that it has made me as peevish as (I want a Comparison.[2] I hope you are gone or going to your Country seat[3] though I think you have a Term[4] upon your Hands. I shall be here long enough to receive your answer, and perhaps to write to you again, but then I shall go further off (if my Health continues) and shall let you know my Stages. I have been for some days as Spleena-tick as ever you were in your Life; which is a bold Word. Remembr I still enjoyn you Reading and Exercise for the Improvement of your Mind and Health of your Body, and grow less Romantick, and talk and act like a Man of the World. It is the saying of the World, and I believe you often say I love my self; but I am so low I cannot say it, tho your new Acquaintance were with you, which I heartily wish for the sake of you and my self.—God send you through your Law and your Reference, and remembr, that Riches are nine parts in ten of all that is good in Life, and Health is the tenth, drinking Coffee comes long after, and yet it is the eleventh, but without the two former you cannot drink it right, and remembr the China in the old house, and Rider Street and the Collonells Journy to France and the London Wedding, and the Sick Lady at Kinsing-ton, and the Indisposition at Windsor, and the Strain by the Box of books at London.[5] last year I writ you Civilityes, and you were angry, this year I will write you none, and you will be angry; yet my thoughts were still the same, and I give you leave to be Carver,[6] and will be answerable for them: I hope you will let me have some of your money when I see you, which I will pay you honestly again; repondez moy si vous entendez bien tout cela, et croyez que je seray toujours tout ce que vous desirerez—adieu—

Address: To Mrs Vanhomrigh

---

[1] Swift wrote 'answer' but he obviously meant 'ask'.
[2] Swift did not close the parenthesis.   [3] To Celbridge.
[4] He alludes to her law business. Trinity term would then just have opened.
[5] Cf. the similar catalogue in the letter of 13 Aug. 1720.
[6] The word is uncertain. Hawkesworth omits the phrase, Scott and Ball leave a blank. Nevertheless, it looks like 'Carver'. For this word the *O.E.D.* gives a seventeenth-century quotation, 'We are ill carvers for ourselves', where the word, as here, has the meaning 'designers' or 'choosers'.

B.M. Add. MS. 39839

Miss Esther Vanhomrigh to Swift

[June 1722.][1]

—, —, —, Cad, I thought you had quite forgot both me, and your promise, of writing to me was it not very unkind to be five weeks absent[2] without sending me one line to let me know you were well and remembered me besides you have had such bad weather that you could have no divertion abroad what then could you do but write and read I know you do not love cards neither is this a time of yeare for that divertion[3] amusement since I saw you I have gone more into this world than I did for some time passed because you commanded me and I do here protest that I am more and more sick of it every day then other one day this week I was to visit a great lady that has been a travelling[4] for some time passed where I found a very great Assembly of Ladys and Beaus (dressed as I suppose to a nicety) I hope you'l pardon me now I tell you that I heartily wished you a Spectator for I very much question if in your life you ever saw the like scene or one more Extraordinary the Lady's behaviour was blended with so many different character's I can not possibly describe it without tireing your patience but the Audience seemed to me a creation of her owne they were so very Obsequious their form's and gestures were very like those of Babboons and monky's they all grin'd and chatter'd at the same time and that of things I did not understand the room being hung with arras in which were trees very well described just as I was considering their beauty and wishing my self in the countrey with — — — one of these animals snatched my fan and was so pleased with me[5] that it seased me with such a panick that I apprehended nothing less than being carried up to the top of the House and served as a friend of yours was[6] but in this one of their owne species came in upon which they all began to

[1] This undated letter is quite clearly a reply to the previous one.
[2] Following 'absent' the words 'which is 35 Days' are struck through.
[3] 'divertion' lightly struck through.
[4] 'a travelling' is written above 'absent' which is struck through.
[5] After 'me' the words 'as I supposed by it's' are struck through.
[6] Vanessa's description of the company she met at the house of the 'great lady' suggests, though not decisively, that some part of the voyage to the country of the Houyhnhnms had been seen by her. On the other hand, the allusion to Gulliver's misadventure with the monkey is evidence beyond question that in some form she had seen chapter five of the voyage to Brobdingnag.

make their grimace's which opportunity I took and made my escape
I have not made one single step in either law or the Reference since
I saw you I meet with nothing but disappointments yet I am obliged
to stay in Town attending on Mr P.¹ &c which is very hard I do
declair that I have so little Joy in life that I don't care how soon
mine endes for God sake write to me soon and kindley for in your
absence your letters are all the joy I have on Earth and sure you are
to good natured to grudge one hour in a week to make any humain
creature happy — — — — Cad think of me and pitty me

B.M. Add. MS. 39839

Swift to Miss Esther Vanhomrigh

Lough-gall. County of Armagh.²
Jul. 13th 1722

I received yrs,³ and have changed places so often since, that I
could not assign a place where I might expect an answer from—
and if you be now in the Country, and this Letter does not reach
you in the due time after the date I shall not expect to hear from
you, because I leave this Place the beginning of August. I am well
pleased with the Account of your Visit and the Behavior of the
Ladyes: I see every day as silly things among both Sexes, and yet
endure them, for the sake of Amusements. The worst thing in you
and me is that we are too hard to please, and whether we have not
made our selves so, is the Question; At least I believe we have the
same Reason. One thing I differ from you in; that I do not quarrell
with my best Friends; I believe you have ten angry passages in your
Letter, and every one of them enough to spoyl two days a piece of
riding and walking. We differ prodigiously in one Point, I fly from
the Spleen to the worlds end, You run out of your way to meet it . .
I doubt the bad weathr has hinderd you much from the Diversions
of your Country house; and put you upon thinking in your Chamber.

¹ Partinton, executor to her father and her brother, against whom the suit
was pending.
² See Swift to Cope, 2 May 1720. There is no evidence that since 1720, if then,
Swift had visited Loughall. See *Poems*, p. 320. The parish, which derives its
name from the white lake, lies about four miles to the north-east of the city of
Armagh.
³ The preceding letter.

The use I have made of it was to read I know not how many diverting Books of History and Travells. I wish you would get yr self a
Horse, and have always 2 Servants to attend you, and visit your
Neighbors, the worse the bettr. There is a pleasure in being rever-
enced, and that is always in your Powers by your Superiority of
Sense, and an easy Fortune. The best Maxim I know in this life is,
to drink your Coffee when you can, and when you cannot, to be easy
without it. While you continue to be spleenatick, count upon it I
will always preach, Thus much I sympathise with you that I am
not chearfull enough to write, for I believe Coffee once a week is
necessary to that. I can sincerely answer all your Questions, as I
used to do, but then I give all possible way to Amusements, because
they preserve my Temper as Exercise does my Health, and without
Health and good humor I had rather be a dog. . I have shifted Scenes
oftener than ever I did in my Life, and I believe, have layn in thirty
Beds since I left the Toun and always drew up the Cloaths with my
left hand, which is a Superstition I have learnt these ten years.[1]—
These Country Post[s] are always so capricious, that we are forced
to send our Letters at a Call, on a sudden, and mine is now demanded, though it goes not out till to morrow, be chearfull and read
and ride and laugh as Cad— used to advise you long ago. I hope
your Affairs are on some better Settlement, I long to see you in
figure and Equipage, pray do not lose that Tast. — farewell

Address: To Mrs Vanhomrigh

Rothschild

Swift to Charles Ford

Lough-Gall. July. 22ᵈ. 1722

I have been here three Weeks with your Old Friend Mʳ Cope,[2]
who is the most domestick man you ever saw, with a Wife whom he
is so silly as to love, and who deserves it as well as a Wife can; and
with nine Children, with whom he troubles himself as much and
his Friends as little as possible I have had little Benefit of Summer
since I left Dublin, the continuall Rains have deprived me of riding
and walking, and I believe the Clymate has not got much Credit

---

[1] Ten years would have carried the practice back to Vanessa's visit to Windsor.
[2] Swift's visit to Loughgall extended from about 1 July to 7 Aug.

with you. My Comfort is, that the People, the Churches and the Plantations make me think I am in England. I mean onely the Scene of a few miles about me, for I have passed through miserable Regions to get to it. I would be glad to know how you have passed your Time, and whether you have cottoned with the Grattans, Jacksons, and College Fellows. Whether you wear out the Walks of Stephens Green, or play at Chess for threepence in the Coffee-house. How the Margoose[1] holds out, and whether you are got into the Train of Rack punch. Whether you sometimes see Sheridan, and grow reconciled to a dull Quibble. Whether the Ladyes at the Japan board[2] continue to be good Company, but I hear that they have taken a Lodging at the Deanry. I writ to Mrs Dingley last Post, and hope my Letter came to her as hers did to me. I presume you and Jervas meet there sometimes, and do you bridle his Eloquence and vanity? As little as you think of us, one of your Acquaintance was here t'other day; it was Archdeacon Morrice,[3] who is a great Builder and Planter, a very honest Gentleman, poor and generous, keeps excellent Wine, has buried his wife, has 2 Children and the Sciatica. What is more, Tisdal[4] lives but 7 miles off, we meet him once a week at a Club. He is fifty times less agreeable than ever, but a great Poet, Writer and Divine, and we fall out every time we meet. The bad Weather has made me read through abundance of Trash,[5] and this hath made me almost forget how to hold a Pen, which I must therefore keep for Dublin, Winter and Sickness. I have been thro the longest Lake in[6] Ireland, and the first fair Weather am to go through the broadest, that turns wood into Stone, and fools into Lyars.

Mr Cope is dispatching his Letters, and desires to present his

[1] Margaux. See Swift's letter to Stella 30 Apr. 1721.
[2] Stella and Rebecca Dingley at the card-table.
[3] Theodore Morris, Archdeacon of Tuam. See Swift to Cope, 9 July 1717.
[4] Stella's old admirer.
[5] The diverting books of history and travels mentioned in his letter to Vanessa of 13 July.
[6] The manuscript has 'and' for 'in'. The 'longest Lake' is Lough Erne, to the west of Clogher, where Swift had been Bishop Stearne's guest before his visit to Loughgall. The broadest is Lough Neagh: 'In some places the waters possess medicinal properties. . . . They have also petrifying powers; but these are supposed to exist in the soil, as petrifications are only found in the lake near the shore of *this* county'—S. Lewis, *Topographical Dictionary of Ireland*, 1846, i, s.v. 'Antrim'. See also Richard Barton, *Lectures in Natural Philosophy*, lecture iii, and John Rutty, *A Methodical Synopsis of Mineral Waters*, 1757, p. 18.—Nichol Smith.

Service to you. You will believe I am not in a Place that breeds much Materials for Letters. Here are neither extraordinary Scenes of Art or of Nature. Our Hay and Barley are quite spoiled, and betwixt you and me, Turf will be very scarce. Oatmeal was never known so dear, Half the poor have already lost half[1] their Itch for want of it.

My most humble Service to Mrs Ford, and Mrs Pen.[2]—and my humble Service to the Ladys: I cannot buy any Linnen for Mrs Dingley it [is] so horrible dear—I wish she would send a Venture of Brimstone, for a dozen of Smocks. I wish you would desire the Ladyes to let Mr Worrall enquire for Saunders[3] Brother and pay him 20^11 taking up my Bond, and a generall Receit.

Address: To Charles Ford Esqr, at | Mrs Ford's House in Dawson | Street, near St Stephen's Green | Dublin
Postmarks: Armagh *and* 27 IY

B.M. Add. MS. 39839

Swift to Miss Esther Vanhomrigh

Aug. 7th. 1722

I am this hour leaving my present Residence,[4] and if I fix any where, shall let you know it, for I would fain wait till I get a little good weather for riding and walking, there never having been such a Season as this rememberd, though I doubt you know nothing of it, but what you learn by sometimes looking out at your back Windows to call yr People, I had yr last with a spleenatick account of yr Law Affairs,[5] you were once a bettr Sollicitor, when you could contrive to make others desire your[6] consent to an Act of Parlmt[7] against their own Interest to advance yours. Yet at present you want neithr Power nor Skill, but disdain to exercise either. When you are melancholy, read diverting or amusing books; it is my Receit, and seldom fails. Health, good humor and Fortune are all that is valuable in this life;

[1] Manuscript 'have'.   [2] Penelope, Ford's sister.
[3] Alexander McGee, Swift's servant. See p. 422, n. 5.
[4] Cope's house at Loughgall.
[5] Vanessa's letter of June *ad fin.*
[6] 'desire your' is written above the line.
[7] A special Act of Parliament in the English legislature had been necessary to enable the sale of the Vanhomrigh estates.

and the last contributes to the 2 former.—I have not rode in all above poor 400 Miles since I saw you, nor do I believe I shall ride above 200 more till I see you again, but I desire you will not venture to shake me by the Hand, for I am in mortal fear of the Itch and have no hope left, but that some ugly vermin called Ticks have got into my Skin, of which I have pulled out some, and must scratch out the rest; Is not this enough to give one the Spleen? for I doubt no Christian Family will receive me. And this is all a man gets by a Northern Journy. It would be unhappy for me to be as nice in my Conversation and company as you are which is the only Thing wherein you agree with Glass-heel,[1] who declares there is not a conversible creature in Ireld except Cad— What would you do in these Parts where Politeness is as much a Stranger as Cleanlyness.—I am stopt; and this Letter is intended to travel with me, so adieu till the next Stage —— Aug 8 Yesterday I rode 28 Miles without being weary, and I wish little Heskinage would do as much. Here I leave this Letter to travel one way while I go another, but where I do not know, nor what Cabbins or Bogs are in my Way. I see you this moment as you are visible at ten in the morning, and now you are asking yr Questions round and I am answering them with a great deal of affected delays, and the same scene has passed forty times as well as the othr from 2 till 7; longer than the first by 2 hours, yet each has ses agremens particuliers—A long vacation, Law lyes asleep, and bad weather, how do you wear away the Time Is it among the Fields and Groves of your Country Seat, or among yr Cosins[2] in Toun, or thinking in a Train that will be sure to vex you, and then reasoning and forming teazing Conclusions from mistaken Thoughts. The best Companion for you is a Philosopher, whom you would regard as much as a Sermon. I have read more Trash since I left you than would fill all your Shelves and am abundantly the bettr for it, though I scarce remembr a Syllable. Go over the Scenes of Windsor, Cleveland row Rider Street, St James's, Kensington, the Sluttery, the Colonell in France &c., Cad thinks often of these, especially on Horseback, as I am assured, What a foolish Thing is Time, and how foolish is Man, who would be as angry if Time stopt as if it passed, But I will not proceed at this rate, for I am writing

---

[1] i.e. Ford.

[2] The only cousin mentioned by Vanessa in her will is the Rev. John Antrobus, who became subsequently a prebendary of Christ Church Cathedral as well as a canon of Kildare (Hughes, *Church of St. John, Dublin*, p. 60).

and thinking my self fast into the Spleen which is the onely thing that I would not compliment you by imitating—so adieu till the next place I fix in, if I fix at all till I return, and that I leave to Fortune and the Weather.

Address: To Mrs. Vanhomrig

Nichols Supplement 1779

Swift to Robert Cope

Dublin, October 9, 1722.

I am but just come to town, and therefore look upon myself to have just left *Loughgall*,[1] and that this is the first opportunity I have of writing to you.

Strange revolutions since I left you: a Bishop of my old acquaintance in *The Tower* for treason,[2] and a doctor of my new acquaintance made a bishop.[3] I hope you are returned with success from your *Connaught* journey, and that you tired yourself more than you expected in taking the compass of your new land; the consequence of which must be, that you will continue needy some years longer than you intended.—Your new bishop *Bolton*[4] was born to be my tormentor; he ever opposed me as my subject, and now has left me embroiled for want of him. The government, in consideration of the many favours they have shewn me, would fain have me give *St. Bride*'s to some one of their hang dogs, that Dr. *Howard* may come

[1] Swift's letter to Sheridan of 22 Dec. shows that after leaving Loughgall he paid a visit to him at Quilca.

[2] The confusion which followed the South Sea scheme favoured the disaffection of the Jacobites. They were still more cheered by the prospect of the birth of an heir to the Pretender which was communicated to them in the spring of 1720. Atterbury hailed this as 'the most acceptable news which can reach the ears of a good Englishman' (Letter to James, 6 May 1720). Charles Edward was born at Rome on 31 Dec. of that year. The streets of London rang to the cries of 'High Church and Stuart!' On 24 Aug. 1722 Atterbury was arrested at his deanery and brought before the Council. After a brief examination he was sent to the Tower.

[3] Theophilus Bolton, no friend to Swift, recently raised to the episcopal bench as Bishop of Clonfert.

[4] The see to which Bolton had been appointed lies in the province of Connaught, and possibly the property which Cope had acquired was situated within the limits of Bolton's diocese.—Ball.

into *St. Werburgh*'s,[1] so that I must either disoblige Whig and Tory in my Chapter, or be ungrateful to my patrons in power. When you come to town, you must be ready, at what time you hear the sound of tabret, harp, &c. to worship the brazen image set up, or else be cast into a cold watery furnace,[2] I have not yet seen it, for it does not lie in my walks, and I want curiosity.—The wicked Tories themselves begin now to believe there was something of a Plot; and every Plot costs *Ireland* more than any Plot can be worth. The court has sent a demand here for more money by three times than is now in the hands of the Treasury, and all the collectors of this kingdom put together. I escaped hanging very narrowly a month ago; for a letter from *Preston*, directed to me, was opened in the post-office, and sealed again in a very slovenly manner, when *Manley*[3] found it only contained a request from a poor curate.[4] This hath determined me against writing treason: however, I am not certain that *this* letter may not be interpreted as comforting his most excellent majesty's enemies, since you have been a state prisoner.[5] Pray God keep all honest men out of the hands of lions and bears, and uncircumcised Philistines.—I hoped my brother *Orrery* had loved his land too much to hazard it on Revolution principles.[6] I am told that a lady of my acquaintance was the discoverer of this plot, having a lover among the true Whigs, whom she preferred before an old battered husband.[7]

[1] It had been suggested to Swift that if he would give St. Bride's to a nominee of the government Howard could be appointed incumbent of St. Werburgh's in place of Bolton. Swift, however, was opposed to Howard, and finally St. Bride's was given to his friend, Robert Grattan.

[2] The allusion is to a bronze equestrian statue of George I erected in this year on a lofty pedestal in the river Liffey. In 1753 the statue was removed to Aungier Street; and in 1798 to the garden of the Mansion House (*Ancient Records of Dublin*, ed. Sir John Gilbert, vii. 187).

[3] Isaac Manley still held the office of postmaster.

[4] Preston was probably discharging Swift's duty at Laracor.

[5] In 1715 by order of the Irish House of Commons.

[6] Charles Boyle, 1674–1731, famous as the editor of the *Epistles of Phalaris* (1695), succeeded to the peerage as fourth Earl of Orrery in 1703. A supporter of Harley's administration, he was admitted a member of the Brothers' Club. In Sept. 1722 he was committed to the Tower on suspicion of complicity in Layer's Jacobite plot (Howell's *State Trials*, xvi. 217, 357–8, 367, 619, 676).

[7] George Granville, 1667–1735, one of the twelve peers created in Dec. 1711, taking the title of Baron Lansdown, married in that same month Mary, widow of Thomas Thynne, daughter of Edward Villiers, first Earl of Jersey, who gained a doubtful reputation (*Portland MSS.* vii. 328).

You never saw anything so fine as my new *Dublin* plantations of elms;[1] I wish you would come and visit them; and I am very strong in wine, though not so liberal of it as you.—It is said that *Kelly* the parson[2] is admitted to *Kelly* the squire,[3] and that they are cooking up a discovery between them, for the improvement of the hempen manufacture. It is reckoned that the best trade in *London* this winter will be that of an evidence. As much as I hate the Tories, I cannot but pity them as fools. Some think likewise, that the pretender ought to have his choice of two caps, a red cap or a fool's cap. It is a wonderful thing to see the Tories provoking his present majesty, whose clemency, mercy, and forgiving temper, have been so signal, so extraordinary, so more than humane, during the whole course of his reign, which plainly appears, not only from his own speeches and declarations, but also from a most ingenious pamphlet just come over, relating to the wicked Bishop of *Rochester*.[4]—But enough of politicks. I have no town news: I have seen nobody: I have heard nothing. Old *Rochfort* has got a dead palsy.[5] Lady *Betty* has been long ill. Dean *Per*— has answered the *other Dean's Journal* in *Grub-street*, justly taxing him for avarice and want of hospitality.[6] Madam *Per*— absolutely denies all the facts; insists that she never made candles of dripping; that Charly never had the chin-cough, *&c.*[6]

My most humble service to Mrs. *Cope*, who entertained that covetous lampooning Dean much better than he deserved. Remember me to honest *Nanty*, and boy *Barclay*. Ever yours, *&c.*

[1] See Swift to Chetwode, 12 Dec. 1721.

[2] Kelly, who had been released, was taken into custody again in the following month.

[3] On Saturday, 28 July, Dennis Kelly, an Irishman, his wife, her mother, and Lady Bellew, sister to the Earl of Strafford, were apprehended on suspicion of being implicated in a Jacobite plot (Boyer, *Political State*, xxiv. 96). On the 30th Kelly was committed to the Tower; but his wife and her mother were set at liberty.

[4] *A Letter to the Clergy of the Church of England on the Occasion of the Commitment of the Right Reverend the Lord Bishop of Rochester to the Tower of London by a Clergyman of the Church of England*, which was reprinted in Dublin.

[5] Chief Baron Rochfort was then seventy. He survived for five years.

[6] Percival, Dean of Emly, was not unnaturally nettled by Swift's description of himself and his wife in 'The Journal', and retorted with 'A Description In Answer to the Journal', which appeared in Dublin in 1722 on the verso of a half-sheet on the recto of which Swift's poem was printed. 'A Description' was reprinted by Scott, *Works*, 1814, i. 272 n.

Swift to Lord Oxford

Dublin. Octr 11th 1722

My Lord[1]

I often receive Letters franked Oxford but always find them written and subscribed by Your Servant Mynett:[2] His meaning is some Business of his own wherein I am his Sollicitor, but he makes his Court by giving me an Account of the State of your Family, and perpetually adds a Clause that Your Lordship soon intends to write to me. I knew you indeed when you were not so great a man as you are now, I mean when you were Treasurer; but you are grown so proud since Your Retirement that there is no enduring you; And you have reason for you never acted so difficult a Part of Life before. In the two great Scenes of Power and Prosecutions[3] you have excelled Man kind, but in this of Retirement you have most injuriously forgot Your Friends. Poor Prior often sent me his Complaents[4] on this Occasion, and I have returned him mine. I never courted your Acquaintance when you governed Europe, but you courted mine, and now you neglect me, when I use all my Insuations to keep my self in your Memory. I am very sensible, that next to receiving Thanks and Compliments I have so much more Merit than any of those[5] thousands whom you have less obliged by onely making their Fortunes without taking them into Your Friendship, as you did me, whom you always countenanced in too publick and particular a Manner to be ever forgotten either by the World or my self, for which never any Man was more[6] proud or less vain.

I have now been ten Years solliciting for your Picture,[7] and if I had sollicited you[8] for a thousand Pounds (I mean of your own

---

[1] The original of this letter is among the Portland papers deposited in the British Museum, List I, vol. xxxiv. In the Forster Collection, no. 542, there is a clerical draft of the letter bearing four corrections by Swift and an endorsement in his hand: 'Oct^{br} 11th 1722 | Copy of a Letter | to the Earl of | Oxford.'

[2] A member of Oxford's household.

[3] Prosecutions] prosecution *draft.*

[4] See Prior's letters to Swift, *passim.*

[5] 'those' written above the line by Swift in the draft.

[6] 'more' written above the line in the draft by Swift.

[7] See Swift's letter to Lord Harley, 9 Feb. 1719–20.

[8] 'you' written by Swift above the line in the draft.

Money, not the publick)¹ I could have prevayled in ten days. You have given me many hundred Hours, can you not now give me a Couple? Have my Mortifications been so few, or are you so malicious to add a greater than I ever yet suffered? Did you ever refuse me any thing I ever asked you? and will you now begin? In my Conscience I believe, that you are too poor to bear the Expence. I ever told you, that I was the Richer man of the two, and I am now richer by five hundred Pounds than I was at the time when I was boasting at Your Table of my wealth before Diamond Pitts.² I have hitherto taken up with a Scurvy Print of you, under which I have placed this Lemma,

> Veteres actus primamque juventam
> Prosequar? Ad sese mentem praesentia ducunt.³

And this I will place under Your Picture whenever you are rich enough to send it me. I will only promise in return, that it shall never lose you the Reputation of Poverty, which to one of your Birth Patrimony and Employments is one of the greatest Gloryes in your Life, and so shall be celebrated by me.

I entreat Your Lordship if your Leisure and my Health will permit, to let me know when I can be a Month with you at Bramton Castle, because I have a great deal of Business with you that relates to Posterity—Mr Minet has for some time led me an uncomfortable Life with his ill Accounts of your Health, but God be thanked, his Style is of late much altered for the better.⁴ My hearty and constant Prayers are for the preservation of you and your excellent Family. Pray My Lord write to me, or you never loved me, or I have done something to deserve your Displeasure. My Lord and Lady Harriette my brother and sister⁵ pretend to attone by making me fine Presents,⁶ but I would have his Lordship know that I would value two of his Lines more than two of his Mannors.⁷ I am ever

---

¹ The allusion is to the thousand pounds from the civil list Swift hoped for to assist him on his installation as Dean of St. Patrick's.

² The Earl of Chatham's grandfather, Thomas Pitt, 1653–1726, Governor of Madras.

³ Claudian, xxi, de consulatu Stilichonis, i. 14–15.

⁴ Oxford had come to London to seek medical advice. His friends considered that he had delayed too long (*Portland MSS.*, vol. vii, *passim*).

⁵ 'my Brother and Sister' written above the line by Swift in the draft.

⁶ See Swift to Lord Harley, 17 May 1718.

⁷ The draft ends at the word 'Mannors'.

with the utmost Truth and Respect | Your Lordships most obedient
humble | Servt | Jon: Swift:

Endorsed: From | Dr Swift Dean of | Dublin Octr: 11. 1722 | Rx Octr. 22

4805

John Gay to Swift

                                                          22 December 1722
Dear Sir.

After every post-day for these 8 or 9 years I have been troubled
with an uneasiness of Spirit, and at last I have resolv'd to get rid of it
and write to you;[1] I dont deserve that you should think so well of
me as I really deserve, for I have not profest to you that I love you
as much as ever I did, but you are the only person of my acquaintance almost that does not know it. Whoever I see that comes from
Ireland, the first Question I ask is after your health, of which I had
the pleasure to hear very lately from Mr Berkeley.[2] I think of you
very often, no body wishes you better, or longs more to see you.
Duke Disney[3] who knows more news than any man alive, told me
I should certainly meet you at the Bath the last Season, but I had
one comfort in being disappointed that you did not want it for your
health; I was there for near eleven weeks for a Cholick that I have
been troubled with of late, but have not found all the benefit I
expected. I lodge at present in Burlington house,[4] and have receivd
many Civilitys from many great men, but very few real benefits.
They wonder at each other for not providing for me, and I wonder
at 'em all. Experience has given me some knowledge of them, so
that I can say that tis not in their power to disappoint me. You find
I talk to you of myself, I wish you would reply in the same manner.
I hope though you have not heard from me so long I have not lost
my Credit with you, but that you will think of me in the same manner

---

[1] Evidently Gay had not written to Swift since Swift had left England. His
last letter was written from Hanover, 16 Aug. [N.S.] 1714. During the same period
Swift does not appear to have written any letter to Gay.

[2] Berkeley had returned to Ireland in the autumn of 1721 and resumed his
fellowship at Trinity College.

[3] Henry Desaulnais, a member of the Society. See p. 125, n. 2.

[4] Gay was provided for by successive noble patrons. At this time he was provided for by Lord Burlington.

as when you espous'd my cause so warmly which my gratitude never can forget. | I am | Dear Sir | Your most obliged & | Sincere humble Servt | J Gay.

London. Decem^r 22. 1722

Mr Pope upon reading over | this Letter desir'd me to tell | you that he has been just in | the same Sentiments with me | in regard to you, and shall never | forget his obligations to you.

Address: To | The Revd Dr Swift Dean of | St Patrick's in | Dublin. | Ireland.
Endorsed by Swift: Mr Gay | Rx Dec^b 28th 1722 (*under address*) *and* Mr Gay | Dec^b 22^d 1722.

Dodsley Miscellany 1745, x. 74.
Swift to the Rev. Thomas Sheridan

Dub. Dec. 22. 1722.

What care we whether you Swim or Sink? Is this a Time to talk of Boats, or a Time to sail in them, when I am shuddering? or a Time to build Boat-Houses, or pay for Carriage?[1] No; but towards Summer, I promise hereby under my Hand to subscribe a (Guinea)[2] Shilling for one; or, if you please me, what is blotted out, or something thereabouts, and the Ladies shall subscribe three Thirteens[3] betwixt 'em, and Mrs. *Brent* a Penny, and *Robert* and *Archy*[4] Half-pence a Piece, and the Old Man and Woman[5] a Farthing each: In short, I will be your Collector, and we will send it down full of Wine, a Fortnight before we go at *Whitsuntide*. You will make eight thousand Blunders in your Planting; and who can help it? for I could not be with you. My Horses eat Hay, and I hold my Visitation on *January* 7. just in the midst of *Christmas*. Mrs. *Brent* is angry, and swears as much as a Fanatick can do, that she will subscribe Six-pence to your Boat.—Well, I shall be a Countryman when you are not; we are now at Mr. *Fad's*,[6] with *Dan*[7] and *Sam*;[8] and I steal

---

[1] Sheridan was evidently spending his Christmas vacation, like his Easter and summer ones, at Quilca, co. Cavan, about forty Irish miles from Dublin.
[2] The word Guinea is struck thro' with a Pen in the Copy.—1745.
[3] The value of an English shilling in Ireland.
[4] His valet and groom.   [5] Other servants.
[6] Sheridan's wife was a Miss MacFadden.
[7] The Rev. Daniel Jackson.   [8] Probably the Rev. Samuel Holt.

cut while they are at Cards, like a Lover writing to his Mistress.—
We have no News in our Town. The Ladies have left us to-day,
and I promis'd them that you would carry your Club to *Arsellagh*,[1]
when you are weary of one another. You express your Happiness
with Grief in one Hand and Sorrow in the other. What Fowl have
you but the Weep? what Hares, but Mrs. *Macfeden's*[2] gray Hairs?
What Pease but your own? Your Mutton and your Weather are
both very bad, and so is your Weather-Mutton. Wild-Fowl is what
we like.—How will this Letter get to you?—A Fortnight good from
this Morning. You will find Quilca not the Thing it was last *August*;[3]
nobody to relish the Lake; nobody to ride over the Downs; no Trout
to be caught; no dining over a Well; no Night Heroics, no Morning
Epics; no stollen Hour when the Wife is gone; no Creature to call
you Names. Poor miserable Master *Sheridan*! No blind Harpers! no
Journies to *Rantavan*![4]—Answer all this, and be my *magnus Apollo*.
We have new Plays and new Libels, and nothing valuable is old but
Stella, whose Bones she recommends to you. *Dan* desires to know
whether you saw the Advertisement of your being robb'd—and so
I conclude, | Yours, &c.

Longleat xiii[5]

Swift to John Gay

Dublin Jan. 8th 1722–3

Coming home after a Short Christmas Ramble, I found a Letter[6]
upon my Table, and little expected when I opened it to read your
Name at the Bottom. The best and greatest part of my Life till these[7]
last eight years I Spent in England, there I made my Friendships
and there I left my Desires; I am condemned for ever to another

---

[1] Stella and Rebecca Dingley had probably gone to spend Christmas with
Peter Ludlow and his wife.

[2] Sheridan's mother-in-law.

[3] When Swift probably stayed with him.

[4] The home, co. Cavan, of Henry Brooke, 1703?–1783, author of *Gustavus
Vasa* and *The Fool of Quality*. See *D.N.B.* He was Sheridan's favourite pupil
and his gifts were held in high esteem by Swift.

[5] The text is here printed from the Longleat transcript, xiii. 92–93. The letter
as printed by Pope in 1741, followed by Faulkner, omits the passages here
placed in half-brackets.   [6] 22 Dec. 1722.

[7] these] those (*error of scribe*) Longleat.

Country, what is in Prudence to be done? I think to be oblitusq;
meorum obliviscendus et illis;¹ what can be the Design of your Letter
but Malice, to wake me out of a Scurvy Sleep, which however is better
than none, I am towards nine years older Since I left you Yet that is
the least of my Alterations: My Business, my Diversions my Conversations are all entirely changed for the Worse, and So are my
Studyes and my Amusements in writing; Yet after all, this humdrum
way of Life might be passable enough if you would let me alone, I
shall not be able to relish my Wine, my Parsons, my Horses nor
my Garden for three Months, till the Spirit you have raised Shall be
dispossessed. I have Sometimes wondred that I have not visited you;
but I have been Stopt by too many Reasons besides years & Lazyness,
and yet these are my good ones; Upon my Return after half a year
amongst you there would be to me Desiderio nec pudor nec modus.²
I was three years reconciling my Self to the Scene and the Business
to which fortune hath condemned me, and Stupidity was what I had
recourse to. Besides, what a Figure Should I make in London while
my Friends are in Poverty, Exile, Distress, or Imprisonment, and my
Enemyes with Rods of Iron. Yet I often threaten my self with the
Journy, and am every Summer practicing to ride and get health to
bear it, The onely Inconvenience is, that I grow old in the Experi-
ment. Tho I care not to talk to you as a Divine Yet I hope you have
not been Author of your Cholick, Do you drink bad Wine? or keep
bad Company, Are you not as many years older as I? It will not be
alwayes et tibi quos mihi dempserit apponet annos.³ I am heartily
Sorry you have any Dealings with that ugly Distemper, and I believe
our Friend Arburthnott will recommend you to Temperance and
Exercise I wish they would have as good an Effect upon the Giddyness I am Subject to and which this Moment I am not free from. I
would have been glad if you had lengthened your Letter by telling
me the present Condition of many of my old Acquaintance, Congreve Arbuthnott Lewis &c, but you mention onely Mr Pope, who I
believe is lazy or else he might have added three Lines of his own.
I am extremely glad he is not in your Case of Needing great Mens
favor, and could heartily wish that you were in his. I have been
considering, why, Poets have such ill Success in Making their Courts
Since they are allowed to be the greatest and best of all Flatterers;

¹ Horace, *Ep.* I. xi. 9.
² Horace, *Odes,* I. xxiv. I. Adapted by Swift.
³ Ibid., II. v. 14-15. Adapted.

The Defect is that they flatter onely in Print or in writing, but not by word of Mouth. They will give Things under their Hand which they make a Conscience of Speaking, besides they are too libertine to haunt Antichambers, too poor to bribe Porters and Footmen, and too proud to cringe to Second hand Favorites in a Great Family. Tell me, are you not under originall Sin by the Dedication to your Eclogues,[1] I am an ill Judge at this distance, and besides, am for my Ease utterly ignorant of the commonest things that pass in the World, but if all Courts have a Sameness in them (as the Parsons phrase it) Things may be as they were in my Time, when all Employments went to Parlment mens Friends who had been usefull in Elections, and there was always a huge List of Names in Arrears at the Treasury, which would take up, at least take up, your Seven years expedient to discharge even one half; I am of Opinion, if you will not be offended, that the Surest Course would be to get your Friend who lodges in your House[2] to recommend you to the next Chief Governor who comes over here for a good Civil Employment or to be one of his Secretaryes which your Parliament men are fond enough of when there is no room at home, The Wine is good and reasonable you may dine twice a week at the Deanry house. There is a Sett of Company in this Town Sufficient for one man, Folks will admire you, because they have read you, and read of you, and a good Employmt. will make you live tolorably in London, or Sumptuously here or if you divide between both Places it will be for your Health. ⌈The D. of Wharton Sattled a Pension on Dr Young,[3] your Landlord is much richer. These are my best Thoughts after three days Reflections Mr Budgill got a very good office here, and lost it by great want of common Politicks[4] If a Recommendation be hearty and the Governor

---

[1] *The Shepherd's Week*, 1714, was preceded by a 'Prologue. To the Right Honourable the Lord Viscount Bolingbroke.'

[2] Swift is jesting. Gay lodged in Burlington House, and his friend ('Landlord' below) was the Earl.

[3] An annuity of £100 had been granted by Wharton to Young, 24 Mar. 1719. This, however, had not been paid, and on 10 July 1722 Wharton granted another annuity of £100. These grants became the subject of litigation. The Lord Chancellor decided in favour of Young's claim to the annuities. *D.N.B.*

[4] Addison procured for Eustace Budgell the office of under-secretary to the Lord-Lieutenant of Ireland. In Aug. 1717 the Duke of Bolton succeeded Sunderland as Lord-Lieutenant. His secretary, E. Webster, quarrelled with Budgell who was superseded. On his return to England he defended himself in a singularly ill-advised pamphlet, *A Letter to Lord —— from Eustace Budgell Esq.*, which was strongly disapproved of by Addison.

who comes here be already enclined to favour you, nothing but fortuna Trojana can hinder the Success If I write to you once a Quarter will you promise to Send me a long Answer in a week, and then I will leave you at rest till the next Quarter day, and I desire you will leave part of a blanck Side for Mr Pope, Has he Some quel [que] chose of his own upon the anvil I expect it from him Since poor Homer helpt to make him rich, why have not I your works? and with a Civil Inscription before it,[1] as Mr Pope ought to have done to his for So I had from your Pridecessors of the 2 last Reigns. I hear yours were Sent to Ben Took, but I never had them, You See I wanted nothing but Provocation to Send you a long Letter, which I am not weary of writing because I do not hear my Self talk and yet I have the Pleasure of talking to you and if you are not good at reading ill hands, it will cost you as much Time as it has done me.⌐ I wish I could do more than Say I love you. I left you in a good way both for the late Court, and the Successors, and by the Force of too much Honesty or too little Sublunary Wisdom you fell between two Stools, Take Care of your Health and Money be less modest and more active, or else turn Parson and get a Bishoprick here, would to God they would Send us so good ones from your Side. | I am ever ⌐with all Friend Ship and Esteem Yours | J.S.⌐

⌐Mr Ford[2] presents his Service to Mr Pope & you. We keep him here as long as we can⌐

Hawkesworth 1766

Swift to the Duke of Grafton

Dublin, Jan. 24, 1722–3.

My Lord,[3]

I received lately from the Dean of *Down*[4] a favourable message from your Grace relating to a clergyman, who married my near

---

[1] *Poems on Several Occasions*, 1720, published by Tonson and Lintot, two quarto volumes, continuous pagination, and generally bound as one.

[2] At this time Ford was in Ireland.

[3] The Duke of Grafton's connexion with Sir Thomas Hanmer promoted doubtless a friendly relationship between Swift and the Lord-Lieutenant. This, however, is the only surviving letter between the two.

[4] After Pratt's death, Dec. 1721, he was succeeded in the Deanery of Down by Charles Fairfax, an English clergyman who had apparently come over as chaplain to the Duke of Grafton.

relation, and whose estate is much encumbered by a long suit at law.[1] I return my most humble acknowledgments for your Grace's favourable answer. I can assure your Grace, that in those times, when I was thought to have some credit with persons in power, I never used it to my own interest, and very rarely for that of others, unless where it was for the public advantage; neither shall I ever be a troublesome or common petitioner to your Grace. I am sorry the Archbishop of *Dublin* should interpose in petty matters,[2] when he has justly so much weight in things of greater moment. How shall we, the humblest of your addressers, make our way to the smallest mark of your favour? I desired your Secretary, Mr. *Hopkins*, whom I have long known,[3] to deal plainly with me, as with a man forgotten, and out of the world, and if he thought my request unreasonable, I would drop it. This he failed to do; and therefore I here complain of him to your Grace, and will do so to himself, because I have long done with court answers.

I heartily wish your Grace full success in all your great and good endeavours for the service of your country, and particularly of this kingdom; and am with the greatest respect, my lord, your grace's most obedient and most humble servant, | Jonath. Swift.

4805

John Gay to Swift

London 3 February 1722–3.

You made me happy in answering my Letter in so kind a manner,[4] which to common appearance I did not deserve, but I believe you guess'd my thoughts, and knew that I had not forgot you, and that I

---

[1] The allusion is to the Rev. Stafford Lightburne, who had married Hannah, a daughter of Willoughby Swift. Earlier Swift had no great opinion of Lightburne, but in course of time he entertained kindlier feelings, and Lightburne served him as curate at Laracor from 1722 to 1733. See Landa, *Swift and the Church of Ireland*, p. 39.

[2] This reads as if King had tried to intervene against Lightburne.

[3] The Right Hon. Edward Hopkins came to Ireland as Chief Secretary to the Duke of Grafton. In the autumn of 1722 he was appointed Master of the Revels with an increase in his salary, which was, apparently, to be obtained from the players. Cf. 'Billet to the Company of Players' (*Poems*, pp. 306–9, 1108), and 'Epilogue to Mr. Hoppy's Benefit-Night' (*Gulliveriana*, pp. 61–65).

[4] Swift's letter of 8 Jan.

always lov'd you. When I found that my Book was not sent to you by Tooke, Jervas undertook it, and gave it to Mr Maxwell[1] who married a neice of Mr Meredith's. I am surpris'd you have heard nothing of it, but Jervas has promis'd me to write about it, so that I hope you will have it delivered to you soon. Mr Congreve I see often, he always mentions you with the strongest expressions of esteem and friendship, he labours still under the same afflictions as to his Sight and Gout,[2] but in his intervals of Health, he has not lost any thing of his Cheerfull temper; I pass'd all the last Season with him at the Bath, and I have great reason to value myself upon his friendship, for I am sure he sincerely wishes me well. we pleas'd ourselves with the thoughts of seeing you there, but Duke Disney,[3] who knows more intelligence than any body besides, chanc'd to give us a wrong information. If you had been there, the Duke promis'd, upon my giving him notice, to make you a visit; he often talks of you, & wishes to see you. I was two or three days ago at Dr Arbuthnot's who told me he had writ you three Letters,[4] but had receiv'd no answer. He charg'd me to send you his advice, which is, to come to England, and see your friends. This he affirms, (abstracted from the desire he has to see you) to be very good for your health. he thinks that your going to Spa, and drinking the waters there, would be of great service to you, if you have resolution enough to take the journey. But he would have you try England first. I like the prescription very much, but I own I have a self interest in it, for your taking this journey would certainly do me a great deal of good. Pope has just now embark'd himself in another great undertaking as an Author; for of late he has talked only as a Gardiner. He has engag'd to translate the Odyssey in three years, I believe rather out of a prospect of Gain than inclination,[5] for I am persuaded he bore his

[1] Probably John Maxwell, created Baron Farnham of Farnham, co. Cavan, 6 May 1756. He married in June 1719 Judith, daughter and heir of James Barry of Newtown Barry, co. Wexford, by his second wife Anne, daughter of Charles Meredyth. Lord Farnham died 6 Aug. 1759, and was buried in Christ Church, Dublin.

[2] Writing to Pope, 13 Feb. 1728–9, shortly after Congreve's death, Swift said that he had the misfortune to squander 'away a very good constitution in his younger days'. Writing to Stella, *Journal*, 26 Oct. 1710, he describes a visit to Congreve, who was then 'almost blind with cataracts' and 'never rid of the gout'.

[3] See p. 125, n. 2.

[4] Probably these letters never reached Swift.

[5] For Pope's agreement with Bernard Lintot in respect of his translation of

part in the loss of the Southsea.[1] He lives mostly at Twickenham,[2] and amuses himself in his house and Garden. I supp'd about a fortnight ago with Lord Bathurst & Lewis at Dr Arbuthnots, whenever your old acquaintance meet, they never fail of expressing their want of you. I wish you would come & be convinc'd that all I tell you is true. As for the reigning Amusement of the town, tis entirely Musick. real fiddles, Bass Viols and Haut boys not poetical Harps, Lyres, and reeds. Theres no body allow'd to say I Sing but an Eunuch or an Italian Woman. Every body is grown now as great a judge of Musick as they were in your time of Poetry, and folks that could not distinguish one tune from another now daily dispute about the different Styles of Hendel, Bononcini, and Attilio.[3] People have now forgot Homer, and Virgil & Caesar, or at least they have lost their ranks, for in London and Westminster in all polite conversation's, Senesino[4] is daily voted to be the greatest man that ever liv'd. I am oblig'd to you for your advice, as I have been formerly for your assistance in introducing me into Business. I shall this year be a commissioner of the state Lottery, which will be worth to me a hundred & fifty pounds; and I am not without hopes that I have friends that will think of some better & more certain provision for me. You see I talk to you of myself as a thing of consequence to you. I judge by myself, for to hear of your health and happiness, will always be one of my greatest satisfactions. Every one that I have nam'd in the Letter, give their Service to you. I beg you to give mine, Mr Popes, & Mr Kent's[5] to Mr Ford. I am | dear S^r |

Your most faithfull | Humble Servt. |JG.

the *Odyssey*, and its financial terms, see British Museum, Eg. Ch., 130, printed in full by Professor Sherburn, *Early Career of Alexander Pope*, pp. 313–16.

[1] Pope's speculation in South Sea stock apparently proved within limits advantageous.

[2] Pope's removal to Twickenham took place towards the end of 1718.

[3] At this time England was enraptured by Handel and other musical stars. Giovanni Battista Bononcini wrote the anthem for the Duke of Marlborough's funeral. Attilio Ariosti wrote operas alternately with Handel for production at the Haymarket.

'Strange! all this Difference should be,
'Twixt Tweedle-*Dum*, and Tweedle-*Dee*!'
Pope and Swift, *Miscellanies. The Last Volume*, 1727.

[4] Francesco Bernardi Senesino, a famous sopranist.

[5] William Kent, 1684–1748, who made his way as a society portrait-painter despite a deplorable absence of talent. He was a better architect and landscape-gardener. *D.N.B.*

London. Feb^r. 3. 1722.

3

My paper was so thin | that I was forc'd to | make use of a cover |
I do not require the | like Civility in return.[1]

Endorsed by Swift: Mr Gay | Feb: 3^d—1722–3

Forster copy

Swift to Knightley Chetwode

Dublin, February 12, 1722–23.

Sir,

Upon my return last October,[2] after five months absence in the
country, I found a letter of yours, which I believe was then two
months old.[3] It contained no business that I remember, and being
then out of health and humour, I did not think an answer worth
your receiving. I had no other letter from you till last Friday,[4] which
I could not answer on Saturday, that being a day when the Bishop[5]
saw no company; however I was with him a few minutes in the
morning about signing a lease and then I had only time to say a little
of your business,[6] which he did not seem much to enter into, but
thought you had no reason to stir in it, and that you ought to stay till
you are attacked, which I believe you never will be upon so foolish
an accusation. On Sunday when I usually see him, he was abroad
against his custom, and yesterday engaged in business and company.
To-day he sees nobody it being one of the two days in the week that
he shuts himself up. I look upon the Whig party to be a little colder
in the business of prosecutions, than they formerly were, nor will
they readily trouble a gentleman who lies quiet and minds only his
gardens and improvements. The improbability of your accuser's
story will never let it pass, and the judges having been so often
shamed by such rascals, are not so greedy at swallowing information.
I am here in all their teeth, which they have shown often enough,
and do no more, and the Chief Justice, who was as venomous as a

[1] The postscript was written by Gay on the verso of the second leaf.
[2] See Swift to Cope, 9 Oct. 1722.
[3] It appears that Swift's last letter to Chetwode was that of 13 Mar. 1721–2.
[4] The 8th. Swift was writing on the following Tuesday.
[5] Archbishop King, who was then one of the Lords Justices.
[6] The Prosecution which Chetwode expected following upon what had
happened at the assizes.

serpent, was forced to consent that a *nolle prosequi* should pass after he had laid his hand on his heart in open court and sworn, that I designed to bring in the Pretender.

Do you find that your trees thrive and your drained bog gets a new coat? I know nothing so well worth the enquiry of an honest man, as times run. I am as busy in my little spot of a town garden,[1] as ever I was in the *grand monde*, and if it were five or ten miles from Dublin I doubt I should be as constant a country gentleman as you. I wish you good success in your improvements, for as to politics I have long forsworn them. I am sometimes concerned for persons, because they are my friends, but for things never, because they are desperate. I always expect to-morrow will be worse, but I enjoy to-day as well as I can. This is my philosophy, and I think ought to be yours; I desire my humble service to Mrs. [Chetwode] and am very sincerely,

Your most obedient humble servant,

J. S.

Address: To Knightley Chetwode, Esq., at Woodbrooke, near Portarlington.

Duncombe

Swift to the Rev. Thomas Wallis

Dublin, February 12, 1722–23.

Sir,

I would have been at Laracor and Athboy before now, if an ugly depending chapter-business[2] had not tied me here. There is a long difficulty that concerns the government, the archbishop, the chapter, the dean, Dr. Howard, and Robin Grattan, and I know not whether it will be determined in a month. All my design is, to do a job for Robin Grattan, but the rest have their different schemes and politics, too deep and too contemptible for me to trouble myself about them. Mean time you grow negligent, and the improvements at Laracor

---

[1] An early reference to Naboth's Vineyard. See Swift to Chetwode, 14 July 1724.

[2] The ugly 'chapter-business' originated when Theophilus Bolton was raised to the episcopal bench as Bishop of Clonfert creating several minor vacancies. Swift's influence did not avail as much as he could have wished, but in the course of the removals he succeeded in obtaining the living of St. Bride's for Robert Grattan and the prebend of Maynooth for Samuel Holt.

are forgotten.—I beg you will stop there for a day or two, and do what is necessary now, before the season is too late, and I will come when this affair is over, and bring down wine (which will not be ready, till then, for it is but just bottled) and we will be merry at your house and my cottage.

I sent your memorial, drawn up by myself, with my opinion on it, and a letter to Dr. Kearney, to recommend it to the primate:[1] I likewise desired Mr. Morgan to second it. I have in vain hitherto sought Dr. Kearney, but shall find him soon; and I intend to engage Dr. Worth[2] and Mr. Cross,[3] and probably all may come to nothing—*Sed quid tentare nocebit?* The ladies are as usually—Mrs. Johnson eats an ounce a week, which frights me from dining with her. My crew has drunk near three hogsheads since I came to town, and we must take up with new when I come down. I suppose you are in the midst of spleen and justice. I have often an ill head, and am so unfortunate as to pick out rainy days to ride in. what is it to you that old Pooley, the painter, is dead?[4] I am ever yours, | J. Swift.

Faulkner 1762

Swift to Archbishop King

Deanery House, 22 February 1722-3.

My Lord,

Mr. *Chetwood* intends to deliver in a Petition to the Government to Day,[5] and entreated me to speak to your Grace before he delivered it, which not having an Opportunity to do, I make bold to inclose his Letter, which your Grace may please to read; and, is the substance

---

[1] John Kearney and Thomas Wallis, as contemporaries at Trinity College, had probably known each other, and hence Kearney was asked to recommend the memorial to the Primate.

[2] Dr. Edward Worth, a leading Dublin physician of the day. He was also a book collector and formed a valuable library.

[3] See p. 349, n. 3.

[4] Thomas Pooley, 1646–1723, a Dublin painter, brother of John Pooley the Bishop of Raphoe, who had died in 1712. See W. G. Strickland's *Dictionary of Irish Artists*, ii. 251. For an elaborate pun on his name see *Journal*, p. 641.

[5] Disregarding the Archbishop's advice (see p. 448) Chetwode had evidently determined to forestall his accusers. Faulkner, misunderstanding the nature of the petition, states in a footnote that Chetwode 'had very good Pretensions to an English Peerage; for which he presented several Memorials, but to no Purpose'.

of what he desired me to say. I am, with the greatest Respect, | My Lord, | Your Grace's most dutiful | and most humble Servant, | J. Swift.

Deanery-House, | Feb. 22, 1722–3.

Forster copy

Swift to Knightley Chetwode

Monday morning, February 25, 1722–23.

Sir,

I was yesterday with the Archbishop, who tells me that it was not thought fit to hinder the law from proceeding in the common form,[1] but that particular instructions were given that you should be treated with all possible favour, and I have some very good reasons to believe those instructions will be observed; neither in this do I speak by chance, which is all I can say. I am, | Yours &c.

Address: To Knightley Chetwode, Esq.

Forster copy

Knightley Chetwode to Swift

[26 February, 1722–23]

I cannot be so wanting to myself as to omit owning my obligations to you in my present affair.[2] You have rendered me great and particular service, and I am convinced of it. The Archbishop, in my opinion, has been kind, but it is through you. I had no interest in him. The first malice was against my life and honour, the present is against my understanding; for my friend Cope tells me now I am attacked for bringing all this upon myself, for that if I had not come to town and stirred in this matter, nobody intended to have attacked or troubled me, though the King's own law servants have told me a warrant was issued to apprehend me, and that I was to have been taken up the very day I fortunately left the country; that indeed

[1] It had evidently been decided to prosecute Chetwode before the petition mentioned in the preceding letter had been received.—Ball.

[2] This letter is to be read as a reply to the preceding one. It is missing from Birkbeck Hill's volume.

orders were sent at the same time to bail me, but it was intended to distress me, for that they were sure the animosity of the country against me was such that I could not find bail there. What you hinted to me in haste[1] in regards to their being mistaken in me and my principles is some argument to me they are either ashamed, if that be possible, of this proceeding, or vexed they cannot compass their wicked ends. But I never trust the devil, wherefore I have got Frank Bernard's[2] promise to go home with me to Woodbrooke, and from there to the Assizes.[3] It was a condition of one of the greatest men's friendship of the age he lived in, I mean the Duke of Espernon,[4] that everybody, even his domestics, should tell him the worst; for otherwise a man could never form a right judgement, and living in suspense is the life of a spider.

I hope you will give me the pleasure of an evening before I leave town, which, I believe, will be this week. I have sent for my horses. Pray lend me your person for the evening, and appoint it yourself; continue to make me happy, I mean continue my friend, which I not only covet but endeavour above all things by every thought, word, and action of my life to merit, as being with all possible attachment, respect and truth, | Your own, | K. C.

Nichols 1779

Swift to Robert Cope

Dublin, May 11, 1723.

I put up your letter so very safe, that I was half an hour looking for it. I did not receive it till a few days before I came to town; for I

---

[1] Probably this was in conversation.

[2] Francis Bernard, 1662–1731, was born in co. Cork. Educated at Trinity College, Dublin, he entered the Middle Temple, and subsequently went to the Irish Bar. A Tory in politics, he was M.P. for Bandon. He became Solicitor-General in 1711. Superseded on the accession of George I. Prime-Serjeant in 1724; and a Justice of the Common Pleas in 1726 (Ball, *Judges in Ireland*, ii. 199). He left issue through whom he became an ancestor of the Earls of Bandon.

[3] In case the government instituted proceedings against him.

[4] Henri de Nogaret, Duc D'Épernon, born 1591, died 11 Feb. 1639. A distinguished, but erratic, French soldier, serving under Louis XIII. See *Nouvelle Biographie Générale* under Candelle.

often changed stages, and my last as well as my first was at *Wood-park* with Mr. *Ford*.[1] This is the first minute of leisure I have had to answer you, which I did not intend to do, till I heard you were come and gone from hence like a spright.[2] I will tell you that for some years I have intended a Southern journey; and this summer is fixed for it, and I hope to set out in ten days.[3] I never was in those parts, nor am acquainted with one Christian among them, so that I shall be little more than a passenger; from thence I go to the Bishop of *Clonfert*, who expects me, and pretends to be prepared for me.[4] You need not take so much pains to invite me to *Loughgall*. I am grown so peevish, that I can bear no other country-place in this kingdom; I quarrel everywhere else and sour the people I go to as well as myself. I will put the greatest compliment on you that ever I made; which is, to profess sincerely that I never found any thing wrong in your house; and that you alone of all my *Irish* acquaintance have found out the secret of loving your lady and children, with some reserve of love for your friends, and, which is more, without being troublesome; and Mrs. *Cope*, I think, excels even you, at least you have made me think so, and I beg you will deceive me as long as I live. The worst of it is, that if you grow weary of me (and I wonder why you do not), I have no other retreat. The neighbours

[1] Swift's movements may be judged from the fact that in March he had attended several meetings of his Chapter, the last on the 18th; and he was evidently back in Dublin for a few days before the date of this letter. We may conclude that he was away from Dublin for five or six weeks. Woodpark, Ford's residence, lay on the road to Trim. Here Swift paid his first and last visit, going and returning. He probably spent some time at Laracor, thence he probably went to Gaulstown, and he may have been at Quilca.

[2] Cope had evidently been in Dublin when he wrote to Swift, and he seems not to have left town until after Swift's return.

[3] Before the date of this letter the final break had taken place between Swift and Vanessa. The last surviving letter from him to her is that of the 7th and 8th of Aug. 1722, nine months earlier than the date of this letter to Cope. The last letter reveals nothing: 'What a foolish thing is Time, and how foolish is man.' What happened during these last months we do not know. Orrery and Deane Swift agree that the final interview took place not long before her death, 2 June 1723. A month earlier, 1 May, she had executed her will. In it Swift had no part and was not mentioned. We can only conclude that it was drafted when she was at enmity with him. Whether his southern journey was planned before the rupture or after cannot be determined; but it has the appearance of being dictated by the desire to escape Dublin gossip.

[4] This reads as if Swift was paying the visit on his own suggestion and not in response to an invitation from his old opponent Bolton.

you mention may be valuable, but I never want them at your house; and I love the very spleen of you and Mrs. *Cope*, better than the mirth of any others you can help me to; it is indeed one additional good circumstance that *T*— will be absent.[1] I am sorry to say so of an old acquaintance; I would pity all infirmities that years bring on, except envy and loss of good-nature; the loss of the latter I cannot pardon in any one but myself. My most humble service to Mrs. *Cope*; and pray God bless your fire-side! It will spare Dr. *Jenney*[2] the trouble of a letter, if he knows from you in a few days that I intend in a week from your receiving this to begin my journey; for he promised to be my companion. It is probable I may be at *Clonfert* by the beginning of *July*. It is abominable that you will get me none of *Prior*'s guineas.[3]—If you want news, seek other correspondents. Mr. *Ford* is heartily weary of us, for want of company. He is a tavern-man, and few here go to taverns, except such as will not pass with him; and, what is worse, as much as he has traveled, he cannot ride. He will be undone when I am gone away; yet he does not think it convenient to be in *London* during these hopeful times.[4] I have been four hours at a commission to hear the passing of accompts, and thought I should not have spirits left to begin a letter; but I find myself refreshed with writing to you.—Adieu; and do me the justice to believe, that no man loves and esteems you more than Yours, *&c.*

[1] Tisdall. During his visits to Loughgall Swift used sometimes to meet him. For a tiresome story of Tisdall's sense of humour see Sheridan's *Life*, p. 431.

[2] Dr. Henry Jenny, a man of some means, became prebendary of Mullabrack, a parish in the county of Armagh not far from Loughgall, in 1690. See Leslie's *Armagh Clergy*, p. 61, *Fasti Eccl. Hib.* iii. 50, and *Poems*, pp. 857, 864, 872.

[3] Evidently Cope had not been assiduous in collecting subscriptions for Prior's poems.

[4] The Bill of Pains and Penalties had passed the House of Commons, and on the very day this letter was written Bishop Atterbury made his defence before the House of Lords. It was on this occasion that Swift wrote the verses 'Upon the horrid Plot', alluding to the lame dog Harlequin, mention of which in clandestine correspondence led to the discovery of Atterbury's part in Jacobite plots (*Poems*, pp. 297–301).

Forster copy

Swift to Knightley Chetwode

[May, 1723.]

Sir,

I was just going out when I received your note.[1] These proceedings make my head turn round. I take it that the government's leave
for you to move the King's Bench must signify something, or else
instead of a dilemma it is an absurdity. I thought you had put in a
memorial, which I also thought would have an answer in form. I
apprehend they have a mind to evade a request which they cannot
well refuse. Will not your lawyer advise you to move the King's
Bench, and will he not say that it was the direction of the government you should do so, and will the government own an advice or
order that is evasive? I talk out of my sphere. Surely the Attorney[2]
could but reconcile this. I imagined your request should [have]
been offered to the Justices[3] in a body, not to one and then to the
other, as that was doing nothing. I am wholly at a loss what to say
further.

Endorsed: Swift, without date, about my prosecution and his sentiments on
several particulars abt it. K.C.

Nichols 1779

Swift to Robert Cope

June 1, 1723.

I wrote to you three weeks ago;[4] perhaps my letter miscarried:
I desired you would let Dr. *Jenney* know that I intended my
journey in ten days after my letter would reach you; and I staid five
or six more, and do now leave this town on *Monday*,[5] and take a long

---

[1] Some fresh development in the proceedings against Chetwode had necessi-
tated his return to Dublin.

[2] The Attorney-General at this time was John Rogerson, who was called to the
Bar at the Middle Temple in 1698, and to the Irish Bar in 1701. He became
Attorney-General in 1720. Like Francis Bernard (see p. 452) he married a sister
of Peter Ludlow. Through a daughter he became an ancestor of the Earls of
Erne (Ball, *Judges in Ireland*, pp. 199–200).

[3] The Lords Justices, Archbishop King, Lord Midleton, and Speaker Conolly.

[4] 11 May.   [5] Swift was writing on a Saturday.

Southern journey, and in five or six weeks hope to get to the Bishop of *Clonfert*'s. My letter to you was very long, and full of civilities to you and Mrs. *Cope*, and it is a pity it should be lost.—I go where I was never before, without one companion, and among people where I know no creature; and all this is to get a little exercise, for curing an ill head. Pray reproach Dr. *Jenney* soundly, if you received my letter, and sent my message; for I know not where to direct to him, but thought you might hear of him once a week. Your friend *Ford* keeps still in *Ireland*, and passes the summer at his country house with two sober ladies of his and my acquaintance.[1] If there be time after my being at *Clonfert*, I will call at Loughgall; though I wish you would come to the bishop's, if Mrs. *Cope* will give you leave. It seems they are resolved to find out Plots here when the Parliament meets, in imitation of *England*; and the chief justice and postmaster[2] are gone on purpose to bring them over and they will raise fifty thousand pounds on the Papists here. The bishop of *Meath*[3] says: 'the bishop of *Rochester* was always a silly fellow.'[4]

I wish you many merry meetings with Tisdall. The graziers will be ruined this year. Praised be God for all things! *Bermudas* goes low.[5] The walk toward the bishop of *Clonfert*'s is full of grass. The college and I are fallen out about a guinea. We have some hangings, but few weddings. The next packet will bring us word of the king and bishop of *Rochester*'s leaving *England*;[6] a good journey and speedy return to one and the other, is an honest Whig wish. And so I remain, ever entirely Yours, *&c.*

[1] Between the latter part of March and the beginning of May 1723 Swift made two brief visits to Woodpark. The latter visit overlapped a long stay at Woodpark by Stella and Rebecca Dingley, extending from April to October. See 'Stella at Wood-Park', *Poems*, pp. 748–52, and notes. From June to August or September Swift was absent from Dublin on his 'long Southern Journey'.

[2] i.e. Whitshed and Manley.

[3] i.e. Evans.

[4] In accordance with the provisions of the Bill of Pains and Penalties Atterbury had been conveyed out of the country never to return.

[5] Berkeley's scheme for the foundation of a university in the Bermudas.

[6] The King left England for Hanover soon after Atterbury's banishment.

Swift to Knightley Chetwode

June 2, 1723.
Past twelve at night.

Sir,

I sent a messenger on Friday[1] to Mr. Forbes's[2] lodging, who had orders if he were not at home, to say that I should be glad to see him, but I did not hear of him, though I stayed at home on Saturday till past two a clock. I think all your comfort lies in your innocence, your steadiness, and the advice of your lawyers.[3] I am forced to leave the town sooner than I expected.[4]

I heartily wish you good success, and am in hopes the consequence will not be so formidable as you are apt to fear. You will find that brutes are not to be too much provoked. They that most deserve contempt are most angry at being contemned, I know it by experience. It is worse to need friends, than not to have them; especially in times when it is so hard, even for cautious men to keep out of harm's way.

I hope when this affair is over you will make yourself more happy in your domestick: that you may pass the rest of your life in improving the scene and your fortune, and exchanging your enemies for friends. I am, &c.

Address: To Knightley Chetwode Esq at his Lodgings in William Street.
Endorsed: About my prosecution at that time.

Transcript at Cirencester[5]

Alexander Pope to Swift

[*August* 1723]

I find a rebuke in a late Letter of yours that both stings & pleases me extreamly. Your saying that I ought to have writt a Postscript to

---

[1] Swift was writing on Sunday.
[2] Presumably the Rev. Thomas Forbes, rector of Dunboyne.
[3] In the legal proceedings then pending.
[4] Vanessa died on this day. The news had probably reached Swift; and he was in haste to leave Dublin. She was buried in St. Andrew's churchyard.
[5] This letter first appeared in Curll's *New Letters of Mr. Pope,* 1736, perhaps secretly communicated by Pope, and in his vol. v of *Mr. Pope's Literary*

my friend Gay's, makes me not content to write less than a whole Letter, & your seeming to receive His kindly gives me hopes you'll look upon this as a sincere effect of friendship. Indeed as I cannot but owne, the laziness with which you tax me, & with which I may equally charge you (for both of Us I beleive have had & one of Us has both had & given[1] a surfeit of writing) so I really thought you would know yourself to be so certainly entitld to my Friendship, that twas a possession, you cou'd not imagine[2] needed any further Deeds or Writings to assure you of it. ⌜It is an honest Truth, there's no one living or dead or whom I think oft'ner, or better than yourself. I look upon You to be, (as to me) in a State between both: you have from me all the passions, & good wishes, that can attend the Living; & all that Respect & tender Sense of Loss, that we feel for the Dead.⌝[3] Whatever you seem to think of your withdrawn & separate State, at this distance, & in this absence, Dr Swift lives still in England, in ev'ry place & company where he woud chuse to live; & I find him in all the conversations I keep, & in all the Hearts in which I would have[4] any Share. We have never met these many Years without mention of you. Besides my old Acquaintances I have found that all my Friends of a later date, were[5] such as were yours before. Lord Oxford, Lord Harcourt, & Lord Harley, may look upon me as one immediately entail'd upon them by You. Lord Bolingbroke is now return'd[6] (as I hope) to take me, with all his other Hereditary Rights; & indeed he seems grown so much a Philosopher as to set his heart upon some of 'em as little as upon the Poet you gave him. Tis sure my particular ill fate, that all those I have most lov'd & with whom I have most liv'd, must be banish'd. After both of You left England, my constant Host was the Bishop of Rochester. Sure this is a Nation that is cursedly afraid of being overrun with too

---

Correspondence, 1737. See further Sherburn, ii. 183, n. 4. This letter in the London editions of 1741–2, and also later, was dated 'Jan. 12, 1723'. The date is not possible, for Bolingbroke did not return from exile till June 1723. This and Bolingbroke's joint letter can safely be dated Aug. 1723.

[1] The allusion is to his large task on Homer.

[2] imagine . . . Deeds] imagine stood in need of further Deeds *1737–42 in Pope's editions*.

[3] The passage in half-brackets is omitted in all Pope's texts; Curll printed it.

[4] wou'd have] desire *1737–42*.

[5] were] are *1737–42*.

[6] Bolingbroke received a pardon in May 1723 enabling him to return to England without fear of arrest.

much politeness, & cannot regain one Great Genius but at the expense of another. I tremble for my Lord Peterborow[1] (whom I now lodge with) he has too much wit, as well as Courage to make a solid General, & if he escapes being banish'd by others, I fear he will banish himself. This leads me to give You some account of my manner of Life & Conversation which has been infinitely more various & dissipated than when You knew me, among all Sexes, Parties & Professions. A Glutt of Study & Retirement in the first part of my Life cast me into this, & this I begin to see will throw me again into Study & Retirement. The Civilities I have met with from Opposite Sets of People have hinder'd me from being either violent or sowre to any Party: but at the same time the observations & experiences I cannot but have collected, have made me less fond of, & less surpriz'd at any. I am therefore the more afflicted & the more angry, at the violences & Hardships I see practis'd by either. The merry vein you knew me in, is sunk into a Turn of Reflexion, that has made the world pretty indifferent to me, & yet I have acquir'd a Quietness of mind which by Fitts improv's into a certain degree of chearfullness, enough to make me just so good humourd as to wish that world well. My Friendships are increas'd by new ones, yet no part of the warmth I felt for the old is diminish'd. Aversions I have none but to Knaves, (f[or] Fools I have learn'd to bear with) & those I cannot be commonly Civil to: For I think those are next of knaves[2] who converse with them. The greatest Man in Power of this sort, shall hardly make me bow to him, unless I had a personal obligation ⌈to him⌉[3] & that I will take care not to have. The Top-pleasure of my Life is one I learnd from you both how to gain, & how to use the Freedomes of Friendship with Men much my Superiors. To have pleasd Great men according to Horace is a Praise; but not to have flatterd them & yet not to have displeasd them is a greater. I have carefully avoided all intercourse with Poets & Scriblers, unless where by great[4] Chance I find a modest one. By these means I have had no quarrels with any personally, & none have been Enemies, but who were also strangers to me. And as there is no great need of Eclaircisse-

---

[1] Pope lodged with Peterborough during Atterbury's trial. Swift, 20 Sept. 1723, seems to assume that Peterborough was involved in Atterbury's plot; though he voted in favour of banishing the Bishop.

[2] those are next of knaves] those men are next to knaves *1737–42 in all Pope's texts except the 1737 quarto and folio.*

[3] Omitted in all texts except Curll's vol. v and the quarto and folio of 1737.

[4] 'great' is omitted in all texts except Curll's.

ments with such, Whatever they writ or said I never retaliated;[1] not only never seeming to know, but often really never knowing any thing of the matter. There are very few things that give me the anxiety of a wish: the strongest I have wou'd be to pass my days with you, & a few such as you. But Fate has dispers'd them all about the world. & I find to wish it is as vain as to wish to live to see the millennium, & the Kingdom of the Just upon Earth.

If I have sinned in my long silence Consider there is One, to whom You yourself have been as great a Sinner. As soon as you see his Hand you'll learn to do me justice, & feel in your own heart how long a man may be silent to those he truly loves & respects. | I am Dear Sir | Your everfaithfull Servant | A: Pope

Curll 1736[2]

Viscount Bolingbroke to Swift

[*August*, 1723]

I am not so lazy as Pope, and therefore you must not expect from me the same indulgence to Laziness; in defending his own Cause he pleads yours; and becomes your Advocate while he appeals to you as his Judge; you will do the same on your Part; and I, and the rest of your common Friends, shall have great Justice to expect from two such righteous Tribunals: You resemble perfectly the two Alehouse-Keepers in *Holland*, who were at the same time Burgomasters of the Town, and taxed one another's Bills alternately.[3] I declare before hand I will not stand to the Award; my Title to your Friendship is good, and wants neither Deeds nor Writings to confirm it; but Annual-Acknowledgments at least are necessary to preserve it; and I begin to suspect by your defrauding me of them, that you hope in time to dispute it, and to urge Prescription against me. I would not

---

[1] retaliated] related *Curll 1737*. There are in the latter half of this letter a few further quite insignificant textual variants.

[2] First published by Curll in his *New Letters*, 1736. This letter was written at the same time as the preceding letter by Pope. Perhaps Pope had shown his letter to Bolingbroke, who was incited to compose a rival treatise. Bolingbroke sailed for the Continent on 14 Aug.

[3] Dutch innkeepers were credited with being extortioners. In this sense Swift alludes to 'a Dutch Reckoning' (*Drapier's Letters*, ed. Davis, p. 84). See *O.E.D.* 'Dutch', 24.

say one Word to you about myself (since it is a Subject on which you appear to have no Curiosity) was it not to try, how far the Contrast between Pope's Fortune and Manner of Life, and Mine may be carried.

I have been then infinitely more uniform and less dissipated, than when you knew me and cared for me; that Love which I used to scatter with some Profusion, among the whole Female Kind, has been these many Years devoted to One Object;[1] a great many Misfortunes (for so they are called, though sometimes very improperly) and a Retirement from the World, have made that just and nice Discrimination between my Acquaintance and my Friends, which we have seldom Sagacity enough to make for Ourselves; those Insects of various Hues, which used to hum and buz about me while I stood in the Sunshine, have disappeared since I lived in the Shade. No Man comes to a Hermitage but for the Sake of the Hermit; a few Philosophical Friends come often to mine, and they are such as you would be glad to live with, if a dull Climate and duller Company have not altered you extreamly from what you was nine Years ago.

The hoarse Voice of Party was never heard in this quiet Place;[2] Gazettes and Pamphlets are banished from it, and if the Lucubrations of Isaac Bickerstaff are admitted, this Distinction is owing to some Strokes by which it is judged that this illustrious Philosopher, had (like the *Indian* Fohu, the *Grecian* Pythagoras, the *Persian* Zoroaster, and others his Precursors among the *Arabians, Magians,* and the *Egyptian* Seres)[3] both his Outward and his Inward Doctrine, and that he was of no Side at the Bottom—When I am there, I forget I was ever of any Party myself; nay, I am often so happily absorbed by the abstracted Reason of Things, that I am ready to imagine there never was any such Monster as Party. Alas, I am soon awakened from that pleasing Dream by the *Greek* and *Roman* Historians, by Guicciardin, by Machiavel, and by Thuanus; for I have vowed to read no History of Our own Country, till that Body of it which you promise to finish appears.[4]

I am under no apprehensions that a Glut of Study and Retirement

---

[1] The Marquise de Villette.
[2] La Source. The 'Hermitage' to which he refers earlier is the same place.
[3] i.e. Seers.
[4] It is doubtful if this can refer to the fragmentary *Abstract of the History of England*, which consists of three distinct parts, first printed by Deane Swift in 1765 and 1768. The allusion is to the *Four Last Years of the Queen*.

should cast me back into the Hurry of the World; on the contrary, the single Regret which I ever feel, is that I fell so late into this Course of Life: My Philosophy grows confirmed by Habit, and if you and I meet again I will extort this Approbation from you, I am *consilio bonus, sed more eo productus, ut non tantum recte facere possim, sed nil non recte facere non possim.*[1] The little Incivilities I have met with from opposite Sets of People, have been so far from rendring me violent or sour to any, that I think myself obliged to them all; some have cured me of my Fears, by shewing me how impotent the Malice of the World is; others have cured me of my Hopes, by shewing how precarious popular Friendships are; all have cured me of Surprize; in driving me out of Party, they have driven me out of cursed Company; and in stripping me of Titles, and Rank, and Estate, and such Trinkets, which every Man that will may spare, they have given me that which no Man can be happy without.

Reflection and Habit have rendred the World so indifferent to me, that I am neither afflicted nor rejoiced, angry nor pleased at what happens in it, any farther than personal Friendships interest me in the Affairs of it, and this Principle extends my Cares but a little Way: Perfect Tranquillity is the general Tenour of my Life; good Digestions, serene Weather, and some other mechanic Springs, wind me above it now and then, but I never fall below it; I am sometimes gay, but I am never sad; I have gained New Friends, and have lost some Old ones; my Aquisitions of this kind give me a good deal of Pleasure because they have not been made lightly: I know no Vows so solemn as those of Friendship, and therefore a pretty long novi-ciate of Acquaintance should methinks precede them; my Losses of this kind give me but little Trouble, I contributed nothing to them, and a Friend who breaks with me unjustly is not worth preserving. As soon as I leave this Town (which will be in a few Days) I shall fall back into that Course of Life, which keeps Knaves and Fools at a great distance from me; I have an aversion to them Both, but in the ordinary Course of Life I think I can bear the sensible Knave better than the Fool: One must indeed with the former be in some, or other, of the Attitudes of those Wooden Men whom I have seen

---

[1] Seneca, *Epistles*, cxx. 10, reads: 'Iam non consilio bonus, sed more eo perductus, ut non tantum recte facere possim, sed nisi recte facere non possim.' Bolingbroke was of course capable of adapting a text, but since Curll was print-ing from a transcript and not from the original, probably Bolingbroke's diffi-cult hand in part misled the transcriber.—Sherburn.

before a Sword-Cutler's Shop in *Germany*, but even in these constrained Postures the witty Rascal will divert me; and he that diverts
me does me a great deal of good, and lays me under an Obligation
to him, which I am not obliged to pay him in another Coin: The
Fool obliges me to be almost as much upon my Guard as the Knave,
and he makes me no amends; he numbs me like the Torpor, or he
teizes me like the Fly. This is the Picture of an old Friend, and more
like him than that will be which you once asked, and which he will
send you, if you continue still to desire it—Adieu, dear Swift with
all thy Faults I love Thee intirely, make an Effort, and love me on
with all mine. | Bolingbroke.

Dodsley Miscellany 1745, x. 76

Swift to the Rev. Thomas Sheridan

Clonfert, Aug. 3. 1723.[1]

No, I cannot possibly be with you so soon, there are too many
Rivers, Bogs, and Mountains between; besides, when I leave this, I
shall make one or two short Visits in my way to *Dublin*, and hope to
be in Town by the End of this Month; tho' it will be a bad Time in
the Hurry of your lowsy P—t.[2] Your Dream is wrong, for this Bishop
is not able to lift a Cat upon my Shoulders; but if you are for a
Curacy of Twenty-five Pounds a Year, and ride five Miles every
Sunday to preach to six Beggars, have at you: And yet this is no ill
Country, and the Bishop has made in four Months, twelve Miles of
Ditches from his House to the *Shannon*,[3] if you talk of improving.
How are you this Moment? Do you love or hate *Quilca* the most of

[1] Swift on his southern journey during the summer of 1723 reached the
parish of Skull in the south-west corner of Cork. The wild scenery of that extremity of Ireland is described in his Latin verses, 'Carberiae Rupes' (*Poems*,
pp. 315–17). Delany in his *Observations*, pp. 135, 136, tells us that Swift's over-
eager curiosity in surveying the cliffs nearly led to an accident. It is possible that
in passing through Cork Swift was entertained by the Corporation (Sheridan,
Life, p. 430); but we have little knowledge of the ground covered by him in the
course of his southern wanderings. He had now arrived in the west of Ireland on
a visit to Bishop Bolton.

[2] i.e. Parliament. The Duke of Grafton returned to Ireland on the 13th of
that month, and opened the Irish Parliament on 5 Sept.

[3] The seat of the Clonfert diocese is situated in co. Galway to the south of
Ballinasloe.

all Places? Are you in or out of Humour with the World, your Friends, your Wife, and your School? Are the Ladies in Town or in the Country? If I knew, I would write to them, and how are they in Health? *Quilca* (let me see) (you see I can (if I please) make Parentheses as well as Others) is about a hundred Miles from *Clonfert*; and I am half weary with the four hundred I have rode. With Love and Service, and so adieu. | Yours, &c.

Longleat xiii (Harleian Transcripts)[1]
Swift to Alexander Pope

Dublin Septemb. 20th 1723

Returning from a Summer Expedition of four Months on Account of health, I found a Letter from you with an Appendix longer than yours, from Ld B[2] I believe. there is not a more universall Malady than an unwillingness to write Letters to our best Friends and a Man might be philosopher enough in finding out Reasons for it. One thing is clear that it shews a mighty difference betwixt Friendship and love; for a Lover (as I have heard) is allways Scribling to his Mistress, if I could permit my self to beleive what your civility makes you say, that I am still rememberd by my Friends in England, I am in the right to keep my self here *Non Sum qualis eram*;[3] I left you in a period of life where one year does more Execution than three at yours, to which if you add the dullness of the Air and of the People it will make a terrible Summ: ⌐I have often made the same remark with you of my Infelicity in being so Strongly attached to Traytors (as they call them) and Exiles, and State Criminalls, I hope Lord Peter with whom you live at present is in no danger of any among those Characters I allways loved him well but of late years the few I converse with have not well known how to describe him⌐[4]—I have no very strong Faith in you pretenders to retirement; you are not of an age for it, nor have you gone through either good or bad Fortune enough to go into a Corner and form Conclusions de

---

[1] The Longleat transcript has been corrected in the hand of Lord Oxford himself in such a fashion as to make one believe it transcribed directly from the original letter. The punctuation is probably not Swift's.—Sherburn.

[2] i.e. Bolingbroke.

[3] Horace, *Odes*, iv. 1. 3-4.

[4] The passage in half-brackets is omitted in all Pope's own texts.

contemptu mundi et fuga Seculi, unless a Poet grows weary of too much applause as Ministers do with too much Weight of Business—Your happiness is greater than your Merit in chusing your Favorites so Indifferently among either party, this you owe partly to your Education and partly to your Genius, employing you in an Art where[1] Faction has nothing to do. For I suppose Virgil, and Horace are equally read by Whigs and Toryes you have no more to do with the Constitution of Church and State than a Christian at Constantinople, and you are so much the wiser, and the happier because both partyes will approve your Poetry as long as you are known to be of neither. ⌜But I who am sunk under the prejudices of another Education, and am every day perswading my self that a Dagger is at my Throat, a halter about my Neck, or Chains at my Feet, all prepared by those in Power, can never arrive at the Security of Mind you possess.⌝[2] Your Notions of Friendship are new to me; I believe every man is born with his quantum, and he can not give to one without Robbing another I very well know to whom I would give the first place in my Friendship, but they are not in the way, I am condemned to another Scene, and therefore I distribute it in pennyworths to those about me, and who displease me least and should do the same to my fellow Prisoners if I were Condemned to a Jayl. I can likewise tolerate knaves much better than Fools because their knavery does me no hurt in the Commerce I have with them which however I own is more dangerous, tho' [not][3] so troublesome as that of Fools, I have often endeavoured to establish a Friendship among all Men of Genius, and would fain have it done. they are seldom above three or four Cotemporaries and if they could be united would drive the world before them; I think it was so among the Poets in the time of Augustus, but Envy and party and pride have hindred it among us I do not include the subalterns of which you are Seldom without a large Tribe under the Name of Poets and Scriblers; I suppose you mean the Fools you are content to see sometimes when they happen to be modest, which was not frequent among them while I was in the world. I would describe you[4] my way of Living if any Method could be called so in this Country, I chuse my Companions among those of least Consequence and most Complyance I Read the

---

[1] where] in which *printed texts 1737–42*.
[2] Omitted in editions 1737–42.
[3] This word occurs in all Pope's printed texts.
[4] describe you] describe to you *1737–42*.

most trifling books I can find, and when ever I write it is upon the most Trifling Subjects.¹ But Reading² Walking and Sleeping take up 18 of the 24 hours. I procrastinate more than I did twenty years ago and have severall things to finish which I put off to twenty years hence Hæc est vita Solutarum³ &c, I send you the Compliments of a Friend⁴ of yours who have⁵ passed four Months this Summer with two grave Acquaintances.⁶ at his Country house without ever once going to Dublin which is but 8 Miles distant, yet when he returns to London, I will engage you shall find him as deep in the Court of Request, the Park, the Operas, and the Coffee house as any man there I am now with him for a few days.

⌐I am going to write to the Person who joyned in your Letter, we are made to fear that he may not Succeed in what will be Attempted for him in Parliament which would leave him in a worse Scituation then he was before.⌐⁷

You must remember me with great Affection to Dr Arburthnet, Mr Congreve, and Gay I think there are no more eodem tertio's between you and me except Mr Jervas to whose house I address this for want of knowing where you live for it is not Clear from your Letter whether you Lodge with Lord P—⁸ or he with you

I am ever ⌐Your Most faithfull humble Servant | J. S.⌐

⌐I never Subscribe my Name et pour cause⌐⁹

Address: To Mr Pope at Mr Jervas's | House in cleveland court | St James's London.
Endorsements: Dean Swifts Letter to mr Pope Sepr 20: 1723—¹⁰

---

¹ As Sherburn observes Swift told Ford in Jan. 1723–4: 'I have left the Country of Horses, and am in the flying Island.' These were among the trifling subjects with which he employed himself.
² Reading] riding *1737–42*. A mistake of the scribe.
³ Horace, *Satires*, i. 6. 128–9.
⁴ Charles Ford.
⁵ 'have' is corrected to 'hath' between the lines of the transcript.
⁶ Stella and Rebecca Dingley.
⁷ Omitted *1737–42*.
⁸ Peterborough.
⁹ The conclusion and postscript were not printed by Pope.
¹⁰ The address and the endorsement are copied on separate sheets in the hand of Lord Oxford.—Sherburn.

Nichols Supplement 1779

Swift to the Rev. Thomas Sheridan

Octobris 12°, 1723, *Saturni* die.

Erudissime Domine,[1]

Mi Sana, Telo me Flaccus; odioso ni mus rem. Tuba Dia pusillanimum: emit si erit mos minimo. Fecitne Latina Sal? I sub me? a robur os. Nantis potatis. Moto ima os illud a illuc? Ima os nega? I dama nam? Memoravi i nos; Ima eris nisi! sit parta.

Si paca eruca? voco Tite nemo! Emerit tono, sit sola ni emit, na edit. Ima ni sum & dum? Ima nil ne ni erim! Tuba nisi no os tegi en parare.

Humillimus, &c.

Excusatum me habeas si subjecti gravitate paululum aliquando emoveor.[2]

When you have puzzled your brains with reading this, you will find it as bad sense as you would desire. | Where do you dine to-day? | To-morrow with me.

Portland MSS.[3]

Swift to the Earl of Oxford

[Dublin, 6 November 1723]

Bussy Rabutin in his exile of twenty years writ every year a letter to the King, only to keep himself in memory, but never received an

[1] This is an early example of one of Swift's games with words. For examples of verses in Mock Latin see *Poems*, pp. 1038–9; and for miscellaneous examples 'Swift's Anglo-Latin Games', *Huntington Library Quarterly*, xvii. 133–59 (Feb. 1954), and 'Swift's Games with Language in Rylands English MS. 659', *Bulletin of the John Rylands Library*, xxxvi. 413–48 (Mar. 1954), both by George P. Mayhew. The following interpretation of the above letter is supplied by Scott, xiii. 481: 'I am an ass; O let me suck calf; O so I do in summer; O but I had mum in all I supt; Minim o' time is tiresome; writes of any tall lass; I buss 'em? O soberer. Nan, sit, sit a top. O Tom am I so dull, I a cully? I so agen? I a madman? I've a memory son. I'm a sinner. 'Tis a part. Is a cap a cure? O covet it O'men, tire me not; 'tis a loss in time and tide. I'm in a musing mood; I am kneeling in mire. A, but I see none, so I never get a rap.

[2] The Latin must be read backwards: Emoveor aliquando paululum gravitate subjecti si habeas me excusatum.

[3] This copy among the Portland MSS. was evidently made for Lord Harley in whose handwriting it is endorsed.

answer.[1] This hath been my fortune, and yet I love you better than ever I did, and I believe you do not love me worse. I ever gave great allowance to the laziness of your temper in the article of writing letters, but I cannot pardon your forgetfulness in sending me your picture. If you were still a first Minister, I would hardly excuse your promise of nine years; I will be revenged, I will put Lord Harley, nay I will put Lady Harriett, upon you. Mr. Minet hath sometimes made me uneasy with his accounts of your health; but he and the public papers being silent in that particular, I am in hopes it is established again.[2] I am recovering mine by riding in hopes to get enough one summer to attend you at Brampton Castle, for I have a thousand things to say to you in relation to somewhat *quod et hunc in annum vivat et plures.* Be so kind in two lines to invite me to your house. You asked me once when you governed Europe whether I was ashamed of your company; I ask you now whether you are ashamed of mine. It is vexatious that I, who never made court to you in your greatness, nor ask[ed] anything from you, should be now perpetually teasing for a letter and a picture. While you were Treasurer you never refused me when I solicited for others, why in your retirement will you always refuse me when I solicit for myself? I want some friend like myself near you to put you out of your play. In my conscience I think that you who were the humblest of men in the height of power are grown proud by adversity, which I confess you have borne in such a manner that if there be any reason why a mortal should be proud, you have it all on your side. But I, who am one of those few who never flattered or deceived you, when you were in a station to be flattered and deceived, can allow no change of conduct with regard to myself, and I expect as good treatment from you as if you were still first Minister.

Pray, my Lord, forgive me this idle way of talk, which you know was always my talent, and yet I am very serious in it, and expect you will believe me, and write to me soon, and comply with everything I desire. It is destined that you should have great obligations to me, for who else knows how to deliver you down to posterity though I

---

[1] From the previous reference to Bussy-Rabutin, Swift to Chetwode, 30 Jan. 1721–2, we may presume that Swift had been reading him. A copy of Bussy-Rabutin's *Histoire amoureuse des Gaules* appears in the sale catalogue of Swift's books, no. 147. This book is listed also in the earlier manuscript catalogue of his books.

[2] The improvement in Oxford's health was, however, only temporary.

leave you behind me, therefore make your court and use me well for I am to be bribed though you never were. I pray God preserve you and your illustrious family, for I hope that title is not confined to Germanes,¹ and that you may live to save your country a second time. For want of another messenger more than for want of manners, I must expect that you will present my most humble respects to my Lord Harley and to Lady Henrietta, whose favours I shall always bear in mind with the highest gratitude.

4805

John Arbuthnot to Swift

[7 November 1723]²

Dear Sir

I have as good a Right to invade your solitude as L B³ Gay or Pope and yow see I make use of it I know yow wish us all at the Devil for Robbing a moment from your Vapors & Vertigo its no Matter for that yow shall have a Sheet of paper every post, till yow come to yourself; by a paragraph in yours to Mr pope⁴ I find yow are in the case of the Man, who held a whole night By a Broom Bush, & found when day Light came he was within two inches of the ground. yow don't seem to know how well yow stand with our great Folks. I my self have been at a great mans table & have heard out of the mouths of violent Irish whigs, the whole table talk; turn upon your commendation;⁵ if it had not been upon the Generall topics of your good qualitys & the good yowdid I should have grown jealous of yow. my intention in this, is not to expostulate but to do yow good. I know how unhappy a vertigo makes anybody that has the misfortune to be troubled with it; (I might have been deep in it myself if Ide had a mind.) & I will propose a cure for yours that Ile pawn my reputation upon. I have of late sent severall patients in that case to the Spaa to drink there of the Geronster⁶ water which

---

¹ i.e. the house of Hanover.
² The date is supplied by the London postmark.
³ Lord Bolingbroke.   ⁴ 20 Sept. 1723.
⁵ The Irish Whigs would be influenced by their knowledge of Swift's support of the Irish interest.
⁶ La Géronstère is one of the springs at Spa in Belgium. The water is not transportable.

will not carry from the spott. it has succeeded Marvelously with them all. there was indeed one who relaps'd a little this last summer because he would not take my advice & return to his course that had been too short the year before. but because the instances of eminent Men are most conspicuous Lord whitworth our plenipotentiary had this disease[1] (which by the way is a little disqualifying for that employment) he was so bad, that he was often forc'd to catch hold of any thing to keep him from falling. I know he was recoverd by the use of that water to so great a degree that he can Ride walk or do anything as formerly. I leave this to your consideration. your freinds here wish to see you & none more than myself, but I really dont advise you to such a jurney to gratify them or myself, but I am allmost confident it would do yow a great dale of good. The Dragon[2] is just the old man when he is Rous'd. he is a little deaf but has all his other good & bad qualitys just as of old. LB[3] is much improvd in knowledge manner & every thing else. the shaver[4] is an honest friendly man as befor. he has a good dale a do to smother his welsh fire which yow know he has in a greater degree than some would imagine. he posts him self a good part of the year in some warm house wins the Ladys' money at ombre, & convinces them that they are highly oblig'd to him L & Ly M[5] M[r] Hill & M[rs] Hill often remember yow with affection.

as for your humble serv[t], with a great Stone in his Right kidney & a family of Men & women to provide for, he is as Chearfull as ever in publick affairs he has kept as Tacitus sayes[6] Medium iter inter vile servitium & abruptam Contumaciam he never rails at a great man, but to his face, which I can assure yow he has had both the opportunity & licence to do.[7] he has some few weak freinds

---

[1] Charles Whitworth, 1675–1725, was envoy extraordinary to Russia, 1704–10. Other diplomatic missions followed; and on 9 Jan. 1720–1 he was created Baron Whitworth of Galway. Arbuthnot's statement that he had cured him of vertigo was belied by his death on 23 Oct. 1725.

[2] Lord Oxford.   [3] Lord Bolingbroke.

[4] Erasmus Lewis had gained the name from Swift's lines:
    'This Lewis is a cunning Shaver,
    And very much in Harley's Favour.'
                                        Poems, p. 171.

[5] Lord and Lady Masham.

[6] Tacitus, *Ann.* iv. 20. 'An sit aliquid in nostris consiliis, liceatque inter abruptam contumaciam et deforme obsequium pergere iter ambitione et periculis vacuum.'

[7] Perhaps the reference is to George I.

& fewer enimys if any he is low enough to be rather despis'd than pusht at by them | I am ffaithfully | Dear Sir | Y^r affectionate | humble Servt | J: Arbuthnott.

Address: For ye Revd Dr Swift, | Deane of St. Patricks, | Dublin. | Ireland.
Postmark: 7 NO
Endorsed by Swift: D. Arbuthn | Novr 17^h 1723 *and* Dr Arb—Rx No^v 17^t—1723

4805

The Duchess of Ormonde to Swift

Decr the 9th 1723

Sir

I find by yrs of the 6th of Nov^{r1} (wch I did not receive till last post) that you have bin so good as to remember yr poor relation[2] here, but as yr three last never came to hand, I think it very happy that you have kept yr liberty thus long, for I can't account for my not receiving them, any other way, than that they were stopt in the post office, & interpreted, as most innocent things are, to mean something very distant from the intention of the writer or actor, I am surprized at the account you give me of the part of Ireland you have bin in,[3] for the best I expect from that gratefull country, is to be forgotten by the inhabitants, for to remember wth any kindness one under the frowns of the Court, is not a gift the Irish are indowed wth, I am very sorry to hear that you have got the Spleen, where a man of yr sence must every day meet wth things ridiculous enough to make you laugh, but I am afraid the jests are too low to do so, change of Air is the best thing in the world for yr distemper, & if not to cure y^r self, at least have so much goodness for y^r freinds here as to come & cure us, for tis a distemper we are overrun wth, I am sure yr company wou'd go a great way towards my recovery, for I assure you no body has a greater value for you then I have, & hope I shall have the good fortune to see you before I dye,

I have no sort of correspondence wth the person you have not seen,[4] & wonder at nothing they do, or do not do,

---

[1] The Duchess's last letter addressed to Swift appears to be that of 1 Sept. 1721; but as will be seen Swift had sent her letters which she had not received.
[2] His sister through the relationship of the Duke and Swift as members of the Brothers' Club.　　　[3] The Ormonde estates in the south of Ireland.
[4] The Duchess refers presumably to the Duke of Ormonde.

I will let y^r Brother[1] & mine know that you remembered him in my letter, he is as good a man as lives,

I am afraid you'l wish you had not encouraged my scribbling to you, when you find I am still such an insipid correspondent, but wth that (wch I hope will make some amends) am wth great sincerity & respect y^r most faithfull | freind & humble servant

Endorsed by Swift: Duchess Ormonde | De^r? 1723

4805

Viscount Bolingbroke to Swift

25 December [O.S. 14] 1723.

Never letter came more opportunely than y^r last.[2] the gout had made me a second visit, and several persons were congratulating with me on the good effect of the waters which had determin'd my former illness to a distemper so desirable.[3] my toe pain'd me, these compliments tir'd me, and I would have taken my feavour again to give the gout to all the Company. att that instant y^r letter was deliver'd to me, it clear'd my brow, diverted my ill humour, and att least made me forget my pain. I told the persons who were sitting round my bed, & who testify'd some surprise att so sudden a change, that this powerful Epistle came from Ireland. att which to say the truth, I did observe that their surprise diminish'd. But the dullest fellow among them, who was a Priest, for that happens to be the case sometimes in this country, told the others that Ireland had been anciently call'd Insula Sanctorum, that by the acquaintance he had at the Irish Colledge he made no doubt of her deserving still the same appellation, and that they might be sure the three pages were fill'd with matière d'édification, et matière de consolation, which he hop'd I would be so good as to communicate to them. a learned Rosycrucian of my acquaintance, who is a fool of as much know-ledge & as much wit as ever I knew in my life, smil'd at the Doctors simplicity, observed, that the effect was too sudden for a cause so heavy in its operations, said a great many extravagant things about

---

[1] The Earl of Arran.

[2] Swift's reply to Bolingbroke's letter of [Aug. 1723], not now forthcoming.

[3] On leaving England, soon after his last letter to Swift, Bolingbroke visited Aix-la-Chapelle and Spa for the benefit of the waters.

the natural and theurgick magick, and inform'd us that, tho' the sages who deal in occult Sciences have been laugh'd out of some countrys, & driven out of others, yet there are to his knowledg many of them in Ireland. I stopp'd these guessers, & others who were perhaps ready, by assuring them that my Correspondent was neither a Saint or Conjuror. they asked me what he was then? I answer'd that they should know it from yr self, and opening yr letter I read them in French the character which you draw of yr self. particular parts of it were approv'd or condemn'd by every one, as every one's own habits induc'd him to judg, but they all agreed that my correspondent stood in need of more sleep, more victuals, less ale, and better company. I defended you the best I could, and bad as the cause was, I found means to have the last word, which in disputes you know is the capital point. the truth is however that I convinc'd no body, not even the weakest of the company, that is my Self. I have but one comfort. I flatter my friendship for you with the hopes, that you are really in the case in which you say our friend Pope seems to be, and that you do not know your own character. or did you mean to amuse yr self like that famous Painter, who instead of copying nature, try'd in one of his designs, how far it was possible to depart from his original? whatever your intention was, I will not be brought in among those friends whose misfortunes have given you an habitual sourness. I declare to you once for all that I am not unhappy, & that I never shall be so, unless I sink under some physical evil. retrench therefore the proportion of peevishness which you set to my account. you might for several other reasons retrench the proportions which you set to the account of others, and so leave yr self without peevishness, or without excuse. I lament & have always lamented your being plac'd in Ireland, but you are worse than peevish, you are unjust, when you say, that it was either not in the power or will of the ministry to place you in England. write minister friend Jonathan, and scrape out the words, *either* [and] *power or*, after which the passage will run as well & be conformable to the truth of things. I know but one Man[1] who had power att that time, & that wretched Man had neither the will nor the skill to make a good use of it. we talk of characters. match me that if you can among all the odd phaenomens which have appeared in the moral world.

I have not a Tacitus by me, but I believe that I remember your quotation; and as a mark that I hit right I make no comment upon

[1] i.e. Oxford.

it. as you describe your publick spirit, it seems to me to be a disease as well as y^r peevishness. y^r proposals for reforming the State are admirable, & y^r schemes concise. with respect to y^r humble servant you judg better than you did in a letter I receiv'd you about four years ago,[1] you seem'd att that time not so afraid of the Nightingals falling into the serpents mouth. this reflexion made me recollect, that I writ you att that time a long epistle in meetre. after rummaging among my papers I found it, & send it with my letter. it will serve to entertain you the first fast-day. I depend on the fidelity of y^r friendship, that it shall fall under no eye but your own Adieu.

Dec: ye 25th 1723

I read in English, for she understands it, to a certain Lady,[2] the passage in your letter which relates to her. the Latin I most generously conceal'd. she desires you to receive the compliments of one who is so far from being equal to fifty others of her sex, that she never found her self equal to any one of them. she says, that she has neither youth nor beauty, but that she hopes, on the long and intimate acquaintance she has had with you, when you meet, if that ever happens, to cast such a mist before y^r eyes, that you shall not perceive she wants either of them.

Forster copy

Swift to Knightley Chetwode

[December, 1723.]

Sir,[3]

I said all I possibly could to Dr. C[oghill][4] and it is your part to cultivate it, and desire that he will make the Archbishop[5] soften the Judges—you want some strong credit with the Lord Lieutenant[6] or

---

[1] 19 Dec. 1719. That letter contains nineteen lines of the 'Long epistle' for which he was searching.

[2] His wife, the Marquise de Villette.

[3] As appears from this and subsequent letters Chetwode had not yet been prosecuted. He had come to town in the hope of obtaining a remission.

[4] As judge of the Prerogative Court Dr. Marmaduke Coghill was in a position to offer advice to ecclesiastical dignitaries.

[5] i.e. Archbishop King.

[6] The Duke of Grafton.

proper methods with those under him. As to putting you off, till the Lieutenant goes, I think that can do no hurt. I suppose it is impossible for the Parl^t to rise till after Christmas,[1] since they are now beginning Bills that will pass with difficulty, and if there be an indemnity, then there will be an end. I believe all people agree with you, that your concern shocks you more than it does others. I am sure I saw my best friends very calm and easy when I was under worse difficulties than you.[2] A few good offices is all we can expect from others.

Archbishop King to Swift

Dublin, *December* 19, 1723.

Sir,[3]

The bearer, Mr. Richardson, is churchwarden of Tallaght and tells me that the chancel of that church lies unfinished for want of your fifteen pounds.[4] You are Rector there and the repair of the chancel is incumbent on you, but inasmuch as it was not ruined in your time, you ought not to be charged with it, but it ought not to lie in the rubbish, and I find the fifteen pounds you promised will finish the repair of it. The churchwarden waits on you to that purpose, and I doubt not but you will answer the expectation of the good people there, and of | Your most humble servant and brother | W.D.

---

[1] This reference has enabled the letter to be dated. After an adjournment of four weeks, as was then customary to allow the bills to be submitted to the Irish and English Privy Councils, the Irish Parliament had reassembled on 14 Dec. Swift's surmise proved correct as the prorogation did not take place until 10 Feb. —Ball.

[2] Probably Swift's thoughts travelled back to the dangerous position in which he found himself after the publication of *The Publick Spirit of the Whigs*.

[3] No copy in King's Letter-Books is now available.

[4] Archbishop King had always shown himself animated by a zeal for church restoration. Fifteen years earlier he had started a fund for the repair of the church and had obtained several subscriptions of fifteen pounds. Apparently Swift had promised a like sum but never paid it.

PRINTED IN GREAT BRITAIN
AT THE UNIVERSITY PRESS, OXFORD
BY VIVIAN RIDLER
PRINTER TO THE UNIVERSITY